Resources, Environment and Agricultural Development

Series Editors

Binlei Gong, Zhejiang University
Hangzhou, China

Scott Rozelle, Stanford University
Palo Alto, CA, USA

"Resources, Environment and Agricultural Development" series aim to provide an in-depth study of the challenges facing the world today, such as resource shortages and environmental pollution, as well as opportunities in agricultural modernization, technological progress, and income distribution, to focus on the critical issues of the balanced development in overall environment. Based on the central theme of overall sustainable and inclusive development in agriculture, the series' coverage includes but is not limited to studies in development economics, environmental & resource economics, agricultural economics, and public administration.

The series are positioned as a collection of scholarly books that aims to explore sustainable and inclusive development of agriculture under the constraints of resources and environmental conditions, under various predisposition of the resource environment and national contexts. We have incorporated many vivid and realistic agricultural development experiences into the book, such as lessons from China's agriculture, which provide a glimpses of China's rich practices and pathways for other countries worldwide.

Wen Lin

Transforming China's Agri-Food System: Government-Market Synergy

Springer

Wen Lin
China Academy for Rural Development
School of Public Affairs
Zhejiang University
Hangzhou, China

ISSN 3059-2216 ISSN 3059-2224 (electronic)
Resources, Environment and Agricultural Development
ISBN 978-981-95-7150-5 ISBN 978-981-95-7151-2 (eBook)
https://doi.org/10.1007/978-981-95-7151-2

This Springer imprint is published by the registered company Springer Nature Singapore Pte Ltd.
The registered company address is: 152 Beach Road, #21-01/04 Gateway East, Singapore 189721, Singapore

Competing Interests This book is supported by the National Natural Science Foundation of China (Grant Nos. 72573155, 72103180, and 72161147001). Given the evolving nature of this field, the book may still have room for improvement. We sincerely welcome comments and suggestions from readers.

Contents

Part I
Introduction

Chapter 1
Introduction

1.1 Overview of China's Agri-Food System

1.1.1 Quantity Dimension of China's Agri-Food System: Securing Food Security

1.1.1.1 The Evolution of China's Food Security Since the Reform and Opening-Up

Prior to the reform and opening-up, China was a net importer of grain and faced significant challenges in achieving food security. In 1977, China's total grain output stood at 282.7 million tons, with net imports of 5.6878 million tons. Per capita grain availability was 297.69 kg, reflecting a relatively low level of supply. Since the reform and opening-up period, China's capacity to ensure food security has steadily improved. This development can be broadly categorized into five stages:

1. **Stage 1 (1978–1984): Enhanced Farmer Incentives and Significant Improvement in Food Security**
   In 1978, China implemented the household contract responsibility system (家庭联产承包责任制) in rural areas, which substantially boosted farmers' production incentives. As a result, grain output increased markedly. By 1984, China experienced its first post-reform bumper harvest, with total grain output surpassing 400 million tons and an average annual growth rate of 5.35%. Per capita grain availability rose to 390.30 kg, improving the basic standard of living for the population. From a trade perspective, China adopted a diversified grain trade strategy, initiating large-scale maize exports. By the mid-1980s, China had established a trade pattern characterized by exports of maize, soybeans, and rice, and imports of wheat, thereby strengthening national food security.

W. Lin, *Transforming China's Agri-Food System: Government-Market Synergy*, Resources, Environment and Agricultural Development,
https://doi.org/10.1007/978-981-95-7151-2_1

2. **Stage 2 (1985–1993): Decline in Policy Emphasis on Grain Production and Resulting Output Volatility**

   During this period, rural reform accelerated, accompanied by a series of emerging issues requiring policy attention. Coupled with the rapid grain output growth in previous years, the government partially relaxed its focus on grain production, leading to fluctuating declines. Although grain output rebounded in 1989, it merely returned to the 1984 level. To address supply shortages, China imported large volumes of grain for three consecutive years (1987–1989), with net imports reaching 10.02 million tons in 1989. Per capita grain availability that year was 361.61 kg, still below the 1984 level. In response, the government refocused on promoting grain production, leading to a recovery. In 1993, total grain output hit a new high of 456.5 million tons, with per capita availability rising to 385.17 kg, reinforcing food security.
3. **Stage 3 (1994–2003): Liberalization of Grain Procurement and Marketing amid Major Food Security Challenges**

   In 1994, China experienced its most severe post-reform inflation, with the Consumer Price Index (CPI) reaching 124.1. In response, China established the Grain Risk Fund, launched the Agricultural Development Bank of China, and expanded the grain reserve system initially set up in 1990, ensuring timely and sufficient disbursement of grain procurement funds to farmers. In 1995, China introduced the provincial governor responsibility system for grain (粮食省长负责制). To reduce the government′s fiscal burden from grain procurement and further incentivize farmers, the 1998 reform implemented monopoly procurement and market-aligned sales policies (粮食垄断收购、顺价销售). These reforms drove grain output to a record high of 512.3 million tons in 1998, with per capita availability reaching 410.62 kg.

   However, from 2001 onward, China began liberalizing grain marketing systems. Many farmers withdrew from grain production, resulting in a sharp decline. Between 1998 and 2003, grain output decreased by 25.79 million tons, with an average annual decline of 3.41%. By 2003, output dropped to 430.7 million tons, and per capita grain availability fell to 333.29 kg, reverting to early-1980s levels and posing severe food security challenges.
4. **Stage 4 (2004–2015): Policy Incentives for Grain Production and Substantial Improvements in Food Security**

   In 2004, China fully liberalized its grain market. Farmers gained complete autonomy in deciding what and how much to produce, and where to sell. Under international trade obligations, the government resorted to market-based regulatory instruments to manage grain supply. To safeguard food security, the central government launched a comprehensive policy package, including direct grain subsidies, seed subsidies, comprehensive input subsidies, agricultural machinery purchase subsidies, the minimum purchase price policy, temporary grain stockpiling, and grain reserve subsidies. These measures not only stabilized grain supply through effective use of international markets but also significantly boosted domestic production.

Despite the global financial crisis, China's grain output grew consistently, achieving 12 consecutive years of increases. By 2015, grain output reached 660.6 million tons, with an average annual growth rate of 3.63%, and per capita grain availability increased to 477.57 kg, firmly securing the "rice bowl" of the Chinese population. Of particular note, the No. 1 Central Document (中央一号文件) focused on agriculture, rural areas, and farmers ("Three Rural Issues") for twenty consecutive years starting in 2004. In 2006, China made an unprecedented move by abolishing the agricultural tax, further stimulating farmers' production incentives.

5. **Stage 5 (2016–Present): Steady Progress in the Grain Sector and a Stable Approach to Food Security**

   Amid continued achievements in reform and development and the ongoing consolidation of food security foundations, the Chinese Communist Party Central Committee introduced a new national food security strategy in 2013. Since then, successive No. 1 Central Documents and agricultural policies have prioritized agricultural productivity and farmers' income growth.

   Even during the COVID-19 pandemic, annual grain output remained above 670 million tons, reaching 686.6 million tons in 2022. As of 2022, China has maintained output above 600 million tons for eleven consecutive years. Per capita grain availability in 2022 reached 486.31 kg, remaining above 470 kg for seven consecutive years, demonstrating the continued resilience and reliability of China's food security system.

1.1.1.2 The Current State of China's Food Security

Overall, China's food security is well ensured. First and foremost, grain production remains the foundation of food security, and both the capacity and resilience of China's grain production system have continued to improve. In 2023, despite adverse impacts from extreme weather events, China's total grain output reached a record high of 695.41 million tons (13.9082 trillion jin), representing a 1.3% increase from 2022. This marked the ninth consecutive year with output exceeding 650 million tons (1.3 trillion jin). Grain procurement volume remained above 400 million tons; standard grain storage facilities nationwide had a total effective capacity of 700 million tons; and grain-related industrial enterprises were expected to achieve a total output value of 4.3 trillion RMB, up 7% year-on-year. The on-farm grain storage loss rate decreased to 2.9%, while the comprehensive loss rate within state-owned grain depots during storage cycles remained below 1%. These indicators reflect continued improvements in China's grain production, distribution, and storage capacities in 2023. Significant progress was made in grain loss reduction and waste prevention, thereby further strengthening the foundation of food security and providing robust support for economic recovery and high-quality development.

Second, grain storage security constitutes a critical pillar of national food security, and China's grain storage standards have continued to advance. Firstly, warehouse management practices have become increasingly standardized, refined, environmentally sustainable, and intelligent. Overall storage conditions are among the most advanced globally, providing effective support for maintaining grain quality and safety during storage. Secondly, macro-level grain regulation has been reinforced, with timely rotations of central and local reserves to adjust supply and demand, and emergency grain logistics and processing capacity now cover nearly all counties and county-level cities. As a result, domestic grain price volatility has remained significantly lower than in international markets, with domestic rice prices notably below global levels. China has also leveraged over 5500 post-harvest service centers to support farmers in reducing losses and increasing income, while also launching demonstration projects integrating green storage technologies and standardization pilots, reducing the on-farm grain loss rate to 2.9% and keeping state reserve loss rates within 1%, thus achieving effective grain conservation. Thirdly, in response to regulatory challenges in managing reserve grain, the government has continuously improved the institutional framework governing grain storage and management. Both goal-oriented and results-based evaluation systems for food security have become more explicit. The enactment of the Food Security Guarantee Law, along with the implementation of the Administrative Measures on Grain Circulation Law Enforcement and the Measures for the Supervision of Grain Quality and Safety, has provided legal safeguards for national food security. Simultaneously, digitization in grain reserve management has been significantly enhanced. All provincial-level grain reserves and reserves at the municipal and county levels in 29 provinces are now fully digitized, with the digital coverage rate across provincial, municipal, and county reserves reaching 95%, laying the groundwork for penetrative, real-time regulatory oversight. Using the Digital Grain Procurement and Sales Regulatory System, the government is piloting a routine video surveillance mechanism, enabling managers to monitor grain storage conditions within their jurisdiction in real time.

In China, the supply conditions of different grain crops vary. Rice, wheat, soybeans, and maize (corn) are classified as major food grains; they can be directly consumed or processed into soy-based products. With protein content around 40%, soybeans are a critical source of high-quality plant protein and play an essential role in Chinese dietary structure (Li et al., 2024).

In recent years, production of rice and wheat has consistently exceeded domestic demand. According to the Ministry of Agriculture and Rural Affairs, "current national reserves of rice and wheat are roughly equivalent to one year's consumption by the entire urban and rural population." A report released by the Food and Agriculture Organization of the United Nations (FAO) in August 2020 indicated that China held the world's largest stockpiles of rice and wheat, with inventories reaching or exceeding annual production volumes. Specifically, wheat reserves totaled 138 million tons, exceeding both the actual production in 2019 (133.6 million tons) and the projected 2020 output (134 million tons). Rice reserves were similarly high and roughly equivalent to the full-year production. Therefore, China does not face shortages of rice or wheat, but rather challenges related to excess inventory and the management of surplus stock.

For maize, both domestic production and consumption have exhibited a rising trend, with imports increasing steadily. Nonetheless, domestic production remains the primary supply source. According to data from the National Bureau of Statistics and the General Administration of Customs, China produced 277.203 million tons of maize in 2022, while total demand reached 297.82 million tons. Since 2020, maize imports have grown rapidly. In 2021, imports surged to 28.348 million tons, an increase of 151% year-on-year, partially bridging the domestic supply-demand gap. In 2022, total maize imports amounted to 20.618 million tons, while exports were negligible at 0.1 thousand tons, underscoring China's continued reliance on maize imports to meet domestic needs.

For soybeans, 2022 marked a significant recovery in domestic production. Sown area reached 153.6566 million mu (approximately 10.24 million hectares), with a total output of 20.2835 million tons. This was the first time both soybean acreage surpassed 150 million mu and output exceeded 20 million tons, making it the largest planting area and highest output since 1958. Despite this, China's domestic demand reached 113 million tons in 2022—the highest in the world. Over 80% of this demand was used for crushing (oil extraction), with the remaining 20% directed toward food consumption. To satisfy this massive demand, China remains heavily dependent on imported genetically modified (GM) soybeans. In 2022, China imported 91.0789 million tons of soybean-related products, exceeding exports by 90.9577 million tons. Total import value reached USD 61.229 billion, resulting in a trade deficit of USD 61.087 billion. China primarily imports GM yellow soybeans from Brazil, the United States, and other major producers, while exporting non-GM yellow soybeans to South Korea, Japan, and other countries.

1.1.1.3 Challenges to China's Food Security

1. **Limited Resilience to Shocks: Pressure on Production Stability and Supply Controllability**

   Despite China's remarkable achievements in sustaining stable and increasing grain output over consecutive years, the country is expected to face mounting risks in the domain of grain production over the coming period. These risks may accumulate or even erupt collectively, posing serious challenges to the stability, sustainability, and controllability of the food system's production capacity. China has shifted from a net exporter to the world's largest net importer of agricultural products, and the trend of net imports across major commodities appears irreversible. According to the General Administration of Customs, China's agricultural trade deficit reached USD 137.8 billion in 2022, up 1.72% year-on-year.

   The convergence of unprecedented global changes—ranging from the COVID-19 pandemic and climate change to geopolitical tensions—has severely disrupted global food markets, reshaping food production and trade patterns and escalating external risks to China's food security. Rising inflation, tighter financial conditions, and lingering pandemic effects have increased the risk of global economic recession. Many international institutions have projected that global economic growth in 2023 will be lower than in 2022, which may further intensify the volatility and unpredictability of international agricultural commodity prices. The pandemic disrupted agricultural trade, logistics, and supply chains, and recovery has been sluggish. Meanwhile, global geopolitical instability and mounting challenges to the multilateral trading system have significantly undermined international grain markets and trade order. These interlocking global factors amplify China's exposure to external shocks and highlight the urgent need to enhance the resilience of the national agri-food system (Cheng & Zhu, 2020).

In addition, the trend of de-globalization presents significant challenges to China's food security. Since the global financial crisis of 2008, imbalances in development and lagging economic governance have contributed to prolonged structural stagnation in the world economy. This has led to deepening inequality in some regions, inequitable resource allocation, and a growing sense of marginalization and insecurity among populations—fostering anti-globalization sentiments (Fan et al., 2019). Recent shifts in global dynamics, including intensifying China–U.S. strategic competition and the disruptive impact of COVID-19, have further eroded trust in international cooperation. The rising tide of de-globalization severely impedes collaborative responses to global challenges, particularly in food system governance.

2. **Low Productivity and Insufficient Integration of Smallholders in the Agri-Food System**

China's agricultural reality is defined by the coexistence of a large national population and a predominance of smallholder farmers. According to the third national agricultural census, smallholders account for 98.1% of all farming households, employ over 90% of agricultural labor, and manage more than 70% of the country's arable land.

However, smallholders are constrained by low productivity, small and fragmented landholdings, and relatively limited human capital. Many lack access to modern technologies for crop cultivation and animal husbandry. For example, in crop farming, they often rely on traditional methods such as manual seeding, fertilization, and irrigation. These methods are not only inefficient but also imprecise. Compared to mechanical seeding, manual sowing is slower and less uniform in depth and density, compromising crop quality and yields. In irrigation, smallholders frequently practice flood irrigation, resulting in wasteful water use and inability to adapt irrigation schedules to crop-specific water demands across different growth stages. This compromises crop stability and productivity.

From a scale perspective, the limited and scattered landholdings of smallholders restrict the potential to achieve economies of scale and hinder large-scale mechanized operations. Consequently, production costs remain high, eroding production incentives and limiting potential yield growth. In terms of labor, rural education levels remain low, and smallholders often lack the knowledge to implement scientific fertilization, integrated pest management, and other modern agronomic practices—constraining productivity and limiting improvements in grain yield and quality.

Beyond production, smallholders face challenges in market access, information acquisition, and value chain integration. Their access to up-to-date information on market prices and consumer demand is limited. In sales, they are in a disadvantaged position: lacking brand awareness and marketing capabilities, most sell their produce as unprocessed raw commodities to grain traders, earning minimal profit margins. Moreover, lacking bargaining power and organizational support, smallholders often accept low procurement prices. Their participation in downstream activities—such as processing and logistics—is minimal, resulting in limited value capture across the agri-food value chain. This further restricts their reinvestment capacity and hinders efforts to improve production quality.

3. **Resource and Environmental Constraints: Meeting Rising Food Demand with Limited Inputs**

Land, water, and labor are essential production factors in food systems. China's per capita arable land is well below the global average, and arable land is increasingly scarce. Rapid urbanization and industrialization have led to the conversion of vast agricultural lands for construction and industrial development. As a result, the total area available for food production has continued to shrink, directly limiting the country's capacity to expand grain output.

Despite progress in reducing chemical fertilizer and pesticide use, overall usage remains high. While such inputs have contributed to yield increases, they have also degraded soil quality, threatening the long-term sustainability of food production.

China has a relatively abundant total water supply, but per capita water availability is only about one-fourth of the global average. Moreover, water resources are unevenly distributed, with northern China—a major grain-producing region—suffering from severe water shortages. For instance, the North China Plain, a key production zone for wheat and maize, heavily depends on overextraction of groundwater, which not only undermines agricultural sustainability but also causes subsidence and other environmental issues, further jeopardizing food security.

Additionally, rural labor shortages have become more pronounced due to the large-scale migration of rural workers to urban areas. The scarcity of young labor exacerbates the problem, as the remaining workforce is predominantly elderly, who often lack the physical capacity and technological adaptability required by modern agriculture.

Climate change further compounds these issues. Global warming and the increasing frequency of extreme weather events have disrupted agricultural production. From 2008 to 2018, climate-related disasters caused cumulative agricultural losses in China totaling 976 billion RMB, accounting for 55% of the world's total agricultural disaster losses during that period (Rosenzweig et al., 2021; FAO, 2020).

Given these severe constraints on land, water, and labor, and in the context of ongoing population growth and dietary transformation, the demand for food in

China is steadily increasing. The fundamental challenge for national food security governance lies in how to use limited resources to sustainably and efficiently meet this growing food demand.

4. Imbalance in the Grain Supply and Demand Structure and the Increasing Pressure of Market Regulation

   At present, grain supply in China fails to meet consumer demand for high-quality staple grains and high-protein foods. In particular, there is a shortage in the supply of mid- to high-end staple grains and soybeans. The upgrading of the consumption structure—from the pursuit of "producing more grain" to "producing better grain"—has imposed new challenges on national food security (Zhou et al., 2020).

   The imbalance in the grain supply and demand structure is mainly reflected in two aspects: regional imbalance and varietal imbalance. First, the regional imbalance in grain supply and demand is prominent. Major grain-consuming regions face significant supply gaps and rely heavily on interregional grain transfers for adjustment. Under normal circumstances, such interregional transfers can be conducted in an orderly manner. However, during major natural disasters or public emergencies, the grain supply capacity of major producing regions and the logistics of interregional grain transportation may be adversely affected. For example, in Northeast China, 59.3% of farmland irrigation water came from groundwater sources in 2016. With the continuous depletion of water resources, the region's grain production capacity is expected to be undermined (Liu et al., 2021). The actual situation shows that grain production in China continues to concentrate in major grain-producing regions. In 2004, these regions accounted for 72.7% of total national grain output; by 2019, this share had risen to 78.9%. In contrast, the shares of grain output from major grain-consuming regions and grain-balanced regions decreased from 20.0% to 16.9% and from 7.4% to 4.2%, respectively, over the same period. Regionally, in 2018, eight regions—including Beijing, Shanghai, Zhejiang, Guangdong, Fujian, Tianjin, Hainan, and Qinghai—had per capita grain outputs below 200 kg. Between 2004 and 2018, per capita grain output declined in ten regions: Fujian, Hainan, Zhejiang, Guangdong, Tibet Autonomous Region, Beijing, Shanghai, Chongqing, Guangxi Zhuang Autonomous Region, and Guizhou. Among the seven major grain-consuming regions, only Tianjin saw an increase in per capita grain output. This growing regional disparity has led to an increase in interregional grain trade, which in turn has exacerbated the pressure on market regulation and coordination (National Bureau of Statistics of China, 2020).

   Second, there is a structural imbalance in grain varieties, particularly a significant gap in soybean supply, which results in a heavy reliance on international markets. Given the increasing complexity of the global economic and trade environment, uncertainties exist regarding the sources of soybean imports. China's demand for soybeans is primarily driven by its need for edible vegetable oil and animal products. However, consumption of these products among residents is characterized by both insufficiency and excess. While some individuals consume excessive amounts of edible oil and animal products—leading to health concerns—others suffer from inadequate intake. This indicates a need for better dissemination of nutritional knowledge and improvements in residents' dietary structures (Wang & Zhang, 2019).

1.1.2 Quality Dimension of China's Agri-Food System: Safeguarding Food Safety

1.1.2.1 The Evolution of China's Food Safety Since the Reform and Opening-up

1. **Stage 1 (1979–1992): Emergence of Food Safety Risks and the Challenge to the Traditional Regulatory System**

   With the deepening of China's reform and opening-up, industries related to food production experienced rapid development. A large number of food producers and operators emerged, particularly characterized by the proliferation of small, fragmented, and individually owned private enterprises. Driven by the rapid pace of economic growth and profound social changes, many of these new actors began to prioritize commercial profit over public health, often operating outside the administrative purview of sectoral regulatory authorities. At the same time, with the gradual reform of state-owned and collectively owned enterprises, significant changes occurred in their management systems and operational mechanisms. Under the new model of autonomous operation and financial self-responsibility, these enterprises developed strong economic incentives. Motivated by profit, many food producers and operators began to engage in fraudulent and adulterative practices, such as substituting inferior ingredients for superior ones or deliberately misrepresenting products. In addition to "pre-market" risk factors, this historical phase witnessed the emergence of man-made food safety risks driven by market competition and profit-seeking behavior.

   In this context, the command-and-control style food hygiene enforcement system inherited from the planned economy became increasingly inadequate. During the economic transition period from 1978 to 1992, China gradually improved and continued to adopt a mixed regulatory model dominated by the health authorities. Although the Ministry of Health retained a leading role in food hygiene supervision, some of its original responsibilities—especially inspection functions—were redistributed to departments such as the Administration for Industry and Commerce, the Ministry of Agriculture (including fisheries), and customs inspection agencies. While traditional regulatory tools such as administrative directives and public education remained prevalent due to the persistence of planned economy institutions, newer mechanisms including legal standards, market-based incentives and penalties, and judicial rulings also began to be employed.

2. **Stage 2 (1993–2012): Evolution of Food Safety Risks and the Exploration of Segmented, Multi-Agency Regulation**

   As China's food industry expanded comprehensively, its boundaries extended across the entire agri-food chain—including primary agriculture, agricultural processing, food manufacturing, distribution, and food services. The ownership structure of food-related entities also experienced profound changes. During this period, food safety governance shifted from post-market hygiene management to a more comprehensive regulatory approach encompassing pre-production, in-process, and post-market stages, covering the entire food supply chain "from farm to fork." The coverage and complexity of food safety regulation significantly increased. In terms of risk typology, the primary threats to food safety transitioned from pre-market risks to market-driven risks—namely, those stemming from opportunistic behavior under market incentives.

   This evolution in risk patterns directly catalyzed deeper institutional reforms in food safety governance. With the increase in regulated actors, product varieties, and risk factors, more regulatory agencies were incorporated into the governance system. During the market reform era from 1993 to 2012, China underwent three major regulatory overhauls—in 1993, 1998, and 2003. These can be divided into two phases: the first (1993–1997), characterized by a multi-agency regulatory structure dominated by health authorities; and the second (1998–2012), marked by the gradual institutionalization of segmented regulation across different stages of the food chain. Traditional administrative interventions such as command-based directives largely phased out, giving way to more modern tools such as technical standards and information disclosure mechanisms, which became increasingly important in this period.
3. **Stage 3 (Since 2013): Escalation of Food Safety Risks and the Construction of a Modernized Governance System**

   China has entered a new era of socialism with Chinese characteristics, where the principal contradiction has evolved into one between the people's growing needs for a better life and unbalanced, inadequate development. Following a prolonged period of rapid expansion, the food industry has become the largest industrial sector in China and a pillar of the national economy. By 2018, the total annual revenue of China's food industry exceeded 9 trillion yuan, with food manufacturing accounting for 10.6% of the total industrial value-added. Agricultural value-added reached 6.47 trillion yuan, growing by 3.5% annually (National Bureau of Statistics of China, 2019). Alongside sustained growth, China is undergoing a critical period of socio-economic transformation. Food safety risks are becoming increasingly severe. Long-standing contradictions—such as environmental pollution—are becoming more pronounced, while new risks continue to emerge due to new technologies and business models. These overlapping traditional and novel risk factors pose major challenges to food safety governance.

   Since the 18th National Congress of the Communist Party of China, the Party Central Committee—with President Xi Jinping at its core—has consistently attached great importance to "ensuring food safety on the tip of the tongue."

Beginning with the reform of the food safety regulatory system in March 2013 and the subsequent revision of the Food Safety Law, China not only pursued vertical regulatory reforms but also explored horizontal governance innovations. Guided by market-oriented reforms, China has sought to harness the power of market mechanisms, social organizations, and public participation, inaugurating a new phase in food safety risk governance. The Fifth Plenary Session of the 18th CPC Central Committee elevated food safety to a national strategic priority, laying the foundation for a uniquely Chinese model of food safety governance. In 2018, a new round of institutional reform was launched and successfully implemented at both central and local levels, marking the beginning of a modernized governance framework characterized by unified authority and societal co-governance. Under the principle of social co-governance, modern, market-based, and digitalized risk governance tools have been widely adopted and continuously innovated, significantly enhancing China's capacity to manage food safety risks.

1.1.2.2 The Current State of China's Food Safety

1. **Overall Improvement in Food Safety and Continued Enhancement of Risk Governance Effectiveness**

   China's food safety status has shown a steady trend of improvement, with notable progress in the effectiveness of food safety risk governance. In terms of food safety inspections, the pass rate for official food safety sampling supervision has remained high in recent years, reflecting the robustness of regulatory oversight (Fig. 1.1). In 2023, adhering to a problem-oriented approach, China's

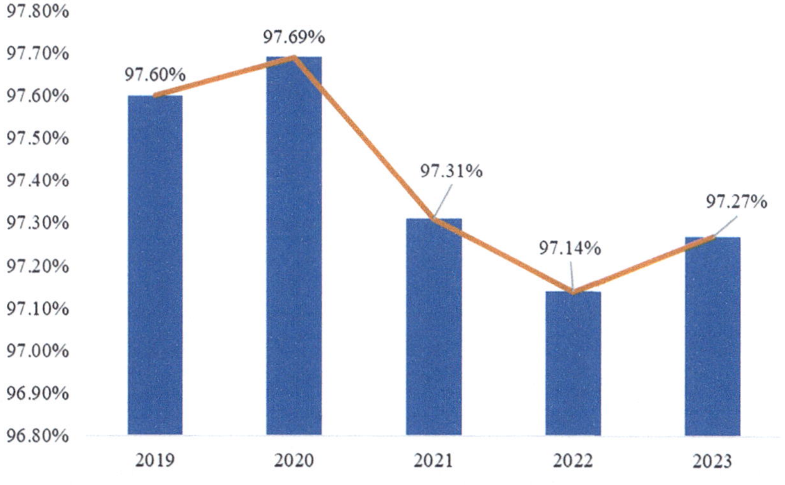

Fig. 1.1 National food safety supervision sampling compliance rate, 2019–2023 (Unit: %). Source: Research report on the state of food safety in China (2024)

national market regulatory authorities completed 6,997,389 batches of food safety supervision sampling, covering 33 major food categories. The overall compliance rate reached 97.27%, representing a 0.13 percentage point increase compared to the previous year. Among the daily staple food categories, the compliance rates for grain products, meat products, egg products, dairy products, and edible oils and fats were 99.48%, 99.19%, 99.86%, 99.87%, and 99.20%, respectively. Among the 33 major food categories tested, the five categories with the highest compliance rates were: Cocoa and roasted coffee products (99.95%), infant formula foods (99.93%), foods for special medical purposes (99.88%), dairy products (99.87%), and egg products (99.86%). Conversely, the five categories with the lowest compliance rates were: Catering foods (93.04%), vegetable products (96.23%), edible agricultural products (96.47%), roasted seeds and nuts (97.68%), and fruit products (98.13%). From 2019 to 2023, the compliance rate for infant formula foods consistently remained above 99.70%, demonstrating stable quality control in a highly sensitive product category. In 2024, the national pass rate for evaluative food safety sampling reached 99.2%, with further improvements observed in specific categories such as livestock and poultry meat, aquatic products, and vegetables. These results reflect the significant progress made by regulatory authorities in ensuring food safety and risk prevention throughout the agri-food supply chain.

Since 2012, the number of food safety incidents nationwide has continued to decline, particularly those resulting from anthropogenic causes. This trend reflects the ongoing enhancement in the effectiveness of China's food safety governance system. According to The Economist, which has published the Global Food Security Index Report annually from 2012 to 2022, China ranked 25th among 113 countries and regions in its 2022 report, released in December. Compared to its 38th place in 2012, China's position rose by 13 spots, placing it within the top 22% globally in terms of food safety assurance capacity. Furthermore, the gap between China's food safety index score and that of the United States has significantly narrowed—from 27.0 points in 2012 to just 3.8 points in 2022.

2. **Progressive Improvement in Food Safety Standards, Legal Frameworks, and Risk Monitoring Systems**

China's food safety standards system consists of national standards and local (regional) standards. National standards cover food safety indicators, quality specifications, and hygiene requirements across various food categories. As of September 2024, a total of 1610 national food safety standards have been issued, involving over 23,000 safety indicators and covering 30 major food categories and 340 subcategories consumed by residents. Local standards serve as supplements to national standards, reflecting the characteristics of region-specific food products. In terms of legal regulation, instruments such as the Food Safety Law of the People's Republic of China provide binding rules and compliance requirements for food production and business operations, thereby offering a robust legal framework to ensure food safety. The continuous improvement of both regulatory standards and legal instruments has significantly contributed to advancing food safety governance in China.

With regard to food safety risk monitoring, by 2023, approximately 9780 secondary and higher-level hospitals had been designated as sentinel hospitals for foodborne disease surveillance, covering all provinces, prefecture-level cities, and 98% of county-level administrative regions. In addition, 32 provincial Centers for Disease Control and Prevention (CDCs) have been appointed as National Food Safety Risk Monitoring Centers (provincial level). The system also includes 27 national reference laboratories for quality control and pathogen identification. A comprehensive, hierarchical, and continuous monitoring system has been established, with the China National Center for Food Safety Risk Assessment (CFSA) serving as the central coordinating body. This system integrates the technical capacities of CDCs, healthcare institutions, and relevant regulatory departments at multiple levels. It conducts risk surveillance on 29 major food categories—including grains and oils, fruits and vegetables, and infant foods—covering 259 specific indicators and encompassing the entire supply chain: primary production, storage, processing, distribution, catering services, and international trade. Major staples under the "grain bag" and "vegetable basket" policy frameworks have been incorporated into the surveillance scope. To date, the system has accumulated 16.4 million data points from food monitoring activities and two million records of food-borne disease cases. Furthermore, a national food safety risk monitoring database, a toxic substance database, and a joint notification and consultation mechanism for surveillance results have been established and widely implemented, enhancing transparency and responsiveness in food safety governance.

1.1.2.3 Challenges to China's Food Safety

1. **Food Safety Issues Induced by Natural Factors such as Pathogenic Microorganisms and Environmental Pollution**

   Contamination by pathogenic microorganisms has long been the foremost cause of food safety incidents. Such contamination frequently occurs on food packaging surfaces, and when packaging is exposed to bacteria or viruses, it significantly increases the risk of foodborne illness or infection outbreaks—particularly in the case of foods consumed directly without cooking. As food travels along the supply chain from farm to table, microbial contamination poses a serious threat to public health. Common pathogenic bacteria in China include Salmonella spp., Staphylococcus aureus, and diarrheagenic Escherichia coli. For instance, Salmonella is often transmitted via raw meat and eggs, leading to diarrhea and fever; Staphylococcus aureus typically contaminates dairy products and leftover foods, causing symptoms such as vomiting and abdominal pain. Viruses (e.g., norovirus and hepatitis A virus) and mycotoxins (e.g., aflatoxins) are also critical food safety hazards. Norovirus is transmitted through contaminated water or food and leads to acute gastroenteritis, while aflatoxins—commonly found in moldy grains—are highly carcinogenic (Wu et al., 2022).

   Environmental pollution is another major challenge to food safety in China. Industrial emissions and the overuse of agricultural inputs (e.g., fertilizers and pesticides) can cause serious soil and water contamination. Heavy metals such as cadmium and lead may bioaccumulate in crops and aquatic products through the food chain. For example, excessive cadmium levels in rice have been frequently reported in certain regions, and long-term consumption may lead to kidney damage and itai-itai disease (painful bone syndrome). Moreover, persistent organic pollutants like dioxins can enter farmland through atmospheric deposition, further threatening food safety.

2. **Food Safety Challenges in Production and Distribution Stages**

   During food production, pesticide residues, additive usage, and processing techniques are major factors influencing food safety. Regarding pesticide residues, chemicals such as organochlorine and organophosphate pesticides can remain on agricultural products. For instance, in 2023, monitoring of pesticide residues in agricultural products indicated that residue exceedance was still occasionally detected in vegetables and fruits. Organochlorine pesticides are particularly concerning due to their long persistence in the environment and potential for biomagnification, posing latent health risks to consumers. In terms of food additives, some enterprises exceed permissible levels or use non-approved additives to improve appearance, flavor, or shelf-life. For example, artificial colorants and preservatives may be excessively added to enhance visual appeal or delay spoilage. Overuse or misuse of such additives may lead to adverse health effects such as allergic reactions or liver toxicity.

   Processing technologies also play a critical role. In order to cut costs, some small-scale producers may adopt outdated or substandard technologies, resulting in inferior product quality. For instance, food produced in small workshops often suffers from poor sanitation and inadequate equipment, increasing the risk of microbial contamination and related foodborne illnesses. Throughout food circulation, storage, and retail, additional risks emerge. Transportation conditions such as inadequate temperature and humidity control can lead to spoilage. For example, cold chain logistics may be poorly implemented, with insufficient refrigeration compromising food quality. Storage environments are equally vital—poor ventilation, humidity, or unclean conditions in warehouses may foster mold growth and microbial contamination. Packaging materials also present a concern; some do not meet hygiene standards and may leach harmful substances into food. For example, certain plastic packaging contains toxic chemicals that may migrate into food during storage. Furthermore, during the retail process, some vendors may, in pursuit of profit, sell expired or spoiled products, thereby introducing additional food safety hazards.

3. **Challenges in Food Safety Regulation**

   First, China's current food safety standards lack scientific rigor and practical applicability. On one hand, a significant proportion of production standards used in the food industry have not been revised for extended periods, reducing their relevance and effectiveness (Zhou & Wang, 2014). On the other hand, some standards are vague and lack of practicality. For example, although the regulatory responsibilities for edible agricultural products are clearly defined—oversight by agricultural authorities before entering the market and by food and drug regulatory agencies once they enter wholesale, retail, or processing stages—the supervision of intermediate processes, such as transport from farm to market, remains ambiguous in terms of responsible authorities and applicable standards (Zhou et al., 2018).

Second, regulatory coordination inefficiencies and resource allocation imbalances present major obstacles. Although the central government emphasizes localized management responsibility (属地管理), the organizational structure of national and provincial regulatory bodies remains unchanged. Discrepancies in regulatory content, standards, and objectives among departments persist, resulting in inter-agency conflicts and misalignment between vertical regulatory hierarchies and local governments tasked with frontline supervision. Furthermore, imbalanced allocation of regulatory resources undermines effective governance. For instance, national performance evaluations often prioritize metrics such as "sampling pass rates" and "number of batches inspected." Consequently, some local governments, driven by short-term performance incentives, concentrate testing resources on food categories with high compliance rates and low testing costs, thereby diminishing the food sampling system's ability to detect actual food safety risks (Li et al., 2021).

Third, limited testing capacity and lax enforcement hinder the implementation of effective food safety oversight. At the grassroots level, the capacity of market supervision agencies remains weak. Frontline inspectors are mostly former personnel from industrial and commercial bureaus, many of whom are older and lack specialized knowledge in food science. Moreover, enforcement remains lenient, and the cost of regulatory noncompliance is relatively low. While the revised Food Safety Law increases the penalties for violations—including license revocation for serious offenders—loopholes remain, such as the ability to reapply for licenses post-revocation. As a result, many violators can still profit despite paying fines.

Fourth, the traceability system remains incomplete. A unified, nationwide food safety traceability system covering the entire supply chain has yet to be established. As a result, information flow between production, processing, distribution, and consumption stages is fragmented, impeding optimal resource allocation. Additionally, low adoption rates are driven by insufficient economic incentives, lack of market entry requirements, absence of premium pricing for traceable products, overly complex record-keeping formats, and time-consuming documentation processes.

4. **Food Safety Risks Arising from the Misuse of New Technologies and Processing Methods**

With rapid technological advancement, emerging technologies and novel materials have introduced new food safety risks. Genetically modified (GM) foods are a prime example. Although GM technologies can enhance crop yields and improve pest and disease resistance, concerns remain regarding their long-term safety. Certain GM crops may introduce novel allergens, potentially affecting human health. Similarly, the application of new food additives may pose safety concerns. Some synthetic additives have been linked to adverse health effects, including carcinogenicity. Moreover, innovative processing techniques such as irradiation and high-pressure processing may alter the nutritional value or sensory attributes of food. Thus, ensuring food safety amid technological innovation remains a key governance challenge.

5. **Insufficient Public Awareness of Food Safety**

   Public perception and awareness significantly influence food safety management outcomes. Many consumers lack sufficient knowledge of food safety and struggle to identify misleading marketing claims. For example, some believe that all "organic foods" are inherently safe, overlooking risks such as pesticide residues or microbial contamination that may still be present. Meanwhile, public concern over food safety continues to grow, accompanied by rising expectations for regulatory performance. This necessitates stronger efforts in public education and communication. Government agencies should promote food safety knowledge through public lectures, awareness campaigns, and media outreach to improve consumer awareness and literacy. Moreover, public participation plays a critical role in food safety governance. Mechanisms such as consumer complaints and social supervision can pressure enterprises to strengthen their food safety management practices, forming a complementary layer to formal regulation.

1.1.3 Quality Dimension of China's Agri-Food System: Enhancing Nutrition and Health

1.1.3.1 Evolution of Food Nutrition in China's Agri-food System Since Reform and Opening-Up

1. **Stage 1 (1978–1993): The Breakthrough from "Hunger" to "Satiety"**

   In the early years of China's reform and opening-up, approximately 80% of residents' food intake came from staple grains. Although grain production increased steadily, the total volume of food consumption did not exhibit a significant upward trend due to the legacy of the state-controlled purchase and distribution system. In fact, consumption of plant-based foods declined, with grain consumption decreasing by 32.7%, while animal-based food consumption steadily increased by 45.5%. Pork dominated the total meat consumption and remained relatively stable at around 17 kg per capita, while the consumption of beef, mutton, and poultry rose rapidly.

   In rural areas, grain consumption increased steadily, with per capita consumption rising by nearly 20 kg over 6 years. Subsequently, with the diversification of food supply, rural per capita grain consumption remained relatively stable. Although cereals and fresh vegetables remained dominant in rural diets during this phase, once basic caloric needs were met, dietary diversity improved. The most prominent trend was the sharp rise in animal-source food consumption. Per capita consumption of meat, poultry, eggs, and aquatic products grew by 102%, 433%, 262%, and 250%, respectively, marking a preliminary improvement in China's historically monotonous dietary structure. The Engel coefficient—a measure of the proportion of income spent on food—declined annually for both urban and rural households, decreasing by 7.2% and 9.6%, respectively.

2. **Stage 2 (1994–2002): The Transition from "Satiety" to "Better Eating"**

   Following 1993, China entered a transitional phase toward a socialist market economy. With continued economic reform, household incomes and consumption levels rose significantly. The Engel coefficient for urban residents fell below 40%, signaling a shift from basic calorie sufficiency toward more diverse and enjoyment-oriented consumption. Urban dietary patterns entered a quality-oriented stage with evident structural upgrades. Per capita grain consumption continued to decline, dropping by more than 20% over 7 years to 79.7 kg in 2002. Per capita fresh vegetable consumption stabilized between 114–120 kg, while fruit consumption increased to 59.9 kg, marking a 49% rise. Although total pork consumption remained stable, its share of total animal-based food declined rapidly from 35.8% in 1994 to 28% in 2002 as other animal-source food supplies grew. Among these, poultry and fresh milk consumption increased most significantly, by 43.2% and 124.5%, respectively.

   In rural areas, grain and fresh vegetable consumption showed slight declines and stabilized at approximately 250 kg and 105 kg, respectively. However, consumption of animal-source foods continued to rise rapidly, particularly for poultry and eggs, which increased by 81.3% and 56.7%, respectively. Despite this progress, rural intake of animal-source foods remained insufficient. As of 2002, rural per capita consumption of beef and mutton, poultry, eggs, and aquatic products was only 1.2 kg, 2.9 kg, 4.7 kg, and 4.1 kg, respectively—less than half the corresponding urban levels. Therefore, while urban residents had entered a stage of quality-oriented consumption, rural residents still lagged behind in dietary upgrading.

3. **Stage 3 (2003–2012): The Development from "Better Eating" to "Eating Well"**

   After China's first national nutrition and health survey in 2002, public awareness of nutrition and health improved substantially through science education and health promotion. As urban food consumption reached a plateau, the intake structure stabilized at a 3:4:3 ratio for grains, vegetables, and animal-source foods, respectively. Urban consumers increasingly emphasized rational dietary structures and individualized food preferences. Changes during this phase were mainly reflected in the internal composition of animal-source foods. Statistics indicate that pork and egg consumption remained stable at approximately 20.5 kg and 10.5 kg per capita, respectively. Meanwhile, the total consumption of fresh milk, poultry, and aquatic products experienced some increase despite fluctuations and gradually stabilized.

   During this period, rural dietary patterns and consumption levels resembled those of urban residents during the 1994–2002 period. The share of plant-based foods declined further, replaced by growing consumption of animal-source foods. Before stabilizing, plant-based consumption continued to decrease, while animal-source food consumption still had room for expansion.

4. **Stage 4 (2013–Present): Advancing Toward a Sustainable Nutrition and Health System**
   In recent years, China has achieved significant progress in ensuring food security and improving national dietary nutrition. In 2022, total grain output reached 687 million tonnes, marking 19 consecutive years of stable production. Per capita grain availability was 483 kg—well above the international food security threshold of 400 kg—ensuring basic grain self-sufficiency and absolute security for staple food. As China entered a stage of high-quality development, the principal social contradiction shifted to the tension between people's growing demand for a better life and unbalanced and inadequate development (Wang, 2020). Consequently, dietary and nutritional expectations have risen significantly. Food consumption patterns have shifted toward diversity and healthfulness (Tian et al., 2021), and both urban and rural residents increasingly prioritize dietary quality. People now aspire not only to "eat a variety" but also to "eat nutritiously" and "eat healthily" (Chou et al., 2022).
   Statistics show that per capita food consumption increased from 515 kg in 1978 to over 1400 kg in 2022. During the same period, per capita raw grain consumption declined from 247.8 kg to 130 kg. A growing number of consumers now emphasize reducing staple food intake, increasing the consumption of non-staple foods, and pursuing dietary diversity and nutritional balance as part of their daily habits.

1.1.3.2 The Current Status of Nutrition and Health in China's Agri-food System

1. **Transitioning to a New Stage: From "Adequate Food" and "Better Food" to "Nutritious and Healthy Diets" and "Diversity Diets"**
   Since 1949, China has made remarkable strides in increasing the supply and diversity of food. The rapid growth of grain and tuber consumption effectively addressed the issue of hunger. Between 1949 and 1978, total grain production increased from 114 million tonnes to 305 million tonnes. After the reform and opening-up, the structure of residents' diets shifted from a grain-and-vegetable-based pattern to a more diversified one including grains, meat, vegetables, and fruits (Tian et al., 2021). From 1978 to 2000, consumption of oil crops grew from approximately six million tonnes to 29.55 million tonnes, with an average annual growth rate of 7.5%. The seasonality of vegetable consumption significantly diminished, and total vegetable consumption increased from 80 million tonnes to 424 million tonnes, growing at 8.7% annually. Fruit consumption rose from 6.793 million tonnes to 62.25 million tonnes (11.7% annually); meat consumption from 12.05 million tonnes to 61.25 million tonnes (8.5% annually); and egg consumption from 2.57 million tonnes to 21.82 million tonnes (11.3% annually).
   Since 2000, dietary health has become a growing concern among residents. The share of grains in the overall diet has continued to decline, while fruit and

dairy consumption have increased significantly. From 2000 to 2020, fruit consumption grew at an average annual rate of 4%, and milk consumption grew by 6.6% annually. It can thus be argued that China has entered a new stage of "nutritious and healthy" eating, one that emphasizes the quantity, quality, safety, and healthiness of food, which is essential for ensuring food security at a higher level.

The structure of the Chinese population's diet from 2000 to 2020 displayed certain changes, as shown in Fig. 1.2a. Total annual per capita food consumption increased from 353.2 kg in 2000–376.6 kg in 2020, and the proportion of starch consumption decreased from 47.1% in 2000 to 37.5% in 2020, implying a weakening of the grain-dominated character of China's diet and an evolution towards a more diversified direction. Meanwhile, the proportion of animal food consumption grew from 10.8% in 2000 to 19.7% in 2020, mainly reflecting a significant increase in the consumption of poultry, aquatic products, eggs, and dairy products, with consumption of poultry and dairy products increasing more than twofold. The regional heterogeneity in the dietary structure and its characteristics was evident from the different provinces (Fig. 1.2b).

2. **Nutritious and Healthy Eating Relies on Imported Food as a Supplement**

China's current food supply structure can be characterized as "no problem with being full, but eating better depends on imports." According to General Administration of Customs data (2000–2022), imported grains and key agricultural products from international markets have become an indispensable supplement to domestic supply. The role of imported food and agricultural products is twofold.

First, imports support domestic production of key agricultural commodities, particularly through feed grain and forage imports. Since 2011, China has become a net importer of grain products, including the three major staple grains, with the net import volume increasing continuously. In 2022, net grain imports reached 143.7 million tonnes, including 20.62 million tonnes of corn (6.9% of

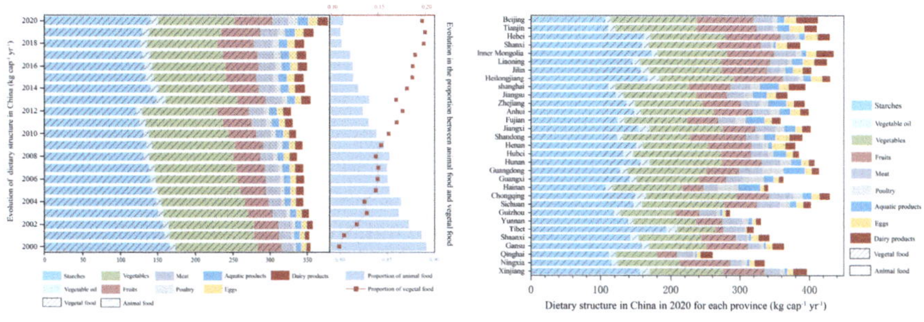

(a) (b)

Fig. 1.2 Evolution of dietary structure in China (**a**) and Dietary structure in China in 2020 for each province (**b**). Source: Xiang, A., Ye, X., Chuai, X., Cai, Y., Wang, T., & Luo, Y. (2024). Heterogeneity analysis of food supply-demand patterns and land carbon loss under different dietary structures in China. Land Use Policy, 145, 107290 total consumption) and 91.08 million tonnes of soybeans (81.5% of total consumption).

Second, imported products meet domestic consumers' growing demand for high-quality, differentiated, and specialty foods. These include large volumes of imported vegetable oils (and oilseeds), sugar crops, meat, dairy, and aquatic products. In 2022, China imported 1.81 million tonnes of rapeseed, 4.93 million tonnes of palm oil, 5.76 million tonnes of dairy products, and 4.54 million tonnes of aquatic products.

3. **The Urban–Rural Gap in Food Consumption Structure Is Narrowing**

From 2013 to 2022, the differences in food consumption between rural and urban residents have narrowed significantly across most food categories. For instance, the per capita gap in grain (raw grain) consumption declined from 57.2 kg to 48.4 kg; in vegetables and edible fungi from 13.2 kg to 6.3 kg; in meat from 6.1 kg to 1.5 kg; in poultry from 1.9 kg to 0.5 kg; in aquatic products from 7.4 kg to 5.5 kg; in eggs from 2.4 kg to 0.7 kg; in dairy products from 11.4 kg to 7.0 kg; and in fresh fruits from 20.5 kg to 13.8 kg. Simultaneously, the urban–rural differences in the proportion of total food consumption accounted for by raw grains, animal-based products, and vegetables and fruits also declined—from 16.7%, 7.8%, and 8.7%, respectively, to 10.8%, 4.6%, and 6.6%. This suggests a significant improvement in rural living standards and the convergence of food consumption patterns across urban and rural populations.

1.1.3.3 Challenges to Nutrition and Health in China's Agri-food System

1. **Consumption-side: Coexistence of Overnutrition and Undernutrition**

Following the achievement of the goal to establish a moderately prosperous society in all respects, residents' demand for both the total volume and diversification of agricultural products has continued to rise. However, the alignment between food supply and nutritional needs in China remains suboptimal, primarily in two respects.

First, excessive intake of dietary fat and salt is common, and the consumption of sugar-sweetened beverages (SSBs) continues to rise. According to the Chinese Nutrition Society, in 2015, the average household daily per capita salt intake was 9.3 g—significantly above the recommended threshold of 5 g. Cooking oil consumption remains high, with rural residents showing a particularly notable increase. Regarding SSBs, consumption rates among children and adolescents exceed 30% and 25%, respectively—substantially higher than among adults. Consequently, the prevalence of overweight and obesity is rising: among children under six, the rate is 10.4%; among those aged 6–17, it is 19%; and among adults aged 18 and above, it exceeds 50%.

Second, the intake of whole grains, dark-colored vegetables, dairy products, and aquatic products remains insufficient. Only about 20% of adults consume the recommended 50 g of whole grains and coarse cereals per day. While vegetable intake is generally adequate, light-colored vegetables dominate the diet; dark-colored vegetables account for only 30% of total vegetable consumption—below the recommended proportion of 50%. For dairy, merely 19.5% of the population meets the recommended intake of 300 mL per day. The average daily intake of legumes is just 25 g, well below the recommended 40 g. In terms of meat consumption, pork, beef, and lamb make up a disproportionately high share, while the intake of poultry and fish remains relatively low. There is a widespread deficiency in micronutrients such as vitamin A, calcium, and iron, contributing to persistent issues of "hidden hunger" that continue to compromise public health.

2. **Consumption-side: Imbalanced Food Consumption among Specific Populations and Regions**

   Significant regional disparities in food consumption patterns are evident and, to a certain extent, hinder coordinated and balanced regional development. Overall, there are large differences in the consumption of major food categories across different regions. For most food types, the gap between the highest- and lowest-consuming regions exceeds the national average consumption level. Even for food categories where regional differences do not surpass the national average—such as grains (raw grains) and vegetables including edible fungi—the absolute differences remain substantial, amounting to 86.9 kg and 89.1 kg, respectively (Table 1.1).

   There are significant disparities in food consumption between urban and rural residents in China. Rural residents tend to consume excessive amounts of grains,

Table 1.1 Regional disparities in major food consumption in 2022 (Unit: kg)

Category	Maximum price	Minimum price	Range	National average	Range/National average
Grains	181.4	94.5	86.9	136.8	0.6
Cereals	172.8	82.5	90.3	123.7	0.7
Edible oils	16.9	6.0	10.9	10.0	1.1
Edible vegetable oils	15.1	5.9	9.2	9.4	1.0
Vegetables and edible fungi	147.3	58.2	89.1	108.2	0.8
Meat	53.0	19.9	33.1	34.4	1.0
Pork	45.8	4.9	40.9	26.9	1.5
Beef	23.0	0.8	22.2	2.5	8.9
Mutton	13.9	0.4	13.5	1.4	9.6
Poultry	26.3	1.0	25.3	11.7	2.2
Aquatic products	30.5	0.5	30.0	13.9	2.2
Eggs	22.4	3.3	19.1	13.5	1.4
Dairy products	22.0	4.5	17.5	12.4	1.4
Fresh fruits	77.3	12.3	65.0	54.7	1.2
Sugar	3.5	0.7	2.8	1.2	2.3

Data Source: Calculated based on the 2023 edition of the China Statistical Yearbook. The range is calculated as the difference between the maximum and minimum values among 31 provinces (autonomous regions and municipalities directly under the central government)

Source: Luo, W. (2023). Research on the Optimization Path for Food Consumption Structure of Chinese Resident. Price: Theory & Practice, (12), 47–51 edible oils, and sugar. From 2013 to 2022, urban residents reduced their consumption of edible oils and sugar by 1.5 kg and 0.3 kg, respectively, whereas rural residents increased their intake of these two items by 0.5 kg and 0.3 kg. In 2022, rural residents consumed 1.4 kg more edible oil and 0.5 kg more sugar than their urban counterparts.

Moreover, dietary imbalances are particularly prominent in the western regions of China. On one hand, the proportion of grain consumption in total food consumption is generally high, while the share of animal-sourced foods is relatively low. In 2022, eight regions—Tibet, Gansu, Qinghai, Shaanxi, Guizhou, Yunnan, Inner Mongolia, and Jilin—reported grain consumption accounting for over 38% of total food intake, seven of which are located in western China. At the same time, regions ranking lowest in the proportion of animal-sourced food consumption are also predominantly located in the west. In Shaanxi, Gansu, Ningxia, and Tibet, meat consumption accounted for less than 17% of total food consumption, placing them at the bottom four nationwide.

On the other hand, the meat consumption structure in western regions is heavily skewed toward red meat, while the intake of aquatic products and poultry remains insufficient. In 2022, the red meat consumption in Tibet, Inner Mongolia, Qinghai, Chongqing, Guizhou, Yunnan, and Sichuan exceeded that of aquatic products and poultry by 36.5 kg, 25.4 kg, 23.8 kg, 23.5 kg, 23.4 kg, 22.9 kg, and 21.5 kg, respectively; in all these cases, the consumption of aquatic products and poultry was less than 60% of red meat consumption. By contrast, in eastern coastal regions such as Jiangsu, Fujian, Shanghai, Zhejiang, Guangdong, and Hainan, the consumption of aquatic products and poultry exceeded that of red meat by 1.3 kg, 3.2 kg, 4.0 kg, 4.8 kg, 5.9 kg, and 20.8 kg, respectively. Although red meat is an important source of iron and protein, it is also high in fat content, and excessive intake is associated with an increased risk of chronic diseases such as hypertension and hyperlipidemia. Therefore, it is crucial to appropriately limit red meat consumption and promote the intake of aquatic products and poultry to achieve a more balanced and health-oriented dietary structure.

3. **Supply-side: A Heavy Burden in Ensuring a Diversified Food Supply**

First, there exists a mismatch between production structure and consumption demand. In recent years, the food consumption structure of Chinese residents has undergone significant changes. The consumption of staple grains has gradually declined, while the demand for high-protein and nutrient-rich foods such as meat, eggs, dairy, fruits, and vegetables has risen markedly. Data show that between 2013 and 2022, per capita grain consumption declined from 148.7 kg to 136.8 kg, while the demand for meat, fruits, and vegetables—key sources of protein and vitamins—continued to grow. This shift has posed challenges to the traditional agricultural production structure, as the existing agricultural production system struggles to accommodate the rising demand for diverse and high-quality food, thereby exacerbating the structural imbalance between supply and demand in agricultural products.

Second, resource constraints coexist with ecological pressures. Arable land, as the foundation of agricultural production, faces increasingly severe challenges. In recent years, China's total arable land area has steadily declined, with notable trends of "non-agriculturalization" and "non-grainization," and a deterioration in overall land quality. Meanwhile, the Third Plenary Session of the Central Committee emphasized the need for a benefit-compensation mechanism for major grain-producing areas. This implies that key grain-producing regions, while safeguarding grain output, may also be burdened with ecological, environmental, and economic pressures. Thus, achieving a balance between food security and diversified food supply within the constraints of limited arable land has become a critical issue.

Third, dependence on international agricultural markets has intensified. China's agricultural import structure is relatively concentrated, with a high degree of dependence on a few countries, particularly for feed crops such as soybeans and corn, as well as meat products. Geopolitical instabilities—such as the China-U.S. trade conflict and the Russia-Ukraine war—have heightened uncertainties in global agricultural markets. The Third Plenary Session proposed integrating both domestic and international markets and improving long-term mechanisms for food conservation and efficiency, further highlighting the imperative of diversifying import sources and ensuring supply chain security amid an increasingly fragile global agricultural supply chain.

Fourth, the coordination between production and marketing, as well as supply chain efficiency, remains low. For example, vegetables, one of the core components of the traditional Chinese diet, are highly susceptible to climate and natural disasters, leading to frequent seasonal supply-demand mismatches. Extreme weather events—such as cold waves, heavy rainfall, and droughts—often cause sharp declines in output in major production areas, resulting in regional supply shortages and price spikes. Furthermore, the disconnect between vegetable production and marketing is pronounced. In large and medium-sized cities, demand for vegetables is rigidly increasing, but local production capacity is inadequate, leading to a heavy reliance on interprovincial transportation. Poor coordination between production and sales has led to frequent occurrences of "difficulty selling at the farm, high prices in the market." The fragmentation of smallholder production is poorly aligned with the demands of a scaled-up market, resulting in significant mismatches in supply-demand information. For instance, during the vegetable surplus crisis in Shouguang, Shandong in 2024, the farm-gate price of Chinese cabbage dropped to 0.2 yuan per jin, while the retail price in Shanghai reached 1.8 yuan per jin—a ninefold difference. Additionally, due to the underdeveloped infrastructure for cold chain logistics, vegetable loss rates in China's distribution chain reach as high as 25%, significantly higher than the 5% average in developed countries. Long-distance transportation not only increases loss rates but also raises prices in major urban consumption centers. For example, more than 70% of vegetables in the Beijing market are sourced from other provinces, with transportation costs accounting for over 30% of the retail price.

1.1.4 Quality Dimension of China's Agri-Food System: Green and Sustainable Development

1.1.4.1 The Evolution of Green and Sustainable Development in China's Agri-Food System Since the Reform and Opening-Up

1. **Stage 1 (1978–1990): Extensive growth phase driven by yield enhancement**

   In the early period of reform and opening-up, China implemented the household contract responsibility system, which decentralized land management rights to individual households. This institutional breakthrough propelled the total agricultural output value from RMB 139.7 billion in 1978 to RMB 766.2 billion in 1990. Grain output increased from 300 million tons to 446 million tons, effectively resolving the long-standing problem of food shortages. However, this phase was characterized by a typical "high input–high output" model: from 1980 to 1990, chemical fertilizer application rose from 12.69 million tons to 25.9 million tons, with an average annual growth rate of 8.4%; pesticide use increased from 530,000 tons to 730,000 tons; plastic film coverage surpassed 33.3 million hectares.

   The extensive growth model led to the initial emergence of non-point source pollution in agriculture. According to environmental monitoring data, by the late 1980s, agricultural sources accounted for 38% of total nitrogen emissions in the Taihu Lake Basin, and the nitrogen loss rate from farmland in the middle and lower reaches of the Yangtze River exceeded 20%. Nationwide, 100 million hectares of arable land had already been polluted by industrial "three wastes." However, environmental governance at this time remained limited to end-of-pipe treatment, and the ecological costs of agricultural production systems were not yet incorporated into policy considerations.
2. **Stage 2 (1990–2000): Construction of the green food system and initial exploration of low-carbon pathways, with steady growth in greenhouse gas emissions**

   In 1990, China's agricultural development reached a significant milestone with the Ministry of Agriculture officially launching the Green Food Initiative. This marked not only the beginning of the greening of China's agri-food system, but also the institutionalization of its green development. The initiative laid a solid foundation for sustainable agriculture and guided production towards more environmentally friendly and health-conscious practices. In 1991, the State Council issued the "Decision on Developing High-Yield, High-Quality, and Efficient Agriculture," which was the first national document to mention "green food." In 1992, the China Green Food Development Center was officially established, further improving the management and certification system of green food. The Center created a dual-grade system for green food—AA-grade (organic) and A-grade—providing clear standards for production and certification, enhancing the credibility and quality of green food, and fostering a healthy market. AA-grade food prohibits the use of synthetic pesticides, fertilizers, and growth regulators, whereas A-grade permits limited use of designated synthetic substances. This classification accommodated diverse consumer preferences and facilitated the diversification of the green food industry.

During this period, China's agri-food system made notable progress in greening, and the green food industry began to expand. Nevertheless, agricultural production was still in a phase of rapid growth, with rising chemical inputs and expanding scale, leading to steady increases in greenhouse gas (GHG) emissions. Despite these trends, the foundational work in green food systems and low-carbon exploration during this period laid a strong groundwork for subsequent green and low-carbon transitions.

3. **Stage 3 (2001–2012): Emergence of ecological agriculture and sustainable development concepts, with rapid growth in greenhouse gas emissions**

   In 2001, China's accession to the World Trade Organization (WTO) marked a historic turning point, integrating Chinese agriculture into the global market and presenting unprecedented opportunities and challenges. After joining the WTO, China's agricultural sector had to face not only global competition but also intensifying pressures from environmental and resource constraints, including land degradation and water scarcity. These challenges drove the transition from traditional extensive agriculture toward ecological and sustainable farming. During this period, the certification systems for green and pollution-free agricultural products became increasingly robust, and market-oriented green production began to take root. The promulgation of the Renewable Energy Law in 2005 encouraged the utilization of agricultural biomass energy. In 2007, the concept of "ecological civilization" was introduced for the first time, reinforcing the importance of sustainable agricultural development and promoting an ecological and sustainability-oriented transformation of the sector. This concept provided new guidance for the development of agriculture, emphasizing environmental protection and sustainable resource use, and encouraged more coordinated interactions between agriculture and the natural environment.

   China made significant progress in ecological and sustainable agriculture during this stage, with growing public acceptance of these concepts and ongoing improvements in relevant technologies and policies. However, the rapid expansion of agricultural scale and accelerating industrialization led to a marked increase in GHG emissions. These increases were largely driven by expanded production, greater use of chemical inputs such as fertilizers and pesticides, and the rapid mechanization of agriculture.

4. **Stage 4 (2013–present): Green and low-carbon development as a national strategy, with a marked deceleration in greenhouse gas emissions**

   Since 2013, China's agri-food system has entered a new phase in which green and low-carbon development has been integrated into the national development strategy, becoming a key driver of sustainable agriculture and contributing to a significant slowdown in GHG emissions. In 2013, the Chinese government explicitly called for accelerating the construction of ecological civilization and promoting a comprehensive green transformation of economic and social development. Subsequently, a series of policy documents were issued to support the green and low-carbon transformation of the agri-food system. For instance, the 2015 "Overall Plan for the Reform of the Ecological Civilization System" emphasized advancing green agricultural development, optimizing agricultural structure, and enhancing resource protection and ecological restoration. In 2017, the State Council released the "Opinions on Innovating Systems and Mechanisms to Promote Green Agricultural Development," which clarified objectives and tasks and advocated for a new agricultural development model featuring harmonious coexistence between humans and nature.

The 2020 national commitment to carbon peaking and carbon neutrality (dual carbon goals) further pushed the agri-food system toward deep emissions reductions. The 2022 "Action Plan for Agricultural and Rural Emission Reduction and Carbon Sequestration" outlined ten key actions, including methane reduction from rice paddies and livestock manure treatment, addressing various stages of agricultural production with specific targets and measures. Soil carbon sequestration (e.g., conservation tillage) and saline-alkali land carbon sinks were also incorporated into national strategies, enhancing the carbon sequestration capacity of agricultural ecosystems and providing new pathways to achieving carbon neutrality. In addition, advances in technology—such as precision sowing, autonomous navigation, and integrated water and fertilizer management—have further improved productivity and resource efficiency, achieving synergy between increased grain output and agricultural emissions mitigation.

According to research from the Institute for Green and Low-Carbon Development (iGDP), in 2019, the agri-food system's GHG emissions in China reached 1.65 billion tons of CO_2e, accounting for 14% of the national total, down about 3 percentage points from 2013. Although the total emissions remained high due to population and consumption growth, the carbon emission intensity per unit of output declined by an average of 2.5% annually between 2013 and 2019, indicating a substantial deceleration in GHG emissions.

1.1.4.2 Current Status of Green and Sustainable Development of China's Agri-food System

1. **China's progress in green and low-carbon development has begun to show results.**

The transformation of food systems is a core agenda within the United Nations' 17 Sustainable Development Goals. In 2021, the UN Food Systems Summit called for the rebuilding of healthier, more sustainable, and more equitable food systems. The nexus between agri-food systems and global climate change mitigation has increasingly become a critical issue in global environmental governance. The relationship between agri-food systems and climate change is characterized by two main aspects: climate change-induced variations in temperature and precipitation may exacerbate instability in agricultural production, and many activities within agri-food systems themselves are sources of greenhouse gas (GHG) emissions. According to the Sixth Assessment Report of the

Intergovernmental Panel on Climate Change (IPCC), from 2010 to 2019, agricultural sector emissions, including those from land use, accounted for approximately 13% to 21% of global GHG emissions; when combined with emissions from food processing, transportation, consumption, and other stages, the entire agri-food system may contribute up to one-third of global emissions. Therefore, only through the green and low-carbon transformation of agri-food systems can agricultural production and consumption patterns be altered to ensure universal access to healthy diets while maintaining the Earth's environment within ecological safety boundaries (He et al., 2016).

China's agricultural carbon emissions peaked at 841 million tons CO_2e in 2016 and declined to 790 million tons CO_2e by 2019. Driven by energy-saving and carbon-reduction policies such as "reduced fertilizer application and pesticide use," China's agricultural carbon emissions have basically reached a peak, and green and low-carbon development in agriculture has begun to show initial achievements (Wang & Zhang, 2022).

2. **Emission Sources and Greenhouse Gas Composition in China's Agri-food System**

Numerous existing studies have systematically reviewed and analyzed greenhouse gas (GHG) emissions resulting from agri-food system activities (Crippa et al., 2021; Li et al., 2016; Poore & Nemecek, 2018; Tubiello et al., 2021). According to research on the scope of GHG emissions from agri-food systems, it was found that in 2019, China's agri-food system emitted approximately 1.65 billion tons of CO_2-equivalent, accounting for about 14% of the country′ s total GHG emissions in that year. Regarding different segments within the agri-food system, agricultural production contributed the highest emissions, comprising approximately 59% of the total agri-food system emissions, followed by food consumption and farm-to-table stages, which accounted for 22% and 19%, respectively.

According to the classification by different greenhouse gases, carbon dioxide (CO_2) accounts for 51% of the emissions in China's agri-food system, while the remaining 49% primarily originates from non-CO_2 greenhouse gases, including methane (CH_4), nitrous oxide (N_2O), and fluorinated gases (F-gases). Among these, methane emissions constitute the largest proportion, mainly deriving from rice cultivation and livestock and poultry farming during agricultural production.

Moreover, since agricultural production represents the largest emission segment within the agri-food system. In 2019, greenhouse gas emissions from agricultural production totaled approximately 970 million tons of CO_2-equivalent. The largest emission source was enteric fermentation in livestock, accounting for 24% of agricultural greenhouse gas emissions, followed by nitrogen fertilizer application and energy consumption primarily from agricultural machinery, accounting for 23% and 20%, respectively. By greenhouse gas type, methane represents the primary emission in agricultural production, contributing about half of the total emissions from this sector.

3. **China's agri-food system carbon emissions still require further control**

   Despite recent declines in carbon emissions from agricultural activities in China, the overall carbon emissions from the agri-food system continue to increase, with a significant rise in the carbon emission share from pre-production and post-production stages. The FAO database accounts for carbon emissions across the entire agri-food system, where emissions from agricultural production include four sources: crop cultivation, animal husbandry, energy use during agricultural production, and soil organic carbon emissions. Pre-production and post-production emissions encompass eight aspects: fertilizer production, pesticide production, household food consumption, food packaging, food processing, food retail, food transportation, and food waste management. With economic development, the agricultural industrial chain has been continuously extended, resulting in a growing proportion of carbon emissions from pre-production and post-production stages. Focusing solely on carbon emissions from agricultural production activities significantly underestimates the agri-food system's role in achieving China's dual carbon (carbon peak and carbon neutrality) goals (Fan & Zhang, 2024).
4. **High dependence on chemical fertilizers and low utilization rate of organic fertilizers**

   Due to declining arable land quality and soil productivity, the contribution of soil fertility to crop yield remains low, leading to a continued high dependence on chemical fertilizers in agricultural production. Since the 1980s, widespread fertilizer use has substantially increased crop yields, but farmers have exhibited a pronounced preference for chemical fertilizers over organic fertilizers. The high cost of commercial organic fertilizers and farmers' greater emphasis on immediate crop yield and economic benefits over soil fertility changes and environmental pollution reduce their willingness to apply organic fertilizers. However, long-term excessive chemical fertilizer application causes soil environmental pollution and decreases soil organic matter content, weakening soil carbon sequestration capacity. Consequently, carbon emissions rise rapidly, making the reduction of nitrous oxide (N2O) emissions from farmland particularly challenging.

1.1.4.3 Challenges in Green and Sustainable Development of China's Agri-food System

1. **Intensifying resource and environmental constraints necessitate an accurate understanding of the relationship between ensuring supply and reducing carbon emissions**

   The agri-food system in China is facing increasingly tight resource constraints, with both scarcity and degradation of water and soil resources. Medium- and low-yield farmland accounts for two-thirds of the total arable land, the effective utilization coefficient of irrigation water is only 0.53, and nearly 20% of agricultural soil is polluted. Climate change is causing shifts in major grain-producing regions, leading to mismatches between resource distribution and grain production capacity. While arable land is decreasing in the south and increasing in the north, the pattern of producing grain in the north and transporting it to the south is becoming more pronounced, indicating a spatial mismatch with resource distribution. Over the past four to five decades, both the area and intensity of drought have shown an upward trend. From 2008 to 2018, the economic losses caused by climate-related agricultural disasters in China amounted to 976 billion yuan, accounting for approximately 55% of global losses. Constrained by the national dual-carbon targets (carbon peaking and carbon neutrality), the agri-food system is under increasing pressure to reduce emissions. However, agricultural carbon emissions are considered subsistence emissions, accounting for a significantly smaller share of national emissions compared to those from energy and industrial production. Thus, a precise balance must be struck between ensuring food supply and achieving emission reductions. In 2014, China's carbon emission intensity per unit of agricultural GDP was 1.42 t CO_2/10,000 yuan, and per capita emissions were 8.93 t CO_2/person—both far lower than those in the United States—reflecting the subsistence nature of China's agricultural emissions. In 2021, the total carbon footprint of food systems related to China's three major staple crops and major livestock and poultry products reached 584 million tons CO_2e. Among these, staple crops accounted for 283 million tons CO_2e, with rice being the highest (66.4%), followed by maize (21.4%) and wheat (12.2%). The total carbon footprint of livestock and poultry production (including pork, beef, mutton, milk, eggs, and chicken) was 301 million tons CO_2e.

2. **The limited level and application of advanced agricultural technologies have undermined the development of green and low-carbon agriculture.**

   The production behavior of smallholder farmers is primarily oriented toward short-term economic returns, leading them to adopt conservative, risk-averse strategies in technology adoption. According to the FAO's "The State of Food and Agriculture 2020" report, fewer than 20% of farmers globally employ high-efficiency agricultural technologies and management practices, such as precision fertilization, drip irrigation, or intelligent machinery. This reflects a broader issue in traditional smallholder-based agricultural systems: inadequate application of advanced technologies, particularly in developing countries where farmers often lack access to modern technology and training and tend to continue using conventional farming methods. At the same time, lagging infrastructure construction has resulted in low levels of resource development and utilization, which conflicts with the goals of improving quality and efficiency in agriculture. Although public investment in small-scale farmland irrigation has increased, including the hardening of irrigation channels down to the field level, systemic issues in agricultural irrigation have yet to be resolved. More than 70% of medium- and low-yield farmland still requires improvement. Under such conditions, current agricultural production relies heavily on traditional means, resulting in inefficient resource allocation and low productivity.

3. **The mechanism for coordinated action among diverse agricultural stakeholders in promoting green and low-carbon development remains underdeveloped.**

   As the most fundamental stakeholders in agricultural production, farmers' interests are closely linked to the pathway of agricultural development. How to guide more actors—including governments, enterprises, and cooperatives—to support farmers' income growth and jointly construct sustainable mechanisms for green and low-carbon agriculture is a key concern for the formulation and improvement of agricultural policy systems. Guided by the objective of healthy and sustainable agricultural development, comprehensive agricultural restructuring, green transformation of production methods, and the integration of primary, secondary, and tertiary industries all require prioritization of farmers' interests. In practice, new agricultural business entities are expected to become the main driving force in applying advanced productive capacity to promote green and low-carbon agricultural development. In recent years, the government has issued a series of policy documents such as the "Opinions on Accelerating the Formation of a Policy System to Foster New Agricultural Business Entities," which has led to rapid growth in their number and size. As the Ministry of Agriculture and Rural Affairs said, at of the end of 2020, the number of legally registered agricultural cooperatives had reached 2.241 million. Nevertheless, the effectiveness of cooperatives remains limited, with problems such as unclear functional positioning, poor internal governance, uneven regional distribution, and weak operational capacity. The uneven performance of new agricultural entities has constrained their ability to serve and benefit farmers. Moreover, with much of the rural labor force aging and lacking education, these issues further weaken the ability of smallholder farmers to contribute to green and low-carbon development. As a result, both new agricultural entities and smallholders face heightened challenges in realizing sustainable agricultural transformation.
4. **The pursuit of high market returns has led to weak green awareness and limited adoption of green and low-carbon production practices among agricultural producers.**

   Agricultural production models oriented toward maximizing market efficiency often drive producers to prioritize short-term yield and economic returns while neglecting green production awareness and environmentally sustainable practices. On the demand side, as household income and consumption capacity continue to grow, consumer preferences are shifting toward product diversification and higher quality, which has spurred rapid growth in demand for green and premium agricultural products. This evolving market demand has had a significant influence on producers' awareness of green production. According to the China Green Food Development Report (2022), the market size for green food products in China has exceeded 400 billion yuan and is projected to grow at an annual rate of 20% over the coming years. Meanwhile, consumers' awareness and attention to green and organic foods are also rising, which has compelled producers to pay more attention to environmentally responsible practices. Nonetheless, due to various constraints, many producers still rely heavily on traditional models involving high chemical input usage. This results in a lag in industrial restructuring relative to the rapid upgrading of consumption structures. In pursuit of higher market efficiency, producers often increase their input of production materials and intensify resource use to maximize output, which runs counter to the objectives of green and low-carbon development.

1.2 Governance in China's Agri-food System Transformation

1.2.1 Governance for the Quantity Dimension: Ensuring Food Security

1.2.1.1 Evolution of China's Food Security Policies Since the Reform and Opening-up

1. **Stage of Rural Economic System Reform (1978–1984)**

   The Third Plenary Session of the 11th CPC Central Committee in 1978 marked the beginning of China's reform and opening up, injecting new vitality into agricultural development. The session initiated the fourth major adjustment in China's agricultural production relations—the household contract responsibility system (Wang et al., 2018). The pioneering implementation of the "work contracted to households (家庭大包干)" in Xiaogang Village, Fengyang County, Anhui Province, heralded the start of rural reforms. This system effectively balanced collective advantages and individual incentives, aligning production relations with the level of productive forces at the time. The reform quickly spread to provinces such as Shandong, Sichuan, Henan, and Shanxi. Farmers not only fulfilled their grain procurement quotas for the state but also retained more grain for personal use. Under the incentive of the reform, the potential of agricultural production was significantly unleashed. Between 1978 and 1984, grain output increased from 304.77 million tons to 407.31 million tons, with an average annual growth of 4.95%; cotton output rose from 2.17 million tons to 6.26 million tons, an annual growth of 19.33%; oil crops grew from 5.22 million tons to 11.91 million tons, averaging 14.74% annual growth (Wang & Zhao, 2022). The household responsibility system and "unified and decentralized management system" played a vital role in agricultural recovery and growth.

   However, the ensuing difficulty in grain sales revealed the rigidity of the state monopoly system of grain procurement and marketing. The enthusiasm of farmers for selling grain surged, compounded by the localized consumption mentality and inadequate storage capacity (Zhang Xuebing, 2007), leading to excessive grain accumulation at state purchasing stations and overstocking of reserves, which eventually halted open procurement. With market circulation restricted, unsold grain piled up in rural areas, prices dropped, and farmers suffered losses—a phenomenon referred to as "cheap grain hurts farmers (谷贱伤农)." This significantly dampened farmers' willingness to grow grain. From 1985 to 1988, grain production remained below the 1984 level, exposing the inflexibility and inefficiency of the existing grain circulation system.

2. **Stage of Market-oriented Reform Exploration (1985–1999)**

   China's No. 1 central document for 1985 proposed replacing state monopoly procurement with contractual purchasing, bringing an end to the 32-year-old system of state monopoly over grain purchases and marking the beginning of market-oriented reform in grain circulation. This reform significantly boosted farmers' enthusiasm for grain cultivation, leading to sustained growth in grain output. However, driven by market forces, grain procurement prices kept rising (Zhou et al., 2018), while the state-controlled selling prices failed to adjust accordingly, resulting in an inverted price structure. At the same time, the circulation system remained underdeveloped, giving rise to recurring problems of "difficulty in selling grain." Grain production fell into a cyclical pattern of "harvest—difficulty in sales—reduced output—readjustment—another harvest" (Huang, 1992).

   To address these challenges, China introduced a series of policy measures in the early 1990s, including a minimum grain protection price mechanism, a dedicated grain reserve system, and a grain risk fund. These initiatives laid the foundation for the current policy framework supporting grain production (Cheng & Zhu, 2012). The minimum grain protection price mechanism was the precursor to today's minimum purchase price policy; the special grain reserve system has evolved into the core of the national grain reserve regulation mechanism; and the grain risk fund became a key source of direct subsidies for grain farmers. In addition, following the 1998 Asian financial crisis, China expanded domestic investment through the issuance of treasury bonds to stimulate domestic demand and sustain economic growth. A significant portion of this investment was channeled into farmland water conservancy and ecological engineering projects, driving rapid increases in grain and agricultural investment.

   With the deepening of rural reform, the environment for grain production continued to improve. In particular, Deng Xiaoping's southern tour in 1992 and the 14th National Congress of the Communist Party of China, which set the goal of establishing a socialist market economy, marked a turning point. Rural factor mobility was gradually liberalized, the industrialization of agriculture accelerated, the grain pricing mechanism was progressively refined, and the circulation system was steadily improved. These reforms contributed to upgrading the grain industry, stabilized farmers' expectations for grain cultivation, and provided a solid foundation for the steady advancement of China's national food security strategy.

1.2.1.2 Current Landscape: Establishment of the National Food Security Policy System (2000–Present)

Since the beginning of the twenty-first century, China has abolished the agricultural tax that had been in place for over two millennia, ushering in a new era of agricultural subsidies. It has gradually established a national food security policy framework characterized by the enhancement of comprehensive production capacity, a food price support system, and a suite of direct subsidy policies.

1. **Enhancing Comprehensive Production Capacity**

   China has developed a green-oriented production support system that channels investments into key areas such as the development of high-standard farmland, pest and disease control, agricultural research and extension, disaster prevention and relief, and the conservation, restoration, and utilization of natural resources. These supportive policy measures aim to bolster the comprehensive production capacity and operational systems of the grain sector and the broader agricultural sector. They are generally not targeted at individual farmers, specific producers, or designated agricultural products, and most are classified as "Green Box" policies under the World Trade Organization (WTO) framework.

   In practice, these policies have been implemented across various phases, with notable shifts since the turn of the century. Driven by rapid economic development, enhanced fiscal capacity, and rural transformation, the support measures have evolved toward more diverse policy objectives, broader areas of concern, expanded coverage, and increasing intensity. According to WTO agricultural notifications, China's investment in agricultural infrastructure rose from RMB 81.8 billion in 2000 to RMB 348.9 billion in 2020. Investment in agricultural R&D increased from RMB 2.7 billion to RMB 11.9 billion, while expenditure on pest and disease control grew from RMB 2.3 billion to RMB 17.1 billion—indicating a marked and sustained expansion.
2. **Establishing a Grain Price Support System**

   China has built a food price support system centered on minimum purchase prices and temporary stockpiling. In 2004, while fully liberalizing the grain market, the government introduced the minimum purchase price mechanism for key grain varieties, to be activated when necessary, and issued detailed implementation plans. Since 2005, this policy has been implemented for early indica rice, mid- to late-season indica rice, and wheat in major grain-producing regions. In 2008, in response to declining international agricultural prices and to safeguard farmers' interests, temporary stockpiling policies for corn and soybeans were introduced in Northeast China and Inner Mongolia (Chen et al., 2009).

   From 2008 to 2014, the government continuously raised minimum purchase prices for rice and wheat as well as temporary stockpiling prices for corn and soybeans, while also reforming the storage mechanisms. However, these policies led to negative effects such as expanding inventories, increasing fiscal pressure, and rising import risks. In 2014, China began decoupling price formation mechanisms from subsidies and launched pilot programs for target price subsidies for soybeans and cotton. In 2016, the temporary corn stockpiling policy was replaced by producer subsidies, and similar temporary stockpiling programs were phased out.

As domestic grain supply shifted from tight to periodically oversupplied and prices moved from below international levels to above them, implementation of support policies became more challenging. Since 2016, the minimum purchase prices for early indica and japonica rice were reduced multiple times, and wheat prices were lowered for two consecutive years after 2018. Following the U.S. complaint to the WTO over China's amber box policies, the government revised the implementation mechanism for minimum purchase prices of rice and wheat by introducing total quantity controls and batch purchases. In light of changes in production costs, market demand and supply, and the development of the grain industry, the minimum purchase prices for rice and wheat entered a new upward adjustment cycle in 2020 and 2021, respectively.

3. **Establishing a Framework for Direct Grain Subsidies**

China has established a direct subsidy system that employs instruments such as agricultural support and protection subsidies, producer subsidies, subsidies for agricultural machinery purchases, and agricultural insurance premium subsidies. These are designed to guide agricultural development toward larger scale, greater intensity, and greener practices. Most of these subsidies are granted directly to farmers or grain producers based on specific eligibility criteria and standards. They may be categorized as income or production subsidies, and either coupled or decoupled from production.

Initially, four types of subsidies were implemented: direct subsidies for grain farmers, comprehensive subsidies for agricultural inputs, improved seed subsidies, and subsidies for the purchase of agricultural machinery. Total funding increased from RMB 14.57 billion in 2002 to RMB 168.05 billion in 2014. In 2015, the first three were consolidated into the Agricultural Support and Protection Subsidy, which was then scaled up nationwide in 2016. Farmland fertility protection subsidies are granted based on contracted land area and are inclusive income subsidies. Moderate-scale operation subsidies prioritize new agricultural business entities and take various forms, including interest subsidies, technical service provision, and direct funding (Xu et al., 2020).

To improve the agricultural insurance system, the central government has subsidized premiums for policy-based agricultural insurance since 2007, covering major grain crops. Over time, this coverage has expanded in both crop types and geographical areas, with enhanced protection levels. In 2018, pilot programs were launched for full-cost insurance and income insurance for grain crops, and were extended to all major grain-producing counties. As alternative measures of the reform of the temporary stockpiling system, a target price subsidy mechanism for soybeans and a producer subsidy mechanism for corn were established. At present, Northeast China and Inner Mongolia apply unified producer subsidies for corn, soybeans, and japonica rice based on actual planting areas. Additional measures include one-time grain planting subsidies, straw incorporation subsidies, and subsidies for crop rotation and fallow practices, forming a coherent, targeted, and performance-oriented subsidy system with complementary functions.

1.2.1.3 Challenges Facing China's Food Security Policy

Despite the establishment of a relatively systematic food security strategy, China's current grain production support policies[1] are now facing multiple challenges as a result of changing international dynamics and the deepening transformation of agriculture and rural areas. These challenges include pronounced market distortions, imbalances in benefit distribution, disruptions in the grain industry and supply chains, and increasing risks of non-compliance with international trade rules.

First, distorted price mechanisms have led to high costs. As the core mechanism for market regulation, any distortion in the price mechanism undermines the efficient allocation of agricultural resources. Although the minimum purchase price policy serves as a price floor, if set too high, it can weaken market signals, result in overproduction, disrupt supply and demand balance, and increase fiscal burdens. For example, from 2014 to 2017, the minimum purchase price for wheat was maintained at RMB 1.18 per jin, and a total of 98.41 million tons of wheat were procured in six major production provinces, with an annual average of 24.6 million tons. During the same period, 127 million tons of rice were purchased at the minimum price, averaging 31.83 million tons annually. Rice, in particular, faced significant price gaps between old and new stocks, which hindered sales; as of 2022, grain from the 2014–2018 inventory was still being used as animal feed. High procurement prices not only increased fiscal pressure but also triggered a chain of additional costs related to storage, interest subsidies, and distribution.

Second, input providers gained more than actual grain producers. Whether through price support or direct subsidies, the benefits of these policies are ultimately redistributed among providers of land, labor, capital, and machinery, as well as actual producers. According to estimates by the Organisation for Economic Co-operation and Development (OECD), the efficiency of price support in developed countries is only 25%, meaning that for every dollar of subsidy, only $0.25 reaches the producer, with nearly one-third captured by input suppliers and 13% by non-farming landowners (OECD, 2002). The income transfer efficiency of area-based subsidies is about 47%, with 47% accruing to landowning farmers and 45% to non-farming landowners (Dewbre, 2001). A similar issue exists in China: as subsidy levels increase, land rental prices rise in parallel, gradually eroding producers' gains. By the end of 2021, 557 million mu of contracted rural land had been transferred, with 324 million mu used for grain cultivation. Between 2016 and 2021, the

[1] Grain production support policies are broadly defined to include not only support and protection for grain producers but also investments in the construction of comprehensive grain production capacity, production systems, business models, and industrial frameworks (such as farmland irrigation and supporting infrastructure, grain technology innovation systems, agricultural extension, and service systems)

land cost per mu for japonica rice increased from RMB 382 to RMB 425 (an 11% increase), while corn and soybean costs rose by 24% and 33% respectively. Excessive land prices and rental costs severely eroded the income and profits of grain producers, making their per-mu earnings significantly lower than the rental income received by land transferors. As a result, a group of "non-farming landlords (不在地主)" has emerged—individuals who own contracted farmland but do not engage in agricultural operations and instead profit from land-related asset income (Zhu & Cheng, 2023).

Third, regional circulation is hindered, and industrial operations are constrained. The separation between production and consumption regions is a key feature of China's grain distribution system. However, imbalanced regional price differences can hinder market-based circulation. Take Heilongjiang Province as an example: although it is a major grain producer, its low population density and weak processing capacity necessitate large volumes of outbound grain shipments. Located in China's northern frontier, the long transport distance to southern markets makes its grain less competitive in terms of logistics costs compared to grain from the Huang-Huai-Hai area or neighboring provinces like Liaoning and Jilin. In remote areas of Heilongjiang, where accumulated temperature is inadequate and quality premiums are difficult to obtain, post-harvest grain sales rely heavily on the minimum purchase price. However, this mechanism leads to price equalization across regions, making it difficult for grain from remote areas to reach logistics hubs or major consumption areas through market-based means. Moreover, the minimum purchase price has adversely affected the operations of grain processing enterprises. Between 2012 and 2021, due to successive increases in the minimum purchase price and sustained market intervention, the domestic selling prices of wheat and rice were 25% and 30% higher than their respective import prices, exacerbating the phenomena of "strong grain but weak rice (稻强米弱)" and "strong wheat but weak flour (麦强粉弱)," and placing heavy pressure on grain processing enterprises.

Fourth, compliance with trade rules faces mounting challenges. Under the WTO framework, support measures are categorized as restricted "Amber Box" policies and non-restricted "Green Box" and "Blue Box" policies. Since 2004, China has implemented minimum purchase price policies, temporary stockpiling, improved seed subsidies, comprehensive agricultural input subsidies, and agricultural insurance premium subsidies, among others. As support intensity increased, policy compliance issues have become more prominent. In 2016, the United States filed a complaint with the WTO Dispute Settlement Mechanism regarding China's Amber Box support for rice, wheat, and corn—a case that attracted attention from 27 members including the European Union and Australia (Wang et al., 2020). In 2019, a WTO panel ruled that China had exceeded its domestic support limits, determining that the production volume of policy implementation areas—rather than actual procurement volume—should be used as the basis for calculation. For example, in 2021, the wheat and rice production volumes of regions implementing the policies accounted for 82% and 81% of national totals, while their actual procurement shares were only 15.7% (data of rice in 2015) and 37% (data of wheat in 2008), respectively. This ruling pushed the minimum purchase price policy to the brink of non-compliance. Although China has since adopted a quota-based and phased procurement mechanism, the Amber Box nature of the policy remains contentious. Moreover, newly implemented mechanisms, such as soybean price subsidies, may also conflict with WTO rules, potentially giving rise to new trade frictions.

1.2.2 Governance for the Quality Dimension: Safeguarding Food Safety

1.2.2.1 Evolution of China's Food Safety Policies Since the Reform and Opening-up

1. **Transitional Stage (1979–1993)**

   In the early years of reform and opening-up, China's institutional framework and policy instruments for food hygiene management remained transitional in nature. **First, in terms of laws and institutional arrangements,** the Ministry of Health officially promulgated the *Regulations of the People's Republic of China on the Management of Food Hygiene* in 1979, based on trial regulations issued in 1965. However, the scope of these regulations was limited to state-owned and collectively owned enterprises. Punitive provisions in these regulations were vague, enforcement powers were weak, and regulatory action mainly relied on persuasion and public education. Local government interference was widespread, while supervisory departments suffered from unclear responsibilities and weak enforcement capabilities. Overall, the regulatory framework lagged behind the pace of industrial development. As a result, food hygiene issues and poisoning incidents increased in frequency in China.

   In 1982, the Standing Committee of the Fifth National People's Congress adopted the *Food Hygiene Law of the People's Republic of China (for Trial Implementation)*—China's first law governing food hygiene. The law specified hygiene requirements for food and related products, licensing procedures, supervision mechanisms, health examinations for personnel, and legal liabilities. It marked the initial establishment of a modern legal framework for food hygiene in China, designating the health administrative authorities as the main supervisory body and making the food hygiene license a prerequisite for business registration. From 1982 to 1994, the compliance rate for food hygiene increased from 61.5% to 82.3%.

   However, this law still retained clear transitional characteristics. It did not fully abolish the supervisory powers of line ministries. For example, departments overseeing food enterprises remained responsible for food hygiene management within their own systems. Urban and rural markets, livestock and poultry quarantine, and export food continued to fall under the supervision of the commerce and industry, agriculture, and foreign trade authorities. Hygiene work within the railway, transportation, and industrial and mining systems was managed by their respective sectors. The Ministry of Commerce continued to oversee food marketing and safety. The State Bureau of Technical Supervision, newly established in 1988, was responsible for the formulation and enforcement of food standards. Although the health department was nominally granted a leading role, the system of combining government and enterprise functions remained in place. Each competent department retained a certain degree of authority, and health administrative agencies only held professional advisory roles within key units. At the local level, six departments—including commerce and industry, metrology, environmental protection, sanitation, animal husbandry, and public health—jointly shared responsibility for food quality supervision.

Second, in terms of food hygiene management tools, with the evolution of the industry base and regulatory system, traditional administrative directives and persuasive approaches became less effective, calling for innovations in food hygiene policy instruments. The government began to adopt legal standards, market-based incentives and penalties, and judicial mechanisms to improve regulatory efficiency. In 1981, the Ministry of Health established the Technical Subcommittee on Food Hygiene Standards and commissioned the Institute of Hygiene under the Chinese Academy of Medical Sciences to formulate a five-year plan for standard development. More than 80 standards were issued, covering seasonings, food additives, packaging materials, and testing methods for microbial and physicochemical indicators. In 1984, China officially joined the Codex Alimentarius Commission and began actively participating in the development of international standards.

2. **Stage of External Supervision (1994–2002)**

During this period, China's food hygiene management advanced toward a more legalized and institutionalized model.

First, in October 1995, the Standing Committee of the Eighth National People's Congress adopted the *Food Hygiene Law of the People's Republic of China*. Building on the earlier trial version, the revised law introduced several important improvements, including the regulation of health foods, more detailed administrative penalties, and strengthened supervision of street food and imported products.

The law reaffirmed the establishment of a national food hygiene supervision system and officially abolished the food hygiene management powers formerly exercised by industry-specific departments under the enterprise-administration integration system. It designated the health administrative department as the principal enforcement authority. In parallel, other departments under the State Council were tasked with food hygiene management within the scope of their respective mandates. For instance, agricultural authorities oversaw primary production; transport and railway departments, as well as the military system, maintained internal hygiene supervisory agencies for their own sectors. Through the establishment of authoritative external food hygiene enforcement and oversight agencies, the government replaced intra-sector food hygiene regulation in most areas, incorporating both regulators and regulated entities into a unified legal framework. Despite some variation in institutional design and division of responsibilities, regulatory authority was essentially transferred to third-party supervisory agencies operating under market economy conditions, thereby establishing a fully externalized food hygiene oversight regime.

In terms of regulatory tools, in line with the socialist market economy framework, traditional administrative interventions were largely phased out. The health authorities continued to strengthen national legislation, technical standards, and administrative enforcement, while also exploring the use of emerging instruments such as quality certification, risk monitoring, and public education (Hu, 2018). **First, more than 90 supporting regulations were issued under the *Food Hygiene Law***, covering areas such as food, raw materials, packaging materials, containers, and penalties for violations. Local governments also formulated and implemented their own supplementary regulations, resulting in a multi-tiered food hygiene regulatory system tailored to China's national conditions. **Second, the standardization system entered a new phase of legal codification.** By the end of 1998, China had issued 236 national food hygiene standards, 227 testing method standards, and 18 industry-specific standards, forming a comprehensive system comprising basic standards, product standards, behavioral standards, and testing method standards. Third, drawing on international experience and adapting it to domestic conditions, **China introduced the Food Safety Action Plan in 2003**. This included the implementation of quantitative and tiered supervision systems, the adoption of Good Manufacturing Practices (GMP) and Hazard Analysis and Critical Control Point (HACCP) management systems, the establishment of surveillance networks for food contaminants and foodborne diseases, and the promotion of risk assessment practices. **Fourth, extensive efforts were made to enhance public awareness and education.** Starting in 1996, China held the "National Food Hygiene Law Awareness Week" campaign for 11 consecutive years. Authorities regularly released food hygiene and food poisoning data to the public and encouraged public participation in social supervision of food hygiene.

The implementation of the *Food Hygiene Law*, along with the new regulatory concepts and institutional arrangements, significantly contributed to the sustained, rapid, and healthy development of China's food industry. The level of food hygiene and safety improved markedly. According to data from successive editions of the *China Health Yearbook* and the *China Health Statistics Yearbook*, the national food hygiene compliance rate reached 90.13% in 2004—up 7 percentage points from 83.1% in 1995, and 29 percentage points from 61.5% in 1982. Meanwhile, the number of nationwide food poisoning outbreaks declined from 1861 in 1991 to 522 in 1997. The number of people affected dropped from 47,367 in 1990 to 13,567 in 1997, and the number of deaths fell from 338 to 132 (see Fig. 1.3).

3. **Stage of Segmented and Multi-agency Regulation (2003–2011)**

During this period, China carried out a series of institutional reforms in food safety supervision. Horizontally, a multi-sector, segmented regulatory system was established; vertically, the distribution of regulatory authority between

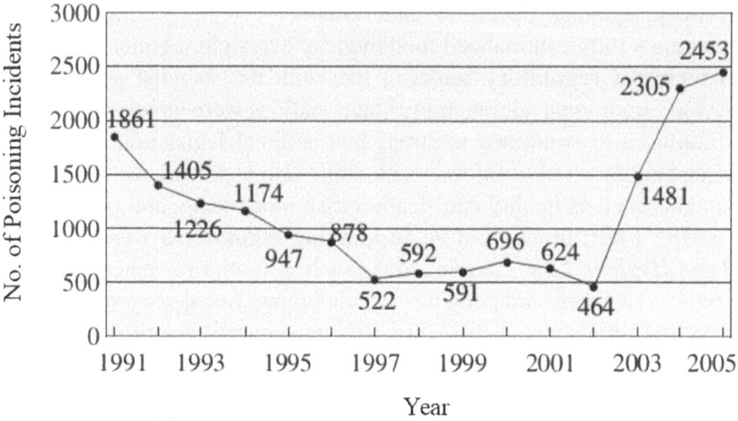

(a) Number of Reported Food Poisoning Cases

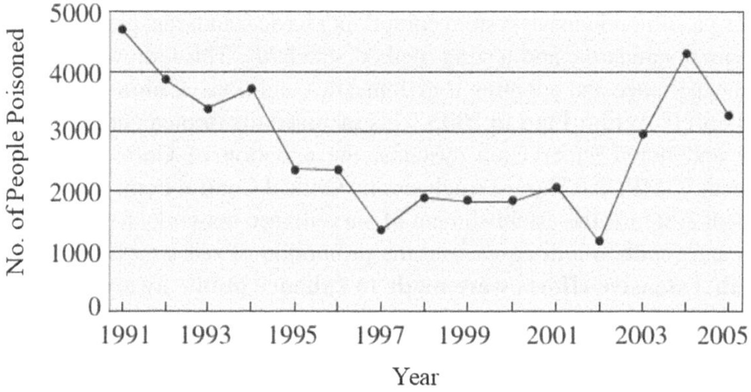

(b) Statistics on the Number of People Affected by Food Poisoning

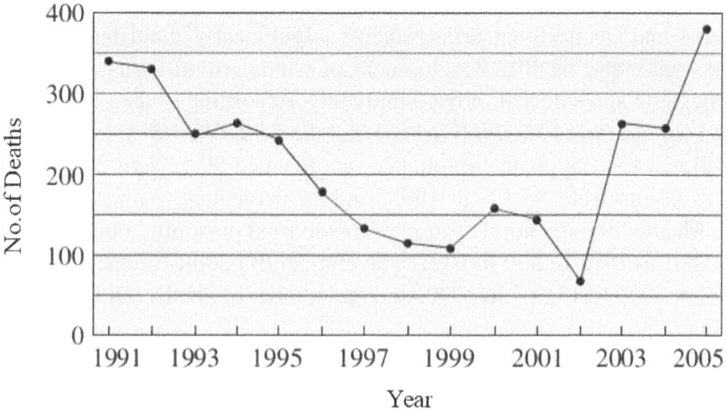

(c) Statistics on Deaths Caused by Food Poisoning

Fig. 1.3 Statistics on Food Poisoning in China (1991–2005). (**a**) Number of Reported Food Poisoning Cases. (**b**) Statistics on the Number of People Affected by Food Poisoning. (**c**) Statistics on Deaths Caused by Food Poisoning. Source: Liu, P. (2010). Chinese Food Safety Regulation: An Empirical Study on Regime Change and Performance Evaluation [J]. Journal of Public Management, 7(02): 63–78 + 125–126. Note: Data sourced from China Health Statistical Yearbook (1992–2006) central and local governments was adjusted. Moreover, the country promulgated its first *Food Safety Law* in response to frequent food safety incidents.[2]

First, in terms of the horizontal setup of regulatory institutions and delineation of responsibilities, the State Food and Drug Administration (SFDA) was established in 2003 to assume overall responsibility for food safety supervision and coordination, though it did not directly engage in law enforcement. In 2004, the *Decision of the State Council on Further Strengthening Food Safety* proposed for the first time the principle of "one regulatory body for one stage of the food chain," clarifying the division of responsibilities: agricultural departments were in charge of primary agricultural production; quality inspection departments, of food processing; industrial and commercial departments, of food circulation; health departments, of food consumption sectors such as catering and canteens; and the SFDA, of overall coordination and investigation of major incidents. This signaled a shift from a health department–dominated regulatory model to one characterized by segmented oversight by multiple departments.

However, since the SFDA was a vice-ministerial-level agency, it lacked sufficient authority and resources to coordinate cross-sector efforts, and loopholes remained in the segmented system. In 2008, a round of institutional reforms elevated the SFDA to a national bureau managed by the Ministry of Health (MOH). Their food safety duties were swapped: the MOH assumed responsibility for overall coordination, the investigation and response to major incidents, formulation of safety standards, risk monitoring, assessment and early warning, the establishment of inspection qualifications and procedures, and the unified release of major information; meanwhile, the SFDA oversaw the catering sector and health-care food regulation. The responsibilities of agriculture, quality inspection, and industrial and commercial departments remained unchanged (see Fig. 1.4 for institutional setup). Simultaneously, the State Council established the Food Safety Commission, responsible for analyzing the food safety situation, guiding efforts across sectors, and proposing major policy measures. Although interdepartmental coordination remained a challenge in practice (Li, Qi, and Liu 2010), this structure nonetheless advanced collaborative governance.

Second, in terms of the vertical allocation of regulatory authority,[3] the food safety regulatory system mainly involved three tiers of local government—provincial, municipal, and county levels—each reporting upward. The hierarchical relationship among regulatory departments is illustrated in Fig. 1.5. Since 2004, the central government has gradually strengthened the accountability of local governments for food safety in their jurisdictions. In September 2004, the State Council issued *the Decision on Further Strengthening Food Safety Work*,

[2] For example, the "inferior milk powder incident" in Fuyang, Anhui in 2003 exposed problems such as overlapping enforcement due to department-specific legislation, lack of accountability, and inadequacies in testing capacity and institutional systems.

[3] The vertical allocation of regulatory authority is referred to the allocation of regulatory power between different levels of government, such as central and local authorities.

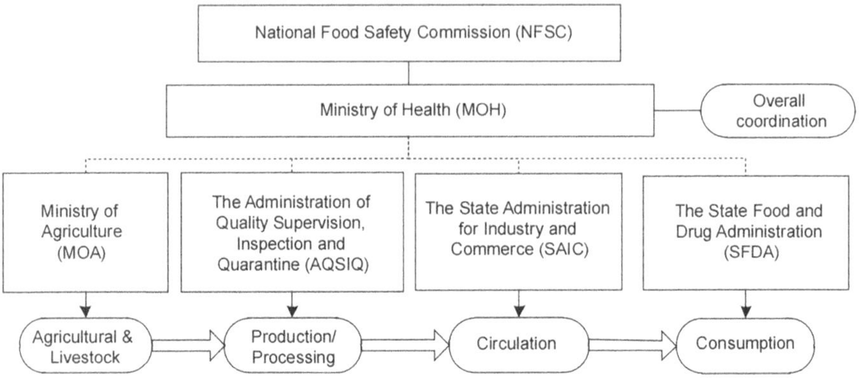

Fig. 1.4 Government authorities involved in food safety supervision and management before March, 2013 in China. Adapted from Jia and Jukes (2013). Chen, K., Wang, X. X., & Song, H. Y. (2015). Food safety regulatory systems in Europe and China: A study of how co-regulation can improve regulatory effectiveness. Journal of Integrative Agriculture, 14(11), 2203–2217

which clearly stipulated that local governments at all levels assume overall responsibility for food safety within their respective administrative regions. They were required to lead and coordinate supervision and rectification efforts and to establish sound mechanisms for coordination. To implement this territorial responsibility, in October 2008 the State Council issued *the Notice on Adjusting the Food and Drug Regulatory System Below the Provincial Level*, changing the vertical management model of SFDA branches below the provincial level to a system of local government oversight. These branches would henceforth be managed by local governments, while receiving professional guidance and supervision from higher-level supervisory bodies and health departments. Personnel management authority, previously held by provincial governments, was transferred to municipal and county levels. Local governments thus assumed responsibility for managing staffing, budgeting, and resource allocation for their local food and drug regulatory agencies. In late 2011, the State Council General Office issued *the Notice on Adjusting the Administrative System of Industry and Commerce and Quality Supervision Below the Provincial Level and Strengthening Food Safety Regulation*, which explicitly abolished vertical management systems for industrial and commercial, and quality supervision departments below the provincial level, replacing them with a decentralized system managed by local governments (Liu & Zhang, 2015).

Third, *the Food Safety Law* was promulgated. With the establishment of the segmented regulatory framework, the revision of *the Food Hygiene Law* was placed on the agenda in September 2004. To avoid departmental interference, the revision process was led by the Legislative Affairs Office of the State Council, which sought broad input from departments, experts, industry associations, enterprises, and international organizations. Meanwhile, the legislative process for *the Law on Quality and Safety of Agricultural Products* accelerated. It was

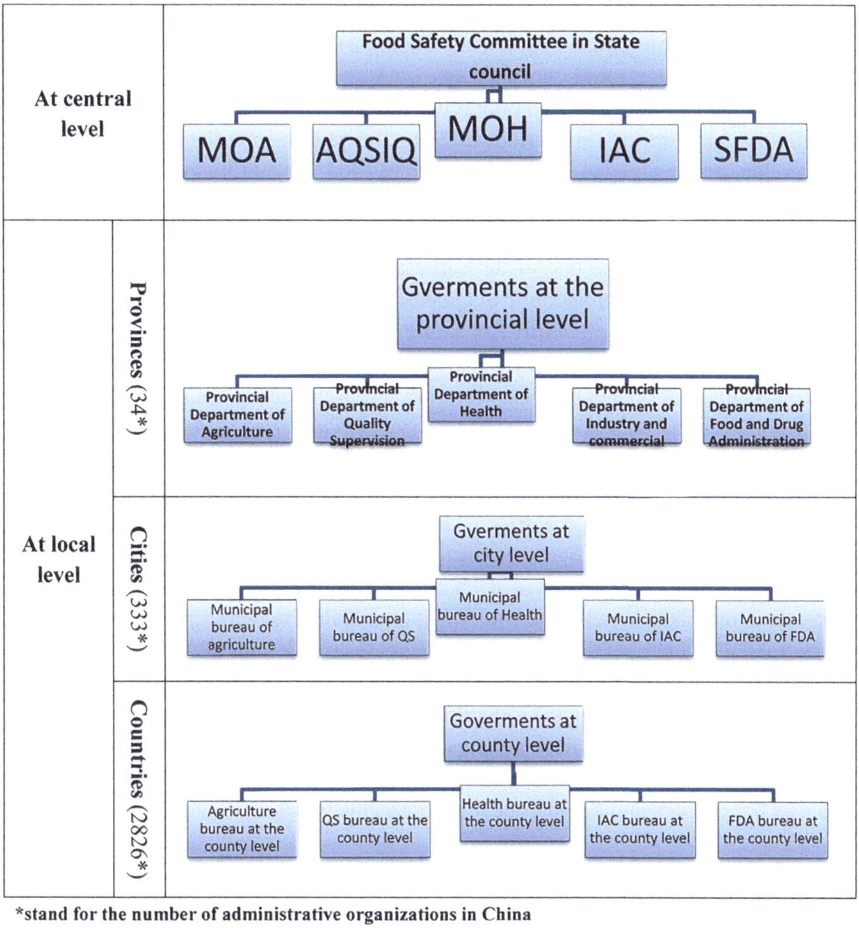

Fig. 1.5 The supervision and administration departments at all levels. Source: Jia, C., & Jukes, D. (2013). The national food safety control system of China–a systematic review. Food control, 32(1), 236–245

passed in April 2006 and came into effect on November 1 of that year. However, *the Food Hygiene Law* only regulated hygiene management along the food industry chain. It did not cover primary agricultural production, nor did it include modern regulatory mechanisms such as risk monitoring, product recalls, and additive regulation. As a result, there was a growing call from various sectors for a higher-level Food Safety Law. A draft of *the Food Safety Law* was submitted to the State Council Executive Meeting in 2006, and to the Standing Committee of the National People's Congress in 2007. After the 2008 "melamine milk powder incident" triggered widespread public concern, the lawmaking process accelerated. On February 28, 2009, *the Food Safety Law* was officially adopted, repealing the *Food Hygiene Law*. This marked a fundamental shift from hygiene-focused regulation to a food safety–centered approach (Jia et al., 2013), enhancing standards, strengthening penalties, and advancing a system that combined segmented oversight with integrated coordination.

In addition, China launched pilot programs for agricultural product quality traceability systems during this period. In 2004, the SFDA, in collaboration with eight other departments, began trial construction of food traceability systems in the meat industry. The Ministry of Agriculture launched a pilot program for the "traceability system for vegetables supplied to Beijing," involving standardized packaging and labeling, which became one of the earliest traceability projects in the country. In 2005, the General Administration of Quality Supervision, Inspection and Quarantine (AQSIQ) issued *the Traceability Procedures for Export Aquatic Products* to address EU trade barriers and also drafted *the Guidelines for Beef Product Traceability* based on international experience. From that year onward, pilot initiatives for food traceability steadily expanded. *The Law on Quality and Safety of Agricultural Products* (2006) established clear standards for agricultural product safety and mandated the development of traceability collaboration mechanisms between agricultural and market regulation departments. In 2010, *the National Meat and Vegetable Circulation Traceability System Construction Standards* were implemented in 10 major cities including Shanghai, Dalian, and Nanjing, laying the foundation for a traceable distribution network. Building a traceability system for agricultural product circulation enabled the government to create an accountability mechanism from the distribution stage, strengthening the awareness and responsibility of food business operators, encouraging production in accordance with safety standards, and enhancing overall food safety assurance. Nationwide pilot projects also facilitated interconnection of regional information systems, improving food safety levels across the country and helping local governments fulfill their responsibilities.

1.2.2.2 Current Landscape: Stage of Unified and Strengthened Regulation (2012–Present)

Since the 18th National Congress of the CPC, food safety regulation in China has entered a new phase of development, becoming an integral part of modernization of China's governance system and capacity.

First, a unified and authoritative regulatory body was established. Horizontally, regulatory functions were consolidated across departments. In March 2013, the "*Plan for Institutional Reform and Transformation of Government Functions of the State Council*" was adopted, aiming to integrate responsibilities, streamline resources, and enhance supervision. Specifically, food safety regulatory functions from the General Administration of Quality Supervision, Inspection and Quarantine (AQSIQ), the State Food and Drug Administration (SFDA), and the State Administration for Industry and Commerce (SAIC) were merged, covering production, circulation, and consumption, to establish the China Food and Drug Administration (CFDA) (Fig. 1.6). This institutional reform marked a shift from segmented, multi-agency supervision to a more centralized model dominated by a single regulatory authority. Meanwhile, the respective responsibilities of the agricultural and food and drug regulatory departments

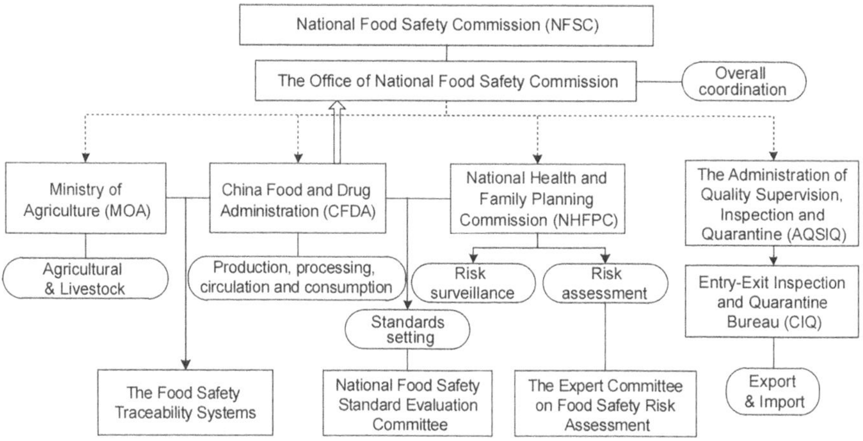

Fig. 1.6 Government authorities involved in food safety supervision and management after March, 2013 (before 2018) in China. Source: Chen, K., Wang, X. X., & Song, H. Y. (2015). Food safety regulatory systems in Europe and China: A study of how co-regulation can improve regulatory effectiveness. Journal of Integrative Agriculture, 14(11), 2203–2217

regarding edible agricultural products were clarified. In 2018, further institutional restructuring integrated the functions of the former SAIC, AQSIQ, and CFDA into the State Administration for Market Regulation (SAMR), consolidating price supervision, anti-monopoly enforcement, and food safety oversight under one body.

Vertically, the allocation of regulatory authority was also refined. The State Council's 2013 "Guiding Opinions on Reforming and Improving the Local Food and Drug Regulatory System" explicitly required that local governments at all levels assume overall responsibility for food and drug safety in their jurisdictions. Leadership of local food and drug regulatory agencies was to be managed by the corresponding level of Party committee, and the appointment and dismissal of their principal officials must be approved by higher-level departments. The long-delayed reform of administrative systems below the provincial level was also launched, with inspection teams and testing institutions transferred to food and drug departments and dispatched agencies established in townships or regions. However, issues such as overstaffing and insufficient funding remained prominent. In response to reform directives, two major institutional models emerged in 2013: one involved merging AIC, AQSIQ, and FDA functions into newly established market regulation bureaus; the other model, adopted by regions such as Inner Mongolia, Hubei, and Shenzhen, retained independent food and drug regulatory authorities. In the 2018 reform, most regions established market regulation administrations, which remain the primary model for unified food safety supervision today.

Second, the Food Safety Law was revised. As economic and social development accelerated, new food safety risks emerged, such as the expired meat incident involving Shanghai Husi Food and the exposure of unlicensed "black workshops" on the Ele.me delivery platform. These posed fresh challenges to regulatory authorities. To address these new issues and adapt to the updated regulatory structure, the revised Food Safety Law was adopted at the 14th session of the Standing Committee of the 12th National People's Congress on April 24, 2015, increasing the number of articles from 104 to 154 and doubling the text to nearly 30,000 characters. Hailed as "the strictest Food Safety Law in history," it came into effect on October 1 of the same year. The new law emphasized prevention, risk management, whole-process control, and social co-governance, and established a rigorous and science-based supervision system. It introduced mechanisms to enhance information disclosure, coordination between administrative and criminal enforcement, risk communication, and punitive damages. It also refined co-governance and market incentives, introducing social oversight tools such as exemplary demonstration, contribution-based rewards, and public education. Moreover, it laid the groundwork for the future development of a professional regulatory workforce, regional coordination of regulatory resources, and scientific delineation of supervisory responsibilities. The law was subsequently amended in 2018 and 2021.

Third, regulatory tools were improved to address the problem of asymmetric information in food safety. The Chinese government focused on strengthening the food sampling inspection and information disclosure system, as well as the food traceability system:

- **Food Sampling Inspection and Information Disclosure System**
- Sampling inspection is a foundational element of food safety supervision and risk monitoring. After its establishment, the CFDA drew upon the experience of its predecessor agencies to formulate the *Administrative Measures for Food Safety Sampling Inspection*. Issued by the CFDA in 2014 and implemented in February 2015, the measures consist of seven chapters and 53 articles, defining the principles, planning, procedures, inspection methods, handling of results, and legal responsibilities. The market regulation authorities are responsible for implementing the sampling inspection, while the State Administration for Market Regulation oversees national inspections and guides local efforts.
- In 2019, the measures were revised to further clarify the scope and classification of food safety sampling inspection. Based on objectives and methodology, inspections were categorized into routine supervision sampling, risk monitoring, and evaluative sampling. Routine supervision involves inspections carried out under legal procedures and food safety standards to identify potential risks. Risk monitoring focuses on detecting hazardous elements for which no existing food safety standard exists. Evaluative sampling assesses the general safety of food products on the market. The revision also enhanced sampling protocols, implemented the the new regulatory mechanism featuring the random selection of both inspectors and inspection targets, and standardized procedures for both on-site and online sampling. Notably, the retesting process was strengthened by clarifying procedures and timelines, improving operational efficiency. Dispute resolution procedures were optimized to protect producers' and traders' rights, and the handling of non-compliance cases was expedited. The revision also enforced stricter standards for sampling management, laboratory qualifications, and data accuracy. Legal responsibilities were reinforced for non-compliance, including

increased penalties, credit-based disciplinary measures, and greater accountability for inspection institutions.

- Since its implementation, the food safety sampling and disclosure system has been significantly expanded. According to official data from SAMR, by 2020, the number of food safety inspection samples reached 6.3874 million, which was 37.07 times, 4.26 times, 2.7 times, 1.9 times, and 1.35 times the number of samples tested in 2015 through 2019, respectively. The frequency of sampling inspections reached 4.52 batches per 1000 people, significantly exceeding the U.S. standard of inspecting high-risk food enterprises once every 3 years (Li & Liu, 2014) (Fig. 1.7).
- **Agricultural Product and Food Traceability System**
- China began developing its agricultural product traceability system relatively early, and has formed a multi-tiered system centered on a national platform and supported by provincial-level platforms. In 2016, the Ministry of Agriculture issued guidelines to accelerate construction of the traceability system, prioritizing large-scale enterprises and specialty industries. By the end of 2018, agricultural departments in 20 provinces had established provincial platforms,

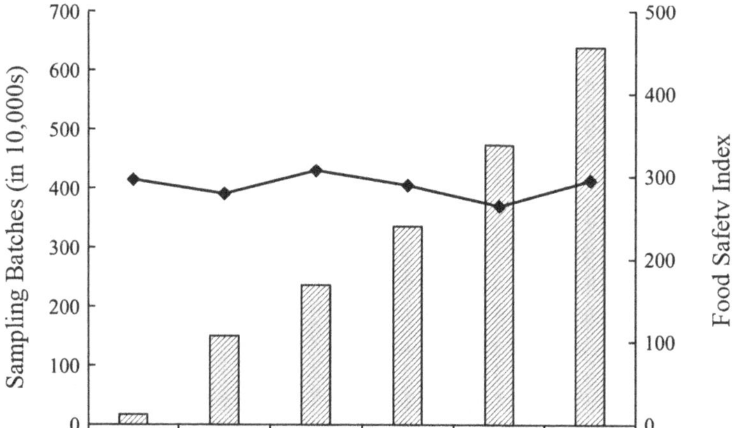

	2015	2016	2017	2018	2019	2020
Sampling Batches	17.23	149.99	236.41	335.59	473.68	638.74
Food Safety Index	296	279	307	289	264	295

Fig. 1.7 National food safety supervision sampling batches and food safety index (2015–2020). Source: Li, T., Fu, H. & Nie, W. (2021). A Study on the Evaluation of Supervision Sampling Efficiency of Food Safety in China: Based on the Perspective of Sampling Batches Distribution under the Pressure of Government Performance Evaluation. Journal of Macro-Quality Research, 9(06), 86–98. Note: The Food Safety Index is an informational index that reflects the overall food quality and safety situation of a country or region during a given period. It is calculated using the bucket effect principle and the golden ratio rule, based on a five-level scale, and integrates multiple types of food safety levels. The index ranges from 0 to 500, with higher scores indicating better food safety conditions (Li, 2017)

incorporating around 130,000 agricultural enterprises. The national system for agricultural reclamation enterprises covered approximately 540 enterprises. The Ministry of Commerce's traceability system for meat and vegetables extended to 58 cities, 15,000 enterprises, and over 300,000 vendors, with 4.2 million traceability data entries submitted daily.[4] In June 2017, the *Administrative Measures on the Traceability of Agricultural Product Quality and Safety for pilot regions* was issued, outlining basic requirements for producer management, information collection, labeling, and QR code transactions.

- The Ministry of Agriculture also launched a national traceability management information platform on a pilot basis in Shandong, Guangdong, and Sichuan, focusing on key categories such as apples, tea, pork, raw milk, and turbot. In 2019, the Ministry of Agriculture required that enterprises with national certifications must implement traceability systems. Certified green, organic, and geographical indication products were required to join the national platform, and from January 1, 2020, uncertified products not registered on the platform would have their certification revoked.
- Although food traceability systems developed later than agricultural product traceability, their growth has been rapid. In 2012, the national food traceability platform was launched. In 2013, the NDRC and Ministry of Finance jointly initiated the IoT-based traceability system for key food products such as dairy and liquor. In 2015, infant formula and edible oils were included in the priority traceability list. The CFDA followed up with technical specifications and management opinions, and in 2016, RMB 700 million in central government funding supported pilot projects in Shandong, Shanghai, Ningxia, and Xiamen. In 2017, the State Council promoted supply-chain-based traceability, expanding coverage to agricultural inputs. In response to the COVID-19 pandemic, a 2020 circular on imported cold-chain food called for closed-loop traceability management. By 2023, China had established 32 cold-chain traceability platforms and 31 provincial-level food traceability platforms, along with more than 50 supporting regulations and 350 related standards.
- **Forth, the Chinese government has continuously intensified its efforts in evaluating and holding local authorities accountable for food safety performance.** In 2012, the State Council issued the *Decision on Strengthening Food Safety Work*, which, for the first time, incorporated food safety into the annual performance assessment system for local governments. It required higher-level governments to conduct annual evaluations of lower-level governments, and to use the results as an important basis for the comprehensive assessment of officials. A "one-vote vetos system(一票否决制)" was applied in regions where major food safety incidents occurred, while outstanding units and individuals

[4] "Authoritative Interpretation by the Ministry of Agriculture and Rural Affairs | Linking Four Aspects in the Traceability of Agricultural Product Quality and Safety," December 2018.
Full text link: http://www.aqsc.org/zlzs/201812/t20181206_328317.htm

were commended. In 2016, the State Council issued the first edition of the *Measures for the Evaluation and Assessment of Food Safety Work*, which served as a key reference for local assessments and remained in use until 2022. The revised version released in 2023 expanded the scope of assessment to include the Xinjiang Production and Construction Corps, refined the evaluation criteria, added real-time tasks and point-based adjustments, introduced a dynamic evaluation mechanism, and established a D-grade level. It also strengthened full-process supervision, emergency response, and incentive and accountability mechanisms, further reinforcing the responsibilities of local governments.

- To implement the requirement that both Party committees and governments share responsibility (党政同责)for food safety, the first internal Party regulation specifically targeting local Party and government leaders—the *Provisions on the Food Safety Responsibilities of Local Party and Government Leading Officials*—was officially issued in February 2019. The regulation stipulated that Party committees and governments at all levels bear overall responsibility for food safety in their jurisdictions, with principal officials serving as the first persons responsible. It incorporated food safety into the comprehensive performance evaluation system for leadership teams and officials, thereby strengthening leadership accountability and territorial management responsibilities. The regulation specifically stated that officials who conceal, falsify, or delay the reporting of food safety incidents, or unlawfully interfere in incident handling or law enforcement, shall be held accountable in accordance with Party discipline, organizational rules, and relevant laws. In September 2022, the Food Safety Commission of the State Council issued the *Opinions on Establishing and Improving a Tiered, Targeted, and Effective Risk Prevention and Control Mechanism at the Terminal Level to Advance the Implementation of Territorial Food Safety Responsibilities*. The document further reinforced territorial responsibility by promoting the establishment of a system in which Party and government leaders at each level are directly responsible for supervising food production and business operators. It also aimed to strengthen the chain of accountability and ensure that responsibilities are clearly assigned, facts are thoroughly investigated, and accountability is effectively enforced in the event of food safety incidents.

1.2.2.3 Challenges Facing China's Food Safety Policies

1. **Problems in the Current Regulatory System**

   China's food safety regulatory system has undergone a transformation from centralized independence to integrated decentralization (Liu Peng, 2020). In the process of merging regulatory agencies and implementing territorial management responsibilities, a large-scale consolidation of institutions took place, and food safety supervision responsibilities were fully devolved, forming a trend toward absolute decentralization. While this move helped to resolve inter-agency coordination issues and reinforced the responsibility of local governments, it also introduced new challenges.

First, the devolution of regulatory authority has conflicted with the limited capacity of grassroots regulators, a problem further exacerbated by institutional mergers. The law stipulates the regulatory responsibilities only in principle, while in practice these responsibilities are passed down layer by layer to the grassroots level, where dispatched agencies often lack the expertise to handle professional matters. Under the territorial management framework, most regulatory tasks fall on grassroots authorities. However, higher-level departments continue to offload responsibilities in a linear fashion, leading to task overload, formalistic enforcement, and the weakening of specialized supervision. After the "multi-in-one(多合一)" institutional integration, grassroots regulatory coverage has expanded, but their professional capacity has failed to keep pace. On one hand, regulatory duties have increased while staff are often required to assume multiple roles; on the other hand, many frontline regulators are former industrial and commercial officials with limited expertise and relatively advanced age. In addition, law enforcement resources are insufficient, with shortages in vehicles, equipment, and personnel severely hampering enforcement efficiency. At a deeper level, gaps persist in the understanding of rule of law and administrative professionalism, and local protectionism continues to interfere with enforcement.

Second, territorial jurisdiction conflicts with the cross-regional nature of food safety risks. With accelerating urbanization and regional economic integration, population is increasingly concentrated in large and medium-sized cities, which rely heavily on external sources for agricultural and food products. As surrounding areas supply these urban centers, associated food safety risks also flow into cities. However, under the current regulatory model, which adheres to the principle of territorial jurisdiction, it is difficult to effectively address cross-regional risks. The *Food Safety Law* and related regulations stipulate that food safety oversight is to be conducted within administrative boundaries—governments at or above the county level and their regulatory agencies are responsible only for food safety within their respective jurisdictions (Fan & Shi, 2023). Consequently, when substandard products from outside a jurisdiction are discovered locally, it is the local government that must respond. Yet administrative law restricts enforcement to within defined territorial boundaries, leaving gaps in food safety oversight.

2. **Problems in the Food Sampling and Inspection System**

Sampling inspection results serve as a primary basis for imposing strict penalties. Inadequate inspection capacity directly constrains the rigor and effectiveness of enforcement. Currently, the sampling inspection system faces two main issues:

First, the allocation of inspection resources does not match the distribution of food safety risks. Sampling quotas are primarily assigned based on the previous year's product qualification rates and population size, with little consideration for risk differences across supply chain stages or between urban and rural areas. In terms of product category, local governments are required in principle to focus on categories with lower qualification rates to improve problem detection. However, since the central government evaluates performance based on sampling qualification rates and number of batches, some local governments, driven by short-term performance goals, prioritize sampling of products with high qualification rates and low testing costs (Li, 2021). This leads to a decline in the proportion of high-risk and high-cost product sampling, ultimately reducing the efficiency of food safety oversight, despite increases in total sampling volume (Li, 2020). Regarding supply chain stages, although risks are concentrated in agricultural production and processing, most inspection resources are directed toward retail and supermarket terminals. For example, fresh products like aquatic foods mainly circulate through wholesale markets, farmers' markets, and catering sectors—yet these high-risk links are often under-sampled (Jin et al., 2021). Resource allocation is also imbalanced between urban and rural areas, where rural regions—often facing more severe food safety risks—suffer from insufficient inspection capacity.

Second, the practical impact of sampling inspection on the market is limited. As a tool for information disclosure, some studies have found that higher inspection intensity and mandatory disclosure may encourage producers to adopt traceability systems. However, food prices are generally unresponsive to government-issued safety information (Lin et al., 2024). As a basis for law enforcement, existing penalties tend to be light, and the cost of violations remains low. The Measures for the Administration of Food Sampling Inspection stipulate that licenses may be revoked for serious violations, but such penalties are reversible upon reapplication, reducing their deterrent effect. Many companies continue to profit significantly even after paying fines. For violations subject to "rectification orders" or "fines," frontline law enforcement often opts for the lower-cost rectification measure, thereby undermining the deterrent power of the regulatory system.

3. **Challenges in Building a Traceability System for Food Quality and Safety**

First, at the institutional level, a unified, end-to-end food traceability system has yet to be established. A national system covering production, circulation, and consumption is still lacking. For instance, wholesale markets do not require producers' records for market entry, and slaughterhouses only request declarations and quarantine certificates without demanding full farming records. This results in fragmented information between upstream and downstream actors. Meanwhile, environmental factors in production areas—such as heavy metal contamination in vegetables or non-point pollution in livestock farming—are closely tied to food safety but are excluded from traceability systems and not integrated into producer records.

Second, there is a lack of motivation among enterprises to participate. For most small and medium-sized food enterprises, establishing traceability systems requires substantial investment in funding and labor, which conflicts with their short-term profit goals. Due to long construction cycles, delayed returns, and cost-benefit mismatches, many businesses exhibit low willingness to participate, hindering the formation of a virtuous cycle (Wu et al., 2023).

Third, traceability technologies and their application remain limited. There is currently no unified database covering the entire food supply chain. Existing platforms operate in silos, lacking a national-level integrated data collection and disclosure system, which increases costs and restricts resource allocation. Additionally, many food supply chains are dominated by small workshops characterized by diverse product categories, numerous participants, wide distribution, and high mobility—making information collection difficult and traceability less effective. System incompatibility and divergent coding standards further cause data fragmentation, duplication, and unverifiability. In the case of imported food, discrepancies in coding systems may also prevent interoperability, disrupting traceability chains.

4. **Shortcomings in the Food Safety Assessment System**

First, result-oriented evaluation distorts regulatory incentives. Under China's current system, local governments at or above the county level are responsible for food safety within their jurisdictions and are held accountable for major incidents. Although responsibilities are clearly defined in law, the emphasis on outcome-based evaluation creates pressure that incentivizes local regulators to collude with enterprises, leading to inflated sampling pass rates and a failure to reflect actual food safety conditions. While penalties exist for concealing information, result-based assessments still encourage data falsification and concealment.

Second, the combination of inspection authority and penalty authority increases the risk of rent-seeking. Regulatory agencies are empowered to conduct both regular and random inspections and to use test results as a basis for penalties. They are also authorized to impose administrative sanctions such as warnings, suspensions, license revocations, and fines. The concentration of both inspection and punishment powers may induce rent-seeking behavior, whereby regulators collude with producers to falsify or suppress results, thereby undermining regulatory fairness and effectiveness.

Third, excessive emphasis on accountability, lack of incentives, and absence of exemption clauses weaken regulatory motivation (Zhou et al., 2018). The current system emphasizes punishment but provides limited incentives and lacks clear immunity provisions. This arrangement places substantial pressure on frontline staff, who may fear being held responsible for oversights and therefore choose to conceal or avoid problems. While enterprises are primarily responsible for food safety incidents, early detection and prevention by regulators can significantly reduce harm to public interests. However, the lack of rewards for proactive problem-solving, combined with the risk of negative media coverage and punitive repercussions, has discouraged regulatory enthusiasm. Although some regions like Hubei and Shanghai have introduced exemption clauses, vague wording and enforcement difficulties have limited their effectiveness in encouraging proactive oversight.

1.2.3 *Governance for the Quality Dimension: Promoting Nutrition and Health*

1.2.3.1 Evolution of China's Nutrition and Health Policies Since the Reform and Opening-up

1. **Stage of Policy Incubation (1978–2000)**

   In the early years of reform and opening up (1978–1984), the central goal of food policy remained ensuring basic supply. As the reform deepened (1984–2000), material abundance gradually increased, and China's food supply policy underwent a marked transformation. In 1985, the state began reforming the compulsory procurement and distribution system for key agricultural and sideline products such as grain, cotton, oil, and vegetables, transitioning to a model dominated by planning with supplementary market regulation. The policy of compulsory grain procurement and sales was eventually abolished. In 1988, the Ministry of Agriculture launched the "Non-Staple Food Project(菜篮子工程)," which promoted the establishment of production bases and supporting service systems for meat, eggs, dairy, aquatic products, and vegetables, aiming to ensure year-round access to fresh food for residents. Meanwhile, the government significantly increased the purchase prices for agricultural products to stimulate farmer enthusiasm for production. These measures helped optimize the dietary structure of residents, shifting from staple-based to more diversified consumption, thereby significantly improving nutritional status. By 1993, the grain ration coupon system was formally phased out, signaling the end of the planned economy-based food supply mechanism and laying the foundation for subsequent dietary transitions. During this period, government focus began shifting toward eliminating hunger and malnutrition, initiating nutritional surveillance and improvement programs. In the 1980s and 1990s, systematic assessments of the population's nutritional status gained increased attention. To support the formulation of public health policies with data, the Ministry of Health commissioned the Chinese Academy of Preventive Medicine to conduct two large-scale national nutrition surveys in 1982 and 1992 (Wang et al., 2019).

   In 1992, the International Conference on Nutrition in Rome adopted the *World Declaration and Plan of Action for Nutrition*, where Chinese delegates pledged to eliminate hunger and malnutrition by 2000. In fulfillment of this commitment, China formulated and implemented the *Outline for the Reform and Development of China's Food Structure in the 1990s* and the *China Nutrition Improvement Action Plan (1996–2000)*, establishing the fundamental strategy for national nutrition improvement.

   In 1993, the *State Council issued the Outline for the Reform and Development of China's Food Structure in the 1990s*, the first national guiding document addressing food consumption, production, processing, circulation, and nutritional improvement. The outline analyzed achievements and challenges in China's food development, proposed guiding principles and basic goals for the

1990s, and laid out relevant policy measures and organizational arrangements. Pursuant to Article 22 of the outline, and with approval from the State Council, the National Food and Nutrition Advisory Committee was established in June 1993. The committee was composed of high-level experts from sectors such as agriculture, health, planning, trade, science and technology, and education. Its primary tasks were to conduct research on food development and nutrition improvement nationwide, provide policy advice and consultancy to the State Council and relevant departments, and propose specific program plans.

The third national nutrition survey in 1992 revealed that rural residents' intake of animal-based foods was only one-third that of urban residents, and their protein intake was also significantly lower. Given the difficulty of rapidly increasing supplies of meat, eggs, milk, and fish, the expert committee proposed a "National Soybean Action Plan(国家大豆行动计划)." In 1996, a leading group was jointly established by the Ministry of Agriculture, Ministry of Health, Ministry of Education, and the China National Light Industry Council. The plan was piloted in 11 counties across 10 provinces and municipalities, covering both urban and rural areas. It utilized existing soybean-processing equipment and traditional methods to produce affordable soybean foods for primary and secondary school students, aiming to address protein deficiencies through high-quality soy protein. The first phase concluded in 1998 and transitioned smoothly into the second phase (Jiang, 1999).

Also in 1993, the State Council instructed the Ministry of Health to lead the drafting of the *China Nutrition Improvement Action Plan for the 1990s*. The drafting group included representatives from the Ministry of Health, State Planning Commission, State Council Leading Group Office of Poverty Alleviation and Development, Ministry of Agriculture, Ministry of Internal Trade, All-China Women's Federation, China National Light Industry Council, Chinese Academy of Preventive Medicine, Chinese Academy of Agricultural Sciences, and the National Food and Nutrition Advisory Committee. Drawing from relevant documents such as the *China National Program for Child Development in the 1990s*, the *Outline for the Reform and Development of China's Food Structure in the 1990s*, the *National 8-7 Poverty Reduction Plan*, and the *China 2000 Iodine Deficiency Elimination Program*, as well as legal instruments like the *Law on the Prevention and Treatment of Infectious Diseases*, the *Water Law*, *China's Agenda 21*, and the *Regulations on Iodized Salt for the Elimination of Iodine Deficiency Disorders,*[5] the draft underwent four rounds of revisions and extensive consultations. The plan was officially issued in 1997, guiding a series of nutrition improvement initiatives.

---

[5] Due to endemic iodine deficiency in many areas, China was among the countries most severely affected by iodine deficiency disorders. As early as the 1960s, the country implemented iodized salt strategies in severely deficient regions. In 1991, the Chinese government committed to eliminating iodine deficiency by 2000. In 1994, the *State Council issued the Regulations on the Elimination of Iodine Deficiency through Iodized Salt.*

In 1999, the Ministry of Health launched a revision of the *Dietary Guidelines for Chinese Residents*.[6] The updated version, issued by the Chinese Nutrition Society in April 1997, emphasized increased intake of dairy and soybean products to address calcium deficiency and introduced dietary recommendations for specific populations, while also strengthening public awareness of food hygiene. To further improve nutrition among primary and secondary school students, the Ministry of Agriculture and six other ministries jointly launched the "National Student Milk Program(中国学生饮用奶计划)" in 2000. This initiative aimed to increase calcium intake and promote healthy bone development by providing students with high-quality milk in schools, thereby fostering healthier dietary habits.

Overall, this phase can be described as the "Incubation Period" of China's nutrition policy. It marked the beginning of nutritional data collection, pilot projects for improvement, and the preliminary development of scientific evidence and policy tools. However, nutrition policy had not yet become a core component of government strategy and remained in the stage of initial exploration and institutional experimentation.

2. **Stage of Policy Formation (2001–2012)**

Entering the twenty-first century, the Chinese government placed increasing emphasis on nutrition and health, formulating and issuing the *Outline for Food and Nutrition Development in China (2001–2010)* to accelerate the establishment of a nutrition policy system. The Outline provided guidance for optimizing dietary patterns and promoting healthy eating habits across the population. Under its guidance, nutrition policies were gradually piloted and promoted in various regions, with government-led initiatives advancing supply-side reforms and improving dietary structures for key population groups.

In 2001, the former Ministry of Agriculture released the *Outline for Food and Nutrition Development in China (2001–2010)*, the first national-level document to systematically plan food and nutrition work in China. The Outline set the overall goal for 2010: to ensure adequate intake of essential nutrients and food for the population, guarantee sufficient food supply, and reduce the incidence of nutrition-related diseases. To achieve these goals, the Outline proposed five major policy measures:

First, structural adjustment and supply capacity enhancement: optimizing the agricultural structure, strengthening the food industry and market systems, and enhancing international competitiveness. Second, legal reinforcement and resource and environmental protection: improving laws, regulations, and standards related to food and nutrition to ensure food safety and hygiene. Third, reliance on science and technology to enhance nutrition awareness: promoting scientific research, disseminating nutrition knowledge, and raising public health awareness. Fourth, dietary improvement and nutrition security: implementing

[6]"Development of the Dietary Guidelines for Chinese Residents" Full text link: http://dg.cnsoc.org/article/lsqy.html

nutrition improvement programs and strengthening nutritional monitoring and risk warning systems. Fifth, enhanced coordination and improved governance mechanisms: promoting tiered management and inter-departmental cooperation to establish a modern food and nutrition governance system.

Guided by the Outline, the Chinese government launched a series of pilot and promotion programs for nutrition interventions, addressing both supply-side reforms and interventions for key population groups. **On the supply side**, food fortification initiatives were introduced to address micronutrient deficiencies. In 2002, the State Grain Administration and the Ministry of Health conducted pilot projects in provinces such as Hebei and Gansu, fortifying subsidized flour with seven micronutrients including iron, zinc, calcium, and vitamin A. This initiative became one of the earliest measures under the National Public Nutrition Improvement Project (RETA). In 2003, the iron-fortified soy sauce program was extended to nine provinces, benefiting over 60 million people and achieving significant results, laying the groundwork for institutionalizing the policy. **For targeted population groups**, multiple nutrition interventions were implemented. From 2001 to 2011, China conducted pilot programs on complementary food supplements **for infants and young children**, providing critical data to support subsequent policy design. In 2012, the central government allocated RMB 100 million to provide nutrient packets to 280,000 children over 6 months of age in 100 poverty-stricken counties. **For school-aged children**, in 2001 the State Economic and Trade Commission, Ministry of Education, and Ministry of Health jointly issued the Guidelines for Promoting Student Nutrition Meals. These guidelines established a mechanism of "government leadership, enterprise participation, school-based implementation, and parental voluntariness," and encouraged local governments to integrate the nutrition meal pilot with the Soybean Action Plan, Student Soymilk Program, and Student Milk Program. Between 2006 and 2007, Du'an County in Guangxi launched a pilot program for nutritional supplementation among boarding students. In 2011, China officially launched the nationwide Nutrition Improvement Program for Rural Compulsory Education Students. In 2012, the former Ministry of Health and Ministry of Education jointly issued the *Monitoring and Evaluation Plan (Trial) for the Nutrition and Health Status under the Rural Compulsory Education Students' Nutrition Improvement Program*, aiming to assess the effectiveness of nutrition interventions. This program received an annual central government investment of RMB 16 billion, covering 680 contiguous poverty-stricken counties and benefiting 26 million students. It led to a significant reduction in childhood anemia and stunting rates. In response to rising rates of **overweight and obesity**, the former Ministry of Health released the Guidelines for Obesity Prevention and Control in Chinese Adults and Children. From 2007 to 2012, China launched the "National Healthy Lifestyle for All Campaign," marking a shift in nutrition policy towards health management throughout the life cycle.

This period may be referred to as the "Formation Stage" of China's nutrition policy. During this time, nutrition policy evolved from early exploration to initial institutionalization: policy coverage became more inclusive, intervention approaches more diversified, and central government funding gradually increased. A basic nutrition policy framework began to take shape. However, compared with countries that had established more institutionalized nutrition systems—such as Japan—China still faced several constraints at this stage. These included the absence of a national-level nutrition law, lack of integration of nutrition targets into national economic and social development plans, weak foundations in basic research and policy evaluation, and inadequate interdepartmental coordination mechanisms. These limitations hindered the systematic, sustained, and operational development of nutrition policy to some extent.

1.2.3.2 Current Landscape: Stage of Rapid Policy Development (2013–Present)

Over the past decade, the living standards of the Chinese people have improved significantly. However, with this rapid improvement came a surge in lifestyle-related and non-communicable diseases. Accelerated pace of life, coupled with unhealthy lifestyles and dietary habits, has led to a marked increase in chronic metabolic disorders, such as overweight and obesity, dyslipidemia, hypertension, and hyperglycemia. These diseases are no longer confined to middle-aged and elderly populations or working professionals, but are increasingly affecting children and adolescents. Meanwhile, the problem of "hidden hunger"—namely micronutrient deficiencies—along with undernutrition among the elderly, has become an issue of growing concern. Against this backdrop, China's nutrition and health policy framework has entered a phase of rapid development, characterized by the release of a series of strategic and programmatic documents.

First, China issued the *National Food and Nutrition Development Outline* (2014–2020) and the *National Food and Nutrition Development Outline* (2025–2030). Following the *Outline for Reform and Development of China's Food Structure* in the 1990s and the *National Food and Nutrition Development Outline (2001–2010)*, the 2014–2020 and 2025–2030 documents constituted the third and fourth sets of strategic blueprints on food and nutrition development. Each reflects the priorities of its era and provides important guidance on fostering healthy diets among the population. The *2014–2020 Outline* emphasized targeted nutrition interventions for key groups—namely, pregnant women and infants, children and adolescents, and the elderly—while highlighting the importance of curbing the rise in nutrition-related diseases. It aligned closely with trends in consumption upgrading and the pursuit of high-quality development in the food sector. The *2025–2030 Outline*, by contrast, underscores the principle of "nutrition-oriented development," advocating for the integration of nutrition and health needs across all stages of food production, processing, distribution, consumption, and product innovation. Greater focus is placed on the development of food products rich in high-quality protein and dietary fiber, and on the promotion of nutritional processing.

Second, the *Healthy China 2030 Planning Outline* was released. In October 2015, the Fifth Plenary Session of the 18th CPC Central Committee first proposed the construction of a Healthy China. In August 2016, the *Healthy China 2030 Planning Outline*, developed under the guidance of this strategic directive, was jointly issued by the CPC Central Committee and the State Council. It became the program of action for advancing the Healthy China initiative over the subsequent 15 years (Xu, 2021). The Outline marked a milestone in China's social development, breaking new ground by elevating Healthy China to the status of a national strategy and formally designating health as a national development priority. According to the Outline, by 2030, the incidence of nutrition-related diseases is to be significantly reduced, the national per capita daily salt intake lowered by 20%, and the growth in overweight and obesity prevalence notably slowed. The overall goal is to achieve health for all through shared efforts and benefits.

Third, the *National Healthy Lifestyle Campaign (2017–2025)* was introduced. In April 2017, the National Health and Family Planning Commission, the General Administration of Sport, the All-China Federation of Trade Unions, the Communist Youth League Central Committee, and the All-China Women's Federation jointly issued the *Action Plan for National Healthy Lifestyles (2017–2025)*. The plan called for four specialized campaigns: "Three Reductions and Three Healths" (reduction of salt, oil, and sugar; promotion of oral health, healthy weight, and strong bones), promotion of moderate physical activity, tobacco and alcohol control, and mental health. These campaigns were implemented through community outreach and engagement in households, schools, workplaces, and medical institutions, helping to popularize healthy lifestyle concepts and provide practical models for adoption.

Fourth, the *National Nutrition Plan* (2017–2030) was released. In June 2017, the General Office of the State Council issued the *National Nutrition Plan (2017–2030)* (hereinafter referred to as the "Plan"), advocating for a life-cycle and whole-process approach to nutrition and health. The Plan aims to embed nutrition into all health policies and enhance public health levels nationwide. It identified six major interventions tailored to six key population groups: the "First 1,000 Days" nutrition action, nutrition improvement for students, nutrition promotion for the elderly, clinical nutrition action, nutrition intervention in poverty-stricken areas, and the balanced diet and physical activity campaign. These efforts have contributed to a more robust nutrition policy system, improved service provision, and a stronger sense of nutritional well-being among the population.

Fifth, the *Healthy China Initiative (2019–2030)* was launched. In July 2019, in accordance with the *Implementation and Evaluation Plan for the Healthy China Initiative* issued by the General Office of the State Council, the Healthy China Action Promotion Committee (hereinafter referred to as the "Promotion Committee") was established and subsequently released the *Healthy China Initiative (2019–2030)*. The document outlines 15 major actions, including the dissemination of health knowledge, promotion of balanced diets, nationwide fitness campaigns, and mental health promotion. It represents a further refinement of the Healthy China strategy. The initiative is notable for two key features: first, it promotes the concept of shared responsibility for health and recognizes individuals as the primary custodians of their own dietary and nutritional well-being; second, it focuses on grassroots implementation, addressing practical health issues and advancing solutions that are actionable and effective.

Sixth, the *14th Five-Year Plan for National Health* was formulated. On May 20, 2022, the General Office of the State Council released the *14th Five-Year Plan for National Health* (hereinafter referred to as the "Plan"), a key national-level special plan for implementing the Healthy China strategy during the 14th Five-Year period. It outlines seven priority tasks, including improving the public health system, promoting full life-cycle health management, and strengthening nutritional interventions for key populations. It also emphasizes the development of nutrition standards, the optimization of nutrition monitoring, and the enhancement of nutritional service capacity, thus providing a top-level design for public health governance in the new era.

In addition, during this period, China issued its first mandatory national standard for nutrition labeling—the *General Rules for Nutrition Labeling of Pre-packaged Foods* (GB 28050-2011), which came into effect on January 1, 2013. **This foundational standard for food safety signaled the full-scale implementation of China's nutrition labeling management system.** The standard mandates that pre-packaged foods must carry a nutrition label, which serves three purposes: promoting public awareness of nutritional knowledge and guiding informed dietary choices; encouraging balanced and healthy eating among consumers; and standardizing enterprises' labeling practices to ensure scientific and accurate nutrition communication, thereby supporting the healthy development of the food industry. In March 2025, the National Health Commission and the State Administration for Market Regulation jointly issued the revised National Food Safety Standard—*General Rules for Nutrition Labeling of Pre-packaged Foods* (GB 28050-2025), scheduled for implementation in 2027. Compared with the 2011 version, the revised standard introduces four major changes: (1) expanding the mandatory nutrients from "1 + 4" (energy, protein, fat, carbohydrate, sodium) to "1 + 6" with the inclusion of sugar and saturated fat; (2) adding a reminder that "children and adolescents should avoid excessive intake of salt, oil, and sugar"; (3) allowing the use of supplementary graphics and text in compliance with the standard to enhance consumer engagement with nutritional information; and (4) introducing reference values for serving sizes, enabling nutrition content to be expressed per 100 g, per 100 ml, or per serving. The rollout of the updated GB 28050 standard will make it easier for consumers to access key nutritional information and make healthier dietary choices.

In summary, over the past decade, China has issued an intensive array of policy documents and development plans related to national nutrition and health (see Table 1.2), reflecting the elevation of "Healthy China" to the level of a national strategy. These policies and plans have collectively underscored an unprecedented prioritization of nutrition and health, evolving over time in both scope and depth. They demonstrate not only the continuity of government commitment but also the dynamism and progressiveness of China's approach to nutrition governance.

Table 1.2 Major nutrition-related laws, policies, and documents since the founding of the people's republic of China

Issuance date	Title	Issuing authority
November 19, 1953	Order on Implementing the Planned Purchase and Planned Supply of Grain	Administrative Council of the Central People's Government
May 27, 1993	Outline of Food Structure Reform and Development in the 1990s	State Council
December 5, 1997	China Nutrition Improvement Action Plan	General Office of the State Council
May 22, 2001	China Women's Development Outline (2001–2010)	State Council
May 22, 2001	China Children's Development Outline (2001–2010)	State Council
November 3, 2001	China Food and Nutrition Development Outline (2001–2010)	General Office of the State Council
April 10, 2008	Nutrition Work Standards	Ministry of Health
February 28, 2009	Food Safety Law	National People's Congress
August 3, 2010	Administrative Measures for Nutrition Improvement Work	Ministry of Health
July 30, 2011	China Women's Development Outline (2011–2020)	State Council
July 30, 2011	China Children's Development Outline (2011–2020)	State Council
January 28, 2014	China Food and Nutrition Development Outline (2014–2020)	General Office of the State Council
June 30, 2017	National Nutrition Plan (2017–2030)	General Office of the State Council
June 24, 2019	Opinions of the State Council on Implementing the 'Healthy China' Initiative	State Council
July 9, 2019	Healthy China Initiative (2019–2030)	Healthy China Initiative Promotion Committee
December 28, 2019	Basic Healthcare and Health Promotion Law	National People's Congress
April 29, 2021	Anti-Food Waste Law	National People's Congress
September 8, 2021	"China Women's Development Outline (2021–2030)"	State Council
September 8, 2021	China Children's Development Outline (2021–2030)	State Council
September 27, 2022	Occupational Classification Dictionary of the People's Republic of China (2022 Edition)	Ministry of Human Resources and Social Security

Source: Fang, H., Deng, T. & Wang, Y. (2024). Promoting nutrition legislation to contribute to building Healthy China. Chinese Journal of Food Hygiene, 36(08), 899–904

1.2.3.3 Challenges Facing China's Nutrition and Health Policies

As China transitions from ensuring food supply and food safety to safeguarding national nutrition and health, public demand for improved nutritional well-being has grown significantly, placing new requirements and challenges on relevant policy efforts. In recent years, the Chinese government has elevated food nutrition and health policies to the level of national strategy, leading to a more comprehensive policy system and notable improvements in national nutrition and health levels. However, compared with other countries, China's progress in nutrition-related legislation remains relatively limited. As early as the 1980s, nutrition experts began advocating for dedicated legislation. A legislative proposal was initiated in 2001, and after 2004, the former Ministry of Health and later the National Health and Family Planning Commission carried out related work. In 2015, a draft version of the *Regulations on Nutrition Improvement* was completed. Yet, the legislation has not proceeded into the formal legislative process at the national level (Fang et al., 2024). The long-term absence of dedicated nutrition legislation has resulted in a lack of institutional safeguards for nutrition improvement efforts, hampering the implementation of nutrition-related plans and the sustained improvement of national health outcomes.

First, a coordinated mechanism featuring government leadership, multi-sector collaboration, and whole-of-society participation has yet to be fully established. As a result, it remains difficult to effectively mobilize stakeholders to formulate and implement nutrition improvement policies. For instance, in the implementation of the National Nutrition Plan, issues persist in the design of constraints, supervision, and incentive mechanisms. Although the policy documents emphasize the importance of oversight and call for the involvement of the National People's Congress, the Chinese People's Political Consultative Conference, supervisory bodies, the media, parents, and organizations such as the All-China Women's Federation, they fail to specify clear penalties and accountability measures for ineffective supervision. This lack of enforceable mechanisms weakens implementation on the ground and leads to recurrent issues in policy execution, including frequent incidents of food poisoning and the misappropriation of nutrition-related funds, thereby undermining policy effectiveness and eroding public trust.

Second, a dedicated financial support mechanism for nutrition work has not been established. Current levels of funding for nutrition and health monitoring, research on nutrition intervention strategies, the development of nutrition and health standards, and the implementation of nutrition plans are inadequate, with development levels falling far behind those of developed countries. Surveys show that the implementation of the National Nutrition Plan suffers from severe shortages of personnel, funding, and physical resources (Shao et al., 2016). Although the central government has earmarked special funds to support student nutrition programs, local governments are required to cover the costs of canteen facilities, staff salaries, utilities, and other operating expenses. In economically underdeveloped regions, limited fiscal capacity has resulted in persistently poor infrastructure in many schools. In extreme cases, schools have resorted to using firewood for cooking due to the high cost of electricity. These conditions not only compromise meal quality but also pose serious safety risks, severely constraining the effective implementation and sustainable development of nutrition policies.

Third, current nutrition efforts are predominantly project-based and temporary, lacking institutionalization, normalization, and long-term continuity.[7] As a result, the effectiveness of nutrition interventions is difficult to sustain, leading to substantial resource waste. Many projects terminate upon the conclusion of pilot phases or when funding expires, without being incorporated into long-term development mechanisms. For example, some pilot schools established dietitian positions and menu review systems during nutrition intervention trials. However, when pilot programs ended, related staffing and funding were withdrawn, resulting in the discontinuation of the intervention mechanism. Moreover, due to the absence of top-level policy design, coordination between central and local governments remains insufficient, and policy fragmentation among departments is widespread. There is no unified management platform or routine coordination mechanism. This project-driven, multi-agency governance model is not only inefficient but also wasteful of resources, ultimately reducing the overall impact of nutrition policies.

Fourth, a national-level nutrition work system has not yet been fully established, and most provinces and municipalities lack dedicated nutrition institutions, with an acute shortage of professional personnel. While China's nutrition research system has taken initial shape—centered around universities and research institutes—the implementation of policies at the grassroots level still faces serious shortcomings. Many provinces and municipalities do not have specialized nutrition offices, and the number of qualified personnel is far from sufficient. Frontline workers often lack professional training, rendering them unable to effectively carry out nutrition guidance and intervention tasks. At the same time, the formulation and implementation of nutrition policies urgently require "policy-oriented professionals" with interdisciplinary capabilities and strategic policy insight. However, the current training and reserve of such professionals in China remains insufficient.[8] A large number of practitioners in the food sector still focus primarily on technical research and product development, lacking systematic understanding of nutrition policy and its social implications. Some policy documents fail to reflect the realities of the industry, leading to confusion among enterprises during implementation. Therefore, it is essential to strengthen research on nutrition and food policy, promote deep integration between scientific research and policy formulation, and improve the current policy framework to build a national nutrition governance system that is more scientific, efficient, and forward-looking.

[7] Li Tao, Guo Min. "Strengthen Nutrition Legislation to Advance National Health Objectives," China Food Safety News, May 23, 2020. https://m.thepaper.cn/baijiahao_7531072

[8] "From a Weak Foundation to Initial Safeguards: From Regional Pilots to National Strategy—China's Growing Nutrition Policy System," China Safe Food Network, September 27, 2019. Full text: http://www.foodscn.cn/dujia/4248

1.2.4 *Governance for the Quality Dimension: Advancing Green and Sustainable Development*

1.2.4.1 Evolution of China's Green and Sustainable Policies in the Agri-food System Since the Reform and Opening-up

The agri-food system is a comprehensive framework encompassing agricultural production, processing, transportation, retail, and consumption. Throughout its operations, greenhouse gas (GHG) emissions are generated across multiple stages (Vermeulen et al., 2012). Major emission sources include agricultural production activities—such as rice cultivation, enteric fermentation in ruminants, manure management, fertilizer application, straw burning, and land tillage—land use change (e.g., deforestation, wetland degradation, and carbon sink losses), the manufacturing of agricultural inputs (such as fertilizers, pesticides, plastic film, and energy), as well as post-production processes including food processing, storage and transport, retail, consumption, and food waste disposal (Wang et al., 2025). While most existing agricultural green development policies in China were primarily designed to address agricultural, water, or air pollution rather than to target emissions directly, they have generated significant co-benefits in terms of GHG reduction within the agri-food system. The development of green and low-carbon policies can be broadly divided into three stages, with the 2002 revision of the *Agriculture Law* and the introduction of the the action plan against pollution in rural areas in 2015 serving as key milestones. These events signaled a transition from the policy's nascent phase toward a more systematic green and low-carbon policy framework for the agri-food sector.

1. **Stage of Conceptual Emergence (1978–2001)**

   From 1978 to 2001, awareness of green transformation in agriculture began to emerge. During this period, policies related to green and low-carbon development primarily focused on three aspects: protection of agricultural resources and ecosystems, certification of green and organic food, and grain-saving initiatives.

   First, with regard to the protection of agricultural resources and ecosystems, the Chinese government began to emphasize the ecological benefits of agricultural development in the early 1980s (Li & Gong, 2020). The No. 1 Central Document for 1982 proposed that agricultural development should be conducive to ecological preservation. In 1984, the State Council called for the prevention and control of agricultural pollution, and the *Environmental Protection Law* in 1989 incorporated "agricultural environment" into the legal framework for the first time. At the same time, pilot programs for eco-agriculture were gradually launched. In the 1990s, the Ministry of Agriculture led pilot projects in eco-agriculture counties, laying a practical foundation for its promotion. In 1998, the Third Plenary Session of the 15th CPC Central Committee proposed sustainable agricultural development, explicitly calling for the protection of arable land, forests, and water resources, as well as the prevention of soil erosion and environmental pollution. Subsequently, the central government allocated special funds for agricultural infrastructure and ecological projects, marking the establishment of a government-supported ecological protection system in agriculture. Beginning in 1999, China launched the Natural Forest Protection Program, followed in 2000 by pilot projects on returning farmland to forest and grassland. These initiatives gradually formed a comprehensive agricultural resource and ecological protection policy system that included forest protection, reforestation, and desertification control. In 2001, a forest ecological benefit compensation mechanism was initiated, and a preliminary financial support framework for ecological conservation was established. In addition, in 1999, China introduced a ban on straw burning and issued the *Administrative Measures for the Prohibition and Comprehensive Utilization of Straw Burning*, delineating prohibited burning zones. While the primary objectives were to protect ecosystems, safeguard human health, and maintain public safety, this policy also contributed significantly to emissions reduction.

Second, in terms of green and organic food certification, the concept of green food was first proposed in 1990 and included in the national "Eighth Five-Year Plan" for land reclamation development. In the same year, the Ministry of Agriculture launched the Green Food Program and established the National Green Food Development Office, which laid out standards and a regulatory framework for green food certification (Zhao et al., 2019). In 1992, the China Green Food Development Center was established to oversee certification and logo management. In 1993, the *Measures for the Administration of Green Food Labels* were issued, and China joined the International Federation of Organic Agriculture Movements. These initiatives laid the institutional groundwork for the subsequent promotion of green food and the realization of its emission reduction potential. The certification process for green food requires strict standards regarding product origin, environmental quality, input use (including pesticides, fertilizers, feed, and veterinary drugs), and packaging and transport, which not only ensure food safety but also indirectly reduce GHG emissions in agricultural production.

Third, regarding grain-saving policies, the government placed high importance on conserving grain and promoting its efficient use, especially at the processing and consumption stages. In the 1980s, China took measures to restrict the grain-intensive operations of the liquor industry and promoted a shift toward lower-alcohol, higher-quality, and more diverse products. Through price reform and production restrictions, the grain use efficiency in the liquor sector significantly improved. Simultaneously, the state encouraged the development of grain-saving livestock and poultry farming and the feed industry. By the 1990s, China had become the world's second-largest feed producer, with a significant increase in feed utilization efficiency—saving approximately 75 million tonnes of grain over a decade. In 1991, China launched "Grain Conservation Awareness Week" to promote a culture of frugality and oppose extravagance and waste. The 1996 white paper *The Grain Issue in China* proposed specific measures to conserve grain, including promoting low-alcohol beverages and discouraging official banquets. During the Ninth Five-Year Plan period, grain-saving policies were included among the core rural development tasks, gradually forming a relatively complete system of public campaigns, regulatory measures, and control mechanisms. In 1997, the government issued the *Provisions on Strict Economy and the Prevention of Extravagance and Waste by Party and Government Organs*, which prohibited the use of public funds for lavish banquets and extravagant consumption (Zhao, 2020). These policies played a vital role in reducing carbon emissions in food processing and consumption.

In conclusion, during the initial phase, although China had not yet formulated a comprehensive emissions reduction policy for the agri-food system, the country accumulated valuable experience and laid a solid institutional foundation for subsequent green and low-carbon transformation through ecological protection in agriculture, the development of green food, and the establishment of grain-saving mechanisms.

2. **Stage of Initial System Development (2002–2014)**

Following its accession to the World Trade Organization, China faced mounting pressure to enhance the competitiveness of its agricultural products, making quality improvement a key focus of policy adjustments. The revised *Agriculture Law of the People's Republic of China* in 2002 incorporated "improving the quality of agricultural products" for the first time into the legal framework. Building on earlier green and organic food policies, green and low-carbon policies in the agri-food system were extended to include agricultural product quality improvement. During this period, policy efforts primarily centered on improving the quality and safety of agricultural products, protecting agricultural resources and the environment, and curbing food waste. A preliminary support system for green and low-carbon development in the agri-food sector began to take shape.

First, in terms of enhancing agricultural product quality, the systems for green food and pollution-free agricultural products were gradually established and improved. In 2002, the Ministry of Agriculture issued the *Opinions on Accelerating the Development of Green Food*, followed by a series of policies promoting the construction of standardized green food production bases. After 2013, efforts were intensified to regulate green food trademark management and brand building. For example, in 2014, the Ministry of Agriculture released the *Implementation Measures for Market Supervision of Green Food Trademarks* and the *Green Food Certification Procedures*. Meanwhile, a certification system for pollution-free agricultural products was established in 2002 and rapidly implemented nationwide, under a "five-unified" approach—unified standards, labels, procedures, management, and supervision. The Action Plan for Pollution-Free Food (无公害食品行动计划) emphasized quality control across the entire production process. In 2005, the Ministry of Agriculture issued the *Opinions on Developing Pollution-Free Agricultural Products, Green Food, and Organic Agricultural Products*, further promoting the coordinated development of the three categories. To regulate pesticide use, the Ministry of Agriculture in 2002 introduced the *Administrative Provisions on Restricted Use of Pesticides*, which incorporated health standards into the restriction criteria, standardized application, review, and issuance procedures, and strengthened safety supervision of agricultural inputs. **Meanwhile, efforts to establish a legal system for agricultural product quality assurance were accelerated.** The 2005 *Animal Husbandry Law* included a dedicated chapter on quality and safety, setting explicit provisions for the supervision and administration of livestock and poultry breeding, trade, and transportation. The 2006 *Law on Quality and Safety of Agricultural Products* clarified standards for quality, place of origin management, product labeling, and supervision mechanisms. The 2009 *Food Safety Law* incorporated edible agricultural products into the national food safety standards system, and its 2015 revision introduced a full-chain traceability system, further strengthening quality management across the entire production process. **In terms of policy support,** the General Office of the State Council and the Ministry of Agriculture successively issued documents such as the *Opinions on the Construction of the "Vegetable Basket" Project*, the *Administrative Measures for the Green Food Label*, and the *Measures for the Administration of Quality and Safety Testing of Agricultural Products*, thereby providing institutional safeguards for the quality supervision of green agricultural products and promoting the establishment of a scientific, systematic, and stringent quality and safety management system.

Second, in the area of agricultural resource and environmental protection, the government increased fiscal investment to promote the implementation and expansion of various agro-ecological projects (Li & Gong, 2020). Starting from natural forest and grassland protection programs, the scope gradually expanded to include fertile soil projects, rural cleanliness initiatives, straw comprehensive utilization, rural biogas, circular agriculture, and the prevention and control of agricultural non-point source pollution. Through project-specific promotion and integrated implementation, a relatively complete engineering system for agricultural ecological and environmental protection was established. In 2008, China began nationwide enforcement of the straw burning ban, prohibiting the open burning of crop residues in the fields. This marked the beginning of a nationwide action on straw burning control that has lasted for more than 17 years. **Relevant laws and regulations were continuously refined to support this effort**. In terms of water resource protection, the revised *Water Law of the People's Republic of China*, *Law on Prevention and Control of Water Pollution*, and the *National Agricultural Water Conservation Outline (2012–2020)* jointly promoted the development of water-saving agriculture. In the area of air pollution control, the *Law on the Prevention and Control of Atmospheric Pollution* clearly prohibited the open burning of straw and specified legal liabilities, thereby providing a legal basis for the straw burning ban. For solid waste management, the 2004 revision of the *Law on the Prevention and Control of Environmental Pollution* by Solid Waste set out requirements for agricultural film recycling and the management of designated no-burn zones for straw. Regarding circular economy development, the enactment of the *Renewable Energy Law*, the *Energy Conservation Law*, and the *Circular Economy Promotion*

Law facilitated the integration of circular economy principles into agriculture. In ecological agriculture, the 2006 release of the *Technical Standards for National Ecological Agriculture Construction* promoted institutionalization and standardization. Concerning pollution from livestock and poultry farming, the 2013 *Regulations on the Prevention and Control of Pollution from the Breeding of Livestock and Poultry*, issued by the State Council, called for comprehensive utilization and harmless treatment of livestock and poultry waste.

Third, in the area of food waste reduction, anti-food-waste policies were progressively strengthened. After the 2008 global food crisis, the Chinese government began to institutionalize food-saving initiatives, starting with curbing catering waste (Zhao, 2020). In the same year, the State Administration of Government Offices and the Administrative Bureau of the Central Committee issued notices requiring regulated official receptions and promoting the practice of packing leftovers. The *Medium- and Long-term Plan for National Food Security (2008–2020)* proposed reducing waste and improving grain utilization efficiency through the adoption of separate dining and green catering standards. In 2010, the *Notice on Further Strengthening Food Saving and Anti-Waste Efforts* explicitly emphasized a dual approach to food security that prioritizes both "increasing production" and "reducing waste." In 2011, the National Development and Reform Commission, together with other departments, launched a nationwide "Anti-Food-Waste Action." After the 18th National Congress of the Communist Party of China, institutional constraints were further strengthened. In 2012, the Party's eight-point frugality code(中央八项规定) were introduced. Between 2013 and 2014, a series of policy documents—such as the *Regulations on Practicing Economy and Combating Waste in Party and Government Organs*, the *Regulations on Official Receptions*, and the *Opinions on Practicing Economy and Combating Food Waste*—were issued to strictly control the use of public funds for lavish banquets. In 2014, the *Grain Law (Draft for Review)* included a dedicated chapter on food saving and loss reduction and proposed establishing a disciplinary mechanism against waste. In the same year, the "Clear Your Plate" campaign (光盘行动), initially a civil initiative, was elevated to a government-led movement to encourage frugal dining habits among the public. The Ministry of Commerce and the National Development and Reform Commission issued the *Measures for Economic Management of the Catering Industry*, encouraging businesses to offer smaller portions and set meals, establish incentive mechanisms for frugal dining, and promote food-saving practices throughout the entire catering process.

In conclusion, during this period, significant progress was made in enhancing agricultural product quality, advancing agricultural ecological and environmental protection, and curbing food waste. These efforts laid the institutional foundation and basic framework for the green and low-carbon transformation of the agri-food system, marking the initial establishment of a policy support system for green and low-carbon development.

1.2.4.2 Current Landscape: Stage of Policy Systematization (2015–Present)

Since 2015, China has gradually developed a green and low-carbon policy system for the agri-food sector, covering multiple stages including agricultural production and land use, food processing, packaging and transportation, food consumption, and waste treatment. This evolution demonstrates a shift from fragmented policy issuance to integrated policy coordination. In particular, at the 75th session of the United Nations General Assembly in September 2020, China announced its targets of peaking carbon emissions before 2030 and achieving carbon neutrality by 2060. At COP28 of the United Nations Framework Convention on Climate Change in 2023, food and agricultural systems were included for the first time as a core component of the climate change agenda. China also endorsed the "*Emirates Declaration on Sustainable Agriculture, Resilient Food Systems, and Climate Action*." The carbon peak and neutrality targets call for achieving deep emission reductions in a shorter timeframe than developed countries. Given the significant role of agriculture in greenhouse gas emissions, promoting green and low-carbon agricultural development is critical for addressing climate change, ensuring sustainable agricultural development, and attaining carbon peak and neutrality objectives.

First, in the stage of agricultural production and land use, efforts to control agricultural pollution have been significantly intensified, and emission reduction and carbon sequestration pathways have become increasingly clear. In 2015, the Ministry of Agriculture issued the *Implementation Opinions on the Campaign to Prevent and Control Agricultural Non-Point Source Pollution*, setting targets to be achieved by 2020, including controlling the total volume of agricultural water use, reducing the application of chemical fertilizers and pesticides, and realizing the basic resource utilization of livestock and poultry manure, crop straw, and agricultural plastic film. In 2017, the Ministry launched five key initiatives for green agricultural development, including the recycling of livestock and poultry manure, substitution of chemical fertilizers with organic fertilizers for fruits, vegetables, and tea, straw management, plastic film recycling, and aquatic biodiversity conservation. The *14th Five-Year Plan for National Green Agricultural Development*, released in 2021, called for building a green and low-carbon agricultural industrial chain, focusing on three priority areas: the conservation and efficient use of agricultural resources, the control of non-point source pollution, and ecological restoration. In 2022, the Ministry of Agriculture and Rural Affairs issued the *Implementation Plan for Agricultural and Rural Emission Reduction and Carbon Sequestration*, which outlined ten major initiatives, including reducing methane emissions from rice paddies, promoting low-carbon livestock and poultry farming, improving the efficiency of fertilizer use, and enhancing farmland carbon sinks. These were further specified in the *Action Plan for Reducing Fertilizer Use by 2025* and the *Action Plan for Reducing Pesticide Use by 2025*, providing clear policy guidance for low-carbon agricultural development. **Fiscal support has been continuously strengthened.** Each year, the central government allocates approximately 100 billion yuan to support the development of high-standard farmland, promoting water-saving irrigation and other green technologies, thereby significantly reducing carbon emission intensity per unit of agricultural output. Data show that in recent years, the per-unit carbon emission intensity of major crops such as soybeans, potatoes, and sugarcane has steadily declined, reflecting a synergy between emission reduction and stable production. **The green technology and standard systems have gradually taken shape**. In 2018, the *Technical Guidelines for Green Agricultural Development (2018–2030)* were issued, emphasizing both production and ecological functions and balancing quality and quantity. The guidelines promoted the establishment of green standards throughout the production chain, including indicators for environmental conditions at production sites, production processes, and product quality. **Systems for ecological restoration and resource conservation have been progressively improved.** In 2016, the *Wetland Protection and Restoration System Plan* was issued to enhance the protection of wetland ecosystems. Since pilot implementation began in 2016, the arable land rotation and fallow system has been gradually incorporated into fiscal support programs, with the pilot area reaching 30 million mu by 2019. In 2021, the Ministry of Ecology and Environment and other departments jointly issued guidance on adopting nature-based solutions to synergize climate change response with ecological and environmental protection.

Second, in the food processing, packaging, and storage and transportation stages, the *14th Five-Year Plan for the Modern Energy System*, released in 2022, called for the electrification of terminal energy use, encouraging electric irrigation, green livestock farming and processing, transformation of rural production and lifestyles, and the adoption of clean energy and energy-saving technologies. In the area of food packaging, the *Guiding Opinions on Accelerating the Transformation of China's Packaging Industry* issued in 2016 emphasized the development of degradable and recyclable materials to improve the environmental performance and safety of packaging. In 2023, the national standard *Requirements for Restricting Excessive Packaging of Commodities—Food and Cosmetics (GB 23350-2021)* came into effect, and in 2024, the *Requirements for Restricting Excessive Packaging of Commodities—Fresh Edible Agricultural Products (GB 43284-2023)* will be implemented, both of which provide technical indicators and evaluation methods for curbing excessive packaging of food products. Regarding logistics and transportation, the *Opinions on Accelerating the Development of Cold Chain Logistics to Ensure Food Safety and Promote Consumption Upgrading*, issued in 2017, called for the use of low-energy, environmentally friendly refrigerants and energy-efficient equipment to develop green cold chain logistics, thereby enhancing the energy efficiency and environmental sustainability of agricultural product transportation.

Third, in the areas of food consumption and waste treatment, policies guiding consumption have been strengthened. The *Anti-Food Waste Law*, implemented in 2021, established a grain-saving system targeting various actors such as restaurants, canteens, supermarkets, and e-commerce platforms. In 2024, the *Action Plan for Grain Saving and Anti-Food Waste* further proposed full-chain grain saving and loss reduction measures from production to consumption, along with establishing a regularized loss statistics system and indicator framework. In terms of dietary structure, the *Dietary Guidelines for Chinese Residents (2022 Edition)* advocated for a diverse, healthy, and sustainable diet, encouraging higher consumption of fruits and vegetables, dairy, and whole grains while reducing intake of highly processed foods rich in fat and salt. The No. 1 Central Document for 2025 also explicitly called for the development of the whole-grain food industry and optimization of dietary structures to support chronic disease prevention and control. In the field of waste management, the *Implementation Plan for Household Waste Sorting System*, issued in 2017, promoted source separation and resource utilization of waste. It required daily collection and special personnel for the transport of kitchen waste, supported by detailed ledger management. The *Law on the Prevention and Control of Environmental Pollution by Solid Waste*, implemented in 2020, established a responsibility system for solid waste governance and incorporated it into the performance evaluation framework.

1.2.4.3 Challenges Facing Green and Sustainable Policies in the Agri-food System

To achieve the goals of carbon peaking and carbon neutrality, the Chinese government has successively introduced the *Action Plan for Reaching Carbon Emissions Peak Before 2030* and a series of sector-specific emission reduction implementation plans, promoting green agricultural development, the improvement of agri-food quality, and dietary transformation, in an effort to facilitate the low-carbon transition of the agri-food system. However, policies aligned with green agricultural development in China remain inadequate, and the current emission reduction outcomes of the agri-food system are still limited. This has dampened the enthusiasm of various stakeholders to engage in carbon mitigation, with challenges mainly reflected in the following two aspects:

First, the agri-food system as a whole lacks a unified strategic emission reduction roadmap and a systematic action framework (Fan & Zhang, 2024). Although the FAO has already issued a global roadmap and timeline for emissions reduction in agri-food systems, and since 2020 the Chinese government has formulated the *Implementation Plan for Agricultural and Rural Emission Reduction and Carbon Sequestration*, which defines key tasks and major actions for agriculture and rural areas, there is still no overarching strategic plan for the entire agri-food system that outlines integrated actions across the whole chain, sets explicit emission reduction targets, or presents a clear timeline for implementation. As the structure of agricultural emissions evolves, carbon emissions from pre-production and post-production stages have now surpassed those from production itself, becoming the key areas for future mitigation efforts. However, since the agri-food system spans multiple sectors and involves diverse objectives—such as food security, nutrition, and rural livelihoods—it remains highly challenging to coordinate across departments and design policies that simultaneously advance multiple goals. This lack of cross-sectoral coherence has become a major constraint on the development of a systemic mitigation strategy.

Second, current macro-level green and low-carbon policies remain detached from practical realities (Jiang et al., 2021). An examination of the green and low-carbon policies issued for agriculture reveals that while they are strategic in orientation, they often lack operational detail and show limited adaptability to local conditions. As a result, local governments may misinterpret or misapply these policies during implementation, leading to policy failures or unintended economic consequences. For instance, the *Implementation Opinions on Effectively Carrying Out the Key Tasks for Agriculture and Rural Affairs* in 2021, issued by the State Council in 2019, placed emphasis on advancing subsidies for the purchase of green agricultural machinery. However, many areas in central and western China still rely heavily on diesel and gasoline-powered equipment, with little support for green machinery procurement. Another example is the *Regulations on the Prevention and Control of Pollution from Large-Scale Livestock and Poultry Farming*, which aim to regulate livestock production. The regulation does not specify the threshold for "large-scale farming," leaving the definition to local governments. In the absence of clear understanding, some local authorities implemented blanket bans on livestock production. This resulted in adverse impacts, and by 2019, the excessive restrictions triggered a nationwide pork supply shortage and sharp price increases. In response, the State Council urgently issued the *Opinions on Stabilizing Pig Production and Promoting Its Transformation and Upgrading*, requiring local governments to immediately revise their policies and restore pork supply as quickly as possible.

Third, the existing policy framework lacks legal safeguards and a comprehensive monitoring and evaluation mechanism (Gao & Zhang, 2022). While the *14th Five-Year Plan for National Green Agricultural Development* marks a milestone as China's first dedicated planning document for green agricultural development, its coverage of carbon peaking and carbon neutrality remains insufficient. There is an urgent need to introduce relevant laws and regulations on agricultural and rural carbon peaking and neutrality that are aligned with the new development paradigm, so as to ensure the stability and sustainability of agricultural "dual carbon" work through legal and institutional means (Niu, 2021). At the same time, current policies concerning agricultural carbon emissions lack clarity on who is responsible for implementation and oversight. In some regions, local governments have used various strategies to transfer or shift carbon emission responsibilities, and the absence of a clearly designated supervisory body has further undermined policy enforcement. These deficiencies have made it difficult to achieve the intended results of green and low-carbon agricultural initiatives (Wang & Tang, 2021).

1.3 Government–Market Synergy in the Quantity and Quality Dimensions of China's Agri-Food System

In addressing the complex and evolving challenges of food, nutrition, health, and the environment in the twenty-first century, the transformation of the agri-food system is not only an urgent task but also a systematic undertaking. China's agri-food system is undergoing a multidimensional transformation aimed at ensuring food quantity security, safeguarding food safety, improving nutritional and health outcomes, and promoting green and low-carbon development. However, these goals are constrained by structural barriers, cross-sectoral conflicts, and coordination difficulties among multiple actors. **Relying solely on either the market or the government cannot effectively drive the transformation**; it is essential to strengthen the coordination between government and market through improved institutional design and policy implementation.

From a market-driven perspective, the market mechanism, as the "invisible hand" in resource allocation, plays an irreplaceable role in adjusting supply-demand structures, promoting product diversification, and meeting consumer preferences within the agri-food system. Nevertheless, a sole reliance on market logic faces numerous constraints. **On the production side, First,** highly fragmented smallholder farmers, as the basic production units in Chinese agriculture, are hindered by limited technical capacity, weak organization, and poor market access. These limitations not only restrict the system's capacity to scale and standardize production but also impede the application of green, low-carbon technologies and nutrition-oriented production practices. The prevailing tendency among smallholders to pursue short-term profits through traditional, input-intensive methods is at odds with the long-term investment and risk-sharing required for green transition. **Second,** small and medium-sized entities dominate food processing, retail, and distribution, posing multiple food safety risks such as pesticide residue exceedances, illegal additives, and cold chain deficiencies. Meanwhile, consumer capacity to identify such risks remains low, and the trust mechanism for food safety is weak. **On the consumption side**, information asymmetry and cognitive biases result in the low market penetration of green and nutritious food. Urban food waste is widespread, rural dietary imbalances persist, and green consumption behaviors remain insufficiently translated into action. Although public awareness of food quality, health, and environmental protection has increased, the absence of consistent institutional incentives and pricing signals undermines the sustainability of green consumer behavior. Food waste further exacerbates carbon emissions. These realities highlight that inherent limitations in the market mechanism—such as incentive failure, insufficient provision of public goods, and the inability to internalize externalities—render it inadequate to independently realize systemic transformation goals.

As the visible hand in institutional supply and resource allocation, the government plays an irreplaceable role in safeguarding basic food security, promoting agricultural modernization, and guiding green, low-carbon, and nutrition-oriented transitions. However, sole reliance on government also faces structural challenges. **In the area of food security,** longstanding reliance on price support and subsidy mechanisms has led to a cycle of distorted price signals, mismatches between production and consumption, and increasing fiscal pressure. In some cases, the benefits of subsidies are captured by rising land rents or capital providers, reducing policy effectiveness. **In food safety regulation**, weak local enforcement capacity, misallocation of inspection resources, and fragmented traceability systems have created blind spots in risk prevention and control. Moreover, performance assessment frameworks may distort incentives, prompting local governments to prioritize superficial compliance rates over substantive governance outcomes, and even to conceal or avoid risks. **In the nutrition and health sector,** although policy attention has grown, legislative frameworks lag behind, fiscal input remains insufficient, interdepartmental coordination is lacking, and local implementation capacity is weak, making it difficult to institutionalize and normalize interventions. Policy sustainability and effectiveness thus remain limited. **In promoting green and low-carbon transition,** there is a prevailing mismatch between abstract macro-level policy targets and the feasibility of micro-level implementation. Systems for agricultural carbon monitoring, post-production control, green machinery adoption, and emission reduction responsibility are still in early stages. At the local level, the absence of legal frameworks, unclear incentive mechanisms, and uneven pressure for accountability frequently result in policy implementation deviations. In some cases, local authorities attempt to evade responsibilities by outsourcing them. Furthermore, fragmented policies and a lack of cross-sectoral coordination mechanisms have significantly constrained the government's capacity to provide systematic guidance across the entire agri-food chain, across regions, and over time.

Thus, in the face of the complex transformation challenge posed by the intersecting goals of food security, food safety, nutrition and health, and green low-carbon development, neither market mechanisms nor government actions alone are sufficient. A deep integration of government and market is essential to achieve full-chain restructuring from production to consumption and from structural adjustment to behavioral transformation. The government should focus on institutional supply, correction of externalities, and the provision of public goods, while improving a toolkit of policies that balances incentives with constraints. The market, in turn, should play a leading role in improving resource allocation efficiency, responding to consumer demand, and fostering product innovation. Particularly in areas of pronounced market failure, such as food safety and green, low-carbon development, effective coordination between government and market is indispensable—not only to fill institutional gaps, but also to jointly shape a sustainable and high-quality future for the agri-food system.

1.4 Summary of the Book

Nowadays, the global situation of food and nutrition security remains severe, with progress stagnating in eradicating hunger, reducing food insecurity, and addressing multiple forms of malnutrition. Both China and the international community have begun to attach greater importance to agri-food system issues, proposing a comprehensive transformation toward systems that are more nutritious and healthy, green and low-carbon, high-quality and efficient, resilient, and inclusive.

The agri-food system serves as a fundamental pillar for achieving national goals related to nutrition and food security, ecological civilization, the "dual carbon" targets, and common prosperity. However, the evolving domestic and international environment presents complex challenges. To effectively respond to overlapping risks and to realize multiple national development objectives, China's agri-food system must undergo a profound transformation. To systematically examine the constraints and challenges currently facing China's agri-food system, and to explore its potential transformation pathways, this volume brings together 12 chapters organized around three key dimensions—quality and safety, nutrition and health, and green and low-carbon development. Collectively, these studies provide a comprehensive analysis of the top-level design, implementation paths, existing challenges, and strategic responses involved in advancing the transformation of China's agricultural and food system.

Food safety constitutes the foundation for achieving agri-food system transformation. Examining the effectiveness and potential shortcomings of food safety regulatory institutions and policy instruments is therefore of great importance. Accordingly, the Part II begins with a discussion on food quality safety. In Chap. 2, Lin and Liang investigate the impact of the decentralization of food safety regulatory authority in China and find that in prefectures where decentralization reform was implemented, the number of food safety incidents significantly declined. While government intervention can effectively improve food safety, government failure is also inevitable in certain contexts. In Chap. 3, Lin et al. provide empirical evidence showing that, during the process of food safety information disclosure, local governments may engage in local protectionism by underreporting or concealing noncompliance information about local enterprises. This behavior is often motivated by promotion incentives or concerns about protecting local economic development. Chapter 4 focuses on the market consequences of government disclosure of food safety information, finding that the disclosure of such information exerts a negative and lagged effect on pork prices in China's wholesale markets. Furthermore, the establishment of a food traceability system represents an effective channel to improve food safety. Understanding consumer demand and preferences for such systems is essential to promoting their development. Chapter 5 shifts the analysis to the individual level and examines consumers' willingness to pay for blockchain-based traceability technologies. The results indicate that consumers are generally willing to pay a premium for blockchain traceability systems, which can enhance consumer trust in food safety and improve the market competitiveness of food products.

Currently, with the rise in residents' disposable income, China's food system is undergoing a transformation from "eating well" to "eating more nutritiously and healthily." During this transition, the structure of household food consumption has changed substantially, with a growing demand for nutritious and health-oriented foods. In the Part III, encompassing Chaps. 6 through 9, examines how different nutritional labels and information interventions influence consumers' healthy food choices. The findings consistently indicate that nutritional labeling and information interventions exert significant effects on consumer decision-making. Chapter 6 shows that providing more detailed information about sweeteners increases consumers' willingness to pay for products containing sweeteners. Chapter 7 employs a discrete choice experiment to investigate respondents' preferences across four dietary patterns differing in healthiness and sustainability—the average diet, the

Chinese Food Guide Pagoda diet**, the EAT-Lancet diet, and the Flexitarian diet. The results suggest that while respondents generally prefer the average diet, raising its relative cost significantly encourages a shift toward healthier dietary patterns. Chapter 8 focuses on another type of nutrition label, the Multiple Traffic Light (MTL) system, and finds that MTL labels significantly reduce calorie, fat, carbohydrate, and sodium intake among Chinese university students, without altering total expenditure. Finally, Chap. 9 investigates how different forms of front-of-pack nutritional labels affect consumers' choices of sugar-sweetened beverages.

In the Part IV, the focus shifts to market mechanisms in providing sustainable foods. This section first examines how trust mechanisms influence consumers' purchasing behavior toward environmentally friendly foods. Then we explore how information and labeling guide consumers in choosing green and low-carbon products, and how consumers' internalized moral values shape their preferences for such products, thereby shedding light on potential pathways for the green and low-carbon transformation of the agri-food system. In Chap. 10, Yuan et al. find that trust in certification agencies and manufacturers effectively reduces the intention–behavior gap in consumers' purchases of environmentally friendly foods. Chapter 11 adopts an international perspective, focusing on U.S. consumers' preferences and willingness to pay for novel carbon labels. The findings in Chap. 12 reveal that green and low-carbon consumption is driven not only by external incentives but also by internalized moral values. Specifically, altruistic consumers assign higher value to sustainable foods. In Chap. 13, Lin and Nayga find that green identity labeling alone is ineffective in increasing consumers' valuation of sustainable products. However, when environmental information interventions are combined with green identity labels, they significantly enhance consumer valuation of existing pro-environmental foods, rather than of novel food products.

References

Chen, K. Z., Yu, L., Lin, W., & Ortega, D. L. (2024). What does it take to revolutionize Chinese diets: Evidence from a choice experiment on urban Chinese consumers. *China Agricultural Economic Review, 16*(4), 850–870.

Cheng, G., & Zhu, M. (2020). COVID-19 Pandemicis affecting food security: Trends, impacts and recommendations. *Chinese Rural Economy, 5*, 13–20.

Chou, H., Lei, X., Leng, G., & Liu, M. (2022). A comprehensive theoretical analysis of grain security in the new era. *Chinese Rural Economy, 7*, 2–17.

Crippa, M., Solazzo, E., Guizzardi, D., Monforti-Ferrario, F., Tubiello, F. N., & Leip, A. (2021). Food systems are responsible for a third of global anthropogenic GHG emissions. *Nature Food, 2*, 1–12.

Fan, S., & Zhang, Y. (2024). Strategic thinking on the low-carbon transformation of agrifood systems in China. *Issues in Agricultural Economy, 12*, 15–23.

Fan, S., Zhang, Y., & Chen, K. (2019). Antiglobalism and global food security. *Issues in Agricultural Economy, 3*, 4–10.

FAO (Food and Agricultural Organization of the United Nations). (2020, July). Crop prospects and food situation-Quarterly global report no. 2. Rome. https://doi.org/10.4060/ca9803en.

Guan, L., Jin, S., & Lin, W. (2024). The role of information in nudging Chinese consumers from choosing sugar to alternative sweeteners. *China Economic Review, 87*, 102233.

Guan, L., Lin, W., & Jin, S. (2025). Effectiveness of front-of-pack nutritional labels: Evidence from sugar-sweetened beverages in China. *Applied Economics, 57*(35), 5344–5358.

He, Y., Yang, X., Xia, J., Zhao, L., & Yang, Y. (2016). Consumption of meat and dairy products in China: A review. *Proceedings of the Nutrition Society, 75*(3), 385–391.

Li, H., Li, M., Huang, X., & Hu, B. (2024). China's soybean supply security under the background of agricultural power strategy: Realistic basis, potential analysis, and strategic selection. *Issues in Agricultural Economy, 7*, 48–58.

Li, H., & Lin, W. (2023). Would altruistic consumers place a higher value on sustainable foods? *Food, 12*(19), 3701.

Li, H., Wu, T., Wang, X., & Qi, Y. (2016). The greenhouse gas footprint of China's food system: An analysis of recent trends and future scenarios. *Journal of Industrial Ecology, 20*(4), 803–817.

Li, T., Bo, H., & Nie, W. (2021). A study on the evaluation of supervision sampling efficiency of food safety in China-based on the perspective of sampling batches distribution under the pressure of government performance evaluation. *Journal of Macro-quality Research, 9*(6), 86–98.

Lin, J., Wang, T., & Lin, W. (2024). Becoming healthier without paying more? Experimental evidence from the impact of multiple traffic lights on Chinese college students. *Nutrients, 16*(13), 2124.

Lin, W., & Liang, J. (2025). Regulatory decentralization and food safety: Evidence from China. *American Journal of Agricultural Economics, 107*(1), 54–80.

Lin, W., Liang, J., Shang, S., & Zhou, J. (2024). Local protectionism, information manipulation, and government disclosure of food safety information. Information manipulation, and government disclosure of food safety information (May 15, 2024).

Lin, W., Ma, B., Liang, J., & Jin, S. (2024). Price response to government disclosure of food safety information in developing markets. *Food Policy, 123*, 102602.

Lin, W., & Nayga, R. M., Jr. (2022). Green identity labeling, environmental information, and pro-environmental food choices. *Food Policy, 106*, 102187.

Lin, W., Nayga, R. M., Jr., & Yang, W. (2024). Preferences and willingness to pay for a novel carbon label: A choice experiment in the United States. *Journal of the Agricultural and Applied Economics Association, 3*(2), 346–357.

Lin, W., Ortega, D. L., Ufer, D., Caputo, V., & Awokuse, T. (2022). Blockchain-based traceability and demand for US beef in China. *Applied Economic Perspectives and Policy, 44*(1), 253–272.

Poore, J., & Nemecek, T. (2018). Reducing food's environmental impacts through producers and consumers. *Science, 360*(6392), 987–992.

Rosenzweig, C., Mbow, C., Barioni, L. G., Benton, T. G., Herrero, M., Krishnapillai, M., et al. (2021). Greenhouse gas emissions from food systems: Building the evidence base. *Environmental Research Letters, 16*(6), 065007.

Tian, X., Long, W., & Fan, S. (2021). Building a diversified food supply system guided by the greater agriculture approach and the greater food approach. *China Development, 24*(1), 35–40.

Wang, X., & Zhang, J. (2022). Basic path and system construction of agricultural green and low-carbon development with respect to the strategic target of carbon peak and carbon neutrality. *Chinese Journal of Eco-Agriculture, 30*(4), 516–526.

Wang, Y. (2020). Changes unseen in a century, high-quality development, and the construction of a new development pattern. *Journal of Management World, 36*(12), 1–13.

Yuan, R., Jin, S., & Lin, W. (2025). Could trust narrow the intention-behavior gap in eco-friendly food consumption? Evidence from China. *Agribusiness, 41*(1), 260–288.

Zhou, J., Wu, Z., & Li, K. (2018). The achievements and prospects of food quality and safety supervision, *2*, 4–14.

Zhou, Y., & Wang, Z. (2014). A study on food safety supervision system in China: Based on the perspective of international comparison, *2*(2), 74–81.

Part II
Government-Market Synergy to Safeguard Food Safety

Chapter 2
Regulatory Decentralization and Food Safety: Evidence from China

2.1 Introduction

Should public goods be provided in a centralized or decentralized system? It is not obvious, a priori, which institutional arrangement is better at providing public goods. A classical argument is that decentralization leads to the efficient production of public goods due to local information advantage (Hayek, 1945), interjurisdictional competition (Tiebout, 1956), and incentives from authority increasing (Besley & Ghatak, 2003). Alternative views include that the decentralized provision is not welfare improving because of lack of scale economy (Prud'Homme, 1995), free riding in public goods with spillover (Oates, 1972), and local capture (Bardhan & Mookherjee, 2000, 2006). This study contributes to the inconclusive literature by investigating how decentralization of regulatory authority affects public good provision, focusing on food safety.

Food safety garners substantial public attention and concern across economies, from developing and transitioning to developed ones (Hamilton et al., 2003; Pouliot & Wang, 2018; Richards et al., 2009; Unnevehr, 2007). An estimated 600 million, almost 1 in 10 people in the world, fall ill after eating contaminated foods, and 420,000 die every year, resulting in the loss of 33 million healthy life years (WHO, 2015).[1] Unsafe food costs low- and middle-income economies about US$110 billion in lost productivity and medical expenses each year (Jaffee et al., 2018).

We examine the effects of regulatory decentralization on food safety and food using a natural experiment in China's food processing and manufacturing sector, the largest and emerging global food market. China has been confronted with significant challenges in food safety, which triggered widespread public concerns and

[1] The Disability-Adjusted Life Year (DALY) is a measure of the overall disease burden, where one DALY represents the loss of the equivalent of 1 year of full health.

W. Lin, *Transforming China's Agri-Food System: Government-Market Synergy*, Resources, Environment and Agricultural Development,
https://doi.org/10.1007/978-981-95-7151-2_2

inflicted economic losses (Bai et al., 2022). In early 2013, the Chinese central government decided to transfer the regulatory authority of food safety in the food processing and manufacturing sector from provincial governments to city-level governments. This decentralization included the delegation of financial and personnel controls over city-level food safety regulation departments from provincial to city-level governments. The reform is a top-down national policy, and its gradual implementation facilitates the application of a staggered difference-in-differences design for our empirical strategy. As official and public data on food safety are unavailable, we compile food safety news and reports and build an externally validated database on food safety incidents in China from 2010 to 2017 (details on data collection and validation in Sect. 2.3).

To estimate the effect of decentralization on food safety, we compare trends in food safety outcomes between the late-treated and early-treated cities using the two-step procedure suggested by Callaway and Sant'Anna (2021) that is robust to treatment timing and treatment effect heterogeneity. We also include covariates prior to decentralization to addresses the potential nonrandomness of decentralization timing. Findings reveal a 51% decrease in the average number of food safety incidents within cities that experienced the reform. We conduct a battery of robustness checks to guard our findings. First, the event study shows that the pretrends in food safety incidents are similar between decentralized and not-yet-decentralized cities, providing evidence in support of the parallel trend assumption. Second, we control for potential confounding policies, such as the selection of food safety demonstration cities. Third, we use the stochastic frontier analyses and sub-sample approach to mitigate the concern of underreporting bias by local governments. Fourth, we employ alternative estimators that rely on less stringent modeling conditions and two-way-fixed-effects difference in differences estimators to assess the decentralization's impact on city-level food safety incidents.

Information and accountability mechanisms are found to explain the improved food safety outcomes from decentralization. The positive effect of decentralization is stronger in provinces where the complexity of food safety information is higher, suggesting that decentralization rectifies information asymmetry in food safety supervision by empowering lower level governments with more information. Meanwhile, decentralization has led to a 28.8% increase in city-level laws and regulations on food safety compared to nondecentralized cities. This is mainly driven by the increased supervision and penalty regulations about food processing and manufacturing industries.

For firm-level analyses, we utilize China's firm registration dataset and merge it with our food safety incident dataset using firm names, resulting in a balanced firm-year panel dataset comprising 3549 firms consistently existing from 2010 to 2017. Similar to the city-level analyses, we employ both the CSDiD and two-way-fixed-effects difference in differences estimations to evaluate the decentralization's impact on the firm-level occurrence of food safety incidents. The findings suggest that decentralization tends to reduced food safety incidents of large-scale and well-established firms.

For industry-level analyses, we use the main revenue generated by the food processing and manufacturing industry as a proxy to assess the economic impact of decentralization. We construct an industry-province-year panel dataset from the China Industrial and Economic Statistics Yearbook and provincial statistical yearbooks, and apply the triple difference method. The results suggest that, at the least, the reform has not negatively impacted the total revenue of large-scale food processing and manufacturing firms while contributing to improvements in food safety.

Our study relates to several strands of literature. First, this research adds to the understanding of decentralization's effects. Existing literature has explored the outcomes of fiscal decentralization (Han & Kung, 2015; Oates, 1993; Thornton, 2007) and political decentralization (Fan et al., 2009; Gallego, 2010; Treisman, 2002). Our research contributes by investigating regulatory decentralization, a form of political decentralization that involves the process of transferring regulatory authority from higher levels of government to lower levels. For regulatory decentralization, we empirically analyze its impacts on public goods, on which existing theories diverge (Bardhan & Mookherjee, 2000, 2006; Besley & Coate, 2003; Prud'Homme, 1995; Tiebout, 1956). Other empirical studies have assessed how decentralization affects the provision of education services (Barankay & Lockwood, 2007; Galiani et al., 2008), health services (Abimbola et al., 2019; Bossert & Mitchell, 2011), workplace safety (Jia & Nie, 2017), and air quality and water quality (Chen et al., 2022; Lipscomb & Mobarak, 2016; Sigman, 2005). Our study presents a novel study to examine decentralization's effect on food safety.

Second, our study is relevant to the literature on the role of information. Although the importance of information on decentralized production and overall organizational performance has been found theoretically (Aghion & Tirole, 1997; Hayek, 1945; Oates, 1972; Tirole, 1986), and several studies showed that higher local information value aligns with increased organizational decentralization (Acemoglu et al., 2007; Aghion et al., 2021; Huang et al., 2017), its impact on the provision of public goods is rarely empirically explored. Although local governments can leverage their superior information to improve regulatory outcomes, the potential for collusion with local firms also exists. It is noted that studying how regulatory decentralization affects food safety provides the right setting for exploring the role of information. Food safety incidents represent market failures from imperfect information, emphasizing the significance of accessible information to regulatory authorities for effective regulatory measures.

There is also a body of studies assessing various food safety regulations, including the obligatory adoption of hazard analysis critical control points (Antle, 2000; Liu & Yue, 2012; Unnevehr & Jensen, 1996), public disclosure of food quality information (Lin et al., 2024; Ollinger & Bovay, 2020), the establishment of maximum residue limits (Fiankor et al., 2021; Hejazi et al., 2022), and food recalls (Ollinger & Houser, 2020; Pozo & Schroeder, 2016; Toledo & Villas-Boas, 2019). Our research studies a different regulation. Concurrently, these studies mainly document how food safety regulations influence firm costs and behaviors, as well as food market outcomes. They over-look the direct exploration of food safety outcomes, except for two recent papers by Ollinger and Houser (2020) and Ollinger and Bovay (2020) that examined the influence of food safety disclosure on Salmonella testing results. This omission would be attributed, in part, to the limited availability of food safety databases over an extended period, in particular in emerging economies. To fill this gap, our paper constructs and presents a novel dataset of 15,897 food safety incidents involving food products processed and manufactured from 2010 to 2017 across 318 prefectural cities. A key advantage of our dataset lies in the inclusion of information on the location of food processing and manufacturing firms involved in food safety incidents. This enables us to trace back the origin city of unsafe food products, thereby providing a more accurate reflection of food safety outcomes.

The remainder of this paper is organized as follows. Section 2.2 provides background on food safety regulation and the decentralization reform in China. Section 2.3 describes the food safety incident database and the source of other variables. Section 2.4 uses the Callaway and Sant'Anna (2021) method and city-level data to show that the decentralization reduced food safety incidents by 51%, followed by robustness checks in Sect. 2.5. Section 2.6 analyzes information and accountability mechanisms underlying the city-level results. Section 2.7 investigates the decentralization's impacts on firm-level food safety incidents and industry-level main revenue. Section 2.8 discusses and concludes.

2.2 Decentralization Reform of Food Safety Regulation in China

In China, food safety is jointly managed by multiple departments (Jia & Jukes, 2013), including the Food Safety Committee of the State Council; the Ministry of Health (MOH); the Ministry of Agriculture (MOA); the Administration of Quality Supervision, Inspection and Quarantine (AQSIQ); the Administration for Industry and Commerce (AIC); and the State Food and Drug Administration (SFDA). The respective roles and responsibilities of these departments at different food supply chain segments are depicted in Fig. 2.1a. Along food supply chains, AQSIQ is responsible for regulating food safety in the food processing and manufacturing segment. The food safety control system at the provincial, city, and county levels follows the same structure as outlined in Fig. 2.1a (Chen et al., 2015).

The Chinese government has made unremitting efforts to address food safety issues, including the implementation of the Food Safety Law in 2009. Another representative effort in this regard is the decentralization reform of food safety regulatory authority. In April 2013, the State Council of China issued the Guiding Opinions of the State Council on Local Reform to Improve the Supervision and Administration of Food and Drugs,[2] and the policy decided to delegate the regulatory authority of the food processing and manufacturing sector from provincial governments to city-level governments (henceforth referred to as the decentralization).

[2]Check the full content in Chinese at https://www.gov.cn/zhengce/content/2013-04/18/content_4394.htm?ivk_sa=1024320u

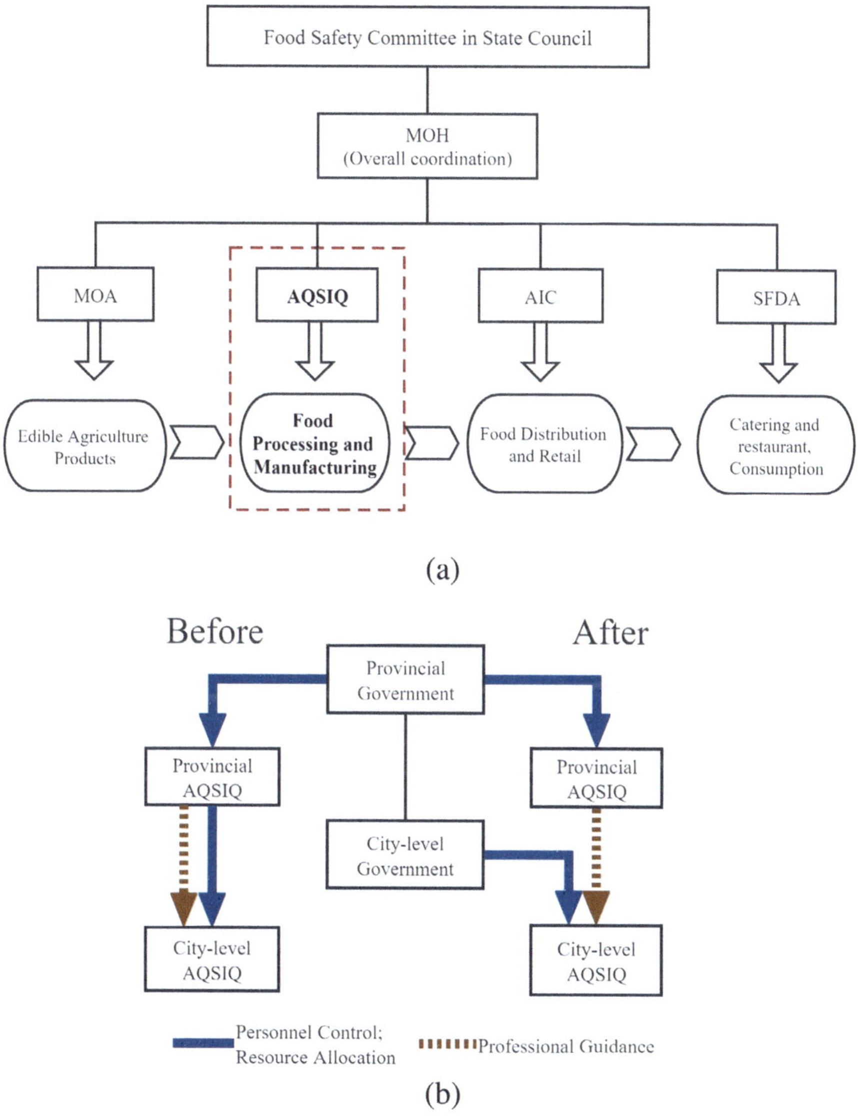

Fig. 2.1 Decentralization reform. Panel (**a**) depicts the food safety responsibilities of each department along food supply chains, and Panel (**b**) depicts the administrative structure of China's local administration of quality supervision, inspection, and quarantine (AQSIQ) before and after the decentralization

AQSIQ was directly involved in the decentralization. Before the decentralization, provincial AQSIQ had control over city-level AQSIQ, and city-level AQSIQ is independent of the corresponding local government. Specifically, for each city-level AQSIQ, its budget and personnel appointments needed to be approved by its provincial AQSIQ. The budget includes funding for food quality tests, specialized equipment procurement, and staff salaries and bonuses, whereas in personnel decisions the provincial AQSIQ has the final say such as appointing a new head of the department. Meanwhile, city-level AQSIQ received professional guidance from the provincial AQSIQ, such as guidance on compliance and legality in the process of food safety supervision and training in food safety monitoring techniques, interpretation of food standards, and food safety risk assessment, which were suggestive and nonbinding for city-level AQSIQ. The decentralization delegates financial and personnel controls over city-level AQSIQ from provincial governments to city-level governments. After the reform, control over city-level AQSIQ is held by its corresponding city-level government, which significantly increases local AQSIQ's dependence on local governments (see Fig. 2.1b). Although the decentralization aims to enhance food safety, the qualitative evidence regarding its impacts remains inconclusive. Some suggested that the reform enhances the local government's accountability in food safety regulation (Wang, 2011), although concerns were raised about the collusion between local governments and food firms as found in other industries (Buntaine et al., 2024; He et al., 2020; Liu & Zhang, 2015).

The decentralization had a staggered rollout, and the time of implementation varied across provinces (Liu et al., 2016). Shanxi province was selected as a pilot site in 2012 before the national rollout.In China's many nationwide policy reforms, it is common to employ policy experimentation through staggered rollout. This approach aims to reduce policy uncertainty and explore the most effective protocols for implementation (Liu et al., 2022). We manually collected the data on the decentralization's implementation time for each of the 31 provinces from the official websites of provincial governments. Appendix A provides the implementation date for each province and the corresponding website sources. Between 2012 and 2015, the decentralization was implemented in 31 provincial administrative regions, and by 2014, 77% of the provinces issued reform notices (Table 2.9).

2.3 DATA

We construct and employ the two main databases in our empirical analysis: the province-level decentralization rollout information aforementioned in Sect. 2.2, and food safety incident data.

2.3.1 Food Safety Incident Data

The primary objective of this study is to examine the decentralization's effects on food safety, using the number of food safety incidents as the dependent variable. The number of food safety incidents has been widely recognized in the literature as a reliable indicator of food safety (Latouche et al., 1998; Piggott & Marsh, 2004;

Spalding et al., 2023). In the absence of publicly accessible and readily available data on food safety incidents in China and other emerging countries, we manually collected the number of food safety incidents before and after the reform. It is common for researchers to use food safety incident data from media sources when official data are unavailable (Holtkamp et al., 2014; Mueller, 1997; Peng et al., 2015; Swinnen et al., 2005).

To enhance the transparency and reliability of data collection, we employ a systematic approach when collecting food safety incident data. The following steps outline the process: (1) The first step involves identifying food safety news articles reported in the Chinese news media between 2010 and 2017. This is achieved by entering keywords such as "food safety" or "food quality" into Baidu, the most popular and largest search engine in China. (2) After retrieving the food safety news articles, we proceed with a thorough reading and screening process. We identify a food safety incident by assessing whether the test result of food fails to meet the national standards. Each news article is carefully assessed to determine its relevance and inclusion in our data collection. To be included, each food safety incident involved in each news article (a news article would report more than one food safety incident) must provide comprehensive details including the media source, report date, specific food product involved, the reason for being identified as unsafe, food processor or manufacturer name and location, and the corresponding date of food processing or manufacturing. The data undergo a cross-validation process in which two separate groups of research assistants independently examine and verify the information. (3) The pertinent details are extracted from the selected news articles and coded according to predefined categories. To be relevant, we only consider food safety incidents that are directly related to the food processing and manufacturing sector. Incidents occurring outside of this sector or not attributable to food processing and manufacturing activities are excluded from the dataset. Finally, we have constructed a dataset consisting of 15,897 food safety incidents that occurred between 2010 and 2017. These incidents involve food products processed or manufactured during that period, spanning 318 city-level administrative regions.

In the food safety incident dataset, each observation captures the food safety incident information at the product and date level, including product name, the name, and location of the processor or manufacturer or retailer, production date, food safety risk factor, and media source. Food safety risk factors refer to the reasons why a food product fails to meet the standard. The types of risk factors identified in food safety incidents are based on the Chinese Implementation Measures for National Food Safety Supervision and Sampling (CFDA, 2018). There are 15 categories of food safety risk factors, including residues of pesticides and veterinary drugs, excessive heavy metals, excessive additives, and microbial contamination. A key advantage of the dataset lies in the inclusion of information on the location of food processors or manufacturers involved in food safety incidents. This feature enables us to trace back the production city of unsafe food products and aggregate food safety incidents at the production city level for formal analyses. We argue that it is crucial to distinguish the production location and the exposure location of unsafe food products as many unsafe foods are detected outside of the places where

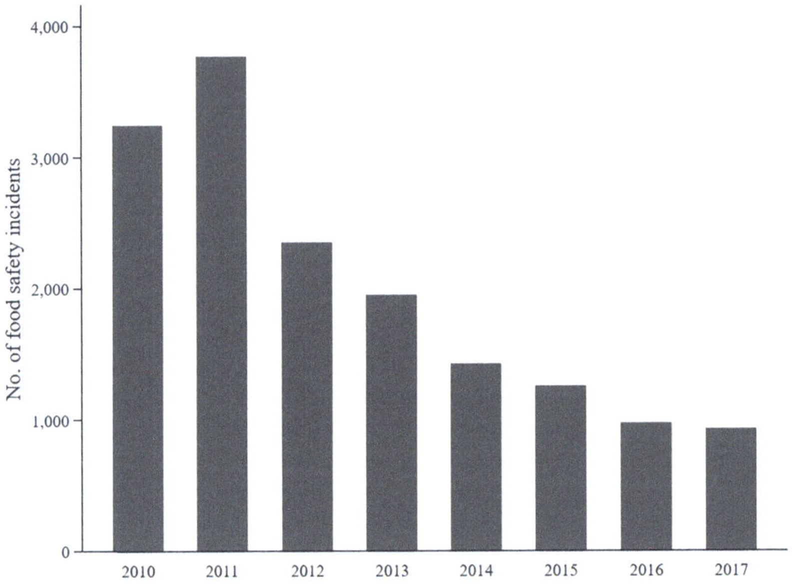

(a)

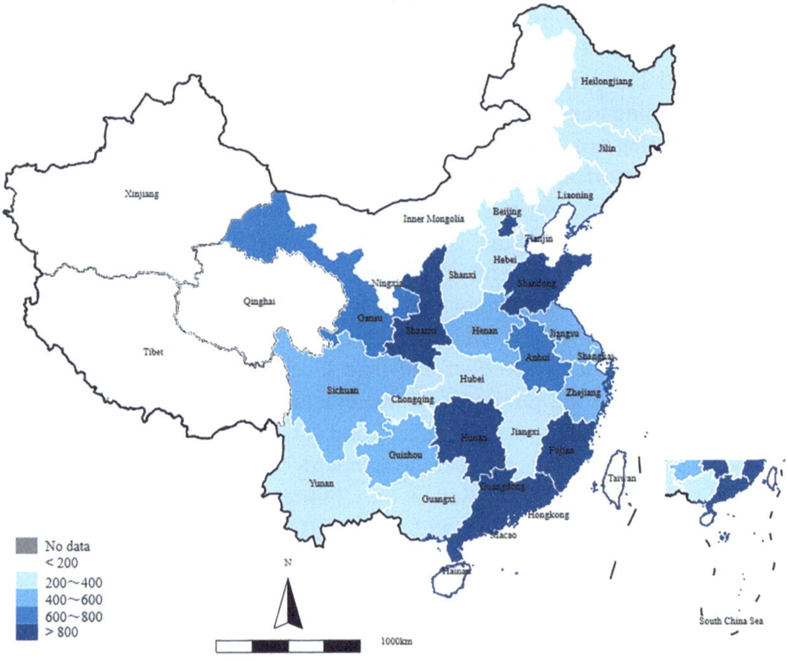

(b)

Fig. 2.2 Food safety incidents distribution by production year and production origin. Panel (**a**) depicts the number of food safety incidents yearly from 2010 to 2017 across 31 provinces, and Panel (**b**) depicts the provincial distribution of food safety incidents across 31 provinces they were originally produced or processed. For example, in the 2008 Chinese milk contamination incident, the melamine-contaminated milk powder was produced in Hebei province, but the incident was initially reported in Zhejiang province. Thus, measuring the number of food safety incidents processed or manufactured by a city provides a more accurate reflection of food safety outcomes. Figure 2.2a presents the temporal distribution of food safety incidents from 2010 to 2017, whereas Fig. 2.2b displays the distribution of food safety incidents across 31 provinces. Food safety incidents reached its peak in 2011, and after the implementation of decentralization reforms, the number of food safety incidents decreased.

Before formal analyses, we ensure the validity of our food safety incident data by providing a detailed description of the dataset and conducting statistical comparisons with existing food safety datasets. Data for this study were collected from a diverse array of media sources that encompass central news portal websites as well as regional portal websites in China (see Appendix B for news media included in our dataset). The food categories included in the dataset encompass all food types specified in China's food production license classification. As a result, the database provides a comprehensive record of food safety incidents across food products in China. This breadth of coverage enhances the reliability and representativeness of the data for our empirical analysis (Table 2.10).

To provide a more accurate assessment of the database's reliability in reflecting the level of food safety in China, we conduct a rigorous comparison between our database and two public datasets, namely the Throw Out the Window database and China's Food Safety Supervision and Sampling Inspection Reports. The reliability and validity of the Throw Out the Window database (referred to as ZCCW), which reports the number of provincial food safety incidents annually from 2004 to 2011, have been verified by both governments and academia (Holtkamp et al., 2014; Liu & Ma, 2016). Table 2.1 exhibits a significant and positive correlation between our manually collected data and ZCCW at the province level, after accounting for the province and year fixed effects. The Food Safety Supervision and Sampling Inspection Reports released by the China Food and Drug Administration (CFDA) for 2016 and 2017 reports contain data on unsafe product categories and food safety risk factors detected through national sampling inspections. Figure 2.3 illustrates a comparative analysis of the distribution of product categories and food safety risk factors between our dataset and the CFDA report. Statistical tests, presented in Appendix C, reveal no differences in the distributions between the two databases (Table 2.11).

2.3.2 Provincial and City-level Controls

Our control variables are obtained from various public statistical yearbooks, such as China Statistical Yearbook, China City Statistics Yearbooks, China Industrial and Economic Statistics Yearbook, China Health Statistics Yearbook, and provincial statistical yearbooks. Additionally, internet penetration rate is sourced from the China

Table 2.1 Correlation between the food safety incident database and ZCCW

	Food safety incident database		
	(1)	(2)	(3)
ZCCW	0.656***(0.057)	0.414**(0.175)	0.722***
p-value			<0.001
Province FE	No	Yes	
Year FE	No	Yes	
Observations	124	124	124
R^2	0.522	0.751	

Note: This analysis is conducted at the province level. The dependent variable represents the ratio calculated from our food safety incidents database, whereas Throw Out the Window database (ZCCW) represents the ratio calculated from the ZCCW dataset. The ratio is the number of food safety incidents in province p, year t divided by the total number of food safety incidents in year t. The sample includes 31 provinces for 4 years. Significance levels are denoted as *** for 1% and ** for 5%

Internet Network Information Center, whereas public concern about food safety is from the Baidu search volume.

Finally, we obtained the panel data for empirical analysis by excluding 5 cities[3] with zero incidents and 35 cities having missing control variables.[4] The panel dataset is sourced from 27 provinces and 278 prefectural cities[5] from 2010 to 2017. Table 2.2 provides the summary statistics for our key variables. The average number of food safety incidents per city is approximately 7 (a standard deviation of 19.25). This indicates significant variation in food safety outcomes across cities, which facilitates the identification of the decentralization effect.

2.4 Baseline Effect of the Decentralization on Food Safety

2.4.1 *Empirical Strategy*

To estimate the effect of the decentralization on food safety, we compare trends in food safety outcomes between the late-treated and early-treated cities using the two-step procedure suggested by Callaway and Sant'Anna (2021) (hereafter CSDiD) that is robust to treatment timing and treatment effect heterogeneity. Equation (2.1) shows how we implemented CSDiD:

[3] There are five cities that have zero incidents in a specific year, which account for only 1.8% of the entire database. The removal of these cities is expected to have little impact on the overall estimate.

[4] Population density and per capita GDP data are unavailable for 35 city-level administrative regions, as these regions are not included in the China Urban Statistical Yearbook.

[5] In the empirical analysis, the panel data include cities that represent 83% of the total cities in China.

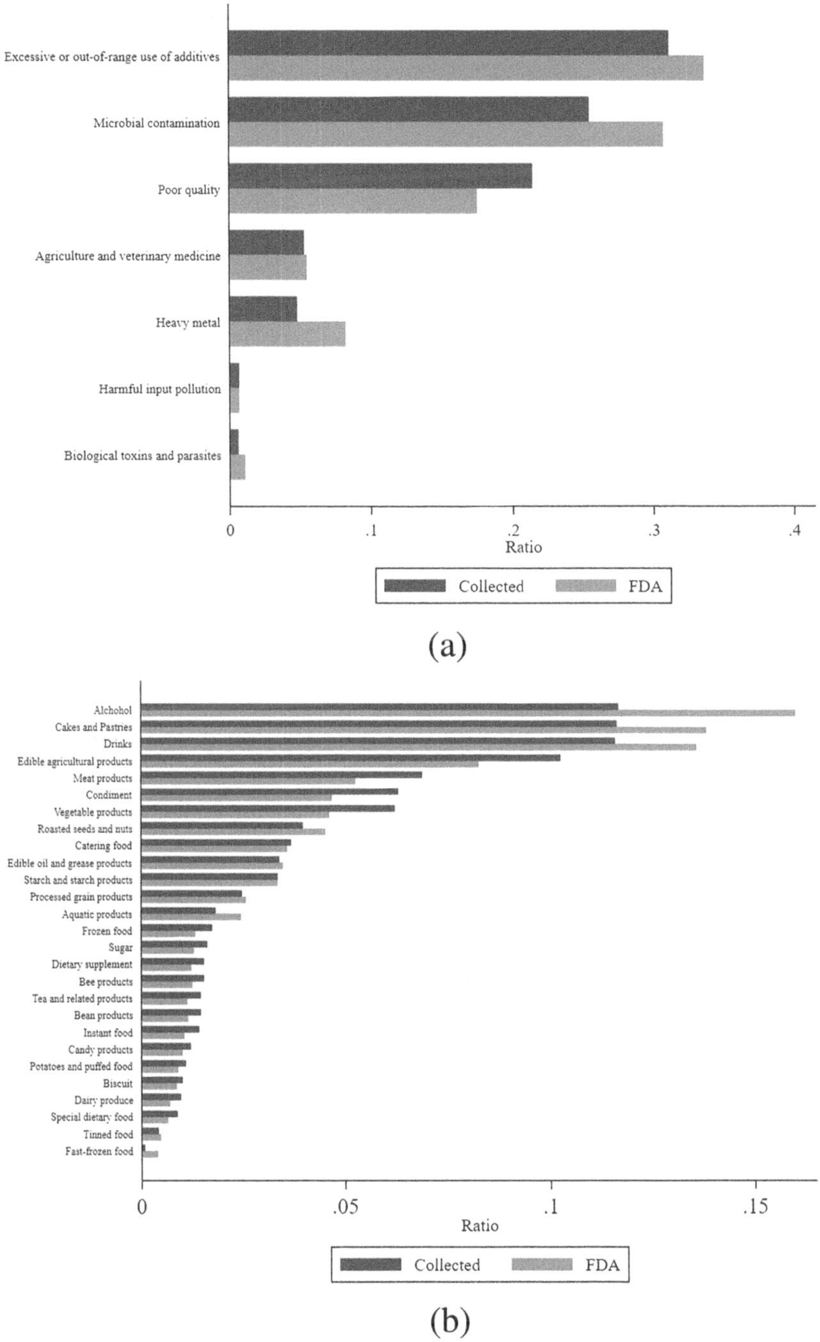

Fig. 2.3 The distribution of product categories and food safety risk factors between our dataset and others. Panels (**a**, **b**) are the distribution of food product categories and food safety risk factors, respectively, between our dataset and the official reports. "Collected" refers to the data that we collected for this study, whereas "FDA" refers to data reported by the China Food and Drug Administration. FDA, Food and Drug Administration

Table 2.2 Summary statistics

Variable	Obs.	Mean	Std. dev.
City-level food safety incidents			
The number of food safety incidents	2224	7.12	19.25
Ln (the number of food safety incidents)	2224	1.05	1.19
City-level controls			
Ln (population density)	2224	5.75	0.91
Ln (GDP per capital)	2224	10.47	0.59
Public concern about food safety measured by Baidu search index	2224	44.36	26.77
Province-level controls			
Ln (consumption expenditure per capita)	216	9.90	0.32
Ln (the number of foodborne illness cases)	216	3.60	1.20
Ln (the revenue of the large-scale food processing and manufacturing industry)	216	7.57	0.97
The number of internet users in 10,000	216	22.42	14.40
Internet penetration rate (%)	216	46.90	13.74

Note: The Chinese Food Safety Supervision and Sampling Inspection Reports released by the China Food and Drug Administration only disclosed food safety incident information for 2016 and 2017, thus we utilized a full sample encompassing 278 cities from 27 provinces from 2010 to 2017 when checking the external validity of our dataset (Sect. 2.3.1) and then using the full sample to run the two-way fixed effect difference-in-differences regressions ($278 \times 8 = 2224$, $27 \times 8 = 216$). But when using the difference-in-differences method described by Callaway and Sant'Anna (2021), as all cities had been decentralized by 2015, we employed the sample from 2010 to 2014

$$ATT(g,t) = E\left[Y_t - Y_{t-1} | G_g = 1\right] - E\left[Y_t - Y_{g-1} | \mathbf{X}, D_t = 0, G_g = 0\right], \qquad (2.1)$$

where Y_t is the outcome variable at year t and g denotes the group first under the decentralization reform at year g. The second term on the right of Eq. (2.1) is the counterfactual with a $D_t = 0$ not-yet-treated comparison group. The identification assumption is that the average outcomes for the group first treated in period g and for the not-yet-treated group would have followed parallel paths in the absence of the decentralization, controlling for a vector of X variables. X includes variables that might affect the timing of policy implementation and simultaneously influence food safety. For example, in regions characterized by a higher public concern regarding food safety, there may be a greater impetus for governments to expedite reforms (Liu et al., 2016). Public concern about food safety is proxied by the Baidu search volume of the term "food safety," internet usage, and the prevalence of food safety incidents.[6] Internet usage can raise public awareness of food safety risks and push the government to implement the reform, such as by promoting greater

[6] Similar to the Google Trends index, the Baidu search index provides public time-series indices based on Baidu search data, which capture how often a search term, like food safety, is entered relative to the total search volume in a given geographical area.

exposure to food safety incidents. Besides, we control factors including city-level per capita GDP and population density, provincial-level per capita consumption expenditure, and the main revenue of large-scale food processing and manufacturing firms. We define $X = Xc \cdot f(t)$. To avoid violating ignorability of treatment (Wooldridge, 2005), *Xc* includes pretreatment values. Last, to flexibly control for the trends in food safety outcomes influenced by the aforementioned factors over time, we interact *Xc* with a third-order polynomial function of time, denoted as Xc .f (t) following Deming (2014), Atkin (2016) and Naritomi (2019). The standard errors are clustered at the province level to account for correlation within provinces.

To aid interpretation, we present individual ATT parameters by group and the aggregates of all average treatment effects on the treated (ATTs). The former is useful because postreform effect estimates allow us to study how the treatment effect changes overtime, whereas prereform effect estimates allow us to visually inspect and formally test whether conditional pretrends in outcomes are parallel.

2.4.2 Impacts of Decentralization on Food Safety

The baseline results are presented in Table 2.3. Columns (1) and (2) provide the estimated average treatment effects of the decentralization on the natural logarithm of the number of food safety incidents under the unconditional parallel trend assumption and conditional parallel trend assumption, respectively. Both coefficients are significantly negative at the 1% level and close in absolute value. Based on Column (2), the point estimate for the aggregated average treatment effect is −0.723, indicating that the decentralization results in a reduction of 51.47%[7] in food safety incidents. Given the sample average of 8.173 safety incidents, the decentralization results in an approximate average reduction of 4.21 incidents per city per year. Considering the nationwide scope of this reform, the impact of the decentralization amounts to a substantial reduction of 1169 food safety incidents in China.

Figure 2.4 presents the point estimates and 95% confidence bands for group-time ATTs of the decentralization on food safety incidents. The estimation is implemented based on Eq. (2.1) under the conditional parallel trend assumption. This figure yields two main findings. First, the plots include pretreatment estimates that can be used as supporting evidence of parallel trends. None of the point estimates in the pretreatment periods (inside of the gray areas) are significantly different from zero, consistent with the parallel trend assumption. Secondly, for cities that initiated reforms in 2012, 2013, and 2014, the estimates of the post-treatment periods (outside the gray area and in white) remain similar, with values of −0.73, −0.75, and – 0.72, respectively, indicating that decentralization decreased the incidence of food safety incidents.

---

[7] Because the dependent variable is ln(incidents) and the regressor is linear, the conversion formula from log points to percentages is (eβ – 1) × 100%. The coefficients are converted in the same manner in the following text.

Table 2.3 Effects of the decentralization on food safety incidents

	D.V. = ln (no. of food safety incidents)	
	Unconditional parallel trends	Conditional parallel trends
	(1)	(2)
Decentralization	−0.722*** (0.112)	−0.723*** (0.116)
Observations	1390	1390
Means of no. incidents	8.173	8.173

Note: This table reports the aggregated treatment effects of the decentralization on the natural logarithm of the number of food safety incidents at the city level. Columns (1) and (2) report the estimators using the difference-in-differences method described by Callaway and Sant'Anna (2021) withoutcome regression estimators under the unconditional parallel trend assumption and conditional parallel trend assumption, respectively. Under the assumption of conditional parallel trends, we include controls consistent with those in Eq. (2.1). Significance levels are denoted as *** for 1%, ** for 5%, and * for 10%. Standard errors are in parentheses clustered by province. The average number of city-level food safety incidents is reported at the bottom of this table. As all cities had been decentralized by 2015, when using CSDiD, we employed the sample from 2010 to 2014 (278 × 5 = 1390)

The event study estimates are displayed in Fig. 2.5. The pretends are similar between decentralized and not-yet-decentralized cities, showing additional evidence in favor of the parallel trend assumption. Since the implementation of decentralization, there has been a significant reduction in the frequency of food safety incidents, persisting steadily into the second year following the reform. Besides, the figure presents ATTs of the decentralization on food safety across all groups in post-treatment periods. When the year since the decentralization equals 0, the effect includes that of all groups (2012, 2013, and 2014); when the year equals 1, the effect includes cities that first implemented decentralization in 2012 and 2013, as those initiated in 2014 only have a contemporaneous ATT (year since decentralization equals 0).

2.5 Robustness Checks

2.5.1 Confounding Policies and Alternative Estimators

In this section, we conduct a series of robustness tests on our baseline findings in Sect. 2.4. We begin by considering three sensitivity tests using the CSDiD method under conditional parallel trends assumption. First, we control for potential confounding policies such as the selection of food safety demonstration cities. In 2017 the China Food and Drug Administration announced the results of the comprehensive evaluation of national food safety demonstration cities, and 15 cities were selected as the first group of national food safety demonstration cities. In Column (1) of Table 2.4 we introduce a dummy variable in Eq. (2.2) to indicate whether the city was designated as a demonstration city. Second, in Column (2) of Table 2.4, we

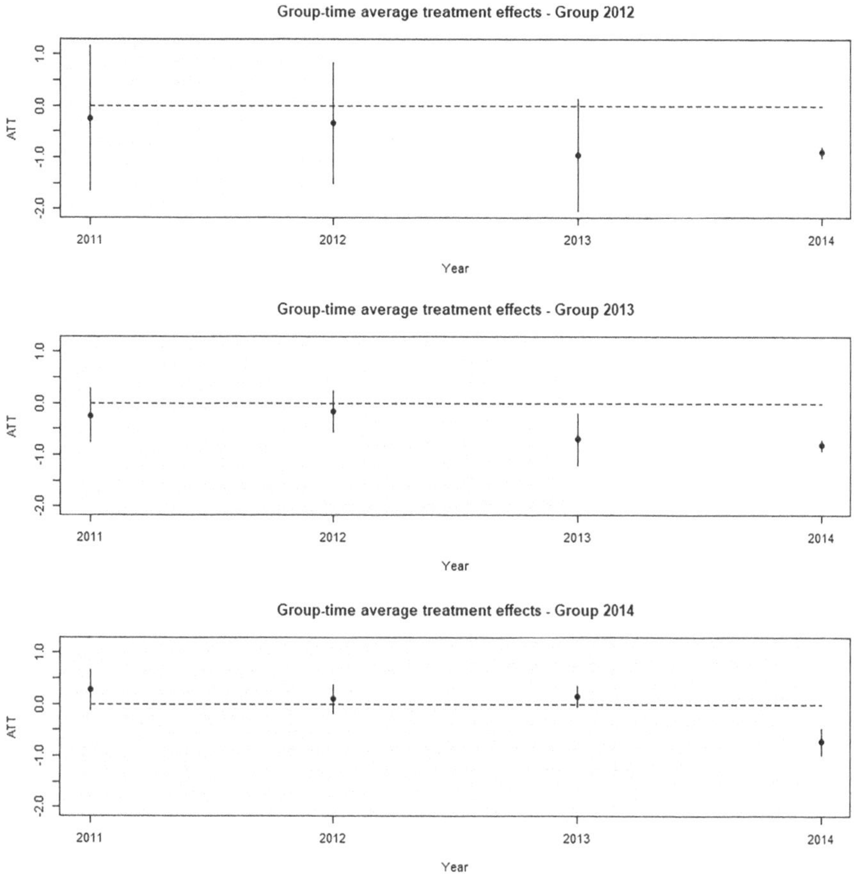

Fig. 2.4 Group-time average treatment effects of the decentralization on food safety incidents. This figure shows the group-time average treatment estimates of the effect of the decentralization on food safety incidents at the city level using the difference-in-differences method described by Callaway and Sant'Anna (2021). Point estimates and 95% confidence bands for pre- and post-treatment periods are inside and outside the gray shaded area, respectively. Confidence bands are constructed using standard errors clustered at the province level. ATT, average treatment effects on the treated

exclude the four municipalities that serve as China's provincial-level administrative regions from the sample. Third, we employ the doubly robust estimators, which rely on less stringent modeling conditions than the outcome regression and the inverse probability weighting procedures (Sant'Anna & Zhao, 2020), and the results are presented in Column (3) of Table 2.4. The estimated coefficient in Columns (1)–(3) remains statistically significant and negative, indicating that our baseline results are robust to the inclusion of confounding policies, the exclusion of special cities, and the use of alternative estimators.

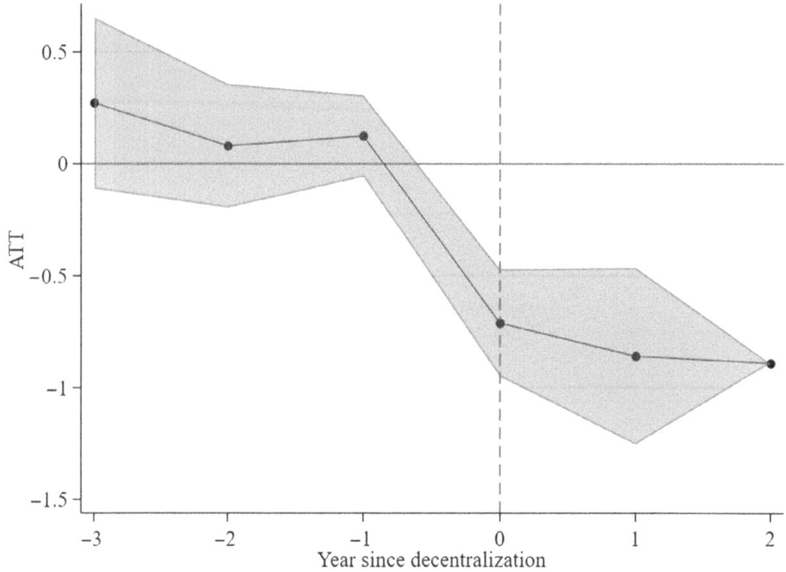

Fig. 2.5 Dynamic effects of the decentralization on food safety incidents. This figure shows the estimates of the overtime effects of the decentralization on food safety incidents at the city level using the difference-in-differences method described by Callaway and Sant'Anna (2021). The black, connected line plot estimates the average effect on food safety incidents in log points, with a 95% confidence interval shown by the gray, shaded area plot. Confidence bands are based on standard errors clustered at the province level. Time (in years) relative to the year of the decentralization runs on the horizontal axis. ATT, average treatment effects on the treated

2.5.2 *Two-Way Fixed Effects Difference-in-Differences Method*

Next, we use the two-way fixed effects (TWFE) difference-in-differences method to further assess the robustness of our baseline results. The model is:

$$Yct = \alpha \cdot Decentralizationpt + \beta' Xc \cdot f\left(t\right) + \varnothing c + \lambda t + \epsilon ct \quad (2.2)$$

where Yct is the natural logarithm of the number of food safety incidents in city c at year t; $\text{Decentralization}_{\text{pt}}$ is a dummy variable that equals 1 if province 1 has already undergone the decentralization at year t, and zero otherwise; and $\varnothing c$ and λt stand for city fixed effects and year fixed effects, respectively. $Xc \cdot f(t)$ is consistent with those in Eq. (2.1). Column (4) of Table 2.4 represents a negative correlation between decentralization and the number of food safety incidents after controlling the city-fixed effects and year-fixed effects, with a significance level of 5%. Column (5) provides the estimated results of Eq. (2.1). Holding other factors constant, decentralized cities experience, on average, a 41% reduction in the number of food safety

Table 2.4 Effects of the decentralization on food safety incidents: Alternative estimators and samples

	D.V. = ln (No. of food safety incidents)							
	CSDiD & conditional parallel trends			TWFE		Skewed measurement error		
	Demonstration	Excluding municipalities	Doubly robust	Without controls	With controls	Local exposure	Non-local exposure	Full
	(1)	(2)	(3)	(4)	(5)	(6)	(7)	(8)
Decentralization	−0.723*** (0.116)	−0.678** (0.337)	−0.446** (0.161)	−0.538** (0.241)	−0.526** (0.242)	−0.178 (0.156)	−0.489** (0.209)	−0.526** (0.240)
Food safety demonstration	Yes							
City FE				Yes	Yes	Yes	Yes	Yes
Year FE				Yes	Yes	Yes	Yes	Yes
Observations	1390	1096	1362	2224	2224	2224	2224	2224
Means of no. incidents	8.173	8.536	8.264	7.117	7.117	0.205	4.270	7.117

Note: This table reports the aggregated treatment effects of the decentralization on the natural logarithm of the number of food safety incidents at the city level, using different estimators, controls and samples. In particular, Columns (1)–(3) report the estimators using the difference-in-differences method described by Callaway and Sant'Anna (2021) under the conditional parallel trends assumption, with controls consistent with those in Eq. (2.1). In Column (1), we introduce a dummy variable to indicate whether the city was designated as a food safety demonstration city; Column (2) excludes the four municipalities under the central government that serve as China's provincial-level administrative regions from the sample; Columns (1) and (2) use outcome regression estimators; Column (3) reports the result using a doubly robust estimator. Under this estimation method, observations were automatically dropped, resulting in a smaller sample size. Columns (4) and (5) report the estimators using the two-way fixed effects difference-in-differences method outlined in Eq. (2.2) without and with controls, respectively. We apply the decomposition (Goodman-Bacon, 2021) and find that the weight of "Later Group Treatment versus Earlier Group Control" is 0.386. Columns (6)–(8) present the estimation result of Eq. (2.3). Local exposure refers to the natural logarithm of the number of food safety incidents reported by media outlets situated in the same location as the food production origin. Significance levels are denoted as *** for 1%, ** for 5%, and * for 10%. Standard errors are in parentheses clustered by province. The average number of city-level food safety incidents is reported at the bottom of this table incidents relative to cities that have not yet decentralized. The absolute value of the TWFE estimated coefficient is smaller than the absolute value of the CSDiD estimator, given the potential negative weights affecting the TWFE estimator.

2.5.3 *Underreporting Tests*

Finally, we perform analyses to examine the potential of food safety incident underreporting. The first type of underreporting would be due to measurement errors, whereas the other type involves intentional underreporting by local governments.

The actual number (Y^*_{ct}) is likely to exceed the observed number (Yct), namely Y^*_{ct} > Yct. This type of nonclassical measurement error potentially leads to biased estimates. We follow the approach by Millimet and Parmeter (2022) and Cuadros-Meñaca et al. (2023) to address this issue with stochastic frontier analysis. The stochastic frontier model is:

$$Yct = \alpha.Decentralizationpt + \beta' Xc.f\left(t\right) + \varphi c + \lambda t - uct + \epsilon ct, \tag{2.3}$$

Where $Y_{ct} = Y^*_{ct} - u_{ct}$. We assume that the error term, u_{ct}, follows a one-sided normal distribution.

Second, given that our food safety incidents are from media articles, there are concerns that the reduction in food safety incidents after the decentralization may be influenced by city-level governments restricting local media from reporting such incidents. Chinese local governments are found to hide incidents to protect their political career or collude with local industries for personal interests (Jia & Nie, 2017; Liu et al., 2022). This could lead to underreporting of the actual food safety situation within their jurisdiction and being even restrictive after decentralization. To address this, we analyzed the impact of the decentralization on food safety incidents covered by local media versus nonlocal media.

The results of underreporting tests are reported in Columns (6)–(8) of Table 2.4. The estimation result using the stochastic frontier analysis to account for general underreporting is consistent with those using TWFE models reported in Column (5), which suggests that skewed measurement error does not lead to a significant bias in the estimation of the decentralization effect. Looking at Columns (6) and (7), we find that the decentralization decreased food safety incidents reported by nonlocal media instead of local media. This implies that the reduction in reporting of food-safety incidents does not appear to be driven by local authorities suppressing information in local media.

2.6 Potential Mechanisms

This section examines how the decentralization improved food safety through the information and accountability mechanisms.

2.6.1 Information Mechanism

Food safety issues arise as a consequence of information asymmetry existing not only between food suppliers and consumers but also between food suppliers and regulators, where food suppliers possess superior knowledge about their products. The latter form of information asymmetry may impede the efficacy of regulatory oversight, potentially leading to insufficient monitoring and enforcement of food safety standards (Hoffmann et al., 2019). This issue would be exacerbated in China and other developing countries where the food value chain comprises numerous fragmented small-scale farmers, traders, and processors (Gereffi & Fernandez-Stark, 2016). Through the process of decentralization, the regulatory authority of food safety in the food processing and manufacturing sector has been shifted from provincial governments to city-level governments, who may be more knowledgeable about local food industries. Lower level governments possess local informational advantages that go beyond that which higher level governments have access Aghion and Tirole (1997), Bardhan (2002), Hayek (1945), and Huang et al. (2017). The declining transparency of food safety regulation information across different administrative levels in China, including central, provincial, and city levels, presents challenges for higher level governments in making well-informed decisions (CPPSS, 2016). Hence, the decentralization could improve food safety more within cities experiencing higher levels of the predecentralization information asymmetry between food suppliers and regulators.

Measuring the magnitude of information asymmetry between governments and stakeholders directly presents challenges (Bo et al., 2021), so we proxy the information asymmetry between food suppliers and regulators by the complexity of local food safety information. When city-level food safety information becomes more complex, relative to city-level governments, provincial governments face greater costs in acquiring and processing relevant information. This increased complexity indicates greater information asymmetry between food suppliers and provincial regulators, impeding effective food safety regulations. Specifically, prior to the decentralization, if one city demonstrates a wider range of product categories involved or a higher prevalence of risk factors associated with these incidents, there could be related to increased information complexity. Additionally, the higher the number of food processing and manufacturing firms within a city before decentralization, the greater the complexity of food safety information. Therefore, we measure the information asymmetry between food regulators and producers based on three indicators: the number of unsafe food categories,food safety risk factors, and food processing and manufacturing firms. Our approach of the information proxy follows prior research, including the studies arguing that a greater geographical distance between firms and regulators escalates the costs associated with regulators acquiring firm-related information (Coval & Moskowitz, 1999; Giroud, 2013; Huang et al., 2017).

The identification of these three indicators is as follows: First, there exist 28 food product categories in total based on the Chinese Food Classification Table for

Market Access of Food Quality and Safety (AQSIQ, 2006) including cakes, drinks, alcoholic beverages, meat products, condiments, roasted seeds and nuts, edible oils, and so forth. Second, we categorize the type of risk factors in food safety incidents based on the Chinese Implementation Measures for National Food Safety Supervision and Sampling (CFDA, 2018). There are 15 types of food safety risk factors, such as residues of pesticides and veterinary drugs, excessive heavy metals, excessive additives, and microbial contamination. We also control for the interaction term between the decentralization and pretreatment food safety incidents. This ensures a comparison between cities with the same level of food safety incidents, thereby eliminating the influence of food safety incidents on the decentralization effect. Third, we calculate the number of food manufacturing and processing firms in each city based on China's firm registration dataset.

As the CSDiD does not produce coefficients on covariates, we divide the city sample into two subsamples and implement Eq. (2.1) for each subsample. The subsamples are divided depending on whether a city is above the sample median of predecentralization indicators. The estimation results are reported in Table 2.5. In Columns (1)–(2), the estimated ATTs of the decentralization on food safety incidents are significantly negative in both the subsample above and below the median

Table 2.5 Examining the information mechanism

	D.V. = ln(no. of food safety incidents)					
	Unsafe food categories		Food safety risk factors		Food processing andmanufacturing firms	
	Abovemedian	Below median	Above median	Below median	Above median	Below median
	(1)	(2)	(3)	(4)	(5)	(6)
Decentralization	−0.948***	−0.935**	−0.962***	−0.883**	−0.881***	−0.242
	(0.140)	(0.292)	(0.162)	(0.277)	(0.144)	(0.587)
Observations	685	564	690	560	695	556
Means of no. incidents	13.832	2.777	13.947	2.520	12.253	4.464

Note: This table reports the differentiated effects of the decentralization on the natural logarithm of the number of food safety incidents at the city level. All columns report the estimators using the difference-in-differences method described by Callaway and Sant'Anna (2021) with outcome regression estimators under conditional parallel trend assumption, with controls consistent with those in Eq. (2.1). In Columns (1)–(2), "above median" includes the city subsample whose number of unsafe product categories for 2010 and 2011 is above the sample median. In Columns (3)–(4), "above median" refers to the city subsample where the count of food safety risk factors for 2010 and 2011 exceeds the sample median. In Columns (5)–(6), "below median" refers to the city subsample where the number of incumbent food firms for 2010 and 2011 exceeds the sample median. The number of unsafe food product categories and food safety risk factors are measured as the number of product categories exposed, and the number of risk factors associated with food safety incidents, respectively. The sample size for Columns (2) and (4) is lower than the original sample size due to the absence of cities decentralized in 2012, whereas the sample size for Column (6) is lower than the original sample size due to the absence of cities decentralized in 2015. Significance levels are denoted as *** for 1%, ** for 5%, and * for 10%. Standard errors are in parentheses clustered by province. The average number of city-level food safety incidents is reported at the bottom of this table of unsafe food categories. However, the point estimate of the above median subsample suggests a larger reduction in food safety incidents than the corresponding number for the below median subsample. The results in Columns (3)–(4), which divide the sample according to the city-level number of food safety risk factors, mirror those of Columns (1)–(2). Columns (5)–(6) report the estimated ATTs for the subsample above and below the median of food processing and manufacturing firms, respectively. The decentralization exerts a 59% significant reduction in food safety incidents within cities with a greater number of food processing and manufacturing firms. Conversely, in cities with a lower number of such firms, the ATT is statistically insignificant. Collectively, the table reveals that in cities with a high level of information complexity (above the median group), both the magnitude and significance of the ATTs are greater compared to cities with low information complexity (below the median group).

2.6.2 *Accountability Mechanism*

We also investigate whether the decentralization improved food safety by enhancing the accountability of local governments in food safety regulation. Prior to the decentralization, city-level governments assumed the responsibility for food safety, yet their capacity to enforce food safety regulations was limited; meanwhile,provincial governments possess regulatory authority but evade accountabilityin this matter. When food safety problems arise, local governments and provincial governments engage in free-riding behavior, where they rely on the efforts and resources of others to address the issues, instead of taking full responsibility themselves (Liu & Zhang, 2015). The decentralization addressed this issue by delegating the regulatory authority to local governments, which would bolster the accountability of local governments because their performance assessment becomes contingent upon the welfare within their specific jurisdictions (Bardhan, 2002; Bardhan & Mookherjee, 2005). Hence, the decentralization is expected to increase the commitment of city-level governments in ensuring effective food safety regulation.

Empirically, we evaluate city-level government's commitment to ensuring effective food safety measures by analyzing the number of city-level food safety-related laws and regulations implemented for at least three reasons. First, governments would choose to enact strict and specific laws and regulations to achieve their goals. This extends beyond the regulation of food safety to areas including environmental protection, resource conservation, and innovation promotion (Kang, 2019; Li et al., 2013; Long & Wang, 2019; Yu et al., 2014). Second, the laws and regulations at higher levels lack the necessary specificity to effectively govern cities with distinct characteristics and needs (Zheng, 2018). Lower level laws and regulations can more effectively address the specific needs of individual cities. Besides, the number of laws and regulations is one of the most important indicators to measure government efforts and performance (Ehler, 2003; Fukuyama, 2013).

To capture this regulatory landscape, we leverage the Law and Regulation dataset provided by Peking University (Beida Fa Bao in Chinese),[8] renowned for its comprehensive collection of policies and regulations in China. We examine four types of food safety laws and regulations. Examples of each type of food safety laws and regulations are shown in Appendix E. The first type encompasses all local regulations directly addressing food safety, identified through a search using the keyword "food safety." The subsequent three types of laws and regulations specifically target the food processing and manufacturing sector. The second type focuses on laws and regulations with titles related to "food safety" and "supervision." The same title keywords are used to collect the third and fourth types of regulations, with the keywords "supervision" replaced by "punishment" and "credit system," respectively. The subsequent three types reflect the supervision, postsupervision, and presupervision laws and regulations, respectively.

Table 2.6 displays the results of implementing Eq. (2.1) to examine the decentralization's impacts on local food safety laws and regulations targeting the food processing and manufacturing sector. Note that in Table 2.6, we incorporate the number of food safety laws and regulations at the provincial level as an additional control variable in the estimations to account for the potential influence of provincial food safety laws and regulations on the laws and regulations at the city level.

Table 2.6 Effects of the decentralization on food safety laws and regulations

	D.V.=ln(no. of food safety laws and regulations)			
	General	Supervision	Penalty	Credit system
	(1)	(2)	(3)	(4)
Decentralization	0.253***(0.043)	0.213***(0.030)	0.189***(0.042)	−0.012(0.014)
Observations	1390	1390	1390	1390
Means of no. of laws and regulations	9.735	4.032	1.289	1.023

Note: This table reports the aggregated treatment effects of the decentralization on the natural logarithm of the number of food safety laws and regulations at the city level. All columns report the estimators using the difference-in-differences method described by Callaway and Sant'Anna (2021) withoutcome regression estimators under the conditional parallel trends assumption, with controls consistent with those in Eq. (2.1) except that we add an additional control variable, the natural logarithm of the number of food safety laws and regulations at the provincial level. Columns (1)–(4) report the effects on food safety general laws and regulations, food safety supervision specific laws and regulations, food safety penalty specific laws and regulations, and food safety credit-system building laws and regulations, respectively (for details please see Appendix E). Significance levels are denoted as *** for 1%, ** for 5%, and * for 10%. Standard errors are in parentheses clustered by province. The average number of city-level food safety incidents is reported at the bottom of this table

[8] Website: http://www.pkulaw.cn/. This dataset encompasses a wide range of legal documents, including currently effective laws, authoritative judicial interpretations, and policy provisions dating back to 1949. The Beida Fa Bao dataset offers valuable resources for researchers and analysts to access and examine relevant policies, regulations and judicial cases, enabling in-depth content research, and empirical analysis (Wang et al., 2018; Zining, 2015).

This control aims to mitigate confounding effects and isolate the specific impact of decentralization on local food safety laws and regulations at the city level (Fig. 2.6).

Results from Table 2.6 reveal that the decentralization has led to a 28.8% increase in city-level laws and regulations on food safety compared to nondecentralized cities. Decentralized cities have seen an approximately 23.7% rise in supervision regulations and a 20.8% increase in penalty regulations for the food processing and manufacturing industry, whereas the number of regulations on credit system building remains unchanged. These findings indicate that the decentralization promoted more local regulations on food safety, with a greater emphasis on supervision and penalty instead of proactive management. To further establish the accountability mechanism, we analyze the correlation between the city-level numbers of new regulations and food safety incidents. As expected, after controlling for city-fixed effects and year-fixed effects, there is a significantly negative correlation (from −0.176 to −0.096) between the number of food safety incidents and food safety regulations, except for credit-system-related laws and regulations. The dynamic effects of Table 2.6 and the correlation analysis are shown in Appendix E (Figs. 2.7 and 2.8).

2.7 Firm and Industry-Level Analysis

This section extends the investigation to the firm level by considering the impacts on food processing and manufacturing firms. This extension serves as a robustness check for our city-level analysis and allows us to explore the heterogeneity of the decentralization effects across firm types, such as firm ownership, size, and experience. Understanding the differential responses of firms is important given their direct involvement in food processing and manufacturing.

For the firm-level analysis, we employ the most comprehensive firm registration dataset provided by the State Administration for Industry and Commerce of China.[9] Each firm record in this dataset includes the information on firm name, location, start-up time, ownership, registration capital, and products. We merge this dataset with our food safety incident dataset using firm names and construct abalanced firm-year panel data including 3549 firms continuously in existence from 2010 to 2017. We excluded firms with missing names and those that entered and/or exited during the study period for consistency. Parallel with the city-level analyses, we perform CSDiD (following Eq. (2.1)) and TWFE estimation techniques, but we introduce an additional firm-level control variable (firm age). We use TWFE DID, which provides a robustness check for CSDiD estimators to explore moderating effects. The balanced panel data are used to estimate Eq. (2.4),which modifies Eq. (2.2) by incorporating firm-level controls.

[9] The food processing and manufacturing industry is divided into three subindustries according to the 2017 National Economy Industry Classification Standard and includes agricultural byproduct processing, food manufacturing and wine, beverage, and refined tea manufacturing.

$$Yit = \alpha.\frac{Decentralizationpt + Ageit + \beta}{Xc}.f(t) + \mu i + \lambda t + \epsilon ct, \tag{2.4}$$

where *Yit* is a dummy variable, indicating whether firm i was involved in food safety incident(s) by producing unsafe foods at year t. The firm-level regression includes city-level regression control variables *Xc* and firm age (Age_{it}) as additional controls. μ_i and λt stand for firm fixed effects and year fixed effects, respectively. This equation is estimated using a linear probability model.

Firm-level results are presented in Table 2.7. Columns (1) and (2) employ the CSDiD method with unconditional and conditional parallel trend assumptions, respectively. The two columns report significantly negative and similar point estimates of the ATT of the decentralization on the firm-level occurrence of food safety incidents. In particular, Column (2) suggests that there is an additional 9.5 percentage points reduction in the probability of food safety incidents for firms under the decentralization, compared to those that have not been under the decentralization. The dynamic aggregated ATTs under the conditional parallel trend assumption are presented in Appendix F (Table 2.14). Columns (3) and (4) employ the TWFE DID method without and with controls, respectively, and Column (4) includes city-level independent variables and firm age as controls. The TWFE DID estimators are close to the CSDiD estimators. Results of Columns (1)–(4) highlight that the decentralization reduces the prevalence of food safety incidents at the firm level, reinforcing our city-level findings in Table 2.3.

To inform the heterogeneity of the decentralization effect across firms, Columns (5) and (7) of Table 2.7 build on Eq. (2.4) and include interaction terms between the decentralization and firm characteristics, including registration capital, ownership, and firm age, respectively. We treat registration capital and firm age as continuous variables, whereas the ownership variables are represented as dummies indicating whether a firm is state-owned, private, foreign, or others. Column (5) indicates that every 100 million RMB increase in a firm's registration capital leads to an additional 0.7 percentage points drop in the prevalence of food safety incidents. The standard deviation of registration capital is 1.46, so the probability of food safety incidents decreases by 1.02 percentage points for every standard deviation increase in registration capital. Column (6) reports that both state-owned firms and foreign firms are more likely to reduce food safety incidents after the decentralization, relative to other firms. Experienced firms respond more positively to the decentralization. One year increase in firm age corresponds to an additional 0.8 percentage points reduction in the probability of food safety incidents for firms in the decentralization provinces (Column 7). In sum, large-scale and experienced firms demonstrate a more pronounced response to the decentralization.

As larger and more established firms demonstrate a more pronounced reduction in food safety incidents after the decentralization, it prompts consideration of potential trade-offs between economic gains and food safety. These firms, in the short run, may need to prioritize food safety by investing in infrastructure, technology, and staff training, temporarily hurting their financial performance. We investigate

Table 2.7 Effects of the decentralization on firm-level food safety incidents

	D.V.=occurrence of food safety incidents(=1, incidents occurred;=0, no occurrence)						
	CSDiD		TWFE				
	Unconditional parallel trend	Conditional parallel trend	Without cor	trols	With controls		
	(1)	(2)	(3)	(4)	(5)	(6)	(7)
Decentralization	−0.088*** (0.024)	−0.095*** (0.025)	−0.106** (0.048)	−0.089** (0.040)	−0.087** (0.041)	−0.094* (0.044)	−0.098**(0.043)
Decentralization x Registration capital					−0.007*** (0.002)		
Decentralization x SOE						−0.089** (0.039)	
Decentralization x Private						0.010 (0.017)	
Decentralization x Foreign						−0.034* (0.018)	
Decentralization x Firm age							−0.008***(0.002)
City FE			Yes	Yes	Yes	Yes	Yes
Year FE			Yes	Yes	Yes	Yes	Yes
Observations	17,745	17,745	28,392	28,392	28,392	28,392	28,392
Means of occurrence of food safety incidents	0.166	0.166	0.137	0.137	0.137	0.137	0.137

Note: This table reports the aggregated treatment effects of the decentralization on the occurrence of food safety incidents at the firm level, using different estimators and controls. In particular, Columns (1)–(2) report the estimators using the difference-in-differences method described by Callaway and Sant'Anna (2021) withoutcome regression estimators under the unconditional and conditional parallel trends assumption, respectively. Columns (3)–(7) report the estimators using the two-way fixed effects difference-in-differences method outlined in Eq. (2.4) without and with controls. Registration capital and firm age are continuous variables, capital is in 100 million RMB and firm age is in year. SOE, Private, and Foreign are three dummies, equal one if a firm is state owned, privately owned and foreign owned, respectively, and zero otherwise. Significance levels are denoted as *** for 1%, ** for 5%, and * for 10%. Standard errors are in parentheses clustered by province

Abbreviation: TWFE, two-way fixed effects

how the decentralization impacts the economic performance of large-scale food processing and manufacturing firms. Ideally, we would collect the economic performance of each food processing and manufacturing firm for analysis, which however is not available. Alternatively, werely on the main revenue generated by the food processing and manufacturing industry as a proxy to assess the economic impact of the decentralization. The revenue data are from the China Industrial and Economic Statistics Yearbook and provincial statistical yearbooks. To analyze the impact, we construct industry–province–year panel data and use the triple difference method. This allows us to compare revenue changes between the food processing and manufacturing industry affected by decentralization and the other industries unaffected before and after the decentralization. The model specification:

$$Revenuefpt = \lambda 0 + \lambda 1 Provincep \times Industryf \times Yeart + \tau\, ft + \rho\, pt + \sigma\, fp + \varepsilon\, fpt, \quad (25)$$

where Revenuefpt is the natural logarithm of the main revenue of industry fat province p and year t; $Province_p \times Industry_f \times Year_t$ is equal to 1 if industry f is the food processing and manufacturing industry and the province p already implemented the decentralization at year t, and zero otherwise. Tft are industry-year fixed effects capturing time-constant industry characteristics and shocks to the industry. Σfp are province-industry fixed effects allowing differences across provinces and industries. ρ_{pt} are province-year fixed effects capturing the time effect across province and year. ε_{fpt} is the error term. To control for potential correlations between error terms, we cluster standard errors at the province level.

Table 2.8 reports the estimation result of Eq. (2.5), with the dependent variable being the natural logarithm of the main revenue at the industry–province–year level. The result indicates that the decentralization leads to a 3.8% increase in the average

Table 2.8 Effect of the decentralization on industry-level main revenue

	D.V.=ln(main revenue)
ProvincepxIndustryfxYeart	0.037*(0.020)
Industry by year FE	Yes
Province by year FE	Yes
Industry by province FE	Yes
Observations	7344
R^2	0.960

Note: This table reports the estimated treatment effect of the decentralization on the natural logarithm of the main revenue of food industry

The model specification is in Eq. (2.5). This analysis is conducted at the industry-province-year level. The data comprise 7344 samples from 34 industries × 27 provinces × 8 years (2010–2017). Significance levels are denoted as *** for 1%, ** for 5%, and * for 10%. Standard errors are in parentheses clustered by province revenue of the food processing and manufacturing industry, with a marginal significance level of 10%. This implies that food safety regulations following the decentralization are at least not vulnerable for large-scale and experienced food firms.

2.8 Discussions and Conclusions

Decentralization has been at the center stage of policy experiments over the last 2 decades in many developing and transition economies. Yet, both theoretically and empirically, the question of whether decentralization is socially welfare improving remains equivocal. We add to the decentralization literature by studying how decentralization of regulatory authority may affect public good provision, in the context of food safety.

This study leverages a natural decentralization experiment that unfolded in China, the world's largest food market, to investigate the effects of decentralization on food safety and food industries. In early 2013 the Chinese central government made the decision to transfer food safety regulatory authority over the food processing and manufacturing sector from provincial to city-level governments. We compile food safety news from numerous media sources in China over 2010 to 2017 and construct an externally validated database of food safety incidents. Results indicate that on average, the number of food safety incidents decreased significantly by half in cities that underwent the decentralization reform. This finding remains robust across alternative samples and model specifications, controlling for potential confounding policies and underreporting of food safety incidents.

Our result differs from studies that cautioned against the decentralized provision of environmental goods and workplace safety due to local capture, regional competition, and spillovers (Chen et al., 2022; Jia & Nie, 2017; Lipscomb & Mobarak, 2016). However, we align with previous research favoring decentralization in education and employment service delivery (Barankay & Lockwood, 2007; Galiani et al., 2008; Mergele & Weber, 2020). Possible reasons include the incentive for local governments to stimulate economic development and tax revenue, potentially leading them to ease oversight of profitable yet polluting firms engaged in emissions (Chen et al., 2022; Han et al., 2021). But for food firms in economies like China, characterized by small-scale and less lucrative, such leniency might not extend to food safety regulations.

We explore two channels underlying the beneficial effects of decentralization. First, the decentralization improved food safety more within cities facing higher levels of predecentralization information complexity, revealing the importance of information advantage in regulating food safety. Although local information is outed as a key advantage of decentralization in the literature, its impact lacks empirical evidence. Our result mirrors qualitative studies arguing efficient food safety regulation relies on the information available to regulatory authorities (Gong et al., 2013; Henson & Caswell, 1999; Zhou & Yang, 2002). Further, the result is consistent with theoretical work that highlights the significance of local information in the decentralized provision of public goods (Hayek, 1945; Oates, 1972), and more broadly, research emphasizing that delegating authority to agents with superior information would lead to improved outcomes within organizations (Acemoglu et al., 2007; Huang et al., 2017). Second, the decentralization heightened the determination and efforts of local governments in food safety regulation as demonstrated by the increased number of relevant regulations and laws within their jurisdictions. This aligns with the finding that arise in the level of decentralization motivates subnational governments to exert greater effort (Aghion & Tirole, 1997; Che et al., 2017). It is noted that the decentralization's impact on different types of food safety laws and regulations differs. The number of laws and regulations on food safety penalties and supervision demonstrate a more pronounced increase, whereas those concerning credit system do not exhibit a significant rise. This discovery implies that city-level governments may prioritize regulatory approaches that result in more immediate impacts on food safety.

Findings from firm-level and industry-level datasets suggest that although the decentralization has yielded greater responsiveness among large-scale and experienced firms, it has not adversely affected the total revenue of large-scale food processing and manufacturing firms. This means that there might not be a trade-off between ensuring food safety and facilitating the growth of food industries. Given the greater receptiveness of large-scale and experienced firms to the reform, they are consequently less susceptible to media exposure due to food safety incidents, which would boost their reputation and market demand (Bovay, 2023; Dou et al., 2015; Smed & Jensen, 2005). Nevertheless, due to data limitation, our revenue analysis focuses on large-scale and experienced firms in the food processing and manufacturing sector, which might lead to the overestimation of the decentralization's impact on revenue. Small-scale firms and individual businesses facing strict regulations might be forced to shutdown. Regulations on food safety disproportionately impact small-scale food processors (Buckley, 2015; Worosz et al., 2008) as regulations can act as entry barriers favoring larger manufacturers (Antle, 1996; Klapper et al., 2006). The DDD result could not be interpreted without caution.

Formulating effective food safety regulations emerges as a critical policy concern in rapidly developing economies as food safety remains and will continue to be of importance (Unnevehr, 2022). The economic burden from foodborne illness is estimated to be at least \$110 billion in 2016 dollars for low- and middle-income countries in Asia and Africa (Jaffee et al., 2018). Our study has implications for effective food safety regulations, particularly with developing and transitioning food markets.

Last, several avenues are pointed out for future research. There exist other possible mechanisms that warrant exploration, such as the role of regulatory resources on the decentralization'simpact on food safety. Although our primary focus has been on the city-level responsiveness to the decentralization reform, there is room for microlevel analyses that delve into how regulatory decentralization influences firms' behaviors when detailed firm-level databases become accessible. We also note that the decentralization, on average, reduced city-level food safety incidents; although this finding is robust to different estimators, sample sizes, and others, we acknowledge the possibility that the decentralization may not enhance food safety situation for all cities (Tables 2.12, 2.13, and 2.13).

Acknowledgments Many thanks to Ran Sun, Tingyu Wang, Shengping Shang, Wenxin Hou, and Wenfeng Fang for their data collection efforts on this project. Editor Dr. Jesse Tack and three anonymous reviewers made insightful comments that helped improve the manuscript. Authors also thank seminar participants at AAEA, CES, CAER-IFPRI, Tsinghua University, Renmin University of China, and China Agricultural University. This work was supported by the National Natural Science Foundation of China (Nos. 72103180; 72273128) and the Fundamental Research Funds for the Central Universities and Key Research Projects of Humanities and Social Sciences under the 14th Five-Year Plan of the Ministry of Education (No. 22JJD790079). All errors remain ours.

Appendices

Appendix A: Information on the Implementation Time for Each Province and the Corresponding Website Sources

Table 2.9 The time of the decentralization reform

Province	Reform time	Source
Anhui	2013/9/26	https://www.ah.gov.cn/szf/zfgb/8128581.html
Beijing	2013/10/13	http://www.beijing.gov.cn/zhengce/zfwj/zfwj/bgtwj/201905/t20190523_75320.html
Chongqing	2013/7/25	https://www.pkulaw.com/lar/a7fc22a7f51226cbdd7c9964de062227bdfb.html
Fujian	2013/11/20	http://www.fujian.gov.cn/zwgk/zxwj/szfbgtwj/201312/t20131203_1415977.htm
Gansu	2013/6/17	http://www.reformdata.org/2013/0619/20170.shtml
Guangdong	2013/8/27	https://www.pkulaw.com/lar/b329fa44d20b609c1beda5dfe1c69b3dbdfb.html
Guangxi	2013/9/27	http://www.gxzf.gov.cn/zwgk/zfwj/zzqrmzfbgtwj/2013ngzbwj/20131226-427433.shtml
Guizhou	2013/7/18	http://www.reformdata.org/2013/0718/20186.shtml
Hainan	2013/7/8	http://www.reformdata.org/2013/0718/20200.shtml
Hebei	2013/3/24	https://www.hbysw.org/contents/44/210.html
Heilongjiang	2013/12/3	https://www.pkulaw.com/lar/85ebf2ab33af7591d20fddd231d295bfbdfb.html
Henan	2013/9/16	http://www.henan.gov.cn/2013/10-12/245742.html
Hubei	2013/7/8	http://www.hubei.gov.cn/zfwj/ezbf/201307/t20130715_1713161.shtml
Hunan	2013/10/15	http://www.hunan.gov.cn/szf/hnzb_18/2013_98309_18/2013nd21q_18/szfbgtwj_98342_18/201311/t20131122_4700773.html
Inner Mongolia	2013/9/26	http://www.reformdata.org/2013/0926/20184.shtml
Ji Lin	2013/8/14	https://www.pkulaw.com/lar/ad73ca640474afbea428f4a3b14a9edcbdfb.html
Jiangsu	2013/9/9	http://www.jiangsu.gov.cn/art/2013/9/24/art_46144_2545200.html
Jiangxi	2013/7/9	http://www.jiangxi.gov.cn/art/2015/12/5/art_4975_212637.html
Liaoning	2013/11/11	https://www.ln.gov.cn/web/zwgkx/zfwj/szfbgtwj/zfwj2011_99989/5732F256C30B4073ADA298DE13BA9698/index.shtml
Ningxia	2014/7/17	https://www.pkulaw.com/lar/1daea75f211306b91b5aed2a882a054ebdfb.html
Qinghai	2013/12/17	https://www.pkulaw.com/lar/b67ba73aa90f05983a1b616f4e2e7a3bbdfb.html
Shaanxi	2012/1/1	https://www.pkulaw.com/lar/3b855ba57373dca340f04c60f29afdd0bdfb.html
Shandong	2013/9/3	http://www.shandong.gov.cn/art/2013/9/12/art_107851_89001.html

(continued)

Table 2.9 (continued)

Province	Reform time	Source
Shanghai	2013/12/19	https://www.pkulaw.com/lar/4d3bea0949896268dc2bbddb04ea5e89bdfb html
Shanxi	2013/6/26	http://www.shanxi.gov.cn/sxszfxxgk/sxsrmzfzcbm/sxszfbgt/flfg_7203/bgtgfxwj_7206/201310/t20131018_161316.shtml
Sichuan	2013/7/29	http://www.sc.gov.cn/10462/10883/11066/2013/7/29/10270947.shtml
Tianjin	2014/7/30	https://www.gov.cn/xinwen/2014-07/30/content_2726945.htm
Tibet	2014/5/6	https://www.pkulaw.com/lar/6688e67a23922063570ff4324baddab2bdfb.html
Xinjiang	2015/6/15	http://mpa.xinjiang.gov.cn/xjyjj/tzgg/201506/afabd075c1dd403f8ba9be5fa1f4c5b8.shtml
Yunnan	2014/5/12	http://www.yn.gov.cn/zwgk/zcwj/yzfb/201606/t20160620_144084.html
Zhejiang	2013/11/25	http://www.zj.gov.cn/art/2013/12/5/art_1229591320_56959.html

Appendix B: Media Source List

Table 2.10 Examples of food safety incidents news media sources

Type	Website	Address
Central	People's Daily Online	http://www.people.com.cn/
	China Quality News Network	https://www.cqn.com.cn/
	China News Network	https://www.chinanews.com/
	Huanqiu News	https://www.huanqiu.com/
	Xinhuanet	http://www.news.cn/
	China Food Supervision Network	http://www.cnfdn.com/
	China Economic Net	http://www.ce.cn/
	ChinaNet	http://www.china.com.cn/
	China National Radio	https://www.cnr.cn/index_c.html
	Legal Daily	http://www.zgswbwz.com/
Provincial	Peninsula Network	http://www.bandao.cn/
	Qilu Network	http://www.iqilu.com/
	New Express	https://epaper.xkb.com.cn/
	Qilu Evening News	https://www.qlwb.com.cn/
	Nanfang Daily	https://epaper.southcn.com/
	Chutian Metropolis Daily	https://ctdsbepaper.hubeidaily.net/
	Yangcheng Evening News	http://www.ycwb.com.cn/
	QianLong	https://www.qianlong.com/
	Straits Metropolitan News	https://www.hxdsb.com/
	Golden Sheep Net	https://www.ycwb.com/
City	Beijing Times	http://www.jinghua.cn
	Beijing Morning Post	http://www.bjcbgw.com/
	Jinan Daily	http://jnrb.e23.cn/
	Guangzhou Daily	https://www.gzdaily.cn/
	Daily Business	https://hzdaily.hangzhou.com.cn/
	Xinmin Network	https://www.xinmin.cn/
	City News	http://xinbao.qdxin.cn/
	Beijing Daily	https://www.bjd.com.cn/
	Jiujiang News Network	https://www.jjxw.cn/
	Qingdao News Network	https://www.qingdaonews.com/

(continued)

Table 2.10 (continued)

Type	Website	Address
Other	Sina	https://www.sina.com.cn/
	Sohu	https://www.sohu.com/
	Tencent	https://www.qq.com/
	NetEase	https://www.163.com/
	Phoenix	https://www.ifeng.com/index.shtml
	Consumer Guide Network	http://www.315oca.com/
	Food Industry Network	http://www.foodqs.cn/
	Food Science and Technology Network	https://www.tech-food.com/
	Food Safety Net	https://www.cfsn.cn/
	First Food Network	https://www.foods1.com/

Notes: The table lists the top 10 media names and websites by the coverage of food safety incidents. A full list of media websites is available upon request. Central media refers to news outlets that are affiliated with the Chinese central government like the Central Publicity Department, the State Administration of Radio, Film, and Television, and the National Press and Publication Administration. Local media includes provincial and city-level outlets, which are guided and directed by enterprises or provincial and municipal units. Other media refers to entities that do not fall into the aforementioned categories; they provide a certain type of comprehensive internet information resource, similar to Google, with a news section

Appendix C: Food Safety Data Validation

Figure 2.3 illustrates a comparative analysis of the distribution of food product categories and food safety risk factors between our dataset and the official reports. To further compare the difference between our data and the official reported data, we conducted a series of difference significance tests. The results are shown in Table 2.11. According to the Shapiro-Wilk W test, it was found that the food

Table 2.11 Differences between the collected data and FDA data

	Unsafe food product categories		
	(1) Shapiro–Wilk W test	(2) Variance ratio test	(3) Wilcoxon signed-rank test
Z-value	3.592		1.177
F-value		0.723	
P-value	0.0002***	0.414	0.239
Observations	14	14	14
	Food safety risk factors		
	(4)	(5)	(6)
	Shapiro–Wilk W test	Variance test ratio	Paired t test
Z-value	−0.931		
F-value T-value		0.874	−1.016
P-value	0.824	0.875	0.349
Observations	7	7	7

product categories of the two datasets did not obey the normal distribution (P-value = 0.0002), while the distribution of food safety risk factors follows the normal distribution (P-value =0.824). According to the results of the Variance ratio test, we found that the differences both in product categories and risk factor structures between the two data sources are variance homogeneous. Therefore, we used the Wilcoxon signed-rank test to compare the median values of the two datasets in terms of product categories and found no significant difference between the data we collected and the official data (P-value = 0.239). Regarding risk factors, we used the paired t-test, and we also found that there was no significant difference between our data and the official reported data (P-value = 0.349).

Appendix D: City-Level Food Safety Laws and Regulations

We have collected four kinds of city-level laws and regulations, and the time range is from 2010 to 2017.

The first type is the number of all local regulations related to "food safety". The screening method is to search within the full text with the keyword "food safety". When collecting the second to fourth types of regulations, the scope was further narrowed to the supervision and management of the food industry by setting the keywords of title and full text. The second to fourth types of laws and regulations are the daily supervision regulations, the penalty regulations and the credit information management system construction regulations.

In the second type, the keywords of the titles of the regulations for daily supervision include "food safety", "food enterprises", "food industry" and "food production", and the relationship between each keyword is "or". The keywords of the full text include "supervision", "food enterprise", "food industry", and "food production". The relationship between "supervision" and other keywords is "and". The relationship between keyword groups containing "supervision" is "or". The relationship between title keywords and full-text keywords is "and". The title keywords used for collecting punishment regulations are the same as above. The keywords in the full text replace the above-mentioned "supervision" with "punishment", and other keywords remain the same, and the relationship between keywords remains unchanged. When collecting credit information management system construction regulations, the only difference from the second screening condition is to replace "supervision" with "credit system" in the full-text keywords, and the relationship between keywords remains unchanged.

Table 2.12 Examples of food safety laws and regulations

Title	City	Website
Interim Provisions of Jinan Fresh Milk Bar Food Safety Supervision and Administration	Jinan	https://www.pkulaw.com/lar/a8efcb1092e1e731376b9d29e09e8c21bdfb.html
The Implementation Plan for Promoting the Institutionalization of Credit Construction in the Food and Drug Industry	Dongying	https://www.pkulaw.com/lar/b51b33000f51233082e4a49214684d77 bdfb.html
Standardized Management Guidelines on Food Safety of Beijing Chain Catering Service Enterprises	Beijing	https://www.pkulaw.com/lar/0b280c9dfbd1107ada0c68493f453e68bdfb.html
Guidelines of the FDA on the Work of Food Production and Processing Workshops	Beijing	https://www.pkulaw.com/lar/faafa70541e9dfa48ab4558257256bd9bdfb.html
Provisions on Duties and Responsibilities of Safety Production of Governments and Departments at All Levels in Shenyang	Shenyang	https://www.pkulaw.com/lar/e4052aea5937a2111bad3aa3fa8d7bd bdfb.html

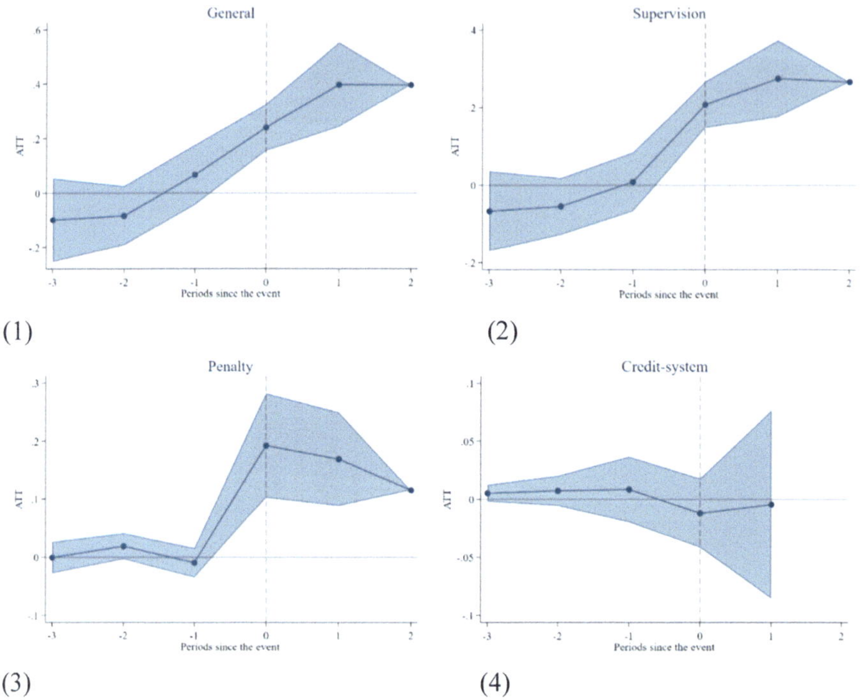

Fig. 2.6 Dynamic average treatment effects of decentralization on local laws and regulations. Notes: This figure shows the estimates of the over-time effects of the decentralization on food safety laws and regulations at the city level using the difference-in-differences method described by Callaway and Sant'Anna (2021), under the conditional parallel trend assumption. Panels (1)–(4) report the dynamic effects of the decentralization on local laws and regulations, corresponding food safety regulations, daily supervision, penalty, and credit system building of the food processing and manufacturing sector. The blue, connected line plot estimates the average effect on food safety incidents in log points, with a 95% confidence interval shown by the gray, shaded area plot. Confidence bands are based on standard errors clustered at the province level. Time (in years) relative to the year of the decentralization runs on the horizontal axis.

Table 2.13 Correlation between the food safety incident and relative laws and regulations

D.V. =Ln (No. of food safety incidents)				
	(1)	(2)	(3)	(4)
General	−0.096***			
Supervision	(0.033)	−0.138*** (0.050)		
Penalty			−0.176* (0.090)	
Credit-system				−0.136 (0.220)
Controls	Yes	Yes	Yes	Yes
City FE	Yes	Yes	Yes	Yes
Year FE	Yes	Yes	Yes	Yes
Observations	2224	2224	2224	2224

Notes: This table reports the correlation between the natural logarithm of the number of food safety incidents and the natural logarithm of the number of food safety laws and regulations at the city level. Column (1)–column (4) display the correlation coefficients between general law, supervision, penalty, and credit-system and the number of food safety incidents, respectively. The coefficients are obtained through ordinary least squares regression with city fixed effects and year fixed effects. Control variables are consistent with those in Equation (1) except that we add an additional control variable, the natural logarithm of the number of food safety laws and regulations at the provincial level. Significance levels are denoted as *** for 1%, ** for 5%, and * for 10%. Standard errors are in parentheses clustered by province

Appendix E: Group-time Average and Dynamic Aggregated Treatment Effects at the Firm Level

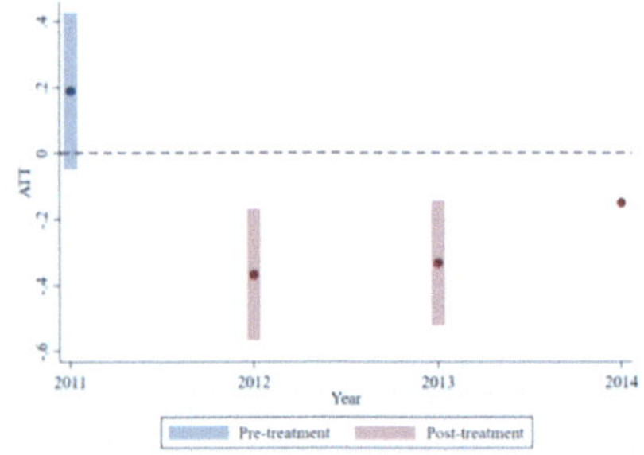

(a) Group 2012

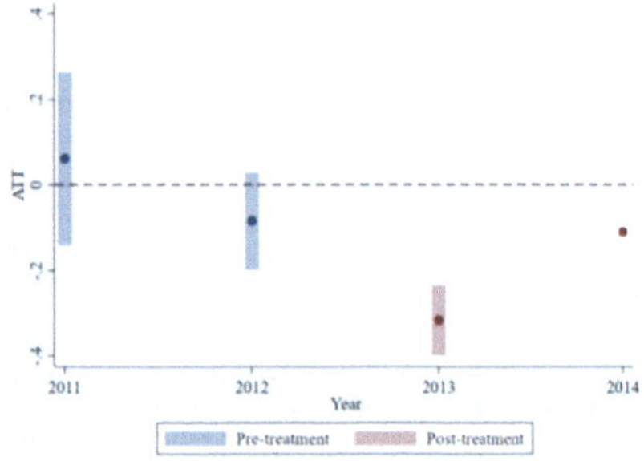

(b) Group 2013

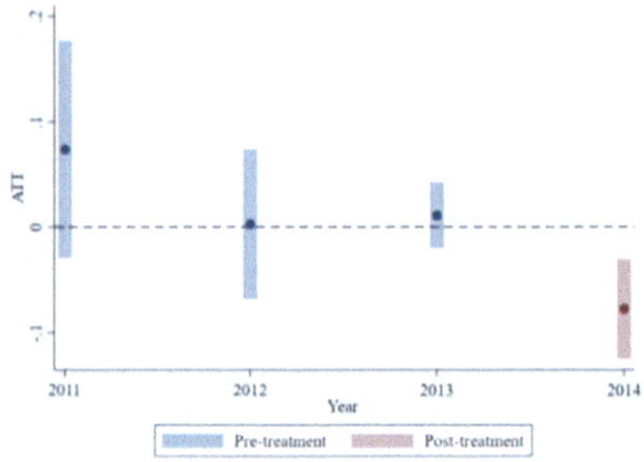

(c)Group 2014

Fig. 2.7 Group-time average treatment effects. Notes: This figure shows the group-time average treatment estimates of the effect of the decentralization on food safety incidents at the firm level using the difference-in-differences method described by Callaway and Sant'Anna (2021), under the conditional parallel trend assumption. Panels (**a**)–(**c**) show the decentralization effects of firms whose provinces began decentralization in 2012, 2013, and 2014, respectively. Confidence bands are based on standard errors clustered at the province level. Blue shadows give point estimates and 95% confidence bands for pretreatment periods. Red shadows provide point estimates and 95% confidence bands for the treatment effect of decentralization

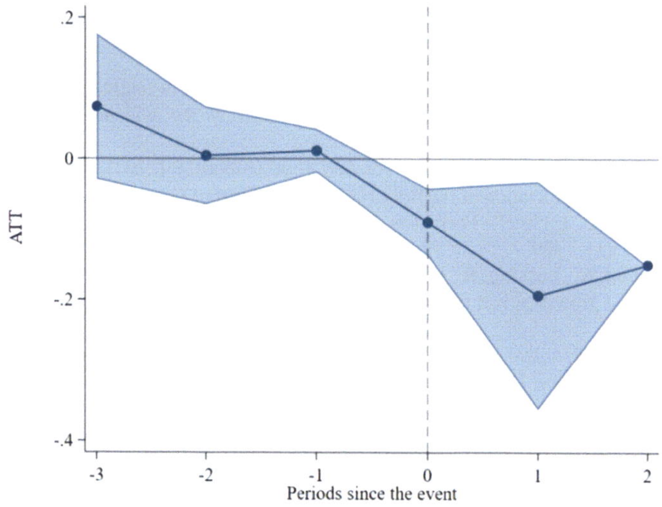

Fig. 2.8 Dynamic effects. Notes: This figure shows the estimates of the over-time effects of the decentralization on food safety incidents at the firm level using the difference-in-differences method described by Callaway and Sant'Anna (2021), under the conditional parallel trend assumption. The blue, connected line plot estimates the average effect on food safety incidents in log points, with a 95% confidence interval shown by the gray, shaded area plot. Confidence bands are based on standard errors clustered at the province level. Time (in years) relative to the year of the decentralization runs on the horizontal axis.

Appendix F: Summary Statistics About Data Used in Sections 6 and 7

Table 2.14 Summary statistics about data used in sections 6 and 7

Variable	Obs.	Mean	Std. Dev.
City-level information mechanism			
The number of product categories	2224	4.19	4.30
The number of risk factors	2224	3.29	2.56
The number of food processing and manufacturing firm	2224	580.25	539.49
City-level accountability mechanism			
Ln (the number of general regulations on food safety)	2224	1.92	1.03
Ln (the number of daily supervision regulations)	2224	0.13	0.34
Ln (the number of penalty regulations)	2224	0.04	0.17
Ln (the number of credit-system building regulations)	2224	0.02	0.13
Ln (the number of provincial food safety laws and regulations)	2224	4.04	0.72
Firm-level dependent variable			
occurrence of food safety incidents (=1, incidents occurred; =0, no occurrence)	28392	0.137	0.344
Industry-level dependent variable			
Ln(main revenue)	7344	5.54	1.99

References

Abimbola, S., Baatiema, L., & Bigdeli, M. (2019). The impacts of decentralization on health system equity, efficiency and resilience: A realist synthesis of the evidence. *Health Policy and Planning, 34*(8), 605–617.

Acemoglu, D., Aghion, P., Lelarge, C., Van Reenen, J., & Zilibotti, F. (2007). Technology, information, and the decentralization of the firm. *Quarterly Journal of Economics, 122*(4), 1759–1799.

Aghion, P., & Tirole, J. (1997). Formal and real authority in organizations. *Journal of Political Economy, 105*(1), 1–29.

Aghion, P., Bloom, N., Lucking, B., Sadun, R., & Van Reenen, J. (2021). Turbulence, firm decentralization, and growth in bad times. *American Economic Journal: Applied Economics, 13*(1), 133–169.

Antle, J. M. (1996). Efficient food safety regulation in the food manufacturing sector. *American Journal of Agricultural Economics, 78*(5), 1242–1247.

Antle, J. M. (2000). No such thing as a free safe lunch: The cost of food safety regulation in the meat industry. *American Journal of Agricultural Economics, 82*(2), 310–322.

AQSIQ. (2006). *Chinese food classification table for market access of food quality and safety*. http://law.foodmate.net/show-47260.html

Atkin, D. (2016). The caloric costs of culture: Evidence from Indian migrants. *American Economic Review, 106*(4), 1144–1181.

Bai, J., Gazze, L., & Wang, Y. (2022). Collective reputation in trade: Evidence from the Chinese dairy industry. *Review of Economics and Statistics, 104*(6), 1121–1137.

Barankay, I., & Lockwood, B. (2007). Decentralization and the productive efficiency of government: Evidence from Swiss Cantons. *Journal of Public Economics, 91*(5–6), 1197–1218.

Bardhan, P. (2002). Decentralization of governance and development. *Journal of Economic Perspectives, 16*(4), 185–205.

Bardhan, P. K., & Mookherjee, D. (2000). *Corruption and decentralization of infrastructure delivery in developing countries*. Boston University, Institute for Economic Development.

Bardhan, P., & Mookherjee, D. (2005). Decentralizing antipoverty program delivery in developing countries. *Journal of Public Economics, 89*(4), 675–704.

Bardhan, P., & Mookherjee, D. (2006). Decentralisation and accountability in infrastructure delivery in developing countries. *Economic Journal, 116*(508), 101–127.

Besley, T., & Coate, S. (2003). Centralized versus decentralized provision of local public goods: A political economy approach. *Journal of Public Economics, 87*(12), 2611–2637.

Besley, T., & Ghatak, M. (2003). Incentives, choice, and accountability in the provision of public services. *Oxford Review of Economic Policy, 19*(2), 235–249.

Bo, S., Deng, L., Sun, Y., & Wang, B. (2021). Intergovernmental communication under decentralization. *Journal of Economic Behavior and Organization, 184*, 606–652.

Bossert, T. J., & Mitchell, A. D. (2011). Health sector decentralization and local decision-making: Decision space, institutional capacities and accountability in Pakistan. *Social Science and Medicine, 72*(1), 39–48.

Bovay, J. (2023). Food safety, reputation, and regulation. *Applied Economic Perspectives and Policy, 45*(2), 684–704.

Buckley, J. A. (2015). Food safety regulation and small processing: A case study of interactions between processors and inspectors. *Food Policy, 51*, 74–82.

Buntaine, M. T., Greenstone, M., He, G., Liu, M., Wang, S., & Zhang, B. (2024). Does the squeaky wheel get more grease? The direct and indirect effects of citizen participation on environmental governance in China. *American Economic Review, 114*(3), 815–850.

Callaway, B., & Sant'Anna, P. H. (2021). Difference-in-differences with multiple time periods. *Journal of Econometrics, 225*(2), 200–230.

CFDA. (2018). *Chinese implementation measures for national food safety supervision and sampling*. https://www.gov.cn/xinwen/2018-01/24/content_5260165.htm?eqid=ec2b50f600005134000000464770d2c

Che, J., Chung, K.-S., & Lu, Y. K. (2017). Decentralization and political career concerns. *Journal of Public Economics, 145*, 201–210.
Chen, K., Wang, X.-X., & Song, H.-Y. (2015). Food safety regulatory systems in Europe and China: A study of how co-regulation can improve regulatory effectiveness. *Journal of Integrative Agriculture, 14*(11), 2203–2217.
Chen, J., Shi, X., Zhang, M.-A., & Zhang, S. (2022). *Centralization of environmental administration and air pollution: Evidence from China* available at SSRN 4092137. https://papers.ssrn.com/sol3/papers.cfm?abstract_id=4092137
Coval, J. D., & Moskowitz, T. J. (1999). Home bias at home: Local equity preference in domestic portfolios. *Journal of Finance, 54*(6), 2045–2073.
CPPSS. (2016). *The report said 29 provincial capitals in China failed in food safety information opacity*. https://www.cqn.com.cn/cj/content/2016-03/16/content_2663998.htm
Cuadros-Meñaca, A., Thomsen, M. R., & Nayga, R. M., Jr. (2023). School breakfast and student behavior. *American Journal of Agricultural Economics, 105*(1), 99–121.
Deming, D. J. (2014). Using school choice lotteries to test measures of school effectiveness. *American Economic Review, 104*(5), 406–411.
Dou, L., Yanagishima, K., Li, X., Li, P., & Nakagawa, M. (2015). Food safety regulation and its implication on Chinese vegetable exports. *Food Policy, 57*, 128–134.
Ehler, C. N. (2003). Indicators to measure governance performance in integrated coastal management. *Ocean and Coastal Management, 46*(3–4), 335–345.
Fan, C. S., Lin, C., & Treisman, D. (2009). Political decentralization and corruption: Evidence from around the world. *Journal of Public Economics, 93*(1–2), 14–34.
Fiankor, D.-D. D., Curzi, D., & Olper, A. (2021). Trade, price and quality upgrading effects of agri-food standards. *European Review of Agricultural Economics, 48*(4), 835–877.
Fukuyama, F. (2013). What is governance? *Governance, 26*(3), 347–368.
Galiani, S., Gertler, P., & Schargrodsky, E. (2008). School decentralization: Helping the good get better, but leaving the poor behind. *Journal of Public Economics, 92*(10–11), 2106–2120.
Gallego, F. A. (2010). Historical origins of schooling: The role of democracy and political decentralization. *Review of Economics and Statistics, 92*(2), 228–243.
Gereffi, G., & Fernandez-Stark, K. (2016). *Global value chain analysis: A primer*. https://www.researchgate.net/publication/265892395_Global_Value_Chain_Analysis_A_Primer
Giroud, X. (2013). Proximity and investment: Evidence from plant-level data. *Quarterly Journal of Economics, 128*(2), 861–915.
Gong, Q., Zhang, Y., & Yu, J. (2013). Incentives, information and food safety regulation. *Economic Research Journal, 3*, 135–147.
Goodman-Bacon, A. (2021). Difference-in-differences with variation in treatment timing. *Journal of Econometrics, 225*(2), 254–277.
Hamilton, S. F., Sunding, D. L., & Zilberman, D. (2003). Public goods and the value of product quality regulations: The case of food safety. *Journal of Public Economics, 87*(3–4), 799–817.
Han, L., & Kung, J. K.-S. (2015). Fiscal incentives and policy choices of local governments: Evidence from China. *Journal of Development Economics, 116*, 89–104.
Han, C., Sun, X., & Li, J. (2021). Emission reduction effect of vertical management reform of environmental regulation—Evidence from the reform of environmental protection system in prefecture level cities. *Economics, 21*, 335–360.
Hayek, F. (1945). The use of knowledge in society. *American Economic Review, 35*(4), 519–530.
He, G., Wang, S., & Zhang, B. (2020). Watering down environmental regulation in China. *Quarterly Journal of Economics, 135*(4), 2135–2185.
Hejazi, M., Grant, J. H., & Peterson, E. (2022). Trade impact of maximum residue limits in fresh fruits and vegetables. *Food Policy, 106*, 102203.
Henson, S., & Caswell, J. (1999). Food safety regulation: An overview of contemporary issues. *Food Policy, 24*(6), 589–603.
Hoffmann, V., Moser, C., & Saak, A. (2019). Food safety in low and middle-income countries: The evidence through an economic lens. *World Development, 123*, 104611.

Holtkamp, N., Liu, P., & McGuire, W. (2014). Regional patterns of food safety in China: What can we learn from media data? *China Economic Review, 30*, 459–468.

Huang, Z., Li, L., Ma, G., & Xu, L. C. (2017). Hayek, local information, and commanding heights: Decentralizing state-owned enterprises in China. *American Economic Review, 107*(8), 2455–2478.

Jaffee, S., Henson, S., Unnevehr, L., Grace, D., & Cassou, E. (2018). *The safe food imperative: Accelerating progress in low-and middle-income countries*. World Bank Publications.

Jia, C., & Jukes, D. (2013). The national food safety control system of china–A systematic review. *Food Control, 32*(1), 236–245.

Jia, R., & Nie, H. (2017). Decentralization, collusion, and coal mine deaths. *Review of Economics and Statistics, 99*(1), 105–118.

Kang, Y. (2019). Food safety governance in China: Change and continuity. *Food Control, 106*, 106752.

Klapper, L., Laeven, L., & Rajan, R. (2006). Entry regulation as a barrier to entrepreneurship. *Journal of Financial Economics, 82*(3), 591–629.

Latouche, K., Rainelli, P., & Vermersch, D. (1998). Food safety issues and the BSE scare: Some lessons from the French case. *Food Policy, 23*(5), 347–356.

Li, H., Long, R., & Chen, H. (2013). Economic transition policies in Chinese resource-based cities: An overview of government efforts. *Energy Policy, 55*, 251–260.

Lin, W., Ma, B., Liang, J., & Jin, S. (2024). Price response to government disclosure of food safety information in developing markets. *Food Policy, 123*, 102602.

Lipscomb, M., & Mobarak, A. M. (2016). Decentralization and pollution spillovers: Evidence from the re-drawing of county borders in Brazil. *Review of Economic Studies, 84*(1), 464–502.

Liu, P., & Ma, L. (2016). Food scandals, media exposure, and citizens' safety concerns: A multilevel analysis across Chinese cities. *Food Policy, 63*, 102–111.

Liu, L., & Yue, C. (2012). Investigating the impact of SPS standards on trade using a VES model. *European Review of Agri-cultural Economics, 39*(3), 511–528.

Liu, P., & Zhang, S. (2015). Toward regulatory federalism: A study on the vertical power distribution of China's food safety regulatory system. *Journal of Central China Normal University (Humanities and Social Sciences Edition), 54*(1), 28–34.

Liu, P., Ma, L., & Liu, Z. (2016). Central-local relations and government reform: An empirical study of reform progress of the China food regulatory institution at the municipal level. *Public Administration Review, 9*(5), 24–42.

Liu, E., Lu, Y., Peng, W., & Wang, S.. (2022). *Judicial independence, local protectionism, and economic integration: Evidence from China NBER working paper*. https://www.nber.org/papers/w30432

Long, C. X., & Wang, J. (2019). China's patent promotion policies and its quality implications. *Science and Public Policy, 46*(1), 91–104.

Mergele, L., & Weber, M. (2020). Public employment services under decentralization: Evidence from a natural experiment. *Journal of Public Economics, 182*, 104113.

Millimet, D. L., & Parmeter, C. F. (2022). Accounting for skewed or one-sided measurement error in the dependent variable. *Political Analysis, 30*(1), 66–88.

Mueller, C. (1997). Media measurement models of protest event data. *Mobilization: An International Quarterly, 2*(2), 165–184.

Naritomi, J. (2019). Consumers as tax auditors. *American Economic Review, 109*(9), 3031–3072.

Oates, W. E. (1972). *Fiscal federalism*. Harcourt Brace Jovanovich.

Oates, W. E. (1993). Fiscal decentralization and economic development. *National Tax Journal, 46*(2), 237–243.

Ollinger, M., & Bovay, J. (2020). Producer response to public disclosure of food-safety information. *American Journal of Agricultural Economics, 102*(1), 186–201.

Ollinger, M., & Houser, M. (2020). Ground beef recalls and subsequent food safety performance. *Food Policy, 97*, 101971.

Peng, Y., Li, J., Xia, H., Qi, S., & Li, J. (2015). The effects of food safety issues released by we media on consumers' awareness and purchasing behavior: A case study in China. *Food Policy, 51*, 44–52.

Piggott, N. E., & Marsh, T. L. (2004). Does food safety information impact us meat demand? *American Journal of Agri-cultural Economics, 86*, 154–174.

Pouliot, S., & Wang, H. H. (2018). Information, incentives, and government intervention for food safety. *Annual Review of Resource Economics, 10*, 83–103.

Pozo, V. F., & Schroeder, T. C. (2016). Evaluating the costs of meat and poultry recalls to food firms using stock returns. *Food Policy, 59*, 66–77.

Prud'Homme, R. (1995). The dangers of decentralization. *World Bank Research Observer, 10*(2), 201–220.

Richards, T. J., Nganje, W. E., & Acharya, R. N. (2009). Public goods, hysteresis, and underinvestment in food safety. *Journal of Agricultural and Resource Economics, 34*, 464–482.

Sant'Anna, P. H. C., & Zhao, J. (2020). Doubly robust difference-in-differences estimators. *Journal of Econometrics, 219*(1), 101–122.

Sigman, H. (2005). Transboundary spillovers and decentralization of environmental policies. *Journal of Environmental Economics and Management, 50*(1), 82–101.

Smed, S., & Jensen, J. D. (2005). Food safety information and food demand. *British Food Journal, 107*(3), 173–186.

Spalding, A., Goodhue, R. E., Kiesel, K., & Sexton, R. J. (2023). Economic impacts of food safety incidents in a modern supply chain: E. Coli in the romaine lettuce industry. *American Journal of Agricultural Economics, 105*(2), 597–623.

Swinnen, J. F., McCluskey, J., & Francken, N. (2005). Food safety, the media, and the information market. *Agricultural Economics, 32*, 175–188.

Thornton, J. (2007). Fiscal decentralization and economic growth reconsidered. *Journal of Urban Economics, 61*(1), 64–70.

Tiebout, C. M. (1956). A pure theory of local expenditures. *Journal of Political Economy, 64*(5), 416–424.

Tirole, J. (1986). Hierarchies and bureaucracies: On the role of collusion in organizations. *Journal of Law, Economics, and Organization, 2*(2), 181–214.

Toledo, C., & Villas-Boas, S. B. (2019). Safe or not? Consumer responses to recalls with traceability. *Applied Economic Perspectives and Policy, 41*(3), 519–541.

Treisman, D. (2002). *Decentralization and the quality of government*. Unpublished paper. Department of Political Science, UCLA.

Unnevehr, L. J. (2007). Food safety as a global public good. *Agricultural Economics, 37*, 149–158.

Unnevehr, L. J. (2022). Addressing food safety challenges in rapidly developing food systems. *Agricultural Economics, 53*(4), 529–539.

Unnevehr, L. J., & Jensen, H. H. (1996). HACCP as a regulatory innovation to improve food safety in the meat industry. *American Journal of Agricultural Economics, 78*(3), 764–769.

Wang, C. (2011). What does the "Restructuring" of industry and commerce and quality inspection Departments below the provincial level mean? *China Youth Daily*. https://zqb.cyol.com/html/2011-11/08/nw.D110000zgqnb_20111108_1-05.htm

Wang, P., Cho, L.-F., & Li, R. (2018). An institutional explanation of media corruption in China. *Journal of Contemporary China, 27*(113), 748–762.

WHO. (2015). *WHO estimates of the global burden of foodborne diseases: Foodborne disease burden epidemiology reference group 2007–15*. WHO. https://www.who.int/publications/i/item/9789241565165

Wooldridge, J. M. (2005). Violating ignorability of treatment by controlling for too many factors. *Econometric Theory, 21*(5), 1026–1028.

Worosz, M. R., Knight, A. J., Harris, C. K., & Conner, D. S. (2008). Barriers to entry into the specialty red meat sector: The role of food safety regulation. *Journal of Rural Social Sciences, 23*(1), 8.

Yu, W., Gao, N., & Gong, Q. (2014). Public demands, local officials' incentive and environmental governance. *Zhejiang Social Sciences, 5*, 23–35.
Zheng, S. (2018). *The number of local laws and regulations in China amounts to 12600 at present.* http://www.rmzxb.com.cn/c/2018-03-11/1990617.shtml
Zhou, D., & Yang, H. (2002). Information asymmetry and government supervision mechanism in food quality and safety management. *Chinese Rural Economy, 6*, 29–35.
Zining, J. (2015). Environmental impact assessment law in China's courts: A study of 107 judicial decisions. *Environmental Impact Assessment Review, 55*, 35–44.

Chapter 3
Local Protectionism in China's Government Disclosure of Food Safety Information

3.1 Introduction

While government interventions to address market failures, such as those stemming from imperfect information, are widely accepted, the literature also recognizes the limits of government intervention (Gradstein, 1993). One frequently discussed cause is rent-seeking (Krueger, 1990; Helm, 2010). Given that the costs of the failure of intervention are typically greater than the costs of the interventions themselves (Stiglitz, 2009), understanding the causes of intervention failure and their implications for public policy design is essential.

This study investigates the potential intervention failure resulting from local protectionism, characterized by local governments favoring firms within their jurisdiction. Local protectionism hinders market integration and leads to substantial welfare losses (Bai et al., 2004; Donaldson, 2015). Previous research has documented various forms of local protectionism, including procurement preferences (Fang et al., 2022), subsidies (Barwick et al., 2021), discriminatory regulations (Eberhardt et al., 2016), and internal trade restrictions (Tombe & Zhu, 2019). We, however, distinguish by examining how regional governments 'manipulate' public information to favor local firms, which reduces the effectiveness of information-based interventions.

Empirically, this study examines whether prefectural governments influence the public reporting of food safety information to protect local firms from negative disclosures in China. Food safety remains a significant public concern in China (Wang et al., 2019; Yang et al., 2019; Liu et al., 2020; Tian et al., 2024). The implementation of food safety sampling and information disclosure in 2014, as part of the China Food Safety Laws, aims to address market failure in the provision of food safety resulting from asymmetric information (Unnevehr, 2015). These measures mandate

W. Lin, *Transforming China's Agri-Food System: Government-Market Synergy*, Resources, Environment and Agricultural Development,
https://doi.org/10.1007/978-981-95-7151-2_3

both central and local administrations to regularly and randomly sample food products, conduct food safety tests and disclose testing outcomes (Sect. 3.2.1 for details). While limited empirical studies have quantified the presence of local protection in public information disclosure, anecdotal evidence suggests that local governments tend to downplay negative reports within their jurisdiction, including food safety issues (Southern Daily, 2016; Ni et al., 2019).

To identify the impact of local protectionism on food safety information disclosure, we utilize product-level data from government websites and compare food safety testing results conducted by local and national administrations for the *same product within the same manufacturing firm and year*. This *within-firm, within-product comparison* allows us to control for many confounding factors, such as firm or product-level selection biases and external shocks (i.e. the pandemic). We construct a panel dataset on product-level food safety sampling and testing information from the websites of national and prefectural market regulation administrations, with 3104 product-level observations from 2020 to 2021. Our results indicate that the likelihood and number of food safety testing failures are significantly lower when products are sampled by local prefectural administrations, compared to the same product from the same manufacturing firm sampled by the national administration within the same year. This suggests the presence of local favoritism in food safety data reporting. The finding remain robust across various model specifications and are substantiated when controlling for multiple fixed effects including product category, sampling segment, year, and prefecture. Food safety testing outcomes may vary depending on the segment of food supply chains where the product is sampled, and we account for this by adding sampling segment fixed effects. The evidence also persists when accounting for potential collusions between independent inspection agencies and food manufacturing firms, the difference in testing capabilities between national and prefectural administrations and the disruptions that COVID-19 may have caused to food production and inspection activities.

Heterogeneous analyses reveal that significantly lower failure rates reported by the local prefectural authority are more likely among food manufacturing firms with higher registration capital and those in local key industries. Further, in prefectures with higher GDP growth targets, local administrations disclose lower testing failure rates compared to the national authority. These imply that local governments tend to favor firms important to local economies, especially when under greater economic growth pressure.

This paper is naturally linked to the study of local protectionism, which traditionally examines provincial convergence patterns or border effects estimated from provincial input-output tables as evidence of protectionism (Young, 2000; Bai et al., 2004; Poncet, 2005). But this approach has limitations (Bai & Liu, 2019). Recent studies, instead, have turned to micro-level datasets to quantify local protectionism in various forms and industries, for example, Barwick et al. (2021), Fang et al. (2022), Liu et al. (2020) and Eberhardt et al. (2016). Our contribution is to demonstrate information manipulation as an important yet overlooked channel through which local protectionism operates. Using data on information-based food safety regulation in China, we provide the first empirical evidence of local protectionism in the agricultural-food market, where prefectural administrations report lower food safety testing failure rates for local firms relative to the national authority.

The paper also relates to the literature that studies how local governments respond to central incentives in China. The central government incentivizes local governments through an economic tournament to stimulate local economic development (Li & Zhou, 2005). However, this system also leads to short-termist behaviors among local governments (Xiong, 2018), such as overleverage through shadow banking, local protectionism (Fang et al., 2022), and manipulating economic statistics (Chen et al., 2019). Our paper finds that local governments tend to favor firms strategic to the local economy, particularly when under greater pressure to meet economic growth targets. This adds to the research by highlighting information manipulation as a hitherto understudied strategy by local governments in tournament competition to protect local economies. Furthermore, our research contributes to the understanding of government data manipulation. Existing studies have focused on various aspects such as GDP manipulation in China (Chen et al., 2019, 2021) and other economies (Briviba et al., 2024), air pollution data (Ghanem & Zhang, 2014; Ghanem et al., 2020), and grain yields (Fan et al., 2016). Our research sheds light on government manipulation in food safety data, another negative consequence of the political competition in China.

Finally, we add to the research on government information disclosure designed to correct information-related market failures. Information mandate has become an important policy instrument for policymakers due to its low cost and intrusiveness, thus motivating studies to assess market responses across economic sectors, including energy, health, food, finance (Bollinger et al., 2011; Seira et al., 2017; Carter & Schaefer, 2019; Myers et al., 2022). In particular, some examined how government disclosure of food safety information affects consumer and producer behaviors and market prices (Toledo & Villas-Boas, 2019; Ollinger & Bovay, 2020; Lin et al., 2024). All these studies implicitly assume the information disclosed by governments is reliable. Our paper complements this strand of literature by examining the reliability of government-disclosed information, a critical question that needs to be addressed before evaluating its effectiveness. Focusing on government disclosure of food safety information in China, we find that information disclosed by local governments, intended to mitigate food safety issues, is manipulated to favor local food firms.

The remainder of the paper is organized as follows. Section 3.2 discusses the public disclosure of food safety tests and information in China and the potential information distortion. Section 3.3 details the empirical strategy and data. Section 3.4 presents the baseline results as well as robustness checks. Section 3.5 conducts heterogeneous analyses to assess the incentive of local protectionism while Sect. 3.6 concludes.

3.2 Institutional Background

3.2.1 Food Safety Sampling Test and Information Disclosure

Governmental provision of food safety information is an essential strategy in addressing food safety issues worldwide, including the United States, the European Union, Canada, Brazil, and China. The China Food and Drug Administration promulgated the "Management Measures for Food Safety Sampling and Testing" in December 2014, initiating the implementation of food sampling tests and information disclosure nationwide. It has since evolved into one of the most important institutions for food safety governance in China. The food safety sampling tests and information disclosure include several stages: planning, sampling, inspection and result submission, the disposal of unqualified foods and corresponding punishment and information disclosure (State Administration for Market Regulation, 2019a).

Annually, the State Administration for Market Regulation (SAMR) formulates a top-down sampling plan delineating the total number of food sampling tests and specifying products to be tested within each product category (Zhou et al., 2022). This national food sampling plan allocates tests between the central and regional administrations. Across all levels of administration, these plans have been crafted based on potential food safety risks and population size (Lin et al., 2024). The categorization of food sampling tests and information disclosure is: (1) activities overseen or authorized by the central administration, specifically the State Administration for Market Regulation, are denoted as *national sampling*; (2) those conducted or authorized by provincial administrations, such as the Administration for Market Regulation in Zhejiang province, are referred to as *provincial sampling*; (3) similarly, tests conducted or authorized by prefectural agencies, like the Administration for Market Regulation in Fuzhou, Fujian province, are designated as *prefectural sampling*. Each level of administration conducts food sampling tests independently.

As per the policy requirement, foods must undergo random sampling in all cases (State Administration for Market Regulation, 2019b). This mandates the random selection of food product, its supplier, and the sampling staff, with suppliers including food manufacturers, wholesalers, retailers, and restaurants or dining halls.

After sampling, the food sample is either examined by the administration directly or sent to an inspection agency for quality tests. The inspection items include microbiological tests, pesticide residue tests, veterinary drug residue tests, heavy metal tests, food additive tests, and quality-related indicators, among others. Normally the test results should be available within 7 business days. In accordance with "China's Food Safety Law and the Implementation Rules for National Agricultural Product Quality and Safety Supervision and Check", when a food product fails safety tests, like pork identified with excessive chloramphenicol use, the administration will impose fines on the food supplier and, in severe cases, revoke the business licenses.

The final step is the public disclosure of food sampling test results, online via government official websites, as mandated by "China's Regulations on the

Disclosure of Government Information and the Management Measures for Food Safety Sampling and Testing". The disclosed information includes the name and production date of the food product, its supplier and location, its producer or manufacturer and location, the result of the safety tests, the sampling administration and inspection agency (if applicable). The workflow of China's food safety sampling tests and information disclosure is shown in Fig. 3.1.

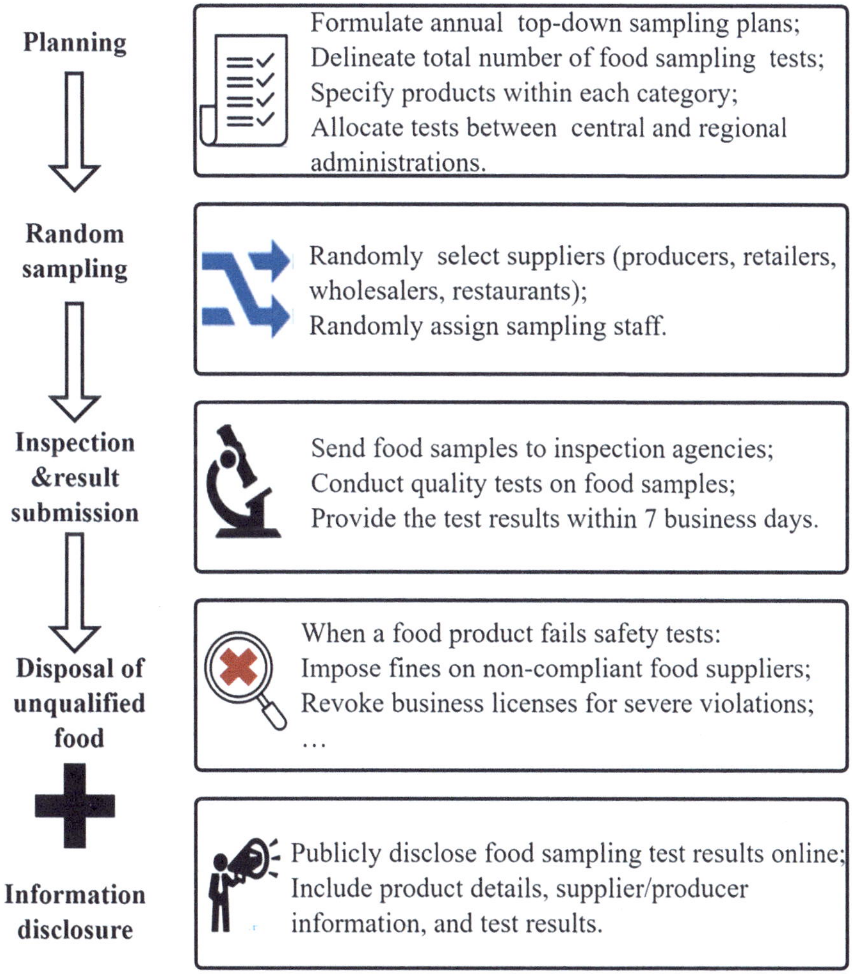

Fig. 3.1 The workflow of food safety sampling test and information disclosure across all administrative levels. Notes: This flowchart illustrates the entire process of food safety testing and information disclosure, from the State Administration for Market Regulation (central level) to local administrations for market regulation (local level). The figure was prepared by the authors themselves. The specific sampling inspection procedures are based on the *Administrative Measures for Food Safety Sampling Inspection* issued by the State Administration for Market Regulation (For details, see the following link: https://www.gov.cn/zhengce/2022-10/08/content_5723511.htm)

3.2.2 *Potential Distortion in Food Safety Information Disclosure*

While food safety sampling tests and information disclosure alleviate pressure on the national administration by assigning some sampling tasks to the local administrations, it meanwhile provides opportunities for local administrations to manipulate food safety data.

In China, food safety, particularly the volume and outcome of food safety sampling tests, is an important determinant for the performance and promotion of local government officials. The Measures for Evaluation and Assessment of Food Safety Work, issued by China's State Council in 2016, highlights the importance of indicators, such as the ratio of food sampling test failures and the number of sampling tasks, in evaluating local food safety governance. In 2019, the Regulations on the Responsibility System for Food Safety of Local Party and Government Leading Cadres reiterated that the selection and appointment of government officials are influenced by their performance in food safety regulation, including the number and passing rate of food safety sampling tests (Shi, 2019). To improve the pass rate of food products, local administrations may manipulate food safety information at multiple stages of the sampling process. First, during the sampling stage, some local officials may notice in advance food producers and operators selected for inspection, thereby reducing the likelihood of detecting problematic products at the source. Second, in the inspection and result submission stage, local administrations may manipulate testing results of food products within their jurisdiction, as even a single food safety incident could damage the collective reputation of all food manufacturers in that area (Bai et al., 2022). This reputational damage can lead to reduced tax revenue, employment, and output, creating economic incentives for local administrations to underreport failed tests to protect their local interests. Third, during the information disclosure stage, staff of prefectural administrations have been found to delay or conceal information during food safety incidents (Ni et al., 2019), raising concerns that local administrations may distort sampling test outcomes to serve their own interests.

It is also important to note that, after sampling, the product is sent to an inspection agency for quality testing (Fig. 3.1). Differences in inspection agencies used for prefectural and national sampling would introduce biases in prefectural sampling test outcomes. In general, inspection agencies can be categorized into two types: those operating as departments within the administration and those that are independent of the administration and privately operated (Lin & Chen, 2020). Food inspection agencies that function as government departments are headed by officials appointed by local authorities. Third-party testing agencies account for a relatively small share among inspection agencies (Lin & Chen, 2020), so the inspection outcomes of local agencies are likely to be influenced by local governments. The selection of inspection agencies for quality testing is made through public bidding and ultimately decided by the administration (Zhao, 2015). Figure 3.2 presents a comparison of inspection agency types used in national and prefectural sampling. Panel

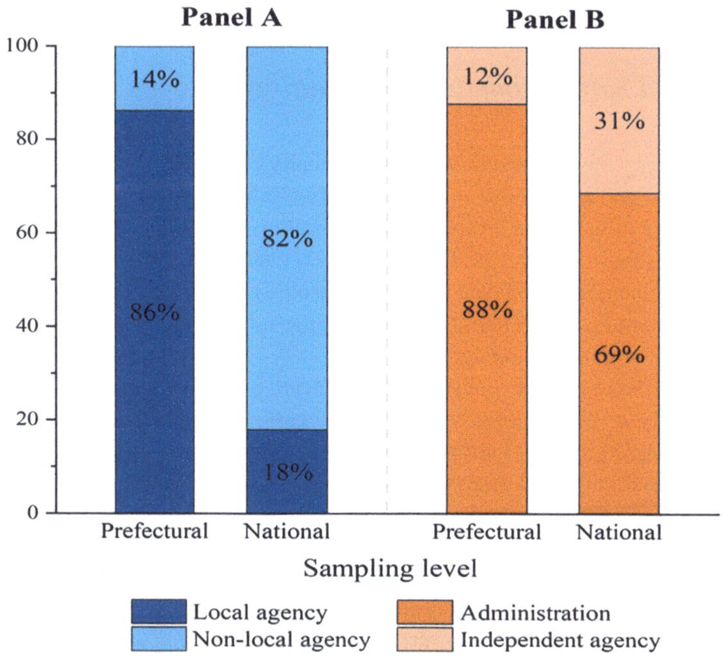

Fig. 3.2 The proportion of different inspection agencies in prefectural sampling and national sampling. Notes: The horizontal axis in the figure represents the sample levels, divided into prefectural sampling and national sampling. The vertical axis shows the percentage of samples inspected by different inspection agencies. Inspection agencies refer to the professional food quality testing agencies. We classified inspection agencies into local and nonlocal agencies based on their name and location in our dataset. Local inspection agencies indicate the agencies located in the same prefecture as the sampling administration. In panel (**a**), the dark blue color represents the proportion tested by local inspection agencies, while the light blue color represents the proportion tested by non-local inspection agencies. In panel (**b**), the dark orange color represents the proportion of tests conducted by the administration itself, while the light orange color represents the proportion tested by independent agencies. The sample sizes for each group in the figure are as follows: prefectural-local agency (794), prefectural-non-local agency (128), national-local agency (12), national-non-local agency (55); prefectural-administration (809), prefectural-independent agency (113), national-administration (46), national-independent agency (21)

A shows the percentage of quality tests conducted by inspection agencies located within the same prefecture as the prefectural administration (referred to as 'local') versus non-local agencies. In prefectural sampling, 86% of the sampled products were tested by local inspection agencies, compared to only 18% in national sampling. Panel B illustrates the percentage of tests conducted by the administration itself versus independent agencies, and 12% of the products in prefectural sampling were tested by independent inspection agencies, while 31% were tested in national sampling. Prefectural sampling relies more on local and non-independent inspection agencies, which are more likely to be influenced by local administrations, so the testing failure rates in prefectural sampling may be lower than national sampling.

3.3 Data and Empirical Strategy

3.3.1 Food Safety Sampling Test Data

Our food safety sampling test database is manually collected from official websites of the national and prefectural market regulation administrations. The data covers comprehensive information on food safety sampling tests conducted by prefectural and national authorities from 2020 to 2021. Each observation in the dataset includes the name and manufacturing date of the food product, where and when the food was sampled, its manufacturer's name and address, the safety test outcome, the sampling administration and inspection agency.

From this database, we construct a balanced product-year panel dataset for empirical analyses. We retain observations where products from the same manufacturer were sampled by both national and local prefectural sampling within the same year. In the final empirical analysis dataset, each product (defined as a company–product category pair) has at least four inspection records: one national and one local sampling inspection in 2020, and one national and one local inspection in 2021. Due to random sampling by national and prefectural administrations, the final dataset comprises 3104 product–year observations, involving 776 products from 750 manufacturers, 26 food categories, spanning 12 provinces which contributed to over half of the national food industry output.

We then identify key variables in this study. First, when a product is sampled by prefectural administration, and its manufacturer is located in the same prefecture as the administration, $local\_samp_{ipt}$ is designated as 1; if the product is sampled by national sampling, $local\_samp_{it}= 0$. The dependent variables are derived by calculating the annual number of testing failures for each product. The variable *Failure* equals 1 if product p in year t failed at least once, and 0 otherwise. The variable N_failure is the total number of failures. For example, if Company M's dairy products were tested five times under the national program in 2021 and three tests failed, then Failure = 1 and N_failure = 3. Sampling segments are grouped into several types, such as production/manufacture, distribution and retail. For instance, a food product sampled at a food processing belongs to the production/manufacture segment; a food sampled at a wholesale market falls under the distribution segment. Table 3.1 describes all variables.

3.3.2 Empirical Strategy

As discussed earlier, we hypothesize that, in the presence of local protectionism, food products manufactured within the prefecture conducting the sampling will exhibit lower failure rates compared to those tested under national sampling, *ceteris paribus*. To empirically test this hypothesis, we compare food safety testing outcomes conducted by local and national administrations for *the same product,*

Table 3.1 Summary Statistics

Variable	Description	Mean	S.D.	Min.	Max.
Dependent variable					
N_failure	The number of failures in sampling tests	0.051	0.308	0	5
Failure	=1, a product fails sampling tests ; =0, otherwise	0.037	0.188	0	1
Independent variable					
Local_samp	=1, a product is sampled by local prefectural administration; =0, if national sampling	0.500	0.500	0	1
Heterogeneous variable					
Covid-19	Standardized city-level daily average COVID-19 case counts	0	1	−1.15	16.73
Register_ capital	Registration capital of a food manufacturing firm, ten thousand RMB	2929.589	13586.150	3	261,614
Key_indus	=1, if a firm belongs to provincial key food industries; =0, otherwise	0.427	0.495	0	1
Target_GDP	Prefectural GDP growth rate target, %	7.138	0.747	5	11
Observations		3104			

Notes: The final dataset comprises 3104 product-level sampling test observations, involving 776 products from 750 manufacturers, 26 food categories and spanning 12 provinces from 2020 to 2021. Table 3.13 in Appendix shows the list of key food industries for each province in our sample

produced by the same manufacturer, within the same year. Our analysis uses two outcome variables: a binary indicator of whether a product fails the test and a count of the number of failures. For the binary outcome, we employ a generalized linear logit model with fixed effects. Linear regression would violate key assumptions in this setting and may produce biased estimates or predicted probabilities outside the [0,1] range (Wooldridge, 2016). At the same time, fixed-effects logit models are subject to estimation bias, particularly in short panels (Katz, 2001). Therefore, we adopt a generalized linear modeling framework with the logit link function. For the count outcome, we use a zero-inflated Poisson (ZIP) model to capture both the discrete nature of the data and the excess zeros.[1] This approach follows prior studies including Cho et al. (2018), Peterson et al. (2013), Lambert (1992), and Gurmu et al. (1999).

First, we use the generalized linear model with the logit link function to estimate the treatment effects of local prefectural sampling on the likelihood of a sampled product failing the test. The generalized linear model (GLM) is:

$$\text{Logit}\, P_{ipft} = \ln\left(\frac{P_{ipft}}{1-P_{ipft}}\right) = \beta_0 + \beta_1 local\_samp_{it} + \mu_{p,f} + \gamma_c + \mu_t + \delta_s + \varepsilon_{ipft} \quad (3.1)$$

[1] The excess zeros in observations are consistent with the fact that the pass rate of food safety sampling tests in China exceeded 97% (Beijing News, 2022).

Where P_{ipft} is the probability that food product p manufactured by firm f fails the test conducted by the level of administration i in year t; $local\_samp_{it}$, is a dummy variable and equals 1 if the product p is manufactured in the prefecture conducting the sampling in year t, and equals 0 if the product p belongs to national sampling. Importantly, we include product-manufacturer fixed effects ($\mu_{p,f}$) and year fixed effects (μ_t) to account for potential confounding factors arising from product and manufacturer sampling selection bias. Prefectural administrations may allocate more tasks to products with lower failure rates and to manufacturer easier to reach (Li et al., 2021). Besides, the testing results may vary depending on the stage of the food supply chain at which the food product is sampled, including production, processing, wholesale, retail, and catering (Jin et al., 2021). Food products under national sampling are often sampled and tested outside their manufacturing origins. To mitigate the potential concern caused by different sampling stages, we introduce sampling segment fixed effects δ_s. Eq. (3.1) also includes prefecture fixed effects γ_c to control for prefecture-specific factors that affect the testing outcome. Standard errors are clustered at the firm level to adjust for correlations among error terms within firm.

In addition to the GLM model, we also investigate how local prefectural sampling affects the number of testing failures using the zero-inflated Poisson (ZIP) model. Let Y_j denote the count of testing failures, where j denotes the jth observation in our product-year panel dataset. ZIP model assumes Y_j from a mixture of two data-generating processes: one generates only zeroes with a probability P_j, and the other follows a Poisson distribution. Y_j can be written as:

$$Y_j = \begin{cases} 0, \text{with the probability } P_j \\ \text{Poisson}\left(\mu_j\right), \text{with the probability } 1 - P_j \end{cases}$$

Where μ_j is the Poisson distribution's mean, P_j is the probability that the observation has zero failure. The ZIP model is:

$$logit\left(P_j\right) = \ln\frac{P_j}{1-P_j} = \boldsymbol{X}_j'\boldsymbol{\theta} \tag{3.2a}$$

$$\ln\left(\mu_j\right) = \boldsymbol{X}_j'\alpha \tag{3.2b}$$

Where $\boldsymbol{X}_j$ represents the vector of variables consistent with those in Eq. (3.1), $\boldsymbol{\theta}$ and $\boldsymbol{\alpha}$ are the corresponding parameter vectors to be estimated in Eqs. (3.2a) and (3.2b), respectively. The log-likelihood function of our ZIP model is:

$$lnL\left(\alpha,\theta|\boldsymbol{Y}_j,\boldsymbol{X}_j\right) = \sum_{Y_j=0} \ln\left(e^{X_j'\theta} + \exp\left(-e^{X_j'\alpha}\right)\right)$$

$$+\sum_{Y_j>0} \ln\left(Y_j X_j'\alpha - e^{X_j'\alpha} - \ln\left(Y_j!\right)\right) - \sum_{j=1}^{n} \ln\left(1+e^{X_j'\theta}\right)$$

Last, we note that the GLM and ZIP models, chosen to fit the nature of our dependent variable (which consists of nonnegative integers, with a majority of observations being zeros), failed to converge when including product-manufacturer fixed effects. This is likely due to the non-linear nature of the model specification. So we estimate both models with product fixed effects instead of product-manufacturer fixed effects as our baseline results. As a robustness check, we also perform linear ordinary least squares (OLS) regression, accounting for product-manufacturer, manufacturer-year, product-year, and sampling-stage fixed effects described in Eq. (3.1).

3.4 Baseline Results and Alternative Specification

Table 3.2 presents the impact of local prefectural sampling on food safety testing outcomes. Columns (1)–(3) examine the extensive margin by estimating Eq. (3.1), while columns (4)–(6) examine both the extensive and intensive margins by estimating Eq. (2). In column (1), the marginal effect of "local_samp" is −0.673, significant at the 5% level, indicating that, for the same product within the same

Table 3.2 Effects of local prefectural sampling on food safety testing outcome

	Failure			N_Failure		
	GLM			Zero-inflated Poisson		
	(1)	(2)	(3)	(4)	(5)	(6)
Local_samp	−0.673**	−0.673*	−0.659**	−0.057**	−0.057**	−0.059***
	(0.295)	(0.355)	(0.287)	(0.027)	(0.029)	(0.011)
Prefecture FE	Yes	Yes	Yes	Yes	Yes	Yes
Year FE	Yes	Yes	Yes	Yes	Yes	Yes
Product FE	Yes	Yes	Yes	Yes	Yes	Yes
Sampling Segment FE	Yes	Yes	Yes	Yes	Yes	Yes
Production-Sampling province FE			Yes			Yes
Observations	2103	2103	2043	3104	3104	3104

Notes: "Local_samp" equals 1 if the sampled product is produced within the prefecture conducting the sampling, and 0 if it is from national sampling. Columns (1)–(3) report the results of general linear logit model (GLM) with fixed effects where the dependent variable equals 1 if a product fails the test. Columns (4)–(6) report zero-inflated Poisson (ZIP) results where the dependent variable is the number of failures. All coefficients are average marginal effects. Columns (3) and (6) include production–sampling province-pair fixed effects. Standard errors are clustered at the prefectural level in Columns (2) and (5), and at the manufacturer level otherwise (in parentheses). *, **, and *** denote significance at the 10%, 5%, and 1% levels, respectively. General linear logit models drop groups without within-group variation, so sample sizes differ across columns manufacturer and year, the likelihood of testing failure(s) in local prefectural sampling is 67.3 percentage points lower than that in national sampling, holding others factors constant. The result of column (4) suggests that the number of test failures in local prefectural sampling is lower by 0.057 compared with national sampling. This effect is substantial considering that the mean value of test failures under national sampling is 0.076 (a decrease of about 75%). In the baseline regressions, since both the outcomes and "local_samp" are defined at the product level, we cluster standard errors at the manufacturer level. However, given that inspections are conducted by prefecture-level agencies, observations within the same city may be correlated. Therefore, we cluster standard errors at the prefectural level in Columns (2) and (5). The results indicate that changing the clustering level does not materially affect the significance of the estimates. Columns (3) and (6) build upon columns (1) and (4) respectively, incorporating fixed effects for production–sampling province pairs of the product. In prefectural sampling, products sampled and tested are predominantly manufactured locally, whereas the majority of products under national sampling are examined outside their production origins. Given that food is perishable and its quality may be influenced by transportation distance between production and sampling locations (Southern et al., 2006), the increased failures observed under national sampling would be attributed to longer distances traveled by the food, rather than local protectionism. To control for this, we introduce pair fixed effects between production province and sampling province. Results from columns (2) and (4) show that the estimated effects of local prefectural sampling on food safety testing outcomes are robust.

We conduct some robustness checks by using alternative model specifications (Table 3.9 in appendix). For the dependent variable denoting the count of testing failures, we assess the robustness using the ordinary least squares (OLS) and Poisson models. The marginal effect of local prefectural sampling remains statistically significant, and the effect size derived from the OLS model is smaller than that of the baseline, whereas the effect size from the Poisson model exhibits a similar magnitude. Besides, given the convergence issues arising from accounting for high-dimensional fixed effects in non-linear models, we evaluate the robustness of our baseline results using linear models such as LPM and OLS. These linear models enable us to simultaneously control for high-dimensional fixed effects, including manufacturer by year, manufacturer by product, product by year and sampling segment fixed effects, mitigating concerns related to omitted variables and sampling selection bias. Our findings indicate that with the additional inclusion of different fixed effects, the impact of local prefectural sampling on food safety testing outcomes remains robust.

3.5 Alternative Explanations for Differences in Food Safety Testing Outcomes Between National and Local Prefectural Sampling

3.5.1 Collusion Between Food Manufacturers and Independent Inspecting Agencies

One potential counterargument to the hypothesis of local protectionism is that the observed lower testing failure rates in local prefectural sampling compared with national-level sampling might stem from the collusion between food manufacturers and independent inspecting agencies, instead of government protection. This means that manufacturers might directly conspire with local inspectors to avoid regulatory penalties and reputation damage, influencing food safety testing results. The food products are either sampled and tested directly by the administration or delegated to independent inspection agencies, and only 12% of the products subjected to prefectural sampling are investigated by independent inspection agencies (Fig. 3.2), which in part alleviates our collusion concern. To formally examine this possibility, we replicate the analysis in Table 3.2 using these two inspection subsamples, and report the findings in Table 3.3. If food manufacturers collude with independent inspectors, we anticipate that the subsample tested by independent inspection agencies shows lower failure rates under local prefectural sampling. However, Table 3.3 indicates that local prefectural sampling reduces the incidence and count of testing failures within the administration inspection subsample, rather than the other subsample. These findings suggest a strong correlation between food safety testing

Table 3.3 Control for potential collusion between firms and independent inspection agencies

	Failure		N_Failure	
	Administration	Independent	Administration	Independent
	(1)	(2)	(3)	(4)
Local_samp	−0.632***	−0.236	−0.370**	−0.422
	(0.116)	(0.146)	(0.179)	(0.640)
Prefecture FE	Yes	Yes	Yes	Yes
Year FE	Yes	Yes	Yes	Yes
Product FE	Yes	Yes	Yes	Yes
Sampling Segment FE	Yes	Yes	Yes	Yes
Observations	515	121	855	134

Notes: "Local_samp" equals 1 if the sampled product is produced within the prefecture conducting the sampling, and 0 if from national sampling. Columns (1)–(2) report the results of general linear logit model (GLM) with a binary dependent variable equal to 1 for failed tests. Columns (3)–(4) report zero-inflated Poisson (ZIP) results with the number of failures as the dependent variable. All coefficients are average marginal effects. "Administration" refers to samples tested by agencies within food safety administrations, and "Independent" to those tested by external inspection agencies. Standard errors (in parentheses) are clustered at the manufacturer level. *, **, and *** denote significance at the 10%, 5%, and 1% levels, respectively. Smaller sample sizes result from fixed effects and missing inspection information outcomes and local administration practice, mitigating the confounding effect of collusions between independent agencies and manufacturers.

3.5.2 Testing Capabilities Between National and Prefectural Administrations

An alternative explanation for the lower failure rate in local prefectural sampling is that local inspectors may lack the same technological resources as national inspectors, rather than deliberate manipulation by local governments. However, based on discussions with staff from market regulation administrations and field experts, food safety testing typically relies on relatively basic methods and does not require advanced equipment. Both central and local authorities possess sufficient capacity to conduct these tests. To account for potential differences in local testing capacity, we include prefecture fixed effects in Eqs. (3.1) and (3.2a, 3.2b). In addition, there is a concern that differences in testing outcomes between national and local inspections may arise from variations in the technical capacity of provincial and prefectural agencies. That is, since local sampling is mostly tested by prefectural agencies while national sampling is primarily conducted by provincial agencies, and given that prefectural agencies may lag behind provincial ones in technical capacity, some substandard samples might not be detected. To rule out this possibility, we conduct additional analyses comparing the results of prefectural inspection agencies under local prefectural sampling and under national sampling (Table 3.8). Results show that, even when all tests are conducted by prefectural inspection agencies, national sampling continues to show lower food safety failure rates compared to local prefectural sampling.

3.5.3 The Disruptions of COVID-19

Our sample period coincides with the outbreak of COVID-19 in China, which may have influenced inspection activities or food production processes, and thus potentially interfered with our results. To assess the impact of the pandemic, we collected data from news media on the daily average number of confirmed COVID-19 cases in each city during the sample period, which serves as a measure of the local severity of the pandemic. We standardized these case counts and interacted them with the key variable "local_samp", incorporating the interaction term into the baseline regression. As shown in Table 3.4, neither the number of COVID-19 cases nor its interaction with "local_samp" has a significant effect on the probability or frequency of inspection failures. Moreover, the average marginal effect of "local_samp" remained very close to that in the baseline regression. These results suggest that the pandemic is unlikely to have materially affected the main conclusions of this study.

Table 3.4 Effects of COVID-19 on the relationship between local prefectural sampling and food safety testing outcomes

	Failure	N_Failure
	GLM	Zero-inflated Poisson
	(1)	(2)
Local_samp*Covid-19	−0.200	−0.033
	(0.267)	(0.050)
Local_samp	−0.674**	−0.060**
	(0.292)	(0.027)
Covid-19	−0.875	0.026
	(1.191)	(0.042)
Prefecture FE	Yes	Yes
Year FE	Yes	Yes
Product FE	Yes	Yes
Sampling Segment FE	Yes	Yes
Observations	2103	3104

Notes: "Local_samp" equals 1 if the sampled product is produced within the prefecture conducting the sampling, and 0 if from national sampling. "Covid-19" represents the standardized city-level daily average of confirmed cases, indicating local pandemic severity. Column (1) reports GLM results with a binary dependent variable equal to 1 for failed tests. Column (2) reports ZIP results with the number of failures as the dependent variable. All coefficients are average marginal effects. Standard errors (in parentheses) are clustered at the manufacturer level. *, **, and *** denote significance at the 10%, 5%, and 1% levels, respectively. Smaller sample sizes result from fixed effects and missing inspection information

3.6 Incentives of Local Protectionism

This section explores the incentives of local administration to underreport testing failures of local products. A common argument for local protectionism is that local governments prioritize local firms or industries, driven by the desire to improve economic performance and increase their chances of promotion (Li & Zhou, 2005; Bai et al., 2020; Chen et al., 2021). In the food sector, negative quality shocks about one manufacturing firm's products could reduce demand for products from other firms within the same origin area and hurt the overall economy due to reputation spillovers (Bai et al., 2022). In particular, larger firms are more important to the local economy and penalizing the largest firms will harm economic growth targets. Thus we expect food safety information manipulation tends to be evident within larger firms that are critical to the local economy, as penalizing these firms could harm local growth objectives.

We proxy the salience of food manufacturing firms to the local economy in two ways: by considering a firm's scale and its classification within local key industries. First, we use registration capital obtained from the Chinese Administration for Industry and Commerce's business registration database as an indicator of firm

Table 3.5 Heterogeneous effects of local prefectural sampling on food safety testing outcome by firm registration capital

	Failure		N_Failure	
	Below Median	Above Median	Below Median	Above Median
	(1)	(2)	(3)	(4)
Local_samp	−0.556	−0.717*	−0.132	−0.033*
	(0.472)	(0.404)	(2.120)	(0.018)
Prefecture FE	Yes	Yes	Yes	Yes
Year FE	Yes	Yes	Yes	Yes
Product FE	Yes	Yes	Yes	Yes
Sampling Segment FE	Yes	Yes	Yes	Yes
Observations	677	1181	996	2108

Notes: "Local_samp" equals 1 if the sampled product is produced within the prefecture conducting the sampling, and 0 if from national sampling. Columns (1)–(2) report GLM results with a binary dependent variable equal to 1 for failed tests. Columns (3)–(4) report ZIP results with the number of failures as the dependent variable. All coefficients are average marginal effects. "Above median" refers to products from firms with registered capital above the sample median. Standard errors (in parentheses) are clustered at the manufacturer level. *, **, and *** denote significance at the 10%, 5%, and 1% levels, respectively

scale. Based on whether a firm's registration capital exceeds the sample median we divide the sample and replicate Table 3.2 using a subsample approach. Table 3.5 suggests that the reduced incidence of testing failures attributed to local prefectural sampling primarily stems from the above-median registration capital subsample. Secondly, key food industries at the provincial level are determined based on the national ranking of output within a food industry, as reported in the China Food Industry Yearbooks (Table 3.13 provides a list of key food industries for each province in our sample). Likewise, we employ a subsample approach to replicate Table 3.2, distinguishing between food manufacturing firms belonging to key industries and those that do not. The results are shown in Table 3.6. We find that among firms belonging to key industries, both the probability and frequency of testing failures in local prefectural sampling are significantly lower than in national sampling. However, within non-key industry firms, the testing results between local prefectural sampling and national sampling show no significant difference. Collectively, these findings suggest that local administrations downplay negative reports concerning large-scale firms and key food industries.

Table 3.7 examines which local governments, in terms of economic incentives, are more likely to underreport food safety testing failures. Economic incentives are captured by prefectural GDP growth rate targets collected from government official websites following the studies by Jin et al. (2005), Ma (2016), and Liu et al. (2020). Considering political competition among prefectural officials, which involves officials from other prefectures within the same province, we evaluate the expectation of GDP growth rate relative to other prefectures within the same province. This allows us to determine whether a local government exhibits a high economic

Table 3.6 Heterogeneous effects of local prefectural sampling on food safety testing outcome by key food industry

	Failure		N_failure	
	Non-key industries	Key industries	Non-key industries	Key industries
	(1)	(2)	(3)	(4)
Local_samp	−0.575	−0.784**	−0.009	−0.110***
	(0.440)	(0.392)	(0.031)	(0.057)
Prefecture FE	Yes	Yes	Yes	Yes
Year FE	Yes	Yes	Yes	Yes
Product FE	Yes	Yes	Yes	Yes
Sampling Segment FE	Yes	Yes	Yes	Yes
Observations	866	1061	1780	1324

Notes: "Local_samp" equals 1 if the sampled product is produced within the prefecture conducting the sampling, and 0 if from national sampling. Columns (1)–(2) report GLM results with a binary dependent variable equal to 1 for failed tests. Columns (3)–(4) report ZIP results with the number of failures as the dependent variable. All coefficients are average marginal effects. "Key industries" refers to products in provincial key food industries based on nationwide output ranking (see Table 3.13 in Appendix). Standard errors (in parentheses) are clustered at the manufacturer level. *, **, and *** denote significance at the 10%, 5%, and 1% levels, respectively

Table 3.7 Heterogeneous effects of local prefectural sampling on food safety testing outcome by prefectural GDP growth target

	Failure		N_Failure	
	Low target	High target	Low target	High target
	(1)	(2)	(3)	(4)
Local_samp	−0.504	−0.955*	−0.051	−0.052*
	(0.375)	(0.504)	(0.086)	(0.027)
Prefecture FE	Yes	Yes	Yes	Yes
Year FE	Yes	Yes	Yes	Yes
Product FE	Yes	Yes	Yes	Yes
Sampling Segment FE	Yes	Yes	Yes	Yes
Observations	1287	636	1820	1284

Notes: "Local_samp" equals 1 if the sampled product is produced within the prefecture conducting the sampling, and 0 if from national sampling. Columns (1)–(2) report GLM results with a binary dependent variable equal to 1 for failed tests. Columns (3)–(4) report ZIP results with the number of failures as the dependent variable. All coefficients are average marginal effects. "High target" refers to products from prefectures whose governments set GDP growth targets above the provincial median. Standard errors (in parentheses) are clustered at the manufacturer level. *, **, and *** denote significance at the 10%, 5%, and 1% levels, respectively

incentive for local protectionism. Table 3.7 shows that there is no significant difference in food safety testing outcomes between local prefectural sampling and national sampling for prefectures with a low expectation of GDP growth rate. However, prefectures that set higher GDP growth targets exhibit significantly lower rates of testing failures relative to national sampling, implying that local governments in the face of greater economic growth pressures tend to underreport food safety testing failures. Lastly, to check the robustness of all the heterogeneity analyses by ZIP model, we present corresponding results using alternative model specifications in Tables 3.10, 3.11, and 3.12.

3.7 Concluding Remarks

Government interventions aim to correct market inefficiencies caused by information frictions, but such interventions may themselves fail. Our study illustrates how the manipulation of public data by local governments, driven by local protectionism, represents a critical yet understudied mechanism through which information-based interventions can be undermined. Using China's information-based regulation of food safety, we provide the first empirical evidence of local protectionism in the agri-food market, which results in unreliable and ineffective information disclosure intended to regulate food safety. Given the vast number and wide geographic distribution of food producers in China, the central authorities rely heavily on test results reported by local regulatory agencies. The majority of inspections are conducted solely by local governments -- in 2024, the number of city-level inspections was over 23 times that of national inspections. Therefore, investigating the existence of local protectionism in the field of food safety is of critical importance.

Our analysis shows that, *for the same product from the same manufacturer and year*, food safety testing conducted by local prefectural administrations exhibits significantly lower failure rates compared to tests conducted by national administrations. This result is consistent across various model specifications, with the addition of product by manufacturer, manufacturing province and sampling-province pairs fixed effects. It also holds when considering potential collusions between independent inspection agencies and manufacturing firms, accounting for technical differences in testing between prefectural and national sampling, as well as possible disruptions to food production and inspection activities caused by COVID-19. This reinforces a local bias in government food safety reporting, potentially at the expense of accurate and transparent disclosure of food safety information. Furthermore, food manufacturing firms with higher registration capital and those critical to local economies are less likely to have testing failures reported by local administrations. This tendency is more pronounced in prefectures with aggressive GDP growth targets. Conversely, in prefectures with lower economic goals, the difference in testing outcomes between local and national administrations is insignificant. These findings imply that regional competition drives local governments to protect industries within their jurisdictions.

Based on the findings of this study, several policy directions can be proposed to further enhance the effectiveness and credibility of China's food safety governance. First, the performance evaluation system for local governments in food safety enforcement should be reformed by shifting from outcome-oriented to process-oriented indicators. Under the current system, a lower failure rate in food sampling tests is often interpreted as better performance, which may incentivize local authorities to conceal noncompliance rather than disclose and address it. Such distorted incentives weaken the overall governance capacity. Future evaluations should instead emphasize the detection rate, the transparency of enforcement processes, and the timeliness of corrective actions. Second, local protectionism can be further mitigated by strengthening external oversight through cross-regional joint regulation and public supervision. Implementing cross-regional enforcement mechanisms and increasing the frequency of non-local inspections can help weaken collusion between local governments and local enterprises, thereby improving the independence and credibility of enforcement. In addition, regional food safety collaboration mechanisms—such as the initiative in the Yangtze River Delta, could be developed to institutionalize cooperation in enforcement, information sharing, and joint sanctions. Meanwhile, greater public and media oversight, supported by transparent in time disclosure of inspection results, open data platforms and monetary rewards for reporting violations, can amplify these effects by enhancing transparency, raising the social costs of concealment, and promoting more trustworthy food safety governance.

Future research could use longer inspection level panel data to and explore designing unbiased information-based interventions, taking information manipulation driven by local protectionism into consideration, particularly within the framework of tournament-style political competition, as seen in China. Moreover, previous studies evaluating public information disclosure may be interpreted with caution, and re-examining these impacts while controlling for local protectionism would be one future area for empirical research.

Appendix

Table 3.8 Difference in testing outcomes from prefectural inspection agencies in local prefectural and national sampling

Variable	Failure		N_Failure	
	Local prefectural sampling	National sampling	Local prefectural sampling	National sampling
Mean	0.032	0.167	0.035	0.267
	(0.176)	(0.379)	(0.007)	(0.126)
P-value	<0.001		<0.001	
Observations	878	30	878	30

Notes: This table shows the T-test results of the local prefectural and national sampling tested by the prefectural agencies. The numbers in parentheses are standard deviations. "Failure" is a binary variable and equals 1 when a sampled product fails food safety tests and 0 otherwise. "N_Failure" is the number of testing failures

Table 3.9 Alternative model specification

	N_Failure		
	OLS	Poisson	OLS
	(1)	(2)	(3)
Local_samp	−0.037***	−0.060**	−0.043***
	(0.015)	(0.029)	(0.019)
Prefecture FE	Yes	Yes	
Year FE	Yes	Yes	
Product FE	Yes	Yes	
Sampling Segment FE	Yes	Yes	Yes
Manufacturer-Year FE			Yes
Manufacturer -Product FE			Yes
Product-Year FE			Yes
Observations	3104	2103	3104

Notes: "Local_samp" equals 1 if the sampled product is produced within the prefecture conducting the sampling, and 0 if from national sampling. All coefficients are average marginal effects. Columns (1)–(3) use OLS and Poisson models with the number of failures as the dependent variable. Standard errors (in parentheses) are clustered at the manufacturer level. *, **, and *** denote significance at the 10%, 5%, and 1% levels, respectively. Poisson models exclude groups without within-group variation, leading to smaller effective sample sizes

Table 3.10 Heterogeneous effects of local prefectural sampling on food safety testing outcomes by firm's registration capital

	Registration capital			
	OLS		Poisson	
The dependent variable: N_failure	Below median	Above median	Below median	Above median
	(1)	(2)	(3)	(4)
Local_samp	−0.039	−0.032*	−0.055	−0.062*
	(0.031)	(0.017)	(0.061)	(0.034)
Prefecture FE	Yes	Yes	Yes	Yes
Year FE	Yes	Yes	Yes	Yes
Product FE	Yes	Yes	Yes	Yes
Sampling Segment FE	Yes	Yes	Yes	Yes
Observations	996	2108	677	1181

Notes: This table reports the robustness check results of column (3) and (4) in Table 3.6. The dependent variable is the number of a product fails sampling tests and we employ the Ordinary Least Squares (OLS) in column (1)–(2) and Poisson model in column (3)–(4), respectively. "Above median capital" means the registration capital of sampled firms exceeds the median of our research sample. We control the city, year, product and sampling segment fixed effects. Standard errors are in parentheses clustered at the manufacturer-level; This table shows the average marginal effects; *, **, and *** indicate significance at the 10%, 5%, and 1% levels, respectively

Table 3.11 Heterogeneous effects of local prefectural sampling on food safety testing outcomes by key food industries

	Key industry			
	OLS		Poisson	
The dependent variable: N_failure	Non-key	Key	Non-key	Key
	(1)	(2)	(3)	(4)
Local_samp	−0.009	−0.085**	−0.013	−0.114**
	(0.011)	(0.036)	(0.026)	(0.050)
Prefecture FE	Yes	Yes	Yes	Yes
Year FE	Yes	Yes	Yes	Yes
Product FE	Yes	Yes	Yes	Yes
Sampling Segment FE	Yes	Yes	Yes	Yes
Observations	1780	1324	866	1061

Notes: This table reports the robustness check results of column (3) and (4) in Table 3.7. The dependent variable is the number of a product fails sampling tests and we employ the Ordinary Least Squares (OLS) in column (1)–(2) and Poisson model in column (3)–(4), respectively. "Key" means the product belongs to a key industry in the province of production. The key food industries in the province of production are determined by the food production volume. If a certain product from a province ranks within the top 5 nationally in terms of production volume, its industry is defined as a key industry in that province. Table 3.13 in Appendix shows the list of key food industries for each province. We control the city, year, product and sampling segment fixed effects. Standard errors are in parentheses clustered at the manufacturer-level; This table shows the average marginal effects; *, **, and *** indicate significance at the 10%, 5%, and 1% levels, respectively

Table 3.12 Heterogeneous effects of local prefectural sampling on food safety testing outcomes by prefectural GDP growth target

	The expectation of GDP growth rate			
	OLS		Poisson	
The dependent variable: N_failure	Low target	High target	Low target	High target
	(1)	(2)	(3)	(4)
Local_samp	−0.027	−0.044*	−0.038	−0.106*
	(0.019)	(0.023)	(0.033)	(0.058)
Prefecture FE	Yes	Yes	Yes	Yes
Year FE	Yes	Yes	Yes	Yes
Product FE	Yes	Yes	Yes	Yes
Sampling Segment FE	Yes	Yes	Yes	Yes
Observations	1820	1284	1287	636

Notes: This table reports the robustness check results of column (3) and (4) in Table 3.8. The dependent variable is the number of a product fails sampling tests and we employ the Ordinary Least Squares (OLS) in column (1)–(2) and Poisson model in column (3)–(4), respectively. "High expectations" means the producing city's GDP growth rate target is above the provincial median. We control the city, year, product and sampling segment fixed effects. Standard errors are in parentheses clustered at the manufacturer-level; This table shows the average marginal effects; *, **, and *** indicate significance at the 10%, 5%, and 1% levels, respectively

Table 3.13 The list of key Food Industries for each province or municipalities

Province	Count	Industry
Shandong	16	Dairy products, grains, sugar, meat products, fruit products, vegetable products, seafood, starch and starch products, eggs and egg products, canned goods, health products, condiments, baked goods, edible oils and their products, food additives, and expanded foods
Guangdong	16	Sugar, fruit products, seafood, beverages, candies and chocolate products, convenience foods, health products, cocoa and roasted coffee, bee products, condiments, baked goods, edible oils and their products, potatoes and expanded foods, food additives, starch and starch products, roasted and nut products
Henan	12	Dairy products, grains, meat products, fruit products, vegetable products, beverages, eggs and egg products, convenience foods, bee products, food additives, potatoes and expanded foods, starch and starch products
Sichuan	11	Meat products, vegetable products, beverages, beans and bean products, tea, candies and chocolate products, alcoholic beverages, bee products, condiments, cocoa and roasted coffee products, roasted and nut products
Hebei	8	Dairy products, meat products, vegetable products, eggs and egg products, convenience foods, edible oils, expanded foods, starch and starch products
Jiangsu	8	Dairy products, vegetable products, seafood, eggs and egg products, baked goods, food additives, cocoa and roasted coffee products, health supplements
Hunan	8	Meat products, canned goods, tea, candies and chocolate products, convenience foods, condiments, baked goods, roasted and nut products
Hubei	6	Beverages, canned goods, tea, candies and chocolate products, bee products, alcoholic beverages
Yunnan	6	Sugar, legumes, tea, cocoa and roasted coffee products, alcoholic beverages, roasted and nut products
Zhejiang	5	Seafood, beverages, bee products, cocoa and roasted coffee products, baked goods
Fujian	5	Seafood, canned goods, tea, candies and chocolate products, edible oils
Heilongjiang	4	Dairy products, grains, beans and bean products, alcoholic beverages
Anhui	4	Grains, beans and bean products, convenience foods, condiments
Guangxi	4	Sugar, fruit products, bee products, starch and starch products
Shaanxi	3	Convenience foods, fruit products, beverages
Inner Mongolia	3	Dairy products, sugar, beans and bean products
Liaoning	2	Eggs and egg products, health supplements
Jilin	2	Grains, expanded foods
Guizhou	2	Alcoholic beverages, health supplements
Shanghai	2	Candies, food additives
Xinjiang	2	Sugar, canned goods
Beijing	1	Roasted and nut products

Notes: There are 32 food industries in total according the Food Production Permit Classification Catalog. Provincial key food industries are determined through the analysis of provincial food production statistics obtained from 2017–2021 China Food Industry Yearbooks, focusing on the top five provinces with the highest production nationwide for each food category

References

Bai, J., & Liu, J. (2019). *The impact of intranational trade barriers on exports: Evidence from a nationwide vat rebate reform in china*. National Bureau of Economic Research.

Bai, C., Du, Y., Tao, Z., & Tong, S. Y. (2004). Local protectionism and regional specialization: evidence from China's industries. *Journal of International Economics, 63*(2), 397–417.

Bai, C., Hsieh, C., & Song, Z. (2020). Special deals with Chinese characteristics. *NBER Macroeconomics Annual, 34*(1), 341–379.

Bai, J., Gazze, L., & Wang, Y. (2022). Collective reputation in trade: Evidence from the Chinese dairy industry. *Review of Economics and Statistics, 104*(6), 1121–1137.

Barwick, P. J., Cao, S., & Li, S. (2021). Local protectionism, market structure, and social welfare: China's automobile market. *American Economic Journal: Economic Policy, 13*(4), 112–151.

Bollinger, B., Leslie, P., & Sorensen, A. (2011). Calorie posting in chain restaurants. *American Economic Journal: Economic Policy, 3*(1), 91–128.

Briviba, A., Frey, B., Moser, L., & Bieri, S. (2024). Governments manipulate official Statistics: Institutions matter. *European Journal of Political Economy, 82,* 102523.

Carter, C. A., & Schaefer, K. A. (2019). Impacts of mandatory GE food labeling: A quasi-natural experiment. *American Journal of Agricultural Economics, 101*(1), 58–73.

Chen, W., Chen, X., Hsieh, C.-T., & Song, Z. (2019). *A forensic examination of China's national accounts*. National Bureau of Economic Research.

Chen, S., Qiao, X., & Zhu, Z. (2021). Chasing or cheating? Theory and evidence on China's GDP manipulation. *Journal of Economic Behavior and Organization, 189*, 657–671.

Cho, D., Hwang, Y., & Park, J. (2018). More buzz, more vibes: Impact of social media on concert distribution. *Journal of Economic Behavior and Organization, 156*, 103–113.

Donaldson, D. (2015). The gains from market integration. *Economics, 7*(1), 619–647.

Eberhardt, M., Wang, Z., & Yu, Z. (2016). From one to many central plans: Drug advertising inspections and intra-national protectionism in China. *Journal of Comparative Economics, 44*(3), 608–622.

Fan, Z., Xiong, W., & Zhou, L.-A. (2016). *Information distortion in hierarchical organizations: A study of China's Great Famine*. Fordham University. *Unpublished Working Paper.* https://wxiong.mycpanel.princeton.edu/papers/Famine.pdf

Fang, H., Li, M., & Wu, Z. (2022). *Tournament-style political competition and local protectionism: Theory and evidence from China*. National Bureau of Economic Research.

Ghanem, D., & Zhang, J. (2014). 'Effortless Perfection:' Do Chinese cities manipulate air pollution data? *Journal of Environmental Economics and Management, 68*(2), 203–225.

Ghanem, D., Shen, S., & Zhang, J. (2020). A censored maximum likelihood approach to quantifying manipulation in China's air pollution data. *Journal of the Association of Environmental and Resource Economists, 7*(5), 965–1003.

Gradstein, M. (1993). Rent seeking and the provision of public goods. *The Economic Journal, 103*(420), 1236–1243.

Gurmu, S., Rilstone, P., & Stern, S. (1999). Semiparametric estimation of count regression models. *Journal of Econometrics, 88*(1), 123–150.

Helm, D. (2010). Government failure, rent-seeking, and capture: The design of climate change policy. *Oxford Review of Economic Policy, 26*(2), 182–196.

Jin, H., Qian, Y., & Weingast, B. R. (2005). Regional decentralization and fiscal incentives: Federalism, Chinese style. *Journal of Public Economics, 89*(9–10), 1719–1742.

Jin, C., Levi, R., Liang, Q., Renegar, N., Springs, S., Zhou, J., & Zhou, W. (2021). Testing at the source: Analytics-enabled risk-based sampling of food supply chains in China. *Management Science, 67*(5), 2985–2996.

Katz, E. (2001). Bias in conditional and unconditional fixed effects logit estimation. *Political Analysis, 9*(4), 379–384.

Krueger, A. O. (1990). Government failures in development. *Journal of Economic Perspectives, 4*(3), 9–23.

Lambert, D. (1992). Zero-inflated Poisson regression, with an application to defects in manufacturing. *Technometrics, 34*(1), 1–14.
Li, H., & Zhou, L.-A. (2005). Political turnover and economic performance: The incentive role of personnel control in China. *Journal of Public Economics, 89*(9–10), 1743–1762.
Li, T., Bo, H., & Nie, W. (2021). A study on the evaluation of supervision sampling efficiency of food safety in China--Based on the perspective of sampling batches distribution under the pressure of government performance evaluation. *Journal of Macro-quality Research, 9*(6), 86–98.
Lin, R. H., & Chen, Z. J. (2020). Construction of food inspection and testing institutions for first-class public welfare. *Journal of Food Safety and Quality, 11*(13), 4424–4427.
Lin, W., Ma, B., Liang, J., & Jin, S. (2024). Price response to government disclosure of food safety information in developing markets. *Food Policy, 123*, 102602.
Liu, D., Xu, C., Yu, Y., Rong, K., & Zhang, J. (2020). Economic growth target, distortion of public expenditure and business cycle in China. *China Economic Review, 63*, 101373.
Ma, L. (2016). Performance feedback, government goal-setting and aspiration level adaptation: Evidence from Chinese provinces. *Public Administration, 94*(2), 452–471.
Myers, E., Puller, S. L., & West, J. (2022). Mandatory energy efficiency disclosure in housing markets. *American Economic Journal: Economic Policy, 14*(4), 453–487.
Ni, G., Niu, X., & Liu, Q. (2019). Can "Keeping Secret" for food safety incidents protect the food industry? Based on the empirical analysis of 2896 Food Safety Incidents. *Journal of Agrotechnical Economics, 7*, 91–103.
Ollinger, M., & Bovay, J. (2020). Producer response to public disclosure of food-safety information. *American Journal of Agricultural Economics, 102*(1), 186–201.
Peterson, E., Grant, J., Roberts, D., & Karov, V. (2013). Evaluating the trade restrictiveness of phytosanitary measures on US fresh fruit and vegetable imports. *American Journal of Agricultural Economics, 95*(4), 842–858.
Poncet, S. (2005). A fragmented China: Measure and determinants of Chinese domestic market disintegration. *Review of International Economics, 13*(3), 409–430.
Seira, E., Elizondo, A., & Laguna-Müggenburg, E. (2017). Are information disclosures effective? Evidence from the credit card market. *American Economic Journal: Economic Policy, 9*(1), 277–307.
Shi, J. (2019). Ensure the "tip of the tongue safety"——Interpretation of the provisions on food safety responsibility system for local party and government leading cadres. *China Quality Supervision, 3*, 24–25.
Southern Daily. (2016, December 22). *Shenzhen: The pass rate of pesticide residue sampling by the government is 99%, representing the pass rate of 80%*. Website link: http://health.people.com.cn/n1/2016/1222/c14739-28968667.html?from=timeline&isappinstalled=1
State Administration for Market Regulation. (2019a). *Measures for the Administration of sampling inspection of food safety*. Website link: https://www.samr.gov.cn/zw/zfxxgk/fdzdgknr/fgs/art/2023/art_e916b7ff0aff4d04ad1bd26674a304a6.html
State Administration for Market Regulation. (2019b). *Notice of the General Administration of Market Supervision on comprehensively promoting the supervision work of "double random and one open"*. Website link: https://www.gov.cn/zhengce/zhengceku/2019-11/07/content_5449656.htm
Stiglitz, J. (2009). Regulation and failure. *New perspectives on regulation, 576.*
Tian, G., Wang, Y., Gong, Y., et al. (2024). The contagion mechanism and governance strategy of corporate social irresponsibility of Chinese food companies. *Food Policy, 122*, 102569.
Toledo, C., & Villas-Boas, S. B. (2019). Safe or not? Consumer responses to recalls with traceability. *Applied Economic Perspectives and Policy, 41*(3), 519–541.
Tombe, T., & Zhu, X. (2019). Trade, migration, and productivity: A quantitative analysis of china. *American Economic Review, 109*(5), 1843–1872.
Unnevehr, L. (2015). Food safety in developing countries: Moving beyond exports. *Global Food Security, 4*, 24–29.

Wang, E., Gao, Z., Heng, Y., & Shi, L. (2019). Chinese consumers' preferences for food quality test/measurement indicators and cues of milk powder: A case of Zhengzhou, China. *Food Policy, 89*, 101791.

Wooldridge, J. M. (2016). *Introductory econometrics a modern approach*. South-Western Cengage Learning.

Xiong, W. (2018). *The mandarin model of growth*. National Bureau of Economic Research.

Yang, L., Zhu, J., Huang, Z., & Geng, J. (2019). A systematic review of China's food safety management since reform and opening up. *Emerging Markets Finance and Trade, 55*(15), 3472–3489.

Young, A. (2000). The razor's edge: Distortions and incremental reform in the People's Republic of China. *The Quarterly Journal of Economics, 115*(4), 1091–1135.

Zhao, X. (2015). Thoughts on the responsive promotion of the market-oriented development of third-party food inspection institutions. *Food Research and Development, 36*(8), 139–144.

Zhou, J., Jin, Y., & Liang, Q. (2022). Effects of regulatory policy mixes on traceability adoption in wholesale markets: Food safety inspection and information disclosure. *Food Policy, 107*, 102218.

Chapter 4
Price Response to Government Disclosure of Food Safety Information in Developing Markets

4.1 Introduction

Theoretical perspectives generally align on the effectiveness of providing quality information as a means to address food safety concerns. When food safety information is disclosed, consumers can distinguish between safe and unsafe products from various suppliers. Consequently, there may be an increase in the demand for safe food products and adecrease in the demand for unsafe ones, leading to higher market prices for safe products and lower prices for unsafe ones. However, for this information-based policy to work effectively, certain assumptions must hold. It is assumed that market buyers are sufficiently aware of disclosed food safety information and that they respond to it by exerting pressure that forces unsafe food products out of the market.

Empirical evidence, primarily from developed countries, supports the notion that the disclosure of food safety information reduces food consumption (Piggott & Marsh, 2004; Shimshack et al., 2007; Schlenker & Villas-Boas, 2009; Arnade et al., 2009). For instance, a detailed scanner-level dataset analysis by Toledo and Villas-Boas (2019) showed decreased sales of both affected and unaffected egg brands following three consecutive egg recalls in California. This, in turn, incentivizes higher compliance with safety standards among food suppliers (Jin & Leslie, 2003; Ollinger & Bovay, 2020; Zhou et al., 2022).

Despite these promising findings, limited research has explored how *developing markets* respond to food safety information disclosure. On one hand, food safety information in developed societies tends to gain greater visibility through a process of "social amplification" by which affected parties bring increased attention to the problem (Ortega & Tschirley, 2017; Hoffmann et al., 2019). Relative to food security, food safety has a lower priority in developing countries than in developed countries (Nait Mohand et al., 2017). This implies potentially lower responsiveness to food safety information in a developing market context, regardless of its high

W. Lin, *Transforming China's Agri-Food System: Government-Market Synergy*, Resources, Environment and Agricultural Development,
https://doi.org/10.1007/978-981-95-7151-2_4

prevalence of food safety events (Henson, 2003). On the other hand, disclosure of unsafe foods in developing markets may gain a stronger response as a result of collective reputation (Bai et al., 2022). In these markets, agricultural suppliers are often small-scale and primarily deal in homogeneous goods, making it challenging to trace food products back to individual traders or producers. Thus if one producer is revealed to supply unsafe foods, other suppliers in the same market may also suffer.

Moreover, prior studies exploring consumer preferences and valuation for safe foods in developing countries indicate that individuals express concern and are willing to pay additional prices for access to food safety information (Ehmke et al., 2008; Ortega et al., 2012; Wongprawmas & Canavari, 2017; Liu et al., 2019; Wang et al., 2019). Although these studies imply strong responses to food safety information by developing markets, it is worth noting that these results were derived from hypothetical stated preference methods (Birol et al., 2010), which may be influenced by hypothetical bias (Penn & Hu, 2021) and demand effects (Carlsson et al., 2018).

This study presents a novel investigation of whether and to what extent markets respond to government disclosure of food safety information, in a *real* developing market setting. Governments play a key role in the provision of public goods including food quality information (Hamilton et al., 2003; Wu et al., 2016, 2022), and this role is particularly important for developing countries where food supply chains are characterized by a large number of small-scale and informal actors, with low traceability levels. As a practical application, we focus on China, the largest food market worldwide, which has been chosen carefully. China's food safety has been a prominent public issue (Alcorn & Ouyang, 2012; Wang et al., 2019; Yang et al., 2019; Liu et al., 2020). Government disclosure of food safety information in China in this study refers to a national policy instrument that mandates the central and local government regulatory agencies to make all the information about food sampling test records and outcomes public on a regular basis. Effective in 2014 as part of the China Food Safety Laws (Jin et al., 2021a), this policy disclosed over 638 million of food sampling test results in 2020, compared to 150 million in 2016 (SAMR, 2020), imposing significantly increased fiscal resources annually. Recent food scandals, including the one discovered in the largest pork processor in this country, Shuanghui,[1] however, may not fully convince the public that food safety in China has improved. This study evaluates the impact of government disclosure of food safety information in China on market outcomes, specifically, market prices, whose fluctuation influences the welfare of numerous agricultural producers, traders, and buyers.

With regard to the empirical strategy, we constructed a panel dataset of weekly pork wholesale prices and pork sampling test result variables[2] at the city level for the period between 2018 and 2020. Results from an event study approach reveal a lagged negative price response to government disclosure of pork safety information in

[1] https://www.scmp.com/news/people-culture/trending-china/article/3,170,567/china-food-scandal-meat-producer-exposed-using.

[2] We discussed in the background section reasons for choosing wholesale prices and pork products.

Chinese agricultural wholesale markets. Average pork wholesale prices began to decrease by 5% 2 weeks after the information disclosure. Besides, disclosure of unsafe pork products exerts some negative impacts on local beef prices and on neighboring cities' pork prices, especially when nearby cities are in the same province as treated cities. We also find that the negative information effects on pork prices are largely driven by negative pork demand shocks, in particular in the main pork consumption cities. Negative pork demand shocks and therefore pork price reduction is more evident in the treated cities with higher internet penetration rate, the incidence of foodborne illness, and food safety regulatory resource, which are used to proxy information accessibility and salience. We note that the estimated average information treatment effects are consistent with different model specifications such as different event windows and difference-in-difference specification. Results from this study contribute to a better understanding of the nationwide information-based food quality regulation, and importantly, inform the efficacy of public information interventions that tackle food safety issues in other developing markets.

Our research inquiry relates to several strands of the literature. First, we inform a stream of research investigating the effect of food safety information on market outcomes. Related work has dominantly focused on the U.S. and other developed contexts, and finds that food safety information may have industry-wide impacts on sales and prices depending on consumers' response to the information (Piggott & Marsh, 2004; Taylor et al., 2016; Shang & Tonsor, 2017). The food safety information is typically indexed by constructed media indices (Piggott & Marsh, 2004), and the presence and intensity of food recall (Lusk & Schroeder, 2002; Toledo & Villas-Boas, 2019; Neill & Chen, 2021) and food safety events (Shimshack et al., 2007; Arnade et al., 2009; Schlenker & Villas-Boas, 2009). This study complements the literature by studying the effects of food safety information in a different setting. We focus on the results of food safety sampling tests made public by the Chinese government regularly. Second, the study relates to the literature on the driving forces of food prices. Previous studies have examined the impacts of weather anomalies (Headey & Fan, 2008; Letta et al., 2022), increased transaction cost (Dillon & Barrett, 2016), trade restriction (Abbott, 2012), supply chain disruption (Ruan et al., 2021; Dietrich et al., 2022), biofuel production (Mitchell, 2008; Zilberman et al., 2013) and quality signals (Mérel et al., 2021) on food prices. This study highlights the impact of information disclosure on market outcomes.

4.2 Background and Mechanism

4.2.1 China' Spork Wholesale Market

This study examines market responsiveness to the disclosure of food safety information within the Chinese pork wholesale market. We focus on pork products for several reasons. First, meat is one of the most frequently tested agricultural products by the food safety regulation organizations in China, due to the abuse of additives and antibiotics in meat production. Second, pork, relative to other meat products, tends to receive more market attention when the safety test results are disclosed. This heightened attention stems from two facets. On one hand, recurring food safety scandals, including those involving China's largest pork firms, underscore the necessity of rigorous scrutiny (Wang et al., 2018). On the other hand, China boasts the title of being the world's largest pork producer (Carriquiry et al., 2019), with numerous hog producers whose livelihoods are closely intertwined with pork market dynamics. Pork also plays an important role in Chinese consumers' daily diet, evidenced by the fact that pork meat carries a substantial weight in the consumer price index calculation (Yu & Abler, 2014).

In emerging economies like China and India, wholesale markets play a pivotal role as intermediary components within agri-food value chains, making substantial contributions, accounting for approximately 30–40% of both value addition and associated costs (Reardon, 2015). Additionally, these wholesale markets have drawn attention as high-risk areas for food safety and adulteration within China's intricate food supply chains (Jin et al., 2021b).

This significance extends to pork wholesale markets, which occupy a critical position within China's meat supply chain. They serve as vital intermediaries that bridge the gap between producers and consumers, facilitating avast volume of transactions. According to data provided by the Chinese Ministry of Agriculture and Rural Affairs in 2019, China's annual pig production reached an astonishing 541 million heads, with over half of these transactions taking place within wholesale markets. The prevalence of pork wholesale markets spans the entirety of China, as data from the Ministry of Agriculture and Rural Affairs in 2020 reveals a total of 23,770 such markets nationwide, covering all 31 provinces. The highest concentrations of these markets are observed in regions such as Jiangsu, Shandong, Henan, and Hebei.

In pork wholesale markets, participants encompass wholesalers, supermarkets, traditional wet markets, specialized pork stores, and institutional buyers such as schools, government agencies, and other organizations. Regarding pork supply, wholesalers primarily source their pork from designated pig slaughter and processing enterprises. Although China's pig slaughter and processing industry has become centralized, the challenge lies in tracing the pork's origins back to the numerous and scattered upstream pig producers. Indeed, the adoption of traceability systems in China'spork wholesale markets remains limited, with less than one-third of these sellers implementing such systems (Jin et al., 2021b). In terms of pork demand, wet markets and supermarket chains emerge as the two main purchasers in pork wholesale markets. In China, approximately 70% of the agricultural products in supermarkets and wet markets originate from wholesale markets (Yuan et al., 2021).

4.2.2 Food Safety Sampling Tests

Food safety sampling tests serve as a pivotal tool for regulatory authorities to oversee food quality and safety. In China, both central and local governments meticulously devise plans for these inspections. The State Administration for Market

Regulation (SAMR) annually formulates a Food Supervision Sampling Plan based on risk analysis and resident population. Provinces, cities, and counties also create their respective plans with varying food safety priorities. At the national level, SAMR focuses on inspecting large-scale supermarkets, agricultural markets, and key production firms nationwide. Provinces handle central-to-local transfers and provincial-level inspections, emphasizing large and medium-sized supermarkets, agricultural markets, production firms, and school campuses. City and county-level regulatory departments supervise small-scale supermarkets, agricultural wholesale markets, small food stores, and workshops.

Sampling inspections are divided into two categories: regular and special. Regular sampling involves inspections conducted according to the annual sampling inspection plans established at the beginning of each year. In contrast, special sampling goes beyond these plans and is typically carried out during holidays, for high-risk products, or in response to food safety incidents. Regular sampling involves a significantly larger quantity of tests compared to special sampling. Local regulatory departments are usually assigned regular and weekly sampling inspections for vegetables, fruits, livestock, and poultry meat.

In accordance with China's Food Safety Law and the Implementation Rules for National Agricultural Product Quality and Safety Supervision and Checks, when a food product, like pork with excessive chloramphenicol use, fails safety sampling tests, regulatory authorities are empowered to take certain actions on its supplier. These include the confiscation of illegal gains from food suppliers and the oversight of product recalls. Additionally, fines are levied, and in severe cases, business licenses maybe revoked. However, an exception is made if the food supplier can demonstrate fulfillment of their obligations to inspect purchased products, provide substantial evidence indicating a lack of awareness regarding safety risks, and furnish traceability information for the products. Under these conditions, the penalty may be waived, and responsibility for the failed tests is typically shifted to the upstream supplier identified in the traceability information. Nevertheless, due to the limited adoption of traceability systems in China's agricultural supply chains, executing large-scale recalls of non-compliant food products is logistically challenging. Fines, thus, remain the prevalent punitive measure, and the specific penalty amounts may differ across regions.

4.2.3 Food Safety Information Disclosure

Beyond food safety sampling tests, information disclosure serves as an additional regulatory mechanism utilized by the government to monitor and enforce food safety in China. According to the Regulations of the People's Republic of China on the Disclosure of Government Information and the Management Measures for Food Safety Sampling and Testing, it is imperative for food safety regulatory authorities to promptly disseminate information pertaining to food safety sampling. Presently, this dissemination occurs primarily through two channels: online and offline.

Firstly, the National Food Sampling Information Platform[3] is responsible for publicly disclosing comprehensive food sampling records and test results. Additionally, at the provincial, municipal levels, food safety regulatory authorities typically use their official websites to disseminate relevant sampling information, which includes details such as the sampling entity, sampled unit address, product's name and production date, producer's name and location, testing agency, test results, and instances of non-compliance. Recently, some local governments have expanded the dissemination of this information through their official social media accounts and news media outlets like Sohu and other self-media accounts, increasing accessibility. However, consumer engagement with this online channel remains limited, as noted by Zhou et al. (2022), primarily due to perceived complexity and insufficient publicity.

Secondly, wholesale markets prominently display food safety information within the physical market premises, providing a more convenient and broadly embraced method for accessing this information. Wholesale markets equipped with information disclosure facilities typically share details from their sampling test records. Information bulletins are typically positioned at the market entrance, ensuring visibility to all entering the market. These records typically include details such as the identification number of the trader in and/or outside the market, product name and test outcomes, etc. Thus, traders who fail in these tests may experience reputational damage due to the public disclosure of this information.

4.2.4 Potential Mechanisms

Considering the background of food sampling tests and information disclosure, we propose that the public disclosure of pork safety information in cities where pork test failures are disclosed would lead to a reduction in pork prices, because of a decrease in pork demand in those cities. The drop in pork demand could be attributed to the fact that buyers avoid pork purchases once they become aware of pork products from a specific wholesaler being disclosed as non-compliant. This behavior would be exacerbated by the limited traceability of agricultural products in China, potentially leading consumers to abstain from buying pork from the entire wholesale market. The reason buyers avoid purchasing such pork is that those who shop in wholesale markets are typically retailers and food service businesses. If their pork is found and disclosed to be non-compliant in inspections, it could harm their reputation and consequently financial well-being.

However, it's worth noting that the impact of public disclosure of pork safety information on pork prices is expected to be smaller, compared to studies conducted in developed markets such as Dillaway et al. (2011). This is not surprising, given the

[3] Website: https://sac.nifdc.org.cn

nature of informational regulation and the characteristics of food supply chains in developing economies. First, the way that the food safety information is disclosed in our context differs from that in the previous studies, making our information less popularized for the market to react. Other than the official website and the offline disclosure, food sampling test outcomes and failures rarely got media coverage in China. In contrast, in the previous work focusing on developed markets, food safety information has been widely popularized by the media. This can be evidenced by the common use of media indices to proxy food safety information (Piggott & Marsh, 2004; Mazzocchi, 2006; Wang & de Beville, 2017). In our case, the moderate information treatment effects would be driven by the unpopularized outcomes of food safety sampling tests, and wholesale markets may be less aware of the information even though they are available online. A recent survey based in Shanghai found that 52% of food suppliers including wholesalers, processors, and retailers didn't know where to find food sampling test results, and the ratio increased to 80% among household consumers (An, 2020).

Second, the food safety information we investigate, that is, the failure of pork safety sampling tests, delivers different content and therefore has different implications from those in the related literature. Most existing work on the US markets used food recalls (Lusk & Schroeder, 2002; Neill & Chen, 2021) or food safety events (Arnade et al., 2009; Schlenker & Villas-Boas, 2009) as indicators of food safety related information, and almost at the sametime the Center for Disease Control and Prevention identified and announced health risks associated with consuming these unsafe foods. For example, Toledo and Villas-Boas (2019) examined how contaminated egg recalls and related safety information (Salmonella infections) affect egg sales. In our case, the information reveals whether a pork product passed the safety tests and why it failed (if failed), without any follow-up information such as health consequences. This could make the information difficult for the public to interpret, hampering its dissemination.

Last and remarkably, the differences underlying food supply chains between developing and developed countries could also potentially contribute to the moderate treatment effect. Food suppliers in developed markets tend to be large-scale and concentrated which would lead to system-wide impacts (Ma & Lusk, 2021), while small-scale food supply chain actors dominate in developing countries. Approximately 75% of agricultural products in China have been supplied by a large number of small-scale wholesale markets (Ren & An, 2010). Diseconomies of scale implies that a low traceability adoption rate in China's agricultural supply chain. A prior survey on Chinese agricultural traders suggests only 30% have adopted traceability (Jin et al., 2021b). Once a seller's product was discovered to be unsafe, products from the same source would be recalled and confiscated by the local market regulation administrator, according to the Food Safety Laws. But in reality, limited traceability adoption makes product recalls difficult, causing little supply shocks.

4.3 Data

Our study investigates whether and how government disclosure of unsafe pork affects pork market prices. We combine two datasets, one related to pork prices, and the other pork safety information disclosure. First, pork price data refers to city-level and weekly wholesale prices of pork products, constructed using the National Agricultural Products Price Database. The database, supported by the Chinese Ministry of Agriculture, covers China's major wholesale markets of agricultural products (Ruan et al., 2021). Second, pork safety information disclosure refers to the records of safety sampling tests conducted and announced by the Chinese Central and Provincial Administration for Market Regulation. Each sampling test record includes whether or not a product fails the safety test, the sampling date and location, information announcedate and the source of the product. Regarding pork products, approximately 90% of the safety test failures in our sample are attributable to the abuse of additives and antibiotics. To match the pork safety records to wholesale price information, we exclude the records (i) whose sampling location is not at wholesale markets, (ii) the pork is not sourced from wholesale markets. Meanwhile, to avoid confounding effects of Asian Swine Flu and Covid-19 on pork prices, observations on two periods, namely 2018 August to 2019 March, and 2019 December to 2020 March (Delgado et al., 2021; Ruan et al., 2021), are dropped from our sample. In addition, other datasets are combined and used to conduct heterogeneous analyses of our treatment effects, including the China city statistical yearbook, China public health statistical yearbook, and fiscal investment on food safety regulation available at the official websites of the provincial Administration for Market Regulation.

Finally, we obtained a city-level and weekly panel dataset, with a time span from January 2018 to March 2021, and 103 prefecture-level cities in 26 provinces of China. Cities in our sample accounted for over 53% of China's GDP in 2018. Figure 4.1 illustrates provinces that have announced pork safety test failure, with darker red denoting more safety failure announcements.

4.4 Empirical Strategy

We used the event study method to investigate the dynamic effects of disclosure of pork sampling test results on pork wholesale prices. The model specification can be expressed:

$$\ln y_{cw} = \alpha_0 + \sum_{j=-5}^{10} \beta_j D_c \times treat_{cw}^{j} + u_c + u_w + \tau_{py} + \tau_{cy} + \varepsilon_{cw} \tag{4.1}$$

where c denotes city, p is province, $w$is week, and$y$ means year. lny_{cw} is the pork price of city c in week $w$in log form. The key variables include a series of dummy

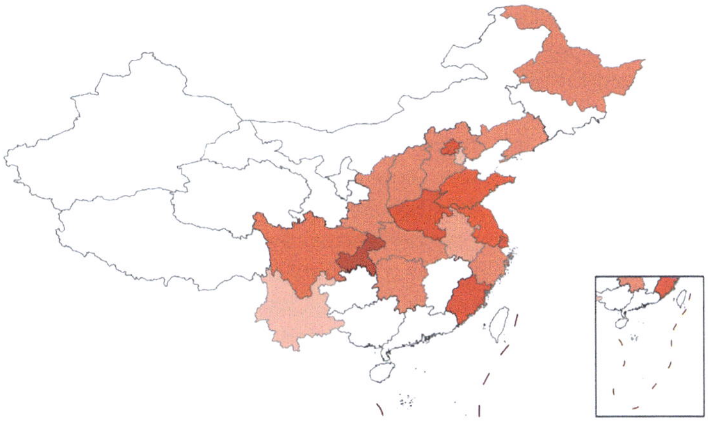

Fig. 4.1 Provinces in the treatment group

variables: D_c is a dummy variable that equals to 1 when city c belongs to the treatment group, that is, city c disclosed pork safety test failure(s) in our study period, and 0 otherwise; $treat_{cw}^{j}$ is also a dummy indicator, with a value of 1 if week w is j weeks after the disclosure of pork safety test failure(s) in city c, and zero otherwise. In the case that j is negative, it means that | j | weeks before the information disclosure. To illustrate, $treat_{cw}$ equals to 1 if week wis at least 5 weeks prior to the information disclosure week in city c, and $treat_{cw}^{9}$ if week wis 9 weeks following the disclosure of pork safety test failure(s) in city c. The parameters, β_j, govern the causal effect of the disclosure of pork safety test failure(s) on pork prices, which are the focus of our study. When $j < 0$, we would expect β_j to be not significantly different from zero. Intuitively, this implies that there has no systematic differences in pork prices between the treatment and control groups prior to the information disclosure intervention, which underlies the validity of our identification strategy. β_{-1} is omitted from Eq. (4.1) such that the information treatment effects are relative to one week before the information disclosure. When $j = 0$, β_0 denotes the immediate impact of the information disclosure on pork wholesale prices; β_j, if $j > 0$, denotes such effect in aj-week lag.

We also included several control variables in Eq. (4.1), such as city fixed effect (u_c), week fixed effects (μ_w), province by year fixed effects (τ_{py}), and city by year fixed effects (τ_{cy}). μ_c captures time-invariant city specific effects on pork prices, including pork production condition and consumption habit; and μ_w captures the weekly trends of pork prices that are common across all cities, such as holiday week. τ_{py} and τ_{cy} are considered in Eq. (4.1) to account for confounding factors that vary by year and province, year and city respectively, for example, annual GPD per capita and annual population in each province or city. ε_{cw} denotes random error terms unobservable to researchers.

Several robustness checks were conducted to guard our findings. First, cities may announce pork safety test failure for several times, but only the first disclosure would be considered for Eq. (4.1). If the time interval between announcements is close, β_j, if $j > 0$, is potentially overestimated. This is because estimated β_j includes not only the impact of the first disclosure of unsafe pork, but also that of the succeeding disclosure. We investigated how the succeeding information disclosure affects pork prices for relevant cities. Second, we estimated Eq. (4.1) with j ranging from −5 to 5, which allows us to explore whether our results are robust to different event windows. Last, given the fact that a minority of the sample has reported multiple pork safety test failures, we use the De Chaisemartin and d'Haultfoeuille (2020) estimator (DIDM) to obtain unbiased estimates of dynamic treatment effects.

4.5 Results

In discussing our empirical findings, we first focus on the average treatment effect of government disclosure of food safety information on pork wholesale prices, followed by the spillover effect results and robustness checks.

4.5.1 Impact of Food Safety Information Disclosure on Pork Prices

Table 4.1 reveals the average treatment effects of government disclosure of food safety information on pork wholesale prices. In the table, Model 1 controls for week and city fixed factors that affect pork prices, Model 2 builds on Model 1 by including province-by-year fixed effects, and Model 3 adds to Model 1 with city-by-year fixed effects. The coefficients, βj, when $j < 0$, across different model specifications, are close to zero and are not statistically significant. This suggests no systematic differences in pork wholesale prices between the treatment and control groups prior to the government information disclosure about unsafe pork products. As Model 3 performs best in terms of goodness offit, we refer to this model when discussing the baseline results.

Several points can be made from the estimation result of Model 3. First, cities that have failed pork safety tests experienced pork wholesale price drops after such information was made public by governments, though the coefficients are significant at the level of 5%. Second, local wholesale prices in the treatment group didn't decrease immediately after the information disclosure. Instead, the local pork prices declined 2 weeks later. The coefficient, $\beta 3$ equals −0.05, indicating that the information disclosure significantly decreases pork prices by 5%, relative to the control group.

Table 4.1 Average treatment effects of government information disclosure on pork prices

	Model1	Model2	Model3
β_{-5}	0.003	−0.020	−0.033
	(0.024)	(0.018)	(0.023)
β_{-4}	−0.007	−0.034	−0.036
	(0.028)	(0.022)	(0.024)
β_{-3}	0.007	−0.012	−0.015
	(0.033)	(0.027)	(0.030)
β_{-2}	0.019	−0.004	−0.006
	(0.043)	(0.038)	(0.040)
β_0	0.016	0.012	0.014
	(0.022)	(0.022)	(0.022)
β_1	−0.012	−0.013	−0.012
	(0.023)	(0.022)	(0.023)
β_2	−0.013	−0.014	−0.007
	(0.025)	(0.024)	(0.023)
β_3	−0.057**	−0.066**	−0.050**
	(0.026)	(0.027)	(0.026)
β_4	−0.030	−0.061*	−0.040
	(0.038)	(0.034)	(0.028)
β_5	0.025	−0.001	0.006
	(0.033)	(0.026)	(0.025)
β_6	−0.019	−0.044	−0.033
	(0.042)	(0.035)	(0.038)
β_7	0.029	0.005	0.013
	(0.038)	(0.033)	(0.034)
β_8	−0.026	−0.053**	−0.051**
	(0.033)	(0.026)	(0.025)
β_9	−0.044	−0.066**	−0.055*
	(0.035)	(0.032)	(0.032)
β_{10}	−0.016	−0.044*	−0.017
	(0.027)	(0.023)	(0.016)
WeekFE	Yes	Yes	Yes
City-YearFE	No	No	Yes
Province-YearFE	No	Yes	No
CityFE	Yes	Yes	Yes
Observations	8492	8492	8492
R^2	0.912	0.916	0.930

Note: ***, ** and * denote statistical significance at the 1%, 5% and 10% levels, respectively. Robust standard errors clustered at province level are in parentheses

4.5.2 Spillover Effects on Nearby Cities and Non-pork Products

Table 4.2 indicates the estimation results on the spillover effects of pork safety information disclosure. Column (1) in Table 4.2 concerns how pork safety information disclosure affects pork prices of all cities adjacent to the treatment group, while column (2) focuses on the adjacent cities within the province. If a city announced the safety test failure of pork products, the average wholesale pork price of the city's all neighboring cities will experience a drop of nearly 12% in the eighth week, although the coefficient is marginally significant. The estimated spillover effects become stronger when restricting neighboring cities to be in the same province as the treated cities, and on average, among these adjacent cities, pork wholesale prices declined 7% and 10% in the second and third weeks after the event, respectively. Column (3) in Table 4.2 reports the estimation results about how pork safety information disclosure affects wholesale prices of other meat products, namely beef. We chose beef prices for several points. Ideally, chicken prices, instead of beef prices, would be investigated as chicken is found to be a major substitute for pork in China (Ma & Lusk, 2021). But chicken prices in our dataset are not feasible for such analysis. On the other hand, beef is the fastest-growing meat consumed in China surpassing the demand growth of pork, and beef consumption per capita in China reached 8.5 lb. in 2019 (Lin et al., 2022). It reveals that government disclosure of pork safety information decreased local beef prices by approximately 6% 3 and 4 weeks later, despite that the estimated effect is of marginal statistical significance.

4.5.3 Robustness Checks

In this subsection, we adopt the three aforementioned approaches to guard the estimated treatment effects of government disclosure of food safety information, whose results are presented in Table 4.3. First, in the benchmark, we explore the impact of the first disclosure of pork safety information during our study period. But pork safety test failure(s) could happen more than once in a city within our sample period.[4] This implies that our baseline results are likely to be confounded by the second and third disclosure of pork safety test failure(s). To rule out such a possibility, we focus on a subsample where cities had announced pork safety test failure at least three times and then investigate how the third disclosure of pork safety failure affects local pork prices (Column (1) of Table 4.3). Results reveal that the effect of the third disclosure ($\beta4 = -0.12$) largely parallels that of the first disclosure of pork safety test failure, which is discussed in the baseline results subsection. Besides, we generate another subsample where the cities announced

[4]Over 80% of the cities announced one and only one pork safety test failure in the sample period, and less than 10% of the cities announced pork safety test failure three times.

Table 4.2 Spillover effects of government information disclosure

	All neighboring cities	Neighboring cities within province	Beef prices
β_{-5}	0.005	0.019	−0.006
	(0.064)	(0.049)	(0.021)
β_{-4}	0.046	−0.018	−0.026
	(0.067)	(0.047)	(0.028)
β_{-3}	0.054	0.010	−0.007
	(0.072)	(0.037)	(0.026)
β_{-2}	0.042	0.051	0.000
	(0.054)	(0.036)	(0.039)
β_0	0.004	0.038	0.014
	(0.076)	(0.048)	(0.025)
β_1	−0.009	0.026	−0.012
	(0.061)	(0.043)	(0.025)
β_2	0.050	0.044	−0.009
	(0.069)	(0.047)	(0.028)
β_3	−0.042	−0.074*	−0.055*
	(0.079)	(0.043)	(0.031)
β_4	−0.022	−0.097*	−0.060*
	(0.070)	(0.053)	(0.032)
β_5	−0.016	0.030	0.006
	(0.061)	(0.048)	(0.029)
β_6	0.010	0.013	−0.042
	(0.056)	(0.044)	(0.034)
β_7	−0.009	0.027	0.015
	(0.057)	(0.052)	(0.029)
β_8	−0.117*	−0.053	−0.039
	(0.066)	(0.045)	(0.035)
β_9	0.002	−0.018	−0.059
	(0.069)	(0.043)	(0.037)
β_{10}	−0.020	0.009	−0.038
	(0.068)	(0.044)	(0.023)
Week FE	Yes	Yes	Yes
City-Year FE	Yes	Yes	Yes
Province-Year FE	No	No	No
City FE	Yes	Yes	Yes
Observations	8492	8492	8492
R^2	0.913	0.916	0.750

Note: ***, ** and * denote statistical significance at the 1%, 5% and 10% levels, respectively. Robust standard errors clustered at province level are in parentheses

Table 4.3 Robustness checks

	(1)	(2)	(3)	(4)
β_{-5}	0.022	0.001	−0.020	
	(0.043)	(0.032)	(0.020)	
β_{-4}	0.010	−0.007	−0.034	
	(0.059)	(0.046)	(0.036)	
β_{-3}	0.059	0.029	−0.012	
	(0.059)	(0.036)	(0.025)	
β_{-2}	0.039	−0.017	−0.004	
	(0.063)	(0.071)	(0.031)	
β_0	0.035	0.009	0.013	
	(0.061)	(0.052)	(0.024)	
β_1	0.047	0.021	−0.013	
	(0.058)	(0.045)	(0.022)	
β_2	0.046	0.013	−0.014	
	(0.059)	(0.037)	(0.026)	
β_3	0.041	−0.063*	−0.067***	
	(0.064)	(0.033)	(0.017)	
β_4	−0.126**	−0.032	−0.061	
	(0.064)	(0.067)	(0.042)	
β_5	−0.050	0.042**	−0.042**	
	(0.061)	(0.016)	(0.014)	
β_6	0.058	−0.020		
	(0.067)	(0.063)		
β_7	−0.064	0.025		
	(0.067)	(0.046)		
β_8	−0.018	−0.033		
	(0.069)	(0.029)		
β_9	0.017**	−0.033*		
	(0.008)	(0.024)		
β_{10}	0.004	−0.052		
	(0.045)	(0.029)		
didcw				−0.021** (0.009)
Week FE	Yes	Yes	Yes	Yes
City-Year FE	Yes	Yes	Yes	Yes
Province-Year FE	No	No	No	No
City FE	Yes	Yes	Yes	Yes
Observations	8492	6789	8492	8492
R^2	0.916	0.913	0.916	0.750

Note: ***, **, and * denote statistical significance at the 1%, 5%, and 10% levels, respectively. Robust standard errors clustered at the province level are in parentheses one and only one pork safety test failure in our dataset, andre-estimated Model (3) in Table 4.1. The estimated treatment effects, shown in Column (2) of Table 4.3, are robust. Second, we test whether our baseline results are sensitive to the study time window specified in the event study. We adopted the specification of Model (3) in Table 4.1 but shorten the postevent time window (Column (3) of Table 4.3). The result indicates that the announcement of pork safety test failure dropped pork wholesale prices 3 and 5 weeks later, at a rate of about 5%. Third, we also explore whether the baseline results remain robust to model specification by using a staggered difference-in-difference approach. Results in column (4) of Table 4.3 suggest that the estimated treatment effect of pork safety information disclosure on pork prices is about −2.1% at a 5% significance level, which is again consistent with our previous findings.

4.6 Heterogeneity

In this section, we investigate several heterogeneity that could explain the information treatment effects on pork wholesale prices documented in Sect. 4.4. Changes in pork prices depend on the ways that information shifts pork demand versus pork supply. Thus we examine the roles of (i) supply chain position, (ii) information accessibility, and (iii) information salience. We note that our goal is not to disentangle and quantify the impact of each role, but instead, we investigate whether a particular force has bite.

4.6.1 Supply Chain Position

Wholesalers in main pork production areas are at a larger scale than those in main consumption areas (Xie et al., 2020), whose average registered capital is two million RMB higher (self-calculated based on the Chinese enterprise registration dataset by the year 2021). Larger vendors and those close to farms in the supply chain have lower transaction costs in obtaining traceable information, resulting in higher adoption of traceability (Zhou et al., 2022). When a wholesaler failed a pork safety test, her pork product will be confiscated, causing a supply decline for large-scale wholesalers common in major pork production regions. Thus we expected the information treatment effects on pork prices to be mainly driven by reduced pork supply among main production cities, while this supply channel would be limited for main consumption cities. The estimation results were derived from the estimation of Model 3 in Table 4.1 using the main pork production and consumption sub-samples, respectively. We generated the sub-samples based on the 2019 hog production action plan by the Ministry of Agriculture and Rural Affairs of China.[5] In the plan, cities in

[5] See the document at the official website: https://www.moa.gov.cn/gk/zcfg/qnhnzc/201912/t20191206_6332872.htm

Sichuan, Henan, Shandong, Hunan, and Yunnan provinces belong to the main pork production areas, including 37% of the national pork production in 2019. Beijing, Tianjin, Shanghai, and cities in Fujian, Zhejiang, and Guangdong provinces were taken as the main consumption regions, whose pork consumption occupied 24% of China'spork consumption in 2019 (National Bureau of Statistics of China, 2021).

Table 4.4 Effects of government information disclosure: main pork production versus consumption subsamples

	Main pork production	Main pork consumption
β_{-5}	−0.022 (0.034)	0.030 (0.032)
β_{-4}	0.020 (0.039)	−0.067 (0.044)
β_{-3}	−0.007 (0.048)	0.037 (0.026)
β_{-2}	0.038 (0.115)	−0.007 (0.031)
β_0	0.063* (0.029)	0.041 (0.033)
β_1	−0.055 (0.046)	−0.025 (0.032)
β_2	0.040 (0.057)	−0.059* (0.034)
β_3	−0.037 (0.058)	−0.100** (0.038)
β_4	0.005 (0.048)	−0.161*** (0.026)
β_5	0.073 (0.067)	−0.044* (0.025)
β_6	−0.029 (0.054)	0.036 (0.062)
β_7	0.011 (0.085)	0.032 (0.060)
β_8	−0.023 (0.036)	−0.090 (0.064)
β_9	−0.034 (0.065)	−0.121** (0.052)
	0.007 (0.034)	−0.041** (0.019)
Week FE	Yes	Yes
City-Year FE	Yes	Yes
Province-Year FE	No	No
City FE	Yes	Yes
Observations	6017	5266
R^2	0.916	0.923

Note: ***, ** and * denote statistical significance at the 1%, 5% and 10% levels, respectively. Robust standard errors clustered at the province level are in parentheses

Table 4.4 presents the information treatment effects of main pork production cities versus main pork consumption cities. Food safety information disclosure yields differentiated influences on pork wholesale prices between major pork production and consumption subsamples. Expectedly, the information effects on major pork production cities are driven by a reduction in pork supply. Among cities located in major hog production regions, β0 equals to 0.063 at a 5% significance level, meaning that they experienced immediate and significant wholesale pork price increases, at a rate of 6% when pork products at or from local wholesale market failed sampling tests and the failure was announced. In contrast, the information disclosure causes a significant decline in pork prices of the main pork consumption subsamples, which would be attributed to negative pork demand shocks. For example, β3 and β4 equal to −0.10 and − 0.161, respectively, with at least a 5% significance level, indicating that after being affected by the safety information disclosure, pork prices for cities who are pork net buyers were 10% and 16% lower than the control group, during the third and fourth weeks, respectively. The downward trend in pork prices was mitigated following the fourth week (β5 = − 0.04), but rebounded in the ninth week (β9 = − 0.12). This somewhat parallels the previous results using the full samples.

4.6.2 *Information Accessibility*

To examine formally whether information accessibility could be one explanation for the estimated average treatment effects, we separated our sample into subgroups with high and low internet penetration rates. Internet penetration rate[6] was used to proxy information accessibility because all results of food safety sampling tests have been first published on the Administration for Market Regulation's websites. Note that all cities in the main consumption subsample were identified to have high internet penetration levels. Table 4.5 illustrates the estimation results using the high and low information accessibility subsamples. Cities having better access to information, experienced over 7% pork price drop after the failure of the pork safety test was announced, which is slightly higher than the average treatment effect (5%). This however fails to hold for the low information accessibility subgroup, whose estimated information treatment effects were statistically insignificant.

[6]The internet penetration rate was calculated following Shi et al. (2022). Cities above and below the median internet penetration rate were grouped into the high and low internet penetration subsamples, respectively.

Table 4.5 Effects of government information disclosure: different internet penetration rate subsamples

	High internet penetration	Low internet penetration
β_{-5}	−0.014 (0.022)	−0.026 (0.029)
β_{-4}	−0.033 (0.029)	−0.023 (0.044)
β_{-3}	−0.017 (0.036)	−0.005 (0.033)
β_{-2}	0.020 (0.039)	−0.115 (0.088)
β_0	0.014 (0.021)	−0.011 (0.086)
β_1	−0.008 (0.026)	−0.055 (0.070)
β_2	−0.020 (0.032)	0.011 (0.018)
β_3	−0.076** (0.033)	−0.007 (0.054)
β_4	−0.073* (0.042)	−0.035 (0.044)
β_5	−0.021 (0.031)	0.057 (0.034)
β_6	−0.071 (0.042)	0.078 (0.049)
β_7	0.007 (0.040)	−0.006 (0.025)
β_8	−0.046 (0.035)	−0.067 (0.048)
β_9	−0.102** (0.038)	0.077 (0.059)
$\beta 10$	−0.049** (0.023)	0.035 (0.070)
Week FE	Yes	Yes
City-Year FE	Yes	Yes
Province-Year FE	No	No
City FE	Yes	Yes
Observations	5450	2875
R^2	0.932	0.904

Note: ***, ** and * denote statistical significance at the 1%, 5% and 10% levels, respectively. Robust standard errors clustered at the province level are in parentheses

4.6.3 Information Salience

In addition to information accessibility, the extent that consumer awareness and attention would affect information treatment effect through informationsalience. We examined whether market awareness and attention to food safety information could be another explanation for our moderate estimated treatment effects. People in places with high incidence already have experience with foodborne diseases, and the unpleasure experience made them more responsive to food safety information (Kariuki & Hoffmann, 2021). To do so, we used the case of foodborne diseases to reflect market awareness and attention as food safety incidents in China have pushed consumers to become more aware of food safety information (Liu & Niyongira, 2017). We generated two subsamples with high and low incidences of foodborne illness, taking the median incidence per capita of the sample as a cut-off. Per capita incidence controls for population size's impact on total cases of foodborne illness. Estimation results between high and low foodborne illness incidence subgroups were presented in Table 4.6. We find that among cities with more cases of foodborne illness, government disclosure of food safety information significantly decreased pork prices by 2.7% and 8.1% in the second and third weeks after the event, respectively. Oppositely, the information disclosure was ineffective in the other subgroup.

We also explored whether the information treatment effects are heterogeneous between cities with strong and weak capabilities and resources on food safety regulation (Table 4.7). The capability and resource are proxied by budgetary expenditure on food safety regulation (Ma & Liu, 2019). For cities with more food safety regulatory resources, local governments may invest more in information disclosure and salience. Again, the median fiscal expenditure per capita was used to split the data into two subsamples. 42 cities fell in the high fiscal expenditure subgroup including Shanghai, Beijing, and those in Sichuan and Yunnan provinces, while 61 cities from Inner Mongolia, Anhui, Henan and Shandong and other provinces belong to the low expenditure subsample. Table 4.7 reveals that, within cities rich in food safety regulatory resources, pork wholesale prices dropped almost 10% after the pork test failure has been announced, relative to the control group. The safety information has yet to exert insignificant impacts on pork prices for cities having relatively weak food safety regulatory resources.

4.7 Discussions and Conclusions

Using an event study approach and a city-level weekly panel dataset including pork wholesale prices and pork safety test outcomes, this study investigateshow government disclosure of food safety information affects market outcomes, in particular, market prices. We focus on the largest developing market, China, and a nationwide food safety information disclosure program. No other studies have examined *actual*

Table 4.6 Effects of government information disclosure: different incidence of foodborne illness subsamples

	High incidence	Low incidence
β_{-5}	−0.005 (0.037)	−0.004 (0.055)
β_{-4}	−0.001 (0.038)	−0.021 (0.071)
β_{-3}	−0.048 (0.053)	0.028 (0.071)
β_{-2}	0.002 (0.060)	0.023 (0.075)
β_0	0.025 (0.024)	−0.006 (0.072)
β_1	−0.037 (0.029)	0.019 (0.074)
β_2	−0.027* (0.014)	−0.016 (0.075)
β_3	−0.081*** (0.024)	−0.026 (0.078)
β_4	0.008 (0.051)	−0.086 (0.076)
β_5	0.032 (0.045)	0.014 (0.071)
β_6	−0.025 (0.065)	−0.023 (0.069)
β_7	0.004 (0.042)	0.045 (0.071)
β_8	−0.013 (0.039)	−0.056 (0.072)
β_9	0.021 (0.049)	−0.121 (0.074)
$\beta 10$	0.011 (0.039)	−0.054 (0.056)
Week FE	Yes	Yes
City-Year FE	Yes	Yes
Province-Year FE	No	No
City FE	Yes	Yes
Observations	3774	4715
R^2	0.931	0.907

Note: ***, ** and * denote statistical significance at the 1%, 5% and 10% levels, respectively. Robust standard errors clustered at province level are in parentheses

market responses to food safety information disclosure based on developing markets. Our findings contribute to the understanding of the effectiveness of information-based food safety regulation and have policy implications for other developing countries facing food safety issues.

Table 4.7 Effects of government information disclosure: different food safety regulatory resource subsamples

	Strong regulatory resource	Weak regulatory resource
β_{-5}	−0.041 (0.040)	−0.001 (0.042)
β_{-4}	−0.006 (0.032)	−0.041 (0.056)
β_{-3}	0.015 (0.035)	−0.020 (0.057)
β_{-2}	−0.026 (0.067)	−0.000 (0.060)
β_0	−0.021 (0.034)	0.053 (0.057)
β_1	−0.008 (0.033)	−0.013 (0.057)
β_2	−0.002 (0.048)	−0.033 (0.058)
β_3	−0.095** (0.053)	−0.041 (0.059)
β_4	−0.091* (0.046)	−0.015 (0.059)
β_5	−0.015 (0.047)	0.028 (0.060)
β_6	−0.069 (0.051)	−0.027 (0.056)
β_7	−0.013 (0.057)	0.024 (0.057)
β_8	−0.016 (0.038)	−0.081 (0.057)
β_9	−0.075* (0.044)	−0.057 (0.058)
$\beta 10$	−0.066* (0.039)	−0.026 (0.042)
Week FE	Yes	Yes
City-Year FE	Yes	Yes
Province-Year FE	No	No
City FE	Yes	Yes
Observations	3347	5142
R^2	0.911	0.921

Note: ***, ** and * denote statistical significance at the 1%, 5% and 10% levels, respectively. Robust standard errors clustered at province level are in parentheses

Results reveal that lagged price response to government disclosure of unsafety pork in China. Average pork wholesale prices began to decrease by 5% 2 weeks after the information disclosure. Disclosure of unsafe pork has a limited spillover effect on local beef prices and on pork wholesale prices of neighboring cities unless the cities are restricted to be within the same province. Heterogeneity analyses indicate that the negative information effects on pork prices found in the main pork consumption cities are largely driven by negative pork demand shocks. Pork price reductions are more evident in the treated cities with higher information accessibility and salience, measured by internet penetration rate, the incidence of foodborne illness, and food safety regulatory resources.

Most of the findings are expected and align with existing literature. Negative and lagged price responses to food safety information are generally consistent with the exited studies (Dillaway et al., 2011), despite the small magnitude of our treatment effects. Possible reasons include reduced demand for pork products in the treatment group after the information about unsafe local pork was made available to the general public, which ultimately led pork prices to drop. Lagged treatment effects on pork prices maybe explained by that it takes a while for wholesalers to learn and respond to the safety information disclosure by governments, thus negative shocks in pork demand would not appear promptly. Besides, significant pork price decreases have been seen in 8 and 9 weeks after the information disclosure, which is potentially caused by further dissemination of food safety information among wholesale market actors, such as non-local traders. The spatial spillover effects of pork safety information disclosure are more evident for cities within the province. This is in part consistent with Toledo and Villas-Boas (2019) who showed that the recalls of contaminated eggs in Northern California reduced egg sales in Southern Californian stores as well. In addition to spatial spillovers, we also test for product spillovers and show that government disclosure of pork safety information decreased local beef prices by approximately 6% 3 and 4 weeks later, despite the estimated effect being of marginal statistical significance. The observed beef price drop may be driven by consumers' overall safety concern about meat products, which is triggered by pork safety test failure.

In assessing the heterogeneous effects of public disclosure of food safety information, we find evident pork price decreases in main pork consumption cities, which could be explained by at least two points. First, cities in the main pork consumption subsample, such as Beijing, Shanghai, and Tianjin, are more developed and urbanized than almost all other parts of China. People in these cities have better access to information and stronger abilities to interpret the information. On the other hand, pork wholesalers in these cities sell products to retailers, restaurants, and educational facilities (Reardon, 2015), who are direct pork buyers and may be more attentive to food safety information, relative to their counterparts (pork traders) in main hog production areas. Secondly, the effect of government disclosure of food safety information on pork wholesale prices is almost led by the high information accessibility subsample, instead of the low information accessibility subsample. This is in line with the previous results showing that the effectiveness of red meat warnings depends on individual exposure to and interpretation of information (Carrieri & Principe, 2022). Thirdly, within cities rich in food safety regulatory resources, pork wholesale prices dropped almost 10% after the pork test failure was announced, relative to the control group. However, the safety information fails to exert significant impacts on pork prices for cities having relatively weak food safety regulatory resources. One plausible explanation is that cities with greater food safety regulatory resources may allocate more investment to information disclosure and visibility. Consequently, this could lead to an enhanced responsiveness of the wholesale market to food safety information and then a more evident drop in pork prices. This is in part consistent with the finding by Zhou et al. (2022) that government disclosure of food safety information promoted traceability adoption among agricultural producers, especially in cities with more regulatory resources.

In light of our findings, this study highlights the importance and necessity of extending the research focus to emerging agricultural markets using actual market data and also has important policy implications for regulating food safety in developing countries whose food safety issues are evident and urgent. First, our results imply that the Chinese government's disclosure of food safety information is, to some extent, useful, as the program significantly reduces pork wholesale prices by approximately 5% (although the price response is lagging). Effective food safety information-based regulation crucially depends on whether and how the market responds to that information. Our baseline result highlights that a potential policy instrument for tackling food safety problems in developing countries for public policymakers is to invest in food safety information collection and disclosure.

Second and admittedly, the magnitude of our average treatment effects is not substantial, indicating that there is potential for enhancing the effectiveness of government food safety disclosures in developing economies like China.[7] Given the substantial financial and personnel resources allocated in food safety sampling tests and their result disclosure in China, a more efficient allocation of public resources that improves social welfare would be warranted. To this end, our heterogeneous analyses inform several possible avenues. For informational public policy to be effective, information disclosure alone is insufficient; ensuring accessible and interpretable information is at least equally important, which probably has more implications for developing rather than developed markets. The effect of government disclosure of food safety information on pork wholesale prices is mainly driven by the high information accessibility subsample, relative to the low information accessibility subsample. This echoes a recent study showing that 52% of food suppliers including wholesalers, processors, and retailers didn't know where to find food sampling test results, and this ratio increased to 80% among household consumers (An, 2020). Together this implies inefficient use of food safety information due to limited market awareness and attention. Furthermore, enhancing public understanding of food safety test outcomes could not be ignored. In our study, the disclosed

[7]A reviewer kindly suggests us to distinguish between inadequate informa- tion exposure and a weak response to enough information. While we acknowledge the merit of this suggestion, we believe the suitable approach would be a randomized field experiment involving two groups of wholesale markets with varying levels of information exposure. However, this is currently outside the scope of our study.

information specifies whether a pork product passed or failed safety tests, but lacks follow-up details on health consequences which might hinder public comprehension and dissemination.

It is worth noting that our results suggest that when one pork wholesaler was disclosed to fail pork safety sampling tests, the pork price in the city where the wholesaler was located declined. This implies that the information disclosure imposes a negative externality on other pork wholesalers within the city, suggesting a collective reputation for food safety in developing markets (Bai et al., 2022; Adalja et al., 2023). Without government interventions to address this externality, pork wholesalers would engage in free-riding behavior with regard to food safety, potentially leading to market failures. To internalize the externality, governments in developing markets are encouraged to disclose more details in a more significant place, for example, to put a warning label at the front of the failed pork wholesaler. Meanwhile, more actions need to betaken to push food supply chain players to adopt traceability or even blockchain traceability systems and to have third-party quality certifications. A caveat on our findings is that they could be contingent on the use of the product, i.e. pork, and of wholesale prices. Future research should test the robustness of our findings to variations in these contexts, including testing our spillover effects on chicken prices whenever the data becomes feasible (Table 4.8).

Financial Disclosure Statement

This work was supported by the National Natural Science Foundation of China (No. 72103180, 72273128).

CRediT Authorship Contribution Statement

Wen Lin: Writing – review & editing, Writing – original draft, Validation, Resources, Conceptualization. Baojie Ma: Writing – review & editing, Visualization, Software, Investigation, Formal analysis. Jiangyuan Liang: Writing – review & editing, Investigation. Shaosheng Jin: Writing – review & editing, Project administration.

Declaration of Competing Interest

The authors declare that they have no known competing financial interests or personal relationships that could have appeared to influence the work reported in this paper.

Appendix

Table 4.8 Descriptive statistics

Variable	Unit	Level	Observation	Mean	S.D
Pork prices (*yuan/kg*)	Yuan/kg	Market-Week	8492	28.18	12.36
Beef prices (*yuan/kg*)	Yuan/kg	Market-Week	8492	67.51	8.63
Number of pork test failure		Market-Week	8492	0.05	0.10
Internet penetration (%)	%	City-Year	349	36.70	19.50
Budgetary expenditure on food safety regulation	Million yuan	Province-Year	93	22.59	19.09
Case of foodborne disease	10,000 persons	Province-Year	93	0.32	0.23

References

Abbott, P. C. (2012). Export restrictions as stabilization responses to food crisis. *American Journal of Agricultural Economics, 94*(2), 428–434.

Adalja, A., Lichtenberg, E., & Page, E. T. (2023). Collective investment in a common pool resource: Grower associations and food safety guidelines. *American Journal of Agricultural Economics, 105*(1), 144–173.

Alcorn, T., & Ouyang, Y. (2012). China's invisible burden of foodborne illness. *Lancet, 379*(9818), 789–790.

An, Y. K. (2020). Regulatory information disclosure as a tool of risk regulation: The case of food safety regulation. *Nanjing University Law Journal, 3*, 129–146. in Chinese.

Arnade, C., Calvin, L., & Kuchler, F. (2009). Consumer response to a food safety shock: The 2006 food-borne illness outbreak of E. coli O157: H7 linked to spinach. *Applied Economic Perspectives and Policy, 31*(4), 734–750.

Bai, J., Gazze, L., & Wang, Y. (2022). Collective reputation in trade: Evidence from the Chinese dairy industry. *The Review of Economics and Statistics, 104*(6), 1121–1137.

Birol, E., Roy, D., & Torero, M. (2010). *How safe is my food?: Assessing the effect of information and credible certification on consumer demand for food safety in developing countries* (No. 1029). The International Food Policy Research Institute (IFPRI).

Carlsson, F., Kataria, M., & Lampi, E. (2018). Demand effects in stated preference surveys. *Journal of Environmental Economics and Management, 90*, 294–302.

Carrieri, V., & Principe, F. (2022). WHO and for how long? An empirical analysis of the consumers' response to red meat warning. *Food Policy, 108*, 102231.

Carriquiry, M., Elobeid, A., Hayes, D. J., & Zhang, W. (2019). *Impact of african swine fever on US and world commodity markets*. Iowa State University, Center for Agricultural and Rural Development (CARD).

De Chaisemartin, C., & d'Haultfoeuille, X. (2020). Two-way fixed effects estimators with heterogeneous treatment effects. *The American Economic Review, 110*(9), 2964–2996.

Delgado, M. S., Ma, M., & Wang, H. H. (2021). *Exploring spatial price relationships: The case of african swine fever in china* (No. w29141). The National Bureau of Economic Research.

Dietrich, S., Giuffrida, V., Martorano, B., & Schmerzeck, G. (2022). COVID-19 policy responses, mobility, and food prices. *American Journal of Agricultural Economics, 104*(2), 569–588.

Dillaway, R., Messer, K. D., Bernard, J. C., & Kaiser, H. M. (2011). Do consumer responses to media food safety information last? *Applied Economic Perspectives and Policy, 33*(3), 363–383.

Dillon, B. M., & Barrett, C. B. (2016). Global oil prices and local food prices: Evidence from East Africa. *American Journal of Agricultural Economics, 98*(1), 154–171.

Ehmke, M. D., Lusk, J. L., & Tyner, W. (2008). Measuring the relative importance of preferences for country of origin in China, France, Niger, and the United States. *Agricultural Economics, 38*(3), 277–285.

Hamilton, S. F., Sunding, D. L., & Zilberman, D. (2003). Public goods and the value of product quality regulations: The case of food safety. *Journal of Public Economics, 87*(3–4), 799–817.

Headey, D., & Fan, S. (2008). Anatomy of a crisis: The causes and consequences of surging food prices. *Agricultural Economics, 39*, 375–391.

Henson, S. (2003). The economics of food safety in developing countries. In *ESA Working Paper*. Food and Agriculture Organization No. 03–09.

Hoffmann, V., Moser, C., & Saak, A. (2019). Food safety in low and middle-income countries: The evidence through an economic lens. *World Development, 123*, 104611.

Jin, G. Z., & Leslie, P. (2003). The effect of information on product quality: Evidence from restaurant hygiene grade cards. *Quarterly Journal of Economics, 118*(2), 409–451.

Jin, C., Levi, R., Liang, Q., Renegar, N., Springs, S., Zhou, J., & Zhou, W. (2021a). Testing at the source: Analytics-enabled risk-based sampling of food supply chains in China. *Management Science, 67*(5), 2985–2996.

Jin, C., Retsef, L., Liang, Q., Renegar, N., & Zhou, J. (2021b). Food safety inspection and the adoption of traceability in aquatic wholesale markets: A game-theoretic model and empirical evidence. *Journal of Integrative Agriculture, 20*(10), 2807–2819.

Kariuki, S. W., & Hoffmann, V. (2021). Can information drive demand for safer food? Impact of brand-specific recommendations and test results on product choice. *Agricultural Economics*.

Letta, M., Montalbano, P., & Pierre, G. (2022). Weather shocks, traders' expectations, and food prices. *American Journal of Agricultural Economics, 104*(3), 1100–1119.

Lin, W., Ortega, D. L., Ufer, D., Caputo, V., & Awokuse, T. (2022). Blockchain-based traceability and demand for US beef in China. *Applied Economic Perspectives and Policy, 44*(1), 253–272.

Liu, A., & Niyongira, R. (2017). Chinese consumers food purchasing behaviors and awareness of food safety. *Food Control, 79*, 185–191.

Liu, R., Gao, Z., Nayga, R. M., Jr., Snell, H. A., & Ma, H. (2019). Consumers' valuation for food traceability in China: Does trust matter? *Food Policy, 88*, 101768.

Liu, R., Gao, Z., Snell, H. A., & Ma, H. (2020). Food safety concerns and consumer preferences for food safety attributes: Evidence from China. *Food Control, 112*, 107157.

Lusk, J. L., & Schroeder, T. C. (2002). Effects of meat recalls on futures market prices. *Agricultural Economics Research Review, 31*(1), 47–58.

Ma, L., & Liu, P. (2019). Missing links between regulatory resources and risk concerns: Evidence from the case of food safety in China. *Regulation Governance, 13*(1), 35–50.

Ma, M., & Lusk, J. L. (2021). *Concentration and resilience in the US meat supply chains, no. w29103*. National Bureau of Economic Research.

Mazzocchi, M. (2006). No news is good news: stochastic parameters versus media coverage indices in demand models after food scares. *American Journal of Agricultural Economics, 88*(3), 727–741.

Mérel, P., Ortiz-Bobea, A., & Paroissien, E. (2021). How big is the "lemons" problem? Historical evidence from French wines. *European Economic Review, 138*, 103824.

Mitchell, D. (2008). *A note on rising food prices*. World bank policy research working paper (4682).

Nait Mohand, N., Hammoudi, A., Radjef, M. S., Hamza, O., & Perito, M. A. (2017). How do food safety regulations influence market price? A theoretical analysis. *The British Food Journal, 119*(8), 1687–1704.

National Bureau of Statistics of China. (2021). *2020 China statistical yearbook*. China Statistics Press.

Neill, C. L., & Chen, S. E. (2021). Food safety events versus media: Nonlinear effects of egg recalls on US egg prices. *Journal of Agricultural and Resource Economics, 47*(1), 23–37.
Ollinger, M., & Bovay, J. (2020). Producer response to public disclosure of food-safety information. *American Journal of Agricultural Economics, 102*(1), 186–201.
Ortega, D. L., Tschirley, D. L. (2017). Demand for food safety in emerging and developing countries: A research agenda for Asia and Sub-Saharan Africa. *Journal of Agribusiness in Developing and Emerging Economies.*
Ortega, D. L., Wang, H. H., Olynk, N. J., Wu, L., & Bai, J. (2012). Chinese consumers' demand for food safety attributes: A push for government and industry regulations. *American Journal of Agricultural Economics, 94*(2), 489–495.
Penn, J. M., & Hu, W. (2021). The extent of hypothetical bias in willingness to accept. *American Journal of Agricultural Economics, 103*(1), 126–141.
Piggott, N. E., & Marsh, T. L. (2004). Does food safety information impact US meat demand? *American Journal of Agricultural Economics*, 154–174.
Reardon, T. (2015). The hidden middle: The quiet revolution in the midstream of agrifood value chains in developing countries. *Oxford Review of Economic Policy, 31*(1), 45–63.
Ren, Y., & An, Y. (2010). Efficient food safety regulation in the agro-food wholesale market. *Agriculture and Agricultural Science Procedia, 1*, 344–353.
Ruan, J., Cai, Q., & Jin, S. (2021). Impact of COVID-19 and nationwide lockdowns on vegetable prices: Evidence from wholesale markets in China. *American Journal of Agricultural Economics, 103*(5), 1574–1594.
SAMR. (2020). *Notice on issuing the 2020 food safety supervision sampling inspection plan by the of the State Administration for Market Regulation*, 2020-01-31. http://www.samr.gov.cn/spcjs/cjjc/qtwj/201902/t20190226_291363.html
Schlenker, W., & Villas-Boas, S. B. (2009). Consumer and market responses to mad cow disease. *American Journal of Agricultural Economics, 91*(4), 1140–1152.
Shang, X., & Tonsor, G. T. (2017). Food safety recall effects across meat products and regions. *Food Policy, 69*, 145–153.
Shimshack, J. P., Ward, M. B., & Beatty, T. K. (2007). Mercury advisories: Information, education, and fish consumption. *Journal of Environmental Economics and Management, 53*(2), 158–179.
Taylor, M., Klaiber, H. A., & Kuchler, F. (2016). Changes in US consumer response to food safety recalls in the shadow of a BSE scare. *Food Policy, 62*, 56–64.
Toledo, C., & Villas-Boas, S. B. (2019). Safe or not? Consumer responses to recalls with traceability. *Applied Economic Perspectives and Policy, 41*(3), 519–541.
Wang, H. H., & de Beville, P. G. (2017). The media impact of animal disease on the US meat demand. *Agribusiness, 33*(4), 493–504.
Wang, H. H., Chen, J., Bai, J., & Lai, J. (2018). Meat packaging, preservation, and marketing implications: Consumer preferences in an emerging economy. *Meat Science, 145*, 300–307.
Wang, E., Gao, Z., Heng, Y., & Shi, L. (2019). Chinese consumers' preferences for food quality test/measurement indicators and cues of milk powder: A case of Zhengzhou, China. *Food Policy, 89*, 101791.
Wongprawmas, R., & Canavari, M. (2017). Consumers' willingness-to-pay for food safety labels in an emerging market: The case of fresh produce in Thailand. *Food Policy, 69*, 25–34.
Wu, L., Wang, H., Zhu, D., Hu, W., & Wang, S. (2016). Chinese consumers' willingness to pay for pork traceability information—The case of Wuxi. *Agricultural Economics, 47*(1), 71–79.
Wu, L., Chen, Y., & Chen, X. (2022). Evolution of policy instruments for food safety risk management: Comparing China and Western countries. *The Journal of Agriculture and Food Research, 8*, 100311.
Xie, D., Zhuo, L., Xie, P., Liu, Y., Feng, B., & Wu, P. (2020). Spatiotemporal variations and developments of water footprints of pig feeding and pork production in China (2004–2013). *Agricu lture, Ecosystems and Environment, 297*, 106932.

Yang, L., Zhu, J., Huang, Z., & Geng, J. (2019). A systematic review of China's food safety management since reform and opening up. *Emerging Markets Finance and Trade, 55*(15), 3472–3489.

Yu, X., & Abler, D. (2014). Where have all the pigs gone? Inconsistencies in pork statistics in China. *China Economic Review, 30*, 469–484.

Yuan, Y., Si, Z., Zhong, T., Huang, X., & Crush, J. (2021). Revisiting China's supermarket revolution: Complementarity and co-evolution between traditional and modern food outlets. *World Development, 147*, 105631.

Zhou, J., Jin, Y., & Liang, Q. (2022). Effects of regulatory policy mixes on traceability adoption in wholesale markets: Food safety inspection and information disclosure. *Food Policy, 107*, 102218.

Zilberman, D., Hochman, G., Rajagopal, D., Sexton, S., & Timilsina, G. (2013). The impact of biofuels on commodity food prices: Assessment of findings. *American Journal of Agricultural Economics, 95*(2), 275–281.

Chapter 5
Blockchain-based Traceability and Demand for U.S. Beef in China

5.1 Introduction

Current price volatility and stagnant per capita consumption in the U.S. has increased the importance of identifying alternative markets for the beef industry to remain profitable. China's increasingly affluent consumer base of 1.4 billion people presents lucrative market opportunities for U.S. agricultural products. Beef, historically a less-sought-out protein, is now the fastest-growing meat consumed in China, surpassing the demand growth of more widely eaten meats like pork (Liu et al., 2009).

Beef consumption in China increased by 22.3%, from 6.45 million tons in 2011 to 7.89 million tons in 2017, with per capita consumption reaching 8.5 pounds in 2019 (Li et al., 2018; OECD, 2019). Due to the fast-growing Chinese demand and limited domestic production, China has emerged as the world's second-largest beef importer, with both the quantity and value of imports more than doubling since 2014. China imported approximately one million tons of beef in 2018, a 51% increase over its total beef imports in 2017, and a 160-fold increase since 2000 (UN Statistics Division, 2018). Despite the uncertainty surrounding trade with China created by the Trump administration's trade policies, the potentially profitable opportunities for American producers warrant the analysis of the Chinese beef market. In particular, information regarding Chinese consumer preferences for U.S. beef and strategies to capitalize on China's growing beef demand is needed given the absence of U.S. beef in the Chinese market for nearly 14 years. This study fills this void by providing an updated understanding of Chinese consumers' preference towards U.S. beef and assessing the potential for U.S. beef in the Chinese market.

How to cite this article: Lin W, Ortega DL, Ufer D, CaputoV, Awokuse T. Blockchain-based traceability and demand for U.S. beef in China. Appl Econ Perspect Policy. 2022;44: 253–272. 10.1002/aepp.13135

W. Lin, *Transforming China's Agri-Food System: Government-Market Synergy*, Resources, Environment and Agricultural Development,
https://doi.org/10.1007/978-981-95-7151-2_5

Along with growing beef demand, Chinese consumers have become increasingly discerning about the safety of food products (Ortega et al., 2011, 2012; Wang et al., 2008). Food safety issues arise, in large part, because of asymmetric information between consumers and producers, providing incentives for agents in the food industry to behave opportunistically (Akerlof, 1970; Hölmstrom, 1979; Ollinger & Bovay, 2020; Starbird, 2005). Traceability, which allows for a product to be traced back to the point of origin, has been a recognized tool tomitigate information asymmetry and improve food safety (Hobbs, 2004; Pouliot & Sumner, 2008). As such, investment in traceability systems could be an avenue for meeting Chinese consumers' food safety concerns and therefore capturing market share. However, in practice, conventional centralized traceability systems may not be technically reliable in ensuring food safety, as evidenced by recent and well-publicized food scares and data breaches (Lin et al., 2019a; Tian, 2017; Yiannas, 2018). Centralized traceability systems are managed and maintained by a centralized authority; if that institutional oversight is compromised, data tampering and information fraud may occur (Bodkhe et al., 2020).

Recent advancements in distributed ledger technology (discussed in more detail by Griffin et al., 2020, in this issue) provide a solution to this problem. Blockchain technology, a type of distributed ledger technology, is a decentralized digital ledger used to record information that has been approved by all connected parties, rather than an authority (Sander et al., 2018). Instead of being controlled by a single entity, blockchain-based food traceability systems enable transaction data along the supply chain to be shared and agreed upon by relevant stakeholders, promoting greater trust and transparency. Another distinguishing feature of blockchain is that data written on it cannot be altered without detection. This increases confidence in the data's authenticity and creates incentives for all stakeholders to ensure data accuracy (Yiannas, 2018). These features make food traceability systems based on blockchain technology more capable of advancing food safety by providing authentic information about the food products. Blockchain-based food traceability holds promise in addressing food safety concerns; however, its successful adoption will ultimately depend on acceptance in the consumer market.

To identify alternative markets for the U.S. beef industry, this study utilizes a hypothetical discrete choice experiment to investigate Chinese consumers'demand for U.S. beef and evaluate their acceptance of blockchain-based traceability. We classify Chinese consumers into different segments with consumer willingness to pay (WTP) for beef attributes and socio-demographic characteristics to inform marketing strategies that will enable the U.S. beef industry to capture market share. Our cluster analysis reveals that 63% of Chinese consumers have a negative valuation for U.S. beef relative to domestic beef, indicating a dire need for impactful marketing strategies if U.S. beef is to be successful in the Chinese market. The use of blockchain-based traceability may assist in these efforts, with consumers willing to pay an average premium of approximately $0.60 per pound for beef traced using blockchain technology compared to conventional digital traceability. Consumers who prefer U.S. beef and blockchain-based traceability are more likely to purchase beef online with large quantities per purchase.

This paper contributes to the literature in various ways. First, we provide an updated assessment of Chinese consumers'preference towards U.S. beef. To the best of our knowledge, we are the first academic research study to examine Chinese consumers' attitudes towards U.S. beef and their purchasing behaviors since the U.S. beef industry regained access to the Chinese market after a 14-year ban. This piece of information is timely and essential for the industry to design and implement effective marketing strategies in China. Second, although blockchain traceability can technically address Chinese consumers' food safety concerns, whether and to what extent they respond to the novel technology is unknown. Thus, we evaluate Chinese consumers' acceptance of this type of product traceability to inform the decision of whether to implement blockchain-based traceability in the U.S. beef industry and capitalize on China's growing beef demand. Previous efforts to implement an industry-wide traceability system and standards have proven difficult in the U.S., impeded in part by producer concerns over cost and technological reliability (Schroeder & Tonsor, 2012; Schulz & Tonsor, 2010). With many of the U.S.'s primary Chinese beef market competitors already having adopted traceability systems, identifying and implementing an appropriate traceability system is critical for the U.S. beef industry to remain internationally competitive. How food shoppers react to this nascent food safety practice is also of interest to a broader audience in the food sector. Like Walmart in the U.S. and Jingdong (JD) in China, food retailing giants have already initiated blockchain technology in food traceability systems tracing products such as mangoes, pork, and beef[1] (see Collart and Canales 2020 in this issue for a list of other food companies that have initiated blockchain-based traceability software). Lastly, we inform marketing strategies for the U.S. beef industry by characterizing consumer segments who place a significant price premium on U.S. beef and blockchain-based traceability.

The remainder of the paper is structured as follows. In the next section, we provide a brief overview of the Chinese beef import market and traceability, which are integral to our study design. Then, we give an overview of our methodology detailing the experimental design and econometric models. Next, we discuss the data, followed by a summary of the empirical results from the study. The last section contains a discussion of the implications of our findings for the beef industry and the marketing of beef products in China.

5.2 Background

5.2.1 China's Beef Import Dynamics

China's beef imports are expected to grow to 2.6 million tons in 2020 (USDA FAS, 2019). Figure 5.1 reports the market share of the main beef imports into mainland China since 2000.

[1] For a complete list of food products that could be tracked by blockchain-based traceability in Walmart, check the website https://www.hyperledger.org/learn/publications/walmart-case-study

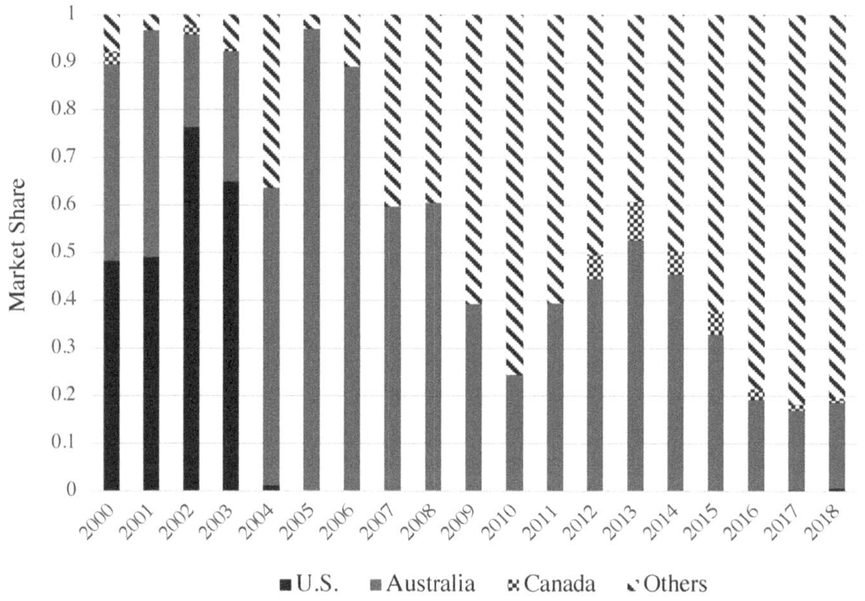

Fig. 5.1 Market share of main beef imports to mainland China, 2000–2018. Source: UN Comtrade

In recent years, Chinese beef imports have mainly originated from five countries: Uruguay, Brazil, Australia, Argentina, and New Zealand (UN Statistics Division, 2018). All beef exported to China is subject to the same traceability requirements (AQSIQ, 2020). Aside from Brazil, each of these countries already has a government-mandated traceability system in place, making all of their beef eligible for export to China under the traceability requirement (Gregg et al., 2018). However, none of these mandated systems require blockchain technology, and China's traceability requirement does not necessarily extend to the provision of that information to consumers.

Canada and Australia have historically been significant trade partners with China. Mao (2008) shows that Chinese tastes are similar to Western tastes for beef quality traits, with high intramuscular fat (marbling) being preferred, followed by tenderness and juiciness. Also, flavor ranks highly among the set of quality traits desired by food consumers. As such, U.S. beef production is well-situated to meet Chinese consumers' demands in terms of beef quality. This places the U.S. among Canada and Australia as primary competitors, given their ability to produce similarly high-quality beef with such desirable traits. Canada does so with a grain-based finishing system similar to the U.S. (Lim et al., 2013), while Australia's largely grass-based system has a world-renowned reputation for high-quality beef products (MLA, 2020). In recent years, the Australian beef industry is partly shifting towards a grain-fed system to cater to the Chinese market (USMEF, 2012). Though other competitors also produce and export high-quality beef, Canada and Australia are most closely positioned in the market with U.S. beef, a position demonstrated by the tendency for these three countries of origin to be highlighted on packaging and marketing materials, in contrast to the other major exporting countries (Hansen et al., 2017). Despite the competitiveness of U.S. beef in the Chinese market as a high-quality product, the American beef industry lost access to Chinese markets in 2003 and has not been able to capitalize on China's growing beef demand because of the negative impact of the bovine spongiform encephalopathy (BSE) outbreak and the ensuing ban (Greene, 2017).

Following the lifting of the 2003 ban on U.S. beef imports in 2017, stringent conditions were placed on beef imports by the Chinese government. According to the USDA-FSIS (2018), beef eligible for export to China must come from cattle less than 30 months of age and be traceable such that it can be proven that the cattle were either (1) born, raised, and slaughtered in the U.S.; (2) imported from Canada or Mexico, raised and slaughtered in the U.S.; or (3) imported from Canada or Mexico for direct slaughter in the U.S. Also, exporters are required to participate in the USDA Agricultural Marketing Service (AMS) Export Verification Program for Bovine for China. Such traceability requirements generally exceed current cattle production standards in the U.S. These additional conditions may require substantial investment by U.S. beef producers to capture Chinese market opportunities. The stringency of these traceability requirements reflects the Chinese government's efforts to ensure high food safety standards for its consumers and protect a population that has been subject to an unsafe and unreliable food system for decades which has only begun to be seriously addressed in the last 10 years (Ortega, 2018).

5.2.2 *Food Traceability System Based on Blockchain Technology*

Blockchain technology offers novelty in food traceability by, among other things, providing full access to authentic information on a product's journey from farm to retailer directly to the consumer. While previous or more conventional food traceability systems have largely maintained records for public safety officials in the event of outbreaks, the consistent and consolidated nature of the information contained in a blockchain allows consumers and any other interested parties to verify the origin and movement of a product through the supply chain. This is achieved by creating a unique tag or identifier beginning when the animal is still on the ranch, which then follows it through the entire processing system, being logged or scanned by supply chain members as it goes. The blockchain system can record and track the temperatures at which the product was held during transport, further improving its utility as a food safety guarantor. Information is then provided by using quick response (QR) codes on end product packaging or even restaurant menus, which the consumer can simply scan with a mobile device to receive a ledger of the product's movements at every step along the supply chain (Biele, 2019). This makes the technology and information extremely accessible to consumers. In addition to the logistics of the product's movement, current blockchain tracing efforts are even proposing means by which the consumer can receive information on the original producer, including the story of the ranch, messages directly from the rancher, and a greater understanding of the operation's safety and sustainability practices (Bandoim, 2019). These sorts of consumer accessibility trials are already underway for startup blockchain tracing firms such as HerdX in the U.S. and BeefLedger in Australia (Bandoim, 2019; Foth & McQueenie, 2019).

5.3 Methods

5.3.1 Experimental Design

To elicit consumer preferences for U.S. beef products and blockchain traceability, we administered an online choice experiment survey that presented a purchase decision for a beef plate (牛腩[2]) to Chinese consumers. Choice experiments remain by far the most used stated preference technique for various reasons: theoretical consistency, flexibility in allowing participants to opt-out of making a choice, and the ability to elicit trade-offs among a broad set of attributes (Hanley et al., 2001; Louviere et al., 2000, 2010; Lusk & Schroeder, 2004). This approach presents participants with multiple decision scenarios or tasks and asks them to select the product option or alternative that they most prefer. Each decision comprises two product alternatives, with experimentally designed attribute levels and a no purchase option.

In addition to whether the product was blockchain traceable, we also evaluate country of origin as one of the product attributes to capture consumers' perception of beef imports, which is a significant source of China's beef supply. Levels for country of origin include domestic (China) and three major beef trading partners of China (U.S., Australia, and Canada). Australia and Canada were chosen due to their similar positions in the Chinese market, offering high-quality imported beef. Additionally, Canadian, Australian, and U.S. beef tend to be the most common country-of-origin distinctions used in the Chinese beef market as these labels connote the presence of those traits desirable to the Western and Chinese palettes, namely marbling, tenderness, juiciness, and flavor. Furthermore, we explicitly assess preferences for tenderness, which is the most important eating quality trait for Chinese beef consumers (Mao et al., 2016). As income rises, consumers will increasingly demand both safety- and quality-assured beef products (Liu et al., 2009). Other studies have also emphasized the importance of tenderness in beef purchasing decisions (Caputo et al., 2016; Gao & Schroeder, 2009; Loureiro & Umberger, 2007; Lusk et al., 2001). Finally, product price is included as it is a significant determinant of product choice, and it can be used to derive a monetary

[2] Beef plate (牛腩) is a common cut of beef in China, mainly used for stewing or braising. The most similar American equivalent cut from the plate is short ribs.

Table 5.1 Attributes and attribute levels in the experiment

Attributes	Levels
Country of origin	Domestic U.S. Australia Canada
Blockchain traceability	Blockchain traceable Traceable
Price (RMB/500 g)	28, 43, 58, 73
Tenderness	Has tenderness claim Does not have tenderness claim

Fig. 5.2 An example of a choice task [Color figure can be viewed at wileyonlinelibrary.com]

evaluation of willingness to pay. Price levels used in the design range from 28 RMB/500 g to 73 RMB/500[3] g. These prices reflect the low-end and high-end market prices at the time of this study. Table 5.1 provides a summary of the selected product attributes and attribute levels.

A full factorial design with two alternatives would require 4096 ($4^{2\times2} \times 2^{2\times2}$) different choice tasks given our design specifications. To reduce the number of choice tasks shown to respondents during the survey, using the generators described by Street and Burgess (2007), we obtained a practical set of 16 choice sets, with a D-efficiency 95.82%. The 16 choice sets were then randomly grouped into two blocks (eight choice tasks per block), and the participants were randomly assigned into one of the two blocks. Each choice task includes two product alternatives with experimentally designed attribute levels and an opt-out option. The inclusion of an opt-out alternative better simulates a real market situation. The order in which the eight choice tasks were presented was randomly varied across subjects. A sample choice task is presented in Fig. 5.2.

Before the choice tasks, we also provide information about blockchain traceability to respondents (see Appendix). The information shown to respondents briefly describes blockchain technology, blockchain traceability, and its advantages over conventional digital traceability systems. Considering that blockchain technology is novel, and its application in food traceability systems is not commonly known, the provision of information helps respondents better evaluate product alternatives in the choice tasks.

[3] 1 US dollar = 6.96 RMB at the time of this study.

5.3.2 Technology Readiness Measurement

To measure consumers' propensity to embrace novel technologies such as blockchain traceability, we implement the Technology Readiness Index (TRI) scale originally developed by Parasuraman (2000). Technology readiness refers to a person's propensity to embrace and use new technologies for accomplishing goals in home life and at work (Parasuraman, 2000). Significant technological changes have occurred since the original version of the TRI was published about two decades ago. Therefore, we adopt an updated version, TRI 2.0, which is a reliable and effective tool for consumer segmentation (Parasuraman & Colby, 2015). The TRI score ranges from 1 to 5, with higher scores indicating higher levels of technology readiness. The index has been widely used to assess consumers' attitudes towards self-service technologies such as online shopping and mobile payment in developed and developing countries (Mummalaneni et al., 2016; Wiegard & Breitner, 2019; Zulkifly et al., 2016).

The index consists of four dimensions: optimism, innovativeness, discomfort, and insecurity. Optimism and innovativeness are drivers of technology adoption, measuring the degree to which individuals believe that technology can benefit their lives and the desire to try new technologies. In contrast, discomfort and insecurity are inhibitors. Discomfort assesses the extent to which respondents feel they lack control of and confidence with technology, and insecurity measures distrust and skepticism of technology.

To elicit the four dimensions of consumer technology orientation, the TRI 2.0 was adopted through a 16-item measurement scale. Each dimension has 4-item scale questions, and each question asks respondents to evaluate an attitude statement about technology using a Likert-type scale from 1 (strongly disagree) to 5 (strongly agree). For example, a statement that measures the dimension of optimism is "New technologies contribute to a better quality of life." The order of the 16 statements' presentation was randomized following Parasuraman and Colby (2015). We calculated a respondent's score of each dimension by taking the mean value of the responses to the four items measuring that dimension. The overall TRI score is the mean score on the four dimensions after reverse coding the scores on discomfort and insecurity.

5.3.3 Econometric Model and Willingness-To-Pay

An indirect utility function based on Lancaster's theory of consumer demand was specified (Lancaster, 1966) to model consumers' beef purchasing decisions. Following random utility theory (McFadden, 1974), choice experiments rely on the assumption that the utility of individual n choosing alternative j in choice situation t can be expressed as:

$$U_{njt} = V_{njt} + \varepsilon_{njt} \tag{5.1}$$

where U_{njt} denotes the utility consumer n obtains from the j_{th} alternative in choice scenariot.

Vnjt is the representative portion of the utility function, which depends on the experimentally designed product attributes for alternative j, and ε_{njt} is the stochastic and unobservable (to researchers) component.

We estimate a mixed logit model with utilities specified in WTP space with correlated parameters. Models specified in WTP space relax the assumption of a fixed price coefficient (Scarpa et al., 2008), and the estimated coefficients can directly be interpreted as marginal WTP values (Scarpa & Willis, 2010). Consumers' preferences for a given attribute are likely to be correlated with their preferences for another attribute (Hess & Train, 2017). In our case, the preference for traceability may correlate with the desire to buy imported beef products. As such, we impose correlations among taste coefficients when estimating our model. The utility function in WTP space can be described as:

$$U_{njt} = \theta_n \begin{pmatrix} -PRICE_{njt} + \beta_{n1} Block_{njt} + \beta_{n2} Tender_{njt} + \beta_{n3} USA_{njt} \\ +\beta_{n4} CAN_{njt} + \beta_{n5} AUS_{njt} + ASC \end{pmatrix} + \varepsilon_{njt} \tag{5.2}$$

where θn is a random positive scalar representing the *price/scale* parameter; *PRICEnjt* is a continuous variable populated with the four price levels in the design; $\text{Block}_{\text{njt}}$ and $\text{Tender}_{\text{njt}}$ are dummy variables for the blockchain traceability and tenderness attributes; *USAnjt*, *CANnjt* and AUS_{njt} are also dummy variables, and they take a value of 1 when the product originates from the U.S., Canada, or Australia, respectively, and 0 otherwise; ASC is the alternative specific con- stant of the no-purchase option; the βs are the random coefficients of the estimated WTP values; ε_{njt} is the random error term, which follows a Type I Extreme Value distribution.

5.3.4 Market Segmentation and Cluster Analysis

To assess the Chinese market potential for U.S. beef and inform business decisions, we conduct segmentation analysis through clustering. Cluster analysis is a statistical method that builds homogeneous groups out of a heterogeneous population (Hair et al., 1998) by sorting on a set of multivariate data. After sorting, the observations within each cluster should have similar characteristics, while the clusters themselves are dissimilar. Clustering techniques have been widely used for segmentation analyses in different fields such as biology, psychology, marketing, and economics.

We use a two-stage clustering method following Petrovici and Gorton (2005) and Van den Broeck et al. (2017). First, Ward's clustering method is applied to determine the optimal number of clusters, maximizing heterogeneity across clusters and minimizing heterogeneity within clusters. Ward's method is a hierarchical clustering procedure where the squared Euclidean distance between points is minimized. The second step is K-means cluster analysis to correct possible misclassification of observations at the boundaries between clusters (Jansen et al., 2006). As one of the most popular and efficient clustering techniques, the K-means method organizes similar groups by minimizing the mean squared distance from each point to its nearest center (Jain, 2010). For our study, the set of variables used in this cluster analysis are Chinese consumers' WTP values for U.S. beef and blockchain traceability, TRI scores, beef consumption and purchasing habits, and demographics. To better understand which aspects characterize the different groups, statistical tests (e.g., F-test or Chi-square test) are used to determine significant differences invariables between clusters.

5.4 Data

A sample of urban Chinese consumers was recruited by Qualtrics, a professional market research company, in November 2018. All respondents were excluded a priori if they were younger than 18 years of age, were not the primary household grocery shopper, or had not purchased beef in the last month. A total of 383 valid observations were collected. Responses were geographically diverse, being spread across different regions of China.[4] Nearly 60% of respondents were female, had an average age of 35 years, and reported having four to five people in their households (Table 5.2). The majority of the study participants had a college degree, a monthly household income of more than RMB 13,000. The average respondent purchased beef at least once a week in a traditional retail channel (wet market or domestic supermarket). Compared to Ortega et al. (2016), who studied beef consumers in Beijing, there is a moderate over-representation of female and younger respondents in our sample. This is expected as we required our respondents to be primary household grocery shoppers, and in China, women are mainly responsible for household food shopping and preparation. Our sample is comparatively young as these individuals are usually more open and willing to participate in online surveys. This might be considered an advantage when assessing potential markets (Sanjuán-López & Resano-Ezcaray, 2020). Descriptive statistics of consumer sociodemographics, beef purchasing and consumption habits, and blockchain purchasing information are presented in Table 5.2. Chinese consumers stated a preference for domestic beef, followed by beef from Australia, Canada, and the U.S. This descriptive ranking reflects the absence of U.S. beef for almost 14 years due to the beef import ban after the BSE disease outbreak. Knowledge was elicited using a single

[4]The regional distribution of our sample generally corresponds to the distribution of the urban population in China, with North 31% (our sample) vs. 22% (the population), East 38% vs. 32%, Central 5% vs. 14%, South 15% vs. 18%, and West 10% vs. 14% (National Bureau of Statistics of China 2019), with slightly more respondents in the North, and fewer from the central provinces.

Table 5.2 Descriptive statistics

Variables	Years	Sample Data
Demographics	%	
Age		35.20 (8.56)
Female		58.22
Household income	%	
	Low	5.48
	Medium	52.48
	High	42.04
College	%	84.86
Household size	Persons	4.49 (1.29)
Region of residence	%	
	North	30.96
	Central	5.67
	East	38.60
	South	15.02
	West	9.75
Purchasing and consumption habits		
Beef purchase frequency	%	
	Daily	3.13
	Every other day	6.27
	2-3 times per week	39.95
	Weekly or less	50.65
Beef purchase location	%	
	Wet market	31.07
	Domestic supermarket	38.64
	International supermarket	18.54
	Online store	11.75
Most preferred origin	%	
	China	43.34
	U.S.	15.93
	Canada	16.45
	Australia	24.28
Heard about blockchain technology	%	85.9
Bought blockchain-traced products	%	44.15
Blockchain traceability knowledge		5.38 (2.16)
Beef quantity per purchase	Grams	808.70 (391.48)
Beef weekly consumption	%	
	Low	30.03
	Medium	60.83
	High	9.14
No. of individuals		383

Table 5.3 Technology Readiness Index (TRI) statistics

	Our sample (2018)	U.S. sample (2012)	Taiwan sample (2016)
Optimism	4.27	3.75	3.66
Innovativeness	3.81	3.02	3.28
Discomfort	2.89	3.09	2.40
Insecurity	3.09	3.58	2.89
Overall TRI	3.51	3.02	N/A

Note: U.S. and Taiwan sample statistics are from Parasuraman and Colby (2015) and Chen and Lin (2018), respectively. Chen and Lin (2018) used a seven-point scale; thus, the values in Table 5.3 for the Taiwan sample are converted to a four-point scale for comparison purposes

self-reported question, "How knowledgeable would you say you are about blockchain traceability?" on a Likert-type scale from 1 (not at all knowledgeable) to 9 (extremely knowledgeable). Our sample is knowledgeable about blockchain traceability to an extent, with an average self-reported score of 5.38. Regarding purchase experience, approximately 45% of consumers have purchased products with blockchain traceability, though the majority (86%) of our respondents claimed that they had heard about blockchain technology. This corresponds to the high TRI scores found in our sample. In Table 5.3, we report the calculated means for TRI and its four dimensions and values obtained from relevant studies for comparison purposes (Table 5.3). TRI's overall value is 3.51, showing that consumers have a relatively strong propensity to embrace novel technologies. Specifically, optimism scored highest (4.27) among the four TRI dimensions, while discomfort scored lowest (2.89), which indicates that Chinese consumers have a very positive view of technology and believe that technology offers people increased control, flexibility, and efficiency in their lives. Compared with the U.S., Chinese consumers are more optimistic and innovative, with a higher level of technology readiness. U.S. respondents are generally more skeptical and distrustful of technology's ability to work properly, often feeling over-whelmed by it (Meng et al., 2009). Interestingly, the story was different 10 years ago—U.S. consumers were more likely to embrace new technologies than Chinese consumers in terms of overall TRI and its four dimensions (Hmielowski et al., 2019; Meng et al., 2009; Wang et al., 2017).

We generate heat maps with follow-up questions to the choice experiment asking respondents to indicate the level of importance that they assigned to various product pack-aging areas (Fig. 5.3). The left and right panels of Fig. 5.3 are identical in terms of beef package size, price, tenderness, and blockchain traceability, except that the left package denotes domestic beef while the right one originates from the U.S. Consumers were asked to evaluate the panels separately. In both the packages, 10% of consumers indicated the country of origin as the most important factor when considering beef purchase. Our data reveals that consumers consider tenderness (34%) and blockchain traceability (31%) as the most important factors in their purchasing decisions. In the two scenarios, approximately 10% of respondents note price to be the driving force in beef purchases. An important finding is that relative to domestic beef, fewer consumers indicated price as being the dominant factor (18% vs. 12%), implying that consumers may be less sensitive to costs when buying

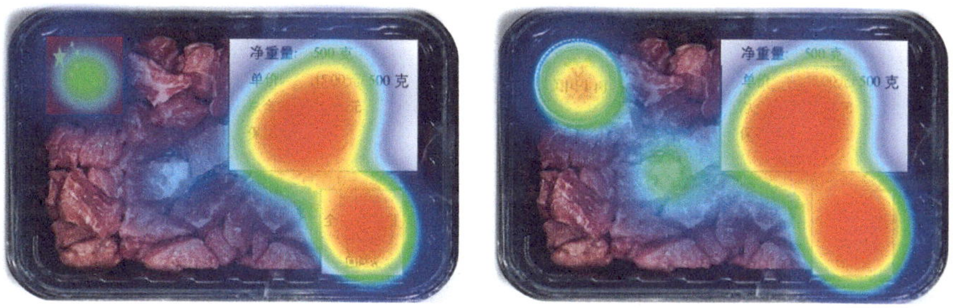

Fig. 5.3 Heat map analysis. The left panel is domestic (Chinese) beef, and the right is imported U.S. beef [Color figure can be viewed at wileyonlinelibrary.com]

the U.S. beef products, which implies promising profit opportunities for the U.S. beef industry.

5.5 Results

Estimates from the mixed logit model in WTP space with correlated parameters are reported in Table 5.4. Mixed logit models allow for random taste, but such power significantly relies on a prior distributional assumption about the preferences (Balcombe et al., 2009). As such, we test various distributions before specifying normally distributed parameters for blockchain traceability, tenderness, and country of origin coefficients, and one-sided triangular distribution for the scale/price coefficient.

The estimation of Eq. (5.2) (Table 5.4) indicates strong heterogeneity in consumer preferences for blockchain traceability and country of origin as the estimated standard deviations for these attributes differ significantly from zero. In terms of country of origin, Australian beef received the highest price premium from consumers. On average, Chinese consumers are willing to pay $1.11 per pound to "upgrade" domestic beef to Australian beef. This finding deviates from the descriptive rank analysis in which consumers preferred domestic products most.[5] Still, it is consistent with other studies that found that Chinese beef shoppers are willing to pay more for Australian beef products over U.S. or domestic beef (Ortega et al., 2016). Our estimation results indicate that consumers, in general, value U.S. and Canadian beef in a way similar to domestic beef. While the mean point estimate for U.S. beef is not statistically significant, there is strong preference heterogeneity around consumer preference for U.S. beef (see Fig. 5.4). Consumer valuation for U.S. beef ranges

[5] This result is not surprising, as research has shown that the descriptive rank question and choice experiment yield different choice outcomes (Caparros et al., 2008; Merino-Castello, 2003). Adamowicz et al. (1994) empha- size results from choice experiments since they are closer to real-market decisions.

Table 5.4 Willingness to pay results ($/lb. equivalent)

Variables	Mean	SD
Blockchain	0.63**	1.31***
	(0.31)	(0.49)
Tender	0.32	1.23
	(0.28)	(0.96)
U.S.	−0.42	6.54***
	(0.60)	(0.81)
Australia	1.11**	4.66***
	(0.49)	(1.19)
Canada	0.44	4.83**
	(0.51)	(2.09)
ASC	−3.78***	
Model statistics		
No. of parameters	22	
No. of choices	3064	
No. of individuals	383	
Log-likelihood	−2492	
AIC/N	1.64	

Note: Asterisks ***, and ** indicate significance at the 0.01, and 0.05 levels. Standard errors are in parentheses. Models were estimated in local currency and quantity units. The exchange rate at the time of this study was 1 US dollar = 6.96 RMB

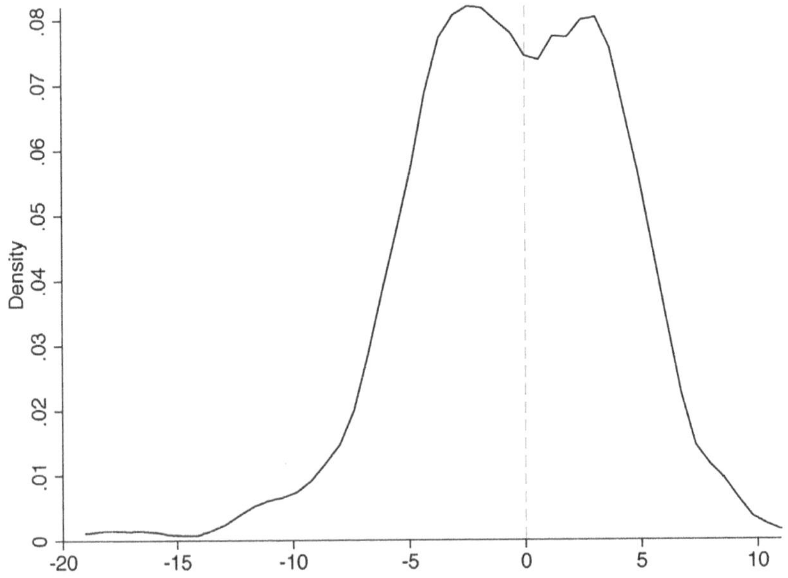

Fig. 5.4 WTP distribution of U.S. beef, $/lb. equivalent

from −$18 to $10 per pound. Slightly over half of the respondents (54%) require compensation before being indifferent between U.S. beef and domestic beef, and, conversely, the remaining 46% are willing to pay more for U.S. beef. In general, our current results are consistent with the finding of Ortega et al. (2016) that Chinese consumers prefer Australian beef over U.S. beef. This is likely due to the proliferation of Australian beef in China after the U.S. BSE outbreak, which led to the ban of U.S. beef in China from 2003 to 2017. Moreover, the recent tariff dispute between the U.S. and China has resulted in higher U.S. meat prices relative to competitors. Our results indicate that despite capturing consumers' attention, tenderness is not an important driver of beef purchases in China (insignificant mean and standard deviation estimates).

We find that blockchain-based traceability exhibits a statistically significant influence on consumers' overall utility. Consumers are willing to pay approximately $0.60 per pound for blockchain traceable beef compared to beef supported with a regular digital traceability system, which is standard for imported meat products. By quantifying consumer preference and valuation for blockchain traceability, we provide a baseline statistic that can be used for market feasibility and investments in blockchain traceability along Chinese meat supply chains. We also find a significant positive correlation (0.89) between individual WTPs for U.S. beef and blockchain-based traceability. Individuals who favor U.S. beef are willing to pay a high premium for blockchain traceability, and vice versa. The complementarity between U.S. beef and blockchain traceability reveals that adopting blockchain traceability would benefit the U.S. beef industry by generating more revenues from exporting beef to China.

We further employ cluster analysis to inform market segmentation for U.S. and blockchain traceable beef. Table 5.5 shows the differences in WTPs, demographics, and beef purchasing characteristics for three consumer segments. The largest cluster, accounting for 38% of respondents, is referred to as "Blockchain curious" as they have a modest willingness to pay for blockchain traceability ($0.52 per pound). While not willing to pay a premium for U.S. beef, consumers in this class tend to purchase beef more from emerging retailers such as online stores and have some blockchain purchasing experience and knowledge. Roughly 25% of the sample belongs to the cluster whom we label as "traditionalists." These consumers have a negative valuation for both blockchain traceability and U.S. beef, preferring domestic products. Compared to other segments, "traditionalists" have the lowest income, purchase the lowest amounts of beef during each grocery shopping trip, and lack knowledge or experience about blockchain-based trace-ability. In contrast, "blockchain enthusiasts" (37% of the sample) are willing to pay a significant premium for blockchain traceability and U.S. beef. Their average WTP is almost $4.00 per pound for beef originating from the U.S. and $1.39 per pound for blockchain-traced beef, which implies the greatest market potential for U.S. beef. This segment has a fairly high level of technology readiness, household income, and subjective knowledge regarding blockchain traceability. Consumers in this group are also more educated, purchase beef in larger quantities more frequently and patronize online retailers. This implies that consumers who buy beef online may be target customers for

Table 5.5 Clustering Results

	Cluster 1	Cluster 2	Cluster 3	
Variables	"Blockchain Curious"	"Blockchain Enthusiasts"	"Traditionalist"	Δp-value
WTP Blockchain ($/lb. equivalent)	0.52	1.39	−0.39	0.05
WTP US ($/lb. equivalent)	−1.13	3.90	−6.00	0.05
TRI	3.48	3.61	3.47	0.24
Age	35	36	35	0.08
Female (%)	63	57	52	0.18
College (%)	83	90	81	0.27
Household income	7.98	8.85	7.52	0.33
Beef quantity per purchase (g)	806	837	768	0.09
Bought beef weekly (%)	28	24	31	0.51
Bought beef from online store (%)	10	15	9	0.02
Bought Blockchain products (%)	50	50	34	0.03
Blockchain subjective knowledge	5.43	5.69	4.82	0.06
Clusters composition No. of individuals Market share	145 38%	143 37%	95 25%	

Note: WTP Blockchain (RMB/500 g) and WTP US (RMB/500 g) are average willingness to pay values for 500 g of blockchain traceable beef and U.S. beef, respectively. Household income was included as a continuous variable in the analysis. For reference, a value of 7 denotes that monthly income falls in the range of RMB 13,000–14,999, a value of 8 RMB 15,000–16,999, and a value of 9 RMB 17,000–18,999

U.S. and blockchain traceable beef products. This parallels findings from previous research that has identified e-commerce as a promising retail channel for premium meat products in China (Lin et al., 2019b).

5.6 Implications and Conclusion

In this paper, we examine how much value Chinese consumers place on blockchain-based traceability in their demand for domestic and imported (U.S., Canada, Australia) beef products using a discrete choice experiment. We further classify consumers into different market clusters based on their valuations for beef products and sociodemographic characteristics. Our segmentation analysis suggests that 63% of Chinese consumers have a negative valuation for U.S. beef relative to domestic beef, indicating a dire need for impactful marketing strategies if U.S. beef is to be successful in the Chinese market. The use of blockchain-based traceability may assist in these efforts, given that blockchain traceability is a significant driver of beef purchasing decisions, with consumers willing to pay an average premium of $0.63 per pound compared to regular digital traceability.

Data from our heat map illustrates that 31% of consumers in our sample consider blockchain-based traceability the most important factor when buying beef, and our market segmentation analysis suggests that there is a group of respondents (37%) who would pay significant premiums for both U.S. beef and blockchain traceable beef products. This implies promising opportunities for the U.S. beef industry and blockchain traceability investors, given the current traceability requirements for exporting U.S. beef to China. A complementary relationship between U.S. beef and blockchain-based traceability provides support for the use of blockchains by the U.S. beef industry to gain market share in China. Our market segmentation analysis also finds that consumers who are willing to pay a premium on U.S. beef consistently prefer blockchain traceability. Thus, if the U.S. beef industry is to successfully market their product in China, the employment of blockchains may significantly improve their ability to reach the most receptive consumers.

Moreover, we find that consumers who prefer these two attributes are more likely to purchase beef online. Imported meat makes up a considerable portion of online meat sales, with imports comprising nearly a third of the meat sold through JD.com in 2016 (Patton, 2017). This result is encouraging for U.S. beef exporters as Chinese online grocery sales continue to grow. Since online sales are already a major outlet for imported beef, and online beef purchasers tend to view U.S. beef more favorably, then a focus on online beef sales could increase the ease with which U.S. beef exporters may be able to capture market share in the Chinese market. Additionally, these online purchases tend to occur in relatively large quantities per purchase, which has implications for how U.S. beef exporters may target potential customers. To gain more exposure and compete directly with Australian products, the U.S. beef industry could increase its marketing activities, for example hosting American barbecue day with large retailers in China. U.S. beef products could also benefit from being featured in China's giant e-commerce platforms, especially during the Chinese New Year. Other studies have also found that product ratings and the number of reviews are important determinants of Chinese online shoppers' product choices (Lin et al., 2019b). These determinants may have consequences for the U.S. beef industry entering the online grocery market in China. It would be beneficial for U.S. beef companies to direct marketing efforts to increase product ratings and incentivize consumers to share their experiences on online platforms. To this end, developing a base of consumer reviews soon after the product launch would provide consumers with valuable information and help increase market share.

The results of this study further inform the U.S. beef industry as they increase promotional efforts following a nearly 14-year trade ban in China by contextualizing their market potential relative to major competitors. Our results provide important information on Chinese consumers' beef preferences for country of origin and indicate that Chinese consumers prefer Australian over domestic and North American beef. With some Australian beef exports already employing blockchain technology (Smith, 2017) and Chinese consumers having an established preference for Australian beef, U.S. beef exporters must carefully position themselves alongside their competitors to effectively win a larger market share. Adopting blockchain traceability technology may be imperative to this positioning.

We do not exclude the possibility that our results may be subject to hypothetical bias. Although our survey does not explicitly include hypothetical bias mitigation methods, we carefully select our respondents to be experienced food purchasers and also provide blockchain information to help respondents better evaluate their choices. The literature has suggested that hypothetical bias mitigation techniques appear to be ineffective and redundant among experienced participants or when product information is provided (Fifer et al., 2014; List, 2001), in part because hypothetical bias is less likely to exist in these contexts. We also note that, while our sample composition is comparable to other studies', our sample size is insufficient to explore regional heterogeneity. Additional work focused on regional preferences for beef products is recommended to develop region-specific positioning strategies. Our results provide evidence that a suitable market for blockchain traceable U.S. beef exists in China; however, future research is needed to understand American producers' attitudes towards this particular market opportunity. Traceability efforts have historically been met with some resistance in the U.S. (Schroeder & Tonsor, 2012; Schulz & Tonsor, 2010). Future studies may aim to investigate whether blockchains will be viewed any differently, particularly in the context of its potential to enhance accessibility to the Chinese food market. Additionally, the implications of blockchain-based traceability adoption in the U.S. for American consumers merits investigation. Blockchain traceability adoption in the U.S. may be especially important as sufficient interest from American consumers may safeguard against losses in an unstable trade environment with China.

Acknowledgments This work was supported in part by the USDA National Institute of Food and Agriculture, Hatch project 04189, and Michigan State University's AgBioResearch. The authors acknowledge comments and suggestions from two anonymous reviewers.

Appendix A Information Presented to Respondents Before Choice Tasks

Before evaluating the choice tasks, please read the information regarding blockchain food traceability.

Blockchain is a decentralized shared, programmable, cryptographically secure, and therefore trusted ledger which no single user controls and which can be inspected by anyone. Each record on a blockchain is agreed upon by all members of the network, and then it becomes a permanent record; it cannot be altered (World Economic Forum).

The food industry has taken advantage of Blockchain technology to trace food products in its supply chain. Information is digitally connected to a food product and entered into the blockchain at every step of its journey—from farm gate to retail store. Blockchain traceability is a novel tool compared to traditional digital traceability systems. The use of blockchain traceability would provide real-time product information, enhance transparency and trust as well as deter food fraud in the food system.

References

Adamowicz, W., Louviere, J., & Williams, M. (1994). Combining revealed and stated preference methods for valuing environmental amenities. *Journal of Environmental Economics and Management, 26*(3), 271–292.

Akerlof, G. A. (1970). The market for 'lemons': Quality uncertainty and the market mechanism. *Quarterly Journal of Economics, 84*(3), 488–500.

AQSIQ. (2020). *Meat registration application*. Accessed July 6, 2020. https://www.aqsiq.net/application/meat-registration

Balcombe, K., Chalak, A., & Fraser, I. (2009). Model selection for the mixed logit with bayesian estimation. *Journal of Environmental Economics and Management, 57*(2), 226–237.

Bandoim, L. (2019). Can blockchain and chip technology improve beef sourcing transparency? *Forbes*. Accessed July 8, 2020. https://www.forbes.com/sites/lanabandoim/2019/04/30/can-blockchain-and-chip-technology-improve-beef-sourcing-transparency/#441ecf473284

Biele, C. (2019). *UPS and HerdX Deliver blockchain-verified beef from U.S. to Japan*. UPS Press Release, November 11, 2019. Accessed July 8, 2020. https://pressroom.ups.com/pressroom/ContentDetailsViewer. page?ConceptType=PressReleases&id=1573245679338-340&WT.mc_id=UPSCOM_NEWSANDINFO_HERDX_PRESSRELEASE_111119

Bodkhe, U., Tanwar, S., Parekh, K., Khanpara, P., Tyagi, S., Kumar, N., & Alazab, M. (2020). Blockchain for industry 4.0: A comprehensive review. *IEEE Access, 8*, 79764–79800.

Caparros, A., Oviedo, J. L., & Campos, P. (2008). Would you choose your preferred option? Comparing choice and recoded ranking experiments. *American Journal of Agricultural Economics, 90*(3), 843–855.

Caputo, V., Scarpa, R., & Nayga, R. M. (2016). Cue versus independent food attributes: The effect of adding attributes in choice experiments. *European Review of Agricultural Economics, 44*(2), 211–230.

Chen, M. F., & Lin, N. P. (2018). Incorporation of health consciousness into the technology readiness and acceptance model to predict app download and usage intentions. *Internet Research, 28*(2), 351–373.

Collart, A. J., & Canales, E. (2020). How might broad adoption of blockchain-based traceability impact the U.S. fresh produce supply chain? Forthcoming in *Applied Economic Perspectives and Policy*.

Fifer, S., Rose, J., & Greaves, S. (2014). Hypothetical bias in stated choice experiments: Is it a problem? And if so, how do we deal with it? *Transportation Research Part A: Policy and Practice, 61*, 164–177.

Foth, M., & McQueenie, J. (2019). Creatives in the country? Blockchain and agtech can create unexpected jobs in regional Australia. *The Conversation*, June: 1–5.

Gao, Z., & Schroeder, T. C. (2009). Effects of label information on consumer willingness-to-pay for food attributes. *American Journal of Agricultural Economics, 91*(3), 795–809.

Greene, J. L. (2017). *U.S. beef: It's what's for China*. Congressional Research Report no. IN10724. U.S. Foreign Agricultural Service. July 22, 2017. Accessed October 4, 2019. https://fas.org/sgp/crs/row/IN10724.pdf

Gregg, D., Juday, D., & Herrington, M. (2018). *Comprehensive feasibility study: U.S. beef cattle identification and traceability systems*. World Perspectives, Inc.

Griffin, T. W., Harris, K. D., Ward, J. K., Goeringer, P., & Richard, J. A. (2020). Three digital agriculture problems in cotton solved by distributed ledger technology. Forthcoming, *Applied Economic Perspectives and Policy*.

Hair, J. F., Black, W. C., Babin, B. J., Anderson, R. E., & Tatham, R. L. (1998). *Multivariate data analysis*. Prentice Hall.

Hanley, N., Mourato, S., & Wright, R. E. (2001). Choice modelling approaches: A superior alternative for environmental valuation? *Journal of Economic Surveys, 15*(3), 435–462.

Hansen, J., Marchant, M. A., Tuan, F., & Somwaru, A. (2017). US agricultural exports to China increased rapidly making China the number one market. *Choices, 32*(2), 1–6.

Hess, S., & Train, K. (2017). Correlation and scale in mixed logit models. *Journal of Choice Modelling, 23*, 1–8.

Hmielowski, J. D., Boyd, A. D., Harvey, G., & Joo, J. (2019). The social dimensions of smart meters in the United States: Demographics, privacy, and technology readiness. *Energy Research and Social Science, 55*, 189–197.

Hobbs, J. E. (2004). Information asymmetry and the role of traceability systems. *Agribusiness, 20*(4), 397–415.

Hölmstrom, B. (1979). Moral hazard and observability. *The Bell Journal of Economics, 10*(1), 74–91.

Jain, A. K. (2010). Data clustering: 50 years beyond K-means. *Pattern Recognition Letters, 31*(8), 651–666.

Jansen, H. G., Pender, J., Damon, A., Wielemaker, W., & Schipper, R. (2006). Policies for sustainable development in the hillside areas of honduras: A quantitative livelihoods approach. *Agricultural Economics, 34*(2), 141–153.

Lancaster, K. J. (1966). A new approach to consumer theory. *Journal of Political Economy, 74*(2), 132–157.

Li, X. Z., Yan, C. G., Sen, L., & Zan. (2018). Current situation and future prospects for beef production in China—A review. *Asian-Australasian Journal of Animal Sciences, 31*(7), 984.

Lim, K. H., Wuyang, H., Maynard, L. J., & Goddard, E. (2013). US consumers' preference and willingness to pay for country-of-origin-labeled BeefSteak and food safety enhancements. *Canadian Journal of Agricultural Economics/Revue Canadienne d'agroeconomie, 61*(1), 93–118.

Lin, Q., Wang, H., Pei, X., & Wang, J. (2019a). Food safety traceability system based on blockchain and EPCIS. *IEEE Access, 7*, 20698–20707.

Lin, W., Ortega, D. L., & Caputo, V. (2019b). Are ex-ante hypothetical bias calibration methods context dependent? Evidence from online food shoppers in China. *Journal of Consumer Affairs, 53*(2), 520–544.

List, J. A. (2001). Do explicit warnings eliminate the hypothetical bias in elicitation procedures? Evidence from field auctions for sportscards. *American Economic Review, 91*(5), 1498–1507.

Liu, H., Parton, K. A., Zhou, Z. Y., & Cox, R. (2009). At-home meat consumption in China: An empirical study. *Australian Journal of Agricultural and Resource Economics, 53*(4), 485–501.
Loureiro, M. L., & Umberger, W. J. (2007). A choice experiment model for beef: What US consumer responses tell us about relative preferences for food safety, country-of-origin labeling and traceability. *Food Policy, 32*(4), 496–514.
Louviere, J. J., Hensher, D. A., & Swait, J. D. (2000). *Stated choice methods: Analysis and applications*. Cambridge University Press.
Louviere, J. J., Flynn, T. N., & Carson, R. T. (2010). Discrete choice experiments are not conjoint analysis. *Journal of Choice Modelling, 3*(3), 57–72.
Lusk, J. L., & Schroeder, T. C. (2004). Are choice experiments incentive compatible? A test with quality differentiated BeefSteaks. *American Journal of Agricultural Economics, 86*(2), 467–482.
Lusk, J. L., Marsh, T. L., Schroeder, T. C., & Fox, J. A. (2001). Wholesale demand for USDA quality graded boxed beef and effects of seasonality. *Journal of Agricultural and Resource Economics, 26*, 91–106.
Mao, Y. (2008). *Study on palatability assurance critical control point of beef*. Master's thesis, Shandong Agricultural University. http://d.wanfangdata.com.cn/Thesis_Y1374525.aspx. Accessed August 12, 2019.
Mao, Y., Hopkins, D. L., Zhang, Y., & Luo, X. (2016). Consumption patterns and consumer attitudes to beef and sheep meat in China. *American Journal of Food and Nutrition, 4*(2), 30–39.
McFadden, D. (1974). *Conditional logit analysis of qualitative choice behavior*. Academic.
Meng, J., Elliott, K. M., & Hall, M. C. (2009). Technology readiness index (TRI): Assessing cross-cultural validity. *Journal of International Consumer Marketing, 22*(1), 19–31.
Merino-Castello, A. (2003). *Eliciting consumers preferences using stated preference discrete choice models: Contingent ranking versus choice experiment*. Economics and Business Working Paper 705, Universitat Pompeu Fabra.
MLA (Meat & Livestock Australia). (2020). *Australia's beef trade with China*. Accessed July 7, 2020. https://www.mla.com.au/news-and-events/industry-news/australias-beef-trade-with-china/#
Mummalaneni, V., Meng, J., & Elliott, K. M. (2016). Consumer technology readiness and e-service quality in e-tailing: What is the impact on predicting online purchasing? *Journal of Internet Commerce, 15*(4), 311–331.
OECD. (2019). *Meat consumption (Indicator)*. Accessed August 12, 2019. https://doi.org/10.1787/fa290fd0-en.
Ollinger, M., & Bovay, J. (2020). Producer response to public disclosure of food-safety information. *American Journal of Agricultural Economics, 102*(1), 186–201.
Ortega, D. L. (2018). *Testimony before the U.S. China Economic Security Review Commission: Hearing on 'China's agricultural policies: Trade, investment, safety, and innovation'*. April 26, 2018. Accessed October 4, 2019. https://www.uscc.gov/sites/default/files/Ortega%20Testimony%204-13-18.pdf
Ortega, D. L., Holly Wang, H., Laping, W., & Olynk, N. J. (2011). Modeling heterogeneity in consumer preferences for select food safety attributes in China. *Food Policy, 36*(2), 318–324.
Ortega, D. L., Holly Wang, H., Olynk, N. J., Laping, W., & Bai, J. (2012). Chinese consumers' demand for food safety attributes: A push for government and industry regulations. *American Journal of Agricultural Economics, 94*(2), 489–495.
Ortega, D. L., Hong, S. J., Holly Wang, H., & Laping, W. (2016). Emerging markets for imported beef in China: Results from a consumer choice experiment in Beijing. *Meat Science, 121*, 317–323.
Parasuraman, A. (2000). Technology readiness index (TRI) a multiple-item scale to measure readiness to embrace new technologies. *Journal of Service Research, 2*(4), 307–320.
Parasuraman, A., & Colby, C. L. (2015). An updated and streamlined technology readiness index: TRI 2.0. *Journal of Service Research, 18*(1), 59–74.

Patton, D. (2017). *Smithfield food foes online to sell U.S. Pork in China*. Reuters (Beijing), October 24. Accessed December 15, 2020. https://www.reuters.com/article/us-china-smithfield-pork/smithfield-foods-goes-online-to-sell-u-s-pork-in-china-idUSKBN1CU07B

Petrovici, D. A., & Gorton, M. (2005). An evaluation of the importance of subsistence food production for assessments of poverty and policy targeting: Evidence from Romania. *Food Policy, 30*(2), 205–223.

Pouliot, S., & Sumner, D. A. (2008). Traceability, liability, and incentives for food safety and quality. *American Journal of Agricultural Economics, 90*(1), 15–27.

Sander, F., Semeijn, J., & Mahr, D. (2018). The acceptance of blockchain technology in meat traceability and transparency. *British Food Journal, 120*(9), 2066–2079.

Sanjuán-López, A. I., & Resano-Ezcaray, H. (2020). Labels for a local food speciality product: The case of saffron. *Journal of Agricultural Economics, 71*, 778–797.

Scarpa, R., & Willis, K. (2010). Willingness-to-pay for renewable energy: Primary and discretionary choice of british households' for micro-generation technologies. *Energy Economics, 32*(1), 129–136.

Scarpa, R., Thiene, M., & Train, K. (2008). Utility in willingness to pay space: A tool to address confounding random scale effects in destination choice to the alps. *American Journal of Agricultural Economics, 90*(4), 994–1010.

Schroeder, T. C., & Tonsor, G. T. (2012). International cattle ID and traceability: Competitive implications for the US. *Food Policy, 37*(1), 31–40.

Schulz, L. L., & Tonsor, G. T. (2010). Cow-calf producer preferences for voluntary traceability systems. *Journal of Agricultural Economics, 61*(1), 138–162.

Smith, G. (2017). Blockchain project sets out to defend Australia's world-class beef. *New Food*, December 13. Accessed August 1, 2020. https://www.newfoodmagazine.com/news/46916/australia-beef-blockchain/

Starbird, S. A. (2005). Moral hazard, inspection policy, and food safety. *American Journal of Agricultural Economics, 87*(1), 15–27.

Street, D. J., & Burgess, L. (2007). *The construction of optimal stated choice experiments: Theory and methods*. Wiley.

Tian, F. (2017). A supply chain traceability system for food safety based on HACCP, Blockchain & Internet of Things. In *2017 International conference on service systems and service management* (pp. 1–6). IEEE.

United Nations (UN) Statistics Division. (2018). *UN Comtrade Database: Trade between China and all reporters*. HS Codes: 0201, 0202, 0203, 0206, 0207. United Nations. https://comtrade.un.org/data/

USDA FAS (United States Dept of Agriculture Foreign Agricultural Service). (2019). *China-people republic of livestock and products annual*. https://gain.fas.usda.gov/Recent%20GAIN%20Publications/Livestock%20and%20Products%20Annual_Beijing_China%20-%20Peoples%20Republic%20of_7-22-2019.pdf

USDA FSIS (United States Dept of Agriculture Food Safety and Inspection Services). (2018). *Export requirements for the People's Republic of China*. https://www.fsis.usda.gov/wps/portal/fsis/topics/international-affairs/exporting-products/export-library-requirements-by-country/Peoples-Republic-of-China

USMEF. (2012). *Australia's cattle on feed up sharply; Grain-fed exports shift toward China, EU*. https://www.usmef.org/australias-cattle-on-feed-up-sharply-grain-fed-exports-shift-toward-china-eu/

Van den Broeck, G., Swinnen, J., & Maertens, M. (2017). Global value chains, large-scale farming, and poverty: Long-term effects in Senegal. *Food Policy, 66*, 97–107.

Wang, Z., Mao, Y., & Gale, F. (2008). Chinese consumer demand for food safety attributes in milk products. *Food Policy, 33*(1), 27–36.

Wang, Y., So, K. K. F., & Sparks, B. A. (2017). Technology readiness and customer satisfaction with travel technologies: A cross-country investigation. *Journal of Travel Research, 56*(5), 563–577.

Wiegard, R. B., & Breitner, M. H. (2019). Smart services in healthcare: A risk-benefit-analysis of pay-as-you-live services from customer perspective in Germany. *Electronic Markets, 29*(1), 107–123.

Yiannas, F. (2018). A new era of food transparency powered by blockchain. *Innovations: Technology, Governance, Globalization, 12*(1–2), 46–56.

Zulkifly, M. M. F., Ghazali, S. E., Din, N. C., Singh, D. K. A., & Subramaniam, P. (2016). A review of risk factors for cognitive impairment in stroke survivors. *The Scientific World Journal, 2016*, 3456943.

Part III
Government-Market Synergy to Enhance Food Nutrition and Public Health

Chapter 6
The Role of Information in Nudging Chinese Consumers from Choosing Sugar to Alternative Sweeteners

6.1 Introduction

Global obesity rates have nearly tripled in the past four decades, affecting both high-income and low- to middle-income countries (Chen et al., 2019; Nie et al., 2019). It is well-established that excessive sugar consumption, especially from sugar-sweetened beverages (SSB), has been linked to an increased risk of obesity and various non-communicable diseases (Bentley et al., 2020; Hirahatake et al., 2019; Singh et al., 2015), which makes these beverages a clear target for policy and regulatory actions (Malik & Hu, 2022; Zhang et al., 2019). In China, SSB consumption is increasing rapidly, with a per capita annual intake of approximately 30 l (Zhai et al., 2022), and SSBs have become an important source of sugar intake for Chinese residents (Chinese Nutrition Society, 2021). Thus, the health authorities have accelerated the development of interventions and programs, such as the National Nutrition Plan (2017–2030) (State Council of China, 2017) and Healthy China Action (2019–2030) (State Council of China, 2019). These interventions all emphasize the importance of a healthy diet and recommend replacing sugary beverages with low-sugar or sugar-free beverages to reduce health problems such as obesity.

To reduce sugar consumption, policymakers worldwide have already taken actions or are considering interventions including taxation, the reduction of sugary product availability, public educational campaigns, and front-of-package nutrition labels. However, their effectiveness in cutting sugar intake among consumers remains inconclusive (An et al., 2021; Drugova et al., 2020; Hagmann et al., 2018; Neuhofer et al., 2020). In recent years, more restrictive interventions such as taxation on the consumption of SSBs have been implemented mainly in developed countries such as France, Britain, and part of America. However, existing studies have different conclusions about the impact of taxation on making consumers

W. Lin, *Transforming China's Agri-Food System: Government-Market Synergy*, Resources, Environment and Agricultural Development,
https://doi.org/10.1007/978-981-95-7151-2_6

change their choice from SSBs to healthier diet drinks (Hagmann et al., 2018; Doble et al., 2020; Powell et al., 2020).

In response to these sugar reduction policies as well as consumer demand for lower-sugar foods, another tool that can be considered is to encourage the use of low-calorie sweeteners (LCS) as a substitution for sugars (Silva et al., 2021). Low-calorie sweeteners (LCS) provide a sweet taste but with substantially fewer calories, therefore, they are popular alternatives to sugar for food manufacturers to use in food and drink reformulation (Hovhannisyan & Bastian, 2022). A substantial body of evidence attested to the safety of LCS (Ashwell et al., 2020; Farag et al., 2022) and reported favorable effects on energy intake and weight management when LCS is substituted for sugars (Abo Elnaga et al., 2016; Harrold et al., 2023; Laviada-Molina et al., 2020; Rogers & Appleton, 2021). Several organizations such as the American Heart Association, the American Diabetes Association, and the British Dietetic Association issued statements advocating the safety of LCS[1](Gardner et al., 2012). However, some studies carried out in developed countries reported significant public distrust in the safety of LCS, in America (Gardner et al., 2012) and UK (Farhat et al., 2021).

In China, according to the National Food Safety Standard for Prepackaged Food Nutrition Labeling Regulation issued by the National Health Commission[2] (GB 28050–2011), sweeteners are allowed to be added to food or beveragesif their sugar content is no >5 g/100 ml. The National Food Safety Standard for the Use of Food Additives (GB 2760–2014) specified the principles for the use of sweeteners and confirmed the safety of adding sweeteners to food or drinks according to the requirements. An important prerequisite for carefully constructing a LCS encouraging policy is a theory-based understanding of whether and how consumers perceive sugar alternatives. The intention behind replacing added sugar with alternatives requires consumers recognition of the safety and benefits of LCS. However, little has been known about the public beliefs and valuations toward added sugar and sweeteners in emerging markets like China. To fill this void, this study explored Chinese consumers' beliefs and willingness to pay toward sweeteners. Consumers' beliefs about sweeteners were elicited from the aspects of acceptance, risks, benefits, and trust in regulation perceptions, to delve into the underlying mechanisms.

Different from most previous studies exploring consumer choice in settings of providing front-of-package or back-of-package nutritional information indicating the content of nutrients (Guan et al., 2022; da Silva et al., 2022; Zhu et al., 2023), this paper contributes to the literature by evaluating how providing functional and safety information of LCS nudges healthy food consumption. A discrete choice experiment and a between-subject design approach are applied in this study to explore the impact of information interventions on increasing consumers' evaluation of products with low-caloric sweeteners in the choice tasks. Moreover, we

[1] British Dietetic Association. Available online: https://www.bda.uk.com/improvinghealth/health-professionals/policy_statements/sweetners. (accessed on 6 January 2020).

[2] See the website: https://members.wto.org/crnattachments/2021/SPS/CHN/21_6717_00_x.pdf

contribute to a broad literature that studies how governments can help consumers reduce sugar intake. This paper focused on information intervention and showed that it can be an effective tool to improve diet quality. Understanding information effects offers important policy insights when designing educational campaigns or effective labeling policy to more cost-effectively target the public, and to make treatments more responsive. Up to now, the main policy tool the Chinese government is using to combat obesity is the back-of-package Nutrition Facts Panel, which was found little effect in promoting healthier food choices (Guan et al., 2021). Other increasingly popular policy tools such as information intervention can be considered to combat the negative health consequences associated with excessive sugar consumption. This paper has the potential to inform public policy interventions and provide valuable insights for policymakers and food marketers when designing effective intervention policies by Chinese consumers' beliefs and preferences for reducing sugar consumption.

The remainder of this paper is organized as follows. Section 6.2 introduces the between-subject treatments and online choice experiment study design. Section 6.3 is the empirical methods followed by data used in this study in Sect. 6.4. Section 6.5 presents the results. The last section presents the conclusion, discussion, and policy implications of this study.

6.2 Study Design

6.2.1 Between-Subject Treatments

This study employs an online survey incorporating a between-subject design and a discrete choice experiment (DCE) to assess the effect of sweetener information on consumer WTP for added sugar and low-calorie sweeteners. The survey consists of three parts. The first part includes questions related to participants' socio-demographic characteristics, SSB consumption patterns, sugar preferences, and beliefs about sweeteners. In the second part, participants were randomly assigned to one of the two treatment groups. Each treatment group was provided with simplified or detailed sweetener information before the DCE questions. The final part consists of a choice experiment to assess consumers' preferences for sugar-sweetened beverages. The target population for this study comprises Chinese urban consumers aged 18 years and above, who have purchased SSB products within the past 3 months.

Before answering the DCE questions, participants were randomly assigned to one of two groups: simple information group (Control) and detailed information group (Treatment). Simple information is an introduction as follows "Sweeteners are food additives that sweeten foods. They include natural sweeteners such as sweeteners and artificial sweeteners such as sugar alcohols." . Detailed information added function and safety confirmation about sweeteners "Sweeteners are food additives that sweeten foods. They include natural sweeteners such as sweeteners and artificial sweeteners such as sugar alcohols. It provides sweetness with no or minimal calories. And it is safe to use reasonably according to national food safety standards." . These groups were designed to explore if and how consumer willing to pay (WTP) for added sugar and low-caloric sweeteners varies when provided with detailed or simplified sweetener information. To enable respondents to read the information, they were notable to continue with the questionnaire until 30 s had elapsed.

6.2.2 Discrete Choice Experiment

During the online DCE experiment, respondents were asked to select the most preferred alternative between two options of packaged beverages and a no-purchase option. Beverages were chosen in this study because they are in general viewed as a promising application field for reducing sugar intake as they area key source of added sugars in the diet (Lakkakula & Schmitz, 2019; Malik & Hu, 2022). A large body of evidence has linked sugar-sweetened beverages with weight gain and health risks (Bentley et al., 2020; Farag et al., 2022). Importantly, bottled black tea is chosen as the product of interest for this study as they are one of the most frequently purchased beverages among Chinese urban consumers and there is a broad range of health-level bottled black tea in the market.

The attributes and attribute levels of the product in question were selected based on relevant literature (Christiansen et al., 2023; Tang et al., 2021), and a focus group discussion was conducted before the experiment. We include three attributes: added sugar, sweetener, and price, as shown in Table 6.2. Four attribute levels are included for added sugar: zero sugar, low sugar, high sugar, and excessive sugar. According to the National Food Safety Standard for Prepackaged Food Nutrition Labeling Regulation issued by the National Health Commission of China,[3] a beveragecan belabeled as zero-sugar if its sugar content is no >0.5 g/100 ml, and it can be labeled as low sugar if the sugar content is <5 g/100 ml. However, there is no specific regulation for the high sugar category. After examining the sugar content of soft drinks in the Chinese market, this study defined "high sugar" as "5 g/100 ml ≤ sugar content < 10 g/100 ml" and "excessive sugar" as "≥10 g/100 ml". Low-caloric sweeteners, which provide sweetness without adding energy to the diet, are considered important substitutes for added sugar. The sweetener attribute was included in the choice set and applied to zero-sugar and low-sugar products. Finally, three price levels were selected to represent actual market price ranges, namely 3.3 RMB/bottle, 5.0 RMB/bottle, and 6.7 RMB/bottle, which were also validated through a pretest. (See Table 6.1)

To minimize the respondent burden and ensure efficient data collection, a full factorial design with 576 different choice questions $(4^1 \times 2^1 \times 3^1)^2$ was initially

[3] See the website: https://members.wto.org/crnattachments/2021/SPS/CHN/21_6717_00_x.pdf

Table 6.1 Attributes and attribute levels in the choice set design

Attribute	Attribute level	Sugar content (g/100 ml)
Added sugar	Zero sugar Low sugar High sugar Excessive sugar	≤0.5 (0.5, 5) [5, 10) ≥10
Sweetener	Yes, No	
Price (RMB/bottle, 500 ml)	3.3, 5.0, 6.7	

Table 6.2 Balance tests between the control and information groups

	Control	Information	P-value	Population
Demographics				
Age	34.866 (9.803)	35.190 (9.501)	0.476	42.509
Female	0.511 (0.500)	0.496 (0.500)	0.510	0.489
Married	0.607 (0.489)	0.638 (0.481)	0.174	0.721
Education			0.981	
Middle school and below	0.67	0.67		64.17
High school	5.22	4.89		16.35
College	83.11	83.00		18.53
Graduate	11.00	11.44		0.95
Annual individual after-tax income			0.954	
Below 20,000RMB	9.22	9.00		
20,000–49,999 RMB	10.67	10.89		
50, 000–999,999RMB	25.22	23.67		
100,000–199,999 RMB	31.56	31.56		
200,000–299,999 RMB	12.89	14.22		
300,000 RMB and above	10.44	10.67		
Household size	3.350	3.369	0.713	
	(1.070)	(1.110)		
BMI	21.697	21.863	0.233	
	(3.018)	(2.896)		
Bottled beverage consumption				
Bottled beverage purchasing frequency			0.836	
Daily	8.89	10.11		
5–6 times per week	16.33	15.89		
3–4 times per week	34.22	34.33		
1–2 times per week	26.33	26.56		
1–3 times per month	11.56	10.00		
Less than monthly	2.67	3.11		

(continued)

Table 6.2 (continued)

	Control	Information	P-value	Population
Weekly bottled beverage expenditure			0.406	
<5 RMB	6.33	6.00		
5–9.99 RMB	17.33	19.22		
10–29.99 RMB	39.33	36.00		
30–49.99 RMB	27.44	27.22		
> 50 RMB	9.56	11.56		
Zero-sugar beverage purchasing frequency			0.572	
Never	0.89	1.56		
Seldom	51.67	52.67		
Often	43.78	42.33		
Always	3.67	3.44		

Note: P-values from t-tests/chi-square tests the null hypothesis of equality of means/frequencies invariables between two groups. Population statistis is from the 2023 China Statistical Yearbook

considered given the selected attributes and attribute levels. However, following the approach of Street et al. (2005), the design was reduced to 20 choice questions with a D-efficiency of over 85%, considering only the main effects. These 20 choice questions were then divided into two blocks of 10 choice questions each to be presented to the participants during the survey. To prevent any potential ordering effects, the order of the choice tasks within each block was randomized. An example of a choice set is provided in Fig. 6.1. Before the choice questions, respondents were given instructions about the DCE and asked to read a scripted cheap talk statement to ensure their careful attention (see Appendix). To ensure respondents had adequately reviewed the instructions and cheap talk, they were unable to proceed with the questionnaire until at least 40 s had elapsed.

6.3 Empirical Methods

To model consumers' purchasing decisions for tea drinks, we specify an indirect utility function based on Lancaster's theory of consumer demand (Lancaster, 1966). Following random utility theory (McFadden, 1974), choice experiments rely on the assumption that the utility of individual n choosing alternative j in choice situation t can be expressed as:

$$U_{njt} = V_{njt} + \varepsilon_{njt} \tag{6.1}$$

$$= \alpha Price_{njt} + \beta_{n1} ZeroSugar_{njt} + \beta_{n2} LowSugar_{njt} + \beta_{n3} HighSugar_{njt} + \beta_{n4} Sweeten_{njt} * ZeroSugar_{njt} + \beta_{n5} Sweeten_{njt} * LowSugar_{njt} + ASCO_{pt} - out + \varepsilon_{njt}$$

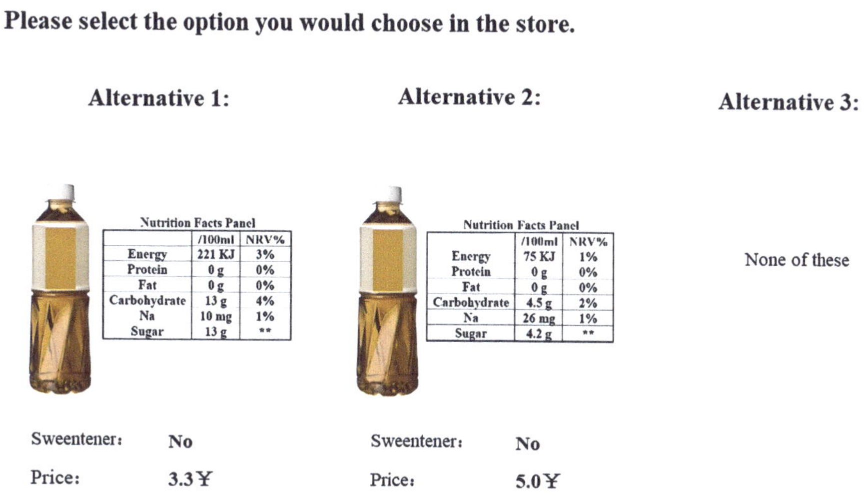

Fig. 6.1 An example of the choice tasks

where V_{njt} is the systematic portion of the utility function, depending on the experimentally designed product attributes of alternative *j*. $Price_{njt}$ is a continuous variable populated with the three price levels in the design; $ZeroSugar_{njt,}$ $LowSugar_{njt}$ and $HighSugar_{njt}$ are dummy variables for the levels of zero sugar, low sugar and high sugar content in tea beverages, and $Sweeten_{njt}$ is also a dummy variable that indicates whether sweetener is included in the production of tea beverages.

If the product exhibits a particular attribute, then all corresponding values are set to 1; otherwise, they are set to 0. $ASCO_{pt-out}$ is the alternative specific constant of the opt-out option; α is price preference and the βs are the non-price taste coefficients. ε_{njt} is the sto- chastic and unobservable (to researchers) component.

We estimate a mixed logit model in which consumer tastes vary concerning unobserved variables, which captures the variability in consumer preferences and provides a more accurate representation of real-world decision-making processes. The model'shigh degree of flexibility allows it to approximate a wide range of random utility models, making it a suitable tool for modeling consumer behavior in various settings (McFadden & Train, 2000). Accordingly, ε_{njt} is the random error term that follows a Type I Extreme Value distribution. To account for the fact that individuals may assign either positive or negative values to non-price product attributes, the model assumes that the coefficients associated with these attributes follow a normal distribution. We specify a fixed price coefficient to obtain reasonable and finite distributions of WTPs (Bliemer & Rose, 2013; Hensher & Greene, 2005; Matthews & Matthews, 2017). To estimate these model parameters, we employ a simulated maximum likelihood estimation technique using 1000 Halton draws.

In our study, we evaluate the impact of sweetener information on consumer valuation of tea beverages by comparing WTPs between the control and treatment groups. We first employ a Monte Carlo simulation technique (Krinsky & Robb, 1986) using the variance-covariance matrix obtained from estimating Eq. (6.1), and then we use a non-parametric complete combinatorial test as suggested by Poe et al. (2005). Further, we match demographic variables with individual-specific or conditional WTPs, as outlined in Train (2003), to identify potential demographic factors that may influence WTPs.

6.4 Data

Data for this study was collected via an online survey in December 2022. Participants were recruited by the professional survey company "PowerCX"[4] in China.They were screened to ensure they were > 18 years old and had purchased the bottled blacktea within the last 3 months. Several trap questions were included in the survey, and participants who failed to answer the trap questions were excluded automatically. Five cities were chosen including Beijing, Guangzhou, Shanghai, Chengdu, and Wuhan, representing the north, south, east, west, and middle China. Finally, a total of 1800 respondents (900 for each group) were employed for the analysis. Table 6.2 reports the balance test across different treatment groups. *P*-values from F-tests/chi-square tests suggest that the null hypothesis of equality in demographic variables between any two treatment groups cannot be rejected at the 10% significance level. Our sample was roughly consistent with the Chinese population in terms of gender, and marital status. The average age of our sample is 35 years old, which is younger than the population mean (42.51). This is somewhat expected because we screened the respondents to ensure that they had purchased the bottled black tea within the last 3 months. Bottled drinks are more popular among young consumers than in their older counterparts. Additionally, it's important to note that our sample consists of individuals with higher education levels and income compared to the general Chinese population. This is due to the recruitment of respondents from five major cities, which are characterized by more advanced economic development and represent significant markets for bottled drinks in China. Overall, the survey results indicate that soft drinks are frequently purchased by respondents, with 34% purchasing them >3 times per week. Additionally, 26% purchase soft drinks 1–2 times per week, 11% purchase them 1–3 times per month, and 3% purchase them <1 time per month. Among soft drinks, tea drinks are the most popular choice, preferred by 76% of the respondents, while only 4% dislike tea drinks. Furthermore, the majority of respondents spend >10 RMB on soft drinks. And 59.78% of the respondents reported that they have a sweet diet or asweet tooth. The results of the chi-square tests suggest that there is no statistically significant difference observed among the treatment groups regarding bottled beverage purchasing frequency and expenditure information. This implies that any variations observed in SSB choices across treatments cannot be attributed to differences in demographic factors, SSB purchasing behavior, or consumption characteristics.

[4]Official website: www.powercx.com

6.5 Results

6.5.1 Impacts of Sweetener Information on Consumer WTPs for SSBs

To assess the impacts of sweetener information on consumer choices of SSBs, we employ mixed logit models to estimate Eq. (6.1) for each treatment. We then generate willingness-to-pay (WTP) values through simulations based on the estimated parameters and variance-covariance matrix derived from Eq. (6.1). The estimation results for the control, treatment, and pooled mixed logit models are summarized in Table 6.7. As expected, most product attributes exhibit significant effects on individual choices of black tea beverages, with coefficients displaying the anticipated signs. In the control group, respondents, on average, show a positive preference for black tea with low sugar content compared to other sugar levels, and they have a significant dislike for sweeteners. In the information treatment group, individual preferences for sugar levels and sweeteners exhibit heterogeneity.

Table 6.3 shows the mean simulated values and 95% confidence intervals for willingness-to-pay (WTP) estimates, as well as the results of the Poe test assessing the equality of WTP distributions across treatments. The table displays the variations in consumer valuations between treatment and control groups and provides a statistical test to evaluate the significance of these differences. Several key findings emerge from our analysis.

Firstly, we find that consumers in the control group exhibit a preference for sugar content in descending order: low sugar without sweetener, zero sugar without sweetener, high sugar, and excessive sugar. On average, respondents are willing to pay an additional 6.04 RMB per bottle to switch from excessive sugar to low sugar without sweetener tea beverages. For an excessive-sugar black tea priced at 5 RMB, the price premium percentage for the low-sugar and sweetener-free level is 120.8%. However, when the sugar content originates from an artificial sweetener, consumers

Table 6.3 Simulated WTP between the control and information groups

	Control	Information
Zero sugar without sweetener	2.192[a] [1.586, 2.797][b]	2.157 [1.572, 2.740]
Low sugar without sweetener	6.040 [5.081, 7.024]	5.386 [4.451, 6.362]
High Sugar	1.915 [1.162, 2.719]	2.372 [1.600, 3.213]
Sweetener on zero sugar	− 0.964 [− 1.828, − 0.082]	0.197 [− 0.679, 1.098]
Sweetener on low sugar	− 3.084 [− 3.554, − 2.610]	− 1.986 [− 2.437, − 1.535]

[a]Indicates the mean of the simulated WTP values using the Krinsky-Robb method
[b]Is 95% confidence interval of the WTP values

in the control group devalue the low-sugar product, assigning a negative valuation of −3.08 RMB per bottle for low-sugar tea beverages with artificial sweeteners. That is, respondents are willing to pay an additional 2.96 RMB per bottle to switch from excessive-sugar to low-sugar with sweetener tea beverages. For an excessive-sugar black tea priced at 5 RMB, the price premium percentage for the low-sugar level with sweetener is 59.2%.

Secondly, consumers have a significant dislike for sweeteners. They value zero sugar without sweetener more than high sugar level products. But when there are sweeteners on the zero-sugar level products, they would prefer high-sugar products. On average, respondents in the control are willing to pay an additional 2.19 RMB per bottle to switch from excessive sugar to zero sugar without sweetener tea beverages. However, when the sugar content originates from an artificial sweetener, consumers in the control group devalue the zero-sugar product, assigning a negative valuation of −0.96 RMB per bottle for zero-sugar tea beverages with artificial sweeteners. That is, respondents in the control are willing to pay an additional 1.23 RMB per bottle to switch from excessive-sugar to zero-sugar with sweetener tea beverages, which is 0.69 RMB lower than that for high-sugar level tea beverages (1.92 RMB).

Thirdly, detailed sweetener information proves effective in increasing consumer valuations of sweeteners on both zero-sugar and low-sugar levels in tea SSBs. Respondents in the treatment exhibit mean WTP values of 0.20 RMB and − 1.99 RMB per bottle for the sweetener on zero-sugar and low-sugar levels, respectively, which is 1.16 RMB and 1.10 RMB higher than those in the control group. On average, respondents in the treatment are willing to pay an additional 5.39 RMB per bottle to switch from excessive-sugar to low-sugar without sweetener tea beverages, and 3.4 RMB per bottle to switch from excessive-sugar to low-sugar with sweetener tea beverages. For zero-sugar tea beverages, they are willing to pay an additional 2.16 RMB per bottle to switch from excessive-sugar to zero-sugar without sweetener beverages, but 2.36 RMB per bottle to switch from excessive-sugar to zero-sugar with sweetener tea beverages. This indicates that sweetener information makes consumers value zero-sugar with sweetener more than zero-sugar without sweetener tea beverages.

Last, to validate the robustness of our findings, we conducted estimations using a pooled sample in the preference space (Table 6.7). Consistent with our previous results, we find that the interaction term between the sweetener dummy and zero-sugar or low-sugar dummy is statistically significant and negatively signed, indicating that consumers devalue sweetener content for both zero-sugar and low-sugar tea beverages. However, the interaction term between the treatment dummy and the sweetener dummy is statistically significant and positively signed for both zero-sugar and low-sugar tea beverages. This suggests that sweetener information intervention effectively increases consumers' WTP for sweetener content in tea beverages.

6.5.2 Consumers' Beliefs About Sweeteners

To shed light on mechanisms, we surveyed respondents and elicited their beliefs about low-calorie sweeteners. Before the information intervention and the discrete choice experiment (DCE), participants were asked to report their beliefs about the acceptance, risk, benefit, and trust in the regulations of sweeteners (Table 6.4). The results of the chi-square tests (all p-values >0.15) suggest that there is no statistically significant difference observed among the treatment group and control group indicating a balanced sample regarding beliefs about sweeteners.

Consumer attitudes toward sweeteners and their trust in regulations are generally positive. Specifically, 60.50% of consumers are open to the idea of certain foods using sweeteners instead of added sugar, while 13.83% hold an unsupportive view, and 25.67% express neutrality. When it comes to taste perception, 40.72% of consumers believe sweeteners taste worse than added sugar, 17.17% hold the opposite view, and 42.11% remain neutral. In terms of regulatory trust, 74.77% of consumers trust the government in regulating sweetener use in food production, with only 3.94% expressing distrust and 21.29% maintaining a neutral stance.

However, consumer beliefs about the risks and benefits of sweeteners are complex, with negative evaluations outweighing positive ones. Regarding risk perception, 70.33% of consumers are concerned about the potential impact of sweeteners on humans, while only 6.94% hold a positive view, and 22.73% remain neutral. Additionally, 61.28% of consumers believe that sweetener consumption is harmful to health, with 10.72% holding the opposite view, and 28.00% expressing neutrality. In terms of benefit perception, 39.83% of consumers think sweeteners are necessary for producing diet products, 25.83% hold the opposite view, and 34.34% remain neutral. Moreover, 51.56% of consumers believe the use of sweeteners can benefit them by reducing calorie intake, while 15.28% hold an opposite view, and 33.16% remain neutral.

Table 6.4 Consumers' beliefs about sweeteners

Beliefs	Description	Control	Information	P-value
Acceptance	I am open to having some foods using sweeteners instead of added sugar	3.556 (0.943)	3.589 (0.925)	0.449
	Sweeteners taste worse than added sugar	3.330 (0.905)	3.303 (0.905)	0.532
Risk	I am concerned about the potential impact of sweeteners on human	3.822 (0.862)	3.789 (0.830)	0.404
	The consumption of sweeteners is harmful to health	3.647 (0.895)	3.612 (0.878)	0.410
Benefit	Sweeteners are necessary to produce diet products	3.17 (1.056)	3.200 (1.002)	0.507
	The use of sweeteners in food can benefit consumers by reducing calorie intake.	3.417 (0.922)	3.478 (0.917)	0.152
Trust in regulations	Government can regulate the use of sweeteners in food production	3.931 (0.803)	3.949 (0.796)	0.637

Note: 1 = totally disagree, 5 = totally agree. P-values from t-tests/chi-square tests the null hypothesis of equality of means/frequencies invariables between two groups

6.5.3 Heterogeneity on the Impacts of Sweetener Information

To examine how consumers' WTPs vary with consumers' beliefs about added sugar and low-caloric sweeteners, and whether the effectiveness of information intervention on consumers' WTPs varies across respondents' beliefs, we conducted heterogeneity analyses by adding cross terms of information intervention and respondents' beliefs including acceptance, risk and benefit perception, and trust in regulations about sweeteners (Table 6.5). Results consistently showed that consumers prefer low-sugar without-sweetener tea beverages most, followed by zero-sugar without-sweetener, high sugar, and excessive sugar (control group). They have a significant dislike for sweeteners both on zero-sugar and low-sugar products.

We found that information effects varied between consumers with different beliefs, especially acceptance of and risk perception about the sweetener. Higher acceptance for LCS makes information intervention more effective in evaluating products with lower sugar level content in comparison to excessive sugar options, and makes consumers willing to pay higher for sweeteners in both zero-sugar and low-sugar products. Specifically, consumers exhibit a positive valuation of 0.941 RMB and 0.349 RMB per bottle for sweeteners in zero-sugar and low-sugar products respectively if they have a higher acceptance of using sweeteners as a substitution for added sugar. In comparison, higher risk perception for LCS makes information intervention less effective in evaluating products with lower sugar level content in comparison to excessive sugar options, and makes consumers willing to pay lower for sweeteners in both zero-sugar and low-sugar products. Specifically,

Table 6.5 Heterogeneity on the impacts of information on WTPs

	Zero sugar without sweetener	Low sugar without sweetener	High Sugar	Sweetener on zero sugar	Sweetener on low sugar
Constant	2.213***	6.083***	1.936***	−0.951***	−3.098***
	(0.206)	(0.196)	(0.114)	(0.148)	(0.095)
Information	0.687	−2.889*	− 1.070	− 1.166	0.762
	(1.710)	(1.625)	(0.946)	(1.225)	(0.785)
Information* Acceptance	0.614**	0.792***	0.615***	0.941***	0.349***
	(0.243)	(0.231)	(0.135)	(0.174)	(0.112)
Information*Risk	−0.489**	−0.315	−0.304**	−0.526***	−0.422***
	(0.240)	(0.229)	(0.133)	(0.172)	(0.111)
Information*Benefit	0.259	0.118	0.114	0.188	0.235**
	(0.247)	(0.235)	(0137)	(0.177)	(0.113)
Information*Trust	−0.542**	0.016	−0.001	0.048	−0.052
	(0.268)	(0.254)	(0.148)	(0.192)	(0.123)
R^2	0.011	0.015	0.025	0.048	0.059
Observations	1800	1800	1800	1800	1800

Note: Numbers in parentheses are standard deviations. *, **, *** indicates statistical significance at the 10%, 5%, and at 1% levels consumers display discounts of −0.526 RMB and − 0.422 RMB per bottle for sweeteners in zero-sugar and low-sugar products respectively if they have a higher concern about LCS on their health. Respondents with higher benefit perception for LCS show a higher valuation (0.235 RMB per bottle) for low-sugar SSBs with sweetener content in comparison to excessive sugar options.

To examine whether the effectiveness of information intervention on consumers' WTPs varies across respondents' demographic characteristics, we conducted heterogeneity analyses by adding cross terms of information intervention and respondents' characteristics including age, education, income, and BMI (Table 6.6). Above_age, Above_edu, Above_incare all dummy variables, taking the value of 1 if an individual score is over the sample median and 0 otherwise. Above_bmi is a dummy and it equals 1 if BMI is >25 and zero otherwise. Results showed that information intervention is more effective for younger and higher income group respondents. Specifically, consumers exhibit discounts of −0.974 RMB and −0.418 RMB per bottle for sweeteners in zero-sugar and low-sugar products respectively if they are over the median age of the sample. In comparison, a higher income level makes information intervention more effective and makes consumers willing to pay higher (0.862 RMB per bottle) for sweeteners in zero-sugar products in comparison to excessive sugar options.

Table 6.6 Heterogeneity on the impacts of information on WTPs

	Zero sugar without sweetener	Low sugar without sweetener	High Sugar	Sweetener on zero sugar	Sweetener on low sugar
Constant	2.213***	6.083***	1.936***	−0.951***	−3.098***
	(0.207)	(0.196)	(0.115)	(0.149)	(0.096)
Information	−0.260	−0.615*	0.523	1.353***	1.222***
	(0.379)	(0.359)	(0.497)	(0.273)	(0.175)
Information* Above_age	0.064	−0.822**	−0.608***	−0.974***	−0.418**
	(0.418)	(0.396)	(0.232)	(0.302)	(0.193)
Information*Above_edu	1.321*	1.764***	−0.812**	0.388	−0.488
	(0.677)	(0.642)	(0.375)	(0.489)	(0.313)
Information*Above_inc	−0.480	0.538	0.453	0.862**	0.262
	(0.499)	(0.472)	(0.277)	(0.360)	(0.230)
Information* Above_bmi	0.684	−0.225	−0.002	0.155	0.219
	(0.645)	(0.612)	(0.358)	(0.465)	(0.298)
R^2	0.007	0.012	0.013	0.026	0.041
Observations	1800	1800	1800	1800	1800

Note: Numbers in parentheses are standard deviations. *, **, *** indicates statistical significance at the 10%, 5%, and at 1% levels

Table 6.7 Mixed logit models in preference-space for each group

	Control		Information		Pooled	
	Estimate	Z-value	Estimate	Z-value	Estimate	Z-value
Mean						
Price	−0.317***	−26.04	−0.319***	−26.27	−0.317***	−26.82
Opt-out	−4.682***	−39.37	−4.487***	−39.94	−4.690***	−40.76
Zero sugar	0.696***	7.11	0.647***	6.87	0.713***	7.49
Low Sugar	1.917***	12.13	1.691***	10.70	1.953***	12.78
High Sugar	0.608***	4.84	0.777***	6.04	0.618***	5.09
Zero sugar*Sweetener	−0.306**	−2.16	0.098	0.67	−0.305**	−2.20
Low Sugar*Sweetener	−0.979***	−13.01	−0.646***	−8.79	−0.996***	−13.21
Price*Information					−0.002	−0.15
Opt-out*Information					0.204	1.32
Zero sugar*Information					−0.043	−0.33
Low Sugar*Information					−0.322	−1.62
High Sugar*Information					0.131	0.81
Zero sugar*Sweetener*Information					0.376**	1.98
Low Sugar* Sweetener*Information Standard deviation					0.360***	3.46
Zero sugar	2.334***	19.64	2.210***	19.84	2.281***	27.85
Low Sugar	1.865***	13.18	2.120***	15.45	2.031***	20.51
High Sugar	0.547***	3.83	0.707***	3.90	0.695***	5.81
Zero sugar*Sweetener	0.453*	1.73	0.591**	2.48	0.489**	2.11
Low Sugar* Sweetener	0.136	0.28	0.226	0.56	0.219	0.43
Model statistics						
Log-likelihood	−6089.890		−6283.374		−12,384.846	
Number of Observations	27,000		27,000		5400	
Number of Individuals	900		900		1800	

Note: all models are estimated via simulation maximum likelihood estimation based on 500 Halton draws. *, **, *** indicates statistical significance at the 10%, 5%, and at 1% levels, respectively

6.6 Conclusion and Discussion

The global effort to reduce free sugar intake faces a critical challenge rooted in consumer beliefs toward sugar and its alternatives. The success of initiatives promoting sugar reduction, whether through encouraging the consumption of low-caloric sweeteners or implementing taxation, hinges on consumer acceptance of these alternatives. If there is resistance to LCS, which is a key component in most diet products, the effectiveness of sugar reduction strategies is compromised. To effectively address and overcome barriers to LCS consumption,a thorough understanding of consumer perceptions and attitudes is essential. Developing communication strategies that resonate with the public is crucial for successful education. This paper aims to delve into consumers' beliefs about added sugar and non-caloric sweeteners, exploring associations between these attitudes and willingness to pay (WTP), using a nationwide Chinese sample. Additionally, the study seeks to evaluate the impact of providing information on altering WTPs of LCS.

Our research reveals a notable inclination among Chinese consumers toward sugar-sweetened beverages (SSBs) with low-sugar content, as opposed to zero-sugar and high-sugar alternatives. This preference is likely rooted in the widespread understanding among Chinese consumers of the health benefits associated with limiting sugar intake. However, it's essential to acknowledge that the innate human preference for sweetness persists from before birth (Mennella & Beauchamp, 1998), and dietary habits are deeply ingrained and resistant to change (Shepherd, 2002). Consequently, despite the potential health advantages of zero-sugar products, the inherent preference for sweetness makes low-sugar content products more appealing. This insight suggests that in the urban Chinese market, low-sugar products may be more effective substitutes for high-sugar items, contributing to an overall reduction in sugar consumption among residents.

Introducing sweeteners into zero-sugar products to replicate the taste of their high-sugar counterparts is a potential strategy. However, our findings reveal a noteworthy aversion among Chinese consumers to sweeteners. They favor zero sugar without sweeteners over high-sugar products. When sweeteners are present in zero-sugar products, consumers switch to high-sugar alternatives. This preference may stem from consumer concerns about the potential health impact of sweeteners. This aligns with previous studies examining the public attitudes toward sweeteners in the UK and the US (Farhat et al., 2021; Gardner et al., 2012; Sylvetsky et al., 2014). For instance, Farhat et al. (2021) surveyed 1589 UK-based adults and found that 25% of the sample considered low-caloric sweeteners harmful. Notably, the percentage of Chinese consumers perceiving sweetener consumption as harmful to health is even larger (61.28% in our case).

Information intervention yielded success in this study, with consumers' demographic characteristics emerging as a pivotal factor influencing the effectiveness of the provided information. Detailed sweetener information indicating the function and safety of the sweeteners proved impactful in enhancing consumer valuations of sweeteners, particularly for both zero-sugar and low-sugar levels in sugar-sweetened beverages. Specifically, the provision of sweetener information led consumers to value zero-sugar beverages with sweeteners more than those without sweeteners. Chinese consumers' preference for sweeteners saw a substantial improvement following information exposure regarding the function and safety of these sweeteners. The improvement will be further enhanced for consumers with higher incomes but will be significantly diminished for elderly consumers.

To delve into the underlying mechanisms, we conducted surveys before the experiment to understand respondents' beliefs about sugar substitutes. In the self-reported acceptance of sweeteners, the reviewer is right in that nearly 60% of our respondents support sweeteners over added sugar, 26% are neutral, and 14% oppose. However, in the discrete choice experiment of bottled tea, when consumers are asked to choose between products with/without sweeteners, they express a strongly negative valuation ofsweeteners in the control group. This implies that our respondents are less favorable toward sweeteners as they had self-reported. On the other hand, while 51.56% believe that the use of sweeteners can be beneficial in reducing calorie intake, 70.33% of consumers express concerns about the potential impact of sweeteners on human health. Chinese consumers reported greater concerns about the use of sweeteners than their counterparts in developed countries. Farhat et al. (2021) surveyed 1589 UK adults and found that 25% of the sample considered low-caloric sweeteners harmful. People with higher concern about the safety of sweeteners are less receptive to sweetener information intervention (Table 6.5). Hence, it is possible that safety concerns about sweeteners play a more significant role than perceived benefits in shaping tea beverage choices.

Our findings may hold implications for the efficacy of sugar taxes, a policy garnering widespread attention from worldwide governments and scholars. Numerous studies have explored the impact of taxes on sugar-sweetened beverage consumption. Some suggest apositive influence of taxes on reducing SSB consumption (Zhai et al., 2022; Zhong et al., 2018), while others argue that the policy has not yielded the desired outcomes (Doble et al., 2020; Powell & Leider, 2020). The crux of our insights lies in the potential ramifications for the effectiveness of sugar taxation policies, especially considering that diet drinks, the primary alternatives to SSBs, often contain low-calorie sweeteners. Beliefs over nutritional content are a primary driver of consumer behavior (Barahona et al., 2023). The effectiveness of the sugar taxation policy maybe reduced if consumers strongly resist LCS in the alternatives of SSBs making them choose SSBs anyway despite the tax. Chinese consumers in this sample exhibited a significantly higher level of perceived concern and risk beliefs about sweeteners compared to those in developed countries, further studies can be conducted to explore if the impact of sugar taxation in China will be less effective than in more developed counterparts.

Our findings give important implications for policymakers to design other effective sugar reduction policies. Firstly, consumers' beliefs about sugar substitutes are the primary drivers of consumer behavior. Chinese consumers are more concerned about the safety of sweeteners compared with those in Western countries. This could be due to miscommunication of information, or a lack of knowledge of the benefits and risks surrounding the use of LCS (Williams et al., 2023). There is a need to develop communications, especially by governments to foster more informed public attitudes toward sweeteners, for example by emphasizing the potential health gains associated with sugar intake reduction and the role of sweeteners in achieving this. The media or other organizations could be provided, for example, with simple explanations and the safety of sweeteners. Secondly, the main policy tool the Chinese government is using now to combat obesity is the back-of-package Nutrition Facts Panel which displays energy, fat, carbohydrate, and sodium content while excluding sugar information (Guan et al., 2021). To restrain sugar intake, some new policy tools can be considered such as promoting sugar substitutes. Information intervention is a promising policy tool to help consumers choose products with lower sugar levels and to increase consumers' evaluation of sugar substitutes. Effective intervention strategies such as simplified front-of-package food labels with sugar information and sugar substitute functional claims should be developed to educate the public about the characteristics and healthiness of sweeteners. Finally,a caveat on our findings is that they could be contingent on the setting being studied, such as hypothetical DCEs and the tea product. Future research should test the robustness of our findings to variations in these contexts, especially using non-hypothetical choice experiments and experimental auctions.

Funding

This study was funded by the National Natural Science Foundation of China (no. 72003175, 72103180, 72273128), Zhejiang Province Philosophy and Social Science Planning Project (no. 23HQZZ05YB), and the fundamental research funds for the central universities.

Declaration of Competing Interest

The authors declare no conflict of i nterest.

Data Availability

The data is available upon request through the corresponding author.

Appendix: Choice Experiment Instruction and Cheap Talk Script

Next, you will be presented with a hypothetical choice involving money. No one will actually be paid money based on the decision you make, but you are asked to make the decision as though it would result in the actual payment. Studies show that people tend to act differently when they face hypothetical decisions. In other words, they say one thing and do something different. We call this a 'hypothetical bias.' For example, in a recent study, several different groups of people made decisions just like the one you are about to make. Payment was real for one group and hypothetical for the other group, as it will be for you. The results of these studies were that on average, more people expressed a willingness to pay money in the hypothetical group than in the real group.

How can we get people to think about their decisions in a hypothetical situation like they think in a real situation?I think that when we hear about a situation that involves doing something that is basically good, for example helping people in need, improving environmental quality, or anything else, our basic reaction in a hypothetical situation is to think: sure, I would do this. I really would spend the money; I really, really, think I would. But when the situation is real, and we would actually have to spend our money, we think a different way. We basically still would like to see good things happen, but when we are faced with the possibility of having to spend money, we think about our options: If I spend money on this, that's money I cannot spend on other things. So, when the payment is real, we act in away that takes into account the limited amount of money we have. We make the decision while realizing that we just don't have enough money to do everything we might like to do.

References

Abo Elnaga, N. I. E., Massoud, M. I., Yousef, M. I., & Mohamed, H. H. A. (2016). Effect of stevia sweetener consumption as non-caloric sweetening on body weight gain and biochemical's parameters in overweight female rats. *Annals of Agricultural Sciences, 61*(1), 155–163.

An, R., Shi, Y., Shen, J., Bullard, T., Liu, G., Yang, Q., et al. (2021). Effect of front-of-package nutrition labeling on food purchases: A systematic review. *Public Health, 191*, 59–67.

Ashwell, M., Gibson, S., Bellisle, F., Buttriss, J., Drewnowski, A., Fantino, M., et al. (2020). Expert consensus on low-calorie sweeteners: Facts, research gaps and suggested actions. *Nutrition Research Reviews, 33*(1), 145–154.

Barahona, N., Otero, C., & Otero, S. (2023). Equilibrium effects of food labeling policies. *Econometrica, 91*(3), 839–868.

Bentley, R. A., Ruck, D. J., & Fouts, H. N. (2020). US obesity as delayed effect of excess sugar. *Economics and Human Biology, 36*, Article 100818.

Bliemer, M. C., & Rose, J. M. (2013). Confidence intervals of willingness-to-pay for random coefficient logit models. *Transportation Research Part B: Methodological, 58*, 199–214.

Chen, Y. J., Peng, Q., Yang, Y., Zheng, S. S., Wang, Y., & Lu, W. L. (2019). The prevalence and increasing trends of overweight, general obesity, and abdominal obesity among Chinese adults: A repeated cross-sectional study. *BMC Public Health, 19*(1), 1293.

Chinese Nutrition Society. (2021). *Scientific research report on dietary guidelines for Chinese residents*. Chinese Nutrition Society.

Christiansen, P., Roberts, C., Radu, C., & Hardman, C. (2023). A validation of a questionnaire to assess consumer attitudes towards artificial sweeteners. *Food Quality and Preference, 103*, Article 104707.

da Silva, C. P., Bento, A. C., & Guaraldo, E. (2022). The impact of front-of-the-packaging nutrition labelling warnings on consumer habits: A scoping review exploring the case of the Chilean food law. *British Food Journal, 124*(13), 66–80.

Doble, B., Ang Jia Ler, F., & Finkelstein, E. A. (2020). The effect of implicit and explicit taxes on the purchasing of 'high-in-calorie' products: A randomized controlled trial. *Economics and Human Biology, 37*, Article 100860.

Drugova, T., Curtis, K. R., & Akhundjanov, S. B. (2020). Are multiple labels on food products beneficial or simply ignored? *Canadian Journal of Agricultural Economics, 68*(4), 411–427.

Farag, M. A., Rezk, M. M., Hamdi Elashal, M., El-Araby, M., Khalifa, S. A. M., & El-Seedi, H. R. (2022). An updated multifaceted overview of sweet proteins and dipeptides as sugar substitutes; The chemistry, health benefits, gut interactions, and safety. *Food Research International, 162*(Pt A), Article 111853.

Farhat, G., Dewison, F., & Stevenson, L. (2021). Knowledge and perceptions of non-nutritive sweeteners within the UK adult population. *Nutrients, 13*(2), 444.

Gardner, C., Wylie-Rosett, J., Gidding, S. S., Steffen, L. M., Johnson, R. K., Reader, D., et al. (2012). Nonnutritive sweeteners: Current use and health perspectives: A scientific statement from the American Heart Association and the American Diabetes Association. *Diabetes Care, 35*(8), 1798–1808.

Guan, L., Zhang, Y., Jin, S., & Zhou, L. (2021). Understanding the low use rate of food nutrition information in China. *International Food and Agribusiness Management Review, 24*(5), 863–876.

Guan, L., Huang, Z., & Jin, S. (2022). Time preference and nutrition label use: Evidence from China. *Economics and Human Biology, 47*, Article 101184.

Hagmann, D., Siegrist, M., & Hartmann, C. (2018). Taxes, labels, or nudges? Public acceptance of various interventions designed to reduce sugar intake. *Food Policy, 79*, 156–165.

Harrold, J. A., Hill, S., Radu, C., Thomas, P., Thorp, P., Hardman, C. A., et al. (2023). Effects of non-nutritive sweetened beverages versus water after a 12-week weight-loss program: A randomized controlled trial. *Obesity (Silver Spring), 31*(8), 1996–2008.

Hensher, D. A., & Greene, J. M. R. W. H. (2005). *Applied choice analysis: A primer*. Cambridge University Press.

Hirahatake, K. M., Jacobs, D. R., Shikany, J. M., Jiang, L., Wong, N. D., Steffen, L. M., & Odegaard, A. O. (2019). Cumulative intake of artificially sweetened and sugar-sweetened beverages and risk of incident type 2 diabetes in young adults: The coronary artery risk development in young adults (CARDIA) study. *The American Journal of Clinical Nutrition, 110*(3), 733–741.

Hovhannisyan, V., & Bastian, C. T. (2022). New insights into the structure of consumer preferences for natural and artificial sweeteners. *American Journal of Agricultural Economics, 105*(5), 1491–1515.

Krinsky, I., & Robb, A. L. (1986). On approximating the statistical properties of elasticities. *The Review of Economics and Statistics*, 715–719.

Lakkakula, P., & Schmitz, A. (2019). US sweeteners: Combating excess consumption with an excise tax? *Agricultural Economics, 50*(5), 543–554.

Lancaster, K. J. (1966). A new approach to consumer theory. *Journal of Political Economy, 74*, 132–157.

Laviada-Molina, H., Molina-Segui, F., Perez-Gaxiola, G., Cuello-Garcia, C., Arjona-Villicana, R., Espinosa-Marron, A., & Martinez-Portilla, R. J. (2020). Effects of nonnutritive sweeteners on body weight and BMI in diverse clinical contexts: Systematic review and meta-analysis. *Obesity Reviews, 21*(7), Article e13020.

Malik, V. S., & Hu, F. B. (2022). The role of sugar-sweetened beverages in the global epidemics of obesity and chronic diseases. *Nature Reviews. Endocrinology, 18*(4), 205–218.

Matthews, R. W., & Matthews, J. R. (2017). The malaise trap: Its utility and potential for sampling insect populations. *The Great Lakes Entomologist, 4*(4).

McFadden, D. (1974). The measurement of urban travel demand. *Journal of Public Economics, 3*(4), 303–328.

McFadden, D., & Train, K. (2000). Mixed MNL models for discrete response. *Journal of Applied Econometrics, 15*(5), 447–470.

Mennella, J. A., & Beauchamp, G. K. (1998). Early flavor experiences: Research update (reprinted from pediatric basics, vol 82). *Nutrition Reviews, 56*(7), 205–211.

Neuhofer, Z., McFadden, B. R., Rihn, A., Wei, X., Khachatryan, H., & House, L. (2020). Can the updated nutrition facts label decrease sugar-sweetened beverage consumption? *Economics and Human Biology, 37*, Article 100867.

Nie, P., Ding, L., & Sousa-Poza, A. (2019). Obesity inequality and the changing shape of the body-weight distribution in China. *China Economic Review, 58*, Article 101348.

Poe, G. L., Giraud, K. L., & Loomis, J. B. (2005). Computational methods for measuring the difference of empirical distributions. *American Journal of Agricultural Economics, 87*(2), 353–365.

Powell, L. M., & Leider, J. (2020). The impact of Seattle's sweetened beverage tax on beverage prices and volume sold. *Economics and Human Biology, 37*, Article 100856.

Powell, L. M., Leider, J., & Leger, P. T. (2020). The impact of the Cook County, IL, sweetened beverage tax on beverage prices. *Economics and Human Biology, 37*, Article 100855.

Rogers, P. J., & Appleton, K. M. (2021). Correction: The effects of low-calorie sweeteners on energy intake and body weight: A systematic review and meta-analyses of sustained intervention studies. *International Journal of Obesity (Lond), 45*(9), 2139–2140.

Shepherd, R. (2002). Resistance to changes in diet. *Proceedings of the Nutrition Society, 61*(2), 267–272.

Silva, P. D., Cruz, R., & Casal, S. (2021). Sugars and artificial sweeteners in soft drinks: A decade of evolution in Portugal. *Food Control, 120*, Article 107481.

Singh, G. M., Micha, R., Khatibzadeh, S., Shi, P., Lim, S., Andrews, K. G., & Mozaffarian, D. (2015). Global, regional, and National Consumption of sugar-sweetened beverages, fruit juices, and Milk: A systematic assessment of beverage intake in 187 countries. *PLoS One, 14*(3), Article e0214344.

State Council of China. (2017). *National Nutrition Plan (2017–2030)*. The State Council of China.

State Council of China. (2019). *The healthy China initiative (2019–2030)*. The State Council of China.

Street, D. J., Burgess, L., & Louviere, J. J. (2005). Quick and easy choice sets: Constructing optimal and nearly optimal stated choice experiments. *International Journal of Research in Marketing, 22*(4), 459–470.

Sylvetsky, A. C., Greenberg, M., Zhao, X., & Rother, K. I. (2014). What parents think about giving nonnutritive sweeteners to their children: A pilot study. *International Journal Of Pediatrics, 2014*, 819872.

Tang, C. S., Mars, M., James, J., de Graaf, K., & Appleton, K. M. (2021). Sweet talk: A qualitative study exploring attitudes towards sugar, sweeteners and sweet-tasting foods in the United Kingdom. *Food, 10*(6), 1172.

Train, K. E. (2003). *Discrete choice methods with simulation*. Cambridge University Press.

Williams, R., Moazzem, M. S., Dees, J., Hayden, M., Traynor, M., & Cho, S. (2023). Consumer acceptability of no added sugar pound cakes under blind and informed testing conditions. *Journal of Food Science, 88*(11), 4677–4692.

Zhai, T. C., Li, L., Wang, J. J., & Si, W. (2022). Will the consumption tax on sugar-sweetened beverages help promote healthy beverage consumption? Evidence from urban China. *China Economic Review, 73*, Article 101798.

Zhang, X., Huang, X., Xiao, Y., Jing, D., Huang, Y., Chen, L., et al. (2019). Daily intake of soft drinks is associated with symptoms of anxiety and depression in Chinese adolescents. *Public Health Nutrition, 22*(14), 2553–2560.

Zhong, Y., Auchincloss, A. H., Lee, B. K., & Kanter, G. P. (2018). The short-term impacts of the Philadelphia beverage tax on beverage consumption. *American Journal of Preventive Medicine, 55*(1), 26–34.

Zhu, C., Lopez, R. A., Zhen, C., & Zhao, Q. (2023). Consumer responses to nutrition labels in China. *Journal of Agricultural and Applied Economics Association, 2*(2), 278–294.

Chapter 7
What Does It Take to Revolutionize Chinese Diets: Evidence from a Choice Experiment on Urban Chinese Consumers

7.1 Introduction

Current dietary patterns have been the leading contributor to the global burden of disease and have posed significant challenges to environmental sustainability. As the world's most populous country, China has achieved remarkable strides in alleviating hunger over the past decades, primarily driven by advancements in economic and social development. However, alongside the improvement, the Chinese diet transition is deviating from the nutritional goal, shifting radually from an absolute quantity shortage to a structural shortage (Han et al., 2020). Specifically, a westernized diet characterized by excessive consumption of meat, fat, salt, sugar and ultra-processed foods is replacing the traditional plant-based one (Huang et al., 2021; Sheng et al., 2021; Zhou et al., 2015). The average daily fat-to-energy ratio among Chinese residents has surpassed the recommended upper limit of 30%, reaching 34.6% (Chinese Center for Disease Control and Prevention, 2021). This diet pattern has generated compounded environmental and health consequences (Afshin et al., 2019; Bloom et al., 2013; Willett et al., 2019). On the one hand, the mortality rate of dietary-related cardiometabolic and metabolic diseases among Chinese adults reached 20.8% in 2012 (Afshin et al., 2019), with associated public health costs predicted to exceed $23 tri by 2030 (Bloom et al., 2013). On the other hand, agri-food systems have been a main source of global greenhouse gas emissions, accounting for approximately 25% of total carbon emissions worldwide (IPCC, 2022). Chinese food consumption has been responsible for emitting an estimated 1.9 bn tonnes of CO_2.[1]

[1] Source: https://www.fao.org/faostat/zh/#data/GT.

W. Lin, *Transforming China's Agri-Food System: Government-Market Synergy*, Resources, Environment and Agricultural Development,
https://doi.org/10.1007/978-981-95-7151-2_7

Promoting sustainable healthy diets has the potential to reduce the burden of heavy healthcare costs and alleviate pressure on resources and the environment (AGFEP et al., 2021; Liu et al., 2021; Springmann et al., 2020). For instance, transitioning toward the Chinese Food Guide Pagoda diet could prevent at least 1.15 m deaths and 425,000 premature deaths in China by 2030, and adherence to the EAT-Lancet diet could prevent over 1.8 m deaths and 665,000 premature deaths (Springmann et al., 2020). Additionally, a shift toward the Chinese Food Guide Pagoda diet or the EAT-Lancet diet could mitigate greenhouse gas emissions associated with food production by 150–200 m tons in 2030 (AGFEP et al., 2021). However, a significant disparity exists between the current Chinese diet and the recommended guidelines outlined in the Chinese Food Guide Pagoda diet or the EAT-Lancet diet. This warrants more research in identifying the factors influencing Chinese residents' diet choices and proposing effective strategies to shift Chinese diets.

Identifying the factors affecting consumer diet choices is the premise for transforming successfully the current Chinese diets toward sustainable healthy ones. Although several previous studies shed light on that several factors affect consumer food choices, such as healthiness, cost, sensory appeal and convenience (Jaeger et al., 2021; Kamphuis et al., 2015; Livingstone et al., 2021; Stroebele & De Castro, 2004), these studies have mainly focused on a single food item or nutrient. This is problematic since consuming a single healthy food item may not lead to overall dietary improvements. Individuals tend to engage in "indulgent" behavior by overcompensating more unhealthy foods after behaving healthily (Raghunathan et al., 2006; Vale et al., 2008).

To fill the gap, this paper focuses on diet selection, a combination of different food products where different food items can act as substitutes or as complements for one another. Diet selection is consistent with real-world grocery shopping situations where consumers purchase various food items as a package. In addition, compared to a single food item, diet selection is a more accurate predictor of disease risks (de Ridder et al., 2017), which is more informative for public health policymaking. Therefore, we aimed to investigate factors influencing the diet choices of urban Chinese consumers and compare the importance of each diet attribute. Furthermore, we simulated Chinese consumer demands for each diet to explore the impact of changes in cost and taste on Chinese consumers' dietselections. Our results inform public policymakers on how to revolutionize urban Chinese diets.

The remainder of the study is organized as follows: Sect. 7.2 introduces the survey and choice experimental design. Section 7.3 describes the empirical methods. Section 7.4 illustrates the data collection and descriptive statistics. Section 7.5 presents the estimation results and heterogeneity analysis. Conclusions and discussions are presented in Sect. 7.6.

7.2 Survey and Choice Experiment Design

7.2.1 Alternative Selection and Experiment Design

We used a Discrete Choice Experiment (DCE) to gain insights into Chinese consumers' diet selections. DCEs could simulate real shopping scenarios under hypothetical situations, facilitating our comprehension of individual behavior and predicting future choices. This approach enables the estimation of the attribute value from stated or revealed choices, even though individuals themselves may not be aware of such values (Lizin et al., 2022). DCEs have found widespread application across various contexts to inform individual food choices (Burton et al., 2001; Kamphuis et al., 2015; Loureiro & Umberger, 2007; Louviere, 1984), which have dominated the currently available valuation literature in the Web of Science on food valuation (Lizin et al., 2022). While choice experiments are particularly valuable in the absence of actual products in the market, they are also frequently utilized to uncover consumer preferences for existing products (e.g. Kamphuis et al., 2015; Livingstone et al., 2021). In this paper, hypothetical choice experiments enable us to include healthy and sustainable diets that are not chosen frequently by Chinese residents.

DCEs provide a framework in which individuals derive utility from the attributes of the available alternatives, and their preferences are revealed through their choices (Lancaster, 1966). In this paper, we utilized labeled choice experiments, a method used in discrete choice experiments, to clarify the attributes and features of the options for participants. Previous studies have consistently revealed the major driving forces leading to food choices (Huang et al., 2022; Jaeger et al., 2021; Kamphuis et al., 2015; Lee et al., 2015; Livingstone et al., 2021; Stroebele & De Castro, 2004). In particular, food healthiness and nutrient content play a crucial role as individuals increasingly prioritize their well-being and seek out options that align with their dietary goals (Huang et al., 2022; Kamphuis et al., 2015). We use four quality-differentiated patterns of "product alternatives" to imply the healthiness and sustainability of diets, including the average diet, the Chinese Food Guide Pagoda diet, the EAT-Lancet diet and the Flexitarian diet. Giving that sensory appeal also influences consumers' perceptions of aparticular food item; they are more likely to select foods they find palatable and enjoyable while avoiding those they find unpleasant or unappealing (Kamphuis et al., 2015; Livingstone et al., 2021). Therefore, we included diet taste as an attribute. Furthermore, price also impacts purchasing decisions. Research has shown that individuals often weigh the cost-effectiveness of a food item against its perceived value and quality (Bai et al., 2022). Low-income consumers are unable to buy healthy diets even if they desire to do so. Therefore, the four diet alternatives were then offered at various cost levels. Table 7.1 presents the selected products and attribute levels employed in experimental design.

First, Table 7.2 displays detailed information about the four diets. The average diet refers to the consumption patterns of an average resident in each surveyed province. Food-group amounts in the average diet were referred to the National Bureau

Table 7.1 Labeled choice experiment design by product

Alternative specific constants
Average diet
Chinese Food Guide Pagoda diet
EAT-Lancet diet
Flexitarian diet
Taste level
Customized taste
Without customized taste
Cost level (RMB per day per person)
20
33
46
59
72

Note(s): 1 RMB ≈ 0.15 dollar at the time of this study (2021.09) Time: 2021.09

Table 7.2 Food type and quantity of various diets (unit: gram)

Diet patterns		Average diet	Chinese Food Guide Pagoda diet	EAT-Lancet diet	Flexitarian diet
Cereals	Whole grains	/	100	232	100
	Other grains	/	225	50	225
	Total grains	303	325	282	325
Animal products	Pork	55	32	7	5
	Beef and lamb	32	7	7	1
	Chicken and other poultry	27	18	29	10
	Eggs	48	45	13	45
	Whole milk or equivalents	102	300	250	300
	Fish	41	58	28	58
Vegetables		377	400	300	500
Fruits		267	275	200	350
Legumes		36	30	75	50
Nuts		/		50	30
Vegetable oils		26	28	47	28

Source(s): The average diet refers to the diet of an average resident in each surveyed province, where the consumption quantity of each food category is computed based on the at-home consumption level from the National Bureau of Statistics of China (2020) and adjusted with the proportion of consumption away from home, which is computed based on the income elasticity of various types of food. This table presents the average diet of urban residents in Beijing. The Chinese Food Guide Pagoda diet refers to the official dietary guideline in China published by the Chinese Nutrition Society in 2016. The EAT-Lancet diet was proposed by the EAT-Lancet Commission in 2019 (Willett et al., 2019). The Flexitarian diet refers to Sheng et al. (2021). The reference amount of legumes is not given directly in the CFGP of Statistics of China (2020) and adjusted with the proportion of consumption away from home, which was computed according to the income elasticity of various types of food. Appendix 1 presents detailed information about the average diet of six surveyed regions. As seen in Appendix 1, although geographical environments and dietary habits in different regions lead to variations in dietary patterns, it is generally observed that residents in various areas had an excessive intake of animal products but lower amounts of milk and fruits. Specifically, the significant deficiency in fruit and dairy product intake was more severe in China's southern, central and southwestern regions. Additionally, severe overconsumption of animal-sourced foods was observed in the southern and eastern regions. Relative to the other three diets, the average diet in each surveyed region is unhealthier according to the computed National Dietary Balance Index (Han et al., 2020). The Chinese Food Guide Pagoda diet is the official healthy diet guideline in China, published by the Chinese Nutrition Society in 2016. The EAT-Lancet diet and the Flexitarian diet are well-recognized sustainable healthy diets worldwide. The EAT-Lancet diet was proposed by the EAT-Lancet Commission in 2019, providing the first diet targets from healthiness and environmental sustainability perspectives (Willett et al., 2019). The Flexitarian diet was first proposed by dietitian Blatner (2009) in his book "The Flexitarian Diet." Scholars have provided general definitions and principles for the Flexitarian diet, emphasizing a reduction in animal-source food consumption and an increase in the consumption of plant-based foods (Springmann et al., 2018). However, they did not prescribe explicit food guidelines regarding quantities of food or food groups. Consequently, we constructed the Flexitarian diet guideline based on the Chinese Food Guide Pagoda diet, with reference to Springmann et al. (2018) and Sheng et al. (2021), despite the absence of strict definitions in their studies. Specifically, in accordance with the Chinese Food Guide Pagoda diet, the intake of livestock meat and poultry was reduced to 1/7 and 1/2, respectively, in the Flexitarian diet. Concurrently, there was an augmentation in the consumption of plant-based sustenance such as fruits, vegetables and soybeans. The overall energy intake was aligned with the standards delineated in the other diets.

Second, defining taste is challenging as it is subjective and varies based on personal preference. Taste perceptions vary among individuals, influenced by genetic factors, cultural backgrounds, ethnicities, personal preferences and environmental factors (Bawajeeh et al., 2020). The inclusion of descriptive taste information is employed by food science communities and economists to address this problem (Livingstone et al., 2021; Moskowitz, 2001). Drawing upon the literature, this study employed descriptive information to operationalize the taste attribute, which was set as a dummy variable (=1, if customized taste) in the experimental design. The concept of customized taste implies that individuals have the ability to select diet tastes according to their personal preferences.

Third, diet cost was set based on the minimum cost of the Chinese Food Guide Pagoda diet and adjusted using actual food prices at the time when the study was implemented. Specifically, this paper utilized the Consumer Price Index (CPI) data published in the China Statistical Yearbook between 2017 and 2021 to adjust the minimum cost of diets following the Food and Agriculture Organization (FAO) and

Yin et al. (2023). The cost attribute had five levels ranging from 20 to 72 RMB per day (roughly from 3.3 to 10.8 US dollars in 2021 September). Our survey showed that 72% of respondents spent 10–70 RMB on their daily diet, meaning that the price level we designed almost covers the range of consumers' daily diet expenditure reported.

7.2.2 *Survey Design*

To simulate real-world shopping scenarios and reduce the number of choice options, an efficient design (Rose et al., 2008) was utilized, resulting in a practical set of six selection tasks for respondents to evaluate (Rose et al., 2008), with a Defficiency of 86%. Each selection task consists of four diet alternatives and one opt-out option. The opt-out options are provided with the following opt-out reminder: "If you don't prefer any of the four diet options, you can choose to keep your current diet." Including this option would potentially mitigate hypothesis bias in DCE responses (Harrison, 2006; Hensher, 2010; Jiang et al., 2022; Ladenburg & Olsen, 2014). Figures 7.1 and 7.2 illustrate a sample choice scenario and a sample diet option, respectively. The order of choice questions and the order of options within a choice question were randomized to avoid ordering effects due to learning or fatigue (Schwappach & Strasmann, 2006). All the choice sets are listed in Appendix 2 (represented as plates to respondents, like Fig. 7.1). We hid the exact names of diet alternatives to prevent consumers from making choices by social desirability bias, although we applied a labeled design in the choice experiment. For example, the average diet was labeled as "option A" in a choice set. Furthermore, we also gave respondents a cheap-talk script (see Appendix 3) to further mitigate potential hypothetical bias. Cheap talk scripts have been used to make consumers aware that people tend to overstate their true willingness to pay (WTP) values in general when estimating from choice experiments. Studies have shown that if consumers are informed about this overstatement, the effect will be reduced or eliminated (Cummings & Taylor, 1999; Farrell & Rabin, 1996; Hensher, 2010; Matthews et al., 2017; Silva et al., 2011).

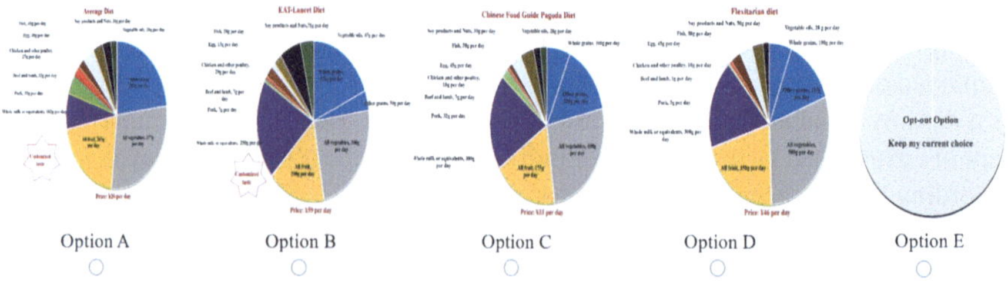

Note(s): The order of choice questions and the order of options within a choice question were randomized. Each option can be enlarged

Fig. 7.1 Asample choice task. Note(s): The order of choice questions and the order of options within a choice question were randomized. Each option can be enlarged

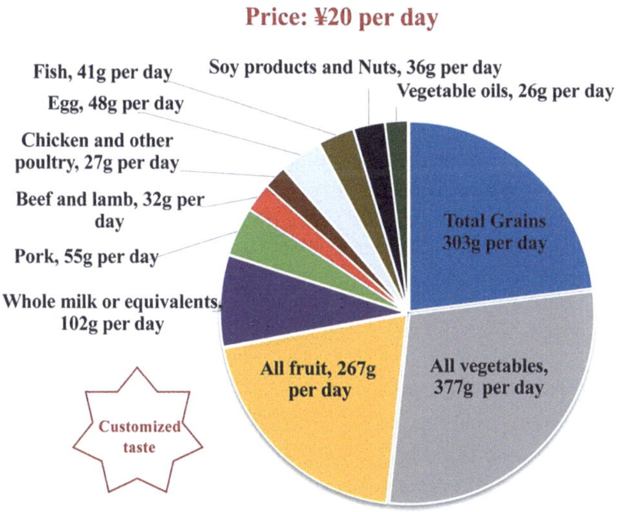

Note(s): To help respondents establish realistic food quantities, before the choice questions, they were asked to compare an estimate of their average daily food consumption and the average consumption of Chinese residents for each food group. Specifically, we provided illustrative examples of each food group to make every consumer understand real food share for comparison. For example, A tomato or a cucumber is about 250g, an apple is about 200 grams, a pack of Tetra Pak milk is about 250g, and an egg is about 50g. Please see Appendix D for specific questions

Fig. 7.2 The average diet of urban residents in Beijing. Note(s): To help respondents establish realistic food quantities, before the choice questions,they were asked to compare an estimate of their average daily food consumption and theaverage consumption of Chinese residents for each food group. Specifically, we provided illustrative examples of each food group to make every consumer understand real food sharefor comparison 200 g, a pack of Tetra Pak milk is about 250 g, and an egg is about 50 g. Please see Appendix 4 for specific questions

In the survey, we employed several strategies to ensure that respondents understand each diet alternative and thus make informed choices in the DCE. First, to help respondents further establish realistic quantities associated with food products, before the choice questions, they were asked to compare their actual diets with the average diet based on the National Bureau of Statistics of China (2022). Additionally, we provided examples to illustrate the quantity of each food product in a diet. For example, a tomato or a cucumber typically weighs 250 g, an apple weighs approximately 200 g, a pack of milk weighs about 250 g and an egg weighs 50 g (Appendix 4 details the comparisons and examples). Third, prior to evaluating the decision task, respondents were presented with a preamble (see Appendix 5) in which we provided examples of food groups to help them better understand and simulate a real-world decision, thereby improving the quality of the data. Finally, we employed pilot testing to make sure respondents understood the meaning of the various diets (represented as plates within the choice tasks).

7.3 Model Specification

Based on Lancaster's theory of consumer demand (Lancaster, 1966) and the random utility theory (McFadden, 1973), we used random parameter logit models with utilities specified in preference space to estimate urban Chinese consumers. Consumer i is assumed to derive the following utility from alternative j: $U_{ijt} = V_{ijt} + \varepsilon_{ijt}$. V_{ijt} is an observable deterministic utility, and V_{ijt} is defined as:

$$\begin{aligned} V_{ijt} &= \alpha_p Price_{ijt} + \beta_{i1} Dieta_{ijt} + \beta_{i2} Dietb_{ijt} + \beta_{i3} Dietc_{ijt} \\ &+ \beta_{i4} Dietd_{ijt} + \gamma_{it} Taste_{ijt} + ASC_{opt-out} \end{aligned} \tag{7.1}$$

where $Price_{ijt}$ refers to the cost of diet, which is a continuous variable populated with five levels. $Dieta_{ijt}$, $Dietb_{ijt}$, $Dietc_{ijt}$ and $Dietd_{ijt}$ are dummy variables denoting the average diet, Chinese Food Guide Pagoda diet, EAT-Lancet diet and Flexitarian diet, respectively. They all take a value of 1 when the diet carries such an attribute and 0 otherwise. $Taste_{ijt}$ represents whether the diet is customized taste or not (1 if yes, otherwise 0). Given our use of the labeled choice experiment, setting the constant for the no-purchase alternative $ASC_{opt-out}$ to zero is common in the literature, as seen in studies by Lusk and Tonsor (2016) and Caputo et al. (2018). This simplifies the estimation of other diet alternatives, as they are measured in relation to this baseline. α_p governs the marginal utility of diet cost and the γ_{it} is the marginal utility of customized taste, β_i means the marginal utility of each experimentally designed diet relative to the opt-out option. The unobserved error term ε_{ijt} follows a Gumbel (extreme value type I) distribution. Simulated maximum likelihood estimation techniques using 1000 Halton draws were used to estimate the models (Train, 2009). We used NLOGIT 6.0 software (Econometric Software; www.limdep.com) to estimate the random parameter logit.

Predicted mean market shares for each alternative were computed based on all individuals' choosing probability (Lusk & Tonsor, 2016). The probability (P_{ij}) of consumer i choosing an alternative j can be expressed using the mixed logit form:

$$P_{ij} = \int \frac{e^{V_{ij}}}{\sum_j e^{V_{ij}}} f(\beta) d\beta \tag{7.2}$$

where V_{ij} is calculated by plugging the estimated coefficients into Eq. (7.1). The assumption regarding the distribution of random parameters $f(\beta)$ is necessary. For identification, the non-price parameters are specified to follow normal distributions, and the price coefficient is specified to follow a constrained triangular distribution. The use of constrained triangular distribution conforms with economic theory (positive marginal utility of income) and has been supported by previous studies (e.g. Ortega et al., 2022; Scarpa et al., 2013).

7.4 Data

7.4.1 Data Collection

To mirror variations in dietary practices and food provisioning attributes, we randomly selected one city from each of the six widely differing regions in China (AGFEP et al., 2023), including Beijing, Shanghai, Shenyang, Wuhan, Chengdu and Guangzhou (excluding the northwest region because of the low coverage of the survey company). Data for this study comes from a larger dataset comprised of 3150 people, whom were randomly assigned into one of nine groups. These nine groups consist of a control group comprised of 350 individuals and eight treatment groups. The purpose of this paper is to understand the factors affecting Chinese diet selections and propose strategies for revolutionizing Chinese diets toward healthy ones. Treatment effect is beyond the scope of this study. To avoid any potential confounding effects on diet choices, we focused on the control group (350 respondents) in this study.[2]

The data were collected online in August 2021 by a professional survey company in China (https://www.lediaocha.com/). Specifically, we first issued informed consent to all participants, and the questionnaire would continue only if the participant agreed with the informed consent; otherwise, it would automatically end. All participants could refuse to participate in the survey and stop filling out the questionnaire at anytime. Additionally, this is an observational study, and we did not collect personally identifiable information. To participate in our study, participants must have been at least 18 years old and be the primary food shoppers in their households. Furthermore, we set up two attention filter questions to screen out inattentive respondents, and those who failed to give the right answer were excluded from our analysis.

7.4.2 Descriptive Statistics

Table 7.3 showed sample characteristics. An average respondent was 38 years old, similar to the median age in China. Around 51% of the sample were female. Most participants were well educated, with a monthly household income of RMB 17,000 (1RMB $\approx$ 0.15 dollars) and above, and they in general did not have any religious beliefs. Our online sample tends to be slightly wealthier and more educated than the population in surveyed cities, although the average years of education of the

[2] We calculated the minimum sample size requirements in terms of the statistical power of hypothesis tests on the estimated coefficients, according to De Bekker-Grob et al. (2015). It needs a minimum sample size of 264 respondents with a statistical power of 0.8 and an $\alpha = 0.10$. Furthermore, several studies have reached effective conclusions based on sample sizes smaller than 300 respondents in the choice experiment of healthcare and food choice (De Bekker-Grob et al., 2015; e.g. Livingstone et al., 2021; Kershaw et al., 2019). This means that obtaining a sample size of 350 will ensure robust estimations.

Table 7.3 Sample description

Variable	Value
Age (year)	38.14 (11.59)
Female (%)	50.57
University degree (%)	82
No religious belief (%)	85.71
The number of adults in household	2.64 (0.94)
The number of children in household	0.83 (0.62)
City of residence (%)	
Beijing	16.57
Guangzhou	16.57
Wuhan	16.86
Shenyang	16.57
Shanghai	16.57
Chengdu	16.86
Monthly household income (%)	
<5000 RMB	0.29
5000–10,999 RMB	14.86
11,000–16,999 RMB	32.57
17,000–22,999 RMB	28.29
23,000–28,999 RMB	14.86
>=29,000 RMB	9.14
Individual daily diet expenditure (%)	
≤30 RMB	12.00
30–50 RMB	29.43
50–70 RMB	20.57
70–100 RMB	28.57
>100 RMB	9.43
Observations	350

Note(s): Values are % or mean (standard deviations) unless otherwise indicated
Source(s): Authors' estimation using online survey data

population aged 15 and above in surveyed cities have reached 12 years. Furthermore, these younger, better-educated, higher-income individuals are becoming the main decision-makers in households. In terms of family structure, the households had, on average, 2.6 adult members and 0.8 children. This is slightly higher than the Chinese average household size. According to the seventh national census released by the National Bureau of Statistics, the average number of family members in China is 2.62. Table 7.4 represented household characteristics of food purchasing behavior. Most (93%) families went grocery shopping more than 2–5 times a week, and half of the families ordered food delivery more than 2–5 times per week. The average daily diet cost per person was between RMB50 and RMB70.

Table 7.4 Food purchasing behavior

Variable	Value
Frequency of food purchasing (%)	
Every day	33.14
2–5 times a week	60.29
Once a week	6.29
Once every 2 weeks	0.29
Less than once every 2 weeks	0.00
Weekly food purchasing expenditure (%)	
<100 RMB	1.43
100–249 RMB	18.86
250–399 RMB	22.29
400–549 RMB	26.57
500–699 RMB	15.71
700–849 RMB	8.29
850–999 RMB	6.29
>1000 RMB	0.57
Frequency of ordering food or grocery delivery (%)	
Every day	4.86
2–5 times a week	49.71
Once a week	27.71
Once every 2 weeks	9.14
Once a month	4.29
Once every 2 months	0.57
Less than once every 2 months	2.57
Never	1.14
Weekly expenditure of ordering food or grocery delivery (%)	
<100 RMB	20.86
100–249 RMB	40.29
250–399 RMB	20.29
400–549 RMB	11.14
500–699 RMB	4.29
700–849 RMB	2.00
>850 RMB	1.14
Weekly expenditure for food-away from home (%)	
<100 RMB	16.86
100–249 RMB	33.14
250–399 RMB	26.29
400–549 RMB	12.57
500–699 RMB	6.86
700–849 RMB	2.86
850–999 RMB	1.43

Variable	Value
>1000 RMB	0.00
Cooking at home (%)	
Never	0.29
Sometimes	88.29
Every meal	11.43
Dietary restriction (%)	
No	88.86
Yes	11.14
Observation	350

Note(s): Values are % unless otherwise indicated
Source(s): Authors' estimation using online survey data

7.5 Results

This section first shows the estimation results of the random parameter logit model and respondents' willingness to pay. Second, we display the estimated impact of change in diet cost or diet taste on Chinese consumers' diet choices, respectively. Lastly, we explore the heterogeneous ranking of food motives for different income subgroups.

7.5.1 Estimation Results of Random Parameter Logit Models

Table 7.5 represents the average estimation results of the random parameter logit model. The coefficients of the four diet alternatives were significantly different from zero, meaning that consumers tend to choose other diets instead of keeping their current diets (or opting out). Among the four experimentally designed diets, the Chinese Food Guide Pagoda diet and the average diet were relatively preferred by respondents. Nevertheless, it is worth noting that the estimated standard deviation around the mean preference for the average diet was large, which meant that there was significant preference heterogeneity in the population. In contrast, the estimated standard deviation for the Chinese Food Guide Pagoda diet was insignificant, indicating that consumer preference for this diet is not heterogeneous. The positive sign for taste indicated that sensory appeal was an important factor in consumers' diet choices. The coefficient of price was negative and statistically significant, showing consumer utility decreased as the cost of a diet increased.

Table 7.6 presents the estimated unconditional mean WTP values and their 95% confidence intervals, The findings indicated that, on average, urban Chinese residents were willing to spend approximately 45, 47, 39, 47 and 16 RMB per day for the average diet, Chinese Food Guide Pagoda diet, EAT-Lancet diet, Flexitarian diet and customized diet taste, respectively. These results indicated that diet patterns were more important than taste for Chinese consumers.

Table 7.5 The estimation results of random parameters logit model

Variable	Coefficient	Standard deviations
Average diet	0.47***	1.24***
	(0.15)	(0.11)
Chinese Food Guide Pagoda diet	0.53***	0.04
	(0.13)	(0.22)
EAT-Lancet diet	0.40***	0.46***
	(0.16)	(0.12)
Flexitarian diet	0.43***	0.68***
	(0.17)	(0.10)
Price	−0.01***	0.01***
	(0.06)	(0.14)
Taste	0.16**	0.24
	(0.00)	(0.00)
Observations	350	
Log-likelihood	−3123.1	
AIC	6268.3	
R2	0.08	

Note(s): Standard deviations indicate the distribution of random parameters as standard deviations. Relative attribute importance was calculated by dividing the difference between the highest and lowest preference weights of that attribute by the sum of all attributes (Kamphuis et al., 2015; Livingstone et al., 2021; Zhang et al., 2022). *, ** and *** denote significance levels at 10%, 5% and 1%, respectively

Source(s): Authors' estimation using online survey data

Table 7.6 Simulated unconditional willingnesstopay

		WTP
Average diet	Mean	45.024
	95% C.I.	[36.918,53.129]
Chinese Food Guide Pagoda diet	Mean	47.229
	95% C.I.	[44.786, 49.672]
EAT-Lancet diet	Mean	39.396
	95% C.I.	[35.650,43.141]
Flexitarian diet	Mean	46.552
	95% C.I.	[31.778, 61.326]
Taste	Mean	15.308
	95% C.I.	[12.666, 17.951]

Source(s): Authors' estimation using online survey data

7.5.2 Results of Predicted Demand Curves

Figure 7.3 displays the predicted demand curves for four diet patterns without customized taste, deriving by incorporating individual marginal utilities. Specifically, these mean demand curves were derived according to the probability of choosing

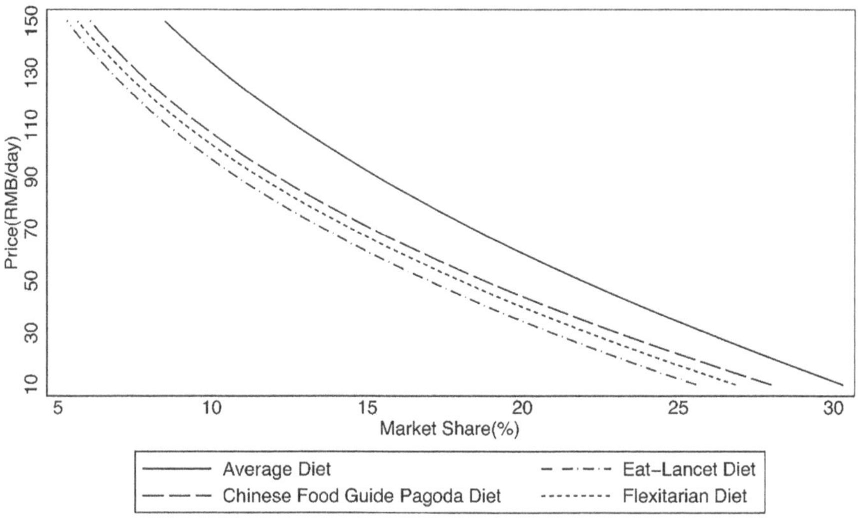

Source(s): Authors' estimation using online survey data

Fig. 7.3 Simulated diet demand curves without customized taste. Source(s): Authors' estimation using online survey data

diet option j for individual i. More specifically, the demand curves were derived with the midpoint of the price levels for each diet, except for the diet of interest, whose price levels were set ranging from 10 to 150 RMB. We found that own price elasticities equaled −0.52, −0.48, −0.45 and −0.48for the average diet, Chinese Food Guide Pagoda diet, EAT-Lancet diet and Flexitarian diet, respectively. That indicated a 10% price increase in the diet (relative to the midpoint price level) reduces its market share by 5%.

Figure 7.4 shows the simulated diet demand curves in two scenarios, namely, with and without customized tastes. Customized taste increased the market share, and the impact of taste remained similar across diets. Taste could, on average, increase about 0.5% of the market share for all four diets. Compared to cost, taste played a less significant role in urban Chinese consumers' diet choices.

7.5.3 Heterogeneity Analysis

Given the significant preference heterogeneity in our sample and the importance of economic status on food choices (Kamphuis et al., 2015), we explored the relative importance of food motives for different income level groups based on subsamples. More specifically, respondents are divided into high- and low-income subgroups according to the sample's median income. Table 7.7 presents the estimated results for different income respondents. The findings indicated that high-income participants prioritized diet healthiness more than low-income participants. They derived

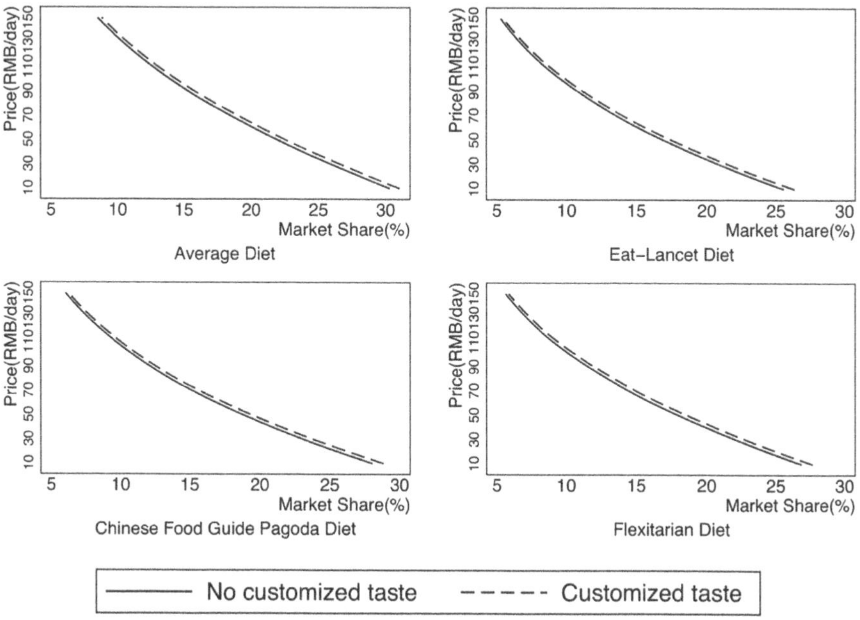

Source(s): Authors' estimation using online survey data

Fig. 7.4 Simulated diet demand curves by taste. Source(s): Authors' estimation using online survey data

significant positive utility from all four diet patterns, with the average diet being their preferred choice. In contrast, low-income participants only derived significant positive utility from the Chinese Guide Pagoda diet. Additionally, low-income consumers demonstrated a significant preference for price and sensory appeal. This indicated that they valued price and taste more than did high-income groups.

7.6 Discussions and Conclusions

The current dietary pattern of Chinese consumers has caused substantial health and environmental challenges (Afshin et al., 2019; Sheng et al., 2021). Our study revealed that in urban China, diet patterns, cost and taste were important factors underlying consumer diet decisions. This is consistent with the findings from the previous studies, which suggest that consumers preferred healthy, cheap, delicious, easy-cooking and purchasing-convenint foods (Jaeger et al., 2021; Kamphuis et al., 2015; Livingstone et al., 2021; Stroebele & De Castro, 2004). This implies that improving the accessibility, affordability and taste of sustainable healthy diets may have the potential to fuel the diet revolution in China.

Specifically, diet patterns, implying the healthiness and sustainability of a diet, were an important factor in urban Chinese diet selection. This is inline with

Table 7.7 The estimation results for different income level respondents

	Low-income	High-income
Means and standard errors		
Average diet	0.093	0.936***
	0.202	0.228
Chinese Food Guide Pagoda diet	0.329*	0.799***
	0.177	0.208
EAT-Lancet diet	0.212	0.700***
	0.206	0.250
Flexitarian diet	0.274	0.663**
	0.212	0.272
Price	−0.017***	−0.008**
	0.003	0.004
Taste	0.253***	0.042
	0.092	0.092
Standard deviations		
Average diet	1.118***	1.309***
Chinese Food Guide Pagoda diet	0.013	0.001
EAT-Lancet diet	0.436**	0.414**
Flexitarian diet	0.467***	0.863***
Price	0.017***	0.008**
Taste	0.459***	0.004
Model statistics		
Log-likelihood	*−1635.42*	*−1475.14*
AIC	3292.80	2972.30
N	183	167

Note(s): Standard deviations indicate the distribution of random parameters standard deviations. *, ** and *** denote significance level at 10%, 5% and 1%, respectively
Source(s): Author's estimation using online survey data

Kamphuis et al. (2015) and Kershaw et al. (2019). However, their experiment designs incorporated a qualitative healthiness attribute characterized by three levels: healthy, neutral and unhealthy. This ambiguous definition of healthiness may pose challenges for participants in connecting healthy foods in surveys with those under real shopping scenarios. As a result, individual preferences for the healthiness attribute could not be accurately estimated. This study used specific and detailed diet patterns, characterized by different food types and corresponding quantities, to indicate healthiness and environmental friendliness. Such an approach may help participants better understand and evaluate diets, leading to a more accurate estimation of individual preferences.

Among the different diet patterns, we found that respondents preferred the average diet most. This is evidenced by the fact that the market share for the average diet was always higher than other diets, regardless of diet cost. A possible explanation for such a result is that, compared to the other three diets, the average diet is closest to the urban Chinese daily diet, which includes more meat and grain but fewer fruits. Nevertheless, the estimated standard deviation around the preference parameter was large, indicating that there was a significant preference variability for the average diet. Considering the heterogeneous preference distribution in the total population, our findings imply that policymakers should hasten efforts to transform the Chinese consumer's diet toward a sustainable healthy diet, particularly for individuals who have strong preferences for the current diet.

In addition, our results show that consumers dislike meatless diets, such as the EAT-Lancet and the Flexitarian diet. Given that high levels of meat consumption would cause burdens and challenges for both public health and the environment (Sheng et al., 2021), our findings highlight that it is crucial to revolutionize urban Chinese diets toward environmentally sustainable and healthy ones. However, shifting toward a meatless diet in China is challenging because consumers are unlikely to reduce their animal product intake, and there is insufficient incentive for businesses to reduce supply without government interventions. In addition, Guo et al. (2022) found that reduced CDG emissions by reducing meat consumption could be offset by the higher emissions from increased fruit, vegetable and dairy product consumption. The production and consumption of these products entail a complex impact on human well-being and environmental concerns. While increasing the consumption of fruits and vegetables could prevent excessive deaths, it also leads to increased NH_3 emissions and water usage (Guo et al., 2022). We should pay more attention to the environmental and human health trade-offs in potential Chinese diet shifts. Extra efforts are warranted to achieve a diet that simultaneously achieves sustainability and health goals.

Our result highlights the importance of prices in promoting healthy food decisions among urban Chinese residents. This is consistent with the related studies derived from laboratory experiments, which suggested that subsidizing healthy foods or taxing unhealthy foods could incentivize consumers to buy healthy foods (French, 2003; Herman et al., 2008; Stuber et al., 2021). Our findings demonstrate that increasing the cost of an unsustainable unhealthy diet has the potential to promote diet shifts among urban Chinese residents. Specifically, if the cost of the average diet increases by 10% with no commensurate increase in the costs of other diets, the market demand would decrease by approximately 5%. Consequently, individuals who were previously inclined to the average diet would likely turn to cheaper and healthier alternatives. In fact, the simulated results suggest that consumers may choose the Chinese Food Guide Pagoda diet as their top choice. Possible reasons maybe that the Chinese Food Guide Pagoda diet is actively promoted by the Chinese government and social organizations, and the diet is more realistic as it compromises the dietary habits and food availability across China. Nowadays, China has issued a range of public health policies such as the Food and Nutrition Development Outline (2011–2020), the National Nutrition Plan (2017–2030) and the Outline of the Program for Health China 2030. In practice, the government has also taken some actions to guide residents to choose a healthy and balanced diet. For example, the Chinese Nutrition Society has issued the 2022 version of the Chinese Dietary Guidelines to popularize nutrition knowledge to the public.

However, it is worth noting that besides the higher-income residents in the large cities focused on in this paper, there are still many low-income groups in China. Our findings demonstrated that consumers with low income valued diets cost more than did high-income groups. Research indicates that there are at least 182.85 million urban households in China whose current diet expenditure is lower than the average minimum cost for a balanced diet, which suggests that low-income populations need to increase their spending by at least 20%–121% to achieve the recommended diet (Yin et al., 2023). What's worse, the COVID-19 pandemic and geopolitical conflicts also have slowed down economic growth and increased food prices, posing unprecedented challenges to the food distribution system. The cost of high-nutrient food groups such as fruits, vegetables and animal-source foods is generally higher than that of low-nutrient foods globally (Bai et al., 2022). Due to the increased cost of nutritious food, low-income and marginalized populations tend to consume cheaper energy-dense foods, which are more affordable and accessible to them (Green et al., 2013; Miller et al., 2016). This highlights the potential need for subsidies targeting vulnerable groups to shift their diets toward healthy ones (Xu et al., 2020). The government needstorecalibrate its agricultural policies and incentives at various levels of the food production and consumption chain to reduce the diet cost for vulnerable consumers and increase their purchasing power and ability to afford sustainable healthy diets.

Last, taste was found to be less important than diet pattern and cost in the high-income groups, while low-income consumers valued taste more importance. Other studies, however, reported that high-income groups rated taste to be significantly more important than their divergent findings could be the different methods of defining taste across studies. Defining taste is challenging as it is subjective and varies based on personal preference. Taste perceptions vary among individuals, influenced by genetic factors, cultural backgrounds, ethnicities, personal preferences and environmental factors (Bawajeeh et al., 2020). Additionally, consumers are normally unable to taste all products when making the purchase decision, whether in reality or in choice experiments. Additionally, results maybe context-specific, as food preferences are heavily influenced by cultural traditions and eating habits of different regions (Yin et al., 2020).

Achieving the goals for sustainable healthy diets will require interdisciplinary collaboration, interagency coordination and international cooperation. This necessitates collaborative efforts among governments, social organizations, businesses and individuals, employing policy guidance, technological innovation, market interventions and consumer education to gradually realize the concept of sustainable healthy diets. Furthermore, it is crucial to establish a comprehensive assessment framework for sustainable healthy diets, enabling the evaluation of different diets' impacts on health, environment and society (AGFEP et al., 2021). Such a framework could provide policymakers and consumers with scientific evidence to make informed choices.

This study also has several limitations. Firstly, our online sample is skewed toward younger, more educated and wealthier consumers; therefore, our results primarily reflect the diet choices of urban Chinese consumers rather than the population. Secondly, this study relied on descriptive information from existing literature to define the taste attribute. Despite our attempts to regulate the quantity of flavor enhancers that could potentially impact taste perception, such as vegetable oil, the quantification of other ingredients, such as sugar and salt, was not adequately controlled. As a result, the definition of taste in this paper makes it challenging to draw comparisons between taste preferences and diet patterns. Thirdly, beyond the scope of this study, we did not conduct further analysis on the impact of information. We leave this as one of the future research topics. Finally, while we employed various strategies to ensure response quality in stated preference surveys, there remains the possibility of hypothetical bias. Recently, researchers have proposed that using "real payment priming" could potentially reduce hypothetical bias in a stated valuation question (Jiang et al., 2022). Future researchers could consider using this method or extending our hypothetical experiments to real-world settings.

Appendices

Appendix 1 The Average Diet in Surveyed Cities (Unit: Gram)

Average diet		Beijing	Guangzhou	Shanghai	Wuhan	Shenyang	Chengdu
Total grains		303	371	327	371	396	451
Vegetables		377	359	336	386	362	403
Fruits		267	147	191	140	210	144
Legumes and nuts		36	29	40	43	50	43
Vegetable oils		26	33	32	41	37	43
Animal products	Pork	55	116	75	89	67	126
	Beef and lamb	32	19	23	12	19	12
	Chicken and other poultry	27	108	55	24	23	55
	Eggs	48	28	41	24	43	30
	Whole milk or equivalents	102	31	73	23	56	41
	Fish	41	116	110	62	63	38

Appendix 2 Choice Sets

The order of options in the choice sets below does not represent the order in the experiment, while each option is presented in random order.

Choice set 1

	Average diet	EAT-Lancet diet	Chinese Food Guide Pagoda diet	Flexitarian diet	
Taste	Customized taste	Customized taste	Without customized taste	Without customized taste	Keep my current diet
Cost of diet (RMB/day)	20	59	33	46	

Choice set 2

	Average diet	EAT-Lancet diet	Chinese Food Guide Pagoda diet	Flexitarian diet	
Taste	Customized taste	Without customized taste	Without customized taste	Customized taste	Keep my current diet
Cost of diet (RMB/day)	46	59	20	72	

Choice set 3

	Average diet	EAT-Lancet diet	Chinese Food Guide Pagoda diet	Flexitarian diet	
Taste	Customized taste	Customized taste	Without customized taste	Without customized taste	Keep my current diet
Cost of diet (RMB/day)	33	20	46	59	

Choice set 4

	Average diet	EAT-Lancet diet	Chinese Food Guide Pagoda diet	Flexitarian diet	
Taste	Customized taste	Customized taste	Without customized taste	Customized taste	Keep my current diet
Cost of diet (RMB/day)	20	33	72	46	

Choice set 5

	Average diet	EAT-Lancet diet	Chinese Food Guide Pagoda diet	Flexitarian diet	
Taste	Without customized taste	Customized taste	Without customized taste	Customized taste	Keep my current diet
Cost of diet (RMB/day)	33	59	20	46	

Choice set 6

	Average diet	EAT-Lancet diet	Chinese Food Guide Pagoda diet	Flexitarian diet	
Taste	Without customized taste	Without customized taste	Without customized taste	Customized taste	Keep my current diet
Cost of diet (RMB/day)	46	72	59	72	

Appendix 3 Cheap Talk Script

Studies have shown that consumers tend to overestimate the price they are willing to pay when answering hypothetical questions. That is, consumers indicated that the price they are willing to pay for a product in the questionnaire is greater than the price they paid for the product in the actual purchase. To avoid the above phenomenon, please assume that you are in the real purchase scenarios when answering the following questions.

Appendix 4 Food Consumption Survey

To help respondents establish realistic food quantities, before the choice questions, they were asked to compare an estimate of their average daily food consumption and the average consumption of Chinese residents for each food group. Questions are as follows:

1. Chinese residents' per capita cereals and potatoes consumption in 2019 was 331 g per day. Cereals and potatoes include rice, wheat food, potatoes, sweet potatoes, and others. 1 Liang (Chinese measurement unit) of rice weighs about 50 g. Could you please estimate your daily cereals and potatoes consumption? Please note: daily food consumption includes three meals, snacks, and midnight snacks.

A. Much higher than the national average
B. Slightly higher than the national average
C. In line with the national average
D. Slightly lower than the national average
E. Much lower than the national average
F. I'm not sure

2. Chinese residents' per capita vegetable consumption in 2019 was 270 g per day. A tomato or a cucumber weighs about 250 g. Could you please estimate your daily vegetable consumption? Please note: daily food consumption includes three meals, snacks, and midnight snacks.

A. Much higher than the national average
B. Slightly higher than the national average
C. In line with the national average
D. Slightly lower than the national average
E. Much lower than the national average
F. I'm not sure

3. Chinese residents' per capita fruit consumption in 2019 was 141 g per day. An apple is about 200 g. Could you please estimate your daily fruit consumption? Please note: daily food consumption includes three meals, snacks, and midnight snacks.

A. Much higher than the national average
B. Slightly higher than the national average
C. In line with the national average
D. Slightly lower than the national average
E. Much lower than the national average
F. I'm not sure

4. Chinese residents' per capita dairy consumption in 2019 was 34 g per day. A pack of milk is about 250 g. Could you please estimate your daily dairy consumption? Please note: daily food consumption includes three meals, snacks, and midnight snacks.

A. Much higher than the national average
B. Slightly higher than the national average
C. In line with the national average
D. Slightly lower than the national average
E. Much lower than the national average
F. I'm not sure

5. Chinese residents' per capita meat and egg consumption in 2019 was 124 g per day. An egg is about 50 g and a chicken leg is about 200 g. Could you please estimate your daily meat and egg consumption? Please note: daily food consumption includes three meals, snacks, and midnight snacks.

A. Much higher than the national average
B. Slightly higher than the national average
C. In line with the national average
D. Slightly lower than the national average
E. Much lower than the national average
F. I'm not sure

6. Chinese residents' per capita aquatic product consumption in 2019 was 37 g per day. A prawn is about 25 g. Could you please estimate your daily aquatic product consumption? Please note: daily food consumption includes three meals, snacks, and midnight snacks.

A. Much higher than the national average
B. Slightly higher than the national average
C. In line with the national average
D. Slightly lower than the national average
E. Much lower than the national average
F. I'm not sure

7. Chinese residents' per capita soy products and nuts consumption in 2019 was 36 g per day. 10 peanuts weigh 8 g. Could you please estimate your daily soy products and nuts consumption? Please note: daily food consumption includes three meals, snacks, and midnight snacks.

A. Much higher than the national average
B. Slightly higher than the national average
C. In line with the national average
D. Slightly lower than the national average
E. Much lower than the national average

Appendix 5 The Wording for Consumers Preceding the Decision Task

Preceding the decision task was the following information:

You will be shown several different diet selection scenarios, please choose the diet you would buy in real life. "If you don't prefer any of the four diet options, you can choose to keep your current diet". In every scenario, each diet product had the same characteristics, except for cost, and taste. The taste label indicates that the diet can be prepared according to your preferred taste. The cost represents the total price of an individual's daily food consumption for a whole day, where daily food consumption includes three meals, snacks, and midnight snacks.

Attention please: 1 jin (Chinese measurement unit) equals 500 g. Generally speaking, an egg weighs about 50 g, a chicken leg weighs approximately 200 g and a cucumber weighs about 250 g.

References

Afshin, A., Sur, P. J., Ferrara, G., Salama, J. S., Mullany, E. C., Abate, K. H., Abbafati, C., Abebe, Z., Aggarwal, A., Agrawal, S., Akinyemiju, T., Bacha, U., Bachman, V. F., Badali, H., Badawi, A., Bensenor, I. M., Biryukov, S. H., Cahill, L. E., Dandona, L., Bernabe, E., Biadgilign, S. K. K., Cahill, L. E., Carrero, J. J., Cercy, K. M., Dandona, R., et al. (2019). Health effects of dietary risks in 195 countries, 1990–2017: A systematic analysis for the global burden of disease study 2017. *The Lancet (British Edition), 393*(10184), 1958–1972. https://doi.org/10.1016/S0140-6736(19)30041-8

AGFEP, CARD, CIFAE, IAED, & IFPRI. (2021). *2021 China and global food policy report.*

AGFEP, CARD, CIFAE, IAED, & IFPRI. (2023). *2023 China and global food policy report.*

Bai, Y., Herforth, A., & Masters, W. A. (2022). Global variation in the cost of a nutrient-adequate diet by population group: An observational study. *The Lancet Planetary Health, 6*(1), e19–e28. https://doi.org/10.1016/S2542-5196(21)00285-0

Bawajeeh, A. O., Albar, S. A., Zhang, H., Zulyniak, M. A., Evans, C. E. L., & Cade, J. E. (2020). Impact of taste on food choices in adolescence—Systematic review and meta-analysis. *Nutrients, 12*(7), 1985. https://doi.org/10.3390/nu12071985

Blatner, D. J. (2009). *The flexitarian diet: The mostly vegetarian way to lose weight, be healthier, prevent disease, and add years to your life.* McGraw-Hill Professional.

Bloom, D.E., Cafiero, E.T., McGovern, M.E., Prettner, K., Stanciole, A., Weiss, J., Bakkila, S., & Rosenberg, L. (2013). *The economic impact of non-communicable disease in China and India: Estimates, projections, and comparisons.* NBER Working Paper No. w19335. https://doi.org/10.3386/w19335.

Burton, M., Rigby, D., Young, T., & James, S. (2001). Consumer attitudes to genetically modified organisms in food in the UK. *European Review of Agricultural Economics, 28*(4), 479–498. https://doi.org/10.1093/erae/28.4.479

Caputo, V., Lusk, J. L., & Nayga, R. M. (2018). Choice experiments are not conducted in a vacuum: The effects of external price information on choice behavior. *Journal of Economic Behavior and Organization, 145*, 335–351. https://doi.org/10.1016/j.jebo.2017.11.018

Chinese Center for Disease Control and Prevention. (2021). *Report on nutrition and chronic disease status of Chinese residents-2020.*

Cummings, R. G., & Taylor, L. O. (1999). Unbiased value estimates for environmental goods: A cheap talk design for the contingent valuation method. *The American Economic Review, 89*(3), 649–665. https://doi.org/10.1257/aer.89.3.649

De Bekker-Grob, E. W., Donkers, B., Jonker, M. F., & Stolk, E. A. (2015). Sample size requirements for discrete-choice experiments in healthcare: a practical guide. *Patient, 8*(5), 373–384. https://doi.org/10.1007/s40271-015-0118-z

de Ridder, D., Kroese, F., Evers, C., Adriaanse, M., & Gillebaart, M. (2017). Healthy diet: Health impact, prevalence, correlates, and interventions. *Psychology and Health, 32*(8), 907–941. https://doi.org/10.1080/08870446.2017.1316849

Farrell, J., & Rabin, M. (1996). Cheap talk. *Journal of Economic Perspectives, 10*(3), 103–118. https://doi.org/10.1257/jep.10.3.103

French, S. A. (2003). Pricing effects on food choices. *The Journal of Nutrition, 133*(3), 841S–843S. https://doi.org/10.1093/jn/133.3.841S

Green, R., Cornelsen, L., Dangour, A. D., Turner, R., Shankar, B., Mazzocchi, M., & Smith, R. D. (2013). The effect of rising food prices on food consumption: Systematic review with meta-regression. *BMJ, 346*(7915), 13–22. https://doi.org/10.1136/bmj.f3703

Guo, Y., He, P., Searchinger, T. D., Chen, Y., Springmann, M., Zhou, M., Zhang, X., Zhang, L., & Mauzerall, D. L. (2022). Environmental and human health trade-offs in potential Chinese dietary shifts. *One Earth, 5*(3), 268–282. https://doi.org/10.1016/j.oneear.2022.02.002

Han, A., Sun, T., Ming, J., Chai, L., & Liao, X. (2020). Are the Chinese moving toward a healthy diet? Evidence from macro data from 1961 to 2017. *IJERPH, 17*(15), 5294. https://doi.org/10.3390/ijerph17155294

Harrison, G. W. (2006). Experimental evidence on alternative environmental valuation methods. *Environmental and Resource Economics, 34*(1), 125–162. https://doi.org/10.1007/s10640-005-3792-9

Hensher, D. A. (2010). Hypothetical bias, choice experiments and willingness to pay. *Transportation Research. Part B: Methodological, 44*(6), 735–752. https://doi.org/10.1016/j.trb.2009.12.012

Herman, D. R., Harrison, G. G., Afifi, A. A., & Jenks, E. (2008). Effect of a targeted subsidy on intake of fruits and vegetables among low-income women in the special supplemental nutrition program for women, infants, and children. *American Journal of Public Health, 98*(1), 98–105. https://doi.org/10.2105/AJPH.2005.079418

Huang, L., Wang, Z., Wang, H., Zhao, L., Jiang, H., Zhang, B., & Ding, G. (2021). Nutrition transition and related health challenges over decades in China. *European Journal of Clinical Nutrition, 75*(2), 247–252. https://doi.org/10.1038/s41430-020-0674-8

Huang, Z., Zhu, Y.-D., Deng, J., & Wang, C. L. (2022). Marketing healthy diets: The impact of health consciousness on Chinese consumers' food choices. *Sustainability, 14*(4), 2059. https://doi.org/10.3390/su14042059

Intergovernmental Panel on Climate Change. (2022). Summary for policymakers. In *Climate change and land: IPCC special report on climate change, desertification, land degradation, sustainable land management, food security, and greenhouse gas fluxes in terrestrial ecosystems* (pp. 1–36). Cambridge University Press. https://doi.org/10.1017/9781009157988.001

Jaeger, S. R., Roigard, C. M., Hunter, D. C., & Worch, T. (2021). Importance of food choice motives vary with degree of food neophobia. *Appetite, 159*, 105056. https://doi.org/10.1016/j.appet.2020.105056

Jiang, Q., Penn, J., & Hu, W. (2022). Real payment priming to reduce potential hypothetical bias. *Journal of Choice Modelling, 45*, 100383. https://doi.org/10.1016/j.jocm.2022.100383

Kamphuis, C., de Bekker-Grob, E., & van Lenthe, F. (2015). Factors affecting food choices of older adults from high and low socioeconomic groups: A discrete choice experiment. *The American Journal of Clinical Nutrition, 101*(4), 768–774. https://doi.org/10.3945/ajcn.114.096776

Kershaw, K. N., Klikuszowian, E., Schrader, L., Siddique, J., Van Horn, L., Womack, V. Y., & Zenk, S. N. (2019). Assessment of the influence of food attributes on meal choice selection by socioeconomic status and race/ethnicity among women living in Chicago, USA: A discrete choice experiment. *Appetite, 139*, 19–25. https://doi.org/10.1016/j.appet.2019.04.003

Ladenburg, J., & Olsen, S. B. (2014). Augmenting short cheap talk scripts with a repeated opt-out reminder in choice experiment surveys. *Resource and Energy Economics, 37*, 39–63. https://doi.org/10.1016/j.reseneeco.2014.05.002

Lancaster, K. J. (1966). A new approach to consumer theory. *The Journal of Political Economy, 74*(2), 132–157. https://doi.org/10.1086/259131

Lee, S. H., Han, D. B., Caputo, V., & Nayga, R. M., Jr. (2015). Consumers' valuation for a reduced salt product: A non-hypothetical choice experiment. *Canadian Journal of Agricultural Economics, 63*(4), 563–582. https://doi.org/10.1111/cjag.12081

Liu, M., McNaughton, S. A., He, Q., & Leech, R. (2021). Longitudinal trajectories of diet quality and subsequent mortality among Chinese adults: Results from the China health and nutrition survey 1997–2015. *International Journal of Behavioral Nutrition and Physical Activity, 18*(1), 51. https://doi.org/10.1186/s12966-021-01118-7

Livingstone, K. M., Abbott, G., Lamb, K. E., Dullaghan, K., Worsley, T., & McNaughton, S. A. (2021). Understanding meal choices in young adults and interactions with demographics, diet quality, and health behaviors: A discrete choice experiment. *The Journal of Nutrition, 151*(8), 2361–2371. https://doi.org/10.1093/jn/nxab106

Lizin, S., Rousseau, S., Kessels, R., Meulders, M., Pepermans, G., Speelman, S., Vandebroek, M., Van Den Broeck, G., Van Loo, E. J., & Verbeke, W. (2022). The state of the art of discrete choice experiments in food research. *Food Quality and Preference, 102*, 104678. https://doi.org/10.1016/j.foodqual.2022.104678

Loureiro, M. L., & Umberger, W. J. (2007). A choice experiment model for beef: What US consumer responses tell us about relative preferences for food safety, country-of-origin labeling and traceability. *Food Policy, 32*(4), 496–514. https://doi.org/10.1016/j.foodpol.2006.11.006

Louviere, J. J. (1984). Using discrete choice experiments and multinomial logit choice models to forecast trial in a competitive retail environment: A fast food restaurant illustration. *Journal of Retailing, 60*(4), 81–107.

Lusk, J. L., & Tonsor, G. T. (2016). How meat demand elasticities vary with price, income, and product category. *Applied Economic Perspectives and Policy, 38*(4), 673–711. https://doi.org/10.1093/aepp/ppv050

Matthews, Y., Scarpa, R., & Marsh, D. (2017). Using virtual environments to improve the realism of choice experiments: A case study about coastal erosion management. *Journal of Environmental Economics and Management, 81*, 193–208. https://doi.org/10.1016/j.jeem.2016.08.001

McFadden, D. (1973). Conditional logit analysis of qualitative choice behavior. In P. Zarembka (Ed.), *Frontiers in econometrics* (pp. 105–142). Academic Press.

Miller, V., Yusuf, S., Chow, C. K., Dehghan, M., Corsi, D. J., Lock, K., Popkin, B., Rangarajan, S., Khatib, R., Lear, S. A., Mony, P., Kaur, M., Mohan, V., Vijayakumar, K., Gupta, R., Kruger, A., Tsolekile, L., Mohammadifard, N., Rahman, O., Rosengren, A., Avezum, A., Orlandini, A., Ismail, N., Lopez-Jaramillo, P., Yusufali, A., Karsidag, K., Iqbal, R., Chifamba, J., Oakley, S. M., Ariffin, F., Zatonska, K., Poirier, P., Wei, L., Jian, B., Hui, C., Xu, L., Xiulin, B., Teo, K., Mente, A., & Institution for Medicine. (2016). Availability, affordability, and consumption of fruits and vegetables in 18 countries across income levels: Findings from the prospective urban rural epidemiology (PURE) study. *The Lancet Global Health, 4*(10), e695–e703. https://doi.org/10.1016/S2214-109X(16)30186-3

Moskowitz, H. (2001). Creating new product concepts for foodservice – The role of conjoint measurement to identify promising product features. *Food Service Technology, 1*, 35–52. https://doi.org/10.1046/j.1471-5740.2001.00004.x

National Bureau of Statistics of China. (2020). *China Statistical Yearbook*. China Statistics Press.

National Bureau of Statistics of China. (2022). *China Statistical Yearbook*. China Statistics Press.

Ortega, D. L., Sun, J., & Lin, W. (2022). Identity labels as an instrument to reduce meat demand and encourage consumption of meat alternatives in China. *Food Policy, 111*, 102307. https://doi.org/10.1016/j.foodpol.2022.102307

Raghunathan, R., Naylor, R. W., & Hoyer, W. D. (2006). The unhealthy tasty intuition and its effects on taste inferences, enjoyment, and choice of food products. *Journal of Marketing, 70*(4), 170–184. https://doi.org/10.1509/jmkg.70.4.170

Rose, J. M., Bliemer, M. C. J., Hensher, D. A., & Collins, A. T. (2008). Designing efficient stated choice experiments in the presence of reference alternatives. *Transportation Research. Part B: Methodological, 42*(4), 395–406. https://doi.org/10.1016/j.trb.2007.09.002

Scarpa, R., Zanoli, R., Bruschi, V., & Naspetti, S. (2013). Inferred and stated attribute non-attendance in food choice experiments. *American Journal of Agricultural Economics, 95*(1), 165–180. https://doi.org/10.1093/ajae/aas073

Schwappach, D. L. B., & Strasmann, T. J. (2006). 'Quick and dirty numbers'? The reliability of a China stated-preference technique for the measurement of preferences for resource allocation. *Journal of Health Economics, 25*(3), 432–448. https://doi.org/10.1016/j.jhealeco.2005.08.002

Sheng, F., Wang, J., Chen, K. Z., Fan, S., & Gao, H. (2021). Changing Chinese diets to achieve a Win–Win solution for health and the environment. *China and World Economy, 29*(6), 34–52. https://doi.org/10.1111/cwe.12393

Silva, A., Nayga, R. M., Jr., Campbell, B. L., & Park, J. L. (2011). Revisiting cheap talk with new evidence from a field experiment. *Journal of Agricultural and Resource Economics, 36*(2), 280–291. https://doi.org/10.22004/ag.econ.117168

Springmann, M., Clark, M., Mason-D'Croz, D., Wiebe, K., Bodirsky, B., Lassaletta, L., Vries, W., Vermeulen, S., Herrero, M., Carlson, K. M., Jonell, M., Troell, M., DeClerck, F., Gordon, L. J., Zurayk, R., Scarborough, P., Rayner, M., Loken, B., Fanzo, J., Godfray, H. C. J., Tilman, D.,

Rockström, J., & Willett, W. (2018). Options for keeping the food system within environmental limits. *Nature, 562*(7728), 519–525. https://doi.org/10.1038/s41586-018-0594-0
Springmann, M., Spajic, L., Clark, M. A., Poore, J., Herforth, A., Webb, P., Rayner, M., & Scarborough, P. (2020). The healthiness and sustainability of national and global food based dietary guidelines: A modelling study. *BMJ, 370*, m2322. https://doi.org/10.1136/bmj.m2322
Stroebele, N., & De Castro, J. M. (2004). Effect of ambience on food intake and food choice. *Nutrition, 20*(9), 821–838. https://doi.org/10.1016/j.nut.2004.05.012
Stuber, J. M., Hoenink, J. C., Beulens, J. W. J., Mackenbach, J. D., & Lakerveld, J. (2021). Shifting toward a healthier dietary pattern through nudging and pricing strategies: A secondary analysis of a randomized virtual supermarket experiment. *The American Journal of Clinical Nutrition, 114*(2), 628–637. https://doi.org/10.1093/ajcn/nqab057
Train, K. E. (2009). *Discrete choice methods with simulation* (2nd ed.). Cambridge University Press. https://doi.org/10.1017/CBO9780511805271
Vale, R. C. D., Pieters, R., & Zeelenberg, M. (2008). Flying under the radar: Perverse package size effects on consumption self-regulation. *Journal of Consumer Research, 35*(3), 380–390. https://doi.org/10.1086/589564
Willett, W., Rockström, J., Loken, B., Springmann, M., Lang, T., Vermeulen, S., Garnett, T., Tilman, D., DeClerck, F., Wood, A., Jonell, M., Clark, M., Gordon, L. J., Fanzo, J., Hawkes, C., Zurayk, R., Rivera, J. A., De Vries, W., Majele Sibanda, L., Afshin, A., Chaudhary, A., Herrero, M., Agustina, R., Branca, F., Lartey, A., Fan, S., Crona, B., Fox, E., Bignet, V., Troell, M., Lindahl, T., Singh, S., Cornell, S. E., Srinath Reddy, K., Narain, S., Nishtar, S., & Murray, C. J. L. (2019). Food in the anthropocene: the EAT-Lancet commission on healthy diets from sustainable food systems. *The Lancet (British Edition), 393*(10170), 447–492. https://doi.org/10.1016/S0140-6736(18)31788-4
Xu, H., Ecker, O., Zhang, Q., Du, S., Liu, A., Li, Y., Hu, X., Li, T., Guo, H., Li, Y., Xu, G., Liu, W., Ma, J., Sun, J., Chen, K., Ma, G., & Abbasalizad Farhangi, M. (2020). The effect of comprehensive intervention for childhood obesity on dietary diversity among younger children: Evidence from a school-based randomized controlled trial in China. *PLoS One, 15*(7), e0235951. https://doi.org/10.1371/journal.pone.0235951
Yin, J., Yang, D., Zhang, X., Zhang, Y., Cai, T., Hao, Y., Cui, S., & Chen, Y. (2020). Diet shift: Considering environment, health and food culture. *The Science of the Total Environment, 719*, 137484. https://doi.org/10.1016/j.scitotenv.2020.137484
Yin, J., Hua, J., Zhang, X., Tuyishimire, A., & Yang, D. (2023). Healthy eating for all? The challenge of adhering to dietary guidelines for low-income groups in China. *Nutrients, 15*(12), 2704. https://doi.org/10.3390/nu15122704
Zhang, M., He, X., Wu, J., & Xie, F. (2022). POSA379 differences in cancer treatment preferences among oncologists, patients and family members: A discrete choice experiment. *Value in Health, 25*(1), S223. https://doi.org/10.1016/j.jval.2021.11.1090
Zhou, Y., Du, S., Su, C., Zhang, B., Wang, H., & Popkin, B. M. (2015). The food retail revolution in China and its association with diet and health. *Food Policy, 55*, 92–100. https://doi.org/10.1016/j.foodpol.2015.07.001

Chapter 8
Becoming Healthier Without Paying More? Experimental Evidence from the Impact of Multiple Traffic Lights on Chinese College Students

8.1 Introduction

The global prevalence of obesity is on the rise due to rapid socio-economic development and significant lifestyle changes among consumers. For example, in 2020, the rates of overweight and obesity among Chinese residents aged 18 years and above were 34.3% and 16.4%, respectively, as reported by the Chinese Nutrition Society in 2021. This phenomenon poses a critical risk factor for cardiovascular disease, diabetes, hypertension, and cancer, highlighting the need for health public interventions.

Nutrition labeling is a crucial tool for enhancing individuals' healthy food choices via the provision of nutritional information on food products (Capacci et al., 2012; Ying, 2020). Specifically, front-of-pack nutrition labeling communicates the nutritional quality of food products using simple icons, enhancing consumers' understanding of food nutritional information and serving as a convenient supplement to traditional back-of-pack nutritional labels (FAO et al., 2020; Food and Agriculture Organization of the United Nations & World Health Organization, 2021; Gomez et al., 2017). One of the most popular front-of-pack labels refers to the traffic light nutrition labeling scheme. The traffic light nutrition-labeling scheme, pioneered by the UK Food Standards Agency, utilizes a color-coded system to denote the levels of various nutrients. Each nutrient is represented by a color—green for low, amber for medium, and red for high levels. The multiple traffic light (MTL) label has been adopted by many developed countries, including the United States, the United Kingdom, France, Switzerland, Canada, and Singapore (Andrews et al., 2021; Bromberg et al., 2022; Egnell et al., 2018; Hagmann & Siegrist, 2020),

W. Lin, *Transforming China's Agri-Food System: Government-Market Synergy*, Resources, Environment and Agricultural Development,
https://doi.org/10.1007/978-981-95-7151-2_8

and some developing countries like Peru, Argentina, and Bulgaria (Defago et al., 2017). No other studies have tested the effectiveness of the MTL scheme in improving individuals' healthy food choices in China despite a large portion of the population being overweight or obese.

In China, the only mandatory nutrition label refers to nutritional content tables on the back of the package (Ying, 2020). Studies have indicated that the effectiveness of the back-of-pack nutritional fact panel is limited in encouraging consumers to make healthy choices due to the challenge residents face in understanding the label (Gong et al., 2015; Li, Xia, & Zhou, 2017b; Li, Zhao, et al., 2017a). On the other hand, China, being one of the world's largest food markets, has seen a significant rise in the consumption of prepackaged foods due to their convenience and easy storage (Zhang et al., 2015). Studies reveal that processed foods contribute substantially to dietary elements that need to be restricted (Weaver et al., 2014). The excessive consumption of prepackaged foods high in sugar, salt, and fat is closely linked to nutrition-related chronic diseases such as obesity and hypertension (Albuquerque et al., 2022; Baker & Friel, 2014; Oikawa et al., 2005; Yuan et al., 2009). Hence, there is an urgent need to design and implement more straightforward and user-friendly labels to guide Chinese residents to consume healthier food.

This study investigates the impacts of theMTL scheme on the healthiness and expenditure of individual food choices using a laboratory experiment in China. The impacts of the MTL scheme on food consumption are not conclusive in the literature. Relevant research has demonstrated the effectiveness of MTL in improving the healthfulness of consumers' food choices compared to other front-of-pack nutrition labeling schemes (Hersey et al., 2013; Koenigstorfer et al., 2014; Lundeberg et al., 2018; Maubach et al., 2014). Research by Crosetto et al. (2018) suggests that nutritional improvements resulting from labeling may come at an economic cost. However, this cost does not exhibit regressive effects compared to other policies such as taxes and subsidies, as indicated by Crosetto et al. (2018). However, another strand of the studies has found that the MTL scheme turns out to be useless in affecting consumer food choices (Gorski Findling et al., 2018; Vasiljevic et al., 2015). While many consumers appreciated the addition of signal light colors to theMTL, some experienced confusion about the label (De la Cruz-Góngora et al., 2017). Moreover, the MTL performs weaker than warning labels in encouraging individual purchases of healthier foods (Khandpur et al., 2018).

This study examines the impact of the multiple traffic light nutrition labels on individual choices of prepackaged food products, with a laboratory randomized control experiment on Chinese consumers. In particular, we focus on college students who are one of the major consumers of prepacked food products. Studies have found that the behavior of students closely mirrors that of non-students in experimental settings. We aim to add to the literature on the effectiveness of the MTL scheme by offering additional empirical evidence on China, the largest food market worldwide.

8.2 Survey Design

This section describes the design of the randomized experiment, traffic light nutritional labels, and the questionnaire in this study.

8.2.1 Experimental Design

To investigate the impacts of traffic light nutritional labels on food choices, we used a between-subject design and randomly assigned subjects into one of two groups: a control group and a labeled group. A between-subject experiment offers several advantages. The controlled setting, careful selection of food products, and randomization of subjects control for confounding factors that could otherwise impact the effectiveness of traffic light labels.

Both the control and labeled groups completed their food purchases within a simulated food shopping platform. The only difference between the two groups lies in the fact that all food products in the labeled group were accompanied by corresponding traffic light labels, adhering to the standards outlined in Table 8.1. Relevant studies have demonstrated that simulated food purchasing environments serve as valuable and practical tools for studying the effects of health interventions, leading to results that closely parallel real-world findings (Braga et al., 2023; Jilcott Pitts et al., 2018; van Herpen et al., 2016; Waterlander et al., 2015).

The simulated food shopping platform of this study included a total of 12 categories and 85 food products, identical for the control and labeled groups. The 12 food categories include chips, bread and pastries, cookies, nuts, jellies, chocolates and marinated seaweeds, dried beans, cereal mixes, dairy products, drinking water and soda, carbonated beverages, fruit juices and tea beverages, and fruits. The food categories and products in the platform were selected from the best-selling prepackaged food items within each respective product category, both online and offline, in the experimental city's grocery stores. In addition to evaluating sales volume, the selection of food products took into account various attributes, such as nutritional content, price, and taste. This approach is tailored to closely replicate the scenarios

Table 8.1 The standard of traffic nutrition labels

	Green	Yellow	Red
Solid food, per 100 g			
Fat	≤3.0 g	3.0–17.5 g	>17.5 g
Carbohydrate	Energy ratio<40%	Energy ratio 40%–70%	Energy ratio>70%
Sodium	≤120 mg	120–600 mg	≥600 mg
Liquid food, per 100 mL			
Fat	≤1.5 g	1.5–8.8 g	>8.8 g
Carbohydrate	≤5.0 g	5.0–11.3 g	>11.3 g
Sodium	≤120 mg	120–300 mg	≥300 mg

faced by consumers in their real food shopping experiences. Figure 8.1 presents the food shopping platform of the control group, where the front and back packaging, price, name, and size of each product were shown to consumers. The food shopping platform of the labeled group was built on the control group's platform, with the addition of a traffic light nutrition label for each product (Fig. 8.2). In both platforms, consumers made their choices by selecting the quantity of food products through a click-based interaction.

8.2.2 *Traffic Light Label Design*

In the absence of official traffic light labels in China, this study crafted the labels by drawing upon official documents and the related literature. These sources include the General Principles for Nutrition Labeling of Prepackaged Foods in China, the Guidelines for Nutrition Claims and Nutrient Functional Claims of Foods in China (National Health Commission of China, 2007), the United Kingdom's Traffic Nutrition Labels from the UK Food Standard Agency, and the study of Seidelmann et al. (2018).

TheMTL scheme, initially devised by the UK Food Standards Agency, employs a color-coded system for various nutrients. In this scheme, the color signifies low (green), medium (amber), or high (red) levels. The green threshold aligns with the standards outlined in Regulation No. 1924/2006 for making low-level nutrition claims. Nutrients receive a red label if their content surpasses 25% and 12.5% of the maximum recommended daily intake for adults in solid and liquid foods, respectively. The color coding is established on a per 100 g basis for solid foods and per 100 mL for liquid foods.

Table 8.1 outlines the precise standards governing our MTL scheme, which is adapted based on the UK's version. These labels provide information on four nutritional elements—calories, fat, carbohydrates, and sodium—for a range of items, including solid foods like cookies, chips, and chocolate, and liquid foods such as

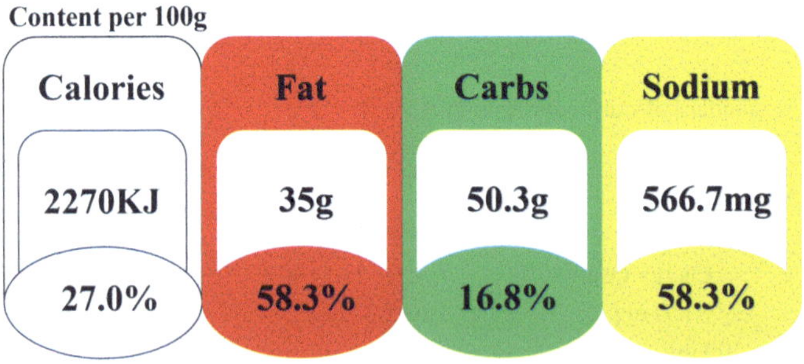

Fig. 8.1 A sample of traffic light nutrition label. Notes: This white panel indicates the amount of energy per 100 g in a food item. The red, green, and yellow panels refer to the amount of fat, carbohydrates, and sodium

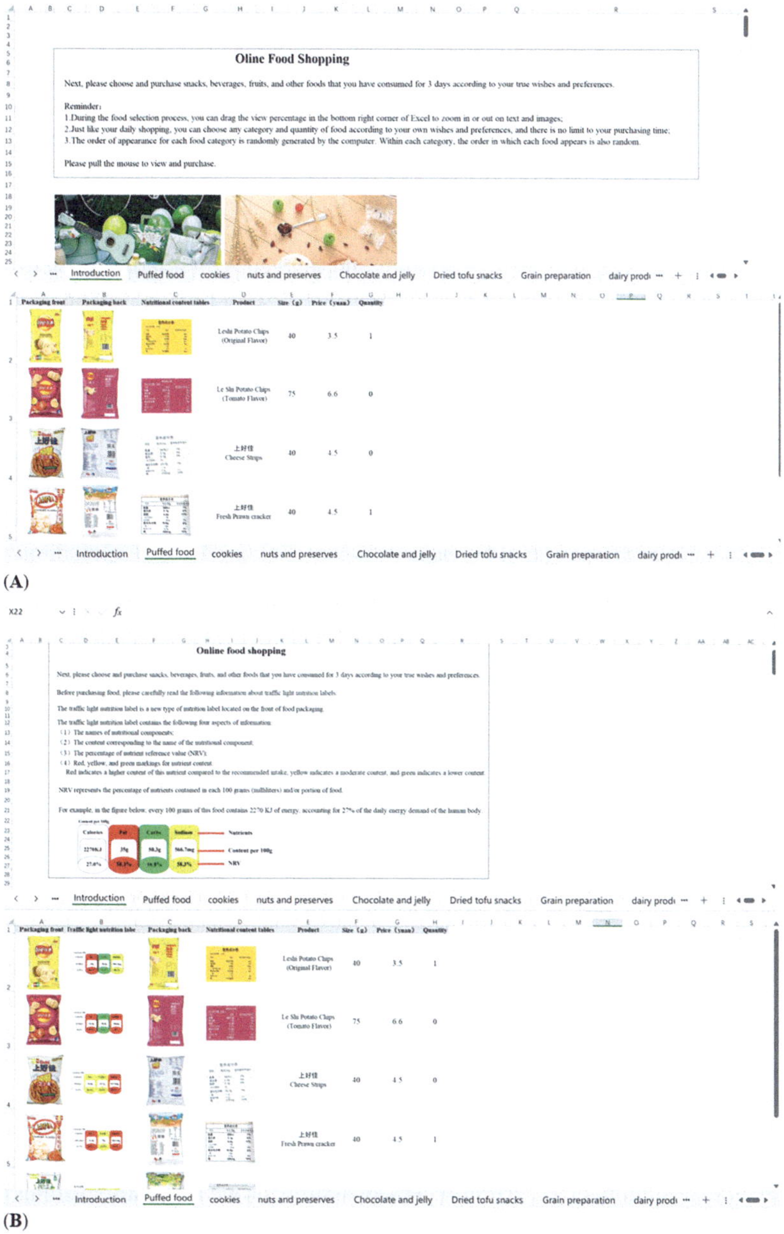

Fig. 8.2 (**a**) The online shopping platform of the control group (Traffic = 0). (**b**) The online shopping platform of the treatment group (Traffic = 1). Notes: the only difference in online shopping platforms between the control group and the treatment group is that the latter included the explanation on traffic nutrition labels, and each food product has been attached with a corresponding traffic nutrition label

fruit juice, yogurt, and soda. In particular, if the fat content per 100 g of solid food is 3 g or below, or the fat content per 100 mL of liquid food is 1.5 g or less, the product is classified as low fat, and the fat panel is marked with the color green. Conversely, if the fat content per unit of a product exceeds 25% of the reference level recommended by the Dietary Nutrient Reference Intake for Chinese Residents, the product is designated as high fat, and its traffic light label includes a red fat panel. Regarding sodium, we define a food item as low in sodium when the sodium content per 100 g of solid food or 100 mL of liquid food is 120 mg or less. Conversely, a food product is classified as high sodium and marked with a red fat panel if the sodium content equals or exceeds 600 mg per unit of solid food or 300 mg per unit of liquid food. While the UK version incorporates sugar content into MTL, China does not mandate the disclosure of sugar content on food products. Instead, China mandates the disclosure of carbohydrates in nutrition labeling. Thus, this study includes carbohydrates instead of sugars in the MTL scheme. Following Seidelmann et al. (2018), foods with less than 40% of calories per 100 g or 100 mL derived from carbohydrates are categorized as low carbohydrate (green). Conversely, foods with more than 70% carbohydrates are designated as high carbohydrate (red), while those with carbohydrate content between 40% and 70% are labeled as medium carbohydrate (yellow). For an illustration of the traffic light label, please refer to Fig. 8.1.

8.2.3 Questionnaire Design

To better understand consumers' food attitudes and choice behavior, we design survey questionnaires before food purchases in the simulated platform. The questionnaire included information on sociodemographic characteristics, usual food purchase and consumption, nutritional knowledge level, and psychological status. First, the sociodemographic part asked for subjects' gender, age, residence, grade, height, weight, household size, pre-tax annual household income from all sources, need to lose or gain weight, etc. The food purchase and consumption part included monthly food expenditures, frequency of eating out and ordering food delivery, food allergies, and chronic diseases. The third part, nutritional knowledge level, was elicited by the General Nutritional Knowledge Questionnaire (GNKQ). GNKQ was first developed by Parmenter and Wardle in the UK in 1999 and then adopted in other countries, such as Australia (Hendrie et al., 2008), Turkey (Alsaffar, 2012), and Japan (Matsumoto et al., 2017). This scale performs well in distinguishing participants' nutrition knowledge levels and predicting their food choice behavior (Gao et al., 2021; Hendrie et al., 2008; Jezewska-Zychowicz & Plichta, 2022; Luo et al., 2023; Mambrini et al., 2023; Manzano-Felipe et al., 2022). Last, cognitive depletion would have a strong effect on food choices (Boswell et al., 2018). So, we assess the subjects' stress and anxiety by using The Depression-Anxiety-Stress Scale

(DASS-21). DASS-21 is a streamlined version of the DASS developed by Lovibond & Lovibond (1995). While keeping the dimensions of the original scale unchanged, seven items were retained for each of the three subscales of depression, anxiety, and stress in order to improve the efficiency of recognizing and assessing the symptoms of the corresponding mood disorders (Gong et al., 2010). Studies have shown that DASS-21 is more suitable than the full version of the DASS (Antony et al., 1998; Crawford & Henry, 2003; Moussa et al., 2016; Thiyagarajan et al., 2022). To ensure the quality of responses, we include two attention checks in the questionnaire. Table 8.2 presents the description of the survey questions.

Table 8.2 Variable definition

Name	Definition
Traffic	=1 if in the nutrition traffic label labeled group, =0 otherwise
Gender	=1 if male, =0 otherwise
Age	Year
Residence	=1 if living in urban, =2 suburb, =3 county, =4 rural
Grade	=1 if fresh year, =2 sophomore, =3 junior, =4 senior, =5 master, =6 doctoral
Height	Meter
Weight	Kilogram
Overweight	=1 if overweight, =0 otherwise
HHsize	Household size
HHinc	Pre-tax total household income in 2021, RMB
Loweight	=1 if on diet, =2 otherwise
Gaweight	=1 if gaining weight, =2 otherwise
Fallergy	=1 if having food allergy, =2 otherwise
Chronic	=1 if having chronic diseases, =2 otherwise
Foodexp	=1 if monthly food expenditure below 600 RMB, =2: 600–1000 RMB =3: 1000–1500 RMB, =4: 1500–2000 RMB, =5: above 2000 RMB
Outfreq	Monthly online food delivery frequency, 0%–100%
Delivfreq	Monthly dining out frequency, 0%–100%
Nutrscroe	Nutrition knowledge score, 1–9
Nutriatten	Attention to food nutrition facts panel, 0%–100%
Nutricomm	=1 if the current nutrition facts panel needs improvement, =2 otherwise
Pressue	Pressure level, 0–14
Anxiety	Anxiety level, 0–10
Certain	Certainty of food choice in the experiment, 0%–100%
Foodnum	Number of food products chosen in the experiment
Texp	Total expenditure in the experiment, RMB
Tcalorie	Total calories from the food products chosen in the experiment, kJ
Tfat	Total fat from the food products chosen in the experiment, gram
Tcarb	Total carbohydrates from the food products chosen in the experiment, gram
Tsodi	Total sodium from the food products chosen in the experiment, milligram

8.3 Survey Procedure

There are three steps in our entire survey.

Upon arrival, participants received a hard copy of the survey instructions and were instructed to thoroughly read them. We further elucidated the instructions and demonstrated to participants how to make purchases on the platform. Participants were encouraged to ask any questions regarding the instructions or the survey. After ensuring clarity on the entire experimental process and details, participants proceeded to sign a consent form, signifying their understanding of the experiment's content, benefits, and potential risks. Specifically, participants were told that they would receive a payment of 15 RMB after finishing the food purchase and questionnaire.

Next, participants proceed with the online questionnaire.

After completing the questionnaire, participants entered the food shopping platform to make food choices. In this segment, participants were tasked with choosing any food products in the platform for their 3-day consumption. There was no time constraint for the subjects, and they could choose any number of food products they desired. To ensure incentive compatibility in food choices, participants were notified that one product from their shopping list would be randomly chosen for an actual transaction, and they would be required to pay the corresponding price. The selected product would then be delivered to them within 24 h. Therefore, food choices made by respondents were subject to individual preferences and budget constraints, close to their actual food purchases.

8.4 Data and Description

We recruited participants from a Chinese university in April and May 2021. Before implementing the survey and experiment, we obtained ethical approval from the university. We released the research recruitment information through the on-campus forum popular among college students, and individuals joined the study voluntarily by completing an enrollment questionnaire, which assessed their eligibility based on criteria such as (1) being over 18 years old and (2) having purchased food products last month. Finally, a total of 100 qualified college students were randomly assigned to one of the two groups, with 47 in the control group and 53 in the labeled group. The size of our control and labeled groups is consistent with other studies using between-subject designs (Lloyd-Smith & Adamowicz, 2018; Xie et al., 2022). The average survey duration was 20 min. Table 8.2 details the variables and their corresponding data.

8.5 Empirical Method and Results

8.5.1 Empirical Model

We used ordinary least-square models to examine the effects of traffic light labels on consumer food choices. The model specification is:

$$Y_i = \alpha_0 + \alpha_1 \text{Traffic i} + \alpha_2 X_i + \varepsilon_i \tag{8.1}$$

where i denotes individual i, Y_i refers to the dependent variables, including the natural logarithm of the total calories, fat, carbohydrates, sodium, and expenditure of the food basketselected by individual i. The key independent variable, Traffic i, is a dummy variable that equals one if individual i was in the labeled group, and zero otherwise. X_i is a vector of control variables, accounting for the impacts of socio-demographics, usual food purchase and consumption habits, and health and nutrition status. The definitions and descriptions of variables are outlined in Tables 8.2 and 8.3.

8.5.2 Baseline Effects

Table 8.3 presents a comparison of differences between the control and labeled groups. In terms of socio-demographic characteristics, approximately 64% of the participants in this experiment were female, with an average age of 21 years and the majority residing in urban or suburban areas. The subjects have an average height of 1.66 m and an average weight of 57.65 kg. Approximately 8% self-reported as overweight, with over half expressing a desire to lose weight. Around 11% of participants reported being lactose intolerant or having allergies, and about 6.67% suffered from chronic conditions such as gastroenteritis and hypoglycemia. Most subjects belonged to families consisting of three-to-four people, with their families reporting an annual income falling within the range of RMB 50,000–120,000. Regarding daily dietary consumption, participants had an average monthly dietary expenditure ranging from RMB 1000–1500. The average weekly frequency of ordering takeaways or eating out for the participants was approximately 26%. Moreover, while most participants demonstrated a certain level of nutrition knowledge, their attention to nutritional labels remained low. Nearly all participants fell within the normal range for stress and anxiety values, with a small proportion of individuals reporting moderate anxiety. In summary, the *t*-test results revealed no significant differences between the control and labeled groups in terms of socio-demographics, food consumption habits, nutrition, and health status.

Data from the food shopping platform included which group a participant was assigned to, the total number of food products chosen by a participant, the total expenditure, and the quantities of calories, fat, carbohydrates, and sodium. The

Table 8.3 Balance test table for students in control and labeled groups

Variable	Traffic = 0 (*N* = 47)		Traffic = 1 (*N* = 53)		
	Mean	S.D.	Mean	S.D.	*t*-Test
Socio-demographics					
Gender	0.364	0.475	0.375	0.434	0.818
Age	21.380	1.963	21.490	2.259	−0.244
Residen	2.297	1.222	2.075	1.207	0.854
Grade	3.081	1.622	3.075	1.530	0.017
Height	1.671	0.078	1.658	0.066	0.804
Weight	59.660	8.787	56.250	9.705	1.703
Overweight	0.081	0.277	0.094	0.295	−0.215
HHsize	3.892	1.022	3.566	0.844	1.652
HHinc	4.324	1.564	3.925	1.426	1.258
Usual food consumption					
Foodexp	3.243	0.830	3.130	0.849	1.092
Outfreq	25.700	19.960	27.110	26.650	−0.273
Delivfreq	27.270	26.040	26.640	28.470	0.107
Loweight	1.459	0.505	1.585	0.497	−1.170
Gaweight	1.919	0.277	1.868	0.342	0.751
Fallergy	1.838	0.374	1.943	0.233	−1.649
Health and nutrition status					
Nutriscore	5.486	1.742	5.245	1.764	0.642
Nutriatten	32.410	28.880	34.910	25.510	−0.433
Nutricomm	1.595	0.498	1.491	0.505	0.968
Chronic	1.946	0.229	1.925	0.267	0.397
Pressure	4.541	3.245	4.755	3.356	−0.302
Anxiety	2.946	2.147	3.340	2.441	−0.790
Food choice in the experiment					
Certain	79.72	19.79	78.72	19.31	0.235
Foodnum	7.514	3.934	6.755	3.486	0.964
Texp	75.870	63.480	61.340	43.300	1.292
Tcalorie	12,023	8937	9160	5594	1.868*
Tfat	84.350	64.650	60.780	40.160	2.132
Tcarb	458.700	360.900	361.600	238.200	1.540
Tsodi	3209	2973	2036	1600	2.418**

Notes: *t*-test scores are obtained from testing equality in each of the variables between the two groups. *, ** denote statistical significance at 10% and 5% level, respectively

quantity of nutrition elements was obtained from the back-of-pack nutritional content table of each product. The participants, on average, chose six-to-seven food items for their shopping baskets. The majority of individuals self-reported a certainty level of nearly 80% regarding their experimental choices. There are no significant differences in the total expenditure and the count of selected food products between the two groups. However, relative to the control group, individuals in the labeled group exhibited significantly lower levels of calories and sodium in their chosen food items, potentially due to the presence of the traffic light labels.

In addition, this subsection presents the baseline effects of the traffic light labels on the healthiness of food choices, followed by an analysis of their impacts on economic costs. All models are estimated using Eq. (8.1).

The average impacts of the traffic light labels on each of the four nutritional elements—calories, fat, carbohydrates, and sodium—are presented in Table 8.4. In general, participants in the labeled group, as compared to the control group, exhibited a tendency to select a basket of food items with lower calories, fats, carbohydrates, and sodium content. This observation holds true even when accounting for control variables. Thus, we focus on the model specification with control variables in discussing empirical results, specifically columns (2), (4), (6), and (8) of Table 8.4.

The results reveal that, on average, the traffic light labels significantly decreased the total calorie intake of an individual in the labeled group by 21%, as compared to the control group. Among the remaining three nutrients, traffic light labels demonstrated the highest effectiveness in reducing sodium intake (30%), followed by fat (25%) and carbohydrates (18%), with statistical significance at the 1% level.

Several studies have suggested that improvements in nutrition induced by labeling often coincide with higher expenditures, disproportionately affecting those with lower incomes in their pursuit of healthier food options (Crosetto et al., 2018). Building upon this, we further investigate the impact of the traffic light labels on the total expenditure (Table 8.5). Table 8.5 reveals that incorporating the traffic light labels into prepackaged foods does not lead to an increase in consumers' food expenditures. Consistent with Crosetto et al. (2018), our study implies that the implementation of MTL does not impose a significant financial burden on consumers, even as it enhances the nutritional quality of their food choices.

8.5.3 Heterogeneity

The utilization of nutrition labels is associated with consumer characteristics. Next, we will investigate how the effects of traffic light labels vary among different genders and levels of nutrition knowledge.

Tables 8.6, 8.7, 8.8, and 8.9 reveal that the effects of MTL vary among groups with different genders and levels of nutritional knowledge. Overall, traffic light labeling has a more significant impact on the female group compared to the male group. In the male subsample, MTL significantly reduced the total calories of food baskets by approximately 39% and total carbohydrate intake by 44%. However, in the female subsample, MTL influenced the intake of all nutritional elements, namely calories, fat, sodium, and carbohydrates. MTL exerted the largest impact on reducing sodium levels in females' food choices (47.8%), followed by fat (30.4%), carbohydrates (24.9%), and calories (20.5%). This difference in the MTL's effects between males and females would be associated with the health awareness and nutritional concepts prevalent in different gender groups. Women are more inclined

Table 8.4 Nutritional impacts of traffic nutrition labels

	Ln(Tcalorie)		Ln(Tfat)		Ln(Tcarb)		Ln(Tsodi)	
	(1)	(2)	(3)	(4)	(5)	(6)	(7)	(8)
Constant	9.190***	7.489***	4.170***	2.344***	5.892***	4.274***	7.716***	4.164***
	(0.104)	(0.664)	(0.126)	(0.769)	(0.113)	(0.742)	(0.147)	(0.967)
Traffic	−0.286**	−0.211**	−0.330*	−0.258*	−0.257	−0.183*	−0.504**	−0.308*
	(0.144)	(0.089)	(0.169)	(0.142)	(0.158)	(0.096)	(0.211)	(0.173)
Control		Yes		Yes		Yes		Yes
R^2	0.041	0.613	0.041	0.483	0.028	0.587	0.057	0.487
Observations	100	100	100	100	100	100	100	100

Notes: The dependent variable takes the natural logarithm form. Control variables are all the variables in Table 8.2, except for those belonging to food choice in the experiment. *, **, and *** denote statistical significance at 10%, 5%, and 1% level, respectively. Standard errors are in parentheses

Table 8.5 Economic impacts of traffic nutrition labels

	Ln(Texp)	Ln(Texp)
Constant	4.079*** (0.112)	2.100*** (0.615)
Traffic	−0.250 (0.162)	−0.121 (0.090)
Control		Yes
R^2	0.024	0.687
Observations	100	100

Notes: The dependent variable takes the natural logarithm form. Control variables are all the variables in Table 8.2, except for those belonging to food choice in the experiment. *, **, and *** denote statistical significance at 10%, 5%, and 1% level, respectively. Standard errors are in parentheses

Table 8.6 Heterogenous impacts of traffic nutrition labels on total calories

	Gender		Nutrition knowledge	
	Female	Male	Below median	Above median
Constant	8.352***	5.376***	7.490***	4.423**
	(0.795)	(1.127)	(0.854)	(1.624)
Traffic	−0.205*	−0.394**	−0.185*	0.106
	(0.103)	(0.179)	(0.098)	(0.588)
Control	Yes	Yes	Yes	Yes
R^2	0.638	0.793	0.660	0.799
Observations	65	25	71	29

Notes: The dependent variable takes the natural logarithm of Tcalorie. Control variables are all the variables in Table 8.2, except for those belonging to food choice in the experiment. *, **, and *** denote statistical significance at 10%, 5%, and 1% level, respectively. Standard errors are in parentheses. Below median refers to the subsample whose nutrition knowledge, indicated by Nutriscore, is below the median of the full sample

Table 8.7 Heterogenous impacts of traffic nutrition labels on total fat

	Gender		Nutrition knowledge	
	Female	Male	Below median	Above median
Constant	2.696**	1.850	1.998*	1.635*
	(1.073)	(1.436)	(1.074)	(0.853)
Traffic	−0.304**	−0.384	−0.190*	−0.374
	(0.134)	(0.356)	(0.098)	(0.517)
Control	Yes	Yes	Yes	Yes
R^2	0.489	0.577	0.509	0.809
Observations	73	27	71	29

Notes: The dependent variable takes the natural logarithm of Tfat. Control variables are all the variables in Table 8.2, except for those belonging to food choice in the experiment. *, **, and *** denote statistical significance at 10%, 5%, and 1% level, respectively. Standard errors are in parentheses. Below median refers to the subsample whose nutrition knowledge, indicated by Nutriscore, is below the median of the full sample

Table 8.8 Heterogenous impacts of traffic nutrition labels on total carbohydrates

	Gender		Nutrition knowledge	
	Female	Male	Below median	Above median
Constant	5.514***	1.322	4.340***	0.818*
	(0.878)	(1.179)	(0.931)	(0.510)
Traffic	−0.249**	−0.441**	−0.181**	0.311
	(0.122)	(0.182)	(0.107)	(0.637)
Control	Yes	Yes	Yes	Yes
R^2	0.603	0.856	0.634	0.785
Observations	73	27	71	29

Notes: The dependent variable takes the natural logarithm of Tcarb. Control variables are all the variables in Table 8.2, except for those belonging to food choice in the experiment. *, **, and *** denote statistical significance at 10%, 5%, and 1% level, respectively. Standard errors are in parentheses. Below median refers to the subsample whose nutrition knowledge, indicated by Nutriscore, is below the median of the full sample

Table 8.9 Heterogenous impacts of traffic nutrition labels on total sodium

	Gender		Nutrition knowledge	
	Female	Male	Below median	Above median
Constant	4.490***	2.712*	4.043***	2.944**
	(1.422)	(1.406)	(1.188)	(1.296)
Traffic	−0.478**	−0.099	−0.082	−0.874
	(0.200)	(0.414)	(0.176)	(0.862)
Control	Yes	Yes	Yes	Yes
R^2	0.481	0.640	0.514	0.802
Observations	73	27	71	29

Notes: The dependent variable takes the natural logarithm of Tsodi. Control variables are all the variables in Table 8.2, except for those belonging to food choice in the experiment. *, **, and *** denote statistical significance at 10%, 5%, and 1% level, respectively. Standard errors are in parentheses. Below median refers to the subsample whose nutrition knowledge, indicated by Nutriscore, is below the median of the full sample

to read nutrition labels compared to men (Campos et al., 2011; Cowburn & Stockley, 2005; Storcksdieck Genannt Bonsmann & Wills, 2012). Expectedly, MTL has more evident impacts among individuals with lower levels of nutrition knowledge. This observation is grounded in the idea that individuals with higher nutrition knowledge may already possess the necessary information to make informed and healthy food choices, rendering the traffic light label less important for their decision-making process. Table 8.10 indicates that the MTL scheme has little impact on food expenditures regardless of gender and nutrition knowledge groups.

Table 8.10 Heterogenous impacts of traffic nutrition labels on total expenditure

	Gender		Nutrition knowledge	
	Female	Male	Below median	Above median
Constant	2.853***	0.431	1.919***	−0.194**
	(0.801)	(1.498)	(0.704)	(0.701)
Traffic	−0.090	−0.254	−0.132	0.207
	(0.105)	(0.315)	(0.097)	(0.714)
Control	Yes	Yes	Yes	Yes
R^2	0.684	0.782	0.722	0.764
Observations	73	27	71	29

Notes: The dependent variable takes the natural logarithm of Texp. Control variables are all the variables in Table 8.2, except for those belonging to food choice in the experiment. *, **, and *** denote statistical significance at 10%, 5%, and 1% level, respectively. Standard errors are in parentheses. Below median refers to the subsample whose nutrition knowledge, indicated by Nutriscore, is below the median of the full sample

8.6 Discussions and Conclusions

More than 50 countries worldwide have implemented front-of-pack nutrition labeling, characterized as a collaborative effort involving governments, food industries, and retailers that ultimately guide consumers to healthier food choices (World Health Organization, 2018). Since half of the adult population in China is overweight or obese, the nutrition labeling scheme, in particular the traffic light nutrition labeling, has growingly received attention and consideration from the Chinese government.

This study offers a novel contribution by assessing the effectiveness of Multiple Traffic Lights (MTL) in guiding Chinese consumers toward healthier food choices through a randomized controlled trial. The insights gained from this research carry implications for the design and implementation of a traffic light labeling scheme in China. Due to the rapid increase in diet-related diseases in recent years, these findings hold significance for addressing and mitigating health concerns in the Chinese population.

The findings reveal that the incorporation of MTL significantly contributes to reducing Chinese consumers' intake of calories, fat, carbohydrates, and sodium. Specifically, the introduction of traffic light labels resulted in a significant 21% decrease in the total calorie intake for individuals in the labeled group, compared to the control group. Among the other three nutrients, traffic light labels exhibited the greatest effectiveness in reducing sodium intake by 30%, followed by fat at 25% and carbohydrates at 18%. Significantly, our research reveals that traffic light labels improve the healthiness of individuals' food choices without adding extra costs. Moreover, the impact of MTL differed across groups, showing larger effects on the female subsample and those with lower levels of nutrition knowledge. This underscores the potential of MTL to enhance and complement China's current back-of-pack nutrition labeling, providing consumers with a more helpful tool for selecting healthy food products. The MTL scheme is especially advantageous for consumers, particularly those who are less knowledgeable about nutrition and nutrition labels since it enables them to choose healthy food products without paying additional costs.

This finding is consistent with several studies showing that front-of-pack labels, such as the MTL scheme, receive more attention from consumers than the existing and classic back-of-pack nutrition panel (Becker et al., 2015, 2016; Graham et al., 2017). Consumers prefer nutrition labels with graphics and symbols, especially those using colors (Campos et al., 2011; Cowburn & Stockley, 2005). Front-of-Pack (FOP) schemes, particularly Multiple Traffic Lights (MTL), are found to be visually appealing, friendly, and easy to understand (Babio et al., 2014; Savoie et al., 2013; Siegrist et al., 2015). Color-coded labels, such as MTL, provide clear visual signals for consumers to recognize healthy and nutritious foods, even without extensive nutrition knowledge. Future research can focus on the application effect of MTL labeling in larger sample sizes and can explore different formats of the MTL scheme, including size, position, and color. Lastly, we acknowledge that this study has some limitations that warrant future research. For example, our focus is on a sample of college students; future research could be extended to investigate the effect of MTL labeling on other demographic groups. Additionally, while we demonstrate the effectiveness of MTL labeling in promoting healthier food choices, other labeling schemes exist. Future research should compare the effectiveness of different nutritional labeling programs to provide a more comprehensive understanding.

Author Contributions Conceptualization, T.W. and W.L.; methodology: T.W. and W.L.; software: T.W.; validation: J.L., T.W. and W.L.; formal analysis, J.L. and T.W.; investigation, T.W.; data curation, T.W.; writing—original draft preparation, J.L. and T.W.; writing—review and editing, J.L., T.W. and W.L.; supervision, W.L.; project administration, W.L. All authors have read and agreed to the published version of the manuscript.

Funding This work was supported by the National Natural Science Foundation of China (No. 72103180) and the Fundamental Research Funds for the Central Universities.

Institutional Review Board Statement This study was approved by IRB of Zhejiang University.

Informed Consent Statement Informed consent was obtained from all subjects.

Data Availability Statement Data will be available upon request.

Conflicts of Interest The authors declare no conflict of interest.

References

Albuquerque, T. G., Bragotto, A. P. A., & Costa, H. S. (2022). Processed food: Nutrition, safety, and public health. *International Journal of Environmental Research and Public Health, 19*, 16410.

Alsaffar, A. A. (2012). Validation of a general nutrition knowledge questionnaire in a Turkish student sample. *Public Health Nutrition, 15*, 2074–2085.

Andrews, J. C., Netemeyer, R., Burton, S., & Kees, J. (2021). What consumers actually know: The role of objective nutrition knowledge in processing stop sign and traffic light front-of-pack nutrition labels. *Journal of Business Research, 128*, 140–155.

Antony, M. M., Bieling, P. J., Cox, B. J., Enns, M. W., & Swinson, R. P. (1998). Psychometric properties of the 42-item and 21-item versions of the Depression Anxiety Stress Scales in clinical groups and a community sample. *Psychological Assessment, 10*, 176–181.

Babio, N., Vicent, P., López, L., Benito, A., Basulto, J., & Salas-Salvadó, J. (2014). Adolescents' ability to select healthy food using two different front-of-pack food labels: A cross-over study. *Public Health Nutrition, 17*, 1403–1409.

Baker, P., & Friel, S. (2014). Processed foods and the nutrition transition: Evidence from Asia. *Obesity Reviews, 15*, 564–577.

Becker, M. W., Bello, N. M., Sundar, R. P., Peltier, C., & Bix, L. (2015). Front of pack labels enhance attention to nutrition information in novel & commercial brands. *Food Policy, 56*, 76–86.

Becker, M. W., Sundar, R. P., Bello, N., Alzahabi, R., Weatherspoon, L., & Bix, L. (2016). Assessing attentional prioritization of front-of-pack nutrition labels using change detection. *Applied Ergonomics, 54*, 90–99.

Boswell, R. G., Sun, W., Suzuki, S., & Kober, H. (2018). Training in cognitive strategies reduces eating and improves food choice. *Proceedings of the National Academy of Sciences of the United States of America, 115*, E11238–E11247.

Braga, B. C., Cash, S. B., Sarson, K., Chang, R., Mosca, A., Wilson, N. L., & W. (2023). The gamification of nutrition labels to encourage healthier food selection in online grocery shopping: A randomized controlled trial. *Appetite, 188*, 106610.

Bromberg, M., Sinai, T., Keinan-Boker, L., Endevelt, R., & Frankenthal, D. (2022). Current use of nutrition facts tables and attitudes towards new red and green front-of-package labels among Israeli consumers. *International Journal of Food Sciences and Nutrition, 73*, 230–237.

Campos, S., Doxey, J., & Hammond, D. (2011). Nutrition labels on pre-packaged foods: A systematic review. *Public Health Nutrition, 14*, 1496–1506.

Capacci, S., Mazzocchi, M., Shankar, B., Macias, J. B., Verbeke, W., Pérez-Cueto, F. J. A., Kozioł-Kozakowska, A., Piórecka, B., Niedzwiedzka, B., D'Addesa, D., et al. (2012). Policies to promote healthy eating in Europe: A structured review of policies and their effectiveness. *Nutrition Reviews, 70*, 188–200.

Cowburn, G., & Stockley, L. (2005). Consumer understanding and use of nutrition labelling: A systematic review. *Public Health Nutrition, 8*, 21–28.

Crawford, J. R., & Henry, J. D. (2003). The Depression Anxiety Stress Scales (DASS): Normative data and latent structure in a large non-clinical sample. *The British Journal of Clinical Psychology, 42*(Pt 2), 111–131.

Crosetto, P., Lacroix, A., & Muller, L., & Ruffieux, B. (2018). *Nutritional and economic impact of 5 alternative front-of-pack nutritional labels: Experimental evidence*. Available at: https://www.semanticscholar.org/paper/Nutritional-and-economic-impact-of-5-alternative-Crosetto-Lacroix/a2295ca059bfbe160e8c1ebc45172a2e9a1ed9a2 (Accessed 1 December 2023).

De la Cruz-Góngora, V., Torres, P., Contreras-Manzano, A., Jáuregui de la Mota, A., Mundo-Rosas, V., Villalpando, S., & Rodríguez-Oliveros, G. (2017). Understanding and acceptability by Hispanic consumers of four front-of-pack food labels. *International Journal of Behavioral Nutrition and Physical Activity, 14*, 28.

Defago, D., Geng, J. F., Molina, O., & Santa María, D. (2017). *Digestible information: The impact of multiple traffic light nutritional labeling in a developing country [MPRA Paper]*. Available at: https://mpra.ub.uni-muenchen.de/79678/ (Accessed 1 December 2023).

Egnell, M., Talati, Z., Hercberg, S., Pettigrew, S., & Julia, C. (2018). Objective understanding of front-of-package nutrition labels: An international comparative experimental study across 12 countries. *Nutrients, 10*, 1542.

FAO, IFAD, UNICEF, WFP, & WHO. (2020). *The state of food security and nutrition in the world 2020: Transforming food systems for affordable healthy diets*. FAO.

Food and Agriculture Organization of the United Nations, & World Health Organization. (2021). Codex alimentarius. In *Guidelines on nutrition labelling CXG 2-1985*. FAO; WHO.

Gao, Z., Wu, F., Lv, G., Zhuang, X., & Ma, G. (2021). Development and validity of a general nutrition knowledge questionnaire (GNKQ) for Chinese adults. *Nutrients, 13*, 4353.

Gomez, P., WerleCO, C., & Corneille, O. (2017). The pitfall of nutrition facts label fluency: Easier-to-process nutrition information enhances purchase intentions for unhealthy food products. *Marketing Letters, 28*, 15–27.

Gong, X., Xie, X., Xu, R., & Luo, Y. (2010). Psychometric properties of the Chinese version of DASS-21 in Chinese colleges students. *Chinese Journal of Clinical Psychology, 4*, 443–446.

Gong, W., Guo, H., Song, C., Yuan, F., Li, X., Liu, W., Wu, X., Luan, D., & Liu, A. (2015). Knowledge and practice regarding food nutrition labeling among primary and secondary students and parents in four cities. *Chinese Journal of School Health, 6*, 847–850.

Gorski Findling, M. T., Werth, P. M., Musicus, A. A., Bragg, M. A., Graham, D. J., Elbel, B., & Roberto, C. A. (2018). Comparing five front-of-pack nutrition labels' influence on consumers' perceptions and purchase intentions. *Preventive Medicine, 106*, 114–121.

Graham, D. J., Lucas-Thompson, R. G., Mueller, M. P., Jaeb, M., & Harnack, L. (2017). Impact of explained v. unexplained front-of-package nutrition labels on parent and child food choices: A randomized trial. *Public Health Nutrition, 20*, 774–785.

Hagmann, D., & Siegrist, M. (2020). Nutri-score, multiple traffic light and incomplete nutrition labelling on food packages: Effects on consumers' accuracy in identifying healthier snack options. *Food Quality and Preference, 83*, 103894.

Hendrie, G. A., Cox, D. N., & Coveney, J. (2008). Validation of the general nutrition knowledge questionnaire in an Australian community sample. *Nutrition and Dietetics, 65*, 72–77.

Hersey, J. C., Wohlgenant, K. C., Arsenault, J. E., Kosa, K. M., & Muth, M. K. (2013). Effects of front-of-package and shelf nutrition labeling systems on consumers. *Nutrition Reviews, 71*, 1–14.

Jezewska-Zychowicz, M., & Plichta, M. (2022). Diet quality, dieting, attitudes and nutrition knowledge: Their relationship in Polish young adults—A cross-sectional study. *International Journal of Environmental Research and Public Health, 19*, 6533.

Jilcott Pitts, S. B., Ng, S. W., Blitstein, J. L., Gustafson, A., & Niculescu, M. (2018). Online grocery shopping: Promise and pitfalls for healthier food and beverage purchases. *Public Health Nutrition, 21*, 3360–3376.

Khandpur, N., de Morais Sato, P., Mais, L. A., Bortoletto Martins, A. P., Spinillo, C. G., Garcia, M. T., Urquizar Rojas, C. F., & Jaime, P. C. (2018). Are front-of-package warning labels more effective at communicating nutrition information than traffic-light labels? A randomized controlled experiment in a Brazilian sample. *Nutrients, 10*, 688.

Koenigstorfer, J., Groeppel-Klein, A., & Kamm, F. (2014). Healthful food decision making in response to traffic light color-coded nutrition labeling. *Journal of Public Policy & Marketing, 33*, 65–77.

Li, N., Zhao, Y., Zhang, M., & Zhu, W. (2017a). Investigation on cognition and behavior of pre-packaged food nutrition labels among students in Peking University Health Science Center. *Occupational Health, 20*, 2795–2799.

Li, X., Xia, Q., & Zhou, Y. (2017b). Cognition and application of food nutrition labeling among residents, Yangpu district, Shanghai city, 2016. *Preventive Medicine Tribune, 11*, 829–832.

Lloyd-Smith, P., & Adamowicz, W. (2018). Can stated measures of willingness-to-accept be valid? Evidence from laboratory experiments. *Journal of Environmental Economics and Management, 91*, 133–149.

Lovibond, P. F., & Lovibond, S. H. (1995). Depression anxiety and stress scales (DASS-42) [database record]. *APA PsycTests, 43*, 13–26.

Lundeberg, P. J., Graham, D. J., & Mohr, G. S. (2018). Comparison of two front-of-package nutrition labeling schemes, and their explanation, on consumers' perception of product healthfulness and food choice. *Appetite, 125*, 548–556.

Luo, M., Liu, Y., Ye, P., Cai, S., Yao, Z., Zhao, L., Luo, J., & Yu, D. (2023). Weight-control behaviors and dietary intake in Chinese adults: An analysis of three national surveys (2002–2015). *Nutrients, 15*, 1395.

Mambrini, S. P., Soranna, D., Averna, E., Di Guglielmo, G., Lucchetti, E., Tinozzi, T., Vinci, C., Barbieri, V., Zambon, A., Bertoli, S., et al. (2023). Development of a questionnaire on nutritional knowledge for the obese hospitalized patient: The NUTRIKOB questionnaire. *Frontiers in Nutrition, 10*, 1232424.

Manzano-Felipe, M. Á., Cruz-Cobo, C., Bernal-Jiménez, M. Á., & Santi-Cano, M. J. (2022). Validation of the general and sport nutrition knowledge questionnaire (GeSNK) in Spanish adolescents. *Nutrients, 14*, 5324.

Matsumoto, M., Tanaka, R., & Ikemoto, S. (2017). Validity and reliability of a general nutrition knowledge questionnaire for Japanese adults. *Journal of Nutritional Science and Vitaminology, 63*, 298–305.

Maubach, N., Hoek, J., & Mather, D. (2014). Interpretive front-of-packnutrition labels. Comparing competing recommendations. *Appetite, 82*, 67–77.

Moussa, M. T., Lovibond, P., & Laube, R. (2016). *Psychometric properties 1 psychometric properties of a Chinese version of the 21-item Depression Anxiety Stress Scales (DASS 21)*. Available at: https://www.semanticscholar.org/paper/Psychometric-Properties-1-Psychometric-Properties-a-Moussa-Lovibond/adc36910fd0df2586b1c8b3d88746a78ba083ab2 (Accessed 1 December 2023).

National Health Commission of China. (2007). Available at: https://www.sciencedirect.com/journal/appetite/publish/guide-for-authors#68000 (Accessed 1 December 2023).

Oikawa, D., Nakanishi, T., Nakamura, Y. N., Yamamoto, T., Yamaguchi, A., Shiba, N., Iwamoto, H., Tachibana, T., & Furuse, M. (2005). Modification of skin composition by conjugated linoleic acid alone or with combination of other fatty acids in mice. *The British Journal of Nutrition, 94*, 275–281.

Savoie, N., Barlow Gale, K., Harvey, K. L., Binnie, M. A., & Pasut, L. (2013). Consumer perceptions of front-of-package labelling systems and healthiness of foods. *Canadian Journal of Public Health, 104*, e359–e363.

Seidelmann, S. B., Claggett, B., Cheng, S., Henglin, M., Shah, A., Steffen, L. M., Folsom, A. R., Rimm, E. B., Willett, W. C., & Solomon, S. D. (2018). Dietary carbohydrate intake and mortality: A prospective cohort study and meta-analysis. *The Lancet Public Health, 3*, e419–e428.

Siegrist, M., Leins-Hess, R., & Keller, C. (2015). Which front-of-pack nutrition label is the most efficient one? The results of an eye-tracker study. *Food Quality and Preference, 39*, 183–190.

Storcksdieck Genannt Bonsmann, S., & Wills, J. M. (2012). Nutrition labeling to prevent obesity: Reviewing the evidence from Europe. *Current Obesity Reports, 1*, 134–140.

Thiyagarajan, A., James, T. G., & Marzo, R. R. (2022). Psychometric properties of the 21-item Depression, Anxiety, and Stress Scale (DASS-21) among Malaysians during COVID-19: A methodological study. *Humanit. Soc. Sci. Commun., 9*, 220.

van Herpen, E., van den Broek, E., van Trijp, H. C. M., & Yu, T. (2016). Can a virtual supermarket bring realism into the lab? Comparing shopping behavior using virtual and pictorial store representations to behavior in a physical store. *Appetite, 107*, 196–207.

Vasiljevic, M., Pechey, R., & Marteau, T. M. (2015). Making food labels social: The impact of colour of nutritional labels and injunctive norms on perceptions and choice of snack foods. *Appetite, 91*, 56–63.

Waterlander, W. E., Jiang, Y., Steenhuis, I. H. M., & NiMhurchu, C. (2015). Using a 3D virtual supermarket to measure food purchase behavior: A validation study. *Journal of Medical Internet Research, 17*, e107.

Weaver, C. M., Dwyer, J., Fulgoni, V. L., King, J. C., 3rd, Leveille, G. A., MacDonald, R. S., Ordovas, J., & Schnakenberg, D. (2014). Processed foods: Contributions to nutrition. *The American Journal of Clinical Nutrition, 99*, 1525–1542.

World Health Organization. (2018). *Better food and nutrition in Europe—Progress report*. Available at: https://iris.who.int/ handle/10665/345370 (Accessed 1 December 2023).

Xie, L., Adamowicz, W., Kecinski, M., & Fooks, J. R. (2022). Using economic experiments to assess the validity of stated preference contingent behavior responses. *Journal of Environmental Economics and Management, 114*, 102659.
Ying, F. (2020). Theoretical understanding and improvement advice on food nutrition label system in China. *Law Science, 2*, 83–102.
Yuan, G., Sinclair, A. J., Xu, C., & Li, D. (2009). Incorporation and metabolism of punicic acid in healthy young humans. *Molecular Nutrition & Food Research, 53*, 1336–1342.
Zhang, J., Li, Z., Huang, F., Zhai, F., Wang, H., & Zhang, B. (2015). Survey on the consumption of pre-package foods among urban adult residents in China. *Acta Nutrimenta Sinica, 21*, 1–9.

Chapter 9
Effectiveness of Front-of-Pack Nutritional Labels: Evidence from Sugar-Sweetened Beverages in China

9.1 Introduction

Due to the negative externalities associated with obesity, which extend beyond the individuals directly affected and economic development, governments implement a range ofpolicies to mitigate and reduce its prevalence. Among others, providing individuals the information that aids in the identification and selection of healthy food options has proven to be one of the most cost-effective policy tools (An et al., 2021; Aranda et al., 2021; Corvalan et al., 2019; Tiboldo et al., 2021). Nutrition Facts Panels (NFP), used worldwide and typically found on the back of food packages, present standardized calorie and nutrition information. However, the effectiveness of NFP in promoting healthier foods has been criticized due to their limited visibility, complexity, and difficulty in comprehension (Guan et al., 2022; Zhang et al., 2022). To tackle these concerns, there has been an emergence of various front-of-pack nutritional (referred to as FOP) labels. The FOP nutrition label formats are interpretive, that is, use words, colours, and symbols to make judgements and be understandable to all population subgroups, empowering individuals to make informed choices and better understand the nutritional value of the products (Grunert & Wills, 2007; Li et al., 2022; Wright et al., 2020).

While studies evaluating the effectiveness of FOP labels have increased recently, several knowledge gaps remain. First, the effectiveness of different types of FOP labelling systems in promoting healthier food choices remains an unresolved question. To optimize the use of FOP labelling for promoting healthier consumption, it is imperative to understand the differential impact of various FOP labels on individual food preferences. Around the world, the most common designs of FOP labels fall into two groups: nutrient-specific labels and summary labels, varying in their graphical presentation (colours, formats, and sizes), and types of emphasized nutrients (critical or positive statements) (Temple, 2020). Nutrient-specific FOP labels highlight the content of energy and of several substances, most commonly saturated

W. Lin, *Transforming China's Agri-Food System: Government-Market Synergy*, Resources, Environment and Agricultural Development,
https://doi.org/10.1007/978-981-95-7151-2_9

fat, sugar, and sodium (or salt), such as traffic light labels, warning labels, and nutrition claims. Summary labels, by contrast, use an algorithm to translate the components of the food into a single value that denotes how healthy or unhealthy it is, such as the health-tick label, or physical activity label. Existing research has primarily examined one or a limited number of FOP labels, resulting in a lack of consensus regarding the efficacy of FOP labels (Oswald et al., 2022; Temple, 2020). There are major differences between the studies, both in the methodology used and the way the results are presented, making it hard to make an exact quantitative comparison of the results of the different studies (Temple, 2020). Consequently, there is a need to construct a unifying framework aiming at identifying the most beneficial FOP labelling type in terms of nutrition information provision and encouraging healthier food choices.

Second, related research has primarily focused on examining consumer perceptions and attention towards FOP labels (Carroll et al., 2021; Ma & Zhuang, 2021; Temple, 2020), and the effectiveness of FOP labelling in individuals' healthy food choices remains a subject of ongoing debate. Some studies argued that FOP labels occasionally mislead consumers, leading to an inaccurate assessment of a product's healthfulness and the increased consumption of unhealthy foods (Eldesouky et al., 2020; Gębski et al., 2019; Melo et al., 2019). For example, the food traffic light FOP labels which have been extensively studied, were perceived as containing more information and had better performance in capturing consumers' attention and facilitating the identification of healthy food options (Defago et al., 2020; Thiene et al., 2018). However, other studies have argued that colour-coded information would make consumers overreact and reduce the individual perception of food healthiness (Nyilasy et al., 2016; Schifferstein et al., 2017). Health-tick label which provides a summary logo of the healthfulness of the food or beverages can save consumers' decision time and help them choose healthier products (Roseman et al., 2018). In contrast, other studies found little improvement in consumers' understanding and food choices under health-tick circumstances (Hodgkins et al., 2015). Some studies confirmed that critical formats indicating unhealthfulness such as warning labels appear more effective in guiding consumers to nutritionally favourable products and promoting reduced consumption of nutrient-poor food and beverages (Machín et al., 2019; Rosenblatt et al., 2019; Silva et al., 2022). However, Egnell et al. (2018) confirmed the weakest performance regarding objective understanding and health rating in the warning system than other FOP label systems.

Thus, this study assesses six kinds of nutrition labels simultaneously (Fig. 9.1), categorized as nutrient-specific FOP labels (traffic light label, warning label, nutrition claims) and summary FOP labels (health-tick label, physical activity labels), and non-interpretative labels (nutrition facts panel), with variations in colours, formats, and wordings. From the graphical presentation, there are three text labels (nutrition facts panel, warning, and nutrition claims), one colour-coded label (traffic light), and two image labels (physical activity, and health tick). Of the types of emphasized nutrients, two of them are positive statements (nutrition claims, health tick), one of them is critical statements (warning label), one of them has both positive and critical statements (traffic light label using red for critical and green for

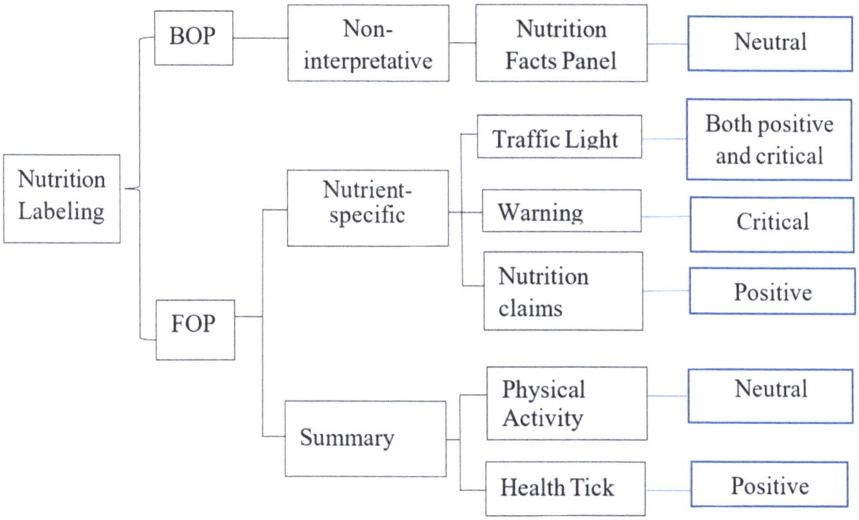

Fig. 9.1 Six kinds of labels selected in this paper

positive), and two of them are neutral (nutrition facts panel, physical activity label). This allows us to assess the effectiveness of different kinds of labels from different perspectives such as interpretation and simplicity, presentation format, and information judgement.

Thirdly, this study contributes to the existing literature by specifically investigating the impacts of FOP labels on sugar-sweetened beverage consumption. SSBs are consumed on a global scale, with intake levels above the recommended daily limits for free sugar in many high-income countries and on the rise in low-income and middle-income countries (Malik & Hu, 2022). It is well-established that excessive sugar consumption, especially from sugar-sweetened beverages, has been linked to increased risk of obesity, diabetes, and cardiovascular disease (Bentley et al., 2020; Singh et al., 2015), which makes these beverages an ideal target for nutritional policy and regulatory actions (Lopez & Fantuzzi, 2012; Malik & Hu, 2022; Zhang et al., 2019). Hence, this study is related to many studies that explored the effectiveness of nutrition labels on SSB purchases (Acton & Hammond, 2018; Neuhofer et al., 2020; Taillie et al., 2020).

The reason we chose China for the empirical context is twofold. On the one hand, the rapid increase in SSB consumption in China, with a per capita annual intake of approximately 30 litres, has contributed significantly to sugar intake and obesity rates nationwide (Yu et al., 2016; Zhai et al., 2022). On the other hand, in developing countries like China, the adoption of simplified and prominent FOP labels is limited, posing challenges in effectively conveying nutritional information to consumers (Downs et al., 2009; Kanter et al., 2018). This study aims to design and assess the impacts of different FOP labels on consumers' valuations regarding sugar-sweetened beverages in the Chinese market. By shedding light on the influence of FOP labels on consumer SSB preferences and willingness to pay (WTP), this research has the potential to inform public policy interventions and provide valuable insights for policymakers and food marketers seeking to promote healthier food choices and combat the negative health consequences associated with excessive SSB consumption.

9.2 Study Design

This study employs an online survey incorporating a discrete choice experiment (DCE) and a between-subject design to evaluate the efficacy of front-of-pack (FOP) labels in influencing consumer willingness to pay (WTP) for SSBs. The survey comprises two sections. The first section collects information on participants' socio-demographic characteristics, SSB consumption patterns, and dietary habits. In the second section, participants are randomly assigned to different treatment groups, with each group exposed to a specific FOP label alongside the conventional Nutrition Facts Panel labels in the DCE questions. The target population for this study comprises Chinese urban consumers aged 18 years and above, who have purchased SSB products within the past three months.

9.2.1 Between-Subject Treatments and Fop Label Design

Prior to answering the DCE questions, participants were randomly assigned to one of six treatment groups, aiming to examine the variations in consumer WTPfor SSBs when presented with different types of nutrition labels. Each nutrition label was assigned to one of the six treatment groups, and examples of these labels can be seen in Table 9.1. The control group utilized the Nutrition Facts Panel placed on the back of food packages, which displayed detailed nutrition information on energy, protein, fat, carbohydrates, sodium, and added sugar. Disclosure of nutritional information has become mandatory since the mandatory labelling system for pre-packaged food products in China was implemented in 2015 by the central government. The first treatment group featured the Traffic Light label, which used colours to indicate high (red), medium (orange), or low (green) content of fat, sodium, and sugar. The coding rules for different nutrients were determined based on the China General Rules for Nutrition Labelling of Pre-packaged Food under the National Standard for Food Safety (refer to Table 9.6 for details). This treatment will be referred to as 'TL' henceforth. The second treatment group employed the Physical-Activity Label, denoted as 'PA', which displayed calorie information in terms of walking steps. Calculations were based on the average weight of Chinese adults aged 18 and above, approximately 65.0 kg, where 1200 kJ is consumed for every 10,000 steps. The activity-equivalent calorie information was determined by dividing the energy content by 1200 and then multiplying by 10,000. As illustrated in

Table 9.1 Examples of designed nutrition labels and treatment groups

Treatment group designed nutrition label		
Control group	Nutrition facts panel/100 mL	NR%
Energy	221 kJ	3%
Protein	0 g	0%
Fat	0 g	0%
Carbohydrate	13 g	4%
Na	10 mg	1%
Sugar	13 g	**
TL	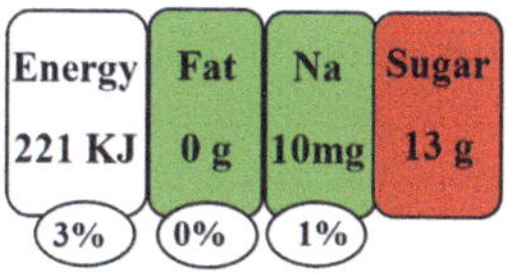	
PA		
WL	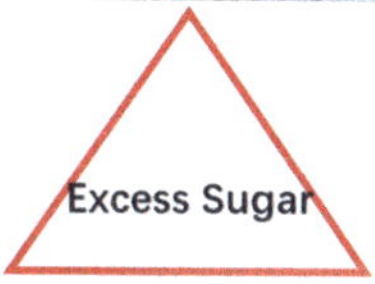	
HT		
NC		

Table 9.1, the physical activity label indicated that for an adult weighing 65 kg, it would require 3170 steps to expend the energy contained in the product. The third treatment group featured the Warning label, denoted as 'WL', which included an 'Excess Sugar' logo if the product had a high sugar content (coding rules are outlined in Table 9.6). The fourth treatment group utilized the Health Tick label, referred to as 'HT', which was assigned to products with low fat, sodium, and sugar content, as per the range specified in Table 9.6. The fifth treatment group employed Nutrition Claims, labelled as 'NC', such as 'sugar-free' or 'low sugar'. According to the China General Rules for Nutrition Labelling of Pre- packaged Food under the National Standard for Food Safety (GB 28,050—2011), a drink can be claimed as 'low sugar' if it contains less than 5 g of sugar per 100 mL, while drinks with sugar content $\leq$0.5 g can be labelled as 'sugar-free'.

9.2.2 SSB Choice Experiment

The respondents were initially provided with introductory information about the specific nutrition label that would be presented in the subsequent discrete choice experiments (see Appendix 2). During the online DCE survey, respondents were asked to make choices between two options of bottle SSBs (500 mL per bottle, which is the most popular size in the Chinese market) and a no-purchase option. SSBs were chosen for this study as they are considered a promising domain for reducing sugar intake and a significant source of added sugars in the diet (Basu et al., 2013). Extensive evidence has linked SSBs to weight gain and increased health risks (Jack, 2017; Malik & Hu, 2022; Yu et al., 2016). Notably, bottled black tea was selected as the focal product for this study, as it is one of the most commonly purchased beverages among Chinese consumers, and there is a wide range of bottled black tea products available in the Chinese market. The attributes and attribute levels of the product under investigation were determined based on relevant literature (Christiansen et al., 2023; Tang et al., 2021) and a preliminary focus group discussion. The three attributes were added sugar, sweetener, and price, as presented in Table 9.2. Four attribute levels were defined for added sugar: sugar-free, low sugar, high sugar, and excessive sugar. According to the National Food Safety Standard for Prepackaged Food Nutrition Labeling Regulation issued by the National Health Commission of China,[1] a beverage can be labelled as sugar-free if its sugar content is not more than 0.5 g/100 mL, and it can be labelled as low sugar if the sugar content is less than 5 g/100 mL. However, there is no specific regulation for the high sugar category. After examining the sugar content of soft drinks in the Chinese market, this study defined 'high sugar' as '5 g/100 mL ≤ sugar content <10 g/100 mL' and 'excessive sugar' as '≥10 g/100 mL'. Low-caloric sweeteners, which provide sweetness without adding energy to the diet, are considered important substitutes for added sugar and are widely used to produce sugar-free and low-sugar beverages.

However, the safety of low-caloric sweeteners is controversial among both literature (Sharma et al., 2016; Suez et al., 2014) and consumers (Farhat et al., 2021), making it an important factor influencing consumers' food choices. Therefore, the sweetener attribute was included in the choice set and randomly applied to

Table 9.2 Attributes and attribute levels in the choice set design

Attribute	Attribute level	Sugar content (g/100 mL)
Added sugar	Sugar free	≤0.5
	Low sugar	(0.5, 5)
	High sugar	[5, 10)
	Excessive sugar	≥10
Sweetener	0, 1	
Price (RMB/bottle)	3.3, 5.0, 6.7	

[1] See the website: https://members.wto.org/crnattachments/2021/SPS/CHN/21_6717_00_x.pdf

sugar-free or low-sugar products. Finally, three price levels were selected to represent cheap, affordable, and expensive in the actual market price ranges, namely 3.3 RMB/bottle, 5.0 RMB/bottle, and 6.7 RMB/bottle, which were also validated through a pre-test.

To minimize the respondent burden and ensure efficient data collection, a full factorial design with 576 different choice questions $(4^1 \times 2^1 \times 3^1)^2$ was initially considered given the selected attributes and attribute levels. However, following the approach of Street et al. (2005), the design was reduced to 20 choice questions with a D-efficiency of over 85%, considering only the main effects. These 20 choice questions were then divided into two blocks of 10 choice questions each to be presented to the participants during the survey. To prevent any potential ordering effects, the order of the choice tasks within each block was randomized. An example of a choice set is provided in Fig. 9.2. Prior to the choice questions, respondents were given instructions about the DCE and asked to read a scripted cheap talk statement to ensure their careful attention (see Appendix 1). To ensure respondents had adequately reviewed the instructions and cheap talk, they were unable to proceed with the questionnaire until at least 40 s had elapsed.

9.3 Empirical Methods

To model consumers' purchasing decisions for tea drinks, we specify an indirect utility function based on Lancaster's theory of consumer demand (Lancaster, 1966). Following random utility theory (McFadden, 1974), choice experiments rely on the assumption that the utility of individual n choosing alternative j in choice situation t can be expressed as:

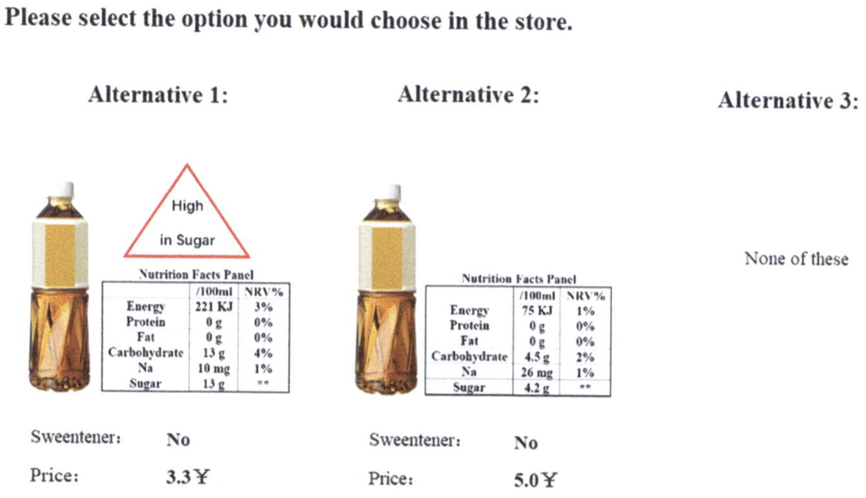

Fig. 9.2 Example choice question in the warning label treatment

$$U_{njt} = V_{njt} + \varepsilon_{njt} = aPrice_{njt} + \beta_{n1}Lowsugar_{njt} + \beta_{n2}Highsugar_{njt} + \beta_{n3}ExcessSugar_{njt} + \beta_{n4}Sweeten_{njt} + ASC_{Opt-out} + \varepsilon_{njt} \quad (9.1)$$

where V_{njt} is the systematic portion of the utility function, depending on the experimentally designed product attributes of alternative j. $Price_{njt}$ is a continuous variable populated with the three price levels in the design; $Lowsugar_{njt}$, $Highsugar_{njt}$ and $OverSugar_{njt}$ are dummy variables for the levels of low sugar, high sugar and excessive sugar content in tea beverages, and $Sweeten_{njt}$ is also a dummy variable that indicates whether sweetener is included in the production of tea beverages.

If the product exhibits a particular attribute, then all corresponding values are set to 1; otherwise, they are set to 0. $ASC_{Opt-out}$ is the alternative specific constant of the opt-out option; α is price preference and the βs are the non-price taste coefficients. ε_{njt} is the stochastic and unobservable (to researchers) component.

We estimate a mixed logit model in which consumer tastes vary concerning unobserved variables, which captures the variability in consumer preferences and provides a more accurate representation of real-world decision-making processes. The model's high degree of flexibility allows it to approximate a wide range of random utility models, making it a suitable tool for modelling consumer preference in various settings (McFadden & Train, 2000). Accordingly, ε_{njt} is the random error term that follows a Type I Extreme Value distribution. To account for the fact that individuals may assign either positive or negative values to nonprice product attributes, the model assumes that the coefficients associated with these attributes follow a normal distribution. We specify a fixed price coefficient to obtain reasonable and finite distributions of WTPs (Bliemer & Rose, 2013; Hensher & Greene, 2005; Matthews & Matthews, 2017). To estimate these model parameters, we employ a simulated maximum likelihood estimation technique using 1000 Halton draws.

In our study, we evaluate the impact of FOP labels on consumer valuation of tea beverages by comparing the distribution of WTP across six treatment groups. To derive this distribution, we employ a Monte Carlo simulation technique (Krinsky & Robb, 1986) using the variancecovariance matrix obtained from estimating Eq. (9.1). To test for WTP equality between the treatments, we use a non-parametric complete combinatorial test as suggested by Poe et al. (2005). Further, we match demographic variables with individual-specific or conditional WTPs, as outlined in Train (2003), to identify potential demographic factors that may influence consumer preferences.

9.4 Data and Sample Description

Data for this study was collected via an online survey in December 2022. Participants were recruited by the professional survey company 'PowerCX'[2] in China. They were screened to ensure they were more than 18 years old and had purchased the

[2] See the website: https://members.wto.org/crnattachments/2021/SPS/CHN/21_6717_00_x.pdf

bottled black tea within the last three months. Several trap questions were included in the survey, and participants who failed to answer the trap questions were excluded automatically. Five cities were chosen including Beijing, Guangzhou, Shanghai, Chengdu, and Wuhan, representing the north, south, east, west, middle China. Finally, a total of 1800 respondents (300 for each group) were employed for the analysis. Table 9.3 reports the balance test across different treatment groups. *P*-values from *F*-tests/chi-square tests suggest that the null hypothesis of equality in demographic variables between any two treatment groups cannot be rejected at the 10% significance level. The sample was roughly consistent with the China Statistics Yearbook (2023) in terms of gender, and marital status (Table 9.3). The respondents were aged 18–70 years, with an average age of 35.03 years, which is younger than the national level (42.51). This is reasonable because we screened the respondents to ensure that they had purchased the bottled black tea within the last three months. Bottled drinks are more popular among young consumers than in their elderly counterparts. Respondents in this sample are better educated and have higher incomes than the national level because they were recruited from five developed cities in China. We focus on consumers in developed cities which is the main concentration area of soft drink consumption so as to provide valuable insights for both policy makers and food marketers when designing effective sugar reduction strategies.

Overall, the survey results indicate that soft drinks are frequently purchased by respondents, with 34% purchasing them more than 3 times per week. Additionally, 26% purchase soft drinks 1–2 times per week, 11% purchase them 1–3 times per month, and 3% purchase them less than 1 time per month. Among soft drinks, tea drinks are the most popular choice, preferred by 76% of the respondents, while only 4% dislike tea drinks.

Furthermore, the majority of respondents spend more than 10 RMB on soft drinks. The results of the Chi-square tests suggest that there is no statistically significant difference observed among the treatment groups regarding bottled beverage purchasing frequency and expenditure information. This implies that any variations observed in SSB choices across treatments cannot be attributed to differences in demographic factors, SSB purchasing habit, or consumption characteristics.

9.5 Results

9.5.1 Impacts of FOP Labels on Consumer WTPs for SSBs

To assess the impacts of FOP labels on consumer choices of SSBs, we employ mixed logit models to estimate Eq. (9.1) for each treatment. We then generate willingness-to-pay (WTP) values through simulations based on the estimated parameters and variance-covariance matrix derived from Eq. (9.1). The estimation results for the six mixed logit models are summarized in Table 9.7. As expected, most product attributes exhibit significant effects on individual choices of black tea

Table 9.3 Balance test across treatment groups

	Control	TL	PA	WL	HT	NC	*P*-value	Country[a]
Age	34.61	34.87	35.10	35.01	35.49	35.10	0.31	42.51
	(9.46)	(9.73)	(9.25)	(9.86)	(10.11)	(9.55)		
Female	0.503	0.507	0.493	0.487	0.527	0.473	0.17	0.49
	(0.50)	(0.50)	(0.50)	(0.50)	(0.50)	(0.50)		
Married	0.643	0.640	0.613	0.593	0.580	0.663	0.26	0.72
	(0.48)	(0.48)	(0.49)	(0.49)	(0.49)	(0.47)		
Education							0.80	
Middle school and below	0.67	0.67	0.33	1.33	0.00	1.00	0.80	64.17
High school	6.00	4.67	3.33	5.33	5.67	5.33		16.35
College	83.67	84.33	85.00	82.67	82.00	80.67		18.53
Graduate	9.67	10.33	11.33	10.67	12.33	13.00		0.95
Annual individual income in RMB							0.34	
<20,000	10.00	9.67	8.33	8.00	8.33	10.33		
20,000–49,999	11.67	9.00	13.00	11.67	6.67	12.67		
50,000–999,999	23.67	26.33	18.67	27.00	27.67	23.33		
100,000–199,999	29.33	31.00	37.00	30.00	32.33	29.67		
200,000–299,999	17.00	13.33	12.67	11.67	12.67	14.00		
≥300,000	8.33	10.67	10.33	11.67	12.33	10.00		
Household size	3.31	3.33	3.32	3.39	3.30	3.51	0.78	
	(1.04)	(1.12)	(1.10)	(1.13)	(1.10)	(1.05)		
BMI	21.68	21.70	21.71	22.03	21.58	21.98	0.79	
	(3.15)	(2.89)	(2.94)	(2.86)	(2.79)	(3.11)		
Bottled beverage purchasing frequency							0.64	
Daily	9.33	10.00	7.00	9.67	11.33	9.67		
5–6 times per week	14.67)	19.67	15.33	16.33	15.00	15.67		
3–4 times per week	33.33	32.00	42.00	32.33	32.33	33.67		
1–2 times per week7	28.67)	23.33	24.00	26.00	29.00	27.67		
1–3 times per month	12.00	12.33	8.67	11.33	9.67	10.67		
Less than monthly	2.00	2.67	3.00	4.33	2.67	2.67		
Weekly bottled beverage expenditure in RMB							0.57	
<5	7.33	5.00	5.67	8.67	5.00	5.33		
5–9.99	16.33	19.33	18.00	19.00	18.67	18.33		
10–29.99	39.67	33.67	36.67	35.00	39.33	41.67		
30–49.99	25.67	27.67	29.33	27.67	26.33	27.33		
>50	11.00	14.33	10.33	9.67	10.67	7.33		

P-values from *F*-tests/Chi-square tests testing the null hypothesis of equality of means/frequencies in demographics and botted beverage purchasing characteristics across treatments. Standard errors are in parentheses

[a]Country-level data are from the China Statistical Yearbook (2023)

Table 9.4 Simulated WTP across treatment

	Control	TL	PA	WL	HT	NC
Low sugar	1.74[a] [0.65, 2.84][b]	3.14*** [1.69, 4.63]	2.08** [0.86, 3.34]	2.89*** [1.14, 4.68]	1.70 [0.15, 3.29]	1.83 [0.71, 2.97]
High sugar	−0.01 [−0.88, 0.84]	−1.95*** [−2.98, −0.95]	0.51** [−0.44, 1.44]	−7.16*** [−8.87, −5.66]	−2.12*** [−3.23, −1.05]	0.02 [−0.83, 0.86]
Excessive sugar	0.38 [−0.34, 1.19]	−3.93*** [−5.15, −2.81]	−1.17*** [−2.02, −0.26]	−8.03*** [−9.95, −6.47]	−2.29*** [−3.32, −1.32]	−0.70** [−1.37, 0.10]
Sweeten	−2.15 [−2.95, −1.42]	−2.27 [−3.14, −1.48]	−2.48* [−3.38, −1.67]	−2.84** [−3.79, −2.00]	−3.20*** [−4.24, −2.27]	−1.15** [−1.91, −0.44]

[a]Indicates the mean of the simulated WTP values using Krinsky-Robb method
[b]Is 95% confidence intervals of the WTP values
*, **, *** indicates statistical significance of the test in WTP difference between the control group (nutrition facts panel) and each of the treatment group suggested by Poe et al. (2005) at the 10%, 5%, and at 1% levels

beverages, with coefficients displaying the anticipated signs. In the control group, respondents, on average, show a positive preference for black tea with low sugar content compared to other sugar levels, and they have a significant dislike for sweeteners. Across the treatment groups, individual preferences for sugar levels and sweeteners exhibit heterogeneity.

Table 9.4 displays the mean simulated values and 95% confidence intervals for willingness-to-pay (WTP) estimates, as well as the results of the Poe test assessing the equality of WTP distributions across treatments. The table captures the variations in consumer valuations across different treatments and provides a statistical test to evaluate the significance of these differences. Several key findings emerge from our analysis.

Firstly, our findings indicate that consumers in the control group exhibit a preference for specific sugar levels,particularly favouring low-sugar content compared to sugar-free tea. On average, respondents are willing to pay an additional 1.74 RMB per bottle to switch from sugar-free to low-sugar tea beverages. For a sugar-free and sweetener-free black tea priced at 5 RMB, the price premium percentage for the low-sugar level is 35%. However, when the sugar content originates from an artificial sweetener, consumers in the control group devalue the product, assigning a negative valuation of −2.15 RMB per bottle for tea beverages with artificial sweeteners.

Secondly, among the five FOP labels, warning labels prove most effective in reducing consumer valuations of high-sugar and excessive-sugar levels in tea SSBs. In comparison to sugar-free content, respondents in the warning label treatment exhibit mean WTP values of −7.16 RMB and −8.03 RMB per bottle for the high sugar and excessive sugar levels, respectively. Following warning labels, traffic light labels, and health-tick labels also discourage consumers from selecting high-sugar and excessive-sugar tea beverages. For example, individuals in the traffic light label treatment exhibit a discount of 3.93 RMB for excessive sugar levels compared to sugar-free content, with a slightly lower discount of 1.95 RMB per bottle for high-sugar content. Similarly, individuals in the health-tick label treatment show a discount of 2.29 RMB for excessive sugar levels and 2.12 RMB for high-sugar levels relative to sugar-free content. In contrast, the impact of physical activity labels on reducing the consumption of sugary tea beverages is less successful compared to the aforementioned labels. While physical activity labels result in a negative valuation of −1.17 RMB per bottle for excessive sugar content, they fail to significantly lower the consumption of high-sugar tea drinks. Additionally, nutrition claims exhibit the lowest effectiveness in reducing consumer WTPs for higher sugar content in tea beverages, with no significant difference in WTP for the high-sugar level between the nutrition claim treatment and the control group.

Thirdly, certain FOP labels encourage the selection of low-sugar tea while reducing the purchase of high-sugar tea, indicating that individuals in these treatments may consider low-sugar content as a substitute for higher sugar levels. Treatments such as traffic light labels, physical activity labels, and warning labels demonstrate this effect, with the traffic light label group exhibiting the largest increase in WTP for low-sugar content (3.14 RMB) compared to the control group (1.74 RMB).

Last, to validate the robustness of our findings, we conducted estimations using a pooled sample in the preference space (Table 9.8). Consistent with our previous results, we find that the interaction term between the treatment dummy and the high-sugar variable is statistically significant and negatively signed in the warning label, traffic light label, and health-tick label treatments. This suggests that these three types of FOP labels effectively reduce consumers' WTP for high sugar content. Similarly, the interaction term between treatment and the excessive-sugar variable is also statistically significant and negatively signed in the five FOP label treatments. This indicates the successfulness of FOP labels in decreasing individual WTPs for excessive sugar content.

9.5.2 Heterogeneity on the Impacts of FOP Labels

To examine whether the effectiveness of FOP labels on consumers' WTPs for low-sugar, high-sugar, and excessive-sugar tea beverages varies across respondent sub-groups, we conducted heterogeneity analyses based on respondents' age, gender, marital status, education, income, BMI status, sugar-sweetened beverage purchasing frequency, and weekly purchasing expenditure. The results of these analyses can be found in Tables 9.9, 9.10, and 9.11 in Appendix.

We analysed the impact of different labels on consumers' WTPs for low-sugar, high-sugar, and excessive-sugar tea beverages across various sub-groups. Results consistently showed that warning labels were most effective in reducing consumer valuations of high-sugar and excessive-sugar levels in tea beverages, followed by traffic light labels and health-tick labels across all sub-groups. For low-sugar content beverages, warning and traffic light labels had a positive effect on WTP across all sub-groups, while physical activity labels positively influenced specific subgroups, including younger, female, non-married, non-graduate, lower BMI, higher purchasing frequency, and higher expenditure people. Nutrition claims only affected WTP among females, and health-tick labels and nutrition facts panels did not significantly impact WTP. For high-sugar-content and excessive-sugar-content tea beverages, warning labels, traffic light labels, and health-tick labels are effective in decreasing WTP across all sub-groups. Physical activity labels showed inconsistent effectiveness in influencing consumer WTPs for SSBs, and both nutrition claims and nutrition facts panels had limited impacts on the WTPs.

Table 9.5 demonstrates the correlation between consumers' willingness to pay for SSBs and demographic as well as SSB purchasing characteristics. Specifically, the elderly population exhibits a negative valuation of −0.02 RMB per bottle for low-sugar beverages when compared to sugar-free options. Females, on the other hand, display discounts of −0.61 and −1.28 RMB per bottle for high-sugar and excessive-sugar beverages respectively, when compared to sugar-free alternatives. Respondents with higher levels of education show a lower valuation (−0.59 RMB per bottle) for SSBs with excessive sugar content in comparison to sugar-free options. Expectedly, consumers with higher BMI tend to prefer sugar-free beverages more and exhibit negative valuations for low-sugar (−0.06 RMB per bottle), high-sugar (−0.10 RMB per bottle), and excessive-sugar (−0.12 RMB per bottle)

Table 9.5 Relationship between demographics/purchasing variables and WTPs

	Low sugar		High sugar		Excessive sugar	
WTP	Mean	S.E.	Mean	S.E.	Mean	S.E.
TL	1.472***	0.247	−1.910***	0.228	−4.310***	0.396
PA	0.319	0.248	0.561**	0.229	−1.569***	0.395
WL	1.197***	0.238	−7.201***	0.228	−8.440***	0.396
HT	−0.012	0.248	−2.081***	0.228	−2.593***	0.397
NC	0.101	0.237	0.031	0.229	−1.110***	0.395
Age	−0.021**	0.007	−0.007	0.008	−0.006	0.013
Female	−0.042	0.156	−0.608***	0.144	−1.279***	0.250
Married	0.081	0.173	−0.119	0.159	−0.294	0.276
Education	0.228	0.159	−0.194	0.147	−0.590**	0.255
Income	0.083	0.059	0.012	0.055	−0.002	0.095
BMI	−0.056**	0.023	−0.095***	0.024	−0.118***	0.042
Household size	0.115*	0.067	0.078	0.061	0.234**	0.107
Purchasing frequency	−0.133*	0.072	−0.014	0.075	−0.159	0.131
Beverage expenditure	0.163**	0.066	0.193**	0.088	0.137	0.153
Constant	1.972*	1.038	2.597***	0.956	5.673***	1.660
Observations	1800		1800		1800	
R^2	0.063		0.480		0.262	

*, **, ***Indicates statistical significance of the test in WTP difference between the control group (sugar-free beverage) and each of the treatment group suggested by Poe et al. (2005) at the 10%, 5%, and at 1% levels

Table 9.6 Coding rules for different nutrients

Nutrients	Low (g/100 mL)	Medium (g/100 mL)	High (g/100 mL)
Fat	≤1.5	(1.5, 8.75]	>8.75
Na	≤0.3	(0.3, 0.75]	>0.75
Sugar	<5	[5, 10)	≥10

content. Interestingly, respondents who spend more on sugar-sweetened beverages on a weekly basis demonstrate a higher WTP for both low-sugar (0.16 RMB per bottle) and high-sugar (0.19 RMB per bottle) options.

9.6 Discussions

Our findings provide evidence that the five FOP labels are effective in discouraging Chinese consumers from selecting tea SSBs with excessive sugar content (≥10 g/100 mL). The effectiveness of these labels, in descending order, was observed as follows: warning label, traffic light label, health-tick label, physical activity label, and nutrition claims. This is possible because compared to the back-of-pack nutrition facts panels in the control group, which provide nutritional information in a standardized format, these five FOP labels are easier for individuals to interpret and understand (Guan et al., 2021; Ma & Zhuang, 2021). For tea SSBs with high sugar content (5 g/100 mL ≤ sugar content <10 g/100 mL), the effectiveness of these labels in descending order was: warning label, health-tick label, and traffic light label. Nutrition claims and physical activity labels failed to discourage consumers from choosing high-sugar content beverages. Consumers were willing to pay more for high sugar content beverages under the physical activity label context, indicating that over-simplified nutrition labels may mislead consumers and fail to make correct food choices.

While previous research has predominantly focused on a limited number of FOP labels (Oswald et al., 2022; Temple, 2020), a consensus on the most effective FOP label has yet to be reached, in particular in China (Eldesouky et al., 2020; Gębski et al., 2019; Melo et al., 2019). Our study found that warning labels were the most effective in reducing consumer valuations of both high-sugar and excessive sugar levels in tea beverages. Importantly, these findings held across all respondent subgroups, including age, gender, marital status, education, income, BMI status, sugar-sweetened beverages purchasing frequency, and weekly purchasing expenditure. The effectiveness of warning labels can potentially be attributed to their explicit warning nature, indicating that an SSB product is unhealthy. Negative information is more influential than positive information in capturing consumers' attention and motivating them to opt for healthier dietary choices (Silva et al., 2022). This finding aligns with previous studies that have shown nutritional warnings to be most effective in terms of attentional capture and promoting healthy food choices (Grummon et al., 2022; Pettigrew et al., 2024; Silva et al., 2022), but inconsistent with some

Table 9.7 Mixed logit models in preference-space for each group

	Control		TL		PA		WL		HT		NC	
	Estimate	Z-value	Estimate	Z-value	Estimate	Z-value	Estimate	Z-value	Estimate	Z-value	Estimate	Z-value
Mean												
Price	−0.33***	16.36	−0.29***	14.87	−0.33**	15.79	−0.30***	13.68	−0.27***	14.15	−0.34***	16.90
Opt-out	−4.46***	26.18	−4.70***	26.80	−4.67***	26.05	−4.45***	26.27	−4.38***	26.64	−4.44***	26.53
Low sugar	0.57***	2.98	0.92***	4.03	0.68***	3.17	0.87***	3.11	0.46**	2.05	0.62***	3.04
High sugar	−0.01	0.03	−0.57***	3.97	0.17	1.06	−2.15***	11.22	−0.57***	4.11	0.01	0.05
Excessive sugar	0.12	0.99	−1.16***	7.21	−0.38***	2.68	−2.41***	10.89	−0.61***	4.89	−0.23*	1.79
Sweeten	−0.70***	6.08	−0.67***	5.99	−0.81***	6.44	−0.85***	7.18	−0.86***	7.24	−0.39***	3.31
Standard deviation												
Low sugar	1.34***	7.70	1.68***	7.92	1.65***	8.79	2.20***	9.50	1.81***	9.60	1.55***	8.05
High sugar	1.11***	6.33	1.18***	6.07	1.38***	7.40	2.06***	9.86	1.04***	5.84	1.20***	7.04
Excessive sugar	1.68***	10.93	2.07***	10.78	1.95***	11.21	2.37***	10.14	1.62***	10.73	1.68***	10.86
Sweeten	1.31***	10.82	1.24***	9.98	1.50***	11.13	1.41***	11.15	1.37***	10.99	1.43***	11.44
Model statistics												
Log-likelihood	−2147.351		−2062.093		−2075.781		−2111.820		−2207.233		−2173.247	
Number of individuals	300		300		300		300		300		300	

Note: all models are estimated via simulation maximum likelihood estimation based on 1000 Halton draws . *, **, *** indicates statistical significance at the 10%, 5%, and at 1% levels

Table 9.8 Mixed logit models in preference-space with pooled sample

	Control & TL		Control & PA		Control & WL		Control & HT		Control & NC	
	Estimate	Z-value	Estimate	Z-value	Estimate	Z-value	Estimate	Z-value	Estimate	Z-value
Mean										
Price	−0.326***	16.30	−0.323***	16.26	−0.326***	16.37	−0.323***	16.42	−0.328***	16.45
Opt-out	−4.473***	26.16	−4.438***	25.96	−4.451***	26.38	−4.438***	26.42	−4.474***	26.40
Low sugar	0.546***	2.85	0.540***	2.86	0.558***	2.97	0.546***	2.90	0.555***	2.95
High sugar	−0.010	0.07	−0.013	0.09	−0.014	0.10	−0..018	0.13	−0.003	0.02
Excessive sugar	0.123	0.98	0.109	0.88	0.116	0.91	0.119	0.95	0.103	0.79
Sweeten	−0.712***	6.32	−0.701***	6.09	−0.698***	6.09	−0.706***	6.13	−0.707***	6.20
Treat*Price	−0.130***	2.62	−0.123***	2.77	−0.121**	2.52	−0.075	1.58	−0.174***	3.64
Treat*Opt-out	−5.137***	7.19	−4.960***	6.73	−3.819***	7.35	−5.665***	5.17	−5.711***	8.14
Treat*Low sugar	0.699**	2.03	0.139	0.42	−0.134	0.40	−0.275	0.91	0.162	0.56
Treat*High sugar	−0.865***	3.46	0.163	0.68	−3.275***	9.98	−0.809***	3.47	−0.006	0.03
Treat*Excessive sugar	−1.635***	6.47	−0.640***	3.00	−3.048***	10.37	−0.871***	4.31	−0.349*	1.72
Treat*Sweeten	−0.274	1.53	−0.239	1.30	−0.439**	2.41	−0.415**	2.25	0.204	1.12
Standard deviation										
Low sugar	1.412***	7.76	1.351***	7.36	1.318***	8.02	1.340***	7.61	1.335***	8.50
High sugar	1.169***	6.71	1.083***	5.66	1.010***	6.42	1.056***	6.37	1.180***	6.46
Excessive sugar	1.665***	10.27	1.638***	11.35	1.726***	9.56	1.649***	10.79	1.765***	10.98
Sweeten	1.245***	11.32	1.306***	9.78	1.306***	12.07	1.313***	11.04	1.288***	11.60
Treat*Price	0.575***	11.31	0.451***	11.21	0.509***	11.62	0.534***	11.59	0.556***	13.11
Treat*Opt-out	3.245***	8.03	3.990***	8.11	3.673***	10.18	4.170***	6.25	3.825***	11.07
Treat*Low sugar	1.189**	2.25	1.634***	4.22	1.483***	4.08	1.292***	2.65	0.474	1.49
Treat*High sugar	1.914***	5.59	1.479***	3.65	2.898***	8.59	1.255***	4.06	1.385***	3.62
Treat*Excessive sugar	2.264***	6.03	1.836***	5.94	2.035***	4.60	1.352***	3.50	1.254***	3.24

	Control & TL		Control & PA		Control & WL		Control & HT		Control & NC	
	Estimate	Z-value	Estimate	Z-value	Estimate	Z-value	Estimate	Z-value	Estimate	Z-value
Treat*Sweeten	0.992***	3.90	1.024***	2.97	0.886***	2.83	1.127***	4.02	1.201***	5.18
Model statistics										
Log-likelihood	−4038.973		−4086.771		−4072.071		−4130.616		−4109.897	
Number of individuals	600		600		600		600		600	

Note: all models are estimated via simulation maximum likelihood estimation based on 1000 Halton draws . *, **, *** indicates statistical significance at the 10%, 5%, and at 1% levels, respectively

Table 9.9 Heterogeneity in WTP for low sugar content across treatment, RMB/bottle

	Control	TL	PA	WL	HT	NC
Above median age	1.683	2.818***	1.841	2.507**	1.612	1.671
	(0.166)	(0.216)	(0.246)	(0.381)	(0.345)	(0.188)
Below median age	1.783	3.730***	2.351**	3.311***	1.873	2.052
	(0.154)	(0.199)	(0.176)	(0.320)	(0.245)	(0.184)
Female	1.585	3.457***	2.033*	2.742**	1.927	1.967*
	(0.172)	(0.230)	(0.258)	(0.408)	(0.273)	(0.196)
Male	1.881	3.012***	2.103	3.040***	1.471	1.717
	(0.147)	(0.191)	(0.184)	(0.307)	(0.348)	(0.183)
Married	1.915	3.229***	1.932	3.079***	1.735	1.820
	(0.128)	(0.192)	(0.200)	(0.316)	(0.285)	(0.163)
Non-married	1.402	3.253***	2.285**	2.641**	1.734	1.865*
	(0.215)	(0.240)	(0.256)	(0.408)	(0.331)	(0.234)
Graduate	2.412	3.835***	2.264	3.791*	2.464	2.346
	(0.201)	(0.357)	(0.326)	(0.947)	(0.638)	(0.303)
Non-graduate	1.659	3.169****	2.044**	2.795***	1.632	1.864
	(0.123)	(0.162)	(0.173)	(0.257)	(0.229)	(0.147)
Above median income	1.995	3.430***	2.471*	3.732***	1.959	1.778
	(0.200)	(0.310)	(0.269)	(0.290)	(0.445)	(0.281)
Below median income	1.643	3.177***	1.948*	2.648***	1.659	1.853
	(0.135)	(0.172)	(0.188)	(0.313)	(0.247)	(0.152)
Above median BMI	1.725	3.023***	1.843	2.811**	1.595	1.750
	(0.177)	(0.208)	(0.241)	(0.329)	(0.351)	(0.174)
Below median BMI	1.739	3.461***	2.316**	3.004***	1.859	1.939
	(0.145)	(0.216)	(0.197)	(0.384)	(0.262)	(0.208)
Above median purchasing frequency	1.766	3.324***	2.389***	3.146***	2.128	1.960
	(0.133)	(0.174)	(0.165)	(0.289)	(0.241)	(0.132)
Below median purchasing frequency	1.687	3.099***	1.490	2.558*	1.176	1.655
	(0.197)	(0.275)	(0.320)	(0.445)	(0.390)	(0.265)
Above median purchasing expenditure	1.792	2.977***	2.322**	3.449***	2.304	1.939
	(0.168)	(0.211)	(0.209)	(0.340)	(0.276)	(0.175)
Below median purchasing expenditure	1.698	3.427***	1.902	2.575**	1.399	1.780
	(0.150)	(0.209)	(0.222)	(0.343)	(0.299)	(0.182)

Note: Numbers in parentheses are standard errors. Asterisks indicate the significance level calculated by the Poe test in WTP difference between the control (T1) and corresponding treatment group within the demographic group. *, **, and *** indicate statistical significance at the 10%, 5%, and 1% levels, respectively

Table 9.10 Heterogeneity in WTP for high sugar content across treatment, RMB/bottle

	Control	TL	PA	WL	HT	NC
Above median age	−0.054	−1.969***	0.521**	−7.312***	−2.391***	−0.282
	(0.160)	(0.172)	(0.192)	(0.401)	(0.176)	(0.163)
Below median age	0.025	−1.841***	0.584**	−7.139***	−1.840***	0.183
	(0.144)	(0.201)	(0.217)	(0.409)	(0.152)	(0.155)
Female	−0.303	−2.047***	0.423**	−7.588***	−2.299***	−0.156
	(0.162)	(0.176)	(0.217)	(0.421)	(0.158)	(0.164)
Male	0.277	−1.769***	0.671*	−6.911***	−1.905***	0.148
	(0.138)	(0.194)	(0.189)	(0.388)	(0.177)	(0.163)
Married	−0.084	−2.021***	0.615**	−7.112***	−2.170***	−0.280
	(0.142)	(0.162)	(0.189)	(0.373)	(0.170)	(0.150)
Non-married	0.110	−1.712***	0.444	−7.395***	−2.081***	0.562*
	(0.160)	(0.222)	(0.218)	(0.446)	(0.157)	(0.164)
Graduate	−0.009	−2.013***	0.993*	−8.560***	−2.488***	−0.494
	(0.357)	(0.443)	(0.368)	(0.820)	(0.257)	(0.281)
Non-graduate	−0.015	−1.898***	0.492**	−7.068***	−2.082***	0.078
	(0.113)	(0.137)	(0.155)	(0.304)	(0.130)	(0.126)
Above median income	−0.016	−1.731***	1.089***	−6.673***	−2.198***	−0.397
	(0.223)	(0.277)	(0.274)	(0.610)	(0.243)	(0.225)
Below median income	−0.014	−1.967***	0.388*	−7.396***	−2.110***	0.130
	(0.123)	(0.149)	(0.166)	(0.323)	(0.136)	(0.134)
Above median BMI	0.029	−2.129***	0.145	−7.141***	−2.244***	−0.269
	(0.152)	(0.180)	(0.208)	(0.403)	(0.186)	(0.155)
Below median BMI	−0.055	−1.682***	0.993***	−7.325***	−2.032***	0.337
	(0.153)	(0.190)	(0.190)	(0.405)	(0.150)	(0.170)
Above median purchasing frequency	−0.051	−1.963***	0.576**	−6.923***	−1.912***	0.006
	(0.144)	(0.162)	(0.175)	(0.367)	(0.140)	(0.139)
Below median purchasing frequency	0.034	−1.825***	0.500	−7.652***	−2.445***	0.001
	(0.162)	(0.222)	(0.251)	(0.454)	(0.203)	(0.201)
Above median purchasing expenditure	0.051	−1.602***	0.620*	−6.552***	−2.118***	−0.041
	(0.172)	(0.204)	(0.230)	(0.485)	(0.189)	(0.200)
Below median purchasing expenditure	−0.053	−2.133***	0.503*	−7.629***	−2.141***	0.027
	(0.138)	(0.169)	(0.184)	(0.351)	(0.152)	(0.143)

Note: Numbers in parentheses are standard errors. Asterisks indicate the significance level calculated by the Poe test in WTP difference between the control (T1) and corresponding treatment group within the demographic group. *, **, and *** indicate statistical significance at the 10%, 5%, and 1% levels, respectively

Table 9.11 Heterogeneity in WTP for excessive sugar content across treatment, RMB/bottle

	Control	TL	PA	WL	HT	NC
Above median age	0.331	−4.034***	−0.931**	−7.775***	−2.552***	−0.956***
	(0.344)	(0.415)	(0.383)	(0.504)	(0.374)	(0.292)
Below median age	0.448	−3.753***	−1.492***	−8.275***	−1.995***	−0.356*
	(0.314)	(0.509)	(0.406)	(0.480)	(0.387)	(0.340)
Female	−0.352	−4.336***	−1.805**	−8.484***	−2.653***	−1.264*
	(0.329)	(0.448)	(0.399)	(0.501)	(0.352)	(0.321)
Male	1.139	−3.463***	−0.574***	−7.614***	−1.796***	−0.189**
	(0.319)	(0.467)	(0.385)	(0.483)	(0.414)	(0.302)
Married	0.095	−3.980***	−0.918**	−7.903***	−2.602***	−1.050**
	(0.300)	(0.397)	(0.361)	(0.471)	(0.356)	(0.274)
Non-married	0.919	−3.771***	−1.600***	−8.191***	−1.860***	−0.004*
	(0.359)	(0.561)	(0.438)	(0.512)	(0.408)	(0.370)
Graduate	0.138	−5.411***	−1.571	−9.150***	−3.571***	−1.370
	(0.851)	(0.837)	(0.761)	(0.923)	(0.674)	(0.618)
Non-graduate	0.416	−3.731***	−1.132***	−7.885***	−2.110***	−0.597**
	(0.241)	(0.347)	(0.300)	(0.373)	(0.291)	(0.238)
Above median income	0.743	−3.270***	−0.135	−7.851***	−2.673***	−1.509***
	(0.502)	(0.726)	(0.618)	(0.747)	(0.582)	(0.442)
Below median income	0.268	−4.105***	−1.494***	−8.071***	−2.162***	−0.442*
	(0.261)	(0.359)	(0.310)	(0.394)	(0.302)	(0.255)
Above median BMI	0.347	−4.110***	−1.471***	−7.839***	−2.520***	−0.807**
	(0.344)	(0.435)	(0.382)	(0.485)	(0.388)	(0.296)
Below median BMI	0.427	−3.692***	−0.863**	−8.227***	−2.084***	−0.564*
	(0.316)	(0.483)	(0.409)	(0.500)	(0.374)	(0.335)
Above median purchasing frequency	0.275	−3.972***	−0.727**	−7.722***	−1.957***	−0.791**
	(0.312)	(0.427)	(0.351)	(0.446)	(0.348)	(0.272)
Below median purchasing frequency	0.541	−3.796***	−2.001***	−8.437***	−2.763***	−0.564*
	(0.349)	(0.495)	0.452)	(0.554)	(0.421)	(0.375)
Above median purchasing expenditure	0.464	−3.278***	−0.552*	−7.354***	−2.361***	−1.030**
	(0.389)	(0.513)	(0.461)	(0.582)	(0.431)	(0.364)
Below median purchasing expenditure	0.345	−4.359***	−1.595***	−8.417***	−2.249***	−0.521*
	(0.291)	(0.415)	(0.347)	(0.432)	(0.345)	(0.279)

Note: Numbers in parentheses are standard errors. Asterisks indicate the significance level calculated by the Poe test in WTP difference between the control (T1) and corresponding treatment group within the demographic group. *, **, and *** indicate statistical significance at the 10%, 5%, and 1% levels, respectively

studies such as Talati et al. (2019) who conducted an experiment on consumers from 12 western countries and found that traffic light label is more effective than warning label. Some studies argued that the experiment settings with outcomes assessed immediately after a single exposure can only capture the short-term effects of the warning label (Clarke et al., 2021; Duran Aguero et al., 2020). Thus, future studies can be conducted to explore if warning labels have a longer-term effect or if customers get acquainted with the information and, after an initial period, return to their original preference habits (Ares et al., 2023).

Colour-coded systems (traffic light labels) and summary labels (health ticks) are also effective in terms of healthier food choices in this study which can be supported by many prior research, which has identified them as one of the most effective FOP labels in catching consumers' attention and helping them identify healthier food options (Balcombe et al., 2009; Defago et al., 2020; Roseman et al., 2018).

And traffic light label seems a bit superior to the health tick label in terms of discouraging the preference for excessive sugar-content beverages. This can be supported by some previous studies that confirmed that nutrient-specific labels such as traffic light labels are perceived as more useful and easier to use than summary labels (Mazzù et al., 2023), and more informative than summary labels in terms of subjective understanding of the product composition (Mazzù et al., 2020). However, it is worth noting that warning labels demonstrated greater effectiveness than both traffic light systems and health-tick in this study. This could be attributed to the negative information disclosure associated with warning labels, which increased consumer concern regarding added sugar.

We found that females, highly educated, and consumers with higher BMI are more receptive to the treatments, and exhibit a more significant decrease in their valuation of high-sugar or excessive-sugar content which parallels the results by Guan et al. (2021) studying the factors on food nutrition information use in China. Possibly because females, highly educated, and consumers with higher BMI, tend to be more health-conscious, and higher education might have generated efficiency gains in health production due to improved health literacy (Celidoni et al., 2023). Interestingly, respondents who spend more on sugar-sweetened beverages every week demonstrate a higher WTP for high-sugar (0.19 RMB per bottle) options. As consumers who spend more on sugar-sweetened beverages tend to have a higher intake of sugar and a higher risk of obesity (Yu et al., 2016; Zhai et al., 2022), these consumers should be specially targeted when designing labelling policies to promote healthy choices.

Our findings indicate a preference among Chinese consumers for SSBs with specific sugar levels, particularly those with low sugar content (0.5 g/100 mL < sugar content <5 g/100 mL), as compared to sugar-free alternatives (≤0.5 g/100 mL). This suggests that low-sugar products might be more successful as substitutes for high-sugar items in the urban Chinese market, promoting a reduction in overall sugar intake among residents. Despite previous studies confirming the efficacy of low-caloric sweeteners as alternatives to sugar (Farag et al., 2022; Hovhannisyan & Bastian, 2022), our research indicates that Chinese consumers have a negative perception of artificial sweeteners. This is in line with Farhat et al. (2021) who conducted a survey of 1589 UK-based adults and found a significant proportion (25%) of participants rated LCS as being harmful, and greater perceived risk was associated with lower reported consumption. Worldwide initiatives currently aim to reduce free sugar intake, but success will depend on consumer attitudes towards sugar and alternatives. Therefore, it is essential for future research to explore consumers' perceptions and attitudes towards artificial sweeteners. Understanding the barriers to sweetener consumption will facilitate the development of effective communication strategies to educate the public about the benefits and drawbacks of sweeteners.

9.7 Conclusions

This study aims to develop various FOP nutrition labels tailored to the Chinese context and investigate their impact on consumers' preferences and WTP for sugar-sweetened beverages. The overall findings suggest that effective FOP label schemes should be implemented to enhance the readability and appeal of nutrition information, thereby encouraging consumers to make healthier food choices. When it comes to sugar content, the most effective FOP labels are likely to be warning labels, followed by traffic light labels and health-tick labels, particularly for products where sugar constitutes a significant portion of the calorie content, such as sugar-sweetened beverages. In contrast, physical-activity labels and nutrition claims have relatively lower effectiveness in reducing the consumption of high-sugar tea beverages compared to the three aforementioned labels, but they still outperform back-of-pack nutrition facts panels.

Our product-specific treatment effects have important policy implications. We conclude that warning labels, traffic light labels, and health-tick labels effectively reduce consumers' WTP for high-sugar and excessive-sugar beverage products. Specifically, the warning label treatment yields the greatest decline in WTP across all sub-groups. This suggests that, in addition to improving readability, consideration should be given to the types of emphasized nutrients (such as critical statements) and graphical presentation (such as colours) to signify unhealthy food products when designing effective nutrition labelling policies. Besides, some studies argued that disclosing negative information can force companies to improve food formulations and improve the health level of food products (Wright et al., 2020). However, considering the company may have limited motivation to highlight negative information, some mandatory FOP label policies can be taken by the government to inform consumers. Compared with negative information labelling systems such as warning labels and traffic light labels, positive information labelling systems such as health-tick labels may be easier to accept and promote in the market. Supporting standards must be formulated and monitored by the government to make the labels more scientific and reliable. Despite consumers reporting nutrition claims, such as 'low sugar' or 'sugar-free', as the easiest to read, our empirical estimation reveals that nutrition claims are the least effective among the five FOP labels in encouraging consumers to choose healthier products. Given that nutrition claims are the primary and only FOP labels in the Chinese market it is crucial to introduce more effective FOP schemes, such as warning systems and traffic light systems, to persuade shoppers to opt for healthier food options in China.

This paper has some limitations and implications for future research. Firstly, our findings could be contingent on the setting being studied, such as hypothetical DCEs and the tea product. Future research should test the robustness of our findings to variations in these contexts, especially using non-hypothetical choice experiments and experimental auctions to capture consumers' food consumption behaviour. Secondly, for the summary FOP labels, this paper chose health tick and physical activity labels in the experiment because it is easier to understand and more suitable for the experiment product sugar-sweetened beverages. More kinds of summary label schemes such as Nutri-Score or Health-Star can be included when experimenting to compare the effectiveness of summary and nutrient-specific FOP labels (Julia & Hercberg, 2017; Mazzù et al., 2021). Thirdly, this paper aims to compare consumers' choices and preferences under different label contexts. Future studies can be conducted to further explore the effect of FOP labels on consumers' cumulative daily intake taking into account the frequency of intake, portions, and so on (Talati et al., 2018).

Disclosure Statement: No potential conflict of interest was reported by the author(s).

Funding: This study was funded by the National Natural Science Foundation of China [grant number No. 72003175; 72103180; 72273128], Zhejiang Province philosophy and social science planning project [grant number No. 23HQZZ05YB].

Data Availability Statement: The data is available upon request through the corresponding author.

Appendices

Appendix 1: Choice Experiment Instruction and Cheap Talk Script

Next, you will be presented with a hypothetical choice involving money. No one will actually be paid money based on the decision you make, but you are asked to make the decision as though it would result in the actual payment. Studies show that people tend to act differently when they face hypothetical decisions. In other words, they say one thing and do something different. We call this a 'hypothetical bias.' For example, in a recent study, several different groups of people made decisions just like the one you are about to make. Payment was real for one group and hypothetical for the other group, as it will be for you. The results of these studies were that on average, more people expressed a willingness to pay money in the hypothetical group than in the real group.

How can we get people to think about their decision in a hypothetical situation like they think in a real situation? I think that when we hear about a situation that involves doing something that is basically good, for example helping people in need, improving environmental quality, or anything else, our basic reaction in a hypothetical situation is to think: sure, I would do this. I really would spend the money; I really, really, think I would. But when the situation is real, and we would actually have to spend our money, we think a different way. We basically still would like to see good things happen, but when we are faced with the possibility of having to spend money, we think about our options: If I spend money on this, that's money I cannot spend on other things. So, when the payment is real, we act in a way that takes into account the limited amount of money we have. We make the decision while realizing that we just don't have enough money to do everything we might like to do.

Appendix 2: Label Description Before the Choice Experiment Questions

In the following, you are presented with several tea beverage purchasing scenatios. Each tea beverage product is characterrized with price, whether it contains sweeteners, and nutrition information presented by labels. All other characteristics of the tea beverage product are identical across the two tea beverage alternatives. Please evaluate each of the following scenarios as you would a real purchading situation.

Nutrition Facts Panel

Nutrition Facts Panel

	/100ml	NRV%
Energy	221 KJ	3%
Protein	0 g	0%
Fat	0 g	0%
Carbohydrate	13 g	4%
Na	10 mg	1%
Sugar	13 g	**

The second column of the table represents the content per 100 mL of the corresponding nutrient in the first column. The third column displays the proportion of the corresponding nutrient content in every 100 mL of the beverage to the daily recommended nutrient intake reference value. Taking energy as an example, the label above shows that the energy content in every 100 mL of the beverage is 221 kJ, accounting for 3% of the recommended daily energy intake reference value.

Traffic Light Label

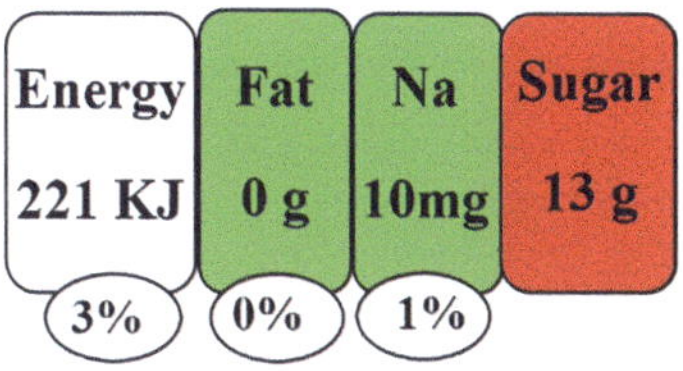

Red, yellow, and green in the above label represent the high, medium, and low levels of nutrient content, respectively. For example, the above figure shows that the product has low fat, moderate sodium content, and excessive added sugar.

The numerical value in the box represents the corresponding nutrient content per 100 mL of beverage. The percentage data in the ellipse represents the proportion of the corresponding nutrient content in every 100 mL of beverage to the daily recommended nutrient intake reference value. Taking sodium as an example, the label above shows that the sodium content in every 100 mL of beverage is 1 0mg, accounting for 1% of the recommended daily sodium intake reference value.

Physical Activity Label

This label shows that the number of jogging steps required to consume the calories in this beverage, calculated using a 65 kg adult as an example, is 3170 steps.

Warning Label

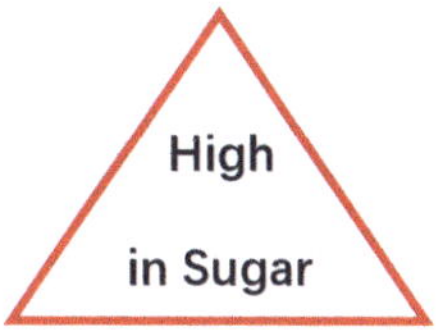

Beverages with this label indicates that the added sugar in this product exceeds the standard.

Health-Tick Label

Beverages with this label indicates that the product is healthy.

Nutrition Claims

Sugar Free

Beverages with this label indicates that the product is sugar-free.

References

Acton, R. B., & Hammond, D. (2018). The impact of price and nutrition labelling on sugary drink purchases: Results from an experimental marketplace study. *Appetite, 121*, 129–137.

An, R., Shi, Y., Shen, J., Bullard, T., Liu, G., Yang, Q., Chen, N., & Cao, L. (2021). Effect of front-of-package nutrition labeling on food purchases: A systematic review. *Public Health, 191*, 59–67.

Aranda, R., Darden, M., & Rose, D. (2021). Measuring the impact of calorie labeling: The mechanisms behind changes in obesity. *Health Economics, 30*(11), 2858–2878.

Ares, G., Antúnez, L., Curutchet, M. R., & Giménez, A. (2023). Warning labels as a policy tool to encourage healthier eating habits. *Current Opinion in Food Science, 51*, 101011.

Balcombe, K., Fraser, I., & di Falco, S. (2009). *Traffic lights and food choice: A choice experiment examining the relationship between nutritional food labels and price*. University of Kent, School of Economics.

Basu, S., Martin McKee, G. G., & Stuckler, D. (2013). Soft drink consumption to global overweight, obesity, and diabetes. *American Journal of Public Health, 103*(11), 2071–2077.

Bentley, R. A., Ruck, D. J., & Fouts, H. N. (2020). US obesity as delayed effect of excess sugar. *Economics & Human Biology, 36*, 100818.

Bliemer, M. C., & Rose, J. M. (2013). Confidence intervals of willingness-to-pay for random coefficient logit models. *Transportation Research Part B: Methodological, 58*, 199–214.

Carroll, N., Perreault, M., Ma, D. W., & Haines, J. (2021). Assessing food and nutrition literacy in children and adolescents: A systematic review of existing tools. *Public Health Nutrition, 25*(4), 1–16.

Celidoni, M., Guzzon, A., & Rebba, V. (2023). Health literacy and education: Evidence from the English longitudinal study of ageing. *Applied Economics, 55*(38), 4441–4454.

Christiansen, P., Roberts, C., Radu, C., & Hardman, C. (2023). A validation of a questionnaire to assess consumer attitudes towards artificial sweeteners. *Food Quality and Preference, 103*, 104707.

Clarke, N., Pechey, E., Kosite, D., Konig, L. M., Mantzari, E., Blackwell, A. K. M., Marteau, T. M., & Hollands, G. J. (2021). Impact of health warning labels on selection and consumption of food and alcohol products: Systematic review with meta-analysis. *Health Psychology Review, 15*(3), 430–453.

Corvalan, C., Reyes, M., Garmendia, M. L., & Uauy, R. (2019). Structural responses to the obesity and non-communicable diseases epidemic: Update on the Chilean law of food labelling and advertising. *Obesity Reviews, 20*(3), 367–374.

Defago, D., Geng, J. F., Molina, O., & Santa María, D. (2020). Can traffic light nutritional labels induce healthier consumer choices? Experimental evidence from a developing country. *International Journal of Consumer Studies, 44*(2), 151–161.

Duran Aguero, S., Araneda, J., Ahumada, D., Silva Rojas, J., Bonacich, R. B., Caichac, A., Salamanca, M. F., et al. (2020). A multicenter study evaluating the stages of change in food consumption with warning labels among Chilean university students. *BioMed Research International, 2020*, 2317929.

Egnell, M., Talati, Z., Hercberg, S., Pettigrew, S., & Julia, C. (2018). Objective understanding of front-of-package nutrition labels: An international comparative experimental study across 12 countries. *Nutrients, 10*(10), 1542.

Eldesouky, A., Mesias, F. J., & Escribano, M. (2020). Perception of Spanish consumers towards environmentally friendly labelling in food. *International Journal of Consumer Studies, 44*(1), 64–76.

Farag, M. A., Rezk, M. M., Hamdi Elashal, M., El-Araby, M., Khalifa, S. A. M., & El-Seedi, H. R. (2022). An updated multifaceted overview of sweet proteins and dipeptides as sugar substitutes; the chemistry, health benefits, gut interactions, and safety. *Food Research International, 162*(Pt A), 111853.

Farhat, G., Dewison, F., & Stevenson, L. (2021). Knowledge and perceptions of non-nutritive sweeteners within the UK Adult Population. *Nutrients, 13*(2), 444.

Gębski, J., Jezewska-Zychowicz, M., Szlachciuk, J., & Kosicka-Gębska, M. (2019). Impact of nutritional claims on consumer preferences for bread with varied fiber and salt content. *Food Quality and Preference, 76*, 91–99.

Grummon, A. H., Reimold, A. E., & Hall, M. G. (2022). Influence of the San Francisco, CA, sugar-sweetened beverage health warning on consumer reactions: Implications for equity from a randomized experiment. *Journal of the Academy of Nutrition and Dietetics, 122*(2), 363–370.

Grunert, K. G., & Wills, J. M. (2007). A review of European research on consumer response to nutrition information on food labels. *Journal of Public Health, 15*(5), 385–399.

Guan, L., Zhang, Y., Jin, S., & Zhou, L. (2021). Understanding the low use rate of food nutrition information in China. *International Food and Agribusiness Management Review, 24*(5), 863–876.

Guan, L., Huang, Z., & Jin, S. (2022). Time preference and nutrition label use: Evidence from China. *Economics & Human Biology, 47*, 101184.

Hensher, D. A., & Greene, J. M. R. W. H. (2005). *Applied choice analysis: A primer*. Cambridge University Press.

Hodgkins, C. E., Raats, M. M., Fife-Schaw, C., Peacock, M., Groppel-Klein, A., Koenigstorfer, J., Wasowicz, G., et al. (2015). Guiding healthier food choice: Systematic comparison of four front-of-pack labelling systems and their effect on judgements of product healthiness. *The British Journal of Nutrition, 113*(10), 1652–1663.

Hovhannisyan, V., & Bastian, C. T. (2022). New insights into the structure of consumer preferences for natural and artificial sweeteners. *American Journal of Agricultural Economics, 105*(5), 1491–1515.

Jack, M. M. (2017). Do sugar-sweetened beverages cause obesity and diabetes? *Annals of Internal Medicine, 167*(1), 72–72.

Julia, C., & Hercberg, S. (2017). Nutri-score: Evidence of the effectiveness of the French front-of-pack nutrition label. *Ernaehrungs Umschau International, 12*, 181–187.

Kanter, R., Vanderlee, L., & Vandevijvere, S. (2018). Front-of-package nutrition labelling policy: Global progress and future directions. *Public Health Nutrition, 21*(8), 1399–1408.

Krinsky, I., & Robb, A. L. (1986). On approximating the statistical properties of elasticities. *The Review of Economics and Statistics, 68*(4), 715–719.

Lancaster, K. J. (1966). A new approach to consumer theory. *Journal of Political Economy, 74*, 132–157.

Li, W., Finkelstein, E. A., & Zhen, C. (2022). Intended and unintended consequences of salient nutrition labels. *American Journal of Agricultural Economics, 104*(2), 853–872.

Downs, J. S., Loewenstein, G., & Wisdom, J. (2009). Strategies for promoting healthier food choices. *The American Economic Review, 99*(2), 159–164.

Lopez, R. A., & Fantuzzi, K. L. (2012). Demand for carbonated soft drinks: Implications for obesity policy. *Applied Economics, 44*(22), 2859–2865.

Ma, G., & Zhuang, X. (2021). Nutrition label processing in the past 10 years: Contributions from eye tracking approach. *Appetite, 156*, 104859.

Machín, L., Curutchet, M. R., Giménez, A., Aschemann-Witzel, J., & Ares, G. (2019). Do nutritional warnings do their work? Results from a choice experiment involving snack products. *Food Quality and Preference, 77*, 159–165.

Malik, V. S., & Hu, F. B. (2022). The role of sugar-sweetened beverages in the global epidemics of obesity and chronic diseases. *Nature Reviews. Endocrinology, 18*(4), 205–218.

Matthews, R. W., & Matthews, J. R. (2017). The Malaise trap: Its utility and potential for sampling insect populations. *The Great Lakes Entomologist, 4*(4), 117–122.

Mazzù, M. F., Romani, S., & Gambicorti, A. (2020). Effects on consumers' subjective understanding of a new front-of-pack nutritional label: A study on Italian consumers. *International Journal of Food Sciences and Nutrition, 72*(3), 357–366.

Mazzù, M. F., Romani, S., Baccelloni, A., & Lavini, L. (2021). Introducing the front-of-pack acceptance model: The role of usefulness and ease of use in European consumers' acceptance of front-of-pack labels. *International Journal of Food Sciences and Nutrition, 73*(3), 378–395.

Mazzù, M. F., Baccelloni, A., & Romani, S. (2023). Counteracting noncommunicable diseases with front-of-pack nutritional labels' informativeness: An inquiry into the effects on food acceptance and portions selection. *British Food Journal, 125*(13), 562–578.

McFadden, D. (1974). The measurement of urban travel demand. *Journal of Public Economics, 3*(4), 303–328.

McFadden, D., & Train, K. (2000). Mixed MNL models for discrete response. *Journal of Applied Econometrics, 15*(5), 447–470.

Melo, G., Zhen, C., & Colson, G. (2019). Does point-of-sale nutrition information improve the nutritional quality of food choices? *Economics & Human Biology, 35*, 133–143.

Neuhofer, Z., McFadden, B. R., Rihn, A., Wei, X., Khachatryan, H., & House, L. (2020). Can the updated nutrition facts label decrease sugar-sweetened beverage consumption? *Economics & Human Biology, 37*, 100867.

Nyilasy, G. A.-O., Lei, J., Nagpal, A., & Tan, J. (2016). Color correct: The interactive effects of food label nutrition colouring schemes and food category healthiness on health perceptions. *Public Health Nutrition, 19*(12), 2122–2127.

Oswald, C., Adhikari, K., & Mohan, A. (2022). Effect of front-of-package labels on consumer product evaluation and preferences. *Current Research in Food Science, 5*, 131–140.

Pettigrew, S., Jongenelis, M., Maganja, D., Hercberg, S., & Julia, C. (2024). The ability of nutrition warning labels to improve understanding and choice outcomes among consumers demonstrating preferences for unhealthy foods. *Journal of the Academy of Nutrition and Dietetics, 124*(1), 58–64.

Poe, G. L., Giraud, K. L., & Loomis, J. B. (2005). Computational methods for measuring the difference of empirical distributions. *American Journal of Agricultural Economics, 87*(2), 353–365.

Roseman, M. G., Joung, H. W., & Littlejohn, E. I. (2018). Attitude and behavior factors associated with front-of-package label use with label users making accurate product nutrition assessments. *Journal of the Academy of Nutrition and Dietetics, 118*(5), 904–912.

Rosenblatt, D. H., Dixon, H., Wakefield, M., & Bode, S. (2019). Evaluating the influence of message framing and graphic imagery on perceptions of food product health warnings. *Food Quality and Preference, 77*, 32–42.

Schifferstein, H. N. J., Howell, B. F., & Pont, S. C. (2017). Colored backgrounds affect the attractiveness of fresh produce, but not it's perceived color. *Food Quality and Preference, 56*, 173–180.

Sharma, A., Amarnath, S., Thulasimani, M., & Ramaswamy, S. (2016). Artificial sweeteners as a sugar substitute: Are they really safe? *Indian Journal of Pharmacology, 48*(3), 237–240.

Silva, C. P. D., Bento, A. C., & Guaraldo, E. (2022). The impact of front-of-the-packaging nutrition labelling warnings on consumer habits: A scoping review exploring the case of the Chilean Food Law. *British Food Journal, 124*(13), 66–80.

Singh, G. M., Micha, R., Khatibzadeh, S., Shi, P., Lim, S., Andrews, K. G., Engell, R. E., Ezzati, M., & Mozaffarian, D. (2015). Global, regional, and national consumption of sugar-sweetened beverages, fruit juices, and milk: A systematic assessment of beverage intake in 187 countries. *PLoS One, 10*(8), e0124845.

Street, D. J., Burgess, L., & Louviere, J. J. (2005). Quick and easy choice sets: Constructing optimal and nearly optimal stated choice experiments. *International Journal of Research in Marketing, 22*(4), 459–470.

Suez, J., Korem, T., Zeevi, D., Zilberman-Schapira, G., Thaiss, C. A., Maza, O., Israeli, D., et al. (2014). Artificial sweeteners induce glucose intolerance by altering the gut microbiota. *Nature, 514*(7521), 181–186.

Taillie, L. S., Hall, M. G., Popkin, B. M., Ng, S. W., & Murukutla, N. (2020). Experimental studies of front-of-package nutrient warning labels on sugar-sweetened beverages and ultra-processed foods: A scoping review. *Nutrients, 12*(2), 569.

Talati, Z., Pettigrew, S., Kelly, B., Ball, K., Neal, B., Dixon, H., Shilton, T., & Miller, C. (2018). Can front-of-pack labels influence portion size judgements for unhealthy foods? *Public Health Nutrition, 21*(15), 2776–2781.

Talati, Z., Egnell, M., Hercberg, S., Julia, C., & Pettigrew, S. (2019). Food choice under five front-of-package nutrition label conditions: An experimental study across 12 countries. *American Journal of Public Health, 109*(12), 1770–1775.

Tang, C. S., Mars, M., James, J., de Graaf, K., & Appleton, K. M. (2021). Sweet talk: A qualitative study exploring attitudes towards sugar, sweeteners and sweet-tasting foods in the United Kingdom. *Foods, 10*(6), 1172.

Temple, N. J. (2020). Front-of-package food labels: A narrative review. *Appetite, 144*, 104485.

Thiene, M., Scarpa, R., Longo, A., & Hutchinson, W. G. (2018). Types of front of pack food labels: Do obese consumers care? Evidence from Northern Ireland. *Food Policy, 80*, 84–102.

Tiboldo, G., Bonanno, A., Lopez, R. A., & Castellari, E. (2021). Competitive and welfare effects of private label presence in differentiated food markets. *Applied Economics, 53*(24), 2713–2726.

Train, K. E. (2003). *Discrete choice methods with simulation*. Cambridge University Press.

Wright, M. A., Beatty, T. K. M., & Chouinard, H. H. (2020). Do firms leverage the FDA nutrient label rounding rules to generate favorable nutrition fact panels or health claims? *Food Policy, 91*, 101807.

Yu, P., Chen, Y., Zhao, A., Bai, Y., Zheng, Y., Zhao, W., & andY. Zhang. (2016). Consumption of sugar-sweetened beverages and its association with overweight among young children from China. *Public Health Nutrition, 19*(13), 2336–2346.

Zhai, T. C., Li, L., Wang, J. J., & Si, W. (2022). Will the consumption tax on sugar-sweetened beverages help promote healthy beverage consumption? Evidence from urban China. *China Economic Review, 73*, 101798.

Zhang, X., Huang, X., Xiao, Y., Jing, D., Huang, Y., Chen, L., Luo, D., Chen, X., & Shen, M. (2019). Daily intake of soft drinks is associated with symptoms of anxiety and depression in Chinese adolescents. *Public Health Nutrition, 22*(14), 2553–2560.

Zhang, Y., Sun, Q., Zhang, M., Mo, G., & Liu, H. (2022). Nutrition literacy measurement tool with multiple features for Chinese adults. *Food and Nutrition Bulletin, 43*(2), 189–200.

Part IV
Government-Market Synergy for Green and Sustainable Agri-Food Development

Chapter 10
Could Trust Narrow the Intention-Behavior Gap in Eco-Friendly Food Consumption? Evidence from China

10.1 Introduction

Due to the negative impacts on the environment and the ecosystem caused by conventional agriculture, eco-friendly agriculture has gained increasing interest worldwide. Eco-friendly agriculture sustains the health of people, the ecosystem, and the soil (Chekima et al., 2019), benefiting both the environment and social welfare. Despite the growing interest, the market share of eco-friendly foods remains low. For instance, the United States is the largest market of organic food in the world, whose an organic market share is 6% of the total market; Switzerland is the highest per capita consumption of organic food, but its organic market share is 10.8% (Willer et al., 2022). The low market share of organic foods is more evident in developing countries including China, whose market share is less than 1% (Willer et al., 2022).

The low market share of eco-friendly foods could be attributed to inconsistent behavior in eco-friendly foods consumption (Aschemann-Witzel & Niebuhr Aagaard, 2014; Frank & Brock, 2018; Nguyen et al., 2019). Inconsistent behavior refers to the inconsistency between what people claim and what they actually behave, including the attitude-behavior gap and intention-behavior gap (ElHaffar et al., 2020). The study focuses on the intention-behavior gap, which has been found in many contexts including the United Kingdom, Canada, Vietnam, Thailand, Italy, and China (Carfora et al., 2019; Frank & Brock, 2018; Nguyen et al., 2019; Nuttavuthisit & Thøgersen, 2017).

Trust would play a role in explaining the intention-behavior gap of eco-friendly food consumption. Eco-friendly foods, such as green and organic foods, include

How to cite this article: Yuan, R., Jin, S., & Lin, W. (2025). Could trust narrow the intention-behavior gap in eco-friendly food consumption? Evidence from China. *Agribusiness, 41*, 260–288. https://doi.org/10.1002/agr.21886.

W. Lin, *Transforming China's Agri-Food System: Government-Market Synergy*, Resources, Environment and Agricultural Development,
https://doi.org/10.1007/978-981-95-7151-2_10

credence attributes, which consumers are difficult to verify even after consumption. For such goods, consumers' trust may give them the confidence to act on their intentions to purchase eco-friendly foods (Macready et al., 2020; Sultan et al., 2020). Consumer trust is negatively associated with their risk perception about food products (Tonsor et al., 2009), and positively relates to perceived benefits of eco-friendly products (Siegrist et al., 2007). Thus the higher the consumer trust, the higher the probability for consumers to choose eco-friendly food products (Grebitus et al., 2015). On the other hand, trust in actors including governments and firms sometimes is considered a sort of heuristic in food purchasing decisions (Ricci et al., 2018), and it positively relates to individual purchases when consumers face knowledge and/or time constraints. Therefore, we would expect that consumer trust contributes to narrow consumer intention-behaviro gap in the eco-friendly foods consumption.

Few studies have explored whether and to what extent trust could narrow the intention-behavior gap in eco-friendly foods consumption. The study aims to investigate the effects of consumer trust in narrowing the intention-behavior gap in eco-friendly food consumption. As a practical application, we focus on Chinese consumers. China is one of the most potential markets for eco-friendly food products worldwide, given its huge market size and currently low retail sales of eco-friendly foods. Eco-friendly foods in this study include green and organic foods. We find that consumers who distrust certifiers are more likely to have the intention-behavior gap in green food consumption, while trust in manufacturers matters in closing the gap in organic food consumption. Besides, trust has a greater impact in narrowing the intention-behavior gap among female, young, well-educated, and environmentally conscious consumers. Our findings highlight the importance of enhancing consumer trust in the eco-friendly food supply chain actors, including manufacturers and certifiers, in promoting eco-friendly food consumption.

Our study makes several contributions to the literature. First, we focus on the intention-behavior gap in eco-friendly food consumption. While the intention-behavior gap is widely discussed by the studies on consumer environmental and ethical behaviors (Gleim & Lawson, 2014; Moser, 2015), the gap in eco-friendly food consumption receives limited attention in the literature. The intention-behavior gap would explain the low market share of eco-friendly foods (Sultan et al., 2020). Some work discusses the intention-behavior gap in consumer eco-friendly consumption (Tung et al., 2012), but they rarely focus on how to narrow the intention-behavior gap. Second, we aim to investigate and compare the roles of consumers' trust in various actors in food supply chains in closing the intention-behavior gap in eco-friendly food consumption. Related studies typically investigate consumer trust in eco-friendly foods themselves, little focus has been given to analyzing consumer trust in those who produce and provide eco-friendly foods, namely various food supply chain actors. Subjects might depend on their trust in the actors of eco-friendly food supply chains to make purchase decisions (Ricci et al., 2018). We investigate consumer trust in four actors in food supply chains, including eco-friendly food regulators, certifiers, farmers, and manufacturers. Last and importantly, this study examines whether and to what extent consumer trust would bridge the intention-behavior gap in eco-friendly food consumption. Limited work has explored the relationship between consumer trust in food supply chain actors and the intention-behavior gap in the context of eco-friendly food consumption. Some have noted that insufficient knowledge about eco-friendly foods among consumers is a critical barrier to eco-friendly consumption (Aertsens et al., 2011). We expect that consumer trust, in particular consumer trust in food chain actors, may enable consumers to compensate for their limited knowledge about eco-friendly food production, processing, and certification (de Jonge et al., 2007).

The remainder of the paper is structured as follows. In the next section, we give an overview of our methodology detailing the experimental design and econometric models. Next, we discuss the data, followed by a summary of the empirical results from the study. The last section contains a discussion of the implications of our findings for the eco-friendly food products industry and the marketing of eco-friendly food products in China.

10.2 Methodology

10.2.1 Trust and Intention-Behavior Gap Measurement

10.2.1.1 Trust

Consumer trust is measured with the previously validated scale developed by de Jonge et al. (2007).[1] The trust scale is frequently applied to measure consumer trust in food contexts in China and other countries (Chen, 2013; Macready et al., 2020; Zhang et al., 2022). Consumer trust in eco-friendly foods is measured in terms of trust-related beliefs about four actors in the food supply chain: eco-friendly food farmer, manufacturer (processing, preserving, and packing eco-products), and certifier (certificating eco-products) and the regulator. Following Poortinga and Pidgeon (2003) and de Jonge et al. (2007), participants are asked to evaluate each of the four actors with respect to four dimensions. The four dimensions include (1) competence, measuring the actor's capability and reliability in performing tasks; (2) benevolence, measuring to which extent the actor behaves in a way that shows concern for the people; (3) openness, assessing to which extent the actor is sufficiently open about the work information; and (4) attention, assessing the degree that the actor gives special attention to related work. Therefore, the trust scale has a total of 16 items. Participants are asked about their level of agreement with each of these

[1] Trust measurement is a debated issue in the literature, but it is certain that trust is multidimensional. The early classical work suggests that trust have three dimensions: ability, benevolence, and integrity (Mayer et al., 1995). In recent years, the trust scale developed by de Jonge et al. (2007) is widely accepted in the literature, this trust scale includes three dimensions: competence, openness, and attention (care). Following de Jonge et al. (2007), meanwhile we consider the dimension of benevolence, therefore, trust in the study is measured by four dimensions: competence, openness, attention, and benevolence.

items on a 5-point scale (1 = Strongly disagree, and 5 = Strongly agree). The trust score of each actor is computed by finding the mean of the relevant four items. Higher score in trust indicates higher level of consumer trust. Table 10.1 shows the trust scales, which is used to measure consumer trust in green food and organic food, respectively. Consumers are randomly assigned to fill in one of the two questionnaires concerning green food consumption and organic food consumption.

Table 10.1 Trust scales

Trust	Items (scale: 1 = Strongly disagree to 5 = Strongly agree)
Regulator	
	Green (organic) food regulator gives special attention to the safety and quality of green (organic) rice
	Green (organic) food regulator has the competence to control the safety and quality of rice
	Green (organic) food regulator is sufficiently open about the safety and quality of green (organic) rice
	Green (organic) food regulator takes good care of the safety and quality of green (organic) rice
Manufacturer	
	Green (organic) food manufacturer gives special attention to the safety and quality of green (organic) rice
	Green (organic) food manufacturer has the competence to control the safety and quality of green (organic) rice
	Green (organic) food manufacturer is sufficiently open about the safety and quality of green (organic) rice
	Green (organic) food manufacturer takes good care of the safety and quality of green (organic) rice
Farmer	
	Green (organic) food farmer gives special attention to the safety and quality of green (organic) rice
	Green (organic) food farmer has the competence to control the safety and quality of green (organic) rice
	Green (organic) food farmer is sufficiently open about the safety and quality of green (organic) rice
	Green (organic) food farmer takes good care of the safety and quality of green (organic) rice
Certifier	
	Green (organic) food certifier gives special attention to the safety and quality of green (organic) rice
	Green (organic) food certifier has the competence to control the safety and quality of green (organic) rice
	Green (organic) food certifier is sufficiently open about the safety and quality of green (organic) rice
	Green (organic) food certifier takes good care of the safety and quality of green (organic) rice

Note: In the trust scale, the eco-products were specified as rice to be consistent within the choice experiment where rice is of interest. Consumers trust for green rice and organic rice are separated into two survey versions, respectively

10.2.1.2 Intention-Behavior Gap

Intention-behavior gap refers to the inconsistency between consumer purchase intention and actual purchase behavior. As such we first describe how consumer purchase intention is measured in our study, followed by actual purchase behavior, and combining the two concepts we discuss the measurement of the intention-behavior gap in eco-friendly food consumption.

First, willingness to pay (WTP) is used as an indicator of consumer purchase intention in the study following Sultan et al. (2020). Compared with other intention measurements such as a commitment to repurchase organic food items, and an attitude to purchase organic food, WTP is a stronger predictor of the behavior (Moser, 2015). We therefore expect WTP might be a better indicator of purchase intention since it conforms the definition of intention, and it has a stronger power to predict behavior.

To elicit consumer WTP for eco-friendly food, a hypothetical choice experiment (CE) about rice purchasing decision was implemented among Chinese consumers. Rice was chosen because it is a staple food in China, and is one of the most common green foods in China. In CE, rice alternatives are varied in four product attributes: certification, brand, country of origin and price (see Table 10.2). We included the certification attribute because we would like to evaluate consumers' WTPs for different eco-friendly certifications. Three levels of the certification attribute are specified: green food certification, organic food certification, and no certifications. Green certification and organic certification are two major eco-friendly certifications in China, while no certification is common in the market. Green-certified food is unique in China, which is produced with limited and safe chemical substances (Yu et al., 2014). Green certification was launched in 1990 by the Chinese Ministry of Agriculture to alleviate severe agricultural environmental pollution caused by chemically intensive farming practices and to seek more sustainable agricultural development (Scott et al., 2014). Different from green certification, organic certification in our context prohibits any chemical use in agricultural production, which has a similar definition and standard to the USDA organic certification. China launched its own national organic product standards in 2005. In 2012, the Administration of Certification and Accreditation of China launched a revised and more stringent set of national organic standards (Scott et al., 2014). In general, organic food certification has more stringent standards in food production and processing than green food certification, and the two separate certifications are approved by different agencies, using different certification labels. Country of origin is also

Table 10.2 Attributes and attribute levels in the choice experiment

Attributes	Levels		
Certification	None	Green	Organic
Origin of country	Thailand	Japan	China
Price (RMB/500 g)	3.60	7.40	13.40
Brand	None	Unknown	Known

included because it plays a critical role in consumers' food choice (Xie et al., 2016). Consumers often use country of origin to infer the quality of a product based on their shopping experiences (Wang et al., 2019; Xie et al., 2016). Three levels of the country of origin are specified in our study, namely China, Japan, and Thailand. Thailand is the largest rice importer of China according to the statistics by Chinese Customs Office in 2019. Japan rice is popular among Chinese consumers due to its good taste. Last, brand is included because it influences consumer food purchasing decisions (Kariuki & Hoffmann, 2021; Liu et al., 2020). Well-known brand products tend to have a higher reputation among consumers, as it gives consumers confidence to choose the products (Lassoued & Hobbs, 2015; Zhou et al., 2017). We included three brand levels, namely known brand, unknown brand, and no brand. Known brand refers to those which have a higher reputation and popularity brands among Chinese consumers, for example, Arawana, Beidahuang, Jinjian, and so forth.[2] Unknown brand refers to those which have a lower reputation and popularity brands. No brand refers to those which have been not branded. (iiii) Finally, the price levels are selected to reflect actual market price ranges. The price level is determined by a collection of online price of green rice and organic rice in 2018, which ranged from 3.60 to 13.4RMB/500 g.

Given the number of attributes and their levels, we generated a D-optimal fractional factorial design with 32 choice sets, blocked into four blocks. Each respondent was randomly assigned to one of blocks and completed eight choice sets. Each choice set includes two rice product profiles and a no purchase option. Fig. 10.1 presents an example of a choice set. Based on the random utility model (McFadden, 1974), random parameters logit (RPL) was used to analyze the choice data, and to simulate consumers WTP for green rice and organic rice, respectively. To operationalizethe RPL, we assume a normal distribution for all non-price attributes and a fixed price attribute (see Appendix).

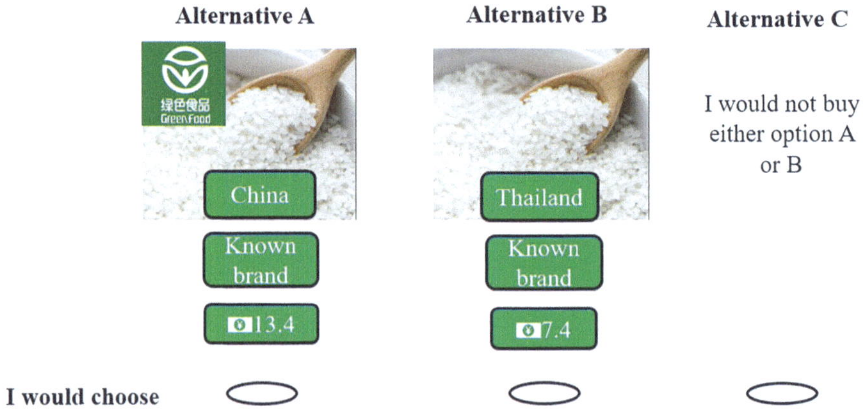

Fig. 10.1 Sample choice set

[2]Arawana: https://www.jinlongyu.cn; Beidahuang: https://www.chinabdh.com; Jinjian: http://www.jjmy.cn.

To identify whether consumers have positive purchase intention of eco-friendly food, we compare the WTP for green rice and organic rice with corresponding actual market prices. If a consumer's WTP for green rice or organic rice is higher than the market price, we could say that the person has positive purchase intention. Otherwise, the consumer has negative intention to purchase eco-friendly foods. Market price is identified by a collection of retailer price of green rice and organic rice online and offline, including the biggest ecommerce platform such as Tmall and Jindong, as well as several offline supermarkets. Average actual market price of green rice and organic rice is 7.4RMB/500 g, and 13.4RMB/500 g, respectively.

Second, consumer purchase behavior of eco-friendly food is measured by respondents' self-reported behaviors. This follows Sultan et al. (2020), which is often used as a proxy measure in the literature to reflect actual behavioral practices (Singh & Verma, 2017; Tandon et al., 2021). The self-reported question asks consumers about the average frequency of purchasing green rice or organic rice, and we provide four response option for consumers: never, one or two times, sometimes, and always. Based on their responses, consumers are grouped into two types: (1) never purchase group, whose answer is never; (2) purchase group, who selects one of the three options, that is one or two times, sometimes, and always.

Lastly, combining consumers' purchase intention and actual purchase behavior, we distinguish four types of the intention-behavior gap in eco-friendly food consumption. The first type refers to (1) behavior gap group, meaning that although consumers have the positive purchase intention, they have never purchased eco-friendly foods previously. The second type is (2) intention gap group, meaning that consumers have the negative purchase intention to purchase eco-friendly foods, but indeed having related purchase experience. The remaining two groups refer to (3) positive consistency group and (4) negative consistency group. Both groups' types have consistent behavior in eco-friendly food consumption, namely their purchase intension is consistent with the purchase experience. In particular, consumers having the positive consistency are those with positive purchase intention and actual purchase experience of eco-foods, while the negative consistency group refers to consumers having the negative purchase intention and accordingly never purchasing eco-foods.

10.2.2 Empirical Model

We use multinomial logit model specification to estimate the impacts of consumer trust on the intention-behavior gap in green and organic food consumption. The dependent variable, denoted by Y, is the type of consumer intention-behavior gap group in eco-friendly foods consumption. We define Y equals to 1 if consumers belong to behavior gap group, 2 if intention gap group, 3 if positive consistency group and 4 if negative consistency group. Consumers belong to one of the four gap groups based on their utilities. The model specification is defined as follows:

$$\ln\left[\frac{p(Y=j)}{p(Y=3)}\right]=\beta_{1i}\text{TRUST}+\beta_{2i}X+\varepsilon_i, \tag{10.1}$$

where $p(Y = j)$ represents the probability that consumers have the jth type of purchase behavior ($j = 1,2,4$), relative to the baseline type (positive consistency group). TRUST denotes consumer trust, and X refers to control variables including consumer sociodemographic characteristics and attitudes. β reflects the effect of explanatory variable on the logarithm of the probability ration between the j type of purchase behavior and the baseline.

10.2.3 Data Collection

Data were collected from ten provinces and cities in China: Beijing, Shanghai, Yunnan, Sichuan, Guangdong, Jiangsu, Hubei, Fujian, Liaoning and Heilongjiang. The study areas include different regions of China, and also developed and less developed areas. The data were collected through an online survey between December 2017 and March 2018. All participants were recruited by BAIDU, a professional market research agency, and were screened to ensure that they were over 18 years of age. Consumers were asked to complete a questionnaire, including the CE tasks, trust scales, consumer attitude, consumption behavior of eco-friendly foods and socio-demographics. Respondents took in general 10 min to complete the survey.

Remember that among a range of eco-friendly food products, our study focuses on green and organic foods. To examine the effect of consumer trust on narrowing the intention-behavior gap in the context of green and organic food consumption, we design two different versions of questionnaire, respectively. Consumers are randomly assigned into one of two surveys. The two surveys only differ in the framing of the consumer trust scale. One surveys measures consumer trust in green food, and the other elicit trust in organic food.

10.3 Results

10.3.1 Descriptive Analysis

10.3.1.1 Sample Demographics

Sample demographics are reported in Table 10.3. A total of 2255 participants completed the survey, with 1314 participants completing the green food version, and 941 participants for the organic food version.

Table 10.3 Demographics of the consumer sample

Variables	Definition	Green group		Organic group		
		Mean	SD	Mean	SD	Census data
Age	Years	33.87	8.28	34.19	8.32	68.6% (15–64 years)
P value = 0.37, *t* value = 0.89						
Gender	Male = 1	0.49	0.50	0.47	0.50	51.24% (male)
	Female = 0					
P value = 0.53, Pearson's $\chi^2(1) = 0.39$						
Marriage	Married = 1	0.64	0.48	0.63	0.48	
	Other = 0					
P value = 0.82, Pearson's $\chi^2(1) = 0.05$						
Education	Under primary school/primary school = 1	3.65	0.89	3.66	0.86	24.77%
	Middle school = 2					34.51%
	High school = 3					15.09%
	Undergraduate = 4					15.47%
	Master/above master = 5					
P value = 0.87, Pearson's $\chi^2(4) = 1.24$						
Income/ RMB	0–3000 = 1;	4.27	1.82	4.30	1.68	9812.75
	3001–5000 = 2;					
	5001–8000 = 3;					
	8001–10,000 = 4;					
	10,001–20,000 = 5;					
	20,001–30,000 = 6;					
	30,001–50,000 = 7;					
	Above 50,000 = 8					
P value = 0.56, Pearson's $\chi^2(7) = 5.83$						

Note: Census data except income comes from the seventh national population census of China, family monthly income calculated according to China Statistical Yearbook. *P* value is the result of balance test of consumer characteristics among four treatment groups. The continuous variable, age is tested using *t* test, while the rest of variables (i.e., gender, marriage, education and income) are tested using a χ^2 test as they are category variable

10.3.1.2 Descriptive Statistics on Intention-Behavior Gap

Table 10.7 shows the consumers WTP results. On average, consumers are willing to pay a premium of 16.24RMB/500 g for green rice, whereas consumers appear unwilling to pay a premium for organic rice (13.15RMB/500 g). The finding is line with previous literature indicating Chinese consumers have a higher WTP for green food than organic food (Jin et al., 2017; Shimokawa et al., 2021). While the finding is contrary to the fact that organic rice price is higher than that of green rice in the market.[3] It is perhaps that consumers are confused about the meaning of the term organic or assume that organic food follows less stringent standards than green food, because Chinese consumers lack of knowledge about organic food (Shimokawa et al., 2021; Yin et al., 2010). According to individual WTPs, consumers whose WTPs for organic rice and green rice are higher than the market price are classified into positive purchase intention group, otherwise in the negative purchase intention group. Table 10.8 shows the results of purchase intention, most of consumers (93.30%) have positive purchase intention for green rice, while only 48.63% of consumers have positive purchase intention for organic rice. Table 10.9 shows the results of consumer purchase behavior of eco-friendly food. 70.85% and 72.05% of consumers have never purchased green rice and organic rice, respectively.

Table 10.4 shows the type of the intention-behavior gap in our sample. The phenomenon of intention-behavior gap in organic food consumption is much severer than that in the green food consumption. In the green food consumption, approximately 31.03% of consumers have inconsistent behavior. 26.14% and 4.89% of consumers are in the behavior gap group and intention gap group, respectively. Turning to the organic food consumption, about half of consumers exhibit inconsistent behavior. 13.47% and 35.69% of consumers are in the behavior gap group and intention gap group respectively. Given the huge market size in China, even a small proportion of intention-behavior gap would have a huge effect on the development of eco-friendly foods market. So the intention-behavior gap in eco-friendly food consumption should be paid much attention in China.

Note that 35.69% of consumers have intention gaps in the organic food consumption, meaning that consumers already making actual purchases of organic

Table 10.4 Consumer behavior types in eco-friendly food consumption

Behavior types	Definition	Green food		Organic food	
		N	%	*N*	%
Type 1: positive consistency	Consistent behavior: having positive intention and actual purchase behavior.	632	67.16	462	35.16
Type 2: behavior gap	Intention-behavior gap: having positive intention but without actual purchase behavior.	246	26.14	177	13.47
Type 3: intention gap	Intention-behavior gap: having negative intention and actual purchase behavior.	46	4.89	469	35.69
Type 4: negative consistency	Consistent behavior: having negative intention but without actual purchase behavior.	17	1.81	206	15.68
Observations		941		1314	

[3] Market price is identified by a collection of retailer price of green rice and organic rice online and offline, including the biggest ecommerce platform such as Tmall and Jindong, as well as several offline supermarkets. Average actual market price of green rice and organic rice is 7.4RMB/500 g, and 13.4RMB/500 g, respectively.

food but with a low intension. Several reasons may explain the intention gap in the eco-friendly food consumption. First, consumer preference for eco-friendly foods is likely to be eroded by fraud labels in market, so in turn they have negative intention to purchase the foods. Second, some individuals' purchase of organic foods is primarily motivated by curiosity (Kushwah et al. 2019), even though those might have a negative intention to organic food. Third, consumers are confused with the meaning of organic food and green food due to lack of knowledge, the confusing makes consumers have a higher WTP for green food than organic food (Jin et al., 2017; Shimokawa et al., 2021). While the price of organic food is higher than that of green food in Chinese market actually. Thus, we observe a higher percentage of negative intention behavior in organic food consumption, then intention gap as well.

10.3.1.3 Descriptive Statistics on Trust and Other Variables

Consumer trust scores are reported in Table 10.10. Cronbach's α reliability coefficients for the four actors in the food supply chain are above 0.70, suggesting that the trust scales are reliable and internally consistent (Nunnally, 1978). Overall, trust levels are rather moderate, with an average score of 3.38. Chinese consumers tend to trust regulator and eco-friendly food label certifiers, relative to the manufacturer and farmer. Consumers have higher trust levels for green food than organic food. Besides, respondents generally rate competence and benevolence higher than attention and openness.

Table 10.11 shows description of control variables. Health awareness was measured by Kraft and Goodell (1993) 3-item health awareness scale which asks participants how much they agreed (1 = Strongly disagree to 5 = Strongly agree) with statements about health habits. Environment awareness was measured by Roberts (1996) 3-items scale which asks participants how much they agreed (1 = Strongly disagree to 5 = Strongly agree). Following de Jonge et al. (2007), food safety risk perception was measured by 3-item scale which asks participants how much they agreed (1 = Strongly disagree to 5 = Strongly agree). Cronbach α values of the three types of awareness are greater than 0.70. Consumer risk perception of food safety is rather moderate (with an average score of 2.90), while consumer health awareness and environment awareness tend to be above the moderate. In terms of knowledge, consumers' knowledge about green rice and organic rice is not high, but consumers tend to have more knowledge of green rice (with an average score of 2.28) than organic rice (with an average score of 1.91). In terms of purchase convenience, consumers express a middle level of convenience to purchase green rice and organic rice. In terms of consumption behavior, most consumers are responsible for buying food at home, and most consumers have experienced of buying imported rice, few consumers have special diets about nutrition and health in the recent year.

10.3.2 Regression Analyses of the Effect of Trust on Intention-Behavior Gap

We use multinomial models to investigate the impact of consumer trust on the intention-behavior gap in eco-friendly food consumption. We first determine whether overall consumer trust affects the intention-behavior gap in eco-friendly food consumption, controlling for other variables. Second, we examine which types of consumer trust in actors affect the intention-behavior gap in eco-friendly food consumption. Lastly, we conduct a sensitivity test by re-grouping strategies, that is, we redefine actual purchase behavior by dividing never purchase, one or two times and sometimes purchase into never purchase group, and other options (i.e., always purchase) into purchase group.

Results indicate that trust indeed have significantly positive impacts on closing consumer intention-behavior gap in the green and organic food consumption (Tables 10.12 and 10.13). Tables 10.12 and 10.13 also show that consumer characteristics affects the intention-behavior gap. Female, infrequent food buyers, infrequent imported food buyers, and inconvenient eco-friendly food buyers are more likely to have intention-behavior gap, in both the green food and organic food consumption.

We then turn to explore the effects of consumer trust in actors on intention-behavior gap in eco-friendly food consumption. Table 10.5 shows results concerning green food consumption. Results indicate that consumer trust in eco-friendly label certifier significantly affects consumer intention-behavior gap in green food consumption. The marginal effect of consumer trust in the certifier is 0.07, meaning that consumer trust in the certifier increases by one unit, the probability for consumers belonging to the behavior gap group will decrease by 7%.

Table 10.6 reports results regarding organic food consumption. We find that consumer trust in organic food manufacturer significantly impacts consumer intention-behavior gap in organic food consumption. Increasing consumer trust in the manufacturer by one unit, the probability for consumer belonging to the intention gap group increases by 8%, relative to the baseline. Trust in organic label certifier also significantly affects consumer purchase behavior in organic food consumption. A one-unit increase of the trust would decrease consumer's probability of falling into the negative consistency group by 3%. The finding once again emphasizes the role of certifier in consumers eco-friendly foods consumption.

In addition, purchase convenience, consumer consumption behavior, consumer environment awareness and health awareness are also found to have significant impacts on intention-behavior gap both in green food and organic food consumption. we take the results of green food regression (i.e., Table 10.5) as an example to discuss. First, if consumer purchase convenience of green food changes from strong convenience to strong inconvenience, the possibility of consumer behavior gap will increase by around 39%. Consumer intention-behavior gap in green food consumption is also affected by consumption behavior. Consumers with special diet are more likely to have positive consistency behavior in green food consumption, the probability would increase 8%. Besides, those who have never purchased imported rice

Table 10.5 Impacts of trust in actors on intention-behavior gap in green food consumption

Variables	B1/2		β1/3		B1/4	
	Coef.	*dy/dx*	Coef.	*dy/dx*	Coef.	*dy/dx*
Regulator	0.03	0.001	0.39	0.01	−0.35	0.001
	(0.16)	(0.03)	(0.29)	(0.01)	(0.48)	(0.06)
Manufacturer	0.20	0.04	−0.36	−0.01	0.02	0.001
	(0.19)	(0.03)	(0.36)	(0.01)	(0.59)	(0.001)
Farmer	−0.03	−0.01	0.28	0.01	0.23	0.001
	(0.18)	(0.03)	(0.35)	(0.01)	(0.54)	(0.04)
Certifier	−0.40**	−0.07**	−0.43	−0.01	−0.25	0.001
	(0.16)	(0.03)	(0.33)	(0.01)	(0.51)	(0.02)
Age	0.001	0.001	0.001	0.001	−0.01	0.001
	(0.01)	(0.001)	(0.02)	(0.001)	(0.03)	(0.001)
Gender	−0.28	−0.05	0.38	0.01	0.62	0.001
	(0.17)	(0.03)	(0.33)	(0.01)	(0.54)	(0.11)
Income	0.04	0.01	0.001	0.001	0.07	0.001
	(0.05)	(0.01)	(0.09)	(0.001)	(0.16)	(0.01)
Education	−0.19*	−0.03	−0.26	−0.01	−0.66**	0.001
	(0.11)	(0.03)	(0.19)	(0.01)	(0.27)	(0.10)
Special diet	−0.41**	−0.08*	0.39	0.02	−0.22	0.001
	(0.20)	(0.04)	(0.33)	(0.01)	(0.62)	(0.02)
Knowledge	−0.08	−0.01	−0.33*	−0.01*	−0.09	0.001
	(0.10)	(0.02)	(0.17)	(0.01)	(0.29)	(0.01)
Purchaser	−0.08	−0.02	0.25	0.01	0.01	0.001
	(0.08)	(0.01)	(0.17)	(0.01)	(0.25)	(0.001)
Import rice						
Sometimes	−0.13***	−0.22***	0.19	0.01	−1.26	−0.01
	(0.23)	(0.04)	(0.54)	(0.01)	(0.81)	(0.01)
Often	−1.39***	−0.26***	0.60	0.03**	−0.92	−0.01
	(0.21)	(0.04)	(0.45)	(0.01)	(0.59)	(0.01)
Always	−1.36***	−0.26***	0.83	0.04	−13.21	−0.02**
	(0.39)	(0.06)	(0.61)	(0.03)	(0.39)	(0.01)
Environment awareness	0.07	0.02	−0.83***	−0.03***	0.02	0.001
	(0.14)	(0.03)	(0.28)	(0.01)	(0.44)	(0.01)
Health awareness	0.25	0.04	0.56*	0.02	0.14	0.001
	(0.15)	(0.03)	(0.31)	(0.01)	(0.47)	(0.01)
Risk perception	−0.12	−0.02	−0.15	0.001	−0.38	0.001
	(0.09)	(0.02)	(0.19)	(0.01)	(0.30)	(0.05)
Convenience						
A little	−1.07***	−0.24**	−0.44	0.001	0.17	0.001
	(0.41)	(0.10)	(0.75)	(0.03)	(1.19)	(0.13)

(continued)

Table 10.5 (continued)

Variables	Β1/2		β1/3		Β1/4	
	Coef.	*dy/dx*	Coef.	*dy/dx*	Coef.	*dy/dx*
Somewhat	−0.99***	0.22**	−0.24	0.01	−0.41	0.001
	(0.38)	(0.10)	(0.70)	(0.02)	(1.15)	(0.01)
More	−1.87***	−0.36***	−1.07	−0.01	−1.37	0.001
	(0.42)	(0.12)	(0.78)	(0.02)	(1.32)	(0.09)
Strong	−2.14***	−0.39***	−1.17	−0.01	−0.50	0.001
	(0.59)	(0.12)	(1.02)	(0.03)	(1.53)	(0.03)
Constant	1.69**		0.23		1.36	
	(0.79)		(1.47)		(2.15)	
Log likelihood	−682.94					
Prob. > χ^2	0					
Observations	941					

Note: Standard deviation is given in parentheses. The estimated coefficients reflect the effect of the independent variables on the log ratio of the dependent variables. Dependent variable is intention-behavior gap (including positive consistency = 1, behavior gap = 2, intention gap = 3, and negative consistency = 4), the baseline type is positive consistency. *dy/dx* is marginal effect at the average level
***, ** and * represent significant at the 1%, 5%, and 10% levels, respectively

have an additional 26% possibility to have behavior gap than frequent imported rice buyers. Those who have purchased imported rice might also prefer high quality food, and country of origin are usually regarded as quality attributes by consumers (Aoki et al., 2017). Third, environment awareness and health awareness also affect consumer intention-behavior gap in green food consumption. Environment awareness increases by one unit, the probability of positive consistency will increase by 3%. In terms of health awareness, health awareness increases by one unit, the probability of intention gap will decrease by 3%.

Table 10.14 shows sensitivity test results regarding organic food consumption, we find that trust in manufacture is positively associated with actual purchase of organic food regardless of intention, trust in certifier is positively associated with high intention purchase and actual purchase of organic food, which confirms the findings of Table 10.5. In the sensitivity test results regarding green food consumption (see Table 10.15), however, we have not found significant relationship between trust in actors and consumer intention-behavior gap in green food consumption. It might be that consumer trust in actors don't have variations among intention-behavior gap groups. Since about 95% of consumers have positive intention to purchase green food, and those population don't show differential trust in actors of green food supply chain.

Table 10.6 Impacts of trust in actors on intention-behavior gap in organic food consumption

Variables	β1/2		β1/3		β1/4	
	Coef.	*dy*/*dx*	Coef.	*dy*/*dx*	Coef.	*dy*/*dx*
Regulator	−0.02	−0.17	−0.17	−0.03	−0.22	−0.02
	(0.17)	(0.13)	(0.13)	(0.03)	(0.16)	(0.02)
Manufacturer	0.20	0.42**	0.42***	0.08**	0.23	0.001
	(0.21)	(0.16)	(0.16)	(0.03)	(0.20)	(0.02)
Farmer	−0.17	−0.13	−0.13	−0.03	0.16	0.03
	(0.18)	(0.14)	(0.14)	(0.03)	(0.18)	(0.02)
Certifier	−0.09	−0.08	−0.08	0.001	−0.31*	−0.03*
	(0.19)	(0.14)	(0.14)	(0.03)	(0.17)	(0.02)
Age	−0.02*	−0.01	−0.01	0.001	0.001	0.001
	(0.01)	(0.01)	(0.01)	(0.001)	(0.01)	(0.001)
Gender	−0.24	−0.09	−0.09	0.001	−0.33*	−0.03
	(0.19)	(0.14)	(0.14)	(0.03)	(0.19)	(0.02)
Income	0.06	0.05	0.05	0.01	0.01	0.001
	(0.06)	(0.04)	(0.04)	(0.01)	(0.06)	(0.01)
Education	−0.17	−0.14	−0.14	−0.02	−0.12	0.001
	(0.13)	(0.09)	(0.09)	(0.02)	(0.12)	(0.01)
Special diet	−0.74***	−0.11	−0.11	0.02	−0.34	−0.02
	(0.24)	(0.15)	(0.15)	(0.03)	(0.22)	(0.02)
Knowledge	−0.01	−0.12*	−0.12*	−0.02	−0.21**	−0.02**
	(0.09)	(0.06)	(0.06)	(0.01)	(0.09)	(0.01)
Purchaser	−0.02	0.09	0.09	0.02	−0.04	−0.01
	(0.10)	(0.07)	(0.07)	(0.01)	(0.09)	(0.01)
Import rice						
Sometimes	−1.24***	−0.09	−0.09	0.16***	−1.84***	−0.22***
	(0.25)	(0.21)	(0.21)	(0.04)	(0.26)	(0.03)
Often	−1.78***	−0.04	−0.04	0.20***	−2.05***	−0.24***
	(0.25)	(0.19)	(0.19)	(0.03)	(0.24)	(0.03)
Always	−2.71***	−0.35	−0.35	0.16***	−2.59***	−0.26***
	(0.64)	(0.29)	(0.29)	(0.06)	(0.52)	(0.04)
Environment awareness	0.10	−0.23*	−0.23*	−0.05**	−0.12	0.001
	(0.17)	(0.12)	(0.12)	(0.02)	(0.16)	(0.02)
Health awareness	0.07	−0.06	−0.06	−0.03	0.25	0.03*
	(0.18)	(0.13)	(0.13)	(0.03)	(0.17)	(0.02)
Risk perception	0.04	0.001	0.13*	0.02	0.13	0.01
	(0.11)	(0.01)	(0.08)	(0.02)	(0.11)	(0.01)
Convenience						
A little	−1.56***	−0.15**	−0.68	0.03	−1.20	−0.08
	(0.53)	(0.07)	(0.47)	(0.08)	(0.52)	(0.06)
Somewhat	−1.22**	−0.12*	−0.40	0.06	−0.98**	−0.08
	(0.50)	(0.07)	(0.46)	(0.08)	(0.50)	(0.06)

(continued)

Table 10.6 (continued)

Variables	β1/2		β1/3		β1/4	
	Coef.	*dy/dx*	Coef.	*dy/dx*	Coef.	*dy/dx*
More	−2.34***	−0.20***	−0.78*	0.06	−2.02***	−0.15**
	(0.53)	(0.07)	(0.46)	(0.08)	(0.53)	(0.06)
Strong	−1.70***	−0.15**	−0.59	0.09	−2.06***	−0.16**
	(0.65)	(0.08)	(0.53)	(0.10)	(0.71)	(0.07)
Constant	2.63***		1.94***		2.38**	
	(1.02)		(0.75)		(0.97)	
Log likelihood	−1519.36					
Prob. > χ^2	0.00					
Observations	1314					

Note: Standard deviation is given in parentheses. The estimated coefficients reflect the effect of the independent variables on the log ratio of the dependent variables. Dependent variable is intention-behavior gap (including positive consistency = 1, behavior gap = 2, intention gap = 3, and negative consistency = 4), the baseline type is positive consistency. *dy/dx* is marginal effect at the average level

***, ** and * represent significant at the 1%, 5%, and 10% levels, respectively

10.3.3 Heterogeneous Analysis

We divide our respondents into different sub-samples by gender, age, education and environment awareness, since these characteristics are found to have significant effects on consumers preference for eco-friendly foods (Aoki et al., 2017). We then estimate logit models with these sub-samples to investigate the heterogeneous effects of consumer trust on the intention-behavior gap in eco-friendly food consumption.

Table 10.16 shows the heterogeneous analysis in green food consumption. Models 1–2 indicate that consumer trust in green food certification significantly impacts the intention-behavior gap among female consumers, while such effect fails to exhibit statistical significance for men. Trust in the certification increases a unit among female consumers, the probability of behavior gap would decrease 14%. The results suggest trust exerts great impacts in bridging the intention-behavior gap for women. Results of models 3–4 indicate that trust exerts great impacts in bridging the intention-behavior gap among the young sample, and the marginal effect is 7%. More educated respondents are more likely to be affected by trust in bridging the intention-behavior gap, as illustrated in models 5–6. Results of model 7–8 indicate that trust exerts great impacts in bridging the intention-behavior gap among more environmental awareness respondents, an increase unit of trust in certification. These findings once again confirm the role of trust in eco-friendly food consumption since trust exerts more influential impact on potential consumers of purchasing eco-friendly foods.

Table 10.17 shows the results of heterogeneous analysis in organic food consumption. Findings in the organic food consumption are consistent with those in the case of green food consumption. It suggests that consumer trust exerts more influential impacts in bridging the intention-behavior gap among female, younger, more educated and environmental awareness respondents.

10.4 Discussion

Consumers usually have positive intentions for eco-friendly foods, but the majority of consumers fail to translate their intentions into actual purchase behaviors in the eco-friendly foods consumption (Chen et al., 2019; Hansen et al., 2018; Padel & Foster, 2005). Prior studies confirmed that trust is a critical factor impacting on consumers intention to buy and actual purchasing behavior of eco-friendly foods (Macready et al., 2020; Sultan et al., 2020). Our results add to the literature by showing that trust also plays an important role in closing the consumer intention-behavior gap in eco-friendly food consumption. Specifically, we revealed that trust in certifiers matters in closing the consumer intention-behavior gap in green food consumption. In China, green food certification is conducted by the China Green Food Development Center under the Chinese Ministry of Agriculture. A series of food safety scandals, such as milk scandals, pesticide residue in fruits and vegetables, and heavy metal residue in rice, happened in China during the past years, these food safety incidents have sparked consumer interest in government certification efforts (Ortega et al., 2012). Therefore, consumers' trust in certifiers plays a critical role in certified food consumption decisions. Turning to organic food consumption, consumers' trust in manufacturers would significantly close the intention-behavior gap. It is likely that consumers' purchase decisions of organic foods is based on their trust in manufacturers, especially when consumers are not knowledgeable about organic labels. Our finding is in line with Macready et al. (2020) who suggests that trust in food manufacturers has the most important impact on building consumer confidence.

In addition, trust has heterogeneous effects on closing consumers' intention-behavior gap in eco-friendly food consumption. Specifically, trust exerts a greater effect on closing the intention-behavior gap among consumers with special diets, consumers with higher environmental awareness and higher health awareness, and individuals who have a higher convenience to buy eco-friendly foods. (i) Consumers with special diets here mean that they have a healthy diet in the last year, so they may put more attention on food quality, nutrition and health. Given that green food is perceived as healthier and more nutritious food (Yu et al., 2014), these consumers with a healthy diet are more likely to buy green food. (ii) Consumers with high environmental awareness tend to have a higher WTP for eco-friendly food (Chekima et al., 2019) because environmental awareness is a major motive for consumers to purchase eco-friendly foods (Bougherara & Combris, 2009; Teng & Wang, 2015). (iii) Health concern is another driver for eco-friendly food consumption. Consumers with higher health awareness would pay more attention to food safety and nutrition, therefore they are more likely to buy green food (Kushwah et al., 2019). In sum, our heterogeneous results again confirmed the critical role of trust in eco-friendly food consumption as we demonstrated that trust is more effective at closing the gap in eco-friendly food consumption among potential eco-friendly foods consumers. Female, younger, more educated and more environmentally conscious consumers are potential eco-friendly foods consumers given that they more likely to buy eco-friendly foods (Aoki et al., 2017).

10.5 Conclusions and Policy Implications

Eco-friendly food consumption is crucial for promoting sustainable food systems. This study investigates the effect of consumer trust in narrowing the intention-behavior gap in eco-friendly food consumption, namely green food and organic food consumption. We find that there exist intention-behavior gaps in green and organic food consumption, with larger gaps found in organic food consumption. Consumer trust is helpful in closing the intention-behavior gap in both green and organic food consumption. Specifically, consumer trust in certifiers affects the intention-behavior gap significantly in green food consumption, while trust in manufacturers is effective in closing the intention-behavior gap in organic food consumption. The role of consumer trust plays in closing the intention-behavior gap in eco-friendly food consumption is not homogenous, with greater effects among female, young, well-educated, and environmentally conscious consumers.

These findings have several policy implications. First, the different impacts of consumers' trust in closing the intention-behavior gap between green food consumption and organic food consumption would be explained by consumer knowledge and misunderstanding about the two eco-friendly foods. Certain Chinese residents consider green food to have higher production standards and qualities, relative to organic food (Yu et al., 2014). Chinese consumers in general are more familiar with green foods (Shimokawa et al., 2021). This calls for more efforts from governments and food industries to help consumers better distinguish between the two eco-friendly labels.

Second, among various actors in food supply chains, consumer trust in food certifiers and manufacturers matters most in translating purchasing intentions of eco-friendly food to actual purchases. Related implications to policy-makers and producers include that consumers would be interested in the food processing practices along food supply chains. Previous studies find that consumers' trust in food manufacturers is positively related to their food safety perceptions (Chen, 2013), which depends on individual perceived openness of food supply chain actors (Macready et al., 2020). Therefore, tools and instruments such as traceability systems and other forms of information disclosure about food production and processing in eco-friendly food systems are encouraged. By making food-related information public to consumers, food manufacturers send signals indicating the reliability of the eco-friendly foods they produce. Besides, more effort is warranted to improve consumer trust in food certifiers, including standardizing the eco-friendly certification system and strengthening certifier supervision. Eco-friendly certifiers supported by governments are likely to be welcomed most by the market because compared with the third-party certifiers, Chinese consumers put more trust in eco-friendly food certified by the government (Ortega et al., 2012). A poorly regulated certification system in China makes consumers distrust eco-friendly foods (Chen et al., 2019). Third, the findings of our heterogeneous analysis bear the implications for effectively targeting consumers who are more likely to translate purchase intention of eco-friendly foods into actual purchases.

Last, our results point out several avenues for future research. Studies that explore why certain Chinese consumers are confused about the two eco-friendly labels, namely, green certification and organic certification would be encouraged. The effectiveness of different approaches in enhancing consumer trust in certifiers and manufacturers in food systems, such as traceability and other forms of information disclosure, needs to be understood. Our study focuses on rice products in China, and other studies focusing on other food products in different and emerging markets are worth investigating.

Acknowledgments We thank the comments from the editor and anonymous reviewers. This study was funded by the National Science Foundation of China (grant numbers: 72103180 and 72273128) and the Food Value Chain Project (jointly conducted by the Japan International Research Center for Agricultural Sciences [JIRCAS] and the Institute of Food and Nutrition Development, Ministry of Agriculture and Rural Affairs of China [IFND, MARA].

Conflict of Interest Statement: The authors declare no conflict of interest.

Data Availability Statement: The data that support the findings of this study are available from the corresponding author upon reasonable request.

Peer Review: The peer review history for this article is available at https://www.webofscience.com/api/gateway/wos/peer-review/10.1002/agr.21886.

Appendix: RPL Model Specified in Preference to Estimate WTP

The study uses a RPL model specified in preference to evaluate consumer WTP for eco-friendly food. The utility function is as follows:

$$U_{ijt} = ASC + \beta_0\, PRICE_{ijt} + \beta_{1i}\, GREEN_{ijt} + \beta_{2i}\, ORGANIC_{ijt} + \beta_{3i}\, KNOWNBRAND_{ijt}$$
$$+\beta_{4i}\, UNBRAND_{ijt} + \beta_{5i}\, CHINA_{ijt} + \beta_{6i}\, JAPAN_{ijt} + \varepsilon_{ijt},$$

Table 10.7 WTP estimates (RMB/500 g)

	Mean	95% CI
Organic	13.25	[11.64, 15.18]
Green	16.23	[14.28, 18.54]
Known brand	9.83	[9.83, 8.54]
Unbranded	1.47	[0.84, 2.18]
China	6.99	[5.93, 8.28]
Japan	−6.88	[−8.19, −5.70]

Abbreviation: CI, confidence interval

Table 10.8 Consumers purchase intention of eco-friendly food

	Green rice	Organic rice
Positive intention	93.30%	48.63%
Negative intention	6.70%	51.37%

Table 10.9 Consumers purchase behavior of eco-friendly food

	Green rice	Organic rice
Never purchase group	70.85%	72.05%
Purchase group	29.15%	27.95%

Table 10.10 Mean values of trust in actors

Item description	α	Green food		α	Organic food		t-Test (P value)
		Mean	SD		Mean	SD	
Government	0.90	3.51	1.16	0.88	3.39	1.12	<0.01
Attention		3.52	1.40		3.37	1.38	<0.01
Competence		3.54	1.28		3.42	1.26	<0.01
Openness		3.45	1.28		3.37	1.24	0.02
Benevolence		3.53	1.32		3.42	1.32	0.02
Manufacturer	0.87	3.41	1.06	0.85	3.29	1.01	<0.01
Attention		3.42	1.35		3.28	1.31	<0.01
Competence		3.43	1.19		3.34	1.17	0.01
Openness		3.33	1.22		3.24	1.16	0.01
Benevolence		3.45	1.24		3.32	1.22	<0.01
Famer	0.86	3.38	1.04	0.84	3.27	0.99	<0.01
Attention		3.38	1.34		3.27	1.28	0.01
Competence		3.43	1.20		3.34	1.17	0.02
Openness		3.35	1.18		3.23	1.17	<0.01
Benevolence		3.36	1.26		3.24	1.24	<0.01
Certifier	0.88	3.41	1.11	0.87	3.35	1.06	0.04
Attention		3.40	1.37		3.32	1.34	0.05
Competence		3.41	1.24		3.38	1.21	0.45
Openness		3.37	1.25		3.29	1.20	0.02
Benevolence		3.47	1.30		3.40	1.27	0.06

Note: Scale 1 = Strong disagree to 5 = Strong agree. P value is the difference t-test results of mean trust value between green food and organic food
Abbreviation: α, Cronbach's α reliability coefficient

Table 10.11 Description of variables

Variables	Definition	Green food		Organic food	
		Mean	SD	Mean	SD
Attitude					
Health awareness	Scale 1 = low to scale to 5 = high	3.68	0.94	3.75	0.85
Risk perception	Scale 1 = low to scale to 5 = high	2.90	0.95	2.84	0.91
Environment awareness	Scale 1 = low to scale to 5 = high	3.88	1.00	3.92	0.91
Knowledge	Knowledge about organic and green food, the score range from 0 = low to 4 = high	2.28	0.88	1.91	1.07
Convenience	Purchase convenience of organic rice and green rice respectively: 0 = inconvenience; 1 = a little; 2 = somewhat; 3 = more; 4 = strong	2.07	0.90	2.09	0.90
Purchase behavior					
Special diet	1 = have a special diet; 0 = no	0.31	0.46	0.31	0.46
Purchaser	Being responsible for purchasing rice at home: 1 = yes; 0 = no	0.79	0.41	0.83	0.38
Import food	Frequency of purchasing import rice. 0 = never; 1 = sometimes; 2 = often; 3 = always	1.16	1.01	1.23	0.97
Observation	Number of respondents	941		1314	

where *ASC* is an alternative specific constant representing the opt-out option; $PRICE_{ijt}$ represents the price levels for per 500 g of rice; $GREEN_{ijt}$ is a dummy variable taking the value 1 if the product carries green certification label, and otherwise 0. Similarly, $ORGANIC_{ijt}$ is a dummy variable taking the value 1 if the product carries organic certification label, and otherwise 0. $KNOWNBRAND_{ijt}$ is a dummy variable taking the value of 1 if the product carries well-known brand, and otherwise 0. $UNBRAND_{ijt}$ is a dummy variable taking the value of 1 if the product carries infamous brand, and otherwise 0. $CHINA_{ijt}$ is a dummy variable taking the value of 1 if the product comes from China, and otherwise 0. $JAPAN_{ijt}$ is a dummy variable taking the value of 1 if the product comes from China, and otherwise 0. Thailand is the baseline. ε_{ijt} represents the random error term which follows a Type I Extreme Value distribution. In the model, the price coefficient θ was assumed to invariant in the population. The coefficients of other attributes: β_{1i}, β_{2i}, β_{3i}, β_{4i}, β_{5i}, β_{6i} were assumed to be random following a normal distribution.

Table 10.12 Impacts of overall trust on intention-behavior gap in green food consumption

Variables	β1/2		β1/3		β1/4	
	Coef.	*dy/dx*	Coef.	*dy/dx*	Coef.	*dy/dx*
Trust	−0.20**	−0.03	−0.11	−0.001	−0.36	−0.001
	−0.1	−0.03	−0.21	−0.01	−0.3	−0.05
Age	0.01	0.001	−0.01	−0.001	−0.01	−0.001
	−0.01	−0.001	−0.02	−0.001	−0.03	−0.001
Gender	−0.30*	−0.06*	0.38	0.01	0.63	0.001
	−0.17	−0.03	−0.33	−0.01	−0.53	−0.12
Income	0.03	0.01	0.01	0.001	0.07	0.001
	−0.05	−0.01	−0.09	−0.001	−0.16	−0.01
Education	−0.19*	−0.03	−0.3	−0.01	−0.66***	−0.001
	−0.1	−0.03	−0.19	−0.01	−0.27	−0.1
Special diet	−0.40**	−0.07*	0.39	0.02	−0.17	−0.001
	−0.2	−0.04	−0.33	−0.01	−0.61	−0.02
Knowledge	−0.07	−0.01	−0.34**	−0.01*	−0.08	−0.001
	−0.1	−0.02	−0.17	−0.01	−0.29	−0.01
Purchaser	−0.1	−0.02	0.25	0.01	0.01	0.001
	−0.08	−0.01	−0.16	−0.01	−0.25	−0.001
Import rice						
Sometimes	−1.08***	−0.21***	0.23	0.01	−1.23	−0.01
	−0.23	−0.04	−0.53	−0.01	−0.81	−0.01
Often	−1.35***	−0.26***	0.61	0.03**	−0.94	−0.01
	−0.2	−0.04	−0.44	−0.01	−0.59	−0.01
Always	−1.33***	−0.25***	0.79	0.04	−13.26	−0.02**
	−0.39	−0.06	−0.61	−0.03	−14.34	−0.01
Environment awareness	0.07	0.02	−0.76***	−0.03***	0.02	0.001
	−0.14	−0.03	−0.28	−0.01	−0.44	−0.01
Health awareness	0.24	0.04	0.53*	0.02	0.11	0.001
	−0.15	−0.03	−0.3	−0.01	−0.47	−0.01
Risk perception	−0.11	−0.02	−0.14	−0.001	−0.39	−0.001
	−0.09	−0.02	−0.19	−0.01	−0.3	−0.06
Convenience						
A little	−1.03***	−0.23***	−0.53	−0.001	0.29	0.001
	−0.41	−0.09	−0.73	−0.03	−1.18	−0.16
Somewhat	−0.95***	−0.22***	−0.3	0.001	−0.32	0.001
	−0.38	−0.1	−0.69	−0.03	−1.15	−0.01
More	−1.82***	−0.35***	−1.06	−0.01	−1.22	−0.001
	−0.41	−0.11	−0.76	−0.03	−1.32	−0.08
Strong	−2.05***	−0.38***	−1.28	−0.02	−0.33	0.001
	−0.59	−0.11	−1.01	−0.03	−1.5	−0.05
Constant	1.66**		0.32		1.41	
	−0.79		−1.47		−2.14	

(continued)

Table 10.12 (continued)

Variables	β1/2		β1/3		β1/4	
	Coef.	*dy*/*dx*	Coef.	*dy*/*dx*	Coef.	*dy*/*dx*
Loglikelihood	−687.67					
Prob. > χ^2	0					
Observations	941					

Note: Standard deviation is given in parentheses. The estimated coefficients reflect the effect of the independent variables on the log ratio of the dependent variables. Dependent variable is intention-behavior gap (including positive consistency = 1, behavior gap = 2, intention gap = 3, and negative consistency = 4), the baseline type is positive consistency. *dy*/*dx* is marginal effect at the average level

***, ** and * represent significant at the 1%, 5%, and 10% levels, respectively

Table 10.13 Impacts of overall trust on intention-behavior gap in organic food consumption

Variables	β1/2		β1/3		β1/4	
	Coef.	*dy*/*dx*	Coef.	*dy*/*dx*	Coef.	*dy*/*dx*
Trust	−0.08	−0.01	0.02	0.02	−0.17	−0.02*
	−0.12	−0.02	−0.09	−0.02	−0.11	−0.01
Age	−0.02*	−0.001*	−0.01	−0.001	0.001	0.001
	−0.01	−0.001	−0.01	−0.001	−0.01	−0.001
Gender	−0.24	−0.02	−0.09	0.001	−0.31	−0.03
	−0.19	−0.02	−0.14	−0.03	−0.19	−0.02
Income	0.05	0.001	0.04	0.01	0.001	−0.001
	−0.06	−0.01	−0.04	−0.01	−0.06	−0.01
Education	−0.16	−0.01	−0.14	−0.02	−0.13	−0.001
	−0.13	−0.01	−0.09	−0.02	−0.12	−0.01
Special diet	−0.75***	−0.07***	−0.12	0.02	−0.34	−0.02
	−0.24	−0.02	−0.15	−0.03	−0.22	−0.02
Knowledge	−0.01	0.01	−0.11*	−0.02	−0.21	−0.02
	−0.09	−0.01	−0.06	−0.01	−0.09	−0.01
Purchaser	−0.02	−0.01	0.09	0.02	−0.03	−0.01
	−0.1	−0.01	−0.07	−0.01	−0.09	−0.01
Import rice						
Sometimes	−1.25***	−0.11***	−0.11	0.15***	−1.82	−0.22***
	−0.25	−0.03	−0.21	−0.04	−0.26	−0.03
Often	−1.78***	−0.15***	−0.05	0.19***	−2.03	−0.23***
	−0.25	−0.03	−0.19	−0.03	−0.24	−0.03
Always	−2.70***	−0.19***	−0.32	0.16***	−2.52	−0.25***
	−0.63	−0.04	−0.28	−0.06	−0.51	−0.04
Environment awareness	0.08	0.02	−0.24**	−0.05**	−0.12	−0.001
	−0.17	−0.02	−0.12	−0.02	−0.16	−0.02
Health awareness	0.09	0.01	−0.05	−0.03	0.25	0.03
	−0.17	−0.02	−0.13	−0.03	−0.17	−0.02
Risk perception	0.03	−0.001	0.13	0.02	0.13	0.01

(continued)

Table 10.13 (continued)

Variables	β1/2		β1/3		β1/4	
	Coef.	*dy*/*dx*	Coef.	*dy*/*dx*	Coef.	*dy*/*dx*
	−0.11	−0.01	−0.08	−0.02	−0.1	−0.01
Convenience						
A little	−1.57***	−0.15**	−0.66	0.03	−1.16	−0.08
	−0.52	−0.07	−0.47	−0.07	−0.52	−0.06
Somewhat	−1.22***	−0.13*	−0.39	0.06	−0.98	−0.08
	−0.5	−0.07	−0.45	−0.07	−0.5	−0.06
More	−2.33***	−0.20***	−0.75	0.07	−2.02	−0.15
	−0.53	−0.08	−0.46	−0.08	−0.53	−0.06
Strong	−1.72***	−0.16**	−0.61	0.08	−2.08	−0.16**
	−0.65	−0.08	−0.52	−0.1	−0.7	−0.07
Constant	2.64***		2.00***		2.49	
	−1.02		−0.75		−0.97	
Log likelihood	−1526.06					
Prob. > χ^2	0.00					
Observations	1314					

Note: The definitions of coefficients are the same with in Table 10.12. Standard deviation is given in parentheses. ***, ** and * represent significant at the 1%, 5%, and 10% levels, respectively

Table 10.14 Sensitivity test of organic food

Variables	β1/2		β1/3		β1/4	
	Coef.	*dy*/*dx*	Coef.	*dy*/*dx*	Coef.	*dy*/*dx*
Regulator	−0.16	0.043	0.26	0.008	−0.364	−0.056
	−0.307	−0.026	−0.412	−0.005	−0.308	−0.026
Manufacturer	0.224	−0.058*	0.959*	0.09	0.458	0.055
	−0.357	−0.032	−0.492	−0.006	−0.357	−0.032
Farmer	−0.082	−0.016	−0.459	−0.006	−0.007	0.021
	−0.331	−0.029	−0.427	−0.005	−0.332	−0.029
Certifier	−0.561*	0.013	−1.116***	−0.008*	−0.622*	−0.017
	−0.331	−0.028	−0.43	−0.005	−0.332	−0.028
Control variables	Yes					
Constant	6.287***		−0.367		7.476***	
	−1.635		−2.179		−1.632	
Log likelihood	−1153.001					
Observations	1314		1314		1314	

Note: The definitions of coefficients are the same with in Table 10.12. Standard deviation is given in parentheses. ***, ** and * represent significant at the 1%, 5%, and 10% levels, respectively

Table 10.15 Sensibility test of green food

Variables	β1/2		β1/3		β1/4	
	Coef.	*dy*/*dx*	Coef.	*dy*/*dx*	Coef.	*dy*/*dx*
Regulator	0.001	−0.003	0.796	0	0.069	0.003
	−0.198	−0.031	−0.652	−0.027	−0.321	−0.012
Manufacturer	−0.006	0.013	0.033	0	−0.357	−0.015
	−0.242	−0.025	−0.831	−0.002	−0.391	−0.014
Farmer	−0.257	−0.035	0.07	0	0.063	0.127
	−0.233	−0.025	−0.864	−0.01	−0.378	−0.014
Certifier	0.13	0.018	−0.922	0	−0.043	−0.007
	−0.203	−0.037	−0.792	−0.036	−0.349	−0.013
Control variables	Yes					
Constant	3.656***		0.015		3.559**	
	−1.064		−3.328		−1.601	
Log likelihood	−529.9					
Observations	941		941		941	

Note: The definitions of coefficients are the same with in Table 10.12. Standard deviation is given in parentheses. *** and ** represent significant at the 1% and 5% levels, respectively

Table 10.16 Results of heterogeneous analysis—Green food

Variables	(1)		(2)		(3)		(4)	
	β1/2		β1/2		β1/2		β1/2	
	Female		Male		Below age		Above age	
	Coef.	*dy*/*dx*	Coef.	*dy*/*dx*	Coef.	*dy*/*dx*	Coef.	*dy*/*dx*
Regulator	−0.05	−0.01	0.09	0.01	−0.12	−0.02	0.2	0.03
	−0.21	−0.04	−0.24	−0.04	−0.2	−0.04	−0.25	−0.05
Manufacturer	0.14	0.03	0.28	0.04	0.28	0.05	0.05	0.01
	−0.26	−0.06	−0.29	−0.06	−0.24	−0.04	−0.32	−0.05
Farmer	0.38	0.01	−0.52*	−0.08*	0.02	0.002	−0.09	−0.02
	−0.24	−0.01	−0.27	−0.04	−0.23	−0.04	−0.03	−0.05
Certifier	−0.75***	−0.14***	0.1	0.02	−0.38*	−0.07*	−0.42	−0.07
	−0.22	−0.05	−0.26	−0.05	−0.22	−0.04	−0.25	−0.06
Constant	2.50**		0.49		0.4		1.06	
	−1.11		−1.22		−1.72		−1.49	
Control variables	Yes		Yes		Yes		Yes	
Log likelihood	−333.13		−330.11		−387.01		−267.88	
Prob. > χ^2	0.00		0.00		0.00		0.00	
Observations	483		458		558		383	

(continued)

Table 10.16 (continued)

Variables	(5)		(6)		(7)		(8)	
	β1/2		β1/2		β1/2		β1/2	
	Below education		Above education		Below environment		Above environment	
	Coef.	*dy*/*dx*	Coef.	*dy*/*dx*	Coef.	*dy*/*dx*	Coef.	*dy*/*dx*
Regulator	−0.12	−0.03	0.04	0.01	0.34	0.05	−0.18	−0.03
	−0.33	−0.06	−0.19	−0.05	−0.28	−0.04	−0.2	−0.04
Manufacturer	0.51	0.1	0.16	0.03	0.08	0.02	0.38	0.07
	−0.4	−0.08	−0.23	−0.14	−0.33	−0.05	−0.25	−0.05
Farmer	−0.51	−0.1	0.08	0.01	−0.41	−0.07	0.08	0.02
	−0.35	−0.07	−0.21	−0.21	−0.33	−0.05	−0.22	−0.04
Certifier	−0.41	−0.08	−0.37**	−0.06**	−0.27	−0.03	−0.49**	−0.09**
	−0.36	−0.07	−0.19	−0.14	−0.27	−0.06	−0.21	−0.04
Constant	1.79		1.93		3.12**		2.81	
	−1.51		−1.58		−1.34		−1.74	
Control variables	Yes		Yes		Yes		Yes	
Log likelihood	−188.58		−453.57		−271.08		−361.42	
Prob. > χ^2	0.00		0.00		0.00		0.00	
Observations	267		674		363		578	

Note: The definitions of coefficients are the same with in Table 10.9. Standard deviation is given in parentheses. Above and below age, education level, and environment awareness are classified according to their mean values respectively

***, **, and * represent significant at the 1%, 5%, and 10% levels, respectively

Table 10.17 Results of heterogeneous analysis—Organic food

Variables	(1)		(2)		(3)		(4)	
	β1/3		β1/3		β1/3		β1/3	
	Female		Male		Below age		Above age	
	Coef.	*dy*/*dx*	Coef.	*dy*/*dx*	Coef.	*dy*/*dx*	Coef.	*dy*/*dx*
Regulator	−0.32**	−0.07*	0.05	0.02	−0.28	−0.06	0.03	0.02
	−0.18	−0.04	−0.19	−0.04	−0.17	−0.04	−0.2	−0.04
Manufacturer	0.63**	0.16**	0.18	−0.01	0.53**	0.11**	0.24	0.03
	−0.24	−0.05	−0.22	−0.05	−0.21	−0.04	−0.24	−0.05
Farmer	−0.43**	−0.10**	0.13	0.03	−0.14	−0.04	−0.09	−0.01
	−0.2	−0.04	−0.21	−0.04	−0.18	−0.04	−0.23	−0.05
Certifier	0.16	0.03	−0.31	−0.04	−0.12	−0.02	−0.06	0.01
	−0.2	−0.04	−0.19	−0.04	−0.18	−0.04	−0.22	−0.05
Constant	1.37		2.22**		2.23		2.48**	
	−1.19		−1.02		−1.59		−1.18	
Control variables	Yes		Yes		Yes		Yes	
Log likelihood	−796.3		−694.63		−841.18		−650.58	
Prob. > χ^2	0.00		0.00		0.00		0.00	
Observations	692		622		745		569	

(continued)

Table 10.17 (continued)

Variables	(5)		(6)		(7)		(8)	
	β1/3		β1/3		β1/3		β1/3	
	Below education		Above education		Below environment		Above environment	
	Coef.	*dy*/*dx*	Coef.	*dy*/*dx*	Coef.	*dy*/*dx*	Coef.	*dy*/*dx*
Regulator	−0.06	0.02	−0.21	−0.05	0.03	−0.003	−0.28	−0.04
	−0.24	−0.05	−0.15	−0.03	−0.2	−0.04	−0.17	−0.03
Manufacturer	0.18	−0.001	0.52**	0.11**	0.25	0.03	0.61***	0.12***
	−0.32	−0.06	−0.19	−0.04	−0.24	−0.05	−0.22	−0.04
Farmer	−0.17	−0.02	−0.13	−0.04	−0.31	−0.05	−0.13	−0.04
	−0.3	−0.06	−0.16	−0.03	−0.24	−0.05	−0.18	−0.04
Certifier	0.19	0.04	−0.17	−0.01	0.01	0.02	−0.14	−0.01
	−0.27	−0.05	−0.16	−0.03	−0.22	−0.03	−0.19	−0.04
Constant	3.36		1.68		1.12		−0.42	
	−1.38		−1.26		−1.11		−1.64	
Control variables	Yes		Yes		Yes		Yes	
Log likelihood	−424.96		−1058.67		−549.86		−927.84	
Prob. > χ^2	0.00		0.00		0.00		0.00	
Observations	373		941		512		802	

Note: The definitions of coefficients are the same with in Table 10.9. Standard deviation is given in parentheses. Above and below age, education level and environment awareness are classified according to their mean values respectively

***, **, and * represent significant at the 1%, 5%, and 10% levels, respectively

References

Aertsens, J., Mondelaers, K., Verbeke, W., Buysse, J., & Van Huylenbroeck, G. (2011). The influence of subjective and objective knowledge on attitude, motivations and consumption of organic food. *British Food Journal, 113*(6), 1353–1378. https://doi.org/10.1108/00070701111179988

Aoki, K., Akai, K., & Ujiie, K. (2017). A choice experiment to compare preferences for rice in Thailand and Japan: The impact of origin, sustainability, and taste. *Food Quality and Preference, 56*(56), 274–284. https://doi.org/10.1016/j.foodqual.2016.03.001

Aschemann-Witzel, J., & Niebuhr Aagaard, E. M. (2014). Elaborating on the attitude-behaviour gap regarding organic products: Young Danish consumers and in-store food choice. *International Journal of Consumer Studies, 38*(5), 550–558. https://doi.org/10.1111/ijcs.12115

Bougherara, D., & Combris, P. (2009). Eco-labelled food products: What are consumers paying for. *European Review of Agricultural Economics, 36*(36), 321–341. https://doi.org/10.1093/erae/jbp023

Carfora, V., Cavallo, C., Caso, D., Del Giudice, T., De Devitiis, B., Viscecchia, R., Nardone, G., & Cicia, G. (2019). Explaining consumer purchase behavior for organic milk: Including trust and green self-identity within the theory of planned behavior. *Food Quality and Preference, 76*, 1–9. https://doi.org/10.1016/j.foodqual.2019.03.006

Chekima, B., Chekima, K., & Chekima, K. (2019). Understanding factors underlying actual consumption of organic food: The moderating effect of future orientation. *Food Quality and Preference, 74*, 49–58. https://doi.org/10.1016/j.foodqual.2018.12.010

Chen, W. (2013). The effects of different types of trust on consumer perceptions of food safety: An empirical study of consumers in Beijing municipality, China. *China Agricultural Economic Review, 5*(01), 43–65. https://doi.org/10.1108/17561371311294757

Chen, M., Wang, Y., Yin, S., Hu, W., & Han, F. (2019). Chinese consumer trust and preferences for organic labels from different regions: Evidence from real choice experiment. *British Food Journal, 121*(07), 1521–1535. https://doi.org/10.1108/BFJ-02-2018-0128

de Jonge, J., VanTrijp, H., Jan Renes, R., & Frewer, L. (2007). Understanding consumer confidence in the safety of food: Its two-dimensional structure and determinants. *Risk Analysis, 27*(03), 729–740. https://doi.org/10.1111/j.1539-6924.2007.00917.x

ElHaffar, G., Durif, F., & Dubé, L. (2020). Towards closing the attitude-intention-behavior gap in green consumption: A narrative review of the literature and an overview of future research directions. *Journal of Cleaner Production, 275*, 122556. https://doi.org/10.1016/j.jclepro.2020.122556

Frank, P., & Brock, C. (2018). Bridging the intention-behavior gap among organic grocery customers: The crucial role of point-of-sale information. *Psychology & Marketing, 35*(08), 586–602. https://doi.org/10.1002/mar.21108

Gleim, M., & Lawson, S. J. (2014). Spanning the gap: An examination of the factors leading to the green gap. *Journal of Consumer Marketing, 31*(06), 503–514. https://doi.org/10.1108/JCM-05-2014-0988

Grebitus, C., Steiner, B., & Veeman, M. (2015). The roles of human values and generalized trust on stated preferences when food is labeled with environmental footprints: Insights from Germany. *Food Policy, 52*, 84–91.

Hansen, T., Sørensen, M. I., & Eriksen, M. L. R. (2018). How the interplay between consumer motivations and values influences organic food identity and behavior. *Food Policy, 74*, 39–52. https://doi.org/10.1016/j.foodpol.2017.11.003

Jin, S., Li, H., & Li, Y. (2017). Preferences of Chinese consumers for the attributes of fresh produce portfolios in an e-commerce environment. *British Food Journal, 119*(03), 817–829. https://doi.org/10.1108/BFJ-09-2016-0424

Kariuki, S. W., & Hoffmann, V. (2021). Can information drive demand for safer food? Impact of brand-specific recommendations and test results on product choice. *Agricultural Economics, 53*, 454–467. https://doi.org/10.1111/agec.12685

Kraft, F. B., & Goodell, P. W. (1993). Identifying the health conscious consumer. *Journal of Health Care Marketing, 13*, 18–25.

Kushwah, S., Dhir, A., Sagar, M., & Gupta, B. (2019). Determinants of organic food consumption. A systematic literature review on motives and barriers. *Appetite, 143*, 104402. https://doi.org/10.1016/j.appet.2019.104402

Lassoued, R., & Hobbs, J. E. (2015). Consumer confidence in credence attributes: The role of brand trust. *Food Policy, 52*(02), 99–107. https://doi.org/10.1016/j.foodpol.2014.12.003

Liu, Y., Chen, X., Rabinowitz, A. N., & Campbell, B. (2020). Demand, challenges, and marketing strategies in the retail promotion of local brand milk. *Agricultural Economics, 51*(February), 655–668. https://doi.org/10.1111/agec.12584

Macready, A. L., Hieke, S., Klimczuk-Kochańska, M., Szumiat, S., Vranken, L., & Grunert, K. G. (2020). Consumer trust in the food value chain and its impact on consumer confidence: A model for assessing consumer trust and evidence from a 5-country study in Europe. *Food Policy, 92*, 101880. https://doi.org/10.1016/j.foodpol.2020.101880

Mayer, R. C., Davis, J. H., & Schoorman, F. D. (1995). An integrative model of organizational trust. *The Academy of Management Review, 20*(03), 709–734. https://doi.org/10.5465/amr.1995.9508080335

McFadden, D. (1974). Conditional logit analysis of qualitative choice behavior. In P. Zarembka (Ed.), *Frontiers in econometrics* (pp. 103–300). Academic Press.

Moser, A. K. (2015). Thinking green, buying green? Drivers of pro-environmental purchasing behavior. *Journal of Consumer Marketing, 32*(03), 167–175. https://doi.org/10.1108/JCM-10-2014-1179

Nguyen, H. V., Nguyen, C. H., & Hoang, T. T. B. (2019). Green consumption: Closing the intention-behavior gap. *Sustainable Development, 27*(01), 118–129. https://doi.org/10.1002/sd.1875

Nunnally, J. C. (1978). *Psychometric theory* (2nd ed.). McGraw-Hill.

Nuttavuthisit, K., & Thøgersen, J. (2017). The importance of consumer trust for the emergence of a market for green products: The case of organic food. *Journal of Business Ethics, 140*(2), 323–337.

Ortega, D. L., Wang, H. H., Olynk, N. J., Wu, L., & Bai, J. (2012). Chinese consumers' demand for food safety attributes: A push for government and industry regulations. *American Journal of Agricultural Economics, 94*(02), 489–495. https://doi.org/10.1093/ajae/aar074

Padel, S., & Foster, C. (2005). Exploring the gap between attitudes and behaviour: Understanding why consumers buy or do not buy organic food. *British Food Journal, 107*(08), 606–625. https://doi.org/10.1108/00070700510611002

Poortinga, W., & Pidgeon, N. F. (2003). Exploring the dimensionality of trust in risk regulation. *Risk Analysis, 23*(05), 961–972. https://doi.org/10.1111/1539-6924.00373

Ricci, E. C., Banterle, A., & Stranieri, S. (2018). Trust to go green: An exploration of consumer intentions for eco-friendly convenience food. *Ecological Economics, 148*, 54–65. https://doi.org/10.1016/j.ecolecon.2018.02.010

Roberts, J. A. (1996). Green consumers in the 1990s: Profile and implications for advertising. *Journal of Business Research, 36*, 217–231. https://doi.org/10.1016/0148-2963(95)00150-6

Scott, S., Si, Z., Schumilas, T., & Chen, A. (2014). Contradictions in state - and civil society-driven developments in China's ecological agriculture sector. *Food Policy, 45*, 158–166. https://doi.org/10.1016/j.foodpol.2013.08.002

Shimokawa, S., Hu, D., Li, D., & Cheng, H. (2021). The urban-rural gap in the demand for food safety in China: The role of food label knowledge. *Agricultural Economics, 52*(2), 175–193. https://doi.org/10.1111/agec.12613

Siegrist, M., Cousin, M.-E., Kastenholz, H., & Wiek, A. (2007). Public acceptance of nanotechnology foods and food packaging: The influence of affect and trust. *Appetite, 49*, 459–466.

Singh, A., & Verma, P. (2017). Factors influencing Indian consumers' actual buying behaviour towards organic food products. *Journal of Cleaner Production, 167*, 473–483. https://doi.org/10.1016/j.jclepro.2017.08.106

Sultan, P., Tarafder, T., Pearson, D., & Henryks, J. (2020). Intention-behaviour gap and perceived behavioural control - behaviour gap in theory of planned behaviour: Moderating roles of communication, satisfaction and trust in organic food consumption. *Food Quality and Preference, 81*, 103838. https://doi.org/10.1016/j.foodqual.2019.103838

Tandon, A., Jabeen, F., Talwar, S., Sakashita, M., & Dhir, A. (2021). Facilitators and inhibitors of organic food buying behavior. *Food Quality and Preference, 88*, 104077. https://doi.org/10.1016/j.foodqual.2020.104077

Teng, C. C., & Wang, Y. M. (2015). Decisional factors driving organic food consumption: Generation of consumer purchase intentions. *British Food Journal, 117*(03), 1066–1081. https://doi.org/10.1108/BFJ-12-2013-0361

Tonsor, G. T., Schroeder, T. C., & Pennings, J. M. E. (2009). Factors impacting food safety risk perceptions. *Journal of Agricultural Economics, 60*, 625–644.

Tung, S. J., Shih, C. C., Wei, S., & Chen, Y. H. (2012). Attitudinal inconsistency toward organic food in relation to purchasing intention and behavior—An illustration of Taiwan consumers. *British Food Journal, 114*(07), 997–1015. https://doi.org/10.1108/00070701211241581

Wang, E., Gao, Z., Heng, Y., & Shi, L. (2019). Chinese consumers' preferences for food quality test/measurement indicators and cues of milk powder: A case of Zhengzhou, China. *Food Policy, 89*, 101791. https://doi.org/10.1016/j.foodpol.2019.101791

Willer, H., Jan, T., Claudia, M., & Bernhard, S. (Eds.). (2022). *The world of organic agriculture. Statistics and emerging trends 2022*. Research Institute of Agriculture FiBL, Frick, and IFOAM-Organics International.

Xie, J., Gao, Z., Swisher, M., & Zhao, X. (2016). Consumers' preferences for fresh broccolis: Interactive effects between country of origin and organic labels. *Agricultural Economics, 47*(2), 181–191. https://doi.org/10.1111/agec.12193

Yin, S., Wu, L., Du, L., & Chen, M. (2010). Consumers' purchase intention of organic food in China. *Journal of the Science of Food and Agriculture, 90*(05), 1361–1367. https://doi.org/10.1002/jsfa.3936

Yu, X., Gao, Z., & Zeng, Y. (2014). Willingness to pay for the "green food" in China. *Food Policy, 45*, 80–87. https://doi.org/10.1016/j.foodpol.2014.01.003

Zhang, Y., Guan, L., & Jin, S. (2022). Trust and consumer confidence in the safety of dairy products in China. *British Food Journal, 124*(4), 3644–3665.

Zhou, J., Liu, Q., Mao, R., & Yu, X. (2017). Habit spillovers or induced awareness: Willingness to pay for eco-labels of rice in China. *Food Policy, 71*, 62–73. https://doi.org/10.1016/j.foodpol.2017.07.006

Chapter 11
Preferences and Willingness to Pay for a Novel Carbon Label: A Choice Experiment in the United States

11.1 Introduction

Carbon neutrality has been one of the world's most urgent goals, with over 110 countries now committing to carbon dioxide emissions reduction. Decarbonizing the food system, despite receiving relatively limited attention, cannot be overlooked in becoming globally carbon neutral. The food system contributes to one-third of the global anthropogenic greenhouse gas emission (Crippa et al., 2021; Tubiello et al., 2021), and even if fossil fuel emissions were removed, emissions from the global food system alone would make achieving the Paris Agreement by 2050 impossible (Clark et al., 2020).

Carbon labels could be a promising policy instrument for the decarbonization of the food system. A carbon label on food products could improve a consumer's ability to make carbon-friendly choices via information provision and may induce producers to provide markets with lower-emission options (Vandenbergh et al., 2011). Prior work on food carbon labeling schemes relies on either a numeric carbon footprint label or a carbon-friendly claim for products (Brunner et al., 2018; Visschers & Siegrist, 2015; Vlaeminck et al., 2014). No other studies, however, have explored alternative carbon labels, such as a label indicating carbon removal technology. Our study focuses on investigating individual preference and valuation for a novel carbon label on food products. Unlike prior carbon labels, the novel carbon label in this study communicates additional information to consumers; it suggests that relative to unlabeled products the labeled product has lower carbon footprint, but also reveals the specific technology to reduce carbon dioxide emissions during food production.

Insight on individual valuation for a new technology-based carbon label is important for several reasons. First, public policymakers are likely interested in whether the market itself could provide agricultural producers with sufficient economic incentive to reduce carbon emissions. A limited understanding of consumer

W. Lin, *Transforming China's Agri-Food System: Government-Market Synergy*, Resources, Environment and Agricultural Development,
https://doi.org/10.1007/978-981-95-7151-2_11

preferences and price premiums for carbon-labeled food products would hinder the voluntary adoption of carbon reduction technology among food producers as the adoption imposes extra costs. A successful voluntary carbon labeling scheme could relieve the pressure on governments to introduce more stringent policy instruments (Elofsson et al., 2016); for example, an emission tax and permit scheme, which could meet substantial resistance from diferent interest groups and even cause welfare loss (Baylis et al., 2013).

Second, the new technology-based carbon label examined in this study has important implications for carbon neutrality as well as food security. Among other carbon dioxide removal and storage technologies, we focus on enhanced silicate rock weathering of crushed basalt (ERW thereafter) applied to croplands. ERW technology amends soils with crushed calcium- and magnesium-rich silicate rocks, such as dunite and basalt, to accelerate the carbon dioxide sequestration process (Cox et al., 2020; Hartmann et al., 2013). Recent studies have shown that basalt, one of the most common rocks on Earth, is a potentially ideal rock for implementing ERW (Goll et al., 2021). Spreading basaltic rock dust on croplands would absorb billions of tonnes of carbon emissions from the air within months. Including the costs of mining, crushing, and grinding of rocks, and transport to and distribution on crop fields, the overall cost of basalt-based ERW ranges from about $80 to $200/ton of carbon dioxide in the current carbon price range (Beerling et al., 2020; Strefler et al., 2018). ERW of basalt, as a result, tends to be cost-efective for large-scale carbon removal, in particular, a prominent option for agricultural carbon sequestration (Goll et al., 2021), in contrast to other carbon removal technologies whose costs are prohibitive. Basalt-based ERW technology implies that reducing carbon dioxide emissions in agricultural and food systems may not hurt food security given that basalt could boost crop yields by increasing soil pH and resupplying depleted soil silica pools (Horton et al., 2021).

With this as backdrop, the present study contributes to the literature by eliciting individual preferences and valuation for the basalt-based ERW technology label using a discrete choice experiment conducted on US respondents. Bread is used as the food product of interest in our study since bread is made from grains planted in the croplands, where basalt dust could be applied to lock the greenhouse gas into carbonates. Our findings show that US consumers in general prefer organic bread most, followed by conventional bread and ERW-labeled bread products. Average willingness to pay (WTP) for ERW-labeled bread is $4, slightly lower than the valuation of organic ($4.76) and conventional ($4.70) bread. This finding implies that US consumers would not be willing to pay a price premium for ERW-labeled bread versus the existing bread products, and US consumers discount ERW-labeled bread to some extent. Nevertheless, consumer preferences and valuation for ERW-labeled bread are not homogeneous across individuals. WTP for ERW-labeled bread is significantly greater among those who are non-White, liberal, more knowledgeable about the causes of climate change and have at least college degrees. Our results highlight that relying in the market itself to promote voluntary adoption of carbon mitigation technology among agricultural producers would not be successful, which calls for extra interventions from public and private organizations.

11.2 Study Design

11.2.1 Experimental Design

We conducted an online choice experiment survey to elicit customer preferences and valuation of the basalt-based ERW technology label in the United States. Given that the basalt-based ERW technology labeled bread is not yet in the market, we conduct a hypothetical choice experiment to assess US consumer bread preferences. Specially, whole-grain bread is chosen as our experimental product. Bread is widely consumed by US households, over 98% US population consuming bread products. With the increasing health-consciousness of consumers, whole grain and multigrain breads have become more and more popular (Mancino & Kuchler, 2012). Three diferent types of whole-grain bread products are included in the experimental design, namely, conventional and unlabeled whole-grain bread, organic-labeled whole-grain bread, and ERW carbon-labeled whole- grain bread. Four price levels are specified based on the range of offline market prices of 20 oz of whole-grain bread and online retail store prices in the United States. The price levels include \$2.37, \$3.27, \$4.19, \$5.09. Table 11.1 details the attributes and attribute levels used in the choice experimental design.

We design a labeled choice experiment using a sequential Bayesian approach (Scarpa & Rose, 2008). First, an efficient design is constructed using theNgene software for a pilot study. A total of 26 individuals are collected for the pilot survey. The estimation results of the multinomial logit model from the pilot survey data are then used as the priors for the final design. In light of the results from our pilot study, and to reflect real market situation, the price of organic whole-grain bread in the final choice tasks is set higher than conventional whole-grain bread's price. Higher organic prices are associated with higher environmental benefits and production costs for organic agriculture. Similarly, one would argue that the price of the basalt-based ERW technology labeled bread may also be higher. We do not constrain the ERW-labeled prices for several reasons. First, despite the basalt dust application imposes extra costs, it could improve crop yields (Horton et al., 2021), which potentially lowers bread production costs. Besides, unlike organic labeled

Table 11.1 Attributes and attribute levels

Attribute	Attribute level
Whole-grain bread	Conventional
	USDA organic labeled
	ERW carbon labeled
Price (\$/20 oz)	2.37
	3.27
	4.19
	5.09

ERW enhanced silicate rock weathering of crushed basalt, *USDA* US Department of Agriculture

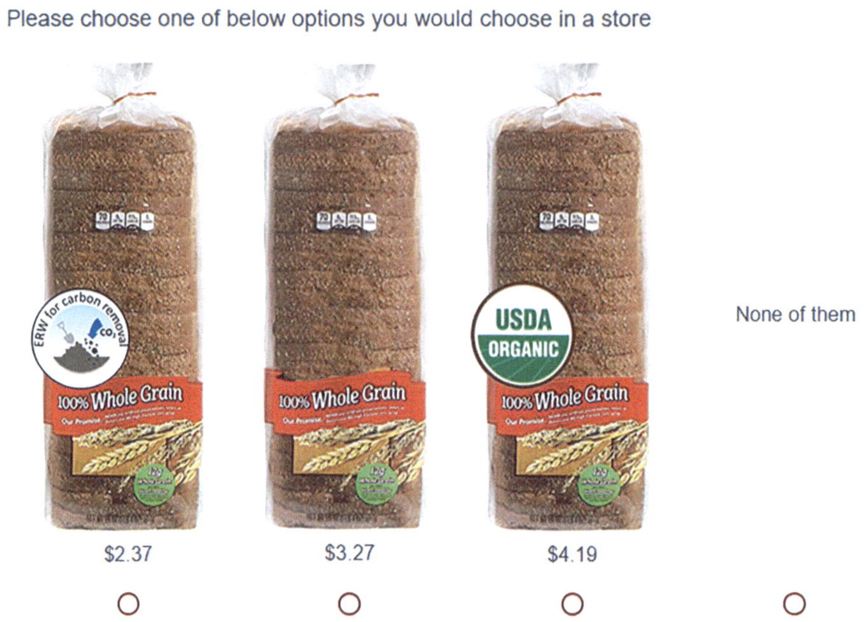

Fig. 11.1 Sample choice set

breads, the ERW-labeled product is not yet in the market. Studies show consumer preferences for novel and controversial food products are uncertain (Ortega et al., 2020), implying that the product can be either positively or negatively valued by individuals. Finally, we use the sequential Bayesian design to construct eight choice sets, and divide them into two blocks of four choice tasks each. The D-e伍ciency is 85.42%. Respondents are randomly assigned into one of the two blocks. Each choice task is composed of three whole-grain bread products aforementioned, plus an opt-out option which is the last alternative in each choice task (Fig. 11.1). The choice tasks are randomized within each block, and the three bread products are also randomized within each choice task. We calculate the minimum sample size required based on the widely used method by Lancsar and Louviere (2008) and de Bekker-Grob et al. (2015), and the minimum sample size for our experimental design is 250 respondents.

11.2.2 Survey Design

Our survey has two main sections, one related to bread choice tasks and the other about demographic and climate knowledge information. In the bread choice task section, before choice task questions, we provide respondents with some information that are common practice for choice experiment research. The information includes the introduction about organic label and carbon removal technology, as well as a cheap talk script to mitigate the possible hypothetical bias in hypothetical choices. After the bread choice tasks, respondents are asked to fill out a questionnaire about their knowledge related to climate change and their demographics. Twelve statements are used to evaluate respondents' overall objective knowledge of climate change (Table 11.8) (Shi et al., 2016). This knowledge scale includes multiple items and is generally thought to be a stronger assessment of knowledge than the previous single-item or self- reported assessment (Wong-Parodi & Rubin, 2022). Each respondent is asked to make a choice about each statement whether it is "correct," "do not know," or "incorrect." If individuals give correct response for a statement, we code the statement as 1, otherwise as 0. The 12 questions can be classified into three scales of climate knowledge that addressed three aspect of climate change, including physical characteristics of climate change, causes of climate change and consequences of climate change. Each climate knowledge scale consists of four questions adopted from Shi et al. (2016). For example, knowledge about the causes of climate change is elicited by statements such as "climate change is mainly caused by human activities" and "The global CO2 concentration in the atmosphere has increased during the past 250 years."

Our survey is programmed in Qualtrics and administered by a consumer panel company, Dynata, to recruit a representative sample. As a professional online market research firm worldwide that maintains over 67 million users, Dynata recruits respondents via email and has been used previously to implement large-scale or nationally representative surveys (Caputo & Lusk, 2020; Milosh et al., 2021; Panzone et al., 2022). The respondents of this study are selected based on their age and bread shopping frequency. The qualified participants are those who are at least 18 years old and have shopped bread in the last 3 months. To ensure response quality, subjects that are not willing to read carefully, reject to provide honest answers, and fail attention trap questions are excluded from the final sample.

11.3 Econometric ModeL

Consumers' bread purchasing decisions are modeled using a utility function, based on Lancaster's theory of consumer demand (Lancaster, 1966). Following random utility theory (McFadden, 1974), choice experiments rely on the assumption that the utility of individual n choosing alternative j in choice situation t can be expressed as:

$$U_{njt} = V_{njt} + \varepsilon_{njt} = \alpha_n Price_{njt} + \beta_{n1} Conventional_{njt} + \beta_{n2} Organic_{njt} + \beta_{n3} ERW_{njt} + ecm_n + \varepsilon_{njt},$$

where V_{njt} is the systematic portion of the utility function, depending on the experimentally designed product attributes of alternative j. $Price_{njt}$ is a continuous variable populated with the four price levels in the design; $Conventional_{njt}$, $Organic_{njt}$, and ERW_{njt} are dummy variables for the conventional, US Department of Agriculture organic labeled, and ERW carbon-labeled bread products, respectively. They all take a value of 1 when the product belongs to that category, and 0 otherwise. α_n is individual n's price preference coefficient and the βs are the nonprice taste coefficients. ecm$_n$ refers to error component accounting for correlation across individual utilities due to extra variance shared by the experimentally designed alternatives, relative to the opt-out option (Caputo, 2020). ε_{njt} is the stochastic and unobservable (to researchers) component of consumer utility. To identify the α and βs, we normalize the utility of choosing the opt-out option to be zero.

We use a mixed logit model to estimate the consumer utility function. Mixed logit models allow consumer tastes to vary with respect to unobserved factors, and thus are highly flexible (McFadden & Train, 2000). We specify the coefficients of the three nonprice product attributes to be random and to follow normal distributions since either positive or negative values would be placed by individuals on these bread products. The price coefficient, α, is set to be negative and one-sided constrained triangularly distributed. Last, we allow for correlations between taste parameters, which may be caused by individual taste as well as scale heterogeneity (Hess & Train, 2017).

To assess preference heterogeneity across demographics, we estimate the model in WTP space using the entire sample and obtain individual conditional mean WTPs. These mean WTPs were later correlated with individual demographics to determine if variations in WTP exist among individuals with diferent demographic characteristics, whose results are shown in Table 11.5.

11.4 Data

The survey is programmed, pretested, and formally administered in December 2020. As previously discussed, to participate in the survey, individuals must beat least 18 years of age. Individuals who could not promise to provide truthful answers, failed the attention check questions, or completed the survey outside of the 95% confidence interval of survey time were excluded from our sample. A final sample of 263 consumers are collected, and the participants, on average, took 8 min to complete the survey.

Table 11.2 describes the demographics and bread choice frequencies of our sample. Around half the sample is female (51%), married (52%), holds a college degree, and has family pretax total annual income ranging from $60,000 to $99,999. Above 60% of the sample is white, nonliberal, and lives in urban areas with 1000–99,999 inhabitants. The demographic characteristics of our respondents are largely in line with that of recent food valuation studies focusing on US consumers (Lin & Nayga, 2022). In terms of individual bread choices in the choice experiment, the conventional and unlabeled bread has been selected most frequently by an average consumer (40%), followed by organic bread (21%), ERW-labeled bread (21%), and opt-out option (17%). Infrequent choices of organic bread could be partly explained

Table 11.2 Sample descriptive analysis

Variable	Definition	Mean
Gender	1 = Female, 0 = Male	0.51 (0.50)
Urban	1 = Less than 1000 inhabitants 2 = 1000–99,999 inhabitants 3 = More than 100,000 inhabitants	2.31 (0.72)
Marriage	1 = Married, 0 = others	0.52 (0.50)
Education	1 = Below college 2 = College 3 = Graduate	1.98 (0.67)
Household annual pretax	1 = Less than$20,000	2.90
Income	2 = $20,000–$59,999	(1.30)
	3 = $60,000–$99,999	
	4 = $100,000–$139,999	
	5 = $140,000 and above	
Political attitude	1 = Liberal, 0 = others	0.27
		(0.44)
Race	1 = White, 0 = non-White	0.62
		(0.49)
Choice frequency of conventional bread	%	40.49(0.35)
Choice frequency of organic labeled bread	%	21.20(0.33)
Choice frequency of ERW carbon-labeled bread	%	20.91(0.25)
Choice frequency of opt-out option	%	17.40(0.32)
Observations	People	263

Note: Standard errors are in parentheses
ERW enhanced silicate rock weathering of crushed basalt

Table 11.3 Climate knowledge scores

Types of climate knowledge	Definition	Our sample	Shi et al. (2016)
Overall knowledge	[0–12]	4.94 (2.75)	7.18
Physical knowledge	[0–4]	1.22 (1.14)	1.96
Causes knowledge	[0–4]	1.82 (1.21)	2.40
Consequences knowledge	[0–4]	1.90 (1.22)	2.82

Note: Higher score indicates higher level of knowledge. Standard errors are in parentheses

by our experimental design where organic bread is set expensive than conventional bread.

Table 11.3 reports individual knowledge concerning climate change, including overall knowledge level and three types of knowledge. The average consumer makes approximately five correct responses among the 12 climate-change-related knowledge questions, suggesting that the subjects are knowledgeable about climate change to some extent. Among three types of climate knowledge, our respondents score highest in consequences knowledge and causes knowledge, followed by physical knowledge. We note that this pattern is similar to the result by Shi et al. (2016), while our climate knowledge scores are lower. A possible reason includes that we focus on US consumers but Shi et al. (2016) used a sample of over 2000 consumers from six countries, including European consumers that are usually found to have higher levels of climate knowledge.

11.5 Results

The estimation results of mixed logit models in preference space and WTP space are presented in Table 11.4. All product attributes and prices significantly afect consumer bread selection in an expected way. In general, ERW-labeled bread is favored least by US subjects, followed by conventional bread and organic-labeled bread, despite strong heterogeneity found in consumer bread tastes.

Table 11.4 Mixed logit models in preference and WTP space

	Preference space		WTP space	
	Coef.	Z value	Coef.	Z value
Mean Price	−2.25*** (0.23)	−9.71		
Conventional	16.51*** (1.74)	9.50	4.62*** (0.30)	15.23
Organic	16.84*** (1.84)	8.72	4.71*** (0.31)	15.22
ERW carbon	16.44*** (1.72)	9.55	4.02*** (0.37)	11.01
Standard deviation				
Conventional	0.605	1.14	0.85***	7.79
	(0.53)		(0.11)	
Organic	1.15***	3.93	0.16	0.50
	(0.29)		(0.33)	
ERW carbon	2.34***	6.35	1.83***	8.62
	(0.37)		(0.21)	
Price	2.25***	9.41		
(0.53)				
ECM	8.60***	7.50	2.06***	7.82
	(1.15)		(0.26)	
Price/scale			13.28***	4.42
(3.01)				
Observations	1188		1188	
Log-likelihood	−1020.31		−1020.31	
AIC/N	1.66		1.67	

Note: Standard errors are in parentheses
ERW enhanced silicate rock weathering of crushed basalt, *WTP* willingness to pay. *$p \leq 0.1$; **$p \leq 0.05$; ***$p \leq 0.01$

Table 11.5 shows the simulated means of WTPs using the full sample and subsamples. We note that the simulated means of WTPs are close to those obtained from mixed logit model in WTP space, suggesting our simulated WTPs are robust to model specification. Looking at the finding from the full sample, average WTP for the ERW-labeled whole-grain bread is smallest, being $4.07/20 oz, followed by the conventional ($4.70) and organic ($4.76) whole-grain bread. Although the WTP of ERW-labeled bread is lower compared to the other two bread products, the price discount on the novel carbon-labeled bread is not substantial. This indicates that US consumers are likely to embrace the novel bread product with certain price discount. The result is consistent with previous studies suggesting that consumers favor carbon labels to some extent (Brunner et al., 2018; Canavari & Coderoni, 2020; Guenther et al., 2012). The result also reveals that US respondents favor organic

Table 11.5 WTP and WTP heterogeneity, $/12 oz

	Obs.	Conventional	Organic labeled	ERW carbon labeled
Full sample	263	4.70 (0.09)	4.76 (0.35)	4.07 (0.90)
By demographics				
Female	135	4.71 (0.08)	4.75 (0.31)	4.05 (0.89)
Male	128	4.71 (0.10)	4.76 (0.39)	4.08 (0.92)
Below 100,000 inhabitants	142	4.71 (0.08)	4.76 (0.33)	3.99 (0.84)
100,000 inhabitants and above	121	4.70 (0.09)	4.75 (0.38)	4.15 (0.96)
Married	136	4.71 (0.09)	4.76 (0.35)	4.01 (0.85)
Not married	127	4.71 (0.08)	4.76 (0.35)	4.13 (0.95)
Below college	61	4.70 (0.07)	4.78 (0.32)	3.88 (0.85)*
College and above	202	4.71 (0.09)	4.74 (0.36)	4.07 (0.92)
Liberal	70	4.72 (0.08)	4.70 (0.36)	4.24 (1.02)**
Nonliberal	193	4.71 (0.09)	4.78 (0.35)	4.00 (0.64)
White	163	4.72 (0.08)***	4.73 (0.28)	3.95 (0.82)***
Non-White	100	4.68 (0.09)	4.80 (0.22)	4.26 (0.99)
By climate knowledge				
Below or equal to median knowledge	149	4.71 (0.09)	4.76 (0.35)	4.04 (0.86)
Above median knowledge	114	4.71 (0.09)	4.75 (0.35)	4.09 (0.96)
Below or equal to median physical knowledge	175	4.71 (0.09)	4.76 (0.37)	4.06 (0.83)
Above median physical knowledge	88	4.72 (0.08)	4.75 (0.31)	4.07 (1.03)
Below or equal to median causes knowledge	174	4.71 (0.08)	4.78 (0.34)	3.97 (0.83)***
Above median causes knowledge	89	4.71 (0.10)	4.72 (0.37)	4.24 (0.10)
Below or equal to median consequences knowledge	183	4.71 (0.09)	4.75 (0.37)	4.09 (0.88)
Above median consequences knowledge	80	4.72 (0.07)	4.76 (0.30)	3.99 (0.94)

Abbreviations: ERW, enhanced silicate rock weathering of crushed basalt; WTP, willingness to pay. *$p \leq 0.1$; **$p \leq 0.05$; ***$p \leq 0.01$, which are calculated using t tests between subsamples bread most, likely driven by consumer perceived health and environmental benefit associated with organic foods.

We then compare the diferences in WTP estimates across diferent demographic subsamples and between consumers with diferent levels of climate knowledge. In general, heterogeneity analysis reveals that consumer valuation of the ERW carbon label tends to be significantly greater among liberal, non- White consumers and those with at least a college degree and those with high level of knowledge about the causes of climate change. Specifically, subjects who self-identify as liberals reveal $0.24 significantly higher WTP for the novel carbon label, relative to those placed by nonliberals. This is partly because liberals tend to be more likely to believe in climate change than those who align themselves with relatively conservative political parties (Hornsey et al., 2016), and thus would like to pay additionally for climate change mitigation. Second, the WTP for ERW-labeled bread is $4.26 among non-White respondents, which is $0.3 significantly higher than the value of white consumers. Third and expectedly, better educated individuals are more receptive to the ERW carbon label, relative to people without college degrees (the WTP for the novel carbon label being $3.88 vs. $4.07). This finding could be explained by the existing literature, which has indicated that education positively correlates with pro-environmental behavior (Meyer, 2015; Panzone et al., 2016), and more educated subjects have greater valuation for environmentally friendly labels (Lin & Nayga, 2022).

Last, we examine whether the diference in individual WTP for ERW-labeled bread would be attributable to the diference in climate change-related knowledge. To do so we divide our sample into two subgroups with above and below median knowledge, respectively. Findings suggest that overall climate knowledge may not be a good predictor for consumer valuation of the novel carbon label. This is because there exists no significant diference in the valuation of ERW-labeled bread between the above- and below-median overall knowledge subsamples. Looking into the three types of climate knowledge, knowledge about the causes of climate change significantly enhances consumer preference and WTP for the novel carbon label. People with the above-median knowledge about climate change causes would like to pay $4.24 for the ERW-labeled bread, in contrast to the value of $3.97 among the below-median subsample. The result somehow mirrors the previous heterogeneity analysis about education, revealing that US consumers less knowledgeable about climate change favor the ERW carbon label-less. We note that this finding is not surprising given that prior research has shown that individual knowledge about climate change leads to environmentally sustainable food choices (Peschel et al., 2016; Schmidt, 2021). But unlike the previous studies, our result not only reinforces the importance of improving public knowledge about climate change, but also highlights which type of climate knowledge is most helpful in improving environmentally friendly food behavior. Climate-related knowledge plays an important role in enhancing consumer preferences for food carbon label, which in turn promotes voluntary adoption of carbon removal technologies.

Our results also indicate that there is no heterogeneity in our results across gender. This finding is somewhat diferent from previous studies showing that men tend to have higher climate knowledge, but are less supportive of climate policies than women (Douenne & Fabre, 2020; Grebitus et al., 2015; Stern et al., 1993). In this regard, whether gender afects the valuation of novel carbon label needs further investigation. Similarly, whether consumers live in populated areas exerts insignificant efects on their valuation of bread products. The valuation of the ERW-labeled bread per 20 oz is just $0.15 higher for individuals in areas with at least 100,000 inhabitants, compared with those below 100,000 inhabitants. Populated areas such as big cities typically produce high carbon dioxide emissions, and are more cost-efective to implement environmental information campaigns, which would let their residents be more aware of the importance of carbon removal.

11.6 Conclusion

Promoting the voluntary adoption of carbon removal technology during agricultural production is a promising tool for decarbonizing the food system, which receives insufficient research focus in the literature. The adoption of carbon removal technology, however, will not be successful unless.

consumer preferences and valuation of technology are understood. This study investigateshow US consumers respond to a new technology-based carbon label on food products, focusing on the basalt-based ERW technology, a prominent option for agricultural carbon sequestration, whose market potential has not been evaluated by prior research.

Our results indicate that on average US consumers would be willing to pay $4/20 oz for the ERW-labeled bread, marginally lower than the WTPs of conventional and organic bread products; implying that the ERW-labeled bread may fail to gain market shares when competing with the conventional and organic bread products. However, consumer valuation of the ERW-labeled bread would be greater if targeted towards certain market segments, including non-White, liberal, well-educated consumers, and those having high level of knowledge about the causes of climate change. Our findings are informative to policymakers since they imply that promoting the adoption of carbon emission mitigation technologies could not count on the consumer market alone. Among others, governmental interventions maybe warranted for successful adoption of ERW basalt carbon emission mitigation technology among agricultural producers, including technology adoption subsidies and climate knowledge education programs. Finally, it is worth noting that while our sample size is adequate given our choice of experimental design, future studies could enhance the robustness of our findings with a larger and more diverse sample of US consumers (Tables 11.6 and 11.7).

Acknowledgments This work was supported by the National Natural Science Foundation of China (No. 72103180).

Data Availability Statement

Data available on request from the authors.

Orcid

Wen Lin http://orcid.org/0000-0001-7695-559X

Appendix

Table 11.6 Choice sets

Choice situation	Price conventional	Price organic	Price ERW Carbon	Block
1	2.37	3.27	4.19	2
2	4.19	5.09	5.09	2
3	3.27	4.19	2.37	1
4	2.37	3.27	5.09	1
5	2.37	4.19	4.19	2
6	4.19	5.09	3.27	1
7	4.19	5.09	2.37	2
8	3.27	4.19	5.09	1

Table 11.7 Instruction and cheap talk script prior to choice experiment

Agricultural food production and provision is a major contributor to carbon emissions and climate change. By removing carbon dioxide gas from the atmosphere and sequestering it for long periods of time, carbon dioxide removal can reduce carbon emissions and therefore mitigate climate change.

Enhanced silicate rock weathering (ERW) is one of the carbon removal technologies, among others. ERW amends soils with crushed calcium- and magnesium-rich silicate rocks to accelerate carbon dioxide sequestration. Recent studies have found that basalt, an abundant fast-weathering rock with the required mineral chemistry, could be ideal for implementing land-based ERW.ERW labeled bread is made from grains planted in the cropland where basalt dust is added to remove carbon from the air.

USDA organic label: products produced without the use of synthetic inputs, including synthetic fertilizers, pesticides, plant growth regulators, nanomaterials and genetically-modified organisms.

Next, you will be presented with a hypothetical choice involving money. No one will actually be paid money based on the decision you make, but you are asked to make the decision as though it would result in the actual payment. Studies show that people tend to act differently when they face hypothetical decisions. On average, more people expressed a willingness to pay money in the hypothetical group than in the real group.

How can we get people to think about their decision in a hypothetical situation like they think in a real situation? When we hear about a situation that involves doing something that is basically good, for example helping people in need, improving environmental quality, or anything else, our basic reaction in a hypothetical situation is to think: sure, I would do this. But when the situation is real and we would actually have to spend our money, we think a different way. We basically still would to see good things happen, but when we are faced with the possibility of having to spend money, we think about our options: If I spend money on this, that's money I cannot spend on other things. So, when the payment is real, we act in a way that takes into account the limited amount of money we have. **We make the decision while realizing that we just don't have enough money to do everything we might like to do.**

Table 11.8 Climate change knowledge items

Physical knowledge
1. Burning oil produces CO2
2. CO2 is harmful to plants
3. Nuclear power plants emit CO2 during operation
4. At the same quantity, CO2 is more harmful to the climate than methane
Causes knowledge
5. The global CO2 concentration in the atmosphere has increased during the past 250 years
6. Climate change is mainly caused by human activities
7. The last century's global increase in temperature was the largest during the past 1000 years
8. Today's global CO2 concentration in the atmosphere has already occurred in the past 650,000 years
Consequences knowledge
9. For the next decades, the majority of climate scientists expect a warmer climate to increase the melting of polar ice, which will lead to an overall rise of the sea level
10. For the next decades, the majority of climate scientists expect an increase in extreme events, such as droughts, floods and storms
11. For the next decades, the majority of climate scientists expect a warmer climate to increase water evaporation, which will lead to an overall decrease of the sea level
12. For the next decades, the majority of climate scientists expect the climate to change evenly all over the world

Source: Shi et al. (2016). For each of the items, respondents selects one of three options, including "A. correct", "B. do not know" and "C. incorrect"

References

Baylis, K., Fullerton, D., & Karney, D. H. (2013). Leakage, welfare, and cost-efectiveness of carbon policy. *American Economic Review, 103*(3), 332–337. https://doi.org/10.1257/aer.103.3.332

Beerling, D. J., Kantzas, E. P., Lomas, M. R., Wade, P., Eufrasio, R. M., Renforth, P., Sarkar, B., et al. (2020). Potential for large-scale CO2 removal via enhanced rock weathering with croplands. *Nature, 583*(7815), 242–248. https://doi.org/10.1038/s41586-020-2448-9

Brunner, F., Kurz, V., Bryngelsson, D., & Hedenus, F. (2018). Carbon label at a university restaurant–label implementation and evaluation. *Ecological Economics, 146*, 658–667. https://doi.org/10.1016/j.ecolecon.2017.12.012

Canavari, M., & Coderoni, S. (2020). Consumer stated preferences for dairy products with carbon footprint labels in Italy. *Agricultural and Food Economics, 8*(1), 4. https://doi.org/10.1186/s40100-019-0149-1

Caputo, V. (2020). Does information on food safety afect consumers' acceptance of new food technologies? The case of irradiated beef in South Korea under a new labelling system and across diferent information regimes. *Australian Journal of Agricultural and Resource Economics, 64*(4), 1003–1033.

Caputo, V., & Lusk, J. L. (2020). What agricultural and food policies do US consumers prefer? A best–worst scaling approach. *Agricultural Economics, 51*(1), 75–93. https://doi.org/10.1111/agec.12542

Clark, M. A., Domingo, N. G. G., Colgan, K., Thakrar, S. K., Tilman, D., Lynch, J., Azevedo, I. L., & Hill, J. D. (2020). Global food system emissions could preclude achieving the 1.5 and 2 C climate change targets. *Science, 370*(6517), 705–708. https://doi.org/10.1126/science.aba7357

Cox, E., Spence, E., & Pidgeon, N. (2020). Public perceptions of carbon dioxide removal in the United States and the United Kingdom. *Nature Climate Change, 10*(8), 744–749. https://doi.org/10.1038/s41558-020-0823-z

Crippa, M., Solazzo, E., Guizzard, D., Monforti-Ferrario, F., Tubiello, F. N., & Leip, A. (2021). Food systems are responsible for a third of global anthropogenic GHG emissions. *Nature Food, 2*(3), 198–209. https://doi.org/10.1038/s43016-021-00225-9

de Bekker-Grob, E. W., Donkers, B., Jonker, M. F., & Stolk, E. A. (2015). Sample size requirements for discrete - Choice experiments in healthcare: A practical guide. *The Patient-Patient-Centered Outcomes Research, 8*, 373–384. https://doi.org/10.1007/s40271-015-0118-z

Douenne, T., & Fabre, A. (2020). French attitudes on climate change, carbon taxation and other climate policies. *Ecological Economics, 169*, 106496. https://doi.org/10.1016/j.ecolecon.2019.106496

Elofsson, K., Bengtsson, N., Matsdotter, E., & Arntyr, J. (2016). The impact of climate information on milk demand: Evidence from a field experiment. *Food Policy, 58*, 14–23. https://doi.org/10.1016/j.foodpol.2015.11.002

Goll, D. S., Ciais, P., Amann, T., Buermann, W., Chang, J., Eker, S., Hartmann, J., et al. (2021). Potential CO2 removal from enhanced weathering by ecosystem responses to powdered rock. *Nature Geoscience, 14*(8), 545–549. https://doi.org/10.1038/s41561-021-00798-x

Grebitus, C., Steiner, B., & Veeman, M. (2015). The roles of human values and generalized trust on stated preferences when food is labeled with environmental footprints: Insights from Germany. *Food Policy, 52*, 84–91. https://doi.org/10.1016/j.foodpol.2014.06.011

Guenther, M., Saunders, C. M., & Tait, P. R. (2012). Carbon labeling and consumer attitudes. *Carbon Management, 3*(5), 445–455. https://doi.org/10.4155/cmt.12.50

Hartmann, J., Joshua West, A., Renforth, P., Köhler, P., De La Rocha, C. L., Wolf-Gladrow, D. A., Dürr, H. H., & Schefran, J. (2013). Enhanced chemical weathering as a geoengineering strategy to reduce atmospheric carbon dioxide, supply nutrients, and mitigate ocean acidification. *Reviews of Geophysics, 51*(2), 113–149. https://doi.org/10.1002/rog.20004

Hess, S., & Train, K. (2017). Correlation and scale in mixed logit models. *Journal of Choice Modelling, 23*, 1–8. https://doi.org/10.1016/j.jocm.2017.03.001

Hornsey, M. J., Harris, E. A., Bain, P. G., & Fielding, K. S. (2016). Meta-analyses of the determinants and outcomes of belief in climate change. *Nature Climate Change, 6*(6), 622–626. https://doi.org/10.1038/nclimate2943

Horton, P., Long, S. P., Smith, P., Banwart, S. A., & Beerling, D. J. (2021). Technologies to deliver food and climate security through agriculture. *Nature Plants, 7*(3), 250–255. https://doi.org/10.1038/s41477-021-00877-2

Lancaster, K. J. (1966). A new approach to consumer theory. *Journal of Political Economy, 74*(2), 132–157.

Lancsar, E., & Louviere, J. (2008). Conducting Discrete Choice Experiments To Inform Healthcare Decision Making: A user's guide. *PharmacoEconomics, 26*, 661–677. https://doi.org/10.2165/00019053-200826080-00004

Lin, W., & Nayga, R. M. (2022). Green identity labeling, environmental information, and pro-environmental food choices. *Food Policy, 106*, 102187. https://doi.org/10.1016/j.foodpol.2021.102187

Mancino, L., & Kuchler, F. (2012). Demand for whole-grain bread before and after the release of dietary guidelines. *Applied Economic Perspectives and Policy, 34*(1), 76–101. https://doi.org/10.1093/aepp/ppr035

McFadden, D. (1974). The measurement of urban travel demand. *Journal of Public Economics, 3*(4), 303–328.

McFadden, D., & Train, K. (2000). Mixed MNL models for discrete response. *Journal of Applied Econometrics, 15*(5), 447–470.

Meyer, A. (2015). Does education increase pro-environmental behavior? Evidence from Europe. *Ecological Economics, 116*, 108–121. https://doi.org/10.1016/j.ecolecon.2015.04.018

Milosh, M., Painter, M., Sonin, K., Van Dijcke, D., & Wright, A. L. (2021). Unmasking partisanship: Polarization undermines public response to collective risk. *Journal of Public Economics, 204*, 104538. https://doi.org/10.1016/j.jpubeco.2021.104538

Ortega, D. L., Lusk, J. L., Lin, W., & Caputo, V. (2020). Predicting responsiveness to information: Consumer acceptance of biotechnology in animal products. *European Review of Agricultural Economics, 47*(5), 1644–1667. https://doi.org/10.1093/erae/jbaa003

Panzone, L., Hilton, D., Sale, L., & Cohen, D. (2016). Socio-demographics, implicit attitudes, explicit attitudes, and sustainable consumption in supermarket shopping. *Journal of Economic Psychology, 55*, 77–95.

Panzone, L., Garrod, G., Adinolfi, F., & Di Pasquale, J. (2022). Molecular marketing, personalised information and willingness-to-pay for functional foods: Vitamin D enriched eggs. *Journal of Agricultural Economics, 73*, 666–689. https://doi.org/10.1111/1477-9552.12489

Peschel, A. O., Grebitus, C., Steiner, B., & Veeman, M. (2016). How does consumer knowledge afect environmentally sustainable choices? Evidence from a cross-country latent class analysis of food labels. *Appetite, 106*, 78–91. https://doi.org/10.1016/j.appet.2016.02.162

Scarpa, R., & Rose, J. M. (2008). Design efficiency for non-market valuation with choice modelling: How to measure it, what to report and why. *Australian Journal of Agricultural and Resource Economics, 52*(3), 253–282. https://doi.org/10.1111/j.1467-8489.2007.00436.x

Schmidt, K. (2021). When less is more–efects of providing simple vs. refined action-knowledge interventions to promote climate-friendly food consumption in German consumers. *Food Quality and Preference, 94*, 104333. https://doi.org/10.1016/j.foodqual.2021.104333

Shi, J., Visschers, V. H. M., Siegrist, M., & Arvai, J. (2016). Knowledge as a driver of public perceptions about climate change reassessed. *Nature Climate Change, 6*(8), 759–762. https://doi.org/10.1038/nclimate2997

Stern, P. C., Dietz, T., & Kalof, L. (1993). Value orientations, gender, and environmental concern. *Environment and Behavior, 25*(5), 322–348. https://doi.org/10.1177/0013916593255002

Strefler, J., Amann, T., Bauer, N., Kriegler, E., & Hartmann, J. (2018). Potential and costs of carbon dioxide removal by enhanced weathering of rocks. *Environmental Research Letters, 13*(3), 034010. https://doi.org/10.1088/1748-9326/aaa9c4

Tubiello, F. N., Rosenzweig, C., Conchedda, G., Karl, K., Gütschow, J., Xueyao, P., Obli-Laryea, G., et al. (2021). Greenhouse gas emissions from food systems: Building the evidence base. *Environmental Research Letters, 16*(6), 065007. https://doi.org/10.1088/1748-9326/ac018e

Vandenbergh, M. P., Dietz, T., & Stern, P. C. (2011). Time to try carbon labelling. *Nature Climate Change, 1*(1), 4–6. https://doi.org/10.1038/nclimate1071

Visschers, V. H. M., & Siegrist, M. (2015). Does better for the environment mean less tasty? Ofering more climate-friendly meals is good for the environment and customer satisfaction. *Appetite, 95*, 475–483. https://doi.org/10.1016/j.appet.2015.08.013

Vlaeminck, P., Jiang, T., & Vranken, L. (2014). Food labeling and eco-friendly consumption: Experimental evidence from a Belgian supermarket. *Ecological Economics, 108*, 180–190. https://doi.org/10.1016/j.ecolecon.2014.10.019

Wong-Parodi, G., & Rubin, N. B. (2022). Exploring how climate change subjective attribution, personal experience with extremes, concern, and subjective knowledge relate to pro-environmental attitudes and behavioral intentions in the United States. *Journal of Environmental Psychology, 79*, 101728. https://doi.org/10.1016/j.jenvp.2021.101728

Chapter 12
Would Altruistic Consumers Place a Higher Value on Sustainable Foods?

12.1 Introduction

Sustainable development poses a significant challenge to human society, and as a response, more than 190 countries signed the Paris Agreement in December 2015 to address climate change mitigation. Recently, achieving carbon neutrality has emerged as one of the world's most pressing goals, with around 110 countries committing to reducing carbon dioxide emissions. Unfortunately, while considerable efforts have been dedicated to non-food sectors and recently some food sectors (Pocol et al., 1973), the role of consumers in promoting sustainable food systems has received relatively less research attention in the literature. This is concerning considering that the food system is responsible for one third of global anthropogenic greenhouse gas emissions, as highlighted by Crippa et al. (2021). Therefore, promoting sustainable food systems is not only crucial but also essential for attaining sustainable development goals.

Sustainable labels have emerged as a promising tool for decarbonizingandenhancing the sustainability of food systems. Through providing information, these labels can empower individuals to make environmentally friendly food choices and incentivize the supply side to offer greener options in the market (Lin & Nayga Jr., 2022). While previous studies have predominantly focused on the adoption behavior of green technologies by the supply side (Bukchin & Kerret, 2018; Devi et al., 2015; Gao et al., 2020), such as food producers, plants, and retailers, there is a growing body of literature that explores the feasibility of promoting sustainable labels among consumers. These studies assess consumer preferences and valuations of different sustainable food products, examining individuals' willingness to pay for

Disclaimer/Publisher's Note: The statements, opinions and data contained in all publications are solely those of the individual author(s) and contributor(s) and not of MDPI and/or the editor(s). MDPI and/or the editor(s) disclaim responsibility for any injury to people or property resulting from any ideas, methods, instructions or products referred to in the content.

W. Lin, *Transforming China's Agri-Food System: Government-Market Synergy*, Resources, Environment and Agricultural Development,
https://doi.org/10.1007/978-981-95-7151-2_12

various green labels, including organic and Fairtrade labels (Becchetti & Huybrechts, 2008; Canavari et al., 2002; Hu et al., 2009; Lazaroiu et al., 2019; Thøgersen & Zhou, 2012; Van Loo et al., 2011, 2015), animal welfare claims (de Boer et al., 2007; Olesen et al., 2010; Verbeke & Roosen, 2009), carbon footprint labels (Echeverría et al., 2014; Gadema & Oglethorpe, 2011; Kimura et al., 2010; Lohmann et al., 2022), and the forage–livestock balance label (Zhang et al., 2023), among others. While several studies have examined individual sustainable labels or compared a limited number of labels (Neuhofer et al., 2023; Sogari et al., 2023), there is a dearth of research that combines multiple sustainable labels within a single context and evaluates consumers' willingness to pay for each label. Understanding the relative market value placed on different sustainable labels and the extent to which consumers value each of them can provide valuable insights for the supply side when considering and planning the adoption of sustainable labels. Conducting research to investigate the market's preferences and valuations of various sustainable labels would contribute to filling this research gap. Such investigations would shed light on which sustainable label(s) are most or least valued by the market and provide valuable information for supply side actors in their decision-making processes regarding the adoption of sustainable labels.

In addition to understanding the factors that influence individual preferences and willingness to pay for sustainable labels, it is crucial to explore various elements in enhancing sustainable food consumption. Existing literature has explored factors such as demographics (Bryant & Sanctorum, 2021; Judge & Wilson, 2019), beliefs (Malek et al., 2019), food consumption habits (Hartmann & Siegrist, 2017; Lemken et al., 2019), and time preferences (De Marchi et al., 2016; Guan et al., 2022). However, one aspect that has received comparatively less attention in the literature is altruism. Altruism, which refers to selfless concern for the well-being of others (Ben-Ner & Hu, 2018), can also have a significantinfluence on individuals' attitudes toward sustainable labels and their willingness to pay for sustainable food products. Altruistic individuals often prioritize the welfare of others and the long-term health of the planet, and these individuals maybe willing to pay a premium for sustainable food products that have the appropriate labels. They see their purchasing decisions as a means to support sustainable practices, promote fairtrade, reduce carbon emissions, and encourage responsible resource management. On the other hand, some studies have demonstrated a positive association between altruism and a series of sustainable behaviors (Wang et al., 2014; Yarimoglu & Binboga, 2019), including the purchases of local foods (Birch et al., 2018) and organic foods (Yadav, 2016). This implies the effect of altruism is likely to be evident in other contexts of food purchases.

Understanding the impact of altruism on consumers' attitudes towards sustainable labels and food choices is therefore crucial for developing effective strategies to promote sustainable food consumption. Through considering individuals' altruistic orientation, policymakers and marketers can tailor interventions and communication strategies to resonate with different altruistic attitudes, thereby encouraging the adoption of sustainable food options. To fill the gap, this study assesses consumers' willingness to pay for different sustainable labels and the role that altruism plays in explaining consumer valuation of sustainable labels, with a discrete choice experiment of a package of 12 oz ground coffee conducted among U.S. consumers. Our study contributes to the literature in several ways. First, we investigate and compare the willingness to pay values for three sustainable labels, namely, organic, Fairtrade, and Carbon Trust labels, on food products under one study. Second, we explain consumers' preferences and valuations of the three green labels with their altruism orientation.

12.2 Materials and Methods

12.2.1 Choice Experimental Design

To assess the value that US consumers place on sustainable food products, we devised and executed a hypothetical online choice experiment. The experiment involved presenting individuals with various decision scenarios or tasks, in which they were asked to select their preferred product option. Each scenario included multiple alternatives of the product, along with a no-purchase option, to simulate real-world market situations. In this study, we focused on a specific product: 12 oz roasted ground coffee, which is a commonly available item in the US market. Through selecting a well-known product, we aimed to ensure familiarity and relevance to participants, enhancing the realism of their decision-making process within the experiment.

Our choice experimental design incorporates four key attributes: USDA organic, Fairtrade, and Carbon Trust labels, as well as price. These attributes were carefully chosen to capture different dimensions of sustainability in the context of coffee products. The USDA organic, Fairtrade, and Carbon Trust labels serve as indicators of sustainable coffee products. Each of these attributes is represented as a binary variable, taking a value of one if the coffee product carries the respective label and zero otherwise. The organic and Fairtrade labels are well-established sustainability certifications, while the Carbon Trust label represents a newer and emerging attribute in the marketplace. Coffee production is known to contribute significantly to carbon emissions within the food system (Poore & Nemecek, 2018) and the inclusion of the Carbon Trust label signifies a commitment by the company to reducing the carbon footprint associated with their coffee products. In addition to the sustainability labels, we also consider price as an attribute in our design. The selected price levels encompass both high-end and low-end prices commonly observed in the real market, ranging from USD 4.95 to USD 12.45. Through including a range of price points, we aim to capture the influence of price sensitivity on consumers' decision-making process. For a comprehensive overview of the chosen product attributes and attribute levels, please refer to Table 12.1

To ensure the efficiency and effectiveness of our choice experiment, we employed a D-efficient design methodology (Burgess & Street, 2005). This approach allowed

Table 12.1 Attributes and attribute levels

Attributes	Levels
USDA organic label	
Fairtrade label	
	No label
Carbon trust label	
Price (USD per 12 oz)	No label 4.95, 7.45, 9.95, 12.45

us to generate a total of 32 choice sets, organized into four blocks, with each block containing eight choice sets. The D-efficiency achieved in our design is an impressive 97.21%, indicating a high level of precision in capturing the relevant information from participants. Within each choice set, two product alternatives were presented, each with experimentally designed attribute levels. Additionally, a no-purchase or opt-out option was included to replicate real-market scenarios where consumers may choose not to make a purchase. To minimize any potential bias or order effects, participants were randomly assigned to one of the four blocks and completed eight choice tasks in a randomized order. This approach ensured a balanced distribution of choice sets across participants and reduced any potential systematic biases. For a visual representation, please refer to Fig. 12.1, which showcases an actual choice set that was used in our experiment.

12.2.2 Altruism Measurement

To assess consumers' altruism orientation, we employed the scale questions developed by Lusk and Briggeman (2009). The psychometricscale consists of five questions listed in Table 12.2, and in each question, respondents were asked to indicate the extent to which they agree with the statement on a scale from 1 (strongly disagree) to 7 (strongly agree). Each statement is easy for respondents to understand and would not cause too much cognitive burden while eliciting their altruism orientation. As a standardized and efficient method for gaining insights into individual attitudes, beliefs, and preferences, multiple-item psychometric scales have been designed and used to quantify risk preferences, time preferences, and environmental beliefs, among others (Malek et al., 2019; De Marchi et al., 2016; Dunlap, 2008).

The order of the questions was randomized.

Fig. 12.1 A sample choice set

Table 12.2 Scale on altruism orientation

Item	Description
1	I am willing to makesacrifices for the good of those around me
2	I enjoy contributing to charities and other non-profit organizations
3	Pay taxes is important because they fund programs such as schools and roads from which everyone benefits
4	I am comfortable receiving benefits even if I don't contribute
5	My personal happiness is more important than the well-being of the average American

12.2.3 Analytical Framework

We employed a mixed logit model to analyze the data obtained from our choice experiment. The mixed logit model offers several advantages in estimating consumer preferences as it accommodates variations in consumer tastes related to unobserved variables. This flexibility enables the model to capture a more realistic substitution pattern among the available alternatives. Adhering to the principles of random utility theory, the utility of individual n selecting alternative j in choice situation t can be represented as follows:

$$U_{njt} = V_{njt} + \varepsilon_{njt} = \alpha Price_{njt} + \beta_{n1} Organics_{njt} + \beta_{n2} Fairtrade_{njt} + \beta_{n3} Carbtrust_{njt} + ASC_{Opt-out} + \varepsilon_{njt} \quad (12.1)$$

In the above equation, Price njt is a continuous variable that includes the four price levels used in the experimental design. $Organics_{njt,}$ Fairtrade njt, and Carbtrust njt are dummy variables indicating the presence (1) or absence (0) of USDA organic,

Fairtrade, and Carbon Trust certifications, respectively, for the specific product. The coefficient α represents individual price sensitivity, while the β coefficients denote the taste coefficients associated with the non-price attributes. The term ASCOpt-out represents the alternative-specific constant for the opt-out option, which remains constant across the population. ε_{njt} represents the random error term, assumed to follow a Type I Extreme Value distribution. To account for heterogeneity in individual preferences, the coefficients of the non-price product attributes are assumed to be random, following normal distributions. This allows for variations in how individuals value these attributes. The price coefficient (α), on the other hand, is specified as a fixed value.

Through considering these components, we can calculate the unconditional choice probability for individual n selecting alternative j in choice situation t:

$$P_{njt} = \int_{\beta} \frac{e^{V_{njt}}}{\sum_k e^{V_{njt}}} f\left(\beta|,\alpha|,ASC_{Opt-out}|,\overline{\beta}\Omega\right) d\beta \tag{12.2}$$

where $f\left(\beta|\alpha, ASC_{Opt-out}, \overline{\beta}\Omega\right)$ is the density function of the vector of random coefficients. The density function of the vector of random coefficients is determined by the parameters β and Ω, which represent the means and the variance-covariance matrix, respectively. These parameters govern the distribution of the random coefficients in the model. To estimate the model, we utilized simulated maximum likelihood estimation with 1000 Halton draws in STATA. This approach allows us to capture the variability in individual preferences and obtain reliable estimates of the model parameters. To compute the mean willingness to pay for the sustainable coffee label k for consumer n, we can use the estimated model. Consumer n's mean willingness to pay for the sustainable coffee label k can be computed as:

$$WTP_{nk} \; = \; , k = 1, 2, 3. \tag{12.3}$$

In our study, we examine and compare the willingness to pay values between groups that exhibit different time preferences. To achieve this, we match the altruism scores with individual-specific or conditional willingness to pay (WTP). Through assessing the relationship between altruism and WTPs, we aim to understand if there are significant differences in WTP based on individuals' altruism orientation. To statistically test for WTP equality between these different groups, we employ the Poe test (Poe et al., 2005). This statistical analysis helps us assess whether the observed differences in WTP between groups are statistically significant.

12.2.4 Data Collection and Quality Control

The survey was conducted in the spring of 2020 utilizing an online opt-in consumer panel sourced from Survey Sampling International. To be eligible for participation, individuals had to beat least 18 years old and have made coffee product purchases within the past two months. To ensure data integrity, respondents who could not commit to providing truthful answers, failed attention check questions or completed the survey outside the 95% confidence interval of the survey time were excluded from the analysis. Ultimately, a sample of 304 US respondents was collected, with the majority completing the survey within a 20 min timeframe.

The survey consisted of three parts: screening questions and the altruism scale questions, eight coffee choice tasks in the second part, and demographic inquiries in the final section. To enhance the reliability of survey responses, a "cheap talk" script was employed in an attempt to minimize potential hypothetical bias. Additionally, at the beginning of the survey, respondents were requested to commit to carefully reading the questions and providing honest answers. Those who could not make such a commitment were not included in the survey. Furthermore, two attention checks were incorporated into the questionnaire to identify and exclude participants who may have been inattentive. Through implementing these measures, we aimed to ensure the validity and accuracy of the collected data, thereby strengthening the robustness of our findings.

12.3 Results and Discussions

12.3.1 Sample Description

Table 12.3 displays the socio-demographic characteristics and choice frequencies of our sample. On average, respondents are around 51 years old, hold a college degree, have a household size ranging from 3 to 4 individuals, hold moderate political views, and have a pre-tax annual household income between 40,000 US to 80,000 US dollars. The majority of respondents identify as white and religious, and they mostly have part-time employment.

This prevalence of part-time work maybe attributed to the survey being conducted during the COVID-19 pandemic. Slightly over half of the sample consists of male participants. Despite the size of our sample, it can be considered broadly representative of the US population. Additionally, we provide an overview of the choices made by our respondents during the choice experimental tasks. Across the eight choice tasks, the average respondent abstains from purchasing any product alternative once, and they favor the more expensive product alternative in almost three out of the eight choice tasks. This suggests that the responses given by participants are reasonably consistent.

Table 12.3 Sample description

Variable definition		Mean
Demographics		
Female	1 = Yes, 0 = No	0.45 (0.50)
Age	Year	50.91 (16.91)
Household Income	1 =< USD 40K, 2 = USD 40K–USD 79K … to 5 => USD 160K	2.30 (1.14)
Education	0 =< College, 1 = College 2 = Graduate	0.67 (0.74)
Household size	Person	3.47 (1.24)
Political view	1 = Liberal, 2 = Moderate 3 = Conservative, 4 = Other	2.05 (0.77)
Religion	1 = Yes, 0 = No	0.77 (0.42)
White	1 = Yes, 0 = No	0.68 (0.47)
Employment	1 = Full time, 2 = Part time, 3 = Unemployed, 4 = Other	2.09 (1.04)
Choice frequency in the choice experiment		
Opt-out option	0–8	1.128 (0.105)
High-priced option	0–8	2.931 (0.076)
Observations	Person	304

Note: numbers in parentheses are standard deviations

12.3.2 Preference and Willingness to Pay for Sustainable Coffee Labels and the Role of Altruism

We begin via examining the results in preference space and subsequently delve into the findings related to willingness to pay (WTP). The estimation results of the mixed logit models in preference space using STATA and 1000 Halton draws are presented in Table 12.4. The benchmark specification, Model (1), focuses on the main effects of product attributes. It includes the fixedcoefficient for price taste and the parameter for non-price attributes, which follows a normal distribution. Model (2) builds upon Model (1) through incorporating interaction terms between altruism scores and product attributes. This addition allows us to investigate how altruism orientation influences individual preferences for sustainable food products.

Model (1) yields several noteworthy findings. Firstly, on average, individuals exhibit a preference for the three sustainable labels, with the USDA organic label

Table 12.4 Preferences for sustainable coffee labels

	(1)	(2)
Mean		
Price	−0.559 *** (0.024)	−0.569 *** (0.024)
ASCOpt-out	−5.265 *** (0.219)	−5.366 *** (0.224)
Organics	0.673 *** (0.115)	0.582 *** (0.124)
Fairtrade	0.411 *** (0.115)	0.372 *** (0.106)
Carbtrust	0.422 *** (0.097)	0.367 *** (0.093)
Organics *Altruism		0.058 ** (0.021)
Fairtrade * Altruism		0.061 *** (0.015)
Carbtrust * Altruism		0.029 * (0.019)
Standard deviation		
Organics	1.603 *** (0.122)	1.373 *** (0.193)
Fairtrade	1.428 *** (0.119)	1.299 *** (0.142)
Carbtrust	1.135 *** (0.116)	0.871 ** (0.120)
Model statistics		
Number of respondents	304	304
AIC	3449.764	3402.054
Loglikelihood	−1716.882	−1683.746

Note: numbers in parentheses are standard deviations. ***, **, and * indicate the 1%, 5%, and 10% significance levels, respectively

being the most preferred, followed by the Carbon Trust label and the Fair Trade claim. Secondly, higher coffee prices result in a decrease in utility, aligning with economic principles. Thirdly, the parameter associated with the opt-out option is significantly negative (−5.3), indicating that individuals tend to choose coffee product alternatives over not purchasing any coffee products. Lastly, there is significant heterogeneity in individual preferences for the three sustainable labels, suggesting that not all participants favor sustainable coffee products, and some individuals even hold a negative valuation of these products. Approximately 34%, 39%, and 35% of respondents express a dislike for the USDA organic, Fair Trade, and Carbon Trust claims, respectively. Possible reasons for this disparity could be the widespread familiarity of the USDA organic and Fair Trade labels in the US market, while the Carbon Trust claim maybe relatively novel for US consumers.

In order to better understand the observed heterogeneity in consumer preferences for sustainable labels, we investigate whether altruism preferences play a role in explaining this variation. This analysis is presented in Model (2) of Table 12.4. We observe a significant improvement in model fit through incorporating the interaction terms between the altruism preference scale and product attributes. This is evident from the increase in log-likelihood (from −1717 to −1684) and the decrease in AIC per person (from 11.35 to 11.19). Furthermore, the inclusion of the interaction terms in Model (2) leads to a reduction in the estimated standard deviations of product tastes, which reflects a decrease in unobserved taste heterogeneity. These statistical findings provide evidence that consumers' preferences for sustainable food products are influenced by their altruism orientation, emphasizing the importance of considering altruism attitudes when studying consumer food choices.

The coefficients of the interaction terms reveal several findings. First, altruism orientation significantly affects consumer choices of organic, Fairtrade, and Carbon Trust-labeled coffee products. Specifically, a person would have stronger preferences for these environmentally friendly coffee products if her altruistic inclination is stronger. This is expected because individuals with stronger altruistic tendencies prioritize the external impacts of their actions. Consequently, they are more inclined to choose products that contribute to broader benefits and positive outcomes beyond their personal interests. Second, among the three sustainable labels, consumer choices of Fairtrade labeled coffee are mostly explained by altruism, followed by the choices of USDA organic and Carbon Trust-claimed coffee products. An individual with an altruism score that is one point higher than the average is expected to derive an additional utility of 0.061 and 0.058 from selecting Fairtrade coffee and organic coffee, respectively. Altruistic individuals, on the other hand, tend to exhibit comparatively weaker preferences for Carbon Trust claims, and those whose altruism scale scored one point higher than the sample mean would have 0.029 higher utility than the average, with a 10% statistical significance level.

We now turn our attention to the willingness to pay (WTP) values derived from the preference-space model estimates in Model (1) of Table 12.4. Table 12.5 presents the average WTPs for sustainable labels in the full sample, as well as in four subsamples categorized according to altruism attitudes. Inline with the findings presented in Table 12.4, the highest WTP is observed for organic coffee (USD 1.2), followed by Carbon Trust-labeled coffee (USD 0.75) and Fairtrade-labeled coffee (USD 0.73). On average, consumers in the United States are willing to pay an additional USD 1.2 for a 12 oz serving of organic coffee compared to unlabeled coffee products. When examining the WTPs for sustainable coffee products across different subsamples, we observe that individuals with lower altruism scores tend to assign lower price premiums for sustainable coffee. To illustrate this, compared to conventional coffee, the valuation of organic coffee is USD 1.48 and USD 1.0 higher per 12 oz in the above-and below-median altruism score subsamples, respectively; the valuation of Fairtrade-labeled coffee is USD 0.63 and USD 0.85 higher in the above- and below- median altruism score subsamples, respectively.

Table 12.5 WTPs for sustainable coffee labels, USD/12 oz

	Full sample	Above median altruism score	Below median altruism score	p-Value
USDA Organics	1.204 (0.251)	1.482 (0.232)	1.053 (0.199)	<0.01
Fair trade	0.735	0.841	0.602	0.039
Carbon trust	(0.186) 0.715	(0.210) 0.820	(0.203) 0.633	0.084
Observations	(0.145) 304	(0.161) 148	(0.175) 156	

Note: numbers in parentheses are standard deviations. p-values are calculated using a t-test examining the equality of WTP between two samples

Additionally, for the two WTP values, the difference between above and below-median score subsamples is significantat least at a 5% level. These findings reinforce the notion that individuals with higher levels of altruism are inclined to select sustainable products that benefit both others and the environment.

12.3.3 Discussions

Our study reveals that among the organic, Fairtrade, and Carbon Trust labels, US consumers display a preference for the organic label, followed by Fairtrade and Carbon Trust labels. Corresponding to this preference ranking, consumers are willing to pay an additional amount of USD 1.20, USD 0.75, and USD 0.73 for organic-, Fairtrade-, and Carbon Trust-labeled coffee, respectively, in comparison to conventional coffee. These values align with the findings of Van Loo et al. (2015), who reported a willingness to pay USD 1.16 for organic coffee and USD 0.68 for Fairtrade coffee among US consumers. Regarding Carbon Trust labels, prior research suggests that their impact on Americans' utility in food productselection is relatively weaker compared to the organic logo, antibiotic-free claims, and even conventional production methods (De Marchi et al., 2016; Asioli et al., 2022). Notably, the higher price premium associated with the organic label maybe attributed to consumers' perception of the health and environmental benefits associated with organic foods (Lusk & Briggeman, 2009; de Magistris & Gracia, 2008; Smed, 2012). For example, Durham and Andrade (2005) proposed that environmental concern holds more influencethan health considerations in consumers' decisions to purchase organic foods, specificallyin the context of US consumer choices of fruits and vegetables.

Additionally, our study uncovers variations in consumer preferences and valuations of the three sustainable labels based on their altruistic orientation. The inclusion of interaction terms between the altruism score and the three labels proves statistically significant, indicating that incorporating altruism orientation in the analysis of food choices provides a better explanation for the heterogeneity surrounding random taste parameters and individuals' decision-making. Expectedly, people with a stronger altruism orientation are more careful about sustainable labels and tend to pay more for them, particularly in terms of Fairtrade labels. Altruistic individuals prefer the Fairtrade label most for several reasons. Fair trade practices are often associated with ethical considerations and social responsibility (Moore, 2004). Altruistic individuals tend to prioritize fairness, justice, and the well-being of others. Through choosing Fairtrade products, they can support producers in developing countries and contribute to reducing poverty and inequality in global supply chains. Secondly, Fairtrade certification ensures that producers receive fair prices for their goods, which can help improve their living standards and empower them economically. Altruistic individuals may be motivated to support fairtrade as a means of promoting economic justice and sustainability in trade relationships. Thirdly, fairtrade practices often involve environmentally sustainable production methods and community development initiatives. Altruistic individuals, who are concerned about the broader impacts of their consumption choices, may view fairtrade as a way to contribute to environmental conservation and community empowerment. Our findings are inline with the studies suggesting that altruistic people tend to have more sustainable behaviors in the context of non-food consumption (Wang et al., 2014; de Morais et al., 2021; Dermody et al., 2018; Mansoor & Paul, 2022; Park et al., 2022) as well as food purchases (Birch et al., 2018; Boobalan et al., 2021; Mesic et al., 2021).

The findings of our study carry implications for advancing sustainability efforts from both the demand side and the perspective of food systems. While previous research has predominantly focused on the supply side, examining the adoption of green technologies by farmers or agricultural firms, it is essential to recognize that the development of sustainable food systems also heavily relies on consumer attitudes and preferences towards environmentally friendly foods. To promote increased sustainable food consumption, policymakers and food suppliers may need to adopt differentiated strategies that cater to the preferences of individuals with different altruistic preferences. For individuals with a strong altruistic orientation, it would be beneficialto highlight the public benefits of green consumption. Conversely, for selfish individuals, emphasizing the private benefits of sustainable food choices would further enhance their inclination toward sustainability. To effectively communicate such messages, the implementation of information provision and targeted marketing campaigns would be instrumental. These strategies can effectively educate consumers about the environmental and societal benefits associated with sustainable food choices, thereby encouraging and facilitating their adoption.

Our study identifies several potential areas for future research. Firstly, while our respondents were geographically diverse, the sample size of our study was relatively small. Future studies could address this limitation through examining our research questions using larger sample sizes and expanding to other contexts. This could include investigating developing countries that face significant environmental challenges and exploring the application of sustainable labels to other food products, such as red meat or even daily dietary choices. Secondly, we employed a hypothetical choice experiment due to the unavailability of Carbon Trust labels in the US market at the time of our study. Although we implemented various strategies to ensure response quality, such as an oathat the survey's outset, a cheap talk script before choice tasks, and attention trap questions, it is important to acknowledge the potential impact of hypothetical bias on our results. Future research could address this issue through investigating individual preferences and willingness to pay for sustainable labels using real experiments or market transaction data once all the sustainable labeled products are available in the market. Thirdly, our study highlights the significance of behavioral factors, beyond monetary mechanisms, in influencing consumers' food choices. It is worth exploring other behavioral factors, such as personality traits and cognitive biases, in future studies to gain a more comprehensive understanding of consumer preferences.

12.4 Conclusions

This research employed a discrete choice experiment to investigate the willingness to pay of US consumers for various sustainable labels on 12 oz ground coffee, while also exploring the role of altruism in shaping consumer preferences for sustainable labels. The study reveals that among the three sustainable labels examined, the USDA organic claim commands the highest price premium compared to unlabeled and conventional coffee, followed by the Carbon Trust and Fairtrade labels. The results obtained from the mixed logit models, which consider both the main effects and interaction terms between altruism score variables and sustainable labels, demonstrate that individuals' altruistic orientation significantly influences their preferences and the associated price premiums for sustainable labels on coffee products. Notably, individuals who are selfless and willing to act for the well-being of others exhibit a stronger preference and valuation for fair trade and organic coffee.

These findings make valuable contributions to the existing literature on consumer choices regarding sustainable foods, particularly through the application of stated preference methods and a specific focus on both established and emerging environmentally friendly labels. Moreover, the study offers insights into how to enhance sustainable food consumption through targeting altruistic consumer subgroups and emphasizing the importance of fairtrade and organic foods over newer green labels. However, it is worth noting that our survey was conducted during the pandemic period, which could potentially impact our empirical findings since consumer preferences for sustainable labels may also have been influenced.

Author Contributions

Conceptualization, H.L.; Methodology, W.L.; Formal analysis, H.L. and W.L.; Investigation, W.L.; Resources, H.L.; Writing—original draft, H.L. and W.L.; Writing—review & editing, W.L.; Visualization, H.L. All authors have read and agreed to the published version of the manuscript.

Funding

This work was supported by the National Natural Science Foundation of China (No. 72003118, No. 72103180, and No. 72141303).

Data Availability Statement

Available upon reasonable request.

Conflicts of Interest

The authors declare no conflict of interest.

References

Pocol, C. B., Amuza, A., Moldovan, M.-G., Stanca, L., & Dabija, D.-C. (1973). Consequences of recent crises on the FLW consumer behaviour: A national wide representative research—The case of Romania. *Foods, 2023*, 12.

Crippa, M. E., Solazzo, D., Guizzardi, F., Monforti-Ferrario, F. N., Tubiello, F. N., & Leip, A. (2021). Food systems are responsible for a third of global anthropogenic GHG emissions. *Nature Food, 2*, 198–209.

Lin, W., & Nayga, R. M., Jr. (2022). Green identity labeling, environmental information, and pro-environmental food choices. *Food Policy, 106*, 102187.

Bukchin, S., & Kerret, D. (2018). Food for hope: The role of personal resources in farmers' adoption of green technology. *Sustainability, 10*, 1615.

Devi, P. I., Solomon, S. S., & Jayasree, M. G. (2015). Green technologies for sustainable agriculture: Policy options towards farmer adoption. *Indian Journal Of Agricultural Economics, 69*, 414–425.

Gao, Y., Zhao, D., Yu, L., & Yang, H. (2020). Influence of a new agricultural technology extension mode on farmers' technology adoption behavior in China. *Journal of Rural Studies, 76*, 173–183.

Becchetti, L., & Huybrechts, B. (2008). The dynamics of fair trade as a mixed-form market. *Journal of Business Ethics, 81*, 733–750.

Canavari, M., Bazzani, G. M., Spadoni, R., & Regazzi, D. (2002). Food safety and organic fruit demand in Italy: A survey. *British Food Journal, 104*, 220–232.

Hu, W., Woods, T., & Bastin, S. (2009). Consumer acceptance and willingness to pay for blueberry products with noncon-ventional attributes. *Journal of Agricultural and Applied Economics, 41*, 47–60.

Lazaroiu, G., Andronie, M., Uța, C., & Hurloiu, I. (2019). Trust management in organic agriculture: Sustainable consumption behavior, environmentally conscious purchase intention, and healthy food choices. *Frontiers in Public Health, 7*, 340.

Thøgersen, J., & Zhou, Y. (2012). Chinese consumers' adoption of a 'green'innovation–The case of organic food. *Journal of Marketing Management, 28*, 313–333.

Van Loo, E. J., Caputo, V., Nayga, R. M., Jr., Meullenet, J. F., & Ricke, S. C. (2011). Consumers' willingness to pay for organic chicken breast: Evidence from choice experiment. *Food Quality and Preference, 22*, 603–613.

Van Loo, E. J., Caputo, V., Nayga, R. M., Jr., Seo, H. S., Zhang, B., & Verbeke, W. (2015). Sustainability labels on coffee: Consumer preferences, willingness-to-pay and visual attention to attributes. *Ecological Economics, 118*, 215–225.

de Boer, J., Hoogland, C. T., & Boersema, J. J. (2007). Towards more sustainable food choices: Value priorities and motivational orientations. *Food Quality and Preference, 18*, 985–996.

Olesen, I., Alfnes, F., Røra, M. B., & Kolstad, K. (2010). Eliciting consumers' willingness to pay for organic and welfare-labelled salmon in a non-hypothetical choice experiment. *Livestock Science, 127*, 218–226.

Verbeke, W., & Roosen, J. (2009). Market differentiation potential of country-of-origin, quality and traceability labeling. *The Estey Centre Journal of International Law and Trade Policy, 10*, 20–35.

Echeverría, R., Moreira, V. H., Sepólveda, C., & Wittwer, C. (2014). Willingness to pay for carbon footprint on foods. *British Food Journal, 116*, 186–196.

Gadema, Z., & Oglethorpe, D. (2011). The use and usefulness of carbon labelling food: A policy perspective from a survey of UK supermarket shoppers. *Food Policy, 36*, 815–822.

Kimura, A., Wada, Y., Kamada, A., Masuda, T., Okamoto, M., Goto, S. I., & Dan, I. (2010). Interactive effects of carbon foot-print information and its accessibility on value and subjective qualities of food products. *Appetite, 55*, 271–278.

Lohmann, P. M., Gsottbauer, E., Doherty, A., & Kontoleon, A. (2022). Do carbon footprint labels promote climatarian diets? Evidence from a large-scale field experiment. *Journal of Environmental Economics and Management, 114*, 102693.

Zhang, Y., Jin, S., & Lin, W. (2023). Would consumers help achieve sustainable development in the Qinghai–Tibet Plateau with a forage– livestock balance certification label? *China Agricultural Economic Review, 15*, 345–374.

Neuhofer, Z. T., Lusk, J. L., & Villas-Boas, S. (2023). Can a sustainability facts label reduce the halo surrounding organic labels. In *Applied economic perspectives and policy*. Wiley.

Sogari, G., Caputo, V., Petterson, A. J., Mora, C., & Boukid, F. (2023). A sensory study on consumer valuation for plant-based meat alternatives: What is liked and disliked the most? *Food Research International, 169*, 112813.

Bryant, C., & Sanctorum, H. (2021). Alternative proteins, evolving attitudes: Comparing consumer attitudes to plant-based and cultured meat in Belgium in two consecutive years. *Appetite, 161*, 105161.

Judge, M., & Wilson, M. S. (2019). A dual-process motivational model of attitudes towards vegetarians and vegans. *European Journal of Social Psychology, 49*, 169–178.

Malek, L., Umberger, W. J., & Goddard, E. (2019). Committed vs. uncommitted meat eaters: Understanding willingness to change protein consumption. *Appetite, 138*, 115–126.

Hartmann, C., & Siegrist, M. (2017). Consumer perception and behaviour regarding sustainable protein consumption: A systematic review. *Trends in Food Science and Technology, 61*, 11–25.

Lemken, D., Spiller, A., & Schulze-Ehlers, B. (2019). More room for legume–Consumer acceptance of meat substitution with classic, processed and meat-resembling legume products. *Appetite, 143*, 104412.

De Marchi, E., Caputo, V., Nayga, R. M., & Banterle, A. (2016). Time preferences and food choices: Evidence from a choice experiment. *Food Policy, 62*, 99–109.

Guan, L., Huang, Z., & Jin, S. (2022). Time preference and nutrition label use: Evidence from China. *Economics and Human Biology, 47*, 101184.

Ben-Ner, A., & Hu, F. (2018). The bright and dark sides of altruism. In *The economics of philanthropy: donations and fundraising*. MIT Press.

Wang, P., Liu, Q., & Qi, Y. (2014). Factors influencing sustainable consumption behaviors: A survey of the rural residents in China. *Journal of Cleaner Production, 63*, 152–165.

Yarimoglu, E., & Binboga, G. (2019). Understanding sustainable consumption in an emerging country: The antecedents and consequences of the ecologically conscious consumer behavior model. *Business Strategy and the Environment, 28*, 642–651.

Birch, D., Memery, J., & de Silva Kanakaratne, M. (2018). The mindful consumer: Balancing egoistic and altruistic motivations to purchase local food. *Journal of Retailing and Consumer Services, 40*, 221–228.

Yadav, R. (2016). Altruistic or egoistic: Which value promotes organic food consumption among young consumers? A study in the context of a developing nation. *Journal of Retailing and Consumer Services, 33*, 92–97.

Poore, J., & Nemecek, T. (2018). Reducing food's environmental impacts through producers and consumers. *Science, 360*, 987–992.

Burgess, L., & Street, D. J. (2005). Optimal designs for choice experiments with asymmetric attributes. *Journal of Statistical Planning and Inference, 134*, 288–301.

Lusk, J. L., & Briggeman, B. C. (2009). Food values. *American Journal of Agricultural Economics, 91*, 184–196.

Dunlap, R. E. (2008). The new environmental paradigm scale: From marginality to worldwide use. *The Journal of Environmental Education, 40*, 3–18.

Poe, G. L., Giraud, K. L., & Loomis, J. B. (2005). Computational methods for measuring the difference of empirical distributions. *American Journal of Agricultural Economics, 87*, 353–365.

Asioli, D., Bazzani, C., & Nayga, R. M., Jr. (2022). Are consumers willing to pay for in-vitro meat? An investigation of naming effects. *The Journal of Agricultural Economics, 73*, 356–375.

de Magistris, T., & Gracia, A. (2008). The decision to buy organic food products in Southern Italy. *British Food Journal, 110*, 929–947.

Smed, S. (2012). Information and consumer perception of the "organic" attribute in fresh fruits and vegetables. *Agricultural Economics, 43*, 33–48.

Durham, C. A., & Andrade, D. Health vs. environmental motivation in organic preferences and purchases. In *Proceedings of the AAEA conference*, Providence, RI, 24–27 July 2005.

Moore, G. (2004). The fairtrade movement: Parameters, issues and future research. *Journal of Business Ethics, 53*, 73–86.

de Morais, L. H. L., Pinto, D. C., & Cruz-Jesus, F. (2021). Circular economy engagement: Altruism, status, and cultural orienta-tion as drivers for sustainable consumption. *Sustainable Production and Consumption, 27*, 523–533.

Dermody, J., Koenig-Lewis, N., Zhao, A. L., & Hanmer-Lloyd, S. (2018). Appraising the influence of pro-environmental self-identity on sustainable consumption buying and curtailment in emerging markets: Evidence from China and Poland. *Journal of Business Research, 86*, 333–343.

Mansoor, M., & Paul, J. (2022). Consumers' choice behavior: An interactive effect of expected eudaimonic well-being and green altruism. *Business Strategy and the Environment, 31*, 94–109.

Park, C., Lee, S., Lee, C. K., & Reisinger, Y. (2022). Volunteer tourists' environmentally friendly behavior and support for sustainable tourism development using Value-Belief-Norm theory: Moderating role of altruism. *Journal of Destination Marketing and Management, 25*, 100712.

Boobalan, K., Nawaz, N., Harindranath, R. M., & Gajenderan, V. (2021). Influence of altruistic motives on organic food purchase: Theory of planned behavior. *Sustainability, 13*, 6023.

Mesic, Ž., Petljak, K., Borovic, D., & Tomic, M. (2021). Segmentation of local food consumers based on altruistic motives and perceived purchasing barriers: A Croatian study. *Economic Research-Ekonomska Istraživanja, 34*, 221–242.

Chapter 13
Green Identity Labeling, Environmental Information, and Pro-environmental Food Choices

13.1 Introduction

Confronted with increased urgency to combat environmental problems, information provision that promotes sustainable behaviors that might improve social welfare have attracted attention in the environmental policy debate as well as in recent literature. Information could foster pro-environmental behavior in several ways, such as by increasing environmental cognitive salience (Kurz, 2018; Wensing et al., 2020; Becchetti et al., 2020; Edenbrandt et al., 2021), by comparing people's behavior with their peers' morally (Allcott, 2011; Ferraro & Price, 2013; Myers & Souza, 2020), and by reducing search cost via ecolabeling (Teisl et al., 2002; Loureiro, 2003; Roheim & Zhang, 2018). There is scant research, however, investigating label information based on green consumer identity. The green identity label communicates that "green" consumers prefer pro-environmental products by stating that "this product is for green shoppers" (Schwartz et al., 2020). There exists two possible impacts of this message on pro-environmental behavior: first, for individuals with implicit pro-environmental perception or preference, a green identity label could steer them into making choices consistent with their self-perception given the postulate by self-perception theory that individuals come to know their own attitudes through their behaviors (Allen, 1982); second, people care about their self-image and prefer to see themselves as "good" (Battaglini et al., 2005), implying that even for those without green preferences, people seeing this label are likely to strive to behave in an environmentally friendly manner.

Despite its potential and ease of implementation, green identity labeling has rarely been applied to promote sustainable behavior, especially in the domain of food consumption. Focusing on non-food settings, existing work has shown inconclusive results on the efficacy of green identity labeling. Some studies have found that providing consumers with a green identity label for their behaviors or preferences increases the choices of eco-friendly products, including compact fluorescent

W. Lin, *Transforming China's Agri-Food System: Government-Market Synergy*, Resources, Environment and Agricultural Development,
https://doi.org/10.1007/978-981-95-7151-2_13

light bulbs, reusable bags, and energy or/and water saving appliances (Schwartz et al., 2020). Another strand of papers, in contrast, concluded limited impact of green identity label on promoting environmental donations (Eby et al., 2019) and environmentally friendly television (Cornelissen et al., 2007).

Whether green identity labels would enhance consumer preferences for sustainable food remains an empirical question to be examined. The purchasing cost of pro-environmental foods is higher relative to conventional ones, implying that the efficacy of the labeling might be undermined by consumer's budget constraint. On the other side, pro-environmental food choices would be more receptive to a green identity label communicating a person's attitudes or actions. Sustainable foods include credence attributes that are difficult to verify even after consumption (Darby & Karni, 1973), whose purchase is largely influenced by individual attitude, value, and perception (Grunert, 2005; Goddard et al., 2013; Lassoued & Hobbs, 2015). To fill this void in the literature, we investigate the effect of green identity labels in nudging carbon emission reduction given the analysis that the food system is responsible for one-third of the global anthropogenic greenhouse gas emission (Crippa et al., 2021; Tubiello et al., 2021).

In addition to exploring the green identity label, this study supplements the literature by evaluating the effectiveness of an environmental information provision and its combined use with green identity labels in promoting green food consumption. The comparison of the efficacy of different types of information provision has important implications for information-based policy design as well as welfare effects. To this end, a discrete choice experiment and a between-subject design approach are employed to assess the impact of information interventions on increasing consumer valuation for sustainable products in the choice tasks. We randomly assign respondents to one of four treatments. The first treatment represents the control group without any information intervention. The second treatment attaches a green identity label to sustainable product in choice tasks, while the third treatment provides environmental information of food products prior to choice questions. The last treatment combines the second and third treatments. Environmentally friendly food behavior is elicited with a discrete choice experiment conducted on US respondents. Prices in choice experiments are varied exogenously across product attributes (referring to USDA organic, fair-trade and carbon trust labels in our case), which enables us to estimate the effect of information provision in a setting where behavioral channels, instead of pecuniary incentives, are the primary mechanisms that affect consumer food preferences. We find that green identity labeling in itself may be ineffective in increasing consumer valuation of sustainable labels in food settings. Nevertheless, our result reveals that provision of environmental information and its combined use with green identity labels can be promising behavioral policy tools that can guide consumers to prefer and value pro-environmental foods more.

Moving beyond studying the average effects of green nudges, this study also explores heterogeneous responses across individuals to our treatments. Understanding such heterogeneity offers important policy insights since the information can assist policy makers to more cost-effectively target the treatments to more responsive subgroups, and meanwhile to avoid subgroups that may react in ways contrary to the policy objective (Heckman et al., 1997; Ferraro & Miranda, 2013). Our findings demonstrate that the treatment has high efficacy among younger, low-income subjects and individuals with graduate degrees. Further, such impacts seem product specific. The valuation of existing sustainable labels such as organic and fair trade certifications is receptive to green nudges while almost null effects are found for the carbon trust label, which remains uncommon in the US marketplace. A better understanding of treatment heterogeneity is important for improving the cost-effectiveness of behavioral policy tools.

13.2 Study Design

13.2.1 Choice Set Design

We design and implement an online choice experiment to elicit US consumers' valuation for environmentally friendly food products. Despite the controversy surrounding choice experiments such as hypothetical bias (Carlsson et al., 2005; Hensher, 2010; De-Magistris et al., 2013), the method is by far the most used stated preference technique for various reasons: theoretical consistency, flexibility in allowing participants to opt out of making a choice, and the ability to elicit trade-offs among a broad set of attributes (Louviere et al., 2000, 2010). Choice experiment enables us to incorporate environmental information treatments in an easy fashion. In the choice experiment, participants are presented with multiple decision scenarios or tasks and are asked to select the product option or alternative that they most prefer. Each decision scenario or choice set is comprised of several product alternatives with experimentally designed attribute levels as well asano-purchase option to simulate real market situation. We use a 12 oz. roasted ground coffee as the product of interest in this study for two reasons. First, the coffee industry is a pioneering industry for environmentally friendly certification schemes, and it has become the model for other commodities (Reinecke et al., 2012). Second, 12 oz. roasted ground coffee is the most common type of coffee consumed in the United States (Van Loo et al., 2015).[1]

In the experimental design, USDA organic, fair trade, and carbon trust labels as well as price have been selected as the product attributes to characterize environmentally friendly coffee. Organic and fair trade labeled coffee are already in the marketplace. The first organic coffee was produced in 1967, and coffee was the first fairtrade labeled product in the market that started in 1989 (Grieg-Gran, 2005). Coffee remains one of the most popular fairtrade products in the market. In addition to the two existing environmentally friendly labels, we introduce a relatively novel label to US consumers, i.e., a carbon trust label. This is because coffee is a significant greenhouse gas emitter among foods, ranked only after beef, lamb, and

[1] We refer readers to Van Loo et al. (2015) for an overview of sustainable labels on coffee.

chocolate (Poore & Nemecek, 2018). Carbon trust labeled coffee indicates that the company commits to reducing the carbon footprint in their coffee products. The three non-price coffee attributes are denoted in the statistical model as dummy variables, taking the value of one when the coffee product carries such an attribute, and zero otherwise. The price levels used in the design include \$4.95, \$7.45, \$9.95, and \$12.45, which reflect the range of market prices at the time of this study. Table 13.1 provides a summary of the selected product attributes and attribute levels.

Given our design specifications, a full factorial design with two product alternatives in a choice set would require 1024 ($4^{2\times1} \times 2^{2\times3}$) different choice scenarios. To reduce the number of choice tasks shown to respondents during the survey, and consequently reduce choice fatigue and improve response quality, we obtained a practical set of 32 choice sets with a D-efficiency 97.21% using the generators described by Burgess and Street (2005) and Street et al. (2005). The 32 choice sets are further randomly grouped into 4 blocks, with eight choice sets per block. Each choice set includes two product alternatives with experimentally designed attribute levels and a no-purchase or opt-out option. To avoid any ordering effects that may confound our result, the 8 choice sets are randomly shown to respondents. The order upon which the two product alternatives within each choice set are also randomly varied as well to mitigate left–right bias (Chrzan, 1994), which has been reported as an effect by stated preference studies (Campbell & Erdem, 2015; Matthews et al., 2017). A sample choice set is shown in Fig. 13.1.

To mitigate potential hypothetical bias, prior to the choice experiment questions, we give respondents a cheap-talk script following Cummings and Taylor (1999) and List (2001) (see Appendix A for the script). We also provide a detailed description of the three non-price attributes to respondents (Appendix B) to help individuals better evaluate the product alternatives.

Table 13.1 Attributes and attribute levels in the choice set design

Attributes	Levels
USDA organic label	USDA ORGANIC
	No label
Fairtrade label	FAIRTRADE
	No label
Carbon Trust label	reducing with the Carbon Trust CO2
	No label
Price (USD per 12 oz)	4.95, 7.45, 9.95, 12.45

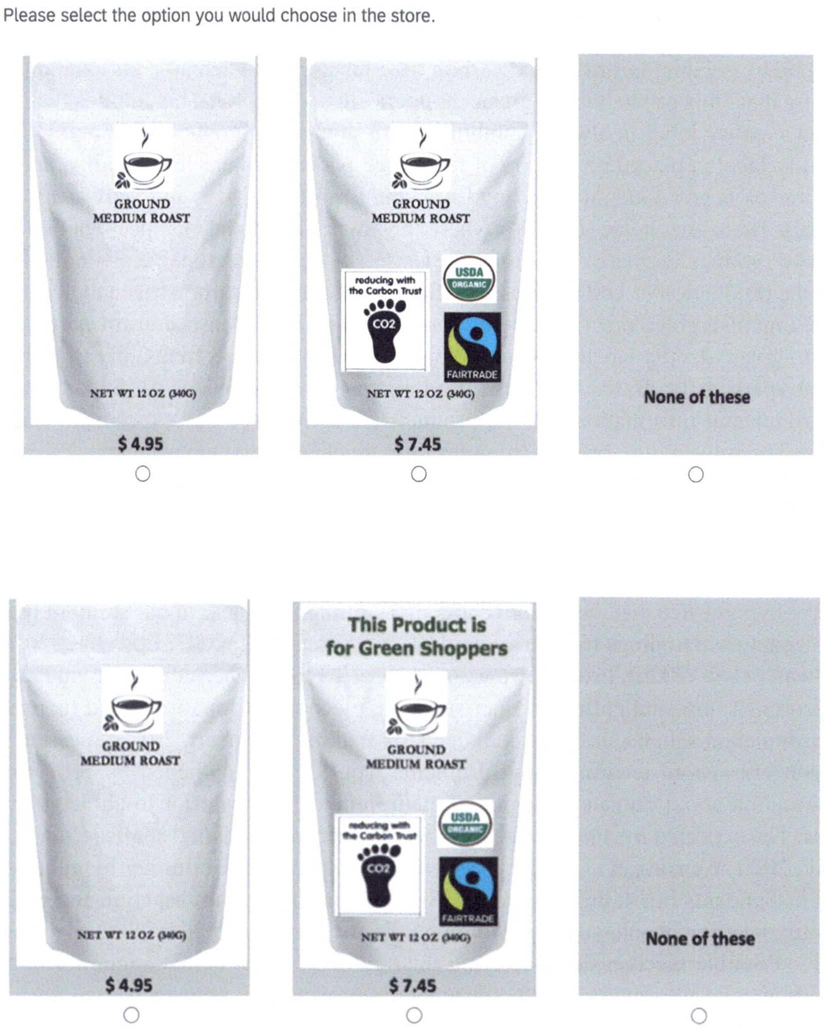

Fig. 13.1 Sample choice sets. Note: the upper panel represents a sample choice set in the control group (T1), and the lower panel shows the sample in T2

13.2.2 Treatment Design and Research Hypotheses

To examine the effectiveness of different environmental information provision, we employed a between-subject approach where respondents are randomly assigned to one of four treatments. The first treatment (T1) refers to the choice experiment described in the above section, without additional information provided. In the second treatment (T2), if the product alternative in a choice task carries at least one of the USDA organic, fairtrade, and carbon trust labels, we attach an additional claim stating that "this product is for green shoppers" in green color. This implies that the green identity label is always combined with non-price product attribute(s). The identity label is placed on the top of the coffee package to ensure visibility, and is referred to as green identity labeling following Eby et al. (2019) and Schwartz et al. (2020). There are choice scenarios where the green identity label appears in both of the two product alternatives within a choice set, but this is reasonable given the fact that the production of USDA organic coffee, fair trade, and carbon trust labeled coffee all involve green practices and/or consequences. In this case, consumers receptive to green identity labeling would select opt-out options less frequently than their counterparts in T1. Based on T1, the third treatment (T3) provides participants with environmental information of food products prior to the choice experiment questions. The information briefly discusses climate change and environmental issues, how food production contributes to these concerns, and how humans could help address them by making environmentally friendly food choices (see Appendix C). In the last treatment (T4), we combine the second and the third treatments, providing subjects with environmental information as well as the green identity label.

We hypothesize that the effectiveness of T2 remains unclear in our study in light of inconclusive findings from prior work (Cornelissen et al., 2007; Eby et al., 2019; Schwartz et al., 2020). Instead, we would expect T3 to enhance consumer valuation of pro-environmental coffee product since the piece of information could increase environmental salience in individual decision-making (Schubert, 2017). Awareness or concerns about environmental problems would be strengthened by providing information about climate change and environmental issues prior to choice questions. The expected treatment effect of T3 is confirmed by existing studies (Van Loo et al., 2020; Wensing et al., 2020; Edenbrandt et al., 2021). We further hypothesize that respondents in T4, the treatment with the environmental information and green identity labeling, would value environmentally friendly food higher relative to those in T3. Possible mechanism underlying the treatment effect is that communicating environmental information with consumers improves their knowledge and awareness about environmental consequences of food production, and that this in turn increases the salience of the green identity label. Respondents might also be more likely and willing to label themselves as green shoppers after being exposed to environmental information.

13.2.3 Survey Design

Our survey consists of two parts. The first part involves hypothetical choice tasks as we describe in the last section, and the second part includes questions on demographics such as age, gender, income, and education. We employ several strategies in the survey to improve the reliability of the responses in hypothetical choice scenarios and overall quality of data. First, we employ a cheap talk script to hopefully reduce potential hypothetical bias as discussed earlier. Second, at the beginning of the survey, we ask respondents to commit to read the questions carefully and provide honest answers, and those who failed to make such a commitment were excluded from our analysis following Elias et al. (2019). We also insert attention checks to screen out inattentive participants. Before survey implementation, we preregistered this research at the Wharton School of the University of Pennsylvania's Credibility Lab[2] for randomized controlled trials.

13.3 Econometric Model

To model consumers' coffee purchasing decisions, we specify an indirect utility function based on Lancaster's theory of consumer demand (Lancaster, 1966). Following random utility theory (McFadden, 1974), choice experiments rely on the assumption that the utility of individual n choosing alternative j in choice situation t can be expressed as:

$$\begin{aligned} U_{njt} &= V_{njt} + \varepsilon_{njt} = \alpha Price_{njt} + \beta_{n1} Organics_{njt} + \beta_{n2} Fairtrade_{njt} \\ &+ \beta_{n3} Carbtrust_{njt} + ASC_{Opt-out} + \varepsilon_{njt} \end{aligned}$$

where V_{njt} is the systematic portion of the utility function, depending on the experimentally designed product attributes of alternative j. $Price_{njt}$ is a continuous variable populated with the four price levels in the design; $Organics_{njt}$, $Fairtrade_{njt}$ and $Carbtrust_{njt}$are dummy variables for USDA organic, fair trade, and carbon trust certifications, respectively. They all take a value of 1 when the product carries such an attribute, and 0 otherwise. $ASC_{Opt-out}$ is the alternative specific constant of the opt-out option, which is invariant in the population; α is price preference and the β s are the non-price taste coefficients. And ε_{njt} is the stochastic and unobservable (to researchers) component.

We estimate amixed logit model in which consumer tastes vary with respect to unobserved variables. It is a highly flexible model that can approximate any random utility model (McFadden & Train, 2000). Accordingly, ε_{njt} is the random error term that follows a Type I Extreme Value distribution. The coefficients of the three non-price product attributes are assumed random following normal distributions since either positive or negative values would expectedly be placedby individuals on the attributes. We specify a fixed price coefficient to obtain reasonable and finite distributions of WTPs (Hensher et al., 2005; Matthews et al., 2017). In addition, we allow for a flexible pattern of correlation between random parameters (Hess & Train, 2017) to account for the cases that a consumer who favors organic labeled coffee

[2] See https://aspredicted.org/, with ID number 39419. The registration form is available on request.

products may also prefer fair trade or carbon trust certifications. Therefore, in a mixed logit model, the unconditional choice probability of individual n choosing alternative j in choice situation t can be expressed as:

$$P_{njt} = \int_{\beta} \frac{e^{V_{njt}}}{\sum_{k} e^{V_{njt}}} f\left(\beta|,\alpha|,ASC_{Opt-out}|,\overline{\beta},\Omega\right) d\beta \tag{13.1}$$

where $f\left(\beta|\alpha, ASC_{Opt-out}, \overline{\beta},\Omega\right)$ is the density function of the vector of random coefficients. β and Ω govern the distributions of random coefficients, denoting the means and the variance–covariance matrix of the vector of random coefficients, respectively. The model is estimated based on simulated maximum likelihood estimation with 1000 Halton draws in R.

We test the treatment effect by comparing the distribution of unconditional WTP across the four groups. The distribution is derived with Monte Carlo simulation (Krinsky & Robb, 1986) using the variance–covariance matrix (Ω) obtained from estimating Eq. (13.1). The non-parametric complete combinatorial test suggested by Poe et al. (2005) is used to test for WTP equality between treatments. We then turn to explore the heterogeneity in the responsiveness of green nudges by matching demographics with individual specific or conditional WTPs.

13.4 Data

The survey was administered in May 2020 using an online opt-in consumer panel drawn from Survey Sampling International. To qualify, individuals must have been 18 years of age and have purchased coffee products in the last 2 months. Individuals who could not promise to provide truthful answers, failed attention check questions, or completed the survey out of 95% confidence interval of survey time are excluded from our analysis. Note that these criteria for sampleselection have been documented in our pre-registration form prior to survey implementation. A nationwide[3] sample of 1034 respondents were collected, with 304 in T1, 323 in T2, 336 in T3, and 341 in T4. The participants, on average, took 13 min to complete the survey, and 95% of the sample finished it in<25 min.

Table 13.2 describes the sample and provides a balance check across treatment groups. Around half the sample is female (47%), employed full-time or part-time (54%), and at least holds a college degree (51%). The average age is 50 years, and average household size is 3.5 persons. The majority of the sample is white and has family income higher than $40,000 (70%). In terms of political orientation, nearly 50% identified themselves as moderate, 27% as liberal, and 26% as conservative. Our sample is comparable to the general US sample in terms of gender and

[3] Participants in our sample live in all 50 states across US, with 22% in the Northeast, 24% in the Midwest, 26% in the South and the remaining 28% in the West.

Table 13.2 Balance test across treatment groups

		T1 = Control	T2 = Green Identity label	T3 = Environmental information	T4 = T2 + T3	p-value[a]
Variable	Definition	Mean	Mean	Mean	Mean	
Female	1 = Yes	0.45	0.43	0.46	0.53	0.038
	0 = No	(0.50)	(0.50)	(0.50)	(0.50)	
Age	Year	50.91 (16.91)	50.98 (17.26)	48.74 (17.51)	49.64 (17.64)	0.285
Income	1 = <$40 K, 2 = $40 K-$79 K …	2.30	2.29	2.28	2.33	0.994
	to 5= > $160 K	(1.14)	(1.17)	(1.12)	(1.18)	
Education	0 = <College, 1 = College,	0.67	0.67	0.69	0.72	0.895
	2 = Graduate	(0.74)	(0.75)	(0.75)	(0.78)	
Household size	Person	3.47 (1.24)	3.64 (1.46)	3.48 (1.24)	3.38 (1.16)	0.295
Political view	1 = Liberal, 2 = Moderate,	2.05	2.06	2.05	1.98	0.468
	3 = Conservative, 4 = Other	(0.77)	(0.80)	(0.78)	(0.77)	
Religion	1 = Yes, 0 = No	0.77 (0.42)	0.81 (0.39)	0.74 (0.44)	0.75 (0.43)	0.143
White	1 = Yes, 0 = No	0.68 (0.47)	0.68 (0.47)	0.72 (0.45)	0.68 (0.47)	0.577
Employment	1 = Full time,	2.09	2.10	2.11	2.11	0.944
	2 = Part time,	(1.04)	(1.02)	(1.04)	(1.06)	
	3 = Unemployed, 4 = Other					
Observations	Person	304	323	336	341	

Note: numbers in parentheses are standard deviations

[a]p-values are from chi-square tests testing the null hypothesis of indifference between groups ofvariables across treatments. We perform Kruskal Wallis tests on most variables except for income, education, political view and employment for which Pearson's chi-squared tests are employed

ethnicity. In the US population, there are 50% female, 76% white, and slightly over 30% holding a bachelor's degree or higher, with a household size of 2.6 persons (US Census Bureau 2019). Compared to the population statistics, our sample is generally older, well-educated, and has a larger household size. Yet this is not unexpected, given that the study recruited adult participants and was conducted online; it is reasonable to expect internet users to be better educated. As a result of random assignment of the treatments, for each of the demographics, the null hypothesis of same distributions across the treatment groups cannot be rejected ($p > 0.100$ for all chi-square tests), with exceptions for gender. Although there are no significant differences in gender among T1, T2, and T3 with a p-value of 0.451, T4 has slightly more female subjects relative to other treatments. Looking at the counts of individuals selecting opt-out and high-priced options across eight choice scenarios (Table 13.3), it can be noted that the respondents in T4 differ significantly from their counterparts in other treatments. They are less likely to purchase neither of the coffee products, and they tend to be less price sensitive with higher frequency of selecting the high-priced option.

13.5 Results

13.5.1 The Effect of Environmental Information Treatments on Consumer WTP

To test the efficacy of our treatments on consumer valuation of pro-environmental coffee labels, we estimate Eq. (13.1) in mixed logit models for each treatment, and then simulate WTP values with the estimates of model parameters and the variance–covariance matrix obtained from estimating Eq. (13.1). Table 13.4 reports the estimation of the four mixed logit models. As conjectured, all product attributes significantly affect consumer coffee selection, with expected signs of all coefficients. Across the four models, organic coffee claim is preferred most by respondents, followed by fair trade and carbon trust labels, despite strong heterogeneity in

Table 13.3 Choice frequency across treatment

	T1 = Control	T2 = Green Identity label	T3 = Environmental information	T4 = T2 + T3
Opt-out option	1.128	1.118	0.991	0.930**
High-priced option	(0.105) 2.931 (0.076)	(0.099) 2.938 (0.076)	(0.095) 3.000 (0.078)	(0.091) 3.182*** (0.076)
Observations	304	323	336	341

Note: Numbers in parentheses are standard errors. Asterisks indicate the significance level calculated by the *t*-test in differences between the control (T1) and corresponding treatment group at the conventional levels of $^{**}p < 0.05$ and $^{***}p < 0.01$

Table 13.4 Mixed logit models across treatments

	T1 = Control		T2 = Green Identity label	T3 = Environmental information	T4 = T2 + T3	
	Coef.	Z-value	Coef. Z-value	Coef. Z-value	Coef.	Z-value
Price	− 0.555***	− 22.636	− 0.535*** − 23.325	− 0.519*** − 22.330	− 0.467***	− 21.537
ASCOpt − out	− 5.435***	− 23.814	− 5.365*** − 24.862	− 5.193*** − 24.080	− 4.818***	− 23.534
Organics	0.689***	5.787	0.748*** 6.766	0.919*** 7.753	0.858***	7.672
Fair trade	0.393***	3.629	0.426*** 4.556	0.558*** 5.992	0.564***	5.760
Carbon trust	0.472***	4.649	0.191** 2.016	0.350*** 3.326	0.461***	4.604
SD. Organics	1.563***	12.484	1.466*** 12.316	1.596*** 13.285	1.550***	13.045
SD. Organics. Fair trade	0.275*	1.797	0.516*** 3.865	0.338** 2.693	0.205	1.423
SD. Organics. Carbon trust	0.576***	4.266	0.533*** 3.981	0.374** 2.548	0.499***	3.569
SD. Fair trade	1.306***	10.771	0.892*** 7.070	0.921*** 7.872	1.186***	10.488
SD. Fair trade. Carbon trust	0.272*	1.855	0.421** 2.453	0.705*** 3.356	0.664***	4.375
SD. Carbon trust	0.893***	7.071	0.764*** 4.866	1.048*** 5.801	0.867***	5.818
Observations	2432		2584	2688	2728	
Log-likelihood	− 1695.7		− 1781.4	− 1815.8	− 1893.9	

Note: models were estimated using 1000 Halton draws for simulations in R. Asterisks indicate significant differences at the conventional levels of *$p < 0.1$, $p < 0.05$, and ***$p < 0.01$

these preferences between subjects. Evidenced by the significant and positive correlation coefficients, consumers who favor carbon trust labeled coffee more would exhibit stronger preferences for organic coffee and fair trade coffee. However, the correlation between the preference of organic label and that of fair trade label is relatively weak.

Table 13.5 reveals the simulated means and 90% confidence interval of the WTP values, as well as the Poe test results for the equality in the WTP distributions between treatments. The table demonstrates several important points. First, on average, consumers in the control group (T1) would like to pay $1.25, $0.70, and $0.85 per 12 oz. for USDA organics, fair trade, and carbon trust labeled coffee, respectively. The values are similar to the result by Van Loo et al. (2015) showing the WTP of US consumers is $1.16 for organic coffee and $0.68 for fair trade coffee. Corresponding with our finding about coffee purchases, previous work reveals that carbon trust certification is less responsible for increasing US respondents' utility in food productselection (De Marchi et al., 2020; Asioli et al., 2018), relative to organic logo, antibiotic-free claim or conventional production method. The significant valuation found in the organic label could be attributed to consumers' perceived health and environmental benefits of organic foods (De Magistris & Gracia, 2008; Lusk & Briggeman, 2009; Smed, 2012). Consumers' perception that organic foods are healthier than the conventional food represents an important motive behind organic food consumption (Hughner et al., 2007). Some suggested that environmental concern is more influential than health in consumers' decision to purchase organic foods, in the context of US consumers' choice of organic fruit and vegetables (Durham & Andrade, 2005).

Second, the provision of environmental information (T3) would promote consumer valuation for organic and fair trade labels. The estimated treatment effect of T3 is $0.50 and $0.40 for organic and fair trade labels, respectively. This result implies that relative to the control group, an average individual in the third treatment increases the valuations by 40% for organic coffee and 57% for fair trade coffee.

Table 13.5 Simulated WTP across treatment, $/12 oz

		Organics		Fair trade		Carbon trust	
	Observations	Mean	90% C.I.	Mean	90% C.I.	Mean	90% C.I.
T1 = Control	304	1.248	[0.856, 1.690]	0.699	[0.357, 1.052]	0.849	[0.546, 1.162]
T2 = Green Identity label	323	1.404	[1.019, 1.792]	0.792	[0.492, 1.099]	0.356***	[0.161, 0.648]
T3 = Environmental information	336	1.769**	[1.342, 2.185]	1.079**	[0.770, 1.400]	0.676	[0.323, 1.037]
T4 = T2 + T3	341	1.833**	[1.355, 2.283]	1.210***	[0.827, 1.605]	0.989	[0.625, 1.373]

Note: Asterisks indicate the significance level of differences between the control (T1) and corresponding treatment group calculated by the Poe test (Poe et al., 2005). *, **, and *** indicate statistical significance at the 10%, 5%, and 1% levels, respectively

Information plays a role because it likely improves consumer environmental knowledge, and/or because it increases consumer sensitivity to pro-environmental products. Our finding is in line with the studies that have shown the impact of information in promoting sustainable food consumption (Lusk et al., 2004; Van Loo et al., 2020; Wensing et al., 2020; Edenbrandt et al., 2021).

Notably, T3 is effective only among existing pro-environmental coffee products rather than novel ones, meaning product specific impact of environmental information. Despite the significant increase exhibited in the WTPs for organic and fairtrade coffee when participants have been exposed to environmental information, consumer valuation of a carbon trust label is similar between T1 and T3. This result is consistent with findings from Kaminski and Caputo (2018) and Wensing et al. (2020) suggesting that environmental information has a stronger effect on consumers' WTP for already established sustainability labels than on a novel label. This could be explained by "familiarity bias", suggesting that individuals prefer familiar goods, others being equal (Tversky & Kahneman, 1974; Lin & Chen, 2006; Cao et al., 2011). Although we provided the description on carbon trust, organic and fair trade claims before the choice experiment, that description may not close the information and/or experience gap between carbon trust label and the others for our subjects. Organic and fairtrade coffee have along history in the marketplace; the first organic coffee was produced in 1967, and coffee became the first fair trade labeled product in 1989. In contrast to organic and fairtrade labels, carbon trust label is novel for US consumers who have not seen and purchased the product previously. It can be inferred from our findings that the environmental information is useful for nudging the purchases of more familiar products; that is, consumers react to information treatments by considering the products familiar to them, rather than those unfamiliar or novel. Our result bears important implications for the design and implementation of environmental information treatments.

Turning to the green identity labeling technique (T2), we find that this treatment is least successful among the three information treatments; moreover, it discourages consumers from purchasing carbon reduced coffee. In the second treatment, consumers' WTP values for organics and fair trade certified coffee products are not differentiated from their counterparts in the control group (T1), but they place a lower price premium on carbon trust label. Relative to the conventional coffee, average valuation for carbon reduced coffee is approximately \$0.36 per 12 oz. in T2, approximately half of that in T1 (\$0.85). This finding is not too surprising given the mixed results suggested by prior research in non-food settings (Cornelissen et al., 2007; Eby et al., 2019; Schwartz et al., 2020). Remember that unlike the provision of environmental information prior to the choice experiment questions, by design, within T2's choice scenarios, products are attached with an additional label, stating that "this product is for green shoppers" if the products carry at least one of the three attributes, that is, organic, fair trade, and carbon reduced claims. Therefore, a possible explanation about the null effect of green identity labels is that providing extra information by including an identity label on the product package distracts respondents' attention. Increased number of green-related labels potentially weakens the effect of green identity labels since it induces competition among labels (Asioli et al., 2020). Another potential explanation includes that respondents employ heuristics in decision-making in the context of choice experiments (Scarpa et al., 2009; Hensher et al., 2018). When confronted with an increased amount of information to be processed, respondents can experience cognitive burden, which can then increase the likelihood that they will use heuristics more frequently in their decision-making. One such heuristic is to stick with the status quo, that is, existing choices or those already known to people. In our case, individualsin T2 may focus more on existing products, substituting organic and fair trade coffee for carbon trust. This in part explains why there is an increase in WTPs for organic and fair trade labeled coffee (though not statistically significant), and meanwhile a reduction in the valuation of carbon trust claim.

Lastly, the joint use of green identity label and environmental information (T4) exerts the largest impact on guiding consumers toward green food consumption, as evidenced by the most notable increases in consumers' WTPs for sustainable coffee products in T4, relative to T1. On average, T4 respondents would place a remarkable amount of money on environmentally friendly coffee, with $1.8 for organic and $1.2 for fair trade coffee. The treatment, nevertheless, fails to achieve the same goal for carbon trust labeled coffee, with no significant difference in the WTP between T4 and T1, suggesting that parallel to the result of T3, T4's impact is again product specific. The impact found in T4 further reveals that the use of environmental information and green identity labels would potentially be complementary. Possible underlying mechanisms include that communicating environmental information with consumers improves their knowledge and awareness about environmental consequences of food production, and that this in turn increases the salience of the green identity label. That is, after being treated by the environmental information, consumers become more aware of the green identity label, and thus they are more likely to take the label as a behavioral cue. Besides, respondents might be more likely and more willing to label themselves as green shoppers as they perceive the importance and necessity to do so after being exposed to environmental information.

13.5.2 Heterogeneity in the Response to Environmental Information Treatments

We next explore whether and to which extent people respond differentially to environmental information treatments by deriving the means of conditional WTPs and testing the equality of the WTPs between subgroups. Table 13.6 in general indicates that the impacts of the third and fourth treatments (T3 and T4) are heterogeneous on consumer valuation of already established sustainable coffee products.

Below we summarize our findings in detail. First, young or low-income subjects are more receptive to the treatments, despite the fact that they place lower value on organic and fair coffee in the control group relative to those above median age or income level. To illustrate, in T1, average WTP for organic coffee is $1.5 and $1 for

Table 13.6 Heterogeneity in WTP across treatment, $/12 oz

		Female	Male	Above median age	Below median age	High income	Low income	Graduate	Non–graduate	Conservative	Liberal
Organics	T1	1.149 (0.202)	1.395 (0.174)	1.485 (0.186)	1.057 (0.186)	1.432 (0.229)	1.198 (0.161)	1.169 (0.307)	1.306 (0.146)	1.158 (0.189)	1.306 (0.212)
	T2	1.278	1.648	1.589	1.382	1.755	1.353	1.831*	1.425	1.316	1.470
	T3	(0.187) 1.784**	(0.167) 1.907**	(0.178) 1.968**	(0.174) 1.745**	(0.211) 1.731	(0.154) 1.917***	(0.334) 2.567***	(0.134) 1.697*	(0.190) 1.612	(0.189) 1.673
	T4	(0.216) 1.837** (0.196)	(0.179) 2.049** (0.222)	(0.206) 1.936** (0.193)	(0.187) 1.938*** (0.223)	(0.221) 1.956* (0.244)	(0.178) 1.927*** (0.185)	(0.338) 2.073*** (0.335)	(0.151) 1.903*** (0.164)	(0.199) 1.747** (0.229)	(0.217) 2.007** (0.220)
Fair trade	T1	0.936 (0.162)	0.719 (0.145)	0.909 (0.153)	0.714 (0.152)	1.040 (0.170)	0.690 (0.139)	0.805 (0.289)	0.820 (0.116)	0.795 (0.146)	0.513 (0.151)
	T2	0.754	0.966*	0.763	1.001*	0.930	0.849	0.647	0.924	0.726	0.736
	T3	(0.129) 0.992	(0.111) 1.107***	(0.119) 1.083	(0.118) 1.028**	(0.146) 1.029	(0.103) 1.068***	(0.214) 1.090	(0.092) 1.046**	(0.122) 0.955**	(0.109) 1.005***
	T4	(0.115) 1.125 (0.148)	(0.091) 1.351*** (0.151)	(0.097) 1.253* (0.142)	(0.106) 1.210** (0.158)	(0.112) 1.098 (0.168)	(0.094) 1.308*** (0.136)	(0.145) 1.350 (0.223)	(0.082) 1.202** (0.120)	(0.103) 0.966 (0.162)	(0.094) 1.119*** (0.146)
Carbon trust	T1	0.725	0.885	0.841	0.780	1.016	0.695	0.726	0.829	0.887	0.849
	T2	(0.108) 0.299**	(0.113) 0.549**	(0.111) 0.387***	(0.112) 0.511	(0.132) 0.495***	(0.097) 0.416**	(0.147) 0.785	(0.090) 0.376***	(0.087) 0.476***	(0.107) 0.571 *
	T3	(0.128) 0.485 (0.157)	(0.098) 0.912 (0.143)	(0.104) 0.837 (0.162)	(0.119) 0.605 (0.140)	(0.138) 0.982 (0.176)	(0.095) 0.564 (0.132)	(0.224) 1.243** (0.221)	(0.083) 0.602 (0.119)	(0.134) 0.483** (0.174)	(0.134) 0.850 (0.153)
	T4	0.952 (0.136)	0.824 (0.154)	0.933 (0.143)	0.850 (0.146)	0.918 (0.175)	0.877 (0.126)	0.943 (0.230)	0.879 (0.114)	0.869 (0.221)	1.021 (0.155)

Note: Numbers in parentheses are standard errors. Asterisks indicate the significance level calculated by the *t*-test in WTP difference between the control (T1) and corresponding treatment group within the demographic group. *, **, and *** indicate statistical significance at the 10%, 5%, and 1% levels, respectively the above and below median age group, respectively. That value has been enhanced by at least $0.7 among the below median age group if being assigned to T3 or T4, yet such treatment effect is $0.3 smaller for people above the median age. Similarly, in contrast to almost the null effects found in high-income individuals, the treatment effectsofT3 and T4 on the WTP for organic and fairtrade labels are largely significant in the low-income group. The evidence suggests that consumers with lower income exhibit more significant improvement in their valuation, which parallels to the result by Akbulut-Yuksel and Boulatoff (2021) studying the effect of green nudge on Canadian households' recycling and municipal solid waste. We note that the finding that our information treatments are more effective to increasing the WTPs among young or low-income respondents should be taken with caution. To enable our treatments instead of pecuniary incentives to be the primary mechanism that affect food choices, WTP for pro-environmental food is drawn from choice experiments where prices are exogenously varied across the three pro-environmental labels. But in real market situations, pro-environmental labeled products are usually priced higher, which implies that our treatment effect for young or low-income subjects could be upper-bound given that this group, at least the low-income people, tends to be more sensitive to prices relative to others.

Second, the provision of environmental information and its combined use with green identity labels exert greater impact on respondents with graduate degrees. In the third or fourth treatments, their valuations of organic relative to the conventional product are statistically higher than their counterparts in T1 as well as non-graduate degree holders in the same treatment. This result, in general terms, is inline with previous studies that show better educated individuals are more responsive to information disclosure in a variety of economically relevant settings (Bollinger et al., 2011; Ortega et al., 2020; Schwartz et al., 2020), and that education positively correlates with pro-environmental behavior (Meyer, 2015; Panzone et al., 2016).

Third, the treatments are more effective to increase the valuation of green products among less conservative individuals. In particular, conservatives respond to green identity labels by significantly reducing their valuation for carbon trust labeled product, while the reduction among liberals is less significant and with smaller magnitude. This suggests that greater political conservatism is associated with greater discounting of carbon trust certified product when the product is labeled for green shoppers, which is in line with the study by Gromet et al. (2013) showing that people identified as conservatives selected energy-saving products less frequently when the product was labeled as a pro-environmental choice relative to when the product carries no labels. Note that the effect of green identity labeling on conservatives is lower WTP for carbon trust label but not for organic and fairtrade labels. This could be partly explained by non-environmental benefits included by organic and fairtrade labels, such as perceived health benefit of organic food. Consumers' perception that organic foods are healthier than the conventional food represents an important motive behind organic food consumption (Hughner et al., 2007; De Magistris & Gracia, 2008; Lusk & Briggeman, 2009; Smed, 2012). Nevertheless, carbon trust label is purely an environmental label and carbon related label.

13.6 Robustness Checks

We assess the robustness of our estimation results in two ways. First, remember that T4 has slightly more females than the other treatments; thus, we want to rule out the possibility that our results are driven by the gender pattern. Second, instead of mixed logit model in preference space, we estimate the pooled sample in WTP space relaxing the assumption of a fixed price coefficient and facilitates the estimation of WTP values (Scarpa et al., 2009; De-Magistris et al., 2013).

Table 13.7 reports the estimation results with the fourth treatment alone and the pooled model with T1. Looking at the first column of Table 13.7, the insignificant coefficients of all interaction terms between female dummy variable and product attributes demonstrate that gender would not affect consumer coffee preferences in T4. We then pool T4 and the control group in the model estimation to explore how consumer coffee preferences in T4 differentiate from those of T1, and whether such differences could be attributable to gender. If gender explains the differences in consumer coffee preferences between treatments, then it is problematic to have more female sample in T4. The pooled model indicates that consumers in the fourth treatment value coffee product attributes significantly differently from their counterparts in T1, but that the differences cannot be explained by gender. Given this result, we confirm that relatively more female subjects in T4 would not be a concern.

Table 13.8 reports the estimated treatment effect using the pooled sample in WTP space and the corresponding p-values of the dummy treatment variables. The results of the robustness test confirm the findings of Table 13.5 in seven out ofnine treatment comparisons. Different from the previous results, no statistically significant impact is found for carbon trust label between T1 and T2, and for fair trade label between T1 and T3. Thus, we find supportive evidence for the treatment effects on organic coffee product.

13.7 Conclusions and Implications

In promoting sustainable behaviors that improve social welfare, researchers have investigated the effect of information provision as a behavioral policy tool that can affect individual decision-making. Much attention in the literature has been focused on non-food settings. No other study, however, has examined the effect of green identity label and its combination with other information intervention on pro-environment food choices. To fill this void, this article expands our understanding by specifically focusing on the efficacy of green identity labels, environmental information, and their joint use in nudging people to value sustainable food products more.

Our results reveal that the provision of environmental information as well as its joint use with green identity labels can increase valuation for existing sustainable food products, but the green identity labeling technique by itself fails to achieve the

Table 13.7 Mixed logit model of T4

	T4	T1&T4		
	Coef.	Z-value	Coef.	Z-value
Price	−0.447***	−15.87	−0.556***	−22.530
$ASC_{Opt-out}$	−4.633***	−17.07	−5.443***	−23.771
Female*Organics	0.269	1.25		
Female*Fairtrade	0.020	0.11		
Female*Carbontrust	0.062	0.33		
Female*Price	−0.043	−1.21		
Female*ASC_{Optout}	−0.396	−1.12		
Female*T4*Organics			0.270	1.215
Female*T4*Fairtrade			0.041	0.197
Female*T4*Carbontrust			−0.086	−0.392
Female*T4*Price			0.004	0.044
Female*T4*$ASC_{Opt-out}$			−0.499	−0.603
T4*Organics			0.238***	5.118
T4*Fairtrade			0.310	1.552
T4*Carbontrust			0.365*	1.794
T4*Price			−0.250***	−2.924
T4*$ASC_{Opt-out}$			−5.026***	−5.421
Organics	0.721***	4.49	0.683***	5.775
Fairtrade	0.546***	3.91	0.397***	3.654
Carbontrust	0.423***	2.99	0.467***	4.529
SD.Organics	1.550***	13.17	1.557***	12.358
SD.T4*Organics			0.438	0.596
SD.Fairtrade	1.174***	10.70	1.316***	10.612
SD.T4*Fairtrade			0.763**	2.209
SD.Carbontrust	0.892***	6.20	0.906***	7.120
SD.T4*Carbontrust			1.482***	4.156
SD.T4*Price			0.633***	10.094
SD.T4*$ASC_{Opt-out}$			1.026***	5.599
Observations	2728		5160	
Log-likelihood	−1890.716		−3295.6	

Note: model is estimated with correlated parameters using 1000 Halton draws for simulations in R. Asterisks indicate significant differences at the conventional levels of *$p < 0.1$, $p < 0.05$, and $p < 0.01$. All coefficients of random parameters are normally distributed. Correlation matrix is available upon request

green goal. This finding is particularly relevant for organizations and policymakers considering toolkits to motivate sustainable food consumption. In past decades, a number of food technological innovations have been proposed to address sustainability challenges in food industries. It is conceivable that there would be more such foods produced with novel technologies in the near future. To encourage the adoption of novel food technologies from the demand side, this study informs policymakers that the use of green identity labels in itself might not be successful, and that

Table 13.8 Robustness test in WTP space ($/12 oz)

	Pooled T2	Pooled T3	Pooled T4
WTP_Organics	0.117 (0.176)	0.286* (0.137)	0.276** (0.108)
p-value	0.506	0.064	0.031
WTP_Fairtrade	0.041 (0.164)	0.107 (0.158)	0.167** (0.063)
p-value	0.803	0.297	0.025
WTP_ Carbontrust	– 0.202 (0.156)	– 0.028 (0.164)	0.013 (0.159)
p-value	0.197	0.863	0.934
Observations	627	640	645

Note: pooled T2 means pooled data with T1 and T2. Numbers in parentheses are standard errors. *, **, and *** indicate statistical significance at the 10%, 5%, and 1% levels, respectively

making the environment and climate change issues salient among the public through information intervention might be cost-effective; for example, having posters or audio programs that communicate the environment and climate change problems to shoppers at retailers. Although combining green identity labeling with environmental information provides comparable impacts with the provision of environmental information alone, it requires additional green labels to be added in the food package, which can add a cost.

Our finding of product-specific treatment effects also has important policy implications. We conclude that environmental information and its joint use with green identity labels are effective for improving the WTP for existing pro-environmental coffee products, such as organic and fair trade coffee, but not for more novel ones like carbon trust labeled coffee. Specifically, our results indicate that green identity labeling can actually reduce consumer valuation for carbon trust labeled coffee. This finding suggests that more caution is needed when considering which food products should be treated since it is possible that environmental information treatments maybe more effective on already existing foods instead of less common foods. We also assess heterogeneous responses to environmental information treatments. Other things being equal, the treatment is more successful when targeting younger, low-income subjects and individuals with graduate degrees. Making the information available to policymakers would improve the cost-effectiveness of green nudge programs.

Lastly, note that it is unlikely to fully rule out the possibility that our treatment effects are driven by demand effects (Carlsson et al., 2018), but the heterogeneous as well as product-specific effects suggest this would be trivial in our study. If the impacts are driven by demand effects, we would expect a smoother increase in WTPs for products. A caveat on our findings is that they could be contingent on the product being studied and the type of environmental information and identity label employed in this present study. Future research should test the robustness of our finding to variations in these contexts, especially regarding the effectiveness of green identity labeling in food settings. Green identity labeling could be regarded as a market segmentation tool that groups consumers into two types: the buyer of the product being green consumers, and non-buyer being non-green consumers. The importance of accounting for market segmentation in food market analysis was highlighted by prior work (McFadden et al., 2021). Alternative designs of informational treatment that improves consumer valuation of sustainable food would also be important avenues for future investigation. For example, a product identity label communicating green preferences or behaviors could be included as a product attribute in choice experiments where individuals could make the trade-off between the identity label and other product attributes.

Acknowledgement This work was supported by the National Natural Science Foundation of China (NSFC) (No. 72103180) and the Fundamental Research Funds for the Central Universities.

CRediT Authorship Contribution Statement
Wen Lin: Conceptualization, Methodology, Formal analysis, Investigation, Writing – original draft, Writing – review & editing. Rodolfo M. Nayga: Conceptualization, Methodology, Writing – original draft, Writing – review & editing.

Declaration of Competing Interest
The authors declare that they have no known competing financial interests or personal relationships that could have appeared to influence the work reported in this paper.

Appendix A: Cheap Talk Script

Please read the information below carefully. Be aware, the "next" button may not appear until you have sufficient time to read the information provided. Next, you will be presented with a hypothetical choice involving money. No one will actually be paid money based on the decision you make, but you are asked to make the decision as though it would result in the actual payment. Studies show that people tend to act differently when they face hypothetical decisions. In other words, they say one thing and do something different. We call this a 'hypothetical bias.' For example, in a recent study, several different groups of people made decisions just like the one you are about to make. Payment was real for one group and hypothetical for the other group, as it will be for you. The results of these studies were that on average, more people expressed a willingness to pay money in the hypothetical group than in the real group. How can we get people to think about their decision in a hypothetical situation like they think in a real situation?

When we hear about a situation that involves doing something that is basically good, for example helping people in need, improving environmental quality, or anything else, our basic reaction in a hypothetical situation is to think: sure, I would do this. I really would spend the money; I really, really, think I would.

But when the situation is real, and we would actually have to spend our money, we think a different way. We basically still would like to see good things happen, but when we are faced with the possibility of having to spend money, we think about our options: If I spend money on this, that's money I cannot spend on other things.

So, when the payment is real, we act in away that takes into account the limited amount of money we have. We make the decision while realizing that we just don't have enough money to do everything we might like to do.

Appendix B: Label Description Before the Choice Experiment Questions

In the following, you are presented with several coffee purchasing scenarios. Each coffee product is characterized with price, whether it is USDA organic, Fairtrade certified, or it has Carbon trust claim. All other characteristics of the coffee product are identical across the two coffee alternatives. Please evaluate each of the following scenarios as you would a real purchasing situation.

USDA organic

Organic coffee refers to coffee produced without the use of synthetic inputs, including synthetic fertilizers, pesticides, plant growth regulators, nanomaterials, and genetically modified organisms.

Fair trade

Fairtrade certification is designed to help producers in developing countries achieve better trading conditions, such as higher export prices. Besides improved social standards, Fairtrade certification requires environmental protection, including carbon emission reduction, soil and water quality, biodiversity protection, and prohibition of genetically modified organisms.

Carbon trust

Company makes a commitment to reduce the carbon footprint of their carbon trust labeled product.

Appendix C: Environmental Information Presented to Participants in T2 and T4

Climate change is one of the most important challenges facing our planet that currently requires humanity's urgent action. For example, carbon dioxide in the Earth's atmosphere has reached a record high.

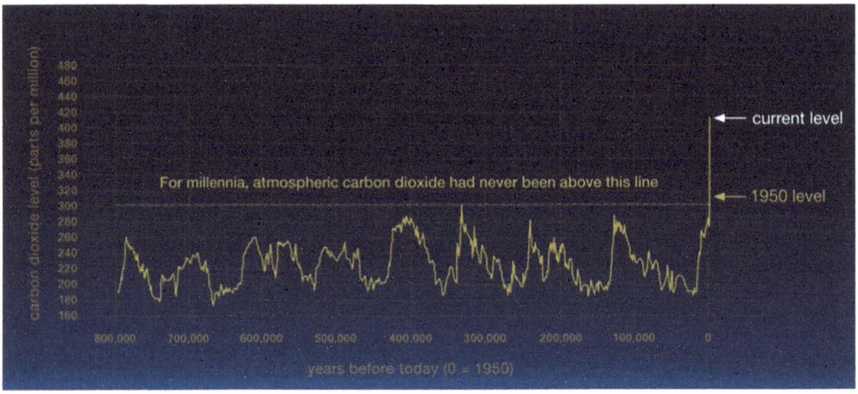

Source: NASA website

Agricultural food production and provision is a major contributor to carbon emissions, ecosystem damage, and the loss of ecosystem services. Environmentally friendly farming methods, such as Fairtrade, organic and low carbon certified production, can mitigate the detrimental environmental impacts of agriculture. By purchasing environmentally friendly food products in your daily life, you support sustainable agriculture, and therefore help combat climate change.

References

Akbulut-Yuksel, M., & Boulatoff, C. (2021). The effects of a green nudge on municipal solid waste: Evidence from a clear bag policy. *The Journal of Environmental Economics and Management, 106*, 102404.

Allcott, H. (2011). Social norms and energy conservation. *Journal of Public Economics, 95*(9–10), 1082–1095.

Allen, C. T. (1982). Self-perception based strategies for stimulating energy conservation. *J. Consumer Res, 8*(4), 381–390.

Asioli, D., Bazzani, C., & Nayga, R. M. (2018). *Consumers' valuation for lab produced meat: An investigation of naming effects*.

Asioli, D., Aschemann-Witzel, J., & Nayga, R. M., Jr. (2020). Sustainability-related food labels. *The Annual Review of Resource Economics, 12*, 171–185.

Battaglini, M., Bénabou, R., & Tirole, J. (2005). Self-control in peer groups. *Journal of Economic Theory, 123*(2), 105–134.

Becchetti, L., Salustri, F., & Scaramozzino, P. (2020). Nudging and corporate environmental responsibility: A natural field experiment. *Food Policy, 97*, 101951.

Bollinger, B., Leslie, P., & Sorensen, A. (2011). Calorie posting in chain restaurants. *American Economic Journal: Economic Policy, 3*(1), 91–128.

Burgess, L., & Street, D. J. (2005). Optimal designs for choice experiments with asymmetric attributes. *Journal of Statistical Planning and Inference, 134*(1), 288–301.

Campbell, D., & Erdem, S. (2015). Position bias in best-worst scaling surveys: A case study on trust in institutions. *The American Journal of Agricultural Economics, 97*(2), 526–545.

Cao, H. H., Han, B., Hirshleifer, D., & Zhang, H. H. (2011). Fear of the unknown: Familiarity and economic decisions. *Review of Finance, 15*(1), 173–206.

Carlsson, F., Frykblom, P., & Lagerkvist, C. J. (2005). Using cheap talk as a test of validity in choice experiments. *Economics Letters, 89*(2), 147–152.

Carlsson, F., Kataria, M., & Lampi, E. (2018). Demand effects in stated preference surveys. *The Journal of Environmental Economics and Management, 90*, 294–302.

Chrzan, K. (1994). Three kinds of order effects in choice-based conjoint analysis. *Marketing Letters, 5*(2), 165–172.

Cornelissen, J. P., Haslam, S. A., & Balmer, J. M. (2007). Social identity, organizational identity and corporate identity: Towards an integrated understanding of processes, patternings and products. *British Journal of Management, 18*, S1–S16.

Crippa, M., Solazzo, E., Guizzardi, D., Monforti-Ferrario, F., Tubiello, F. N., & Leip, A. (2021). Food systems are responsible for a third of global anthropogenic GHG emissions. *Nature Food, 2*(3), 198–209.

Cummings, R. G., & Taylor, L. O. (1999). Unbiased value estimates for environmental goods: A cheap talk design for the contingent valuation method. *The American Economic Review, 89*(3), 649–665.

Darby, M. R., & Karni, E. (1973). Free competition and the optimal amount of fraud. *The Journal of Law and Economics, 16*(1), 67–88.

De Magistris, T., & Gracia, A. (2008). The decision to buy organic food products in Southern Italy. *The British Food Journal.*

De Marchi, E., Cavaliere, A., & Banterle, A. (2020). Consumers' choice behavior for cisgenic food: Exploring the role of time preferences. *Applied Economic Perspectives and Policy.*

De-Magistris, T., Gracia, A., & Nayga, R. M., Jr. (2013). On the use of honesty priming tasks to mitigate hypothetical bias in choice experiments. *The American Journal of Agricultural Economics, 95*(5), 1136–1154.

Durham, C. A., & Andrade, D. (2005). *Health vs. environmental motivation in organic preferences and purchases* (No. 378-2016-21257).

Eby, B., Carrico, A. R., & Truelove, H. B. (2019). The influence of environmental identity labeling on the uptake of pro-environmental behaviors. *Climate Change, 155*(4), 563–580.

Edenbrandt, A. K., Lagerkvist, C. J., & Nordström, J. (2021). Interested, indifferent or active information avoiders of carbon labels: Cognitive dissonance and ascription of responsibility as motivating factors. *Food Policy, 101*, 102036. https://doi.org/10.1016/j.foodpol.2021.102036

Elias, J. J., Lacetera, N., & Macis, M. (2019). Paying for kidneys? A randomized survey and choice experiment. *The American Economic Review, 109*(8), 2855–2888.

Ferraro, P. J., & Miranda, J. J. (2013). Heterogeneous treatment effects and mechanisms in information-based environmental policies: Evidence from a large-scale field experiment. *Resource and Energy Economics, 35*(3), 356–379.

Ferraro, P. J., & Price, M. K. (2013). Using nonpecuniary strategies to influence behavior: Evidence from a large-scale field experiment. *The Review of Economics and Statistics, 95*(1), 64–73.

Goddard, E. W., Hobbs, J. E., Innes, B. G., Romanowska, P. E., & Uzea, A. D. (2013). Risk perceptions and preferences for ethical and safety credence attributes. *The American Journal of Agricultural Economics., 95*(2), 390–396.
Grieg-Gran, M. (2005). *From bean to cup: How consumer choice impacts upon coffee producers and the environment*. International Institute for Environment and Development.
Gromet, D. M., Kunreuther, H., & Larrick, R. P. (2013). Political ideology affects energy-efficiency attitudes and choices. *Proceedings of the National Academy of Sciences of the United States of America, 110*(23), 9314–9319.
Grunert, K. G. (2005). Food quality and safety: Consumer perception and demand. *The European Review of Agricultural Economics, 32*(3), 369–391.
Heckman, J. J., Smith, J., & Clements, N. (1997). Making the most out of programme evaluations and social experiments: Accounting for heterogeneity in programme impacts. *The Review of Economic Studies, 64*(4), 487–535.
Hensher, D. A. (2010). Hypothetical bias, choice experiments and willingness to pay. *Transportation Research Part B-methodological, 44*(6), 735–752.
Hensher, D. A., Rose, J. M., Rose, J. M., & Greene, W. H. (2005). *Applied choice analysis: A primer*. Cambridge University Press.
Hensher, D. A., Balbontin, C., & Collins, A. T. (2018). Heterogeneity in decision processes: Embedding extremeness aversion, risk attitude and perceptual conditioning in multiple process rules choice making. *Transportation Research Part A: Policy and Practice, 111*, 316–325.
Hess, S., & Train, K. (2017). Correlation and scale in mixed logit models. *The Journal of Choice Modelling, 23*, 1–8.
Hughner, R. S., McDonagh, P., Prothero, A., Shultz, C. J., & Stanton, J. (2007). Who are organic food consumers? A compilation and review of why people purchase organic food. *The Journal of Consumer Behaviour: An International Research Review, 6*(2–3), 94–110.
Kaminski, D. M., & Caputo, V. (2018). *Milk produced under certified labor conditions: Are US consumers willing to pay for it and does prior information impact their behavior?*
Krinsky, I., & Robb, A. L. (1986). On approximating the statistical properties of elasticities. *The Review of Economics and Statistics, 68*, 715–719.
Kurz, V. (2018). Nudging to reduce meat consumption: Immediate and persistent effects of an intervention at a university restaurant. *The Journal of Environmental Economics and Management, 90*, 317–341.
Lancaster, K. J. (1966). A new approach to consumer theory. *The Journal of Political Economy, 74*(2), 132–157.
Lassoued, R., & Hobbs, J. E. (2015). Consumer confidence in credence attributes: The role of brand trust. *Food Policy, 52*, 99–107.
Lin, L.-Y., & Chen, C.-S. (2006). The influence of the country-of-origin image, product knowledge and product involvement on consumer purchase decisions: An empirical study of insurance and catering services in Taiwan. *J. Consumer Marketing, 23*(5), 248–265.
List, J. A. (2001). Do explicit warnings eliminate the hypothetical bias in elicitation procedures? Evidence from field auctions for sportscards. *The American Economic Review, 91*(5), 1498–1507.
Loureiro, M. L. (2003). Rethinking new wines: Implications of local and environmentally friendly labels. *Food Policy, 28*(5–6), 547–560.
Louviere, J. J., Hensher, D. A., & Swait, J. D. (2000). *Stated choice methods: Analysis and applications*. Cambridge University Press.
Louviere, J. J., Flynn, T. N., & Carson, R. T. (2010). Discrete choice experiments are not conjoint analysis. *The Journal of Choice Modelling, 3*(3), 57–72.
Lusk, J. L., & Briggeman, B. C. (2009). Food values. *The American Journal of Agricultural Economics, 91*(1), 184–196.
Lusk, J. L., House, L. O., Valli, C., Jaeger, S. R., Moore, M., Morrow, J. L., & Traill, W. B. (2004). Effect of information about benefits of biotechnology on consumer acceptance of genetically

modified food: evidence from experimental auctions in the United States, England, and France. *The European Review of Agricultural Economics, 31*(2), 179–204.

Matthews, Y., Scarpa, R., & Marsh, D. (2017). Using virtual environments to improve the realism of choice experiments: A case study about coastal erosion management. *The Journal of Environmental Economics and Management, 81*, 193–208.

McFadden, D. (1974). The measurement of urban travel demand. *Journal of Public Economics, 3*(4), 303–328.

McFadden, D., & Train, K. (2000). Mixed MNL models for discrete response. *The Journal of Applied Econometrics, 15*(5), 447–470.

McFadden, B. R., Bovay, J., & Mullally, C. (2021). What are the overall implications of rising demand for organic fruits and vegetables? Evidence from theory and simulations. *Q Open, 1*(1), qoab008.

Meyer, A. (2015). Does education increase pro-environmental behavior? Evidence from Europe. *Ecological Economics, 116*, 108–121.

Myers, E., & Souza, M. (2020). Social comparison nudges without monetary incentives: Evidence from home energy reports. *The Journal of Environmental Economics and Management, 101*, 102315.

Ortega, D. L., Lusk, J. L., Lin, W., & Caputo, V. (2020). Predicting responsiveness to information: consumer acceptance of biotechnology in animal products. *The European Review of Agricultural Economics, 47*(5), 1644–1667.

Panzone, L., Hilton, D., Sale, L., & Cohen, D. (2016). Socio-demographics, implicit attitudes, explicit attitudes, and sustainable consumption in supermarket shopping. *The Journal of Economic Psychology, 55*, 77–95.

Poe, G. L., Giraud, K. L., & Loomis, J. B. (2005). Computational methods for measuring the difference of empirical distributions. *The American Journal of Agricultural Economics, 87*(2), 353–365.

Poore, J., & Nemecek, T. (2018). Reducing food's environmental impacts through producers and consumers. *Science, 360*(6392), 987–992.

Reinecke, J., Manning, S., & Von Hagen, O. (2012). The emergence of a standards market: Multiplicity of sustainability standards in the global coffee industry. *OrganizationStudies, 33*(5–6), 791–814.

Roheim, C. A., & Zhang, D. (2018). Sustainability certification and product substitutability: Evidence from the seafood market. *Food Policy, 79*, 92–100.

Scarpa, R., Gilbride, T. J., Campbell, D., & Hensher, D. A. (2009). Modelling attribute non-attendance in choice experiments for rural landscape valuation. *The European Review of Agricultural Economics, 36*(2), 151–174.

Schubert, C. (2017). Green nudges: Do they work? Are they ethical? *Ecological Economics, 132*, 329–342.

Schwartz, D., Loewenstein, G., & Agüero-Gaete, L. (2020). Encouraging pro-environmental behaviour through green identity labelling. *Natrue Sustainability, 3*(9), 746–752.

Smed, S. (2012). Information and consumer perception of the "organic" attribute in fresh fruits and vegetables. *Agricultural Economics, 43*, 33–48.

Street, D. J., Burgess, L., & Louviere, J. J. (2005). Quick and easy choice sets: Constructing optimal and nearly optimal stated choice experiments. *The International Journal of Research in Marketing, 22*(4), 459–470.

Teisl, M. F., Roe, B., & Hicks, R. L. (2002). Can eco-labels tune a market? Evidence from dolphin-safe labeling. *The Journal of Environmental Economics and Management, 43*(3), 339–359.

Tubiello, F. N., Rosenzweig, C., Conchedda, G., Karl, K., Gütschow, J., Xueyao, P., Obli-Laryea, G., Wanner, N., Qiu, S. Y., De Barros, J., & Flammini, A. (2021). Greenhouse gas emissions from food systems: Building the evidence base. *Environmental Research Letters, 16*(6), 065007.

Tversky, A., & Kahneman, D. (1974). Judgment under uncertainty: Heuristics and biases. *Science, 185*(4157), 1124–1131.

Van Loo, E. J., Caputo, V., Nayga, R. M., Jr., Seo, H. S., Zhang, B., & Verbeke, W. (2015). Sustainability labels on coffee: Consumer preferences, willingness-to-pay and visual attention to attributes. *Ecological Economics, 118*, 215–225.

Van Loo, E. J., Caputo, V., & Lusk, J. L. (2020). Consumer preferences for farm-raised meat, lab-grown meat, and plant-based meat alternatives: Does information or brand matter? *Food Policy, 95*, 101931.

Wensing, J., Caputo, V., Carraresi, L., & Bröring, S. (2020). The effects of green nudges on consumer valuation of bio-based plastic packaging. *Ecological Economics, 178*, 106783.

Part V
Conclusion and Outlook

Chapter 14
Conclusion

As one of the world's largest producers and traders of agricultural products, China occupies a significant position in the global agri-food supply chain. Therefore, China's measures in transforming its agri-food system will have profound implications for global agriculture and the food industry, as well as for global climate change mitigation, exerting a demonstrative effect in the global transition toward sustainable agri-food systems. At the international level, the transformation of the agri-food system contributes to promoting global food security, mitigating climate change, fostering sustainable agriculture and fair trade, improving nutritional structures, and enhancing resource efficiency, thereby advancing the realization of the Sustainable Development Goals (SDGs). At the domestic level, such transformation helps optimize the agricultural structure, ensure food and nutrition security, promote green and low-carbon development, and enhance the quality and competitiveness of agricultural products. It also contributes to achieving a moderately prosperous society in all respects, laying the foundation for building a high-quality and sustainable modern agricultural system, and advancing the process of Chinese modernization.

This book provides a systematic discussion of the top-level design, implementation pathways, existing challenges, coping strategies, and key stakeholders involved in China's agri-food system transformation, focusing on three major themes: food safety, nutrition and health, and green and low-carbon development.

1. **Food Safety Governance Transition**

   Food safety serves as a fundamental pillar for promoting the transformation of the agri-food system. A safe food supply is not only a prerequisite for safeguarding public health and social stability but also an essential driver for advancing green agricultural development, upgrading the food industry, and optimizing consumption structures. Improvements in food safety governance contribute to the sustainability of production methods, the normalization of market systems,

W. Lin, *Transforming China's Agri-Food System: Government-Market Synergy*, Resources, Environment and Agricultural Development,
https://doi.org/10.1007/978-981-95-7151-2_14

and the modernization of governance mechanisms, thereby providing a solid foundation for realizing a high-quality, green, and healthy agri-food transformation.

The government plays a dominant role in food safety governance. Globally, it is a widely accepted consensus that governments at all levels safeguard food safety through institutional and policy design. However, what constitutes an optimal institutional arrangement, and through what mechanisms institutional design affects food safety, remain critical questions for analysis and discussion.

For a long time, both academia and policymakers have debated whether public goods should be provided through centralized or decentralized institutional arrangements. On the one hand, decentralization is believed to enhance efficiency in the provision of public goods by leveraging local information advantages, inter-jurisdictional competition, and incentive effects arising from delegated authority. On the other hand, decentralization may not always improve social welfare due to the absence of economies of scale and free-rider problems caused by spillover effects. In Chap. 2, Lin and Liang focus on the design of governmental regulatory institutions and examine how the devolution of regulatory authority affects food safety—a typical public good. Exploiting the quasi-natural experiment of China's food safety regulatory reform, in which authority was delegated from the provincial to the prefectural level, they construct a prefecture-level database of food safety incidents and rigorously validate its internal and external consistency. The empirical results show that, in prefectures where decentralization reform was implemented, the number of food safety incidents significantly declined. The delegation of regulatory authority reduced information costs for grassroots supervision and strengthened accountability among local governments, thereby improving the overall level of food safety governance.

Although, in theory, government intervention can effectively mitigate market failures, one cannot overlook the potential for government failure. In Chap. 3, Liang et al. analyze a common cause of such failure—local protectionism—by examining how it manifests in information-based policy tools and undermines regulatory effectiveness. Their study reveals how local governments manipulate information disclosure to protect local enterprises, distorting information transparency and eroding regulatory credibility. Using publicly available data from China's food quality inspection system, the authors compare test results conducted by local and national authorities for the same product produced by the same firm within the same year to identify the effect of local protectionism in information disclosure. The findings show that local authorities report significantly lower noncompliance rates than national agencies, especially in key local industries, among firms with high registered capital, and in regions facing strong economic growth pressures—demonstrating a clear tendency of local governments to protect domestic enterprises by manipulating public information.

This study offers several insights for improving governmental food safety governance. It suggests revising local government performance assessments to shift away from purely outcome-oriented targets such as high compliance rates, and instead focus on transparency and enforcement quality. Furthermore, it highlights the need to strengthen cross-regional supervision and joint enforcement mechanisms to prevent local protectionism from undermining the effectiveness of public policies.

Beyond macro-level policy guidance, the market—the "invisible hand"—also plays a crucial role in food safety governance. Yet whether driven by government intervention or market mechanisms, food safety governance fundamentally depends on information as a key resource. Food safety inspection and disclosure systems have become essential tools worldwide for controlling risks, assessing compliance, and managing public trust. A growing body of research investigates how disclosure of food safety information affects consumer behavior and market outcomes—ranging from empirical analyses using real market transaction data in developed countries to experimental studies on consumer information preferences in developing countries.

However, evidence on the effectiveness of food safety information disclosure in developing agricultural markets—particularly the extent to which agricultural product prices respond to quality information—remains limited. Price mechanisms are at the core of market operations and serve as the most sensitive and efficient means of resource allocation. The effectiveness of information disclosure can thus be evaluated through market price responses. Effective public disclosure of inspection results enables consumers to identify and purchase safer products, thereby increasing demand for high-quality goods and reducing demand for substandard ones. According to supply-demand theory, this process raises the prices of high-quality products and lowers those of inferior ones, eventually driving the latter out of the market. In Chap. 4, Lin et al. evaluate the impact of food safety information disclosure on market prices. Using pork wholesale market data at the city level and corresponding quality inspection data, they employ an event study approach to examine the effect of publicizing inspection failures. The results indicate that after the government disclosed noncompliance in pork inspections, local wholesale pork prices showed a lagged decline. Furthermore, disclosure not only affected local pork prices but also exerted negative spillover effects on beef prices in the same city and pork prices in neighboring cities. By investigating the responsiveness of agricultural market prices to quality information, this study provides an in-depth assessment of China's food safety information disclosure policy, revealing directions for improving its effectiveness. These findings offer new perspectives for understanding information-based food safety regulation in developing countries and provide valuable policy implications for designing and implementing effective food safety governance in other emerging economies.

Enterprises are the primary entities responsible for food safety. They are obligated to enhance product quality through management and technological innovation, thereby promoting a positive demonstration effect across the industry chain. The food safety traceability system, as an important tool, also plays a vital role in food safety governance. The food safety traceability system, by employing modern information technologies, enables the recording, tracking, and management of the entire process of food production, processing, distribution, and consumption. This system facilitates rapid source identification, accountability determination, and product recall in the event of food safety incidents, thereby minimizing potential harm to public health. However, due to the high costs, long construction periods, and uncertain consumer acceptance, the adoption rate of such systems remains relatively low among numerous small and medium-sized enterprises.

Understanding consumer preferences and responding to market demand is one of the key strategies for enterprises to maximize profits. This, in turn, influences firms' motivation to improve food safety management and adopt advanced management technologies. When consumers exhibit stronger preferences for traceable products and are willing to pay a price premium, enterprises are more likely to adopt traceability systems. With sufficient market scale, unit costs decline, profitability increases, and food safety management is strengthened. Therefore, understanding consumer preferences provides valuable guidance for promoting traceability systems and other innovative management strategies. In Chap. 5, Lin et al. assess Chinese consumers' acceptance of U.S. beef and blockchain-based traceability systems. Given China's rapidly growing demand and limited domestic production, the country has become the world's second-largest beef importer. Using a hypothetical discrete choice experiment (DCE) and analyzing willingness-to-pay (WTP) estimates alongside cluster analysis, the study identifies different consumer groups' preference patterns and socio-economic characteristics. The findings show that consumers are generally willing to pay a premium for blockchain-based traceability systems. Such systems can enhance consumer trust in food safety and strengthen product competitiveness in the marketplace. The study offers policy and practical insights for market positioning in the global beef industry, marketing strategies for entering the Chinese market, and enterprise-level traceability system development, while also providing implications for improving food safety through market-driven mechanisms.

2. **Nutrition and Health Transition**

   The nutrition and health transition constitutes an essential pillar of China's high-quality agri-food system development. With rising income levels and changing lifestyles, consumers' dietary needs have evolved from "eating enough" to "eating well and eating healthy." A health-oriented consumption concept is gradually becoming a shared social consensus. However, the coexistence of caloric surplus and nutritional deficiency remains a pervasive issue, as overweight and obesity rates continue to increase and the contradiction between traditional dietary habits and health goals becomes more prominent. Against this background, the government and the market have jointly fostered an interactive mechanism through information dissemination, institutional innovation, and behavioral guidance, steering dietary structures toward a more balanced, low-sugar, and rational direction. Chapters 6 through 9 systematically elaborate this process, showing that information interventions and nutritional labeling significantly affect consumer decision-making; policy innovations can improve diet quality without increasing overall expenditure; the "information–cognition–behavior" chain forms the key mechanism of health transition; and effective government–market coordination provides institutional assurance for sustained improvement in public health.

Information interventions and nutrition labels have been shown to alter consumer decisions. The effective transmission of information enables consumers to identify both the health risks and nutritional value of food products, thereby correcting their initial preference biases. In Chap. 6, Guan et al. investigate the role of information interventions in guiding urban consumers from sugar-sweetened to sugar-free alternatives. They find that although Chinese consumers generally harbor safety concerns toward sweeteners, exposure to scientific information on the safety and functions of sugar substitutes substantially reduces perceived risk and increases both acceptance and willingness to pay (WTP) for low- and zero-sugar beverages. This result indicates that targeted information interventions can promote healthier consumption choices by improving risk perception and trust. Meanwhile, front-of-pack nutritional labels (FOPL) perform a comparable role in shaping decisions. Chapter 9 uses sugar-sweetened beverages as an example and compares the effectiveness of multiple label designs. The results show that warning labels significantly reduce WTP for high-sugar drinks, while traffic-light and health-tick schemes also decrease the likelihood of purchasing unhealthy products. These findings reveal that the form and presentation of information strongly influence cognitive processing; when nutritional data are conveyed through intuitive, interpretive, and visual cues, their health-guiding effect becomes substantially stronger. Collectively, the empirical evidence on information interventions and nutrition labeling highlights a key direction for health policy—strengthening market discipline through information mechanisms so that healthy choices emerge as spontaneous rational behavior.

Policy innovations have further expanded the feasible boundaries of the health transition. In conventional understanding, healthy diets often imply higher economic costs, posing real constraints for low- and middle-income households. Yet Chaps. 7 and 8 demonstrate that institutional innovations can improve dietary structures without increasing total expenditure. Chapter 7, conducted by Chen et al., applies a Discrete Choice Experiment (DCE) to examine urban residents' preferences for different dietary patterns. Four meal plans are compared: Average Diet, Chinese Food Guide Pagoda Diet, EAT-Lancet Diet, and Flexitarian Diet. The results show that while most consumers still favor familiar average diets, simulated policy scenarios that raise the relative cost of unhealthy diets or reduce the cost of healthy ones significantly increase the selection rate of healthier plans. This finding indicates that popularizing healthy diets depends not only on improving cognition but also on designing appropriate institutional incentives. When the government adjusts relative costs through price levers and fiscal subsidies, structural improvements in diet quality can be achieved without altering budget constraints. Chapter 8 further validates the economic feasibility of such policy tools. In a randomized controlled trial among college students, Lin et al. find that multiple-traffic-light (MTL) labels significantly reduce intake of calories, fat, carbohydrates, and sodium while keeping total spending constant. These results demonstrate that information-based policy interventions can balance health and affordability, realizing a "healthy-yet-not-costly" equilibrium. Together, they show that innovations in information and price mechanisms can deliver a Pareto improvement in nutritional structure even under limited resources.

From a behavioral-mechanism perspective, the "information–cognition–behavior" chain constitutes the core pathway of health transition. Dietary choices are not merely price responses but the outcomes of integrated information processing, cognitive evaluation, and value judgment. Information interventions reshape consumers' belief systems, enabling them to correctly identify the health attributes of food; cognitive updating is then translated into choice intention and WTP, generating collective health preferences in the marketplace. Evidence from Chaps. 6 and 9 indicates that when information is transparent, accurate, and interpretive, consumers actively incorporate health factors into their decision framework, forming sustained preferences for low-sugar and low-fat products. Chapter 8 further shows that the color-coding of MTL labels reduces cognitive load and allows consumers to make faster and more rational judgments under time constraints. This nudge-based mechanism has low cost and strong persistence, making it an important behavioral foundation for promoting public health. By improving the information environment and decision architecture, governments can stimulate intrinsic health motivations among individuals and thereby achieve social-level behavioral transformation without coercive measures.

The continued advancement of nutrition and health transition ultimately depends on the synergy between government and market. The government serves as the "direction-setter" through institutional design, information provision, and standard formulation, while the market translates these policy goals into practice through product innovation, label optimization, and supply adjustment. At the policy level, nutrition and health have been incorporated into the "Healthy China 2030" strategy, which promotes FOPL institutionalization and nationwide health education. Local governments have advanced standardized labeling, information disclosure, and public outreach to build transparent and credible information environments. On the market side, enterprises—motivated by policy incentives—accelerate product reformulation and innovation, lowering sugar, salt, and fat content to avoid unfavorable labels and enhance competitiveness. Changes in consumers' WTP in turn reinforce firms' health-oriented innovation incentives, forming a self-reinforcing triad among policy, market, and behavior. Government institutions correct information asymmetries and externalities, while market competition internalizes public-health objectives into profit motives. Through such mutual reinforcement, healthy dietary patterns become more widespread and public-health outcomes continuously improve.

In sum, the nutrition and health transition is a vital support for China's agricultural modernization and sustainable development. Information interventions and nutrition labels establish the foundation for informed choices; policy innovation broadens the scope of structural improvement without extra spending; the "information–cognition–behavior" mechanism reveals the micro-logic of individual change; and government–market synergy ensures the long-term feasibility of transformation. China's experience demonstrates that health transition need not come at the expense of economic burden—it can be realized through the organic integration of cognitive renewal, information systems, and market incentives. In the future, as nutrition-information standards are refined and labeling institutionalization proceeds, the interaction among government, enterprises, and consumers will become more fluid, laying a solid foundation for achieving the goals of "Healthy China 2030."

3. **Green and Low-Carbon Transition**

The green and low-carbon transition has become a crucial direction for advancing the high-quality development of China's agri-food system. With intensifying climate pressures and the establishment of the carbon-neutrality goal, emission reduction and structural transformation within agriculture and food systems have acquired unprecedented importance. The food system accounts for roughly one-third of global anthropogenic greenhouse-gas emissions, and the greening of consumption behavior represents the most promising field for emission mitigation. Advancing this transition requires not only sustained institutional and technological innovation but also improvements in market mechanisms and social awareness.

Within this process, consumer behavior plays a pivotal linking role. The key challenge lies in transforming individuals from passive responders into proactive participants, making green consumption a widespread social practice rather than a conscious choice of a few. How can institutions cultivate trust? How does information shape decisions? Through what mechanisms can markets, policies, and society generate joint force? These questions are examined in depth in the preceding chapters.

Trust reconstruction forms the prerequisite for realizing green consumption. In Chap. 10, Yuan, Jin, and Lin analyze the role of trust in environmentally friendly food consumption using Chinese consumer data. They find that although most consumers endorse green values, a significant intention–behavior gap persists. The level of trust becomes a decisive factor: institutional trust in certifiers significantly promotes purchase conversion for green food, while relational trust in manufacturers is critical for organic food consumption. The heterogeneity of trust across actors reveals structural constraints in green consumption—when facing complex certification systems and fragmented market information, consumers rely more on verifiable institutional trust and perceivable corporate reputation. The study further shows that women, younger, more educated, and environmentally conscious groups respond more strongly to changes in trust, implying that the accumulation of social capital amplifies green-consumption behavior. Trust is both a psychological foundation and an institutional product; its stability depends on transparency in regulation and credibility of certification systems. By strengthening information disclosure, improving traceability, and standardizing certification procedures, institutional trust can be restored, thereby sustaining low-carbon behavior among market participants.

Building on this foundation, information systems and carbon labeling serve as vital connectors between policy and market. Chapter 11 investigates the influence of carbon labels on food consumption among U.S. consumers. Lin, Nayga, and Yang use a Discrete Choice Experiment to demonstrate that when products display carbon-footprint information, consumers adjust preferences accordingly and exhibit higher WTP for low-carbon options. The experiment also introduces Enhanced Rock Weathering (ERW) carbon labels, showing that respondents with higher education, stronger environmental awareness, and liberal political attitudes react most positively. The interpretability of information and consumers' knowledge jointly determine policy effectiveness: when individuals understand the scientific meaning of carbon information and trust its regulatory source, labels function as credible behavioral signals. This finding reveals the coupling mechanism between information and cognition and underscores that institutionalized carbon-label policies are not merely emission-reduction tools but integral components of market signaling systems. By unifying standards, refining verification systems, and reinforcing government endorsement, the credibility of information disclosure can be significantly enhanced, fostering a stable low-carbon price mechanism at the consumption end.

At the same time, the combination of green identity labeling and environmental information provides strong social motivation for low-carbon behavior. Chapter 13 demonstrates that the interaction between information nudges and identity labeling effectively promotes sustainable choices. Lin and Nayga find through online experiments that green-identity labels alone have limited influence on consumer preference, but when combined with environmental information, their effect strengthens substantially. Environmental information enhances cognitive salience, while identity labeling activates self-consistency motives, encouraging consumers to act in accordance with their "green self-image." The study also notes that the impact is more pronounced among younger, lower-income, and better-educated groups, reflecting the diffusion of social norms and group identity. The integration of environmental information and green identity thus functions not only as a tool of consumption guidance but also as a medium for cultivating green social culture. Through institutionalized information disclosure and symbolic identity expression, policies and markets together build a communication mechanism centered on social recognition of low-carbon values.

On the psychological-mechanism level, Chap. 12 complements these findings by highlighting altruistic motivation in low-carbon consumption. Li and Lin, using sustainable coffee as a case, show through a Discrete Choice Experiment that individuals with stronger altruistic orientation demonstrate higher preference and WTP for sustainability labels such as Organic, Carbon Trust, and Fair Trade. Consumers with stronger environmental awareness and public responsibility view their purchases as contributions to environmental protection and social equity. This result suggests that green and low-carbon consumption is driven not only by external incentives but also by internalized moral values.

When policies and markets institutionalize the value of "consuming for others," altruistic preferences interact with social norms to strengthen the ethical foundation of green transition.

Overall, trust mechanisms, carbon labeling, identity recognition, and altruistic motivation interact within the green-and-low-carbon transition, forming a tripartite pathway of institution–information–society. Institutional trust provides a stable foundation; information disclosure and labeling enhance transparency and behavioral visibility; and social trust and value identification infuse the transition with endogenous motivation. The government plays a directional and institutional role—formulating unified standards, strengthening information governance, and guiding public cognition to establish a trustworthy green environment. The market, through technological innovation and product differentiation, translates low-carbon ideals into concrete supply, while society, through identity diffusion and cultural shaping, normalizes green consumption. This multi-level collaborative mechanism ensures that emission reduction in the agri-food system extends beyond the production end to encompass self-regulation and value reconstruction on the consumption side.

Chapter 15
Outlook

15.1 Institutional Innovation and Multi-Actor Co-Governance

China's agri-food system transformation is shifting from a policy-driven stage dominated by government leadership toward a new phase characterized by collaborative governance among the market, government, and society. The governance model is evolving from a single-centered regulatory system to a multi-actor co-governance framework. The market mechanism has inherent advantages in resource allocation and technological innovation, while the government plays a pivotal role in safeguarding public interests and managing risks. With the increasing participation of social organizations, industry associations, and public supervision, tripartite co-governance involving the market, government, and society is becoming the new norm. The governance of the agri-food system is thus forming a multi-level, multi-actor, and multi-channel interactive pattern.

This reshaping of the governance model is reflected not only in adjustments to institutional arrangements but also in the exploration of collaborative mechanisms at the practical level. For example, the "Let's Discuss Together (大家商量着办)" deliberative governance mechanism introduced in Haidian District, Beijing, offers a vivid example of institutional co-governance innovation at the grassroots level. By establishing inter-departmental coordination groups, community deliberation platforms, and mechanisms for market actors to participate in governance, Haidian has transformed food safety from a government-centric regulatory matter into a public issue jointly addressed by multiple stakeholders. The district promotes a system of community food-safety supervisors in farmers' markets and school canteens, and conducts joint activities such as public voting on testing priorities and real-time information disclosure. These mechanisms deepen transparency and strengthen

W. Lin, *Transforming China's Agri-Food System: Government-Market Synergy*, Resources, Environment and Agricultural Development,
https://doi.org/10.1007/978-981-95-7151-2_15

collaborative governance by embedding citizen participation into decision-making and oversight, demonstrating a viable pathway for institutional innovation in practice.

Internationally, Denmark's food-safety system offers a complementary example of institutionalized co-governance. The clear functional separation between the Danish Veterinary and Food Administration (DVFA) and the National Food Institute at the Technical University of Denmark (DTU)—with the former responsible for risk management and the latter for independent, science-based risk assessment—reduces conflicts of interest and enhances governance credibility. Denmark's co-governance model is further embodied in sector-based self-regulation. Under the "Health Advisory Agreement" mechanism, farms are required to engage certified private veterinary consultants who conduct regular evaluations of biosecurity conditions, emphasizing a cooperative and preventive approach that aligns regulatory objectives with industry incentives. These mechanisms—science-based independence, structured industry participation, and routine professional oversight—provide useful references for China's ongoing institutional reforms, while also highlighting areas where China may develop locally adapted models.

Whether in China's local governance experiments or international institutional arrangements, a common trend is evident: institutional innovation is no longer exclusively a government endeavor but the outcome of coordinated action among multiple actors operating within a shared governance framework. The core challenge is to balance trust, responsibility, and incentives in a dynamic environment. Trust is the precondition for co-governance; responsibility defines its operational boundaries; incentives ensure sustained engagement. To enhance the resilience and efficiency of governance under evolving conditions, future institutional building should strengthen three key mechanisms: (1) Constructing trust-based cooperation structures, supported by transparent information disclosure, consistent enforcement, and robust communication channels; (2) Clarifying the responsibility boundaries of government, enterprises, industry associations, and the public, ensuring clear accountability within a multi-actor system; (3) Enhancing incentives for participation through credit-based rewards, policy support, technological subsidies, and public recognition, transforming governance from external compliance pressure into internal motivation.

The future governance paradigm will not rely solely on administrative commands or market signals but will be shaped by the integrated use of rules, incentives, and transparency mechanisms to achieve a stable pattern of institutionalized co-governance.

15.2 Digital Economy and Intelligent Governance

Technological progress is reshaping the governance model of the agri-food system. The future of food safety and agricultural sustainability will increasingly depend on digitalized, networked, and intelligent infrastructures. The digital economy not only provides new efficiency tools for market operations but also offers innovative governance approaches for government regulation and social oversight.

Recent practices in China offer compelling demonstrations of how digital technologies empower agri-food governance. At Beijing's Xinfadi market, an "AI + blockchain"-based smart traceability system enables real-time tracking and risk identification across the entire circulation chain. With over 300 AI-based imaging devices and advanced recognition algorithms, the system identifies fruit and vegetable categories, verifies weights, and detects anomalies within seconds. Its blockchain ledger records 12 key data indicators allowing consumers to access end-to-end information with a simple scan. Since its launch, the system has identified more than 1200 irregular transactions, reduced product loss rates from 4.7% to 1.9%, and shortened the detection time for problematic goods from 72 h to just 2 h, establishing a replicable model for intelligent governance in high-volume wholesale markets.

Digital governance is also transforming the catering sector. China Telecom's "See - through Kitchen (明厨亮灶)" platform integrates real-time video streaming, AI-powered behavior recognition, and cloud-based alert systems to enable intelligent regulation of key food-handling processes. The system automatically detects risk points such as noncompliant container use, missing headgear, or abnormal temperature and humidity levels, enabling regulators to conduct remote inspections. The platform has been widely implemented in school canteens and small food establishments, easing the burden of limited grassroots regulatory capacity and shifting the model from "traditional inspection" to "digital oversight." These innovations illustrate how digital technologies enhance the visibility, precision, and scalability of food-safety governance.

Beyond improving existing regulatory practices, technology is driving a deeper shift in governance logic. On one hand, big data empowers predictive risk management by identifying temporal and spatial patterns in food-safety risks, facilitating a transition from reactive response to proactive prevention. On the other hand, digitalization improves information symmetry across government agencies, market actors, and consumers, forming a technology-enabled collaborative network that strengthens societal co-governance.

Going forward, it is essential to accelerate the construction of a digital infrastructure covering the entire agri-food value chain, including blockchain traceability systems, real-time IoT monitoring networks, and AI-based quality inspection platforms. Through technological empowerment, it is possible to achieve full-process traceability from farm to table, enhancing the authenticity and verifiability of food safety information. Meanwhile, an open and shared data ecosystem should be established to promote information symmetry and resource coordination among regulatory authorities, market entities, and the public. Moreover, big data should be leveraged to improve the precision of governance. Through data analytics and artificial intelligence algorithms, authorities can realize real-time risk prediction, dynamic monitoring of public sentiment, scientific assessment of consumption trends, and optimized allocation of regulatory resources. These measures enhance public management efficiency, reduce administrative costs, and enable proactive risk prevention.

However, technological progress also introduces new challenges. The expansion of digital platforms and algorithmic power may lead to problems such as "data monopoly" and "algorithmic bias." In the future, mechanisms of cooperation and checks and balances between the public sector and platform enterprises must be established to ensure that digital transformation promotes efficiency while upholding fairness and public interest.

As digital technologies continue to penetrate the entire agri-food chain, the future governance landscape will no longer depend solely on traditional inspection methods or fragmented data flows, but will instead be shaped by the systematic integration of digital infrastructures, intelligent analytics, and interoperable data systems. This transition will support a more anticipatory, transparent, and coordinated governance regime, enabling the agri-food system to evolve toward a resilient and intelligence-driven model of modern oversight.

15.3 Public Participation and Social Awareness

The future governance of the agri-food system involves not only institutional and technological transformation but also the reconstruction of social trust and public consciousness. Achieving food safety, nutritional health, and sustainable consumption requires active public engagement and broad societal collaboration. Only by fostering social consensus and behavioral self-governance can the system evolve from "external regulation" to "social co-governance."

At the county level, the "four-pronged approach" to collaborative food safety governance implemented in recent years by Xiangjiang County, Jiangxi Province, offers an operational and replicable model for grassroots public administration. Local authorities have strengthened regulatory systems, focused on key risk areas, enhanced public education, and improved emergency and sampling capacities. The county conducts extensive food-safety education in communities, schools, and rural areas, and has created an innovative "park + community + market" science-popularization network. Eighteen thematic food-education stations have been established in high-traffic areas, providing targeted information on household nutrition, elderly health, and food selection. This dynamic public-education model aligns content with seasonal and local needs, gradually transforming residents from passive recipients of regulation into active contributors to food-safety governance.

Internationally, Japan's long-standing food-education (shokuiku) system further reveals how public awareness can be cultivated in a systematic, institutionalized manner. Since the enactment of the Basic Act on Food Education in 2005, Japan has built a national–local–school–family "food-education community." Through periodic Basic Plans for Food Education, integration of food-education curricula into compulsory schooling, promotion of family participation, and community-based food-safety activities, Japan has successfully transformed food safety and nutrition into a society-wide endeavor. Knowledge of nutrition, risk awareness, and healthy consumption habits are transmitted through the education system and reinforced through community activities and media channels, forming a culturally rooted and institutionally supported model of public participation.

From Xiajiang's grassroots practices to Japan's national-level food-education system, the impact of public consciousness on food-governance outcomes is evident. Public participation enhances regulatory enforcement: informed consumers who actively report, supervise, or provide feedback extend the reach and effectiveness of governance. Meanwhile, rising social awareness fosters a market environment where enterprises strive to improve quality and build trust-based reputations, driven by both market pressure and societal expectations.

Looking forward, public participation should be further strengthened. First, a multi-layered trust system must be established. Governments should enhance public credibility through transparent information disclosure and consistent institutional enforcement. Enterprises should build long-term trust through brand reputation and corporate social responsibility. Consumers, through supervision, feedback, and rational choice, form a social force that shapes public opinion and constrains behavior.

Social organizations, media, and educational institutions should also play a proactive role in agri-food governance. Social organizations can act as intermediaries in risk communication, public education, and industry self-regulation; media serve to expand information dissemination and shape public perception; educational institutions cultivate healthy, rational, and sustainable consumption habits.

In addition, multi-channel information disclosure, science popularization, and public communication should be strengthened to promote social consensus, turning food safety and green consumption into shared societal values. This transformation—from passive regulation to active participation—will form the most dynamic social foundation of future governance.

Public engagement and social awareness constitute not only a "soft power" but also one of the most dynamic and enduring institutional resources in modern agri-food governance. In the future, as public participation deepens, social consciousness will increasingly shape market norms, encouraging enterprises to prioritize quality and reputation. Ultimately, a society with strong awareness and active participation forms the most enduring foundation for modern agri-food governance.

15.4 Global Cooperation and Knowledge Sharing

The deep transformation of China's agri-food system holds domestic significance while also generating global value through institutional innovation and knowledge spillovers. As China's role in global food trade, agricultural technology, and sustainable development continues to grow, the "China experience" is becoming an important reference for international governance.

In recent years, China has actively promoted international cooperation in agriculture by disseminating institutional practices, technological solutions, and governance concepts—particularly through Agricultural Technology Demonstration

Centers (ATDCs) established across African countries. These centers introduce advanced varieties, promote efficient cultivation techniques, and provide training in processing, mechanization, pest control, and farmer-field-school methodologies. By 2024–2025, China had established around 24 ATDCs in Africa, training more than 50,000 local agricultural technicians and helping several countries develop localized research and extension systems. In parts of East Africa, Chinese-guided demonstration farms have achieved significant yield increases in crops such as maize and cassava, contributing to local food self-sufficiency and supply-chain resilience.

China is also deeply engaged in multilateral food-governance initiatives. Through cooperation with the FAO, participation in global food-security programs, the UN poverty-reduction agenda, and the Belt and Road agricultural cooperation framework, China promotes data-sharing, technological interoperability, and policy coordination. The China–FAO South–South Cooperation Programme, for example, sends Chinese experts to developing countries to provide technical assistance in rice cultivation, vegetable production, and livestock management, while supporting the development of monitoring systems and quality standards. These initiatives facilitate cross-border knowledge transfer and offer practical, scalable solutions grounded in China's governance experience.

Looking ahead, China's role in global food governance is expected to evolve from a technology provider to an institutional participant and co-shaper of global rules. China can deepen capacity-building cooperation with developing countries, support the construction of food-safety monitoring systems and supply-chain management capabilities, and strengthen collaboration on climate adaptation, food-loss reduction, and biodiversity protection—contributing to a greener, more inclusive, and resilient global food system.

China's agri-food system transformation is an integral component of the country's modernization process. It not only concerns food security and public health but also underpins high-quality economic growth and ecological civilization. Future development should aim to balance efficiency, equity, and sustainability, achieving dynamic equilibrium between market vitality and government governance.

Within this synergistic framework, China is expected to progress from ensuring basic food safety to promoting healthy and sustainable development, and ultimately to contributing to global governance innovation. Through continuous policy reform, technological empowerment, and social collaboration, China will contribute distinctive wisdom and institutional experience to the future development of the global food system.

The manufacturer's authorised representative in the EU is Springer Nature Customer Service Centre GmbH, Europaplatz 3, 69115 Heidelberg, Germany. If you have any concerns regarding our products, please contact ProductSafety@springernature.com

Printed and bound by CPI Group (UK) Ltd, Croydon, CR0 4YY
20/10/2026
02236467-0017